HAROLD B. LEE
PROPHET & SEER

L. Brent Goates

Bookcraft
Salt Lake City

First printing in hardbound 1985
First printing in paperbound 2001

Library of Congress Catalog Card Number: 85-72077

ISBN 0-88494-573-1 (hardbound)
ISBN 1-57008-794-6 (paperbound)

Printed in the United States of America   72082-6931
Publishers Press, Salt Lake City, UT

10   9   8   7   6   5   4   3   2   1

HAROLD B. LEE
PROPHET & SEER

Contents

Preface

On October 6, 1972, Harold B. Lee was sustained as President of The Church of Jesus Christ of Latter-day Saints at the Church's semiannual general conference. On that occasion he offered a humble formula for assessing his accomplishments: "The only true record that ever will be made of my service in my new calling will be the record that I have written in the hearts and lives of those with whom I have served and labored within and without the Church."

There is no question that President Lee gained the generous praise of those with whom he labored, and that which he called his "true record" was indeed an enviable one, written on the hearts of those whose lives he touched. Yet the written record between the covers of this book, largely of his own origin, also might be acclaimed as part of that "true record." Hopefully it will be an enduring record of this illustrious prophet's labors.

From the time of his call to the apostleship until his death, Harold B. Lee served for thirty-two years and eight months as a General Authority of the Church. Because little thus far has been published about his early life or his entire career, this record of his preparation for his distinguished career should make an interesting contribution to Church literature. It will show that Harold B. Lee excelled at all he did, usually at an age earlier than his peers. He was destined to greatness.

I have intentionally made this book, as much as possible, an autobiography by quoting extensively from President Lee's own writings. I have therefore restrained my editorial commentary. Included in the panoramic view of his public, adult life are the "men of God" who walked across the common stage to form Church history from President Lee's missionary days in Denver, Colorado in 1920 to his death in 1973. The dominant sources I have drawn upon are the personal diaries, the family and personal histories, and the private letters of Harold B. Lee. For the thirty-three years following his call to the apostleship, President Lee maintained a daily journal. Because he recorded in common pocket-sized planning calendars, with two days allotted on each page, his entries were forced toward brevity. His technique became that of sketching—pen strokes on a drawing he couldn't linger to finish because of lack of time and of lines in his book. Rarely did he examine in depth a person or event, or his reactions to them. After reading all thirty-three diaries, I have come to know the man, who, in these hurried daily entries, has revealed essential insights into the dynamic life he lived.

The biography sources were to have been balanced, however, by many choice firsthand, personal stories telling how lives have been unalterably changed for the good by an intimate experience with President Lee. Obviously this treatment would never be found in the diaries of President Lee. While these anecdotal stories are prepared, the sheer volume of the biography has forced this counterbalancing material to come forth in a later publication.

As in reading most biographies, some readers might hope here for a piquant look into Harold B. Lee's personal life and public service. In an effort to provide a complete report some such treatment has been included, but it rather has been my pronounced objective to provide abundant evidences of his inner spirituality, shown in developing degrees as he moved onward and upward in his leadership climb. In a belief that most Church members seek an identity with their prophet-leaders, this record is prepared so that they might fulfill that desire to better appreciate and admire, for much information is included which is worthy of being cherished. It is hoped that all readers will look well beyond the candid facts to discover and appreciate the creative and spiritual mind of Harold B. Lee and observe how under his leadership some outstanding innovations in the Church were developed. Understanding why the Church operates as it does and scrutinizing the finished works left behind by President Lee is made possible here by his dutiful record keeping and the persistent work of family biographers. These authors are most anxious that the world, and especially the Church membership and historians, come to better appreciate President Harold B. Lee, prophet and seer.

The research for this volume began shortly after President Lee's passing in 1973. It was commenced first from the desire to preserve a true and complete record of his ministry for his progeny; second, from the belief that every President of the Church should be the object of an exhaustive and comprehensive biography; finally, from the wish to share with all the Church membership the multitude of faith-promoting experiences and a review of the concurrent Church history in the Harold B. Lee years. In the end, the final product had to be telescoped to make possible a general distribution. It is hoped that this reduction has not made significant deductions from the spirit of the work or from efforts to achieve the above triad of objectives.

The eleven-year labor of preparing this manuscript for publication has been demanding, its only interruption being my three-year service in the California Arcadia Mission (1975–1978). I express gratitude to my family members, who understandingly substituted for me often because of my preoccupation. There were many compensatory rewards for my efforts. The daily penetration into the spiritual realm of Harold B. Lee's world has helped to shield my family in part from the discordance of a more clamorous world. Perhaps it is not too much to hope that the messages of President Lee's life and labors might also provide this refuge for the readers of these pages.

I express gratitude to the office of the First Presidency of the Church for making available to me the personal correspondence files of Harold B. Lee, which contained all letters he wrote and received during the time he was President. I express appreciation also to the Church Historian's office staff, and to the late Elder G. Homer Durham, Church Historian, for his encouragement in the completion of this project.

All the poetry included in the book, except two cited verses, is the work of the late Elder S. Dilworth Young. On his own initiative, Elder Young sought to learn of President Lee's history and to write and paint it, using his artistic talent to draw near to the President, whom he loved and admired. Long before his death and in the earliest years of the preparation of this book, Elder Young turned over all this poetry to me with permission to use his verses as desired. The Lee family appreciates his work and his devotion.

The chief editor and critic for this manuscript has been my dear wife, Helen Lee Goates, the only survivor of Harold B. Lee's immediate family. She has painstakingly read, reread, and urged many rewrites to bring the text closer to how she perceived her father would have preferred it to be. Although my name alone shows as author, her faithful and extensive labor deserves a large measure of credit for this book.

Trusted and willing typists have worked over this extended period to refine the manuscript copies. I extend appreciation to

Marilyn Lloyd Smith, Irma Hailes, and Carol Steffensen, dear friends and professional colleagues, who became personally interested in this project as they typed this text.

Finally, while it would be convenient to ascribe all responsibility to President Lee for the contents of this book, as though it were indeed his autobiography, such would be far short of the truth. Actually an agonizing judgment was rendered on almost every page as decisions were made on the many possibilities combed from his writings and those of his contemporaries. The dilemma of the historian is probably best explained by Elder B. H. Roberts in his preface to *A Comprehensive History of The Church of Jesus Christ of Latter-day Saints.*

> It need not be said that this course has laid a heavy burden upon the writer of this history. It is always a difficult task to hold the scales of justice at even balance when weighing the deeds of men. It becomes doubly more so when dealing with men engaged in a movement that one believes had its origin with God, and that its leaders on occasion act under the inspiration of God. Under such conditions to so state events as to be historically exact, and yet, on the other hand, so treat the course of events as not to destroy faith in these men, nor in their work, becomes a task of supreme delicacy; and one that tries the soul and the skill of the historian.

I have felt deeply the burden of holding in my hands the "scales of justice," and having to decide, after much soul searching, which events would present a fair and honest portrayal of Harold B. Lee's life and times. To the extent that there is unintended but inevitable bias in this judgment, I accept the responsibility. My plea is the same as the Prophet Moroni's as he prepared the title page of the Book of Mormon, writing: "And now, if there are faults they are the mistakes of men; wherefore, condemn not the things of God. . . ."

L. Brent Goates

Ancestry
and
Early Years

———

CHAPTER 1

Ancestry

A CHILD OF PROMISE

We talk of Margaret's bravery.
Eleven times she placed
Her life upon the block
And offered it that
Children might be born.
No sterile chamber
Where the doctor waits,
The anesthetic cone
And nurse in readiness,
Could be her lot.
The cabin walls absorbed
The agonizing cries.
With Death close by,
He did not claim her life.
Instead, he took each child—
Each little one—to Heaven.
All eleven.

Then came the twelfth.

For her the light burned
Dim, then flickered low,

And out—
But she had filled her life, and
Given all that she could give.
Her mission was performed;
A son was born,
The only child to live.

He was named his father's name—
Samuel Lee.*

Motherhood has produced heroines throughout history. Few women have tried more nobly and with greater persistence to enter the ranks of motherhood than Margaret McMurrin Lee. The family history records:

Samuel Marion Lee, Sr.

Margaret McMurrin Lee

She married Samuel Marion Lee in the Endowment House on November 4, 1863, at the age of seventeen. On the pioneer frontiers of southern Utah, she endured much hardship and her health began to fail soon after her marriage.

By those who knew her, she was described as modest, good-looking, and of a shy, sweet disposition. She was full of fun and was known as a beautiful dancer.

Because of ill health, her first babies were either stillborn or lived but a few minutes. She despaired of ever having a living baby until she received a patriarchal blessing at the hands of Patriarch Abel Lamb of Salt Lake City, which gave her renewed hope and anticipated joy at the thoughts of motherhood fulfillment.

* © S. Dilworth Young 1976. Used by permission.

In this blessing, the patriarch promised:

> Thou shalt be blessed in every good thing in righteousness before the Lord. And your health shall be restored and notwithstanding your severe sickness at this time you shall yet live. . . . And you shall have a son and he shall be a mighty man in Israel and his name shall be the name of his father's; therefore trust in the Lord and have faith in His promises and it shall be fulfilled every whit and the blessings of Sarah of old shall be conferred upon thee in the due time of the Lord and you shall yet be a great blessing upon your parents and your companion; and I seal you up unto eternal life. Amen.

After ten bitter disappointments, with no child of her own to nestle in her arms and to love, the next baby following this blessing also was stillborn. This was but another test to survive, and she wondered at the fulfillment of her promise. Her only answer seemed to be: "for ye receive no witness until after the trial of your faith" (Ether 12:6).

After her trial of faith she did indeed receive a witness; the second child after the patriarch's blessing brought her reward. This promised son was premature, weighing but three and a half pounds at his birth on November 22, 1875, and so tiny that a large finger ring could be slipped over his arm.

Already weakened and in frail condition from the rigors of pioneer life in the arid frontier country, Margaret could not endure the long and arduous travail of bearing her son. She gave her life in the ultimate sacrifice, dying November 30, 1875, at the age of twenty-nine. She was buried at Panaca, Nevada, where the couple lived.

As prophesied by the patriarch, this "son of promise" was given the name of his father—Samuel Marion Lee.

Grief and loneliness filled the heart of Mary, the deceased Margaret's sister, as she undertook the heavy task of caring for the tiny babe after his mother's passing. Mary and Margaret had married two Lee brothers, Samuel Marion and Francis, Jr., and had accompanied their husbands to help settle what was then thought to be the Southern Utah Territory.

Mary McMurrin Lee took the child and for six months nursed him along with her own child, many times wondering if she would be able to keep this tiny baby alive. It seemed futile at times. After a

Samuel Marion Lee, Jr., as a boy

while the strain from this double duty was too great, and she felt her own strength waning. So tiny Samuel was delivered to Grandmother McMurrin, Mary's mother, to have the wee one live with her in Salt Lake City.

Mary would live in Panaca until she died at the age of ninety-five. During all that time she would yearn to return to Salt Lake City, longing for the companionship of another sister, Maggie. Her greatest satisfaction, however, would come from seeing Samuel grow into a kind, stalwart man who always expressed his gratitude and love toward her. Tiny Samuel would prove to be worth every minute of her sacrifice.

> The journey to the City of the Saints
> Was done. For fourteen
> Days the team had pulled the wagon
> Through the sand, the dust, and more.
>
> "I'll give him one last nursing," Mary said.
> Her mother nodded; then, the task completed,

>Mary laid the infant in his bed,
>And went away—back to Meadow Valley.*

Thus, Samuel was raised in the home of his grandparents, Joseph and Margaret Leaing McMurrin. His father, still living in Nevada, assisted in his support and came occasionally to Salt Lake City to see him. At the age of fourteen, Samuel M. Lee went to Panaca, where he visited for a time with his father. There he saw his birthplace and the grave of his mother, and he personally thanked his Aunt Mary for the patient, loving care she had given to him. Without her valiant service this child of promise would not have lived to fulfill his special mission in mortality.

After the death of his grandmother on September 4, 1893, Samuel went to Clifton, Idaho, to live with his uncle and aunt, Riley and Jeanette McMurrin Davis. Here he met and fell in love with Louisa Bingham; they were sealed in marriage in the Logan Temple by Elder M. W. Merrill on May 13, 1895.

They were young at the time of the marriage. Louisa was always somewhat sensitive about this point. She thought it might not be a proper example if her family discovered what a young, little bride she was at age sixteen. They reared a fine family of six children in the little farming community of Clifton.

>When she saw him,
>She knew his story well—
>The twelfth and only child
>Which lived;
>His mother died in
>Giving birth.
>From then until his
>Sixteenth year
>His grandmother had
>Kept her hearth
>Warm to his growing.
>
>And so they came together,
>Drawn by a magnet
>Neither one could see,
>To be the parents of a
>Man of Destiny.*

Theirs was the responsibility to rear a marked, choice spirit in their home, a soul chosen before he was born to become the eleventh President of The Church of Jesus Christ of Latter-day Saints—President Harold Bingham Lee.

* © S. Dilworth Young 1976. Used by permission.

The Lee family's earliest ancestor in America was William Lee. Born on August 15, 1745, in Carrickfergus, one of the ancient capitals of Ireland, William, along with his brother, Francis, and Francis's wife, left their native land and sailed to America in 1770. They landed in Philadelphia.

One wonders now if he understood his unsettled feelings that led him to seek a better life in the New World. Doubtless he could not have known, as we do now, that he really came to start a chosen lineage in a free land so that in time it could match up with foreordained purposes.

Not long after his arrival in America, William married Susannah Chaffings. It must have been an exciting year for him—a new home and a new bride in the same year. Moving southward to North Carolina they established a home where four sons were born. Samuel Lee, the youngest, was born on April 14, 1775. Sorrow followed because shortly after Samuel's birth the young mother passed away.

To support his four sons William Lee left all his holdings with Judge McElroy, likely a close friend, and joined the army to fight in the Revolutionary War. He was wounded and left for dead in the Battle of Guilford County Courthouse, which was fought in the Carolinas in March, 1781. Thanks to the good nursing care he received, he recovered from his wounds, ultimately marrying his nurse, Sarah McMullen. They became the parents of seven children.

The history to be followed here is a lineage through the youngest son by his first marriage, Samuel Chaffings Lee. Samuel's sixth child was named Francis. Harold B. Lee's own account of his paternal ancestry gives more information about this man:

> My great-grandfather, Francis Lee, was born at Wilmington, Ohio, in 1811, in a family of eight children. He joined The Church of Jesus Christ of Latter-day Saints at Randolph County, Indiana, in 1832.
>
> My great-grandmother, Jane Vail Johnson, joined at the same time and they were married in 1835.
>
> They moved with the Saints into Missouri and lived at Liberty and Far West, where they were located in 1838 when the "Exterminating Order" was issued by Governor Boggs, and with their two children were with the 14,000 Saints who were forced thereby to

leave the state. They found refuge at Payson, Illinois, until 1843, when they settled in Nauvoo.

Following the martyrdom of the Prophet Joseph Smith, Francis Lee, with others, made ready to go westward as the presiding brethren had counseled. In company with 225 other Saints, they crossed the Mississippi River on February 14, 1845, arriving at the Missouri on June 14, 1846. In 1850 they reached the Platte River, where cholera broke out and several died, among whom was their son, Jacob Edward. At the Missouri River camp they were by chance joined by Francis's father, my great-great-grandfather, Samuel Lee, who had started on foot to the California gold fields but from this point on accompanied his sons to Salt Lake, where they arrived on September 17, 1850. In 1851, my great-great-grandfather, Samuel Lee, joined the Church at Tooele, Utah.

Scarcely settled in their new community of Tooele, thirty-four miles to the southwest of Salt Lake City, Francis Lee heard his name read at the 1862 general conference of the Church in the Salt Lake Tabernacle, among those called by Brigham Young to leave with their families to settle the Utah "Dixie country." From the Santa Clara and St. George encampment, where the famed missionary to the Indians, Jacob Hamblin, was leader, Francis Lee was asked to settle the Indian Territory in Meadow Valley. That location became Panaca, which they considered at the time to be southwestern Utah, but which actually developed later to be in Lincoln County, Nevada. Here they lived in a dugout house, which consisted of a cubical hole dug in a hillside and covered with a roof of wooden poles, topped with clay.

MEADOW VALLEY
[Panaca, 1864]

The buttes and gray-clad hills
Lie flat and quiet in the
Noonday light.
The sun beats down upon
The sage-clad flats,
Shrinking the shadows
Underneath the sage to
Polka dots upon the valley floor.

One comes upon the valley
Suddenly, and there it lies—
A green oasis in the

Somber hills.
Its spring of water is
Lifeblood to the meadowland,
And to the cultivated
Crops of pioneers,
Sent to claim the land
By Brigham Young.

The lazy smoke drifts slowly
Toward the sky
From 'dobe chimneys,
While in the dark cool light
Of shaded noon, the sombre
Clothing of the women,
Kneeling at their hearths and
Poking at each stubborn blaze,
Blends with the graying floor.
A blackened pot hangs strong
Upon the crane—

It's dinner time in Meadow Valley.

In from the fields the men find
Cooling peace and strength
To face the sun of afternoon.
The food is plain, but appetites
Are strong,
While hunger is as stimulating wine.

And soon more land is plowed,
And seed is planted row on row
To make plants bloom as Eden bloomed,
Long, long ago.

The sun is setting low
Behind the western hills.
The purple shadows deepen
On the sage. The cottonwoods
Along the watercourse
Glow bright,
Then fade,
As day becomes the night.*

The Panaca settlers had so much difficulty with the Indians that the Church authorities gave them permission to abandon the project. Typical of the pluck of these indomitable pioneers,

* © S. Dilworth Young 1976. Used by permission.

however, was Jane Vail Johnson Lee [Francis's wife] who said she was in Panaca to stay and refused to leave. One day two Indians came into her dugout home, and one of them spotted a rifle in the corner of the room. He demanded it, but Jane refused to give it to him. When he started for the gun, she struck him so hard with a piece of stove wood that it knocked him down. He staggered to his feet and drew his bow, attempting to aim an arrow at her. She used another piece of wood in defense, which smashed the Indian's bow and arrow. He and his companion fled for their lives. Francis Lee died in Panaca in 1866. Jane, his wife and Harold B. Lee's great-grandmother, died on July 10, 1875.

The third child of Francis Lee, Samuel Marion, was Harold B. Lee's grandfather and was born at Payson, Illinois, in 1841. He married Margaret McMurrin, and the couple also lived in Panaca, Nevada, where their only child to live more than a few short minutes, Samuel Marion, miraculously survived a premature birth. As earlier recounted, Margaret died on November 30, 1875, at the age of twenty-nine, eight days after the birth of her baby. Grandfather Samuel Marion Lee died in 1890.

Great-Grandfather and Great-Grandmother

Joseph McMurrin, Margaret's father, was born at Crossmaloof, Renfrewshire, Scotland, on July 26, 1822. He was an expert cooper, one who makes barrels and bends wood. Joseph married Margaret Leaing on November 25, 1842. Converted to the Church, the McMurrins crossed the plains in the 1850s with one of the handcart companies. Their arrival in Utah was delayed because his artisanship was required to repair many handcart wheels en route to the Salt Lake Valley.

They settled in Tooele, where two families were twice united —Samuel Marion Lee, Sr., married Margaret McMurrin, and Francis Lee, Jr., married Mary McMurrin, Margaret's sister. Each of the Lee brothers took his bride to Meadow Valley, in Panaca, Nevada.

To Joseph McMurrin and Margaret Leaing were born nine children. The three oldest children died as infants and were all given the name of Elizabeth. Another three children were Margaret [President Lee's grandmother], Mary [Lee] and Jeanette [Davis].

President Lee wrote further of his great-grandparents, Joseph McMurrin and Margaret Leaing:

Grandfather and probably Grandmother were baptized into the Church in 1854 and emigrated to Utah in 1855. The old home was located at Sixth South and Main Street, Salt Lake City. Grandfather married Jeanette Irvine in polygamy in 1869 and raised nine children by this marriage. Grandfather helped install the first telegraph line into Salt Lake City. He served in the bishopric of the Eighth Ward in Salt Lake, during which time he was incarcerated six months in the Utah State Penitentiary for his plural marriage. He was given charge of the Tabernacle grounds for a number of years and met many great personalities among the tourists, one of whom he notably remembered was a Senator McDonald, who gave him a $20 gold piece for the valuable information received from Grandfather. Later he had charge of the tithing-hay barn located where the Presiding Bishop's Office stood, at 40 North Main Street. In this position he came to know people from Canada to Mexico who came to Salt Lake to trade. Grandfather McMurrin was a large man, weighing over two hundred pounds. He died in 1897.

Margaret Leaing was born in Glasgow, Scotland, in 1826, and was endowed in the Endowment House in 1859. She died in 1893.

Of his paternal grandparents President Lee wrote:

Grandfather Samuel Marion Lee, third son of the before-mentioned Francis Lee, who was born at Payson, Illinois, in 1841, settled with his parents in Meadow Valley, a hostile Indian country. Here, in southern Utah, Great-grandfather Francis Lee, with his seven sons and three daughters, became widely known. He was nearly six feet tall, of medium weight, and had jet black hair, which could be mistaken for "Indian hair" when allowed to grow long. He was active in Church work, being a superintendent of the Sunday School for a number of years, and later, a counselor in the bishopric.

After the passing of Margaret Lee in childbirth, Samuel Lee, Sr., married Jane Rice, of Farmington, Utah, on June 29, 1877, and had four daughters and one son. Samuel Lee, Sr., died of yellow jaundice on January 27, 1890.

President Joseph W. McMurrin

One previous General Authority of the Church adds luster to Harold B. Lee's ancestry. President Joseph W. McMurrin, Harold B. Lee's great-grandfather, was appointed a member of the First Council of the Seventy in 1897. He went to Los Angeles to preside over the California Mission immediately after his call as a General Authority. He remained in this position until 1931, when he was released because of ill health that led to his death in Los Angeles on October 25, 1932. At his funeral services held in the Wilshire Ward

While yet a boy he moved with his parents to Clifton, Idaho, where he engaged in farming. He was baptized into the Church on February 8, 1877, by Harvey Dixon and was confirmed the same day by the same Harvey Dixon.

He was married to Rachel Elvira Henderson, December 7, 1875, and they were endowed in the Endowment House at Salt Lake City in September, 1880. They were married in the temple by President Joseph F. Smith.

After his marriage, he spent most of his time freighting into Montana until the railroad was built. After this he engaged in the buying and selling of cattle for a number of years.

In the year 1902, he was elected sheriff of Oneida County, and in 1904 he was elected county assessor for a two-year term. Following this, he was appointed deputy warden of the Idaho State Penitentiary at Boise. It was on the occasion of a visit to Boise about 1906 that I first remember him. In 1909 his health broke and he returned to Clifton, Idaho, where he was an invalid dependent upon Mother and Father for eight years. He died July 17, 1916 at the age of fifty-nine. He held the office of a seventy in the priesthood at the time of his death.

Grandmother

Rachel Elvira Henderson was the daughter of Martin Henderson and Sarah Wheeler and was born at Kaysville, Davis County, Utah, January 25, 1858. Her parents were pioneers in southern Idaho, making their home at Clifton, Idaho. She was baptized and confirmed a member of the Church on August 6, 1876, by Harvey Dixon.

As a girl she was full of life and vigor, but shortly after her marriage to Perry Calvin Bingham, on December 7, 1875, she was broken down in health and was never again able to enjoy good health up to the time of her death. She was faithful in her Church duties, often walking the two miles to her meetings carrying a baby.

Grandmother had long, beautiful, black hair and even at her death it was of sufficient length to reach to her waist. She was a patient sufferer for many years, but a wonderful grandma, and I remember many times hieing away to her home for some luxury or a story. She died at Clifton, Idaho, at the age of forty-nine, on December 10, 1907.

The following children were born to Perry Calvin Bingham and Rachel Elvira Henderson: Sarah Bingham, born 1876, died 1879; Louisa Emeline, born January 1, 1879, died July 27, 1959; Perry Calvin, born 1882, died 1895; Effie Lucretia, born December 28, 1884, died October 22, 1946; and Zeida, died at birth, 1894.

Great-Grandfather and Great-Grandmother

Martin Henderson was born November 10, 1835, in Missouri and was married to Sarah Wheeler, who was born September 20, 1836, in Michigan. After the death of his first wife, Grandfather married Elizabeth Bake.

Martin Henderson was unschooled, as was his father, Samuel Henderson. He could neither read nor write, but is described as a typical pioneer and a hardy frontiersman, ready at a moment to fight for his honor. In his prime he weighed 180 pounds and was of medium build.

From such noble ancestors came a great posterity. Each ancestor has left something in the molding of a heritage that was to include a prophet of God, Harold B. Lee.

1875. The country was preparing to celebrate the centennial of the founding of the nation.

CHAPTER 2

Parentage

"I thank God today for my parentage. My father and mother are listening, either in this great assembly or on the radio, if perchance they did not get into this meeting. I think, perhaps, this is my way of paying tribute to the two family names they gave me at my birth, Bingham and Lee. I trust I shall not disgrace those names. I have been blessed with a splendid father and a grand and lovely mother."

Elder Harold B. Lee spoke this sincere tribute as he responded to his call as a member of the Quorum of the Twelve Apostles on April 6, 1941.

FATHER: SAMUEL MARION LEE

In his personal journal Harold B. Lee wrote the following concerning his father:

Samuel Marion Lee, my father, was born at Panaca, Nevada, November 22, 1875, the "baby of promise" to Margaret McMurrin and Samuel Marion Lee. After the death of his mother, he was nursed for six months by his Aunt Mary Lee and was then taken and raised in the home of his maternal grandparents, Joseph and Margaret Leaing McMurrin.

Grandmothers have a way
With growing boys.
They have learned through rich
Experience with their own.
They give more love,
The discipline is soft
And kind,
The cookie jar more full.
There is more patience
With expanding minds,
When questioning the pull
And tug of growth.
And so this boy
Brought to his grandmother
Joy.
In him she saw her
Girl, her child,
His manner hers, the
Look about the eyes,
The smile,
Surely a look into
Her daughter's paradise.*

Occasionally young Samuel had a visit with his father, who was still living in Nevada. At age seventeen, his beloved grandmother, with whom he was living in Salt Lake City, died in his arms on September 4, 1893. Then he went to Clifton, Idaho, to live with his uncle and aunt, Riley Davis and Jeanette McMurrin Davis. Here Father met Louisa Bingham, and they were married in the Logan Temple by Apostle M. W. Merrill, on May 13, 1895.

Out on the farm
Louisa Bingham
Grew and blossomed
Into girlish womanhood.
Her blue eyes
Caught the color of the
Bright hills in spring,
And in the fall they
Danced with joy
At autumn's coloring.
At home she learned
To wash and cook and sew,
And winter
Saw her

* © S. Dilworth Young 1976. Used by permission.

Skating, sledding, and
Riding in the bobsleigh
Through the snow.

Then Samuel Lee, now
Working on his uncle's farm,
Watched her grow,
Saw with his heart
As well as with his eyes—
The slow unfolding
Of her girlish charm,
The bloom of girlhood
High upon her cheeks,
A budding woman,
Gentle, soft, and warm.*

To Samuel and Louisa, my parents, the following children were born: Samuel Perry, December 5, 1896–August 14, 1979; Harold Bingham, March 28, 1899–[December 26, 1973]; Clyde Bingham, October 12, 1902–September 11, 1953; Waldo Bingham, November 24, 1905–February 14, 1959; Stella Bingham, December 21, 1907–[January 28, 1974]; and Verda Bingham, July 1, 1910-------.

In the winter of 1895–96, Father taught in the Rushville School at a salary of $50 per month. Shortly after his marriage he was chosen assistant superintendent of the Sunday School with Henry J. Howell, and later served as the superintendent for five years. In May 1911 he was chosen second counselor to Bishop James W. Davis, and was sustained as the bishop of Clifton Ward on June 6, 1914. He was released as bishop on April 1, 1923. He was appointed treasurer of the Oneida Irrigation District, January 1909, and held this position until February 1920. He was a school trustee from 1918 to 1922.

On January 1, 1924, he moved with his family to Salt Lake City and lived in the Hawthorne Ward, where he was set apart as a ward teacher. In May 1926, he went to Green River, Wyoming, as manager of the Piggly Wiggly Grocery. During the ten months that he was there he served as the president of the Young Men's Mutual Improvement Association and as a block teacher. Upon his return he worked as a watchman at ZCMI. In due time he advanced to the position of night supervisor and held this position for ten years.

Samuel Marion Lee was an ardent genealogist in his last twenty years of life. By permission of his employers at ZCMI, he took his records to work with him; between rounds of his night watchman duties, he would copy diligently his genealogical records. Because

---

* © S. Dilworth Young 1976. Used by permission.

of his dedication, there are now in existence three sets of copies of over 1,500 sheets of genealogical records, each set in his own handwriting. One set is in the Genealogical Library, one is with his daughter Verda, and one was given to his son Harold.

Personal Characteristics

Samuel Lee was described most often as a quiet, gentle, compassionate, unassuming, thoughtful man. Listening empathetically to his many "boys" at work as they spilled out all their troubles, including social dating woes, Samuel served as a wise counselor to them. He even at times tried his hand successfuly at matchmaking. Kenneth E. Knapp, one of "his boys," who later became a prominent Utah hospital administrator, wrote this character sketch of Samuel M. Lee.

> When first I saw the man who was to be my boss, my impressions were immediate and certain. He was stocky and thick and appeared as solid and firm as the rock he resembled. He projected the image of a "big" man, belying his modest stature.
>
> My eye impressions told me Sam Lee was a stern man who would be a "no nonsense" supervisor. The heavy, once dark mustache, now abundantly streaked with gray, did little to soften the initial impact of the man I saw and was waiting to know as a personality.
>
> When finally introduced to him as "the new man you requested," I expected his words to roll out thunder-like from beneath that heavy mustache.
>
> How wrong I was. Sam Lee was a soft-spoken man, so kind in his speech, I was momentarily caught off-guard. With the passing of time, I marveled often how totally wrong first impressions can be. Mr. Sam Lee was one of the fairest and most thoughtful men I have known. The harshness I anticipated was completely foreign to the man. The men under him loved and admired him, and he made each of us feel he was equally fond of us.
>
> Many called him "Sam"—and I sensed he loved it—but I was not one of them. I was never quite able to address him by his first name. I was but twenty years old, fresh from the mission field, and the respect I had for this well-seasoned man just wouldn't permit that familiarity. To me, and apparently many others, he was "Bishop Lee," a title that somehow seemed so appropriate.
>
> As part of the night force at the ZCMI Department Store, I scrubbed and waxed floors, dusted furnishings, polished the fixtures, and washed windows, display cases, walls and ceilings. Periodic welcomed relief occurred when Bishop Lee would assign

the duty of making security rounds, or punching the security clocks, as we called it.

A dozen or so men were kept busy discharging the tasks and duties that rested on the "night force." There was never an awareness that all we did fell under the watchful eye of Bishop Lee, but, somehow, it must have. Sam Lee was uncanny. Without obviously observing, he knew exactly where we were in our work and where we ought to be at that hour. When it was time to break for our night-time lunch period, he would very kindly remind us where we should be in our assigned duties to complete our work on time and, when necessary, would offer suggestions that would enable us to "catch-up" so our schedules would be completed before the day force reported for duty.

The night-time break was a welcome time everyone looked forward to enjoying. We assembled where the white tile of the grocery met the carpeted floor of the book department in the old store. If Bishop Lee was management's commissioned leader of the night force during our actual working hours, he was our own designated natural leader during our breaks. Sam Lee was a gifted communicator. In delightful ways he regaled us with his reminiscings of days gone by and in making some distant character in history vividly come to life again.

His wisdom seemed limitless and I benefited often from his counsel. He loved the Church and espoused the gospel in a very inoffensive yet impressive way. As he talked to us, and we were a rather interesting array of opposites from every walk of life, his words seemed to register with each man. Always I could see his love of God and His teachings flow through in all he uttered.

The year was 1935 and the country was still in the throes of economic stress from The Great Depression. Bishop Lee was worried about people like me, young folks who were anxious to marry and establish homes and families. But he counseled me that it should only be done when we were ready to so prioritize our lives that we could live within our means. I listened to him then, and I'm still listening to him now, or at least to his teachings.

I remember Bishop Sam Lee, and as I do, I get a warm feeling inside. Like all his men, I wanted to do my best for him and he never failed to let us know he appreciated it when we did. He was easy to love and knew how to love back.

Throughout his life it was necessary for Samuel to conserve his meager financial resources. One exception, however, was food for his table, which was always spread well with good food.

To others, Samuel Lee appeared to be most generous. If he had an obvious fault, it was perhaps his tendency to carry charity to the extreme. Once started, he seemed to seldom know when to stop giving.

His youngest daughter, Verda, remembers well an experience with Inez Henderson, a neighbor in Clifton. Her husband had been killed and she was often without food in the home. One day Samuel was impressed to fill a large basket with the best available food, and when he opened the door to Sister Henderson's home to deliver it, she burst into tears, later explaining to her benefactor that she had been without food and that her only recourse had been to the Lord in prayer. Samuel had come that day in answer to her fervent supplications to God. Samuel M. Lee was a man our Heavenly Father could easily reach when he had a mission of mercy at hand.

He is well remembered as one who loved everyone. He was a man with whom people became easily acquainted. His grandchildren loved him dearly, and many of them still remember how his heavy moustache tickled their noses when he kissed them. His son-in-law, Charles Ross, knew him well for fourteen years before he married Samuel's daughter Verda, and remembers him as the warmest, friendliest man he has ever known.

Characteristic of his personality was the creation of his own "patented" swear word. When he was wont to vent his anger or frustration, he would say, "Oh, nickofishtoe." That always seemed to take care of the situation, with a release that seemed harmless enough to all present.

Despite the fame and prestige which came to his son Harold as an Apostle of the Lord, Samuel never forgot his patriarchal place to preside in honor and dignity over his home and posterity. After the long years of World War II had ended, the Church authorities commissioned Elder Lee to make the first visit of a Church leader to Hawaii since the bombing at Pearl Harbor. Regular passenger transportation was not yet available so Elder Lee was obliged to sail on a freighter ship. It was a dangerous mission, still under war-time conditions and filled with uncertainty.

Elder Lee's diary, under the date of June 24, 1945, contains an entry concerning this visit to Hawaii that captures their father-son relationship:

> I went up to Father and Mother's for dinner and was very much concerned over Father's physical condition. He seemed to be losing weight and strength. He expressed a desire to give me a blessing,

which he did, and reminded me of my lineage, rehearsed my life, and blessed me for the trip to Hawaii.

Samuel Marion Lee died on May 17, 1947, at the age of seventy-one. For over twenty years he had lived with his wife and their youngest daughter, Verda, and during the last year of his life also with Verda's husband, Charles Ross, in Salt Lake City. At the time of his passing he had sixteen grandchildren and six great-grandchildren.

Samuel Marion Lee, Jr.   Louisa Emeline Bingham

MOTHER: LOUISA BINGHAM LEE

Harold B. Lee's journal contains this account of his mother's life:

> Louisa Emeline Bingham was the second child of Perry Calvin Bingham and Rachel Elvira Henderson, and was born at Clifton, Oneida County, Idaho, on New Year's Day, January 1, 1879. She was baptized by William F. Garner on August 8, 1887, and was confirmed by John Sant on the same day.
>
> When my mother was a young child she was obliged to shoulder the responsibility of caring for an invalid mother, as well as the younger children in the family, and to perform all the household duties in the home. In addition to doing the cooking, housework, and sewing, she often performed the outside chores as well. She was so small that she was required to stand on a box to enable her to reach far enough down into the tub to scrub the clothes on a washboard. When she was sewing, her feet would hardly reach the machine treadles.

Her father was away much of the time freighting into Montana, and it became my mother's responsibility to bathe, feed, and care for not only her younger brother and sister, but also her bedfast mother. They lived about a five-minute walk from school, and Mother would arise very early, fix breakfast, dress and care for her brother and sister, bathe and feed her mother, then dash off for school. When all the other children were enjoying their games at recess, Mother would run home to care for her mother and begin preparing lunch. At noon she would hurry home again to take care of the family responsibilities which came upon her early in her life.

Mother owned a famous saddle pony named Maude, which she rode for the cows and on other errands. I often rode Maude in my own childhood.

At the age of fourteen, Mother was sustained as a Sunday School teacher in the Rushville School. In 1908, she became a counselor to Emma Garner in the Young Women's Mutual Improvement Association. She was made the president of this organization in 1914, and in 1920 was sustained as the second counselor to Millie G. Anderson in the stake presidency of the YWMIA of the Oneida Stake. She was released in December 1923. Simultaneously she worked in Primary and Relief Society and was chosen on the sewing committee, having the responsibility of sewing temple clothes for the dead. During all this Church activity she was rearing her family of four sons and two daughters, besides caring for an invalid father and mother.

Mother was an inveterate worker. Before we were old enough to work, Mother went into the fields with Dad and did mowing, raking, and practically everything a man did.

There are two characteristics that stand out in my memory of Mother. With her skill as a seamstress we were always considered well dressed as children, but practically all our outer clothing was made over from second-hand clothes.

Her other outstanding skill was in caring for the sick. She always began with castor oil, and so successful was she that never was a doctor in our home excepting when the babies came. I recall the many weary days and nights when four of us were down in bed at the same time with scarlet fever. Father was away much of the time, and for several days, my brother Clyde, particularly, was at death's door. I remember also Mother's bitterly successful fight to save his life when he suffered with diphtheria. She swabbed his throat constantly for several days and nights to prevent its closing.

Exerting great patience and skill, Louisa sat many long hours by the bedside of other sick persons, too, in the neighborhood and farm communities. Her nursing skills extended occasionally to service as a midwife. She assisted the doctor in the delivery of eight of her own grandchildren.

A further glimpse into this family's home life is seen through Harold's sisters' memories of their growing up in a setting made memorable by their mother's constant, watchful care and concern. Special mothers make special moments for children, and Verda and Stella remember their childhood home with fondness:

> The simple joys created by a loving mother of hot, homemade tomato soup after sacrament meeting on Sundays; the "lumpy-dick," of which Harold was so fond; a very special evening when mother had made new flannel nightgowns for us as little girls; and the nights when we couldn't sleep, because the delicious aroma of baking bread cast its tantalizing aroma through the house to our nostrils in the bedroom—all will never be forgotten. It was on such occasions that, late at night, Father would open our bedroom door quietly, pick up his little girls in his arms, and carry us into the bright light of the kitchen and sit us on the table. Then Mother would place a plate of delectable slices of hot bread and honey on the table, along with a glass of cold milk for each of us. That was a treat for princesses, and we were treated that way. We did have the sweetest childhood.

Personal Qualities

There were times, of course, that little children erred and had to be taught right from wrong. Such lessons were essential in the home of a future President of the Church. Harold's mother supplied the more obvious discipline. Though it was firm, it was never harsh.

This rugged farm mother insisted that her children obey her. She wasn't domineering, but the children didn't argue with her either, because they knew she would support her words with action. She swished around her "little green willow" as a means of lending authority to her instructions.

After one tense moment, when one of the boys disobeyed and then hid in the lucerne patch to avoid the inevitable lashing, this undaunted mother made a speech over the silent field, promising retribution whenever the disobedient lad came home. Though always the hardest act she had to do, she never failed to carry out her pronouncements of justice; however, the application of the "little green willow" was always very light, and it hurt the mother more than the child.

Speaking of this incident, one of the biographers of Louisa Emeline Bingham Lee, Jaynann Morgan Payne, wrote appropriately: "Blessed are the mothers of this earth who will devote such minutes of their precious time awaiting at the edge of eternity for a child to think it over, to repent and learn to do his Father's will. Blessed is she who inspires this fusion of the practical with the spiritual, and points little souls to their eternal destiny."

Louisa would never defend her children if they were wrong or at fault, but if she felt they were unjustly treated or unfairly criticized, she was a little tigress and would defend them to the bitter end. From such an upbringing came Harold's intense family pride and fierce family loyalty.

Verda has reflected on her mother's philosophy of life as follows:

> Although Mother's motto was "You can always do a little bit better," her example was the most potent sermon of all. Her home was shining and she was the most immaculate housekeeper. Daddy once said: "Mother, I do believe that you make dirt just because you enjoy cleaning it up so much!" And her personal grooming was just as neat and tidy as her home. In later years, when poverty no longer stalked our family, she dressed herself tastefully and elegantly in clothes that she created herself. We daughters, especially, remember hearing Mother's voice call to us: "I don't want any of you children to leave this house without a bath and clean underclothes. What if you are in an accident!"
>
> Our home reflected a great love of beauty and fine taste. She was gifted in the art of flower arranging and her beautiful handiwork lent the stamp of her personality in our home. Though our family was poor for many years, we children were always well dressed and well fed because of Mother's thrifty efforts and talents. Our home was a haven of orderliness and beauty.

Harold B. Lee's personal history gives evidence of his respect for his mother:

> I think I came to appreciate her first while teaching at Oxford, Idaho. Mother guessed the dangers that beset an eighteen-year-old school principal, susceptible to temptation and always in danger of a fatal step in such a responsible job. Never did she go to bed at night until I had come home. While I ate the hot lunch she always had for me, she questioned me about the day's work. She had a keen intuition and on some occasions compelled Dad to hitch up a team and go to meet me. This companionship has always con-

tinued, and in my manhood I value greatly Mother's wisdom. Mother was always blunt and outspoken and had a way of correcting that sometimes antagonized, but was always effective.

As with any good mother, she always knew where her children were. Her oldest son, Perry, recalls the unique approach she used:

> Our mother had a system all her own in keeping her brood in line and under surveillance. She always saw to it that we went to our parties and various interests outside the home, two-by-two, secure in the knowledge that when we returned, she was bound to get the whole story—"from the mouths of two witnesses."

Her sense of humor was a recognized trait. Verda suffered with ill health for many years, and one day when she was preparing to go back to work after a particularly severe illness, her mother gave her this advice: "Verda, always remember to never, never look like you feel!"

In later years, after Harold had been called to membership in the Council of the Twelve, Verda recalled that her mother one day was comparing her children's similarities in personality. She said to Verda: "You know, I think you are a lot like your brother Harold in many ways." Then, lest Verda be flattered and be proud of the comparison, she quickly added with a twinkle in her eye, "And there are a lot of things I could improve in the both of you!"

After Louisa had an operation on her right knee, they wheeled her out of the hospital to meet her family. Her husband, Samuel, said to the waiting daughters, "You girls just don't seem to have nearly as pretty legs as your mother does." Louisa's quick reply was, "Now, Father, you know I haven't got a leg to stand on!"

But more important was her profoundly spiritual nature. Her Apostle son commented further on this:

> She was deeply religious, more so than appeared on the surface.
> As just a high school boy, I went away on a high school debating team trip. We won the debate. I called Mother on the telephone only to have her say, "Never mind, son. I know all about it. I will tell you when you get home at the end of the week." When I came home she took me aside and said, "When I knew it was just time for this performance to start, I went out among the willows by the creekside, and there, all by myself, I remembered you and prayed God you would not fail." I have come to know that that kind of love is necessary for every son and daughter who seeks to achieve in this world. (Conference Report, April 6, 1941)

Her sons often came to their mother seeking her counsel. When asked what to say at a particular funeral or speaking commitment, Louisa would reply: "Just preach the gospel!" She told her son Harold that at too many funerals the speakers talked only about the deceased person. She firmly declared to Harold: "When I die, I want the gospel preached. My friends already know me and it won't do them any good to hear more about me; just preach the gospel to them!"

Into the Twilight

In the latter years of Louisa Bingham Lee's life she suffered with heart problems. On more than one occasion her sons and her husband carried her almost unconscious outside her house to give her more air and oxygen to revive her. Yet she would never restrict her Church activity and loved to spend an entire day quilting at Relief Society. With her sparkling, pointed humor, she kept the sisters "in stitches." Sometimes she would be utterly spent after her strenuous sewing days at the Church and would collapse on the bed at home. But when her family and doctors cautioned her about her continuous activity, she would reply spunkily, "I am going to wear out, not rust out!" She was right, too, for she was active to the end of her eighty years.

About one year prior to her husband's death and just before Christmas, Samuel lay dying in the hospital at age seventy. Doctors had told Louisa that her husband had less than three days to live. Without hesitation she responded to that dire prediction with courage and faith: "That's what *they* think. I'm taking Father home!" She called for her sons at 10:30 P.M. to come to the hospital and administer to their father. Her faith was rewarded, for she took her husband home and he lived yet another year.

She remained a slender, attractive, well-groomed lady, whose hair stayed its natural, dark brown color until she was age eighty. This caused her to look years younger. She was alert and active until only a few hours before she died on July 27, 1959.

During the Twenty-fourth of July pioneer celebration in her final year, she sat watching the parade from the curb of a downtown street corner. Three days later, she lay critically ill in the hospital. Tubes were in both arms for intravenous injections, and she was flat on her back in her hospital bed. Verda was caring for her and was reluctant to leave her side even for a moment. Louisa insisted, however, that she go home to eat with her husband.

When Verda asked hesitantly, "But Mother, you'll be here when I get back, won't you?" Her mother perked up and replied with her typical wry humor: "Of course, I will. I can't go anyplace—I'm sewed to the bed!" She died at nine o'clock that night.

Final Tributes

Harold B. Lee's journal entries concerning his mother conclude with this tribute: "She was intensely loyal to her friends and equally vindictive toward her enemies. While never unreasonably upholding her family, she would defend them to her death against slander."

This family loyalty Elder Lee inherited from his mother.

When his mother's biography was being prepared for publication in a Church magazine the author, Jaynann Morgan Payne, came to President Lee's office to obtain his approval. As she turned to leave, President Lee stood and spontaneously offered his final tribute to his mother, saying: "She was an angel from heaven and she passed through the lights and shadows of life with great fortitude. . . . And when everyone else gave up, she didn't."

1899–1910. A decade of confidence. Peace, prosperity, and well-stocked stores. Immigrants came to America looking for work. The Wright brothers took a short but historic flight.

CHAPTER 3

Childhood (1899–1910)

SPRING 1899

The March wind
Shrills its tunes
Along the eaves,
Whistling songs of warning
Of the cold:
"Watch out! It's not yet spring,"
It seems to sing.
The winter's not yet done,
Though it be old.
It's not quite time for spring to be.

The house stands warm
And firm against the cold.
And with the birth of that first day
Of spring,
A son is born, a second son.
A name was given, Harold Bingham Lee.*

* © S. Dilworth Young 1976. Used by permission.

On a blustery March 28, 1899, Harold Bingham Lee was born in a humble cottage in Clifton, Oneida County, Idaho, the second child of Samuel Marion Lee and Louisa Emeline Bingham.

As was to be his nature, he came wide-eyed and questioning into this dreary, hard, pioneer life, without benefit of an attending physician, although aid to his mother was given by a midwife, Aunt Susan Henderson. Harold later wrote: "At the time of my birth, Father was away from home working on a canal and the weather was very stormy. It was necessary to send Bert Henderson with the news of the pending birth. There seems to have been some disappointment when I arrived, Mother having hoped for a girl."

Three years earlier an older brother, Samuel Perry, had become the firstborn of this family. Following Harold came other babies—two more brothers and two sisters. The entry of these children helped to shape that humble little cottage into a home of love and companionship.

After Harold ascended to the highest position in the Church, his brother Perry was asked if the President, as a child, had given any indication of his knowledge of his ultimate destiny as a Church leader. Perry chose to answer by quoting the lines of a Primary song sung by children: "He played as little children played, the pleasant games of youth."

Harold himself recalls his first day in school:

> In 1904, I went with Perry to visit school. Chloe Howell, the teacher, set me at some work to keep me busy, and I surprised her by writing the ABCs and by writing my name. She persuaded Mother to permit me to start school, and although I was only five years of age and the school house was located over two miles from our home, Mother consented. Among the teachers that stand out in my memory are Chloe Howell, Emma Bybee Davis, James W. Davis, and H. Perry Howell.

Perry described his younger brother and playmate in these words:

> Harold had beautiful, heavy, wavy, brown hair, and Mother, I think somewhat disappointed that her firstlings were not girls, took full advantage of his crowning glory to train his hair into dangling ring- lets that reached below his shoulders. The neighborhood ladies would exclaim him a "beautiful picture" in his Lord Fauntleroy

Left to right—Harold, Clyde, and Perry, 1904

ruffles and lace-trimmed sleeves, but no boy could tolerate such a travesty to manhood, nor did he, for too long.

We arrived at the small school every day dressed in knee pants with white starched cuffs folded back over the coat sleeves and white, sailor-collars draped down over the shoulders. And those ringlets were carefully combed and painstakingly curled, dangling down our backs for all the world to see, and pull—and scoff.

When Harold arrived at school still with his mass of beautiful hair, it may have been the first time he went into training for the hard knocks of life to come. Suffice to record that those curls caused more skinned knuckles and black eyes than either politics or religion. Finally, he had had enough. I remember now how our mother wept when he purloined a pair of scissors and literally "sawed" off one of the frontal danglers, spoiling the whole effect, which made it necessary to delete the remainder—a welcomed relief. He was at last a boy—a fat, chubby one and a pet of all the teachers.

Harold's journal concurs with this description and adds that his Grandfather Bingham finished cutting off his curls. Perry recalls:

Grandfather Bingham, who was deputy warden of the Idaho State Penitentiary, prevailed upon one of the inmates who had skill in such art, to braid the curly locks into two watch chains, which Mother kept among her treasures. Later one of them became the prized possession of my brother's wife, Fern.

Harold preserved another childhood memory in his journal:

In 1905, Mother took Perry, Clyde and me to Boise, Idaho, to visit with Grandfather and Grandmother, where I recall some visit happenings during this stay. During that time, a convict escaped from the chain gang and the bloodhounds were sent to track him down, with the traveling guard in the charge of Grandfather, following close behind. He was run down in the mountains, nearly frozen, and when word came that they were returning with the convict, Grandmother took us all in the house and pulled down the blinds lest we should see the return and be unfavorably impressed.

On another occasion, Perry and I were chased out of the guard's kitchen by the cook with a butcher knife when we were meddling in the kitchen. For his pains, the cook was put in solitary confinement and fed on bread and water for three days. One Sunday, Grandfather took me to a prison church service, and I shall never forget the sight of hundreds of prisoners, all dressed in stripes, as was the custom then.

Harold B. Lee's journal contains this brief but significant recollection of his baptism: "I was baptized a member of the Church on June 9, 1907, at Clifton, Idaho by Lester Bybee. The place was known as 'Bybee Pond' at the old lime kiln, located on the Bybee property. This was on a Sunday morning. I was confirmed the same day by Bishop E. G. Farmer."

Another never-to-be-forgotten childhood memory occurred on December 10, 1907, the night his Grandmother Bingham died. Harold recorded: "Following her death, Perry and I stayed a part of the night alone with her, which experience, to one as young as I, was not a pleasant one."

About sixty-five years later, President Lee expressed another early recollection. In an interview by a reporter from the *Church News* just prior to a general conference of the Church—now as

President of the Church—he sat in his beautiful office in the Church Administration Building and recalled his first experience at a general conference. He then had been just a small boy living with his family in Clifton, Idaho.

My father had grown up in Salt Lake City. His parents had both died and his grandmother raised him until she, too, passed away. He then lived with an aunt in Idaho.

Naturally, my father was anxious for his boys to see some of the scenes he had remembered as a boy in Salt Lake City, so it was decided that we would go down to attend general conference. He took his two oldest boys; I was second oldest. Of course, the pending conference, as such, was not our most immediate interest. We wanted to see the sights of the big city.

My earliest recollection—I was just a young lad—was sitting in the south gallery of the Salt Lake Tabernacle and looking down at the pulpit and seeing President Joseph F. Smith sitting there. I was impressed at seeing for the first time the President of the Church.

I still recall, too, that Mother fixed food for us. I remember we had fried chicken, and all we needed, too.

That was my first visit to Salt Lake City.

CACHE VALLEY

Who will dream of Cache Valley,
A jewel hidden in among
The mountains of the Wasatch?
Its lush grass fed the ponies
Of old Washakie
And other Shoshone braves,
While resting in their
Teepees on the trail
Which led
To Ogden's Hole—
And on and on
Past mighty Timpanogos,
Up the Wasatch Valley.
Its streams, swift flowing streams,
Where boys could learn
To shoot a trout
With arrows made with crudely boyish skill,
Or track a beaver to its watery home.

One sees the dust kicked up
By ponies of the braves

Returning from a hunt
In Ogden's Hole,
And sees Jim Bridger
Meet Kit Carson's men
As furs are sold
For liquid lightning.
One year's work is gone
In one summer's frenzied
Rendezvous.

Piercing the hills
From north and east,
The waters of the Bear,
Tired from their
Tumbling hurried rush
From old Bald Mountain's
Heights,
Meander through the
Valley's fertile land.

The firs are far against
The rising hills,
The red-bark willow
Lines the quiet banks,
While here and there
The cottonwoods rise up
To shade the deer and elk.
Wild ducks and geese
Find here a happy resting place
En route to summer—or to winter—
Homes.

Into the valley come the pioneers,
Peter Maughan, that rugged son
Of England, and others with him,
Spreading out upon the valley floor,
Plowing up the fertile bottomland,
Fencing in their pastures
With aspen poles—
Pastures lush with grass.

And after them, plodding
To its northern end,
Go other pioneers
Who clear the land
And make their farms at

Clifton town,
A sleepy pleasant place to live,
Where two score gentle
Kindly men make home,
Their calloused hands the sign
Of honest toil.*

ON THE FARM

A small boy learns of many things
Upon a farm.
He catches pollywogs
And sees that some
Have legs while others don't,
Then wiser folks tell him
That they are baby frogs.
He learns what holds
The water skaters up;
That swimming in an
Irrigation ditch is fun.

He takes the cows to pasture
After milking time,
And brings them in again,
And knows that evening shadows
Are not like those of early morn.
Ofttimes he sees the
Wad come up the gullet
As a cow starts chewing,
And after a while he sees her swallow
And bring up another one,
Then wonders why he can't
Do that himself.

He learns to milk a cow,
And notices the music of this
Act—the harsh metallic sound
Of rhythmic ringing,
Soon changing into softer
Sighing as the foam rises higher,
Higher in the pail.
Then, too, the family cat, ten feet away,
Enjoys a squirt of fresh warm milk.
Some deep
And undefined urge is satisfied.*

Family Life on the Farm

The growing-up years of Harold Lee as a barefoot, overall-clad lad, working with his father and brothers in the field to meet the unrelenting pressures of family life on the farm, were not untypical of the era. He later described that life to his grandchildren:

We lived on a farm of about a hundred acres at the foot of the mountain to the west of us and about two miles north of the ward meetinghouse and schoolhouse. There was a string of houses running from between the meetinghouse and our place, which gave the name "Stringtown" to the string of houses where we lived.

It was necessary for us to work hard on the farm and quite often there was little income to show for it. We did raise all the foodstuffs needed; we had gardens, orchards, cows, chickens, and pigs. We raised enough feed for our cows, whereas they produced the milk and the cream and occasionally cheese and some to market. We couldn't produce some things that were necessary, so we took eggs to the country store and traded for the things that we couldn't have otherwise.

On days of celebration, like the Fourth of July, we were given two or three dimes to spend on such a day, but we knew that if we spent it all on that day, there was a long season ahead of us when we might not have anything to spend, and we usually wound up with a few nickels left over.

We took our grain to a mill at Weston, Idaho, and from the returns we got our flour, our bran and shorts for feed, as well as our cereals.

Perry adds his recollection of their agricultural way of life:

In our family everyone was required to work in some degree, according to his ability. Our father was a firm believer that we were here to literally "work out our salvation," with the emphasis on work. It became an axiom that, if we would eat well, we must labor for the things which we needed. Our garden was one of the main projects, and under the kindly persuasion of a wise father, each was led to do his fair share.

In those days on the farm, food storage for the future, especially in the winter, was a way of life; no last-minute trip to the grocery store or supermarket was possible. Our milk supply, as well as meat, eggs, and potatoes and other vegetables, were produced on the farm.

Milk in the summer was kept fresh and sweet in the sod-covered milk house that spanned a running stream near the house. Six-quart pans of milk were cooled therein and later skimmed. The resulting cream was hand-churned, and molded into pounds of butter to be bartered for groceries or for family use, and was stored in the milk-house to be drawn upon as needed. The by-product of the churning process was honest-to-goodness buttermilk flecked with tiny nodules of butter—a gourmet's delight.

Potatoes and vegetables were stored in an underground earth-topped pit. Eggs were stored in jars of waterglass. Wheat was taken from the thresher at harvest time to the mill and exchanged for fifty-pound sacks of flour—a year's supply. A steer and a hog were butchered in the fall, and then smoked or otherwise preserved to be used through the year.

Haying time brought various jobs. Harold graduated from riding the derrick horse that was used to lift the huge forks of hay onto the growing stack, to pitching the hay onto the wagon from the cured haycocks. He also learned to mow and rake the ripened alfalfa and other fodder grasses. He became adept at driving the four-in-hand team that hauled the lumbering wagonload of sugar beets to the loading dock.

These and other taxing, but interesting, tasks he mastered one by one, which conditioned the growing boy for the man he was to become. In the descriptive language of the scriptures, "He increased in wisdom and in stature and in favor with God and man." (Luke 2:52.)

PROTECTED AND PRESERVED

"Through my childhood there seemed to be a guiding hand over me." So wrote Harold B. Lee in his personal life history.

Perhaps he was recalling a close call he had with death during a bout with pneumonia when he was a young man: His mother bent over her seventeen-year-old son once more to feel his feverish head and listen to his tight, labored breathing. It was after midnight, and Harold's chest disease had not seemed to respond to his mother's mustard plasters. Anxiety clutched at her heart and she knew she must do something quickly, or her son would die in a few hours.

She hurried to the back porch and opened a large sack of onions, filled her apron, and went into the kitchen. After slicing a large panful of onions she dumped them into an empty flour sack and covered her son's chest with that wet, juicy sack. Then she prayed and waited for a miracle.

By morning his breathing was improved, and he was over the crisis. When the family praised Harold's mother for saving his life, she merely said: "Oh, but I didn't save his life. The Lord did. He just expects us to do everything we can do to help."

But this was not the only time that a protective influence seemed to be watching over him through his childhood years on the farm.

"During these years I had two exciting experiences," Harold wrote in his life's history.

> Mother was making soap and had a large tub of lye preparation stored on a high shelf to keep it out of the reach of the younger children. She wanted to take it down, and since I was the only one home she enlisted my help. We climbed up on a chair and began to steady it down. When it was exactly above my head, our hold slipped and the tub and its burning lye water dashed over my face, head, and arms. As quickly as she could act, Mother seized me so I wouldn't run and kicked off the lid from a jar of beet pickles she had just made, and with her right hand cupped, dipped out the reddened, pickle vinegar from the beets over my burning face, neck and arms to stop the eating of the lye and save me from being badly scarred. What could have been a tragedy was averted because of her inspired action. Often she was intuitively led by the Spirit.

> On another occasion, Father was away on the header and Perry and I had just finished doing the morning chores. I had just finished pouring the milk through the separator, which was a machine which separated the milk from the cream. While waiting for the separator to stop, I foolishly and absentmindedly was tapping my fingers on the outside wheel as it turned around. Not paying attention to what I was doing, I unwittingly put my fingers into the cogs and suffered a severe injury that tore the flesh from the first joint of the third finger of my right hand. Mother was sitting at the table under a bowery just outside and I ran out and put my finger, with the bone protruding, in front of her. She turned ill at the sight. Miraculously, Bishop Erastus E. Farmer appeared on the scene at the moment needed and squeezed the mashed flesh around the bone so it would heal. Mother bound up the wounded finger and the flesh began to grow. While my finger in adult life was somewhat disfigured, it never prevented me from playing the piano.

OBEDIENCE

The young boy Harold,
Walking toward a barn,
Heard a voice

'Way down within him say,
"Don't go in that barn
Today!"
And, feeling that
He should obey,
Turned,
And went another way.
In later years
He told the tale
About the voice
He had heard.
Then someone said:
"What was in the barn
To cause you harm?"
"I do not know," was the reply,
"I did not go."*

Harold cited in his journal two more examples of his being protected:

I had accompanied Father to the "flat" below Dayton, where we owned a forty-acre farm. Just over the fence to the east of the property, some old sheds and barns had blown down, and I set out on a tour of exploration. I had just parted the wires to crawl through when I heard a voice as distinctly as a person could speak, command: "Harold, don't go near that lumber over there!" I looked around quickly, wondering where the voice had come from and frightened at the unusual experience, and then ran as fast as possible away from some unknown danger. I have wondered what the danger could have been and have imagined everything from rattlesnakes to rusty nails.

During my early childhood, my grandmother lived in the old home and Mother used to send meals down with my older brother, Perry, and myself. It was a dark, stormy night when we went down this time, and I stood on the porch cleaning my feet, holding onto the sill, but my foot slipped and I fell backwards; my left hand fell on a broken bottle and cut a gash four or five inches long. I bear the scar of that accident. The treatment Mother gave me was to burn a sock and sift the ashes from the sock down into the open wound. Somehow it worked and avoided the possibility of blood poisoning. This injury kept me from attending school most of the year.

In telling these experiences to his grandchildren, Harold B. Lee would often demonstrate the scars on his fingers and his left palm to authenticate his boyhood escapes from near dangerous mishaps.

* © S. Dilworth Young 1976. Used by permission.

Among my earliest recollections was an occasion when my instinctive meddling got me into some trouble. Mother was putting up fruit, and as she finished there were sometimes juices left over which she allowed me to drink. On this occasion, I went to do the same thing, but after taking a few swallows I discovered that this was lye water she had put in to get rid of the burned fruit which was sticking to the inside of the pan. This time I remember my mother and Grandmother Bingham poured olive oil down my throat to save me from being fatally injured.

In my young boyhood there were many occasions, as I recall the earlier years of my life, when my mother's instructive and intuitive understanding prompted her to know that help was needed. Once on a stormy night, she directed my father to go and search for me, only to find that my horse had stumbled while crossing a stream of water and thrown me into a pool of half-frozen mud. My mother had known that help was needed.

One other incident stands out vividly in my memory. There was a severe thunderstorm raging near the mountain where our home was located. Our family, consisting of my grandmother, my mother, and two or three of the younger children, were seated in the kitchen before an open door, watching the great display of nature's fireworks. A flash of chain lightning followed by an immediate loud clap of thunder indicated that the lightning had struck very close.

I was playing back and forth in the doorway when suddenly and without warning, my mother gave me a vigorous push that sent me sprawling backwards out of the doorway. At that instant, a bolt of lightning came down the chimney of the kitchen stove, out through the kitchen's open doorway, and split a huge gash from top to bottom in a large tree immediately in front of the house. Had it not been for Mother's intuitive action, and if I had remained in the door opening, I wouldn't be writing this story today.

My mother could never explain her split-second decision. All I know is that my life was spared because of her impulsive, intuitive nature.

Years later, when I saw the deep scar on that large tree at the old family home, I could only say from a grateful heart, "Thank the Lord for that precious gift possessed in abundant measure by my own mother and by many of the faithful mothers, through whom heaven can be very near in time of need."

Harold B. Lee often used these powerful personal experiences to teach the responsibility of parenthood and to emphasize the spiritual influences which could come to fathers and mothers in directing and protecting the lives of their children. His summary teachings on this point follow:

Within every person born into this world there is a heavenly gift which is called by the Lord in his revelations, "The Light of Christ, or the Light of Truth, or the Spirit of God," which even in early childhood gives to every person the ability to tell the difference between what is right and of the Lord, and that which is of the world. This might be called our conscience, or the voice of the Spirit of God within us.

When a person grows older, added to this first heavenly gift is given the gift of the Holy Ghost, which comes as a blessing from the elders of the Church following baptism. This gift, as explained by the Master, was "to teach us all things, bring all things to our remembrance, and to even show us things to come."

When one becomes a father or a mother, it is especially important that they prepare themselves to receive by these wonderful gifts from the Lord, a greater gift of understanding in raising their children, in order to make certain that their children are taught properly as commanded by the Lord, and to receive heaven-sent instructions or warnings for their family. This might be called intuition or the voice of the Lord coming into one's mind from heavenly sources to safeguard the welfare of the family as long as they are yet in the home. Therefore the parents have the responsibility of teaching and training in correct principles until their children are all old enough and have the stability and responsibility to make mature judgments and right decisions.

1910–1920. The nation became mobile. Men fought the Kaiser Bill, while women got the vote, drank, and smoked. Model T Fords rolled off assembly lines, and Mary Pickford was America's sweetheart. Babe Ruth hit his first major-league home run for the Boston Red Sox.

CHAPTER 4

Youth (1910–1920)

CHILDHOOD

What does the Lord say to his
Chosen servant?
Grow, my son, grow in knowledge
And wisdom.
Know, my son, the ways of the
Wind, blowing from
Gog and Magog,
The ways of the cottontail and
Weasel.
Know the painting of the
Lord upon his easel,
The sky at sunset,
The deep purple across the valley.
Such color cannot be
Matched by man.

My son, you can
See the wind waving
The ripening grain
Across the field.
The yield is yours
For your good
And for your food.
Feel the freedom of
Climbing trees.
Feel the strong branches
Against your knees.
Climb high, and in
Your childhood imagery
Reach and touch the sky
Behind its curtain of
Blue. I am where
You can find me,
If you pray
Every day.

Hear my voice in the
Wind and the rain.
But better—seek the
Still small voice with
Which I speak
To the humble and the meek.
You heard it once and
Remembered well—
To hear it say:
"Don't go in that barn today"—
Now learn to hear it as
You grow,
And know that I the Lord
Am teaching you to
Know of me, the Lord—if you
Would learn the harmony
Of my holy word.

Each spirit comes from paradise
To grace a home upon the earth—
His talents, his desires,
Hopes, and loyalties
Well hidden in the mortal
Clay which is his birth.

> Instinctively this boy
> Shied from the pranks
> And little sins of other boys,
> And so sought other
> Things to occupy his time.
> His mother, wise to his
> Unspoken thoughts,
> Provided music. So he grew,
> Loving the chords,
> Learning, absorbing, as one
> Who hears
> Within his heart
> The vast eternal music
> Of the spheres.
>
> Such music as the Lord
> Would have him learn
> Found echo in his
> Heart;
> Apart from other boys,
> He learned the art.*

Harold B. Lee was ordained to the early offices of the priesthood as follows: Deacon: Dec. 20, 1909, by A. D. Henderson; Teacher: Feb. 23, 1913, by S. M. Lee [his father]; Priest: Jan. 24, 1915, by S. M. Lee [his father]; Elder: Nov. 11, 1917, by James L. Williams.

Because Harold started school nearly two years before other boys his age, he was ordained a deacon along with his classmates, although he was only ten years of age.

Harold remembered in these words his emergence from boyhood to young manhood, as marked by his graduation from the district school:

> I graduated from the district school eighth grade in 1912 at the age of thirteen. My teacher was H. Perry Howell. The graduation exercises were held for the county at Franklin, Idaho. Father, Mother, and I, with Bishop J. W. Davis and his wife, drove a team of horses and a buggy from Clifton to Lewiston the day before the exercises. After staying overnight at the Bybee home, we made the remainder of the trip the next day.

Harold's brother, Perry, with whom he shared many youthful experiences away at school, describes his brother as follows:

Always studious in school and in his auxiliary and priesthood classes, he early displayed a talent for music. He charmed his teachers and had ready rapport with his classmates and a wide circle of friends. He early learned to play the piano under the tutelage of a Scottish lady [Mrs. Sarah Gerard], who was prone to rap knuckles at the sound of a wrong note. Soon he was playing the piano or organ for Primary and Sunday School. Rest-time from farm labors found him at the piano, adding to his skill and to the pleasure and delight of homefolks at the sounds of music which he pleasantly provoked.

Perry also recalls the origin of the musical interest:

Our father surprised us one day as we were convalescing from a bout with scarlet fever by bringing into our sickroom two shining instruments—a baritone horn for Harold and a cornet for me. That cured the fever in jig time, but I'm afraid the raucous sounds that came from those shiny horns in the learning process gave our parents many a headache.

One of Harold's earliest adventures into the world of music resulted when a man named Cox came to town and organized the Clifton Silver Concert Band. From this experience came increasingly more interest with various instruments and musical organizations.

High School Days

Harold's personal history recalls the major change in his life when he went away to school for the first time:

In the fall of 1912, I entered the Oneida Stake Academy at the age of thirteen years. Mother had not yet permitted me to wear long pants, and when I entered high school I was the youngest of the class and was one of the only two in school who were wearing knee pants.

When I entered school I was anxious to continue my music training. The high school band offered the best opportunity. My first instruments were an alto and the French horn. Later in my school, when I had attained a bit more ability, I was invited to join the Preston Military Band, and the second year I took up the baritone. Under the tutelage of Professor Charles J. Engar, I played through the summer and winter with the Preston Band. For these four years we concertized on all patriotic and civic occasions and were paid a fee for our services.

Perry and I were fitted up in a room and started our housekeeping in the home of Robert Daines, located across the street from the Oneida Stake Academy. This was a Church-operated school, which later was donated to the state and became Preston High School.

Living in the same house were a total of thirteen boys, and one could easily guess the impromptu parties staged. Underneath our room were the quarters of the principal of the school, J. Robert Robinson. On various occasions, he appeared and soundly scolded us for the "ceiling-cracking" performance we sometimes staged.

In my second year at high school I became acquainted with Ethel Cole of Fairview, Idaho, and during our high school years and until I went on my mission in 1920, she and I kept up a rather constant, intimate friendship either by correspondence or by occasional visits. I remember her as my first "sweetheart" and the only girl with whom I kept steady company prior to my mission. I always admired her as a genuine friend.

Debater, Sportsman

In my senior year at high school, 1915–16, I was extremely busy with a number of school activities outside of my school work. One of my debating teammates was Sparrel Huff. The Oneida Academy was in a league with the Fielding Academy of Paris, Idaho, and the subject to be debated was "Resolved That the Monroe Doctrine Should Be Abolished." We defended the negative side and Louis Ballif and Irel Lowe the affirmative. Prior to the finals with the Paris teams, we staged debates all over the adjoining counties.

Never in the history of our school had a team won from Fielding Academy at Paris, but we succeeded in turning the tables in a thrilling two-to-one decision over a Paris team, composed of Nellie Parker and George Bateman. They gave us a banquet following the debate, and the next day we returned to Preston as conquering "heroes," where our home team was victorious and our student body gave us a real reception in a special assembly.

My favorite sport was basketball, and at the time I attended high school it was the major athletic sport. In my junior year I was elected athletic reporter for the *Oneida,* the school paper; and in my senior year, I was elected the student manager of athletics, which was the "plum" of all school offices because it carried the privilege of accompanying all athletic teams on their trips to handle the business affairs while en route, all expenses being paid by the school. Art Rynearson was the coach, and we were fortunate in having a team that competed on even terms with college teams like the UAC. Our team played games that took us from Rexburg, Idaho, on the north to Ogden, Utah, on the south. It was often my responsibility, also, to "scout" rival teams.

Besides managing the team, I gained considerable skill as a player. I was a member of the senior team that won the class championship. Following my graduation I continued to play and enjoyed some reputation as a basketball player.

In the graduating class there were but five girls and twenty-five boys; a great bunch of fellows. On the night of Founders' Day we climbed to the top of the flag pole over the Academy and nailed our class colors, and then each in turn climbed to the flag and kissed the colors. After singing and giving class yells we retired to our rooms, and awoke in the morning to discover that during the night our colors were taken down by the junior class. A grand fight followed which was finally stopped by officers.

Teacher Training

In the summer of 1916, at the age of seventeen, I attended the Albion State Normal School at Albion, Idaho, to receive preparatory training to become a teacher. This was a fine school, providing me some of the finest teachers of my lifetime. The laws of Idaho required a rigid test in fifteen subjects in order to qualify, and I spent a very strenuous summer in intensive study, losing twenty pounds in weight, but [I] gained my objective, passing the required examination with an average grade of 89 percent.

Albion was a quaint little old-fashioned town twenty or thirty miles from the nearest railroad at Burley, Idaho. Practically nothing was there but the school, which was splendid. There were no amusements except at the school, and the old board sidewalks indicated the general backwardness of the inhabitants. Removed as it was from all attractions that might detract from school, I think I never absorbed so much knowledge as during the summers of 1916 and 1917 when I earned my second- and third-class certificates. The second year I played in the town band with Lee M. Lockhard, and played baseball on the team from the school.

During both summers I lived at the home of the Burgess family of Albion.

First Teaching Assignment

Although only age seventeen, I was employed to teach my first school during the winter of 1916–17, at the Silver Star School,

Oneida Stake Academy debating team, 1915–16: Sparrel Huff and Harold B. Lee

Oneida Stake Academy basketball team, 1915: Harold, team manager, standing at far right

about five miles south of Weston, Idaho. Here in a one-room school, I had some real experience. With about twenty to twenty-five pupils, I had most of the grades represented from the first to the eighth grade. My program consisted of twenty-eight classes each day. So conscientious was I that I would count the youngsters on the grounds, and if they were all there, I would ring the bell, although it was many times not much after 8:30 a.m. Almost nightly I placed my school problems before the Lord, and although I never worried so much over a work, the Lord never deserted me and I learned some of the most valuable lessons of self-mastery of my life.

When I signed with the school board, I drew lots with them for my compensation. They wanted to pay me $60 and I wanted $65 a month. They flipped a coin and I lost and was paid the $60 a month, but I also was given an extra $15 a month for board and room with the family of Lars Rasmussen. This included furnishing feed for my horse, which I rode back and forth from home on the weekends.

When I came to take over the school, the board cautioned me against allowing the children to walk the picket fence surrounding the school for fear of injury. Within the first week, I looked out of the window and discovered my first-grader standing on his head on the fence. With my Kodak I took his picture, with feet pointing aloft, to show the trustees when they next came to warn me further about the danger of the picket fence.

Apparently this first-grader, the only one in this tiny one-room school, became famous or infamous. All the Lee family knew about him. Perry, Harold's brother, reported fifty-seven years later: "His lone first-grader, Varsal by name, was either his greatest problem or his prize pupil, for I heard his name muttered often in his nighttime dreams as he visited home on weekends. I remember his name still, and I am sure Harold has not forgotten him."

Oxford School

From the Silver Star School, Harold, now eighteen years of age, was promoted to Oxford, Idaho, where he became teacher and principal of a larger school at an increased salary. He led in the activities of the school as well as the sports of the community, of which he became an integral part. Of this year he records:

This one-room school was the community center where all dances were held. A banjo, violin, and a portable organ served as instruments in an orchestra. The dances would go until midnight, when a halt was called while the women prepared their coffee,

Silver Star School, Weston, Idaho, 1916–17—first teaching
appointment

District school at Oxford, Idaho, where Harold (standing at right on steps) became
principal at age eighteen

cake, and sandwiches, and the men went outside to get their whiskey and beer which had been hauled from Utida, the state line, and kept for the occasion. Following this interlude the dance continued until daylight.

In the following year I was employed at $90 per month to become the principal of the district school at Oxford, Idaho, with Velma Sperry and Tressie Lincoln as associate teachers. Oxford had the reputation of having a rough crowd of boys, and the threat had been reported to me that I wouldn't last long in the school as the principal. In solving the situation, my basketball experience stood me in good stead. Because of my good size, I taught these big boys, some of whom were older than I, to play basketball, and during the lunch hours, I dressed in basketball togs and played with and against them, but as fortune would have it, I maintained sufficient dignity to win their confidence as their principal, and also win the kind of friendship that has lasted even to this day.

I was principal of this school for three winters and was there during the severe influenza epidemic of 1918, our school being quarantined for some months. We had just reopened the school when every family but two came down with the disease, and it became necessary for neighboring towns to assist in supplying food and nursing until their recovery.

While I was there we organized the Oxford Athletic Club, composed of the town fellows. I played a forward position on the first team and we traveled into all the neighboring towns to play. This activity gave me some prestige in the town. Those were days when the rules were lax, and I bear today scars of some of those encounters.

Because my father had financed me through school, and I was staying at home, I turned over my paychecks from teaching school to him and then paid my extra expenses by playing in a dance orchestra. A family by the name of Frew had just moved into Oxford, Idaho, and bought a large ranch. Two of the boys had played in the Lagoon Resort Orchestra. One was a violinist and the other was a trap drummer. They auditioned for others to join them, looking for a trumpet player, a piano player, and they also wanted a slide trombone player. They tried out one of the men who had a slide trombone, but he wasn't sufficiently schooled in dance time to gain acceptance, so he urged me to take his trombone and fill the position. I had been taught music in my school days at home by Mrs. Sarah Gerard, so that I played the organ and the piano with enough ability to be the ward organist. Because of my ability to read both bass and treble cleffs, and because I could play a wind instrument, the only other requirement I needed to play the trombone was to learn the various positions on the slide to make the various

Harold B. Lee and his ladies chorus, 1919

notes. This required long hours of practice day and night, mostly nights, to the distraction of my entire family, who was glad when I finally got enough ability to play without this harrowing experience for the family.

We were the only dance orchestra from Logan, Utah on the south to Pocatello, Idaho on the north, and it was not uncommon for us to play two and three nights a week. The roads were muddy, the nights were dark, the automobiles were poor. In the wintertime the roads were hazardous. On occasion it was almost morning before we arrived home. After a few hours' rest I then went back to preside over the school. This, besides playing basketball, began to take its toll, and I came down with a severe case of pneumonia.

For three years I played slide trombone in this five-piece orchestra which played from town to town in our valley. Known as the Frew Orchestra, it was composed of Dick Frew, violin; Chap Frew, the drums; Marion Howell, the cornet; Reese Davis, the piano; and myself on the trombone.

The Frews were always drinking when possible and indulging in conduct at a level far below what it should have been. I know that through those years, my folks "held their breath" lest I allow this kind of association to overcome me.

CHURCH CALLINGS

Practically the only Church activity I engaged in at this time was as president of the elder's quorum, which was composed of the elders of the Clifton, Oxford, and Dayton wards. Walter Hatch and William Hardwick served as my counselors.

For two or three years I was organist of the Clifton Ward, and in connection with this activity in music I organized and trained a group of girls into a ladies' chorus. When I left for my mission, these girls gave me a gold ring.

*Years
of
Preparation*

———

1920–1941

1920–1922. The search for normalcy after the end
of World War I and the Russian Nationalities War.
The Essex automobile was the first expensive
sedan. The Jazz Age began.

CHAPTER 5

Western States
Mission (1920–1922)

A mission is a university,
Teaching not of earth
But things of God,
The Father of us all,
And of his Son,
His well-beloved Son.
One learns to hear the
Whispering,
The Holy Ghost is talking
To him now—
Of where to go and
What to do
To find the hearts
Of those he seeks,
And what to speak,
And when—
Those words which
Burn into the hearts

Of men
To bring them to the truth.
This youth,
Now fully grown,
With confidence went forth
And proved his worth
In bringing God's choice work
To men on earth.*

Having assumed so much responsibility for one so young in years, Harold B. Lee was maturing in personality; his mental training had demanded discipline. Now came his greatest development with the abrupt changes in life-style brought about by his call to the mission field.

In September of 1920, at the age of twenty-one, I received a call to fill a mission in the Western States Mission, with headquarters at Denver, Colorado.

There was no indoctrination for missionaries at that time. I was instructed to obtain my temple ordinances, so on November 6, 1920, Father and I went to the Logan Temple, where I received my endowments and made preparations to leave home to be in Salt Lake City to be set apart on November 9. Mother was at home with a new baby and unable to go to the temple with us. I never realized how great a gap my family filled in my life until I bade them goodbye.

The parting words of my father when I left for the mission field were, "Harold, my boy, your father and mother are looking for big things from you."

No one was "greener" and more unused to city life than I was, and as a result, I lost my bearings and got turned around in Salt Lake. At the hands of the Presiding Patriarch, Hyrum G. Smith, I received my second patriarchal blessing.

After a one-hour meeting at the Church Office Building, I was set apart on November 9, 1920, by Brigham H. Roberts of the First Council of the Seventy. Elder Roberts promised me I would go and return in safety.

In company with Elder Owen H. Martin, of Salt Lake, I left for my mission at 5:30 p.m. on November 10, 1920, over the Union Pacific Railroad. We arrived in Denver the next day, Armistice Day, at noon, and were met at the depot by President John M. Knight and a group of missionaries.

We were taken to the Denver Chapel at the corner of Seventh Avenue and Pearl Street, where a baptismal service was in session. The first missionary work I did was Relief Society visiting with Elder Daniel Peterson and the lady missionaries.

* © S. Dilworth Young 1976. Used by permission.

I was assigned to work with Elder Willis J. Woodbury, of Salt Lake. He was a cello player, and when he discovered I could play the piano, he insisted on regular musical practices.

We often carried his cello and some music with us when we went tracting, and during the day we were invited in to sing and play, thereby opening the way for the preaching of the gospel. With this approach usually we succeeded in being invited into three homes a day, which was about a record for us. In every home we were complimented and invited back again. After playing and preaching, we made real friends at each visit.

HUMBLE BEGINNINGS

It will be comforting to all missionaries who have represented the Church to know that President Lee began his labors in the same humble and discouraging manner as did they. Of his first day of tracting door-to-door in Denver he said: "The first lady we met shut the door in our faces while we were trying to tell her our message. We had eight gospel conversations, one lady promised to attend our church, and only two refused our literature."

What missionary hasn't approached his first priesthood ordinance work with some nervousness and apprehension? It was the same for the young Elder from Clifton, Idaho. His companion, Elder Woodbury, rehearsed with him over and over the anointing prayer as they were en route to bless a little girl. But when the time came to perform his first priesthood ordinance, Elder Lee's careful preparation failed him. He summarized the experience in these words:

> When I began to anoint the girl I forgot the whole prayer and made a mess of things. While we were going home Elder Woodbury asked me if I would get sore at him if he told me something. Reassured, he said, "For pete's sake, don't ever do it like that." I will never forget that lesson.

Months later he was to be introduced to another stern discipline of missionary work, preaching to the public as they passed by at a street meeting. His written recollection of this experience follows:

> We held our first street meeting last Saturday night, and they gave me the "honor" of being one of the speakers, along with Sister Dunn and Elder Bergeson. If you want a thrill you sure want to try street preaching. "Scared," did you say? I thought I would surely faint until I got started, then somehow I forgot myself and everyone

else, I'm afraid. We are preaching on the corner of 19th and Welton Streets in Denver, and succeeded in keeping a few people sticking around all the time. I think if I keep on finding out how little I know, by the time my mission is over I will be convinced I don't know anything. Like the old professor at school used to say: "It's all right to say you don't know if you don't say it too often." But with me, it's getting quite frequent.

Other early tracting experiences were typically humiliating to this inexperienced missionary. His diary records:

> While tracting I sold a lady two small books and promised to bring back to her a Book of Mormon the next day. I was as tickled as a boy with new shoes, but when I went back the lady wouldn't even come to the door. I sure thought I had a convert there.

A month later, the story was not much different. He writes:

> We spent over five hours and never got a decent conversation. One lady, when I told her I was a Mormon, told me to go on down the street, that she had had more arguments with Mormon Elders. I asked her what she disagreed with and she said, "Oh, this faith and works stuff." She believed that "by grace ye are saved." When I attempted to quote from the scriptures, she slammed the door with the invective: "Go on down the street."

These disheartening but strengthening experiences were beginning to mold the leadership qualities of the young missionary. He had baptized several families and now was beginning to love his missionary work, despite its discouragements. After seven months in the mission field, he wrote:

> We have, all totaled in the conference, about fourteen baptisms for this month, and if ever I felt like working, it is now, when I am just beginning to appreciate the responsibility that rests upon me. I am praying that I will always be kept just a "high private in the rear ranks" so that I can continue to do the work I am beginning to love.

Leadership Debut

Elder Lee's desires for obscurity were not granted. When he had been in the field but nine months, his mission president called him into his office and told him that he had been selected to be the next president of the Denver Conference. President Knight's words were, "I am just giving you a chance to show what is in you." Later in his journal Elder Lee wrote:

With companion, Elder Willis J. Woodbury, on first day of tracting

John M. Knight, president of Western States Mission

I know now I have gained what I'm sure Father would call "big things"—the confidence of President Knight.

Only nine short months today since I arrived in Denver; and when I think back on all the wonderful experiences that have been mine in that time, I feel as though it had been but a dream, but I thank the Lord continually. The crying necessities of today wake me up to the fact that I must be working always if God is to accomplish anything through me.

Presiding over a "conference" in those days meant being the presiding authority over all the missionaries, branch presidents, and Saints in a geographical area now referred to as a district in the mission field. Elder Lee's territory extended northward from Denver to the Wyoming line—including Fort Collins, Greeley, Longmont, Boulder, and Steamboat Springs—and from Littleton on the south to the Nebraska border on the east. He had supervision of thirty-five missionaries.

From this time forward to the end of his mission he was constantly engaged in reorganizing the branches, advising the Saints on their personal lives—including marital counseling on pending divorces—administering to and blessing the Saints, solving the problems of the missionaries, and attempting, as much as time permitted, to continue to do active proselyting work. The demands on his time, energy, physical strength, and moral character were heavy and unrelenting. But such burdens were also the training for his amazing leadership skills as they developed and tested the young spiritual giant growing within him.

Many new experiences came to him as a result of his being conference president. His first marriage ceremony was for Oscar A. Anderson and Jennie Voorhees. He wrote the following of his first experience in arranging for and taking charge of a funeral service: "It was the request of the family that I talk, and this was my first attempt in a funeral. Although I felt pretty shaky in the knees, everything went all right and without a 'hitch.' " He added, "From now on, I suppose, the few missionaries that are here will have plenty to do in the way of preaching, with two street meetings every week besides the Sunday night meeting."

Such leadership positions had mundane roles, too, for Elder Lee's diary records that when the Elders went away on other assignments, he made the fire to heat the water for the baptismal services.

In retrospect, knowing that Harold B. Lee conceived of and introduced an improved approach to home teaching during the 1960s, it is interesting to see the earliest emergence of those concepts as they developed in the Denver Conference in 1921. Faced with the immense task of caring for the needs of all the Saints, yet desiring to be actively involved in missionary proselyting work most of the time, Elder Lee devised a new plan to shift to the missionaries the responsibility of "watching over the Saints," instead of attempting to handle the entire job himself as his predecessor had done. He felt certain that the missionaries would take a bigger interest in the work if they knew he was not going to assume all these extra assignments himself. At the same time he organized the Elders into continuing companionships in the firm belief that if they were kept together for designated periods of time, "two by two," they would be more circumspect and many embarrassing predicaments could be avoided. This was to be a firm conviction that would always remain in his leadership philosophy, for in later years he preached the same counsel for even the travels of the General Authorities.

Throughout the conference area the plan developed in the small branches as well as in Denver; instead of having the conference president visit the Saints all the time, he assigned the Elders to call on them once a month, a format similar to the ward teaching practices at that time in the strong stakes in Utah. In this manner, better "watch care" was given as the Saints were urged to attend to their duties, thereby relieving the conference president of much of that burden.

Later, he reported in a letter how the new plan was working:

> We have our visiting districts arranged now so they can be covered in the shortest amount of time by having each missionary study his districts and arrange in rotation those that are near together. We are gradually working in a few of the local members of the priesthood, and someday I hope to be able to step out and leave the visiting entirely to the branch officers. I believe most of the families have given up the idea of having a visit from the conference president once a week, as my predecessor, Harry Jensen, did.

In addition to the heavy burdens he carried for the families under his jurisdiction, with five divorces pending at one point, Elder Lee devoted his major attention to developing the effectiveness of missionary work. One day he recorded in his diary:

> With Elders Kelsey and Allred I had a fine day tracting. I sent them alone and when I got around the block I found them sitting under a tree utterly disgusted because they couldn't talk at the homes. After I preached "Mormonism" to them for fifteen minutes to give them an idea of what to say, they started out and had a very successful time, some of the conversations lasting half an hour.

The remainder of that first year in the mission field was spent in similar leadership and teaching experiences with the missionaries, such as urging them to wear their "derbies" in Denver and locating the elders in Greeley for the winter, where they paid fifteen dollars rent per month for an excellent room. In a letter during this period he expressed his attitude on missionary converts as follows:

> I almost feel as a little kid today and I cannot help but be happy. If all those who have promised to be baptized appear, there will be twelve or fourteen new members of the Church after our baptismal service today. Of course, many have experienced the satisfaction

that comes when you are able to measure the effectiveness of your work by converts. Although our success can't possibly be measured in that way, yet therein is the fascination of missionary work.

One morning during study class, word reached the Elders that a member's little girl was dying. President Knight sent Elder Lee and the matron, Sister Winmill, to go to the home. They arrived just after the babe had died and found everything at the home in confusion. The hearse came while they were there, and they did their best to console the sorrowing mother. The sisters from the mission came and cleaned the house and washed the clothing, while Elder Lee went with the father and mother to make arrangements for the burial. The coffin cost $35, the hearse $15, embalming $20, and a burial lot $250, making a total of $320—more, including burial clothing. The father was making only $20 a week to keep a family of eight. Where would the money come from? Such problems were typical of the struggles of the conference president in Denver in 1921.

At times, such constant responsibility had its depressing side effects. One day he recorded in his journal:

> Felt pretty blue all day because of many griefs and complaints brought by the missionaries and from different Saints. Felt as incapable as a babe and sure acted like one, too. Elders Hood and Peterson both seemed to sense my feelings and pledged the most encouraging kind of support.

Other entries, however, expressed the brighter side of his labors, such as these comments on his attitude toward his leadership appointment and his love for his fellow workers:

> With such a splendid bunch of missionaries, I'm sure the president expects a great deal to be accomplished. Many times have I prayed that God would make me worthy to be a leader among such fine people. When the president selected me as conference president, he told me he was giving me a chance to show what was in me. He certainly has played fair with me, and if I fail it will be because I wasn't a big enough man for Denver.

SECOND YEAR

Friday, November 11, 1921, marked completion of his first year in the mission field. The next month was a busy one as he prepared for a district conference. The first session, on a Friday, featured a priesthood meeting with twenty-seven missionaries in attendance. All had been asked to fast, and the meeting lasted six hours and fifteen minutes, during which time every missionary was asked to express his true feelings. His own reactions were recorded in his journal:

> When conference finally arrived I was as happy as a little child, so much so, in fact, that when my turn came to talk it was very nearly impossible. Through sheer joy I could hardly speak. Never before have I been able to appreciate real people who are doing their best to help in God's great work, and words fail me in expressing my love toward them. We had a force of twenty-seven in attendance, six lady missionaries and twenty-one Elders.

After the conference President Knight and Elder Lee had a "splendid talk," during which President Knight told him how pleased he was with the meetings. Discussing the affairs of the conference, President Knight promised to give Elder Lee two Elders to work in Fort Collins and to maintain a force of thirteen Elders in Denver. Missionary productivity at that time was eight baptisms per Elder, but Elder Lee had hopes of raising that to around ten before Christmas 1921.

On Saturday and Sunday, February 18–19, 1922, the missionaries in Denver were stimulated immensely by a visit from Elder James E. Talmage of the Council of the Twelve. Arriving during a baptismal service on Saturday, Elder Talmage spoke briefly on the bestowal of the Holy Ghost and aided in confirming the newly baptized as members of the Church. He made suggestions freely during the missionary meeting that followed, teaching the Elders how to meet all forms of opposition while proselyting. That night Elder Talmage spoke on "Heaven's First Law—Obedience." Sunday night he spoke on the subject, "Will Many or Few Be Saved?" The Pearl and Seventh Avenue chapel was crowded to overflowing with the largest crowd of Latter-day Saints and their friends ever assembled to that point in Denver. Four hundred and fifty people assembled within the chapel walls. Many were compelled to sit on the floor, and about twenty-five persons were turned away because of lack of space to see and hear. That night Elder Lee played a piano accompaniment for a ladies' vocal duet, and, with President Knight, assisted Elder Talmage in blessing many people after the meeting.

The labors in the Denver Conference continued into 1922 with the usual problems and Elder Lee's persistent growth-through-adversity progress. One day he knew he had not measured up to a street meeting challenge. Of the experience he wrote: "I made a miserable mess of my part of the meeting, apparently because I was relying upon my strength and ability and not upon the Lord."

On a happier day, however, his attitude toward missionary work is revealed by this journal entry:

> I'm as happy, despite the vying of Elders for credit for baptisms, as though it were I who had brought the proper pressure to bear to bring about their conversions, and I rejoice that I am able to erase my own selfish desires and to push loyally for the success of the entire conference—that anyone's success is a big boon to my individual appreciation. I'm going to live up to the expectations made of me to the end that patience and strength will prevail.

A glimpse into the budding personality and leadership qualities of this young churchman is seen by his recording of the comments made by the Denver branch president, President Smart, when he moved to Houston and was paying his parting respects to Elder Lee. The description from a letter says:

> When he left me, he told me he respected me and was glad for the opportunity of working with me, saying that I was a hard one to say that about, because of the peculiar qualities that were distinctly mine that kept people long in the dark as to superior abilities that I might possess. That one fact of my makeup has caused me more misgivings as to my ability to succeed than any other. I wish someone would give me a recipe of instruction so I might overcome.

The work prospered under his leadership. An appraisal of the new plan of having the missionaries serve as monthly home teachers to the members showed good results. "In our meeting the missionaries reported the best of conditions among the Saints because of our visits to them to try to keep them in the path of duty."

On August 6, 1922, Elder Lee made a brief observation in his journal about a fast and testimony meeting in which a Sister Maulden and a Sister Haskan, older members of the ward, spoke of their personal acquaintance with the Prophet Joseph Smith.

Though sobered by the weight of such great responsibility, for one so young, Elder Lee was not devoid of a sense of humor. One entry in his diary refers to a humorous incident that occurred as Sister Knight, wife of the mission president, was conducting the sustaining of Relief Society sisters in their various positions in the branch. In doing so she said: "All who are in favor of sustaining these officers in their various 'dispositions' may make it manifest by raising the right hand." Of this blooper Elder Lee wrote: "Amen, we have to do it daily with our sisters here in Denver."

Another example came after a street meeting one day, which he recorded in his diary: "When Elder Murdock declared 'the heavens were opened,' one old fellow gazed solemnly up at the sky!"

The financial burdens on Elder Lee's family to maintain their first missionary were not out of his mind during these closing months of his mission. In a letter dated August 27, 1922, he wrote:

> I received a most encouraging letter from Father, who told me they would never ask for my release and would only pray God to increase their crops so I can stay until released. I am so appreciative of my people at home. Waldo, my sixteen-year-old brother, just sent me a check for $40, saying he wanted some credit, too, so you see they all consider that they are doing the Lord's work when they help to keep Harold in the mission field. I could cry when I think of it all, and my prayer is that God will make me humble so that I shall not disappoint them when I do go home.

The progress he felt taking place in the last months of his mission among his colleagues is reflected in this comment: "Among the missionaries is growing the knowledge that the Lord is blessing their labors to the extent that many are believing in their testimonies, and we have hopes that in years to come, some of the work we are doing will be felt in the lives of these people." It no doubt came as a product of extensive effort properly directed.

The work schedule and results of these days, as noted in a letter dated September 22, 1922, are summarized as follows:

> I've just returned from choir practice. This week, among other activities, I have done thirty hours tracting, attended three cottage meetings, and preached on the street Wednesday night, and I am slated to preach in church on Sunday night. We have a total of seventy-two baptisms so far this year; one more than for the year 1921 in the Denver Conference.

Perhaps the most trying and personally challenging problem of his mission came through personal conflicts emerging from his competence and unusual leadership abilities. The jealousy and envy of some fellow workers brought much criticism, with which he had to learn to cope. In this early conflict we can see the character developing to meet the adversity as would be required in the years ahead when often he was younger than those he would preside over.

After one such experience, the most stressful of his entire mission, Elder Lee pleaded to his closest missionary friend: "Lend me your courage while I pray always that I might be submissive to authority and forget self in a last effort to go all the way in this sacred work."

THE CLOSING WEEKS

As his mission was coming to a close, the pace quickened. These comments from letters in October 1922 tell of the intense activity in which he was routinely engaged.

> When I tell you we are having to hold eighteen cottage meetings this week, besides street meetings and Mutual and choir practice, and only fifteen missionaries here in Denver, you can know that we have but little spare time if we measure up with our other requirements. There is a healthy spirit of competition among the Elders here now, the very condition I have wanted to see; and as a result the pace is fast and furious and all will be well if someone doesn't weaken. But don't think I'm getting too straight-backed to admit of foolishness at times, because my indulgence in that on occasions has kept me alive. Times are so strenuous that we don't have time to get sick or die. This week, too, I have been fighting off a bad cold, but have been unable to slacken up because of the work demanded of me. A number of the missionaries have likewise had colds, but with twenty-four cottage meetings to hold, we haven't had much time to lose.

In his third November in the missionary field (November 9, 1922), President Knight showed his reliance on the now fully developed Denver Conference president by asking Elder Lee to take his place in conducting a conference in Sheridan, Wyoming. The president was called away suddenly to attend to missionary problems elsewhere and gave Elder Lee but two hours' notice to make the train. Elder Lee's letters indicated his reply:

> I told the president he was giving me a bigger bite than I could chew, but if the best I could do was all right, that I would go. He said there was no one else he would rather trust and the Church would pay my expenses. I did the best I could—preached, played the piano, conducted the singing, and helped settle the difficulties in

the branch. When President Knight arrived on Monday, Elder Scadlock insisted that I talk again, but I graciously declined and played the part of wisdom. While there, the president took me into his confidence more than he has ever done before and took me with him wherever he went. I wish I could tell you more details (letters are unable to convey the thoughts intended) regarding the value of this trip to me, coming, as it has, at the close of my mission when many thoughts have crowded themselves upon me to make me more appreciative and humble in the responsibility that is mine—to determine whether or not I can make good among strangers, etc.

Meanwhile, conditions at home were worrying Elder Lee. A letter from his brother Clyde made him feel despondent for days. He wrote his reactions in these words:

He told how Father seems to be getting much older because of the worries he had. To think that I have caused my parents worry and hardship makes my heart ache. Sometimes I feel as though I couldn't stay to finish under the circumstances, but I've come to know out here that ofttimes when things are the blackest, just then, things begin to happen. Never again, if I know it, will my folks be in the position they are in today. What I shall do in the future is dark and uncertain; my prayer to God is that things will happen for the best.

RELEASE PLANS

Elder Lee didn't have time to anguish long over financial conditions at home, for in two weeks the answers were provided. From his diary this important announcement was recorded:

Before the president left for Omaha, Nebraska, he called me into his office and told me to sit down in an easy chair. He asked about my finances and if it would be possible to get a school contract this late in the year. He told me I would get my release at the December conference, and that he would leave with me for Salt Lake City on December 14, 1922.

Elder Lee enlarged on this discussion in these words:

The president talked to me a long time about the past and the future. He expressed the wish that I might stay until spring, but after I had explained the circumstances he thought it best to go now. Of course, I'm up in the air, and lucky for me there will be so much to do from now on that no time will be granted me to even think of the future or to regret the past. President Knight is urging the hundred baptisms from Denver before January 1, and I hope to get them by conference time. Barring accidents, everything looks promising.

Elder Lee plunged into the work challenge and lost himself and his thoughts of the coming change in his life by a saturating effort. Even the meetinghouse got a final cleaning by the presiding Elder, who wanted to leave everything in proper order: "We declared a housecleaning day and cleaned the church from top to bottom. We scrubbed and oiled the entire upstairs and downstairs, and washed and oiled all the woodwork and the chairs. I crawled up and down the floors on my knees until my knees were calloused and my back ached."

Two days later his final conference in the mission field began. The Saturday priesthood meeting started at 8:00 A.M. and lasted until 4:00 P.M., with twenty-eight missionaries present to help engender a most wonderful spirit. His diary records:

> Each missionary related his experience of the summer, and everyone seemed to radiate a general feeling of good fellowship. When my turn came to speak, after all the others had talked, I found I was up against a hard proposition. I was finally able to control myself after a time, and then say what I wanted. The president likewise experienced the same difficulty when he attempted to speak. He praised the missionaries for what they had done and gave instructions.

RELEASE AND RETURN

At the Sunday sessions of conference a new attendance record was set, with 310 persons in attendance for the evening meeting. Elder Lee's talents were much in evidence—he sang in a mixed quartet and in a male quartet, spoke in the evening, and played the accompaniments for all the musical selections—as the president announced his release to the missionaries and the Saints assembled.

The next day's diary entry (Monday, December 11, 1922), described the missionary meeting as follows:

> When the president announced that I was released, he said that it would bankrupt the English language to tell how much he thought of me and said that I had been on the firing line from the time I had arrived in Denver. Elder Andrew Hood was chosen in my place. He is sixty-two years old. The missionaries presented me with a beauti-

ful watch chain. A total of thirty-three of them had contributed funds to purchase it for me.

There followed a busy week of leave-taking, last-minute converts to baptize, babies of close friends to bless, and many good-byes.

Finally, the day of departure arrived. On a Thursday morning, December 14, 1922, Elder Lee left his work in Denver, where so many spiritually developing experiences had occurred in his life. Traveling with him on the Denver and Rio Grande train was President John M. Knight, who was going to Salt Lake City to attend the Ensign Stake quarterly conference. He had never been released as the second counselor in the stake presidency while serving his mission in Denver. Also accompanying them were Sister Harriet Jensen, who was to be hospitalized in Salt Lake City for surgery. All the missionaries came to the depot to say good-bye to their conference president. Also in the throng was Mabel Hickman, Elder Lee's first convert in Denver. The journey home was uneventful, but was full of anticipation and expectation.

An interesting diary entry for Friday, December 15, 1922 states, "While talking to President Knight about my next mission, he said that someday I would be sent to preside over one of the missions."

Elder Lee attended the Ensign Stake conference on Sunday, December 17, 1922, with his mission president, and surprisingly he was called on to speak for ten minutes. Nearly a thousand people were present, and Elder Lee later discovered, when they complimented him personally on his sermon, that many of the General Authorities were present.

That night Elder Lee had his first insight into reality as he began the adjustment to less spiritual conditions at home. He attended one of the Salt Lake City wards and wrote of the visit, "I discovered a sad falling off from the Spirit manifested in the mission field."

The final chapter of his mission return was written under date of Monday, December 18, 1922, describing how President Knight took him to meet a number of Church officials. Here in the Church Office Building, where he was destined someday to be the presiding officer, the young returned missionary met President Charles W. Penrose; Elders Joseph Fielding Smith, Nephi L. Morris, John W. Wells, Richard R. Lyman, and Andrew Jensen; Louie B. Felt of the Primary Association; and a host of others. If they could have known then how the life and mission of this obscure young missionary was to later be joined with theirs in the service of the Lord, perhaps they would have greeted him differently as they met for the first time.

Elder Lee was given a letter of recommendation that was approved by President Penrose, which permitted him to enter the Salt Lake Temple for ordinances he performed two days later. He officially reported his mission to Elder Harold G. Reynolds at the Church offices. The final introduction made by President Knight was to a Sister Green, who was told by President Knight that "Harold B. Lee was going to be sent back to the Western States Mission to preside, after he himself was released and sent home."

The last mission diary entry records the courtesy visits Elder Lee made to missionary friends and parents of missionaries, and to Freda Jensen, whom his former missionary companion Elder Murdock hoped to make his wife. She could not then know what a profound influence Harold B. Lee would be in her life . . . as her husband some forty years later.

A Special Visit

More than a courtesy call, however, was the visit Elder Lee made to the home of Sister Fern Tanner in the Granger area of Salt Lake City. He wrote of this visit in these words:

> Little did I realize what it meant to face a cold and unsympathetic world after living for two wonderful years in the idealistic atmosphere of the gospel. The president gave me to understand as we reached Salt Lake City that from there on out I must shift for myself and that his responsibility was at an end.
>
> My first thought upon arriving in Salt Lake was to find Fern L. Tanner, with whom I had corresponded practically during our entire mission, she having returned from the Western States Mission in July 1922.
>
> Fern met me with her brother, Bud, and his wife, Ethel, that night at the Kenyon Hotel, and I went to her home, where I first met Daddy and Mother Tanner.
>
> We talked far into the night, I think more as missionary friends than as sweethearts. There was much to ask and much to tell. Both of us had experienced joys and disappointments, but through it all we had gained a deep testimony of the gospel of Jesus Christ, the real value of which we then but little realized.

Back Home to Idaho

After spending a week in the Salt Lake City area, during which time he attended the temple twice, Elder Lee arrived home in Clifton, Idaho, just a few days before Christmas 1922.

The patriarchal blessing given by Presiding Patriarch Hyrum G. Smith on the head of Harold Bingham Lee as he was leaving for the Western States Mission had indeed been fulfilled. In it Patriarch Smith had predicted:

> And, if thou wilt honor the Holy Priesthood which has been given thee, thou shalt be advanced therein in due time, and be called into positions of trust and responsibility and leadership, and shall have an influence for good among thine associates.

Personal Missionary Highlights

In addition to the diary entries and letters written while Elder Lee served as a missionary, he also summarized his mission for inclusion in a family history. In this summary many of the more interesting personality sketches, experiences, and travels are detailed. A few excerpts from this text follow:

First Converts

> The first converts I baptized were Mabel and Florence Hickman, at whose home we were rooming. Mabel was an active member of the First Christian Church, and when she and Florence joined the Church, their family and the Christian Church members accused them of everything from immorality to insanity. They proved their conversion to the gospel and became splendid aids in the Denver Branch. They were both expert stenographers.
>
> During my mission I had the privilege of baptizing 45 converts. Their religions were as follows: Christian Science (2); Methodist (11); Salvation Army (2); Christian (11); Seventh-Day Adventists (3); Catholic (2); Baptist (3); Lutheran (3); no Church affiliation (8). I made a complete list of these converts in the middle of the Bible I used in the mission field.

Missionary Companions

> I was made president of the Denver Conference to succeed Elder Harry Jensen, and my companion at this time—midsummer of 1921—was Vernal Bergeson, of Cornish, Utah. We "batched" for a time and later moved to 740 Grant Street in Denver. "Berg" had

been spending eighty to ninety dollars each month before this time, but immediately cut his expenses to less than half in order to conform to my pocketbook.

Elder David S. Murdock, of Heber City, was one of the most loyal companions I had in the mission field. He was a tireless worker but had a personality that offended some people. He had an unusual knack in making friends, and he baptized many converts.

A Scoutmaster

During the first few months of my mission, I had charge of a scout troop of the Denver Branch of the Capitol Hill District. This troop was made up of boys of ten different denominations and some splendid contacts were made. We took two hikes and overnight outings to Starbuck and up to Boulder Canyon.

Fern L. Tanner

> Working in the mission office
> Was a woman,
> Young, and strong in spirit,
> True to her ideals of gospel truth.
> Gentle was her voice,
> Gracious in her walk
> And talk.
> Her spirit, too, reached back
> Into eternity.
> She saw the need to testify,
> To warn the world,
> To bring souls to repent and
> Serve the Lord.
> And so they met
> And each saw in
> The other one
> Their future destiny,
> But waited till
> Each one had done his part
> Of missionary work
> To speak the thoughts and
> Yearning of the heart.*

Fern L. Tanner arrived in Denver just two weeks before I did, and I met her on her birthday, November 14, 1920, three days after I arrived. From that day, her influence became a power in my life. Little did I dream that some day she would become my wife and the mother of my children. She was transferred to the Pueblo Con-

* © S. Dilworth Young 1976. Used by permission.

Fern Lucinda Tanner, 1920

Harold B. Lee, 1921

ference, and we corresponded during the entire time she labored there. She later returned to the mission office in Denver to work a short period before her release.

F. Elinor Johnson

F. Elinor Johnson, of Benjamin, Utah, was the matron in charge of the work of the lady missionaries when I arrived. She was a most cultured lady, having graduated from the Brigham Young University, yet she was a genial "mixer" with all classes. Fern was assigned to be her companion, and among the three of us there was formed a "trinity" that "sat in judgment" on most of the affairs of the mission during those first few months.

During her mission she was constantly in contact with people who had tuberculosis. Near the close of her mission she became ill with what the doctor diagnosed as stomach trouble. When she arrived home, it was found that she had an advanced case of tuberculosis, and after a lingering sickness, most of the time in the County Hospital at Salt Lake City, she died; her funeral services were held at Payson, Utah, in March 1925.

When she knew the end was near, she began to plan her services and had the entire program worked out when she died, even to the individuals she invited to offer the prayers. I was asked to speak. In the closing moments of her life she wrote her testimony until the stupor of death halted her writing.

Mission President

John M. Knight was the president of the Western States Mission. As president of the Denver Conference, I was close to him. I came to learn his virtues as well as his weaknesses. He was a fearless fighter in his missionary work and was always on the go, visiting the various divisions of the mission, which extended from North Dakota to New Mexico and from West Colorado to East Nebraska. At the time of the Pueblo flood in the month of June 1921, I accompanied him to inquire about the safety of the Saints and missionaries in the Pueblo District, where 1,500 people were estimated to have lost their lives. Losses up to $30 million were reported.

Visit to Nauvoo

One year later, in June 1922, Elder Lee accompanied his mission president on another memorable journey, this time on a tour of the eastern part of the Western States Mission, including a brief extension into the area of Nauvoo and Carthage, Illinois.

This trip made a deep impression on the now matured missionary, for he recorded his every impression with meticulous detail, even taking many photographs to give lasting memory to his written summary. From this unforgettable experience with the historical centers of the early Church, Elder Lee was to draw time after time as he traveled throughout the Church teaching the Saints and missionaries over his thirty-three-year span as a General Authority. He frequently repeated those vivid impressions when testifying of the divine calling of the Prophet Joseph Smith and of his martyrdom with Hyrum, his brother, on June 27, 1844.

1924–1931. Charles Lindbergh completed the first solo, nonstop transatlantic flight from New York to Paris. Valentino died, and the stock market climbed, then plunged. Ford cars sold for $290, but Chevrolet had a successful competitor to the Model T. Transatlantic radio and telephone began, and the first all-talking, full-color motion picture was introduced. The Hawley-Smoot Tariff Act was enacted. The first non-stop transpacific flight was made.

CHAPTER 6

Marriage and
Early Church Callings

It was a happy Christmas in Clifton for the Samuel M. Lee family now that Harold had returned for the 1922 holidays. The young missionary, however, like many of our Lord's servants fresh from the mission field, had mixed feelings, and he especially found it difficult to smile and say he was happy to be home. He discovered that his parents were listening carefully to discover if he was going to express any dissatisfactions with home through suggesting that he was leaving.

Sober thoughts were running through Harold's mind. For the first time, he realized that his parent's home and farm were in financial jeopardy due to the severe economic depression all farmers had experienced in the past two years while he had been gone. The payments on the mortgages had not been made during that time. Harold wrote, "I thank the Lord that my parents didn't tell me all their difficulties." Had he known all, he might have returned early from the mission field to help.

Though no one seemed to have any answers, there was a family solidarity and beautiful spirit in his home. He wrote of that Christmas: "Although people have no money in their pockets, they have bushels of love in their hearts and I believe there has never been a time when there was more of the real Christmas spirit."

Harold tried with pronounced effort to adjust from the spiritual influence of the mission field to the less than ideal circumstances at home. He endeavored to fit himself into those activities by which he could accomplish the most good. To be a companion to his younger brother Clyde, who needed his positive influence, Harold had to take up basketball again, for Clyde was the leading athlete in the town. Basketball with Clyde was not without its risks, however. In the mission field Harold had developed a hernia, which was aggravated by his attempts on the basketball court. Other physical problems ensued.

After being home only three weeks, Harold took part in a basketball game between Clifton and Oxford, the town where he had taught school before his mission. In that game, which was played considerably more physically then than now, Harold sustained a wrenched back that necessitated his being carried off the floor. Two years away from sports had produced a softened condition not to be overcome in just three weeks of activity at home.

Already the townsfolk were urging Harold to qualify to teach in the high school the next year, although a degree from a college would be required of Harold if the high school were to be accredited. He was examining several offers to teach at this time, and knew well that the family's financial condition urged such an investigation.

Church activity in his life was increased when the stake presidency asked Harold to return to his premissionary assignment as president of the elders quorum for Oxford, Dayton, and Clifton wards. Additionally, he was called to be the theological teacher in Sunday School. Characteristic of a faithful missionary, he longingly noted, however, "It doesn't give the satisfaction that missionary work brings."

As January drew to a close, Samuel Lee wondered if he should start plowing soon. It was a frustrating thought, because he and his boys had begun to despair, having worked hard the previous summer only to fail to even cover expenses. Everywhere in the area people were talking about selling their farms.

A cloak of gloom hung over the town of Clifton and the Lee farm, located just two miles from the meetinghouse. Harold was depressed in his valiant efforts to make home better than it was when he rejoined the family, but still he strove to prove he was mature enough to hold on to the success he had achieved in Denver. Word from the mission field thrilled him when he learned that after his departure all records for convert baptisms in the past had been broken when the year-end count was tallied.

A snowy period in early February restored conditions for sleighing, which earlier had melted under unseasonal sunshine. Harold donned his hightop boots and a sweater, pulled on heavy outer clothing, and mused over his uncertain future as he tramped around in the snow, chopping and sawing wood, "a last resort" choice—a necessity for fuel and an outlet for his frustrations. It seemed better than basketball for profitable exercise, as he had painfully discovered.

That same January, Harold took a cold fifteen-mile ride to Preston, Idaho, where he was installed in the elders quorum work at the Oneida Stake quarterly conference. The stimulation from this experience provided the first adequate spiritual experience he had enjoyed since his days in the Denver Conference.

A minstrel show sponsored by the M-Men, which Harold helped to produce, soon brought an outlet for his musical interest. His share was the musical production, and his brother Perry wrote the comic script. His notation about the event was, "I will be qualified after this week to give expert advice on the staging of minstrel shows."

Deeper thoughts filled his mind. He had thought he understood conditions at home well enough to adapt himself without difficulty, but he finally confessed to himself and others that for these past months it was only with intense effort that he could find his way through the maze to a new path of accomplishment and a firm future. A new plan finally emerged. It was only too apparent that he must set his stakes down away from Clifton.

Move to Salt Lake City

"My first move in that direction was made when I went to the Salt Lake City Latter-day Saints Hospital for a hernia operation in February 1923, where I remained for one month. I went to the Tanner home to convalesce after I left the hospital," wrote Harold in summary of his decision to break away and start anew.

In Salt Lake City while recovering from surgery, he received a most distressing letter from his mother, vaguely intimating some problems at home and announcing that his father, who had served ten years as bishop of the Clifton Ward, had been released. His brother Perry soon arrived in Salt Lake City for the annual general conference of the Church in April; afterwards, both Harold and Perry returned to the family farm in Clifton to assist in straightening out the difficulties.

His parents told Harold at that time of their concern about his feelings that his mission might have placed an added financial burden on them, and their fear was that this might have weakened Harold's faith in the gospel and the blessings of the Lord. Harold wrote his reactions:

It gave me a joy I am unable to express to see their pride and satisfaction in my missionary service. I could cry when I think that in the midst of all their trouble and grief they have placed uppermost the spiritual values, and in their great stress, have found peace and rest through the gospel.

Father and Mother have gone through a veritable hell and appear to have aged years since I last saw them. Even in the short time I have been gone to Salt Lake, Father's hair is more gray than ever and I'm sure that only love and hard work will ever make back to them what they have lost.

Then Harold recorded the conclusion that emerged from his visit back home:

We have decided unanimously that I should go to work to get ahead financially, so I will return to Salt Lake and find employment as soon as possible. I'm going to do the right, as the Lord directs.

This same resolute determination would later mark his illustrious career. A formula that never failed to meet all the problems in the life of Harold Bingham Lee was to study the circumstances, search out the solution, apply all one's energies to its accomplishment, and through it all trust continuously and everlastingly in a loving Heavenly Father for guidance and direction.

MARRIAGE

Determined to launch a new future path, Harold B. Lee returned to Salt Lake City to attend school at the University of Utah during the summer of 1923 and to plan for his forthcoming marriage. His springboard for economic independence started with part-time employment at the Paris department store. A few months later, in the fall of that year, he obtained an appointment as the principal of the Whittier School and later of the Woodrow Wilson School in the Granite School District in the Salt Lake City area.

Of those memorable days of marriage and of their becoming a separate family, Harold wrote:

> On November 14, 1923, I was married to Fern L. Tanner in the Salt Lake Temple, with Elder George F. Richards of the Council of the Twelve officiating. Never doubting our ability to get ahead together, we put our full trust in each other and moved into our first home at 1538 West 800 South, owned by Daddy Tanner, and obligated ourselves for $800 of furniture and a used Ford automobile for $300, on my salary of $135 per month.

At the time of his marriage, Harold was teaching school in Hunter, Salt Lake County, in the Granite School District. When he returned to school on a Monday morning, after his wedding announcement was published over the weekend, one ingenious student placed on his desk the newspaper clipping of the bride's photograph and announcement and scrawled at the bottom of the page, "Is November 14 a holiday from school?"

Harold reported in his journal the birth of his only two children, both daughters:

> The first year of our married life was a glorious honeymoon in which we made preparations for our first baby. Despite the fact that we carefully followed the instructions of Dr. A. C. Callister, Fern came near losing her life from a serious hemorrhage when our baby [Maurine] was born.
>
> Maurine was born September 1, 1924. Within fifteen months our second baby came. Fern had been in constant labor pain for sixty hours before Helen was born on November 25, 1925. With her birth we saw the beginning of a sweet companionship of close

Harold and Fern Lee in front of their first home

sisters that developed with each year of their lives. They were both born in the Latter-day Saints Hospital in Salt Lake City.

EMPLOYMENT AND HOMES

During the first years of our married life I struggled to complete my education at the University of Utah by extension study and summer school work while I taught school. I was forced to seek new employment each summer to support my little family until school would begin in the fall. One summer I sold meats and produce for Swift and Company, the next I dispensed gas and oil and checked out equipment at the Salt Lake City Street Department under Commissioner T. T. Burton from 3:00 p.m. to 11:00 p.m. The next two summers I was a watchman and train checker at the Union Pacific north yards under the special agent's department. Some of my choicest friends during these years were Superintendent D. W. Parratt, of the Granite Schools, Commissioner T. T. Burton, and Edward H. Eardley.

Fern was never content that I should remain in the school teaching profession. I sold Nash automobiles one summer, and later worked for the grocery department of ZCMI, and for the Bennett Gas and Oil Company. Finally, in 1928, I was invited by L. A. Ray to become a salesman for the Foundation Press, Inc. I was guaranteed a salary of $50 per week, and an over-writing on all sales of the salesmen whom I had trained. I resigned in the fall of 1928 from the Granite schools. My new work took me into Wyoming, Colorado, Washington, Oregon, and Idaho, and on many of these trips I was accompanied by Fern and our two girls.

In 1930, I was called to Denver by E. H. Ferris, president of the Foundation Press, and notified that I was to continue in the promotion of Master Library sales, and L. A. Ray was to spend his time with the "Pageant of the Nation," a collection of pictures. This move caused friction between myself and Mr. Ray, and consequently, in September 1930, I was designated to continue alone as the Intermountain manager, with offices in the McIntyre Building in Salt Lake City.

Shortly after his marriage in 1923, Harold had sent for his parents to join him in Salt Lake City. At that time, all his family moved from the farm in Clifton, Idaho, to obtain work in Salt Lake City. His father first took work at the Utah Wholesale Grocery; later, when the depression hit hardest, he was obliged to work in Green River, Wyoming, as manager of the Piggly Wiggly Grocery store. The family lived at several Salt Lake City locations before finally establishing a home which his parents occupied until their deaths, located at 213 F Street. Father Samuel M. Lee ultimately gained permanent employment as a night watchman for the ZCMI Department Store in Salt Lake City and eventually became the night supervisor.

In his family history, Harold gave further details of those years of growth and changes:

When Maurine was born we were forced to move into a larger home at 1534 West 8th South Street. In 1928, Fern's father and mother gave up their home at 1310 Indiana Avenue, because of their old age, to live with their daughter, Emily, in Granger, Utah. We purchased the old home for $2,700 at $25 per month at 7 percent interest.

Fern's father, Stewart T. Tanner, died July 23, 1931, and her mother, Janet Coats Tanner, died July 6, 1932.

From the time our two babies were born their Grandpa and Grandma Tanner seemed to take a great interest in their care and never less than once or twice a day did they plan to see the girls. Grandpa Tanner always called Maurine his "pal." They were a lovable father and mother, wise and just, making no distinction between their own children and their sons- and daughters-in-law.

It has been my joy to see perpetuated in Fern many of the fine traits of her mother. Like her mother, Fern is quiet and unassuming and yet vigorous in her denunciation of unfairness and calumny, generous to a fault, sensitive, impressionable, a splendid mother, and an ideal homemaker. Mother Tanner endured the hardships of pioneer life without a murmur, but was not content until their farm house in Granger was the finest in that community. A close parallel is to be found in Fern. No matter how often public duty takes me away from home, there is always an assurance of her loyal support. We began married life on a borrowed $300. Due to her high standards, our present home has all the conveniences possible, and while small and not the most convenient, it has breathed the influence of a charming wife and a loving mother. These sterling qualities were apparent on the first night of our marriage when she reminded me of our family prayers.

CHURCH CALLINGS

Harold B. Lee was on his way to his destined greatness. He accepted calls to serve in Church and community as they came to him with surprising regularity for one so young in years.

His personal record gives the following account of his early Church appointments.

My first Church responsibility after coming to Pioneer Stake was M-Men instructor in the Poplar Grove Ward. We had a fine group of boys who had suffered from lack of leadership. In stake competition our boys were victorious in basketball, debating, male quartet, public speaking, etc. The second year I was made Sunday School Superintendent of Poplar Grove Ward, with Bert Crockett and Wilford Brown as assistants.

After two years in ward work in the Sunday School, I was drafted in 1926 as the superintendent of religion classes in the Pioneer Stake by President D. E. Hammond. This was a pioneer experience with almost a complete rejuvenation and reorganization necessary.

In 1927 I was chosen as a member of the Pioneer Stake high council, along with Joseph Jenkins. I was ordained a high priest and set apart as a high councilor by Elder Richard R. Lyman of the Council of the Twelve.

Upon the release of T. T. Burton in 1928, I was released as superintendent of religion classes and made stake superintendent of Sunday Schools. My counselors were Edwin Bronson and E. Albert Rosenvall.

Before I had been set apart to this position, and while attending the October Pioneer Stake quarterly conference, I was startled to hear my name announced as the selection of President D. E. Hammond for the position of second counselor in the stake presidency. Charles S. Hyde was advanced to first counselor and J. A. Hancock was released.

I greatly enjoyed my association with President Hammond and Charles S. Hyde, and the experience I gained from this association was profitable, for at the Pioneer Stake quarterly conference one year later, in October 1930, President Hammond was released as stake president by Apostles Rudger Clawson and George Albert Smith of the Council of the Twelve.

PRESIDENT OF PIONEER STAKE

On the Friday preceding the quarterly conference, I was called to the office of President Rudger Clawson, where I was told by President Clawson and Elder George Albert Smith that I had been chosen by the First Presidency and the Twelve as the new president of Pioneer Stake. I told them I would much prefer working as a counselor to Brother Hyde, and was bluntly told by George Albert Smith that I had been invited to meet with them, not to tell them what should be done, but to find out if I was willing to do what the Lord wanted me to do. There followed a discussion on the selection of my counselors. Again I was told when I asked if they had any suggestions on that, "We have suggestions, but we are not going to tell you—that is your responsibility. If you are guided by the Spirit of the Lord, you will choose those whom we have in mind."

Seeking spiritual direction in choosing his counselors was another learning experience for this young leader.

I retired that night, or rather early morning, to a fitful sleep, about three o'clock in the morning, after earnest prayer for guidance. During the few hours I tried to sleep it would seem that I had chosen two counselors and was trying to hold council meetings with them. Disagreements, obstacles, and misunderstandings would arise, and I would awake with a start to realize that my first choices were wrong. This process was repeated with ten or twelve of my brethren until, when morning came, I was certain the Lord had guided me to choose Charles S. Hyde and Paul C. Child as my counselors. When I announced to the Brethren my decision the next morning, they smiled their approval. The men whom they had desired had been selected.

On the Saturday night following our conference priesthood convention, I went for a long ride with Brother Hyde, who was many years my senior in age and experience, and informed him of the proposed change and of my desire for him to be my first counselor. It was like a thunderbolt to him, and he deferred his answer until he could think it over and talk with President Clawson the next day. Paul C. Child had been my bishop in the Poplar Grove Ward for seven years, and he was not aware of his selection until his name was placed before the conference.

The reorganization of the stake presidency took place on October 26, 1930. President Lee's new work was before him now and he plunged in with characteristic fervor, as his journal describes:

No sooner had the reorganization been effected than we were faced with many stern and serious problems. The Cannon, Poplar Grove, and Thirty-second wards had been disorganized by the change when their bishops were made high councilors and Bishop Child was appointed a counselor in the presidency. Also the [stake] Genealogical Society and the high priest's presidency underwent a change.

CHURCH COURTS

In requiring an accounting preceding the transfer of leadership in each ward being reorganized, it was discovered that there was a serious shortage in one ward's tithing and building funds. A complete audit was conducted, and, as a presidency, an investigation of the entire matter was undertaken, which resulted in a high council trial in which a former bishop of the ward, who was by then serving as a member of the Pioneer Stake high council, was disfellowshipped from the Church.

This was my first experience in conducting a high council trial. The trial involved the straining of friendships formed over a period of ten years. When the decision of the presidency was announced after the trial had gone on until four o'clock a.m., the high council refused to vote their approval, whereupon I merely announced that the decision of the presidency was not the decision of the council, and promptly dismissed the trial. On the next Sunday morning, the council was reconvened to show why our decision should not be sustained, and we then received their unanimous vote. The suddenness of our decision had seemed to stun them until they could be given a chance to think the matter over more carefully.

Following that stressful experience came many other excommunications for adultery, polygamy, and apostasy. Some of the most trying were the cases of those charged with immorality and adultery, one involving a nineteen-year-old girl, as well as one for alleged dishonesty against a member of the high council.

SEMINARY TEACHING

In 1931 the Church decided to establish a seminary in connection with the newly constructed South High School in Salt Lake City, and I was asked to be associated with Merrill D. Clayson as a teacher. Two classes each day were held, at eight o'clock each morning and three-thirty after school. I worked with some splendid youngsters during two winters and a part of the third. Coming early in the morning I found it possible to teach the morning class before office hours, and this I did without much difficulty until the late fall of 1933 when the demands of my position as city commissioner made necessary my resignation. This was the most enjoyable teaching I ever did. My associate, Merrill Clayson, was a master at directing the social activities, which ranged from bonfire parties to dancing and Sunday night programs. This association to me was life at its best, and I was loathe to leave a work where I saw such possibilities for doing good. The morning Dr. Joseph F. Merrill left for Europe to preside over the European Mission, he called and asked that I consent to at least get the work started at the seminary that fall, 1933.

Thus commenced the intense Church leadership career of Harold B. Lee. At age thirty-one, he was the youngest stake president in the Church at that time. His appointment at such an early age to preside in Pioneer Stake, even compared with his many other attainments, was without doubt one of the highlights of his Church service and laid the foundation for his teaching and leadership for the years to come.

1932–1933. Prosperity ended and the Great
Depression began. So did sit-down strikes. The
New Deal was launched and the gold standard
suspended. Ford introduced a low-priced V-8
rumble-seat model.

CHAPTER 7

Concern for the Poor and Needy

Forerunner to the Church's security program was a
Pioneer Stake plan that emerged from the constant prayers, big
hearts, and bright minds of President Harold B. Lee's stake presidency. Several years before the Church moved to help its general
membership in the Great Depression, Pioneer Stake, where great
numbers of the poor and distressed resided in Salt Lake City, was a
scene of intense action to stave off economic disaster. Because this
program was the embryo of the famed welfare plan to come later,
it is interesting to hear the details of it in Harold B. Lee's own
words, summarizing the imaginative, valiant work of a stake presidency whose action told of their charity, or the true love of Christ,
for those over whom they presided.

THE DEPRESSION

In November 1929 there was ushered in an economic upheaval
that came to be known as the "Depression." Millions of men and

In Pioneer Stake President Harold B. Lee's words, "deplorable 'ghetto' conditions in Redwood Road area" during the Depression

women were thrown out of employment and business houses of long standing closed their doors, as did banks and investment concerns. By 1933 the national jobless rate became a shocking 24.9 percent. Out of a work force of 51,132,000, [approximately] 12,830,000 were unemployed. Some of the most notable businesses to fold in Salt Lake City were Walker Brothers store, Columbia Trust Company, Deseret Savings Bank, Western Building and Loan Company, Consolidated Music Company, Ashton Jenkins Real Estate, and many others. It was no uncommon sight to see dozens of vacant stores along Main Street with a For Rent sign in each window.

My business with the Foundation Press, Inc., suffered along with others, but I was able, by exerting all my energy, to maintain my office and keep up some production until I severed my connections with the Foundation Press, December 1, 1932, when I was appointed a city commissioner of Salt Lake City.

Many of the meetings of the Pioneer Stake presidency were devoted to a prayerful study of our stressful conditions and of plans to cooperate in relieving the economic distress of our Saints. Our study reached a climax when word reached us that Alfons J. Finck, of our high council, was one of the organizers and promoters of the Natural Development Association originated by Ben J. Stringham.

PIONEER STAKE RELIEF PLAN

In response to our invitation, Brother Finck met in council with us. We pointed out the error of his course and outlined our plans for Pioneer Stake. The meeting ended by our appointing Brother Finck as a key man in our program to further perfect our relief organization.

If the story were left with the brief account described above, an important element would be missing. We learn additional information from the writings of Alfons J. Finck himself, which tell of his feelings and the deft handling of a delicate situation by President Lee. A document entitled *The Early Days of the Welfare Plan in Pioneer Stake,* written by Brother Finck, contains this elaboration:

The stakes were advised of President Grant's attitude and pronouncement that the "Natural Government" movement was "radical." . . . I felt that in the absence of any Church effort it was unjust to label the activities of well-meaning men "radical" when thousands of Church members were seriously affected and individual efforts were futile. . . . During our high council meeting we were informed about the decision of President Grant. My personal resentment almost made me resign.

I was invited to a special meeting with the presidency of the stake—President Harold B. Lee, President Charles S. Hyde, and President Paul C. Child. Their meeting was in President Lee's office in the McIntyre Building on Main Street.

When I met with the brethren I was still in a resentful mood. But thanks to God, they did not rebuke me, but offered to me, in a wonderful spirit of love and tolerance, the opportunity to work in the cause of the welfare of our people in the Church, and not outside of it. The manner in which they did this disarmed me, and without hesitation I accepted and thus became a participant in the early struggles of the welfare work in Pioneer Stake. At the same time, I realized that these brethren had not been idle but had sought wisdom and inspiration about this matter, and when they invited me they had already achieved in council the plan which was to become a permanent part of Church activities. Incidentally, the "Natural Government" did not live long after that.

It was under such circumstances that the presidency of Pioneer Stake went into action. Much fasting and prayer went into the organization and work. From their own council meetings the entire high council with the stake presidency formulated principles of the welfare work, which still is the basic plan of today.

President Lee's historical account of the organization of Pioneer Stake's welfare work in 1932 continues:

A stake committee—consisting of President Child as chairman, with C. O. Jensen, Thomas E. Wilding, and Brother Finck and Fred J. Heath—was appointed to secure a storehouse agreeable to our plans and to work out the details of its operation, including a suitable bookkeeping and merchandising system.

Within a week their report was submitted to the stake presidency and high council for approval. A suitable warehouse was secured without cost at 333 Pierpont Avenue, belonging to the Browning interests of Ogden. Bishop Jesse M. Drury of the Fifth Ward, who was unemployed, was selected as manager. Brother Finck was selected as head bookkeeper and Gladys May as stenographer. Bishops C. E. Davey, R. F. W. Nickel, and James Graham, also unemployed, were sent into the country districts adjoining Salt Lake City to enter into contract with the farmers in behalf of Pioneer Stake, by which we agreed to furnish labor to farmers to harvest crops when they were ready, for which we were to receive a share of the harvest.

A census of the unemployed of the stake revealed the startling fact that of our 7,300 people, there were over 4,800 who were wholly or partially dependent upon outside agencies for a livelihood. An employment committee in each ward, consisting of a member of the bishopric and the chairman of the welfare committees of the Melchizedek Priesthood quorums and the Relief Society welfare workers, kept in touch with the available male and female workers. Directed by Fred J. Heath of the stake central committee, workers from all wards were assigned to farm and industrial projects, which were organized from Provo on the south to Layton on the north.

Workers were told that for their services the stake would undertake to see that food and fuel and shelter for themselves and their families would be provided fully. Hundreds of tons of produce soon began to roll in—peaches, tomatoes, fruits, vegetables, and meats. Relief Society women were organized and two canning machines

Pioneer and Salt Lake Stake Bishops' Storehouse, 333 Pierpont Avenue, Salt Lake City, 1933

were purchased for their own use. After exhausting all surplus bottles in the area through a "drive," we purchased ten to twenty thousand cans from the American Can Company at 1.5 cents each.

After supplying our families and stocking our storehouse, we were able to sell considerable surplus to outside people.

The storehouse was known as the Pioneer Stake bishop's storehouse and the bishops of our eleven wards were organized into an executive committee, with Bishop Joseph H. McPhie of the 25th Ward as chairman. They were instructed to meet regularly and to manage and initiate the policies of the storehouse. The First Presidency, after hearing our plan, agreed to permit withdrawals from the tithes to supplement the food received from our own efforts. With these funds we purchased at wholesale prices butter, eggs, flour, sugar, coal, etc., to provide a wide variety of foodstuffs for our people.

The authorization by the First Presidency was more dramatic than attested by President Lee's terse explanation. Some thought the dynamic young leaders in Pioneer Stake had just appropriated the tithing funds for their worthy project of taking care of the poor. An added testimony comes from President Paul C. Child as captured on a tape recording just before his death by Elder Glen C. Rudd of the General Welfare Committee. President Child recalls this tense decision:

No, President Lee just didn't take those funds. We had been authorized to use the tithing, but even this wasn't enough. After appealing to the Presiding Bishop for more money, President Lee asked for a meeting with the First Presidency. We went in and presented our problem to President Grant and his counselors.

President Grant, after listening carefully, turned to President Ivins, his first counselor, and said, "What do you think, Tone?"

President Ivins said, "I think these brethren had better take care of their people."

President Grant turned to President Clark, asking, "What do you think, Reub?"

President Clark said: "I agree with President Ivins. These brethren ought to take care of their people, and we ought to be grateful that we have the one stake presidency in the Church that strongly feels the way they do."

President Grant then banged his fist on the table to emphasize his support for the welfare program of Pioneer Stake, saying: "Brethren, take care of your people, and that is the instruction from the First Presidency of the Church. If you need additional money, more than your tithing and fast offering, you are to come directly to the Presidency of the Church from now on, and get the help you need.''

That was a great moment in the history of welfare in the Church. Thereafter changes were made in all aspects of the work so that the poor people could receive the help they needed.

President Lee included in his personal history an article taken from the *Salt Lake Tribune* of that time to further explain the Pioneer Stake relief program, from which the following is quoted:

Exchange Idea Assures Many Jobs for Idle

Stake Adopts Cooperative
Methods Successful in
Pioneer Days

As in the pioneer days of barter and trade, when a man did a day's work for a quantity of oats, exchange is the basis of the cooperative movement to relieve unemployment now in operation in the LDS Pioneer Stake. The movement is under the direction of Harold B. Lee, president of Pioneer Stake, and eleven ward bishops.

No charity is involved, and the unemployed person works strictly on a no-wage basis, receiving goods and foods necessary for his immediate needs. . . .

For the past month, unemployed carpenters, painters, and other workmen have been working on the building, which includes a storage basement, a mezzanine sewing department for renovating old clothes, a main floor for canned goods and groceries, and a second floor for dry goods and clothing. Pioneer Stake members have donated trucks for transportation of goods from outlying districts and from stake homes. Jesse M. Drury, bishop of the Fifth LDS Ward, is manager of the storehouse, and Miss Gladys May is the stenographer.

Each ward bishop is the chairman of a make-work committee. As many as twenty men a day are being sent out to pitch hay on Salt Lake County farms, or to pick peas in American Fork, or cherries and apricots in Bountiful and other towns, each man receiving his pay in produce as distributed from the storehouse.

Mr. Lee announced that Pioneer Stake men are keeping busy in other ways, too, as in the managing of a community vegetable garden at Second West and Thirteenth South streets. The chief benefit of the plan, Mr. Lee said, is that it keeps unemployed men busy and repays them with their greatest needs.

President Lee's history continues with another newspaper article:

The following information, recorded in a newspaper editorial, relates how thirteen men, who were being employed at the Pioneer Stake bishop's storehouse, were seriously injured in a wreck:

October 27, 1932

The Wreck at the Crossing

With the news that 13 men had been seriously injured, one perhaps fatally, when an interurban car struck a loaded truck in the northern part of this city, the sympathy of the people went out to the injured and their families. The men were among the 20,000 of this county who have no regular work and were being employed through the efforts of the Pioneer Stake organization, whose work in meeting this depression has been most commendable. . . .

Meanwhile the injured men are being cared for, and President Harold B. Lee, of the Pioneer Stake, states that the accident has drawn the people more closely together than he would have believed possible. In the southwestern quarter of the city, where there is a very large proportion of unemployment, the stake authorities have been sending out some 75 to 100 men a day, alternating them in work that they have secured from farmers in different parts of the state. There has been a general spirit of unity to help each other, and he states that last night when the knowledge of this serious accident had spread among the people, prayers were offered in the homes of the wards for those who have had added to their already difficult plight, this sudden and serious misfortune.

A MIRACULOUS ASSISTANCE IN A CRISIS

President Lee's account continues, as he recorded it in his historical account:

In the fall of 1932 it became apparent that the drain upon the finances of the Church was more than the Church could stand, and the tithes of our wards had so decreased that they could not pay the relief needs of the people. We were determined that our promise to the people should be made good, but how was a big question. The government had just launched a huge relief program, known as the Reconstruction Finance Corporation, and the Church sent out word that hereafter, relief of Church members was to come from that source. It seemed that we must break faith with our people.

At this critical juncture, we called a meeting of our bishops. They asked us what they were to do. As though moved by the Spirit of the Lord, President Child said: "We want you to see to it that every one of your people is taken care of. We don't know where the money will come from to pay the bills, but our people must be provided with their needs." I heartily seconded his instruction, but as we left the stake hall we wondered from where our help would come.

The answer came within the next two weeks. Through our efforts, our storehouse, with its entire personnel, was made a county auxiliary storehouse to serve our district and the government agreed to purchase all the produce we had on hand at regular prices. My appointment as city commissioner seemed to come at just the psychological time to give us prestige in accomplishing our objective. With the government purchasing our supplies garnered from the previous summer's effort, we were able to take care not only of those who came within the scope of the Reconstruction Finance Corporation, but all our worthy Latter-day Saints who were entitled to help from the Church. When the RFC discontinued its operations the next spring, we found we had between four and five thousand dollars in the bank and approximately two thousand dollars worth of produce in the storehouse. Certainly the Lord had "ordered" events for the succor of his children.

PIONEER STAKE GYM

The Pioneer Stake gym was undertaken as a work project [in 1933] under our Pioneer Stake relief program. The First Presidency gave us $4,500, the unemployed of the stake furnished us with carpenters, masons, painters, bricklayers, and laborers, and the balance of the cost was taken from funds earned in produce the previous summers. The work on the gymnasium was directed by T. T. Burton and the laborers were organized by Fred J. Heath. Both of these brethren were unemployed and were members of the high council of the stake. When completed, a fine opening social was held, at which President Heber J. Grant and Bishop Sylvester Q. Cannon, Presiding Bishop of the Church and native of our stake, were present. All the rough lumber for the building and all the bricks were secured from old dilapidated buildings which were obtained from the owners for the tearing down and cleaning up the premises. Bishop Nicholas G. Smith, of the 17th Ward, donated an old building that provided most of our large timbers.

The following account, from a newspaper article, gives a description of this project:

Men are busily engaged in putting the roof on the new Pioneer Stake gymnasium at Eighth West between Fifth and Sixth South streets.

Work on this $15,000 building was begun last spring and will be completed by the time winter sets in. The building was carried forward as a make-work project. . . .

Approximately 25 to 30 men have been at work each day for the past six weeks on the new Pioneer Stake gymnasium, to rush it to a completion by the middle of September, it was announced Saturday by President Harold B. Lee, of the Pioneer Stake.

These men, President Lee reports, have donated their time at no cost to the stake, and the building, although approved as a make-work project, has been erected without the aid of the federal funds, as was announced Friday. President Lee said that it was a stake project and that to have accepted the federal make-work funds for the building, they would have been forced to employ men living outside of the stake boundaries.

This gymnasium, which at its completion will be valued at approximately $30,000, will have been erected at a cash expenditure of about $3,000. Those men working on the building are among the unemployed of the stake, and their families have received aid through the facilities of the stake warehouse. . . .

When the gymnasium has been completed it will be operated under the direction of a stake committee.

President Lee's historical record then told how the new gym was used.

Activities of the Gym: 1933–34

The MIA organizations and the Primary were given charge of the activities of the gym, and from October 1933 through the winter, every night from six o'clock until eleven o'clock was programmed with activities involving the various groups, from Primary age to adult women and men. Bleachers seating four hundred people were provided, and it was no uncommon sight to see from four hundred to seven hundred spectators enjoying the evening's contests and sports. In many instances the recreation provided at the gym was the only recreation these people had enjoyed since the depression in 1929.

1934 Recreational Plan

In 1934 we planned to further intensify its use. Our objective for the stake was "to provide fully for the spiritual, physical, educational, and recreational needs of every member of Pioneer Stake." To attain that objective, recreationally, we promoted a uniform stake budget plan by which the purchasers in one ward may be admitted to all events in their ward and in the stake and in every

Pioneer Stake Gymnasium constructed in 1933 as a work project under the Pioneer Stake relief program

other ward in the stake. Those who were able were asked to pay sufficient to provide entertainment for those who were dependent, and, upon the bishop's recommendation, the latter may even receive his budget ticket gratis. All wards were put on a strict budget for all maintenance and organizational needs. All public dances in the stake were held in the gymnasium and participated in by all holders of stake budget tickets in order to control the character of the participants and to provide the highest standard of entertainment.

The building of the gym was a veritable inspiration; had it been started one month later, its success and the ultimate ridiculously low cost would have been jeopardized.

"A MARVEL TO VISITORS"

In our plan for the relief of the people of Pioneer Stake, there was no new organization effected—it was merely the setting of the quorums and organizations of the Church in motion. And, while it was a marvel to visitors not of the Church and unacquainted with the Church organization, it was merely the applying of the Lord's method to the solution of the present problem.

A *Salt Lake Tribune* reporter wrote a news article at the instance of John F. Fitzpatrick, the newspaper's publisher, who, through President J. Reuben Clark, Jr., asked to visit our storehouse. I explained our plan from the issuance of the "pay" slip to the workman to the "pay-off" through the storehouse, and then took him to visit the Second West garden and the gym to see the men actually at work, then to the storehouse to see the Relief Society women canning fruits and vegetables and remodeling and sewing clothes for needy persons.

Several Eastern men also came to visit our projects, among whom was a Mr. Pearmain, from Washington, who was connected with government relief; Mr. Markey, a friend of President Clark's from New York; and a brother of the Reverend Webb, who years ago wrote "The Case Against Mormonism." Each was the same in saying without hesitation: "We dream of these accomplishments being possible in the East, but never hoped to have it worked out as practically as you have it here."

Many a relief worker during those years "thanked God for the storehouse," but through our experience with this cooperative relief plan, we learned first-hand why the people of the Church are not prepared to live the United Order.

LDS SCRIP

At the first of 1933, the Presiding Bishopric reduced its appropriation to wards for ward maintenance. As a consequence there was such an alarming decrease in individual donations for this purpose that the six city stakes, Salt Lake, Ensign, Liberty, Granite, Grant, and Pioneer, entered into an organization known as "Six Salt Lake City Stakes Associated." The purpose of such an organization was to foster a scheme of financing that amounted to a 2 percent sales tax on all purchases made with "Guaranteed Emergency Certificates" issued by the "Six Salt Lake City Stakes Associated." The earnings from the sale of stamps were required to be affixed to the certificate to validate the purchase and was returned to the sixty-six wards of the six stakes in proportion to the participation of each. The sale of the $100,000 issue started briskly, with business houses and ward members cooperating splendidly. Opposition quickly arose from these sources: first, from employees of the Church offices and Church institutions who feared they would receive too much scrip for their salaries; second, from the Church bankers who saw in the plan a danger to their institutions; and third, from non-Mormon institutions who objected to paying into a proposition that had for its objective the paying of ward expenses by the Mormon Church. President A. W. Ivins had favored it in the absence of President Heber J. Grant, but when President Grant returned, he branded it as something that looked too much like "getting something for nothing." Gradually, one institution after another refused to honor the scrip, after first having consented, until it was found advisable to recall all certificates at their full value. President Wilford Beesley was chairman of the organization, with President B. S. Hinckley, President Winslow Farr Smith, President Hugh B. Brown, President Joseph J. Haynes, and myself as associates. Bishop Gordon Taylor Hyde served as secretary.

GOVERNMENT EMPLOYMENT ACTIVITIES

The gigantic work-relief program instituted by the government, known as the Civil Works Administration, will probably go down in history as the most stupendous expenditure of federal funds for direct unemployment relief ever attempted. Under this program money was allocated to the various states as an outright grant based upon the number of unemployed in the state. "Re-employment bureaus" for registering all unemployed men and women were opened in every county. Untrained workers and lack of definiteness in this registration caused much confusion, and it was no uncommon practice for the same men to register four or five times and to receive as many cards calling him for various work projects.

In this program, cash was paid outright, with the wage scale ranging from 50¢ an hour for laborers to $1.25 an hour for skilled mechanics. It was apparently the thought of federal authorities that these billions of dollars poured into the pockets of the consumers of the country would act as a "prime" to revive business. While this continued, all business did flourish, but the revival was apparently but temporary, for after a trial of five months, from December 1932 to May 1933, this program was halted and there came into existence another organization known as the Federal Emergency Relief Administration, or the FERA.

The FERA refused to accept men for work on its accepted projects unless they were adjudged to be in need of relief. Each applicant was compelled to sign an affidavit declaring his assets. Such stipulations were required to be certified before a notary public, and if it were found that the man had money in savings, life insurance policies that might have a surrender value, etc., he was refused help until such time as he had exhausted his last resources. Great consternation followed and I thought surely here was a similar condition to that described in the Bible as the "grinding the faces of the poor." Workers under this program were far less efficient and much dissatisfaction was the result, with groups of Communists staging demonstrations before legislative officials and public office holders.

RIOTS AND COUNTERMEASURES

On one of these occasions, the rioters halted a sheriff's sale on the steps of the City and County Building and forced the sheriff with his deputies back into the building, down the steps to the first floor, where the officers attempted to halt them with streams of water from a fire hose. The Communists promptly took the hose away and the officers resorted to tear gas bombs. These were thrown back at the officers, and they retreated into the sheriff's office and out of the windows while the marchers took possession of the building. All city and county employees were ordered to vacate the offices until order could be restored and the tear gas fumes ventilated from the building. Following the escapade, the Communists became bolder, openly threatening government officials until their demands were met. They marched to the state capitol while the state legislature was in session and demanded a hearing. Oscar Larson, an alien leader, and others were permitted to appear before a joint session of the House and Senate. Here a disgraceful scene was staged, which thoroughly disgusted even those among the lawmakers who had been inclined to be friendly.

In order to combat this menace, a secret meeting of the American Legion was called at the Armory on Fourth East and Fourth South, attended by city and county officials, who explained the purpose of the meeting. All Legionnaires were sworn in as special officers and each one armed with a hickory wagon spoke with a buckskin string through one end to sling upon the wrist. The following day the Communists had planned a second raid upon the City and County Building. At 7:30 a.m., the American Legion began to assemble. First-aid supplies and tear [gas] bombs were deposited on the third floor in the city council chamber. No one was allowed to enter the building except they were properly identified. As the Communists began to gather they encountered the grim-looking men seated on the steps at all entrances to the building. Mass meetings were held throughout the day which were addressed by the leaders. There was no violence whatever, but the Legion men left that day keenly and visibly disappointed that there had been no fight. Shortly thereafter, [the rioters'] leader, Larson, was arrested and deported, and it appeared that sane thinking was to replace un-American tactics in trying to iron out the difficulties of unfortunates who were forced to accept charitable assistance.

A Blessing to the Needy

This record of President Lee's stake presidency years demonstrates his unbounded concern for the poor and the needy during the Great Depression, when a majority of the members of Pioneer Stake were unemployed. Here we can readily perceive the principles that were developing in his mind, concepts that would later become famous in the operation of the Church welfare plan.

When President Lee later instructed Church members on the principles of the welfare program, no one ever doubted the authenticity of his counsel. He had been through the program's travail from its earliest labor pains. His mind, aided by devoted associates, had conceived of the principles, as inspired by heaven and in answer to earnest prayers from an impoverished people. No one in Church history had a more firm understanding of the welfare program than did Harold B. Lee, for his knowledge and conviction was born of personal struggles. Untold thousands of Latter-day Saints throughout the Church have been blessed by those early efforts in Pioneer Stake.

1932–1934. Franklin D. Roosevelt was elected president of the United States and his fireside chats soothed a troubled nation. Frequency-modulation (FM) radio was perfected by a United States scientist named Edwin Armstrong. A United States astronomer, Karl Jansky, invented the science of radio astronomy, allowing men to "see" deep into space. The Security Exchange Act was passed.

CHAPTER 8

Entrance into Politics

Although heavily involved in the stressful endeavors of helping his Pioneer Stake membership survive the economic depression, President Lee also found time to serve his community.

APPOINTMENT TO CITY COMMISSION

Here is his account of his entry into the political arena:

During the latter part of October 1932, Commissioner Joseph H. Lake died following an operation at the Latter-day Saints Hospital.

A day or two after his death I made a casual call upon John M. Knight, Commissioner of Public Safety and my former mission president, at the Public Safety Building to discuss the details of a meeting held a few weeks before in the Pioneer Stake Hall, where I had defended the honor of John M. Knight and T. T. Burton against the accusations of Richard R. Lyman, Gordon T. Hyde, Heber C. Iverson, and others. During our conversation, the death of Commissioner Lake was mentioned and John M. Knight asked if I would accept the appointment if it were offered to me. It was the furthest thing from my mind, and I asked him what chance he thought I would have. He said he thought I had all the chance in the world. He called Police Chief Payne into his office, then he left immediately to make contacts that would start a sentiment in my interest. As I walked out into the lobby, I was met by Clarence Cowan, my brother-in-law, who was then active in city government, who asked the same question as to why I should not seek the vacant appointment on the city commission.

I had business later that day at the Presiding Bishop's Office, and as I walked in the door, I was met by Frank Penrose and Charles S. Hyde, who told me they just had been talking about the possibilities of my being appointed to the city commission.

The coincidence was rather startling, and from that moment it seemed that I was shoved from this place to the other, where I contacted some of the most influential friends, all close to the Board of Commissioners. Among those most active in urging my appointment were Clarence Cowan, Joseph H. Preece, E. C. Davies, Jack Findling, and Lee Lovinger.

One of the most powerful friends I met at this time was John F. Fitzpatrick, manager of the Kearns interests and publisher of the *Salt Lake Tribune* and the *Salt Lake Telegram.*

During the weeks of anxiety and uncertainty as to the outcome of my candidacy, Paul Child said to me, "Well, I have placed the matter before the Lord, and if you're to be the next commissioner, it will be because he wants you there." This statement defined very clearly my own feelings, and it was with that thought in my mind that I accepted the appointment to take office on December 1, 1932.

The following is an announcement of my appointment as city commissioner as recorded in a newspaper clipping:

Board Elects West Side Man To City Office

Appointment Effective Dec. 1
Under Action of Commission

Nominated By Marcus

Officer Due To Be Assigned
To Street Department

Harold Bingham Lee, 34, of 1310 Indiana Avenue, was appointed City Commissioner Wednesday to fill the unexpired term of the late Commissioner Joseph H. Lake.

The appointment is effective December 1. While it was proposed by Mayor Louis Marcus, Commissioners Harry L. Finch, George D. Keyser and John M. Knight unanimously concurred in the appointment. . . .

"I will endeavor to give the people of Salt Lake City the same business-like and efficient service they have been receiving and cooperate fully with other members of the commission," said Mr. Lee.

Mr. Lee was born March 28, 1899, in Clifton, Idaho and moved to Salt Lake ten years ago. He has been a resident of the westside ever since his arrival and joins the commission as a representative of that section. He has been prominent in civic organizations, particularly those interested in building up and improving the westside of the City. He has been the leader in battles before the City Commission for the maintenance of adequate public transportation for westside residents. . . .

The term of office which Mr. Lee will complete begins December 1 and expires January 1, 1934, and will be preceded by the usual municipal primary election in October, 1933, and the regular city election for the purpose of selecting two commissioners and a city auditor in November, 1933.

It is regarded as certain that he will be a candidate for reelection next fall. The availability of a candidate as election timber for the coming year was frequently and openly discussed by members of the City Commission during the consideration of the 30 or more applicants for the position.

It is also regarded certain that Harry L. Finch, commissioner of parks and public property, will be a candidate to succeed himself. Holdover members of the Commission will be Mayor Louis Marcus and Commissioners George D. Keyser and John M. Knight, who are serving their first year of the present administration, though Mr. Keyser was a commissioner many years ago.

The *Salt Lake Tribune* commended Harold B. Lee and the city commission for his selection in an editorial the day following announcement of his appointment:

A Wise Selection

Salt Lake finds a promising executive in Harold B. Lee, who has just qualified for the vacancy in the city commission caused by the death of Joseph H. Lake, commissioner of streets. The commission is entitled to public commendation for its wise and happy selection.

Mr. Lee is well and favorably known throughout the city and state. While he has not been active in politics, his civic interest has

Salt Lake City commissioners and other officials, 1938–39: (left to right) George D. Keyser, Ethel McDonald, Harold B. Lee, Charles Finlayson, William Murdock, P. H. Goggin, and Mayor E. B. Erwin

been keen. He is well acquainted with local problems and is ably qualified for the work which he has undertaken.

The new commissioner is young and vigorous, carrying with him the full courage of his convictions. By reason of these virtues the public may expect a strong and efficient administration of his department.

As a resident of the west side, his selection is entirely compatible with the sectional complexion of the city commission as determined by the election of his predecessor. Mr. Lee, undoubtedly, will be given every measure of public cooperation in his new work. The *Tribune* extends its congratulations to the new commissioner and commends the remainder of the commission for an appointment so promising of sound public service.

WORK AS COMMISSIONER

Harold B. Lee later reflected on those first days of public service:

> I entered upon my new work with considerable fear and many misgivings. Most of my close friends bemoaned my "entrance into politics" as disastrous to my character and standing. Then, too, I was entering the governing body of the city at a time when the finances and business affairs were in a precarious condition. While the demands of the people were the same as formerly, the available funds were the lowest since the inauguration of the commission form of government in about 1915. By the 15th of December, the budgets had to be prepared, and immediately after my taking office I worked day and night in a study of the Departments of Streets and Public Improvements in order to make a fairly intelligent budget of the department's needs for 1933. At the time, John M. Knight and I were the only Mormons on the board. [The others were] Marcus, Keyser, and Finch. . . .

> The year 1933 saw the expansion of government aid in relief as an attempt to stem the depression. Following the demise of the Reconstruction Finance Corporation work relief activities, there followed, with the incoming national Democratic administration under Franklin D. Roosevelt, the Civil Works Administration, by which the city was required to furnish the materials and supervision while the CWA provided the labor.

> A feature story article was written for the *Salt Lake Tribune* under date of January 28, 1934, again at the instance of my old friend, John F. Fitzpatrick. He saw in this project and others under my direction, as Commissioner for Streets and Public Improvements, much to commend. He instructed one of their leading reporters, Monte Wilson, to write the story and obtain photographs telling of our many projects to make Salt Lake City a better place to live.
>
> In his article, Wilson was extremely thorough and took special care to avoid exaggerations.

> Upon taking office, I found it necessary to discharge the supervisor of streets. . . . He threatened me if I should let him go. Because of the lack of finances, I abolished the position of office manager, which was held by Lou Fisher.
>
> The only new appointment I made was that of John S. Corless as foreman of maintenance.

A newspaper article about the new commissioner's first day in office contained the following comments:

> Harold B. Lee voted officially on the motions before the City Commission Thursday when, under an appointment effective December 1, he took his place as a member of the board that governs Salt Lake City.
>
> He voted first in the affirmative on a motion made by Commissioner John M. Knight that Mr. Lee be assigned to the Street Department, the position held by the late Commissioner Joseph H. Lake, whom Mr. Lee succeeds. . . .
>
> Aside from a study of the budget for 1933, Mr. Lee said his experience was as yet insufficient to make any definite announcement as to policy.
>
> So far as political obligations are concerned, he said, he has only those inherited from Commissioner Lake and regards it an obligation to fill the place vacated by the late commissioner.
>
> "There will be no changes in the present personnel of the Street Department to meet any of my personal obligations or favor, even for the friends who have worked for me," he said.
>
> "The streets and sidewalks and the collection of garbage and ashes and other services of the department that spends so much public money, must be maintained. The only duties I have pertain to efficient service and city economy."

FIRST POLITICAL CAMPAIGN

The year 1933, my first in public office, was one full of new experiences and responsibilities. The Department of Streets and Public Improvements employed more men than any other city department except the public safety, which was operated largely under civil service. I found that to be responsible for a half-million dollars annually in the management of the department required intensive study of the organization itself and the personnel. Then, too, I accepted the appointment as city commissioner with the understanding that I would be a candidate for election in the fall of 1933.

My only hope to be successful in the election was to build my department into a political organization that could cope successfully with other political groups. To this end, I began the first of September to segregate my 250 employees into precincts and to hold meetings with them to become better acquainted, to outline plans, to define my position on various questions, to prepare them to answer complaints, and to meet opposition that might come.

In answer to those who declared that the Street Department was "not worth a damn" politically, we were successful in polling 13,336 voters in the primary election, to qualify the highest of the four winning candidates in the primary election.

I had chosen as an advisory committee, Joseph H. Preece, Clarence Cowan, E. C. Davies, and Lauren W. Gibbs, with Parley Eccles as my campaign manager.

There were about twenty candidates for the office of city commissioner and four for the office of city auditor. Among the candidates was my old supervisor, J. Fields Greenwood, who had sworn to defeat me. He polled slightly less than five hundred votes in the primary voting.

The two weeks between the primary and the election was a veritable nightmare, with each of the four qualifying candidates fighting for every advantage. The questions of prohibition and the proposed Municipal Power Plant likewise were to be decided in the same balloting.

In order to push the liquor question into the campaign, the editors of the *Salt Lake Tribune* demanded a statement from each of the candidates as to their position on the prohibition question. I took the position that it was not an issue for the city election, but finally it was thought wise that I prepare such a public statement. Seeking counsel from my old friend, John F. Fitzpatrick, of the Kearns interests, I worded a brief statement to the effect that "I was not satisfied with conditions as they were under prohibition and I certainly could not sanction the old saloon conditions of the past."

My opponents immediately attacked this statement saying I was dry, while others said I had "straddled" the fence, but my good friends upheld and defended me and my position, that I had the courage of my convictions and had taken the only position I could without being a traitor to my professions as a Church man and a known dry.

The Goggin forces were radical wets, and Finch and Mullins were both wet.

I was favored by two natural advantages in the election: first, I was the only Mormon left in the race; and second, I was the only westside candidate.

Admittedly I was in an awkward position as a stake president running for office at the time when Salt Lake City was voting two to one to repeal prohibition. In spite of these handicaps, I led the other three candidates by nearly three thousand votes, the official tabulation giving me 29,336 votes.

Finch blamed the Utah Power and Light Company for his defeat, saying that they had financed Goggin.

There were only three pieces of campaign literature circulated in my behalf, chiefly because there was no source from which money could be obtained for a greater advertising campaign. On one of the handouts there were listed the names of men and women who were a truly representative group from all classes, political parties, and religions. . . . While this group of sponsors are commonly known to politicians as "scenery," I found these persons to be warm friends and splendid backers.

Following is the copy from one piece of campaign literature, which documents the accomplishments of Commissioner Lee in his first year in office:

Harold B. Lee

was appointed City Commissioner on December 1, 1932, to fill the vacancy caused by the death of the late Street Commissioner, Joseph H. Lake.

Some of his first year's accomplishments:

- Has operated his department on $145,682.75 less than in 1931.
- Saved the taxpayers in one year $24,629.03, as certified to by the City Auditing Department.
- Has rendered efficient service in the maintenance of streets, sanitary sewers, and storm sewers.
- Increased efficiency, economy, and sanitation in garbage disposal.
- Maintained 535 miles and resurfaced 70.7 miles of city streets.
- Because of the increased efficiency and consequent savings as above set forth, and regardless of the low budget, has employed more laborers than in 1932, *without reducing the wage scale.*

Instrumental in securing the expenditure of 2½ million dollars of federal and state funds for building cement highways in our community in 1933–34.

Has worked harmoniously with the present Commission to maintain a business-like administration.

A tribute to Commissioner Lee's accomplishments in this regard is well set forth in the following quotation from a local paper:

"The Salt Lake City Commission, . . . despite
the shrinkage in valuations, kept down the levy and

Harold B. Lee (third from left), commissioner of the Salt Lake City Department of Streets and Public Improvements, with officials and employees of that department in front of the City and County Building

> proceeded to cut and carve and save in the operation
> of city government."

Mr. Lee's accomplishments are a tribute to the young man of today.

A vote for Harold B. Lee is a vote for sound, constructive, efficient and economical administration of your public business.

Another interesting sidelight is a visit that the victorious commissioner had with a member of the First Presidency. In his personal journal Harold B. Lee recorded the following excellent advice to men in political office, counsel which he himself passed on to dozens of public figures as they, in time, came to him for advice on how to conduct themselves in office:

> Following the election I called on the First Presidency of the Church and had a visit with President A. W. Ivins. I told him it would be my pleasure to counsel with them on any matters in which they were interested. He [told me] that the only counsel he

had to offer was that I should take the actions I thought were right. He said, "I would ten times rather a man would make a mistake while doing that which he thought was right than to do right just for policy sake." President Heber J. Grant and President J. Reuben Clark, Jr., were in the East during the election, but both came to the county clerk's office and voted. President Clark and his wife came to my office afterward and wished me "good luck."

Because of the utmost importance of this campaign to be elected city commissioner, both from the standpoint of my economic welfare and my political future, or opportunities for a continuance in public life, I kept minute records of election returns, district by district, as they were reported in the public press.

My work brought me in contact with the leaders in every field, and I have formed friendships that wouldn't be possible otherwise. I have had the opportunity to see men at their best and at their worst. One of my choice associations was with John M. Knight. Assigned to the Public Safety Department, he was constantly a target at which everyone was shooting. With a rough exterior, he was always vigorous and at times defiant, and yet in our intimate contacts I found him as pliable as a child.

1934–1948. Amelia Earhart and her plane were missing over the Pacific Ocean. German dirigible *Hindenburg* exploded. German physicist Otto Hahn split atoms of uranium to produce a reaction called "nuclear fission." Invasion of Poland and Austria by Hitler started World War II. The jet age began with the flight of a German Heinkel 178 aircraft, powered by a gas-turbine jet engine. Congress passed draft laws. John Ford's *Stagecoach* was the first adult western movie. The United States found relief in celluloid musicals, radio, and Big Bands.

CHAPTER 9

Family Life

What is it like to grow up in the home of a prophet?

In a small home on Indiana Avenue on the west side of Salt Lake City, where they had moved in 1928, the Lee family—Harold and Fern and their two little girls—continued to build their loving and exemplary relationships. For some reason known only to our Heavenly Father, this was destined to be the permanent size of this little family.

The idealism of these parents immediately began to leave a lasting impression on their children, their friends, and their neighbors. They consistently demonstrated a simple joy and appreciation for each other and the absolute assurance that God was near and would bless their every pursuit.

Helen's childhood memories illustrate the loving relationship of this young father with his little girls:

> We were living in a home my parents had bought from my Grandfather and Grandmother Tanner, my mother's parents. A sleeping porch had been built onto the back of this house where space heaters were supposed to keep it warm in the wintertime; however, they were not very adequate, and it always was cold out there. Our nightly ritual would begin with the four of us kneeling together in prayer in the living room, and then Daddy would take one of us in each of his arms and carry us to our bed so we wouldn't have to walk across the cold floor. As we grew bigger, he would still carry us by putting one of us on his back and the other in his arms, reluctant I suppose to give up that special "togetherness." He always had some endearing words to say to us as he tucked the covers tightly around us.

He knew then, and later was to teach the entire Church, how important it was that children feel their father's love for them. It was through experiences such as this nightly routine that Maurine and Helen grew up knowing of their father's interest and concern for his little girls. Helen reflects even today on that important emotional foundation, saying, "I have often thought about that expression of father love to us and ever will be grateful that love, security, and tenderness were planted deep in our hearts."

FIRST LESSON

Helen's earliest recollection of her father's teachings reach back to the day she first was introduced to her Heavenly Father in an unforgettable lesson. Of course, the girls had been taught from the time they could talk to say their prayers, but on this particular occasion they were to learn from their father what this relationship really meant.

> When my sister and I were still very small we went with Mother and Daddy and several other families on a picnic to hike up to Timpanogos Cave, in American Fork Canyon, near Provo, Utah. We had our lunch and the plan was to then hike up to the cave. Mother, wisely recognizing the limitations on her physical strength, decided not to try to make the climb with us. Knowing she wouldn't be with

us she was full of admonitions and advice, reminding us to stay close to Daddy, not to let go of his hand, not to run, and that we must not get too close to the edge of the trail.

I remember moving up a little closer to Daddy, gripping his hand a bit tighter as I said to Mother when we parted: "Oh, Mommy, you don't have to worry about us. As long as we're with Daddy we'll be just fine. He won't let anything hurt us." My complete confidence in my Daddy's ability to keep us safe must have started him thinking as he realized that there was yet a greater lesson he could teach his little girls as they walked along the trail that day.

He told us that I was right; as long as Daddy was there and was right close by, he would do everything he could to keep us safe from harm. But, he added, there would come a time in our lives when Daddy couldn't be with us, when we'd be away from him, when there would be dangers other than physical dangers that we would encounter. As we grew older we would realize that we needed someone else besides our Daddy to keep us safe. He reminded us about our Heavenly Father, explaining that He loved us every bit as much as did our earthly father, and that He had the power to be with us wherever we were, wherever we went.

Whatever the circumstances, whatever the danger, we could always call upon this unseen Heavenly Father to guide us and to help us. That lesson has never been forgotten and my understanding of my relationship with my Heavenly Father began in that early childhood experience.

On September 16, 1934, President Lee, president of Pioneer Stake, was invited to give the Sunday evening sermon in the Salt Lake Tabernacle. He related this same experience with his girls. He preceded the story by saying, "Obedience and confidence in God, it seems to me, are absolutely necessary to moral safety and spiritual well-being." In conclusion, he added: "If confidence in God is established, love for him and obedience to him will follow. Then, and only then, can the teachings of the scriptures become live symbols to us."

A Practicing Psychologist

This young father practiced a form of modern psychology, known as "the positive reinforcement technique," perhaps without knowing it as anything other than the promptings of the Spirit and the answers to humble, parental prayers. It fits as a perfect application of the "As If" theory popularized by William James of Harvard University, and it seemed to work successfully in the lives of Maurine and Helen. Helen explains as follows the principle she only came to understand fully in her adult years:

> Whatever it was that he wanted us to become he told us that we were already. Because we loved him so much we tried hard to be what he thought we were, what he told us we were, so that we would not disappoint him. We didn't ever want him to find out that we really weren't as good as he thought we were. We always wanted him to be proud of us.
>
> For example, my sister and I started taking music lessons when we were very young. I played the violin and my sister, the piano. He would tell us that there was nothing grander than to have his little girls play for him and that together we made the most beautiful music this side of heaven. In reality, we were squeaking and squawking and playing many wrong notes, but he always made us feel that it was just the loveliest music he'd ever heard. The result was we'd practice when we really didn't want to do so, to perfect our music just for Daddy's sake. Finally, after we had surmounted the initial obstacles, it then became an enjoyable experience for us and we were able to practice for the right reason. But the psychology had worked as he must have known it would. His desire to have musicians in the family was fulfilled, and our lives were made richer because of his wisdom and encouragement.
>
> In our awkward, adolescent years he would tell us often that he was so proud of his beautiful, charming daughters. Well, I knew I was anything but beautiful and charming. My hair was "Dutch" cut, I wore horn-rimmed glasses which I hated, I was pudgy and overweight, and even had to wear corrective shoes. Yet, I reasoned, if Daddy thought I was beautiful, I must try very hard to be what he thought I was, because I just couldn't disappoint him. So every night in my prayers I asked God to help me become what my daddy thought I was already.

Another illustration of his fatherly psychology is the manner in which he resolved the differences of opinion about the seating order at the table. Helen told how she finally was satisfied with her chair for meals:

> Daddy used to sit at the end of the table and Mother sat on his right. My sister and I would contend about who was going to sit on his left. Both of us wanted the honor of sitting closest to Daddy, on the other side of him. Maurine had chosen first to sit by Daddy at this particular meal and I said, "Oh, but you sat there last time and now it's my turn." She countered, "But I chose to first."
>
> Then the master teacher resolved the argument. Turning to me he said, "Now Helen, I need you to sit across the table from me for a

very special reason. You know I have a terrible time with this soup and sometimes I spill it on my tie or on my shirt. Now, if you sit right there across from me you can watch Daddy to make certain I don't spill anything on this nice new tie." After that I was perfectly happy with my place of honor, sitting facing him, contented with the responsibility of watching him and making certain he didn't get any spots on his tie.

A Close Family

There was never a trace of disappointment that he was not blessed with sons. Helen has often stated:

> If he were ever disappointed in not having a son, Maurine and I never knew that. He made us think that having two little girls was just the greatest blessing he could have as a father. I've appreciated that attitude, because, of course, as we grew older we knew that he might have had some regrets. But if he did, we certainly didn't know it at the time we were growing up.

In fact, the subject was never mentioned until two months before his death. At a tribute dinner to honor L. Brent Goates, his first son-in-law, after Brent's twenty-one years of service to the Latter-day Saints Hospital, President Lee said, in his response at the end of the banquet program: "I suppose it is the desire for every father to one day have a son. Daughters, yes, they are wonderful! But to have a son, I suppose, is the hope and desire of every father. When Brent came into my life, I found that son."

Harold B. Lee was blessed to have grandsons and another son-in-law to help fill the void of not having a son of his own. He greatly enjoyed his eight grandsons, as well as his two grand-daughters, because of the enrichment and fulfillment they brought to his life.

The Lee family was a close-knit unit. Maurine and Helen were only fifteen months apart in age and grew up as constant companions. They were taught that sisters didn't ever quarrel, but that they just loved each other.

In those days the Church had no family home evening program, but with a small family of four the purposes of family togetherness were addressed in other ways just as effectively. Much of the time when the girls were small, the family could go with Harold as he made his calls as a salesman for Foundation Press. The principal product that Harold was selling was the Master

Library, a set of beautiful books about the Bible. Helen recalls, "I still can remember fondly turning those pages, reading those great stories, and loving the beautiful photographs in those books."

In the evening when he was making a sale, conducting his business, or delivering a set of books, the family would quickly leave with him after dinner, waiting in the car while he took care of his business. Helen remembers the fun times on the way home:

> There was always an ice cream cone or some other treat when Daddy had finished his business for the evening. We frequently stopped at an A&W Root Beer stand, where Daddy would drive in, roll down his car window, and order, "Two and two." That meant he wanted two large mugs of root beer and two small ones. The half-sized mugs had the same handles on them as the large ones, and we took great delight in drinking from them.

As explained earlier, Harold became the Intermountain Sales Manager of the Foundation Press in 1930, which took him frequently out of state. He never failed to use these trips for family vacation purposes, and in addition to taking his wife and two girls with him, he would often invite his parents to travel with them.

Some of the girls' fondest childhood memories were of these trips. Harold's then unmarried sister Verda would sometimes go with Grandmother and Grandfather Lee, too. The first time the girls ever went to Yellowstone Park, they all went together.

Helen still remembers one particular automobile trip to the Northwest:

> Grandfather Lee found it difficult to sit in the back seat for two or three hours at a time. As a night watchman at ZCMI he was accustomed to doing a lot of walking. So, when we stopped at a service station, Grandpa would get out of the car and say, "Which direction will you take out of town, Harold?" Dad would indicate the way we'd be going, and then Grandpa would say: "Well, pick me up along the way." He would then start off down the highway walking rapidly, and we would find Grandpa quite a way down the road.

The first car Harold and Fern owned was a little Model T Ford. That was when the two girls were babies. The first new car the Lees ever owned came many years later, when Harold was a Salt Lake City commissioner. In later years, however, Harold preferred Buicks and traded them in frequently, always driving a late-model car.

Harold's desire to brighten and bless the lives of his parents is also seen in other family activities. Harold's parents were frequent visitors in his home for dinner, especially on holidays and birthdays. This established a very close relationship among them. Helen further describes these occasions:

> My aunt, my father's youngest sister, Verda, lived with my grandparents for many years after they moved to Salt Lake. My grandfather died shortly after Aunt Verda was married, so Grandmother lived with my Aunt Verda and her husband, Charles J. Ross, until the time of her death. All the time I was growing up it was Grandpa and Grandma Lee and Aunt Verda, and eventually Uncle "Chick," who were with us on every special occasion. Every Christmas they would come and stay overnight with us, from the time Maurine and I were born, until we were married. They were with us often in those years, and it was a happy circumstance for all of us.

TEACHING FROM THE SCRIPTURES

Everyone who has known Harold B. Lee has been aware of his outstanding comprehension of the scriptures. When asked questions he most often answered from the scriptures. Such a scripturalist would, of course, teach his daughters to love the words from God and the prophets as did he; yet he did it so routinely and consistently that his daughters grew up with these sacred books almost unaware of their father's constant teaching. Helen reflects upon her own scriptural development in these words:

> Whenever we had a question as we prepared for a two-and-a-half-minute talk we were to give, or whenever anything was discussed around the dinner table requiring an answer, we'd ask, "What about this, Dad? What do you think?" He would reply, "Get out your scriptures, girls, and let's see what the Lord says about it." He would get his book, too, and have us turn to the right scripture and we'd read together what we needed to know. There were many times when I would think how much easier and quicker it would be if Daddy would just give us the answer. But I came to understand later that he was once again giving us a wonderful opportunity to learn important lessons. In so doing, he taught us that the scriptures were where we turn first for our answers. He didn't go to the intellectual, academic, or philosophical answers of men, or to the beautiful, lofty lines of poets. Those, he told us, were wonderful resources, but they were sought only after we had searched the scriptures and the spiritual essence was understood. These were keys to his profound knowledge of the scriptures, and he wanted us to know and love them, too.

This wise father made certain that his teenage daughters had their own personal sets of the standard works. To make them all the more precious he wrote inscriptions in each book of scripture, which proved to uplift not only his daughters but also others with whom they were shared through the years.

For one of Maurine's books he wrote:

> To my dear Maurine: That you may have a constant measure by which to judge between truth and the errors of man's philosophies, and thus grow in spirituality as you increase in knowledge, I give you this sacred book to read frequently and cherish throughout your life. Lovingly, your father, Harold B. Lee.

Maurine's scriptures also contained the most remembered and most frequently quoted of all the inscriptions:

> The sermons of your father will be no better than the lives of his daughters.

MUSICAL TALENT

Sometimes historical accounts glowingly describe Harold B. Lee's musical ability. One such reference said, "He played musical instruments as a young boy and became an accomplished musician." On one occasion at Brigham Young University, when such a compliment was read he couldn't help but look at his daughter Helen and chuckle while shaking his head. The family alone understood that while he loved music, he could never be described accurately as an "accomplished musician."

In truth, his humble musical career began as he grew up in Clifton, Idaho. An old piano that someone had given to his parents stood in the parlor of their home. During his adolescent years he became more and more interested in that piano as he found himself gradually withdrawing from his group of friends. While these other boys were going off to make mischief, he felt the necessity of finding his own recreation and diversion. He read considerably, but he kept returning to the piano, fingering it and trying to play tunes on it.

Finally, someone moved into town who could show Harold how to put chords together and how to read music. Soon he was spending hours by himself, playing but not really practicing, because he wasn't taking formal lessons. He played for pleasure and was largely self-taught, yet he became skilled enough to perform with a dance band as he grew older, earning pocket money for school. Sometime during those years he also acquired a slide trombone and taught himself to master it. He played the baritone horn for four years in the high school band. In the dance band Harold would play either wind instrument as needed, and sometimes filled in for the piano player. He was almost devoid of any private tutoring, but he loved music; that, more than anything else, probably qualified him as a "good" musician. He wanted music in his life and strove to master his instruments simply because he enjoyed music so much.

Harold frequently played the piano during fun times with the family. His girls loved him to play one of the John Philip Sousa marches, and the louder he banged it out the better they liked it. Another selection, their absolute favorite, was titled "Midnight Fire Alarm," a solo he had learned during his early years in Idaho. These were two of the few numbers he had committed to memory. Of course, he played the hymns as well, and years later he served as the accompanist in the temple meetings of the Council of the Twelve, acting in that capacity along with Elder Spencer W. Kimball, who, he was quick to admit, was more advanced in musical training than was he.

The performances of the "Midnight Fire Alarm" have special memories for his daughters. Helen describes the scene in this manner:

> Maurine and I would dance and prance around the room as Daddy was playing this exciting, loud music. He played with such enthusiasm that the entire house seemed to vibrate, and we loved it! Once he finished a real workout performance with such flourish that he could see he had thoroughly delighted us, as well as some of our little friends who were with us. He felt especially pleased with his exceptional rendition when he overheard Mar's friend say, "Gee, that was really good, wasn't it?" He was quickly deflated, however, when Mar answered honestly, "Uh, huh, and the best part about it is watching the piano shake!"

Harold appreciated fine music, and for that reason he was insistent that his daughters start their musical education at ages seven and eight. He faithfully drove them back and forth from their music teacher's home some distance away, until they could drive themselves. The private music lessons continued until the girls were in college. No doubt it often strained the family's limited

Helen (with violin) and Maurine   Working in the garden

Lee home at 1208 South Eighth West, Salt Lake City

financial resources, but he was most willing to sacrifice for them so that they might obtain the same love for music which he possessed.

Helen expressed her gratitude for his insistence that they learn to perform musically in these words:

> I've always been grateful for his encouragement. Music has added a deep dimension to my life, and it was a wonderful experience to share with my sister. It was one more channel which drew us together. We performed constantly together. We studied with the same teacher, Sister Melba Lindsay Burton, so we'd always go to our lessons together. Each time, after our individual lessons were over, she would teach us to perform together, Maurine at the piano and I playing the violin. By the time we were married we had performed in almost every ward building then existing in the Salt Lake City area. We began responding to such requests when we were still very young and played until 1945, a period of about twelve years. I can remember my father patiently taking us everywhere we had to perform, until we could become more independent. He was a busy man, but never was he too busy to take us where we had to be for our music and come back and pick us up or wait for our performance to end. It was just understood that he would take us anyplace we had to be, and he did so consistently.

Personality and Work Characteristics

Much is revealed about a man's character by the manner in which he conducts his routine responsibilities about the home. Always loaded down with heavy Church and community service burdens, Harold nevertheless worked diligently to improve and upgrade their home surroundings to make life better for those he loved so much. Helen grew up in his home admiring and loving this industrious, driving father:

> My father worked hard to improve each home we lived in and its surroundings, from our smallest home on Eighth South where we were living when I was born, and including the next home at 1208 South Eighth West, where we made so many happy memories.
>
> He was a real "do-it-yourself" man around the house. We have many fond remembrances of him fixing everything that needed his attention. We never knew what it was to hire a carpenter, except for major remodeling projects, or to have any yard work done by others. Only in the last decade of his life did he ever have any gardening help. Of course, without sons that meant that he did all

the work himself; he was the entire yard crew. We girls helped Mother in the home; she needed us there to help her care for our large house. So, routinely, Dad was up early in the morning (five o'clock in the summertime or whenever daylight permitted) so that he could get out and work in his yard, where there was always much for him to do.

When we moved to Eighth West the property in back of our home was completely undeveloped, and extended all the way to the Jordan River, west of our home. It was his dream to develop this to such back yard beauty as to make it enjoyable to us and to our friends and family. He reclaimed it from nothing but weeds. When he completed all his projects, we had a beautiful board fence which divided the formal gardens from a vegetable garden. There were also a few fruit trees planted down next to the river.

The same ingenuity was followed when he laid out this back yard for a sprinkling system. This too was a "do-it-yourself" project. Undoubtedly, he had someone advise him how to go about it and maybe help with the technical aspects of the job, but I can remember that essentially my father laid out the plan and installed it himself, and it served him well, all through those years. He was a real handyman and was most resourceful. As I've grown older I've discovered not all men have those qualities and capabilities around a home.

My father also landscaped this section with very little outside assistance. He skillfully planned for a sunken fish pond, when they were considered stylish, and we had a Japanese pagoda, as well as white-painted benches placed at strategic spots around the yard. He developed a beautiful lawn and added shrubs. Later a large patio also was added where we did our entertaining, including dancing.

As we grew older and had many parties at our home in our teen-age years, he realized that we needed a barbecue in the back yard. I suppose most men would have had some expert come and build a brick fireplace with a barbecue, but this was never the route Dad took. He made some inquiry and looked at a few barbecue arrangements which other people had installed. Before we knew it Dad had purchased the materials and built it himself, and it suited our purposes very well. It may not have been as fancy as some others we had seen, but it provided what we needed for entertaining our friends.

He didn't end his enjoyment of his handiwork there, for when we had our parties he was out cooking the hamburgers for us. What more could we ask? It was his personality and character to be involved, and he always delighted in playing the role of the genial host.

Another interesting view of my father that I took for granted as I was growing up was that my father learned in those early married years that if he was going to accomplish all that he wanted to do, he was going to have to move fast. I mean that literally. He moved like lightning. His movements always were very quick, and I suppose that as he became busier, and his life became more complicated, he compensated by just running at top speed to accomplish everything. This was especially true of the care demanded by the big yard around our home. He could cut a lawn faster than any man I ever knew, including our young, vigorous sons. He'd just tear back and forth, up and down, and if you had to deliver a message to him or say something to him, you would have to run along with him back and forth across the lawn, because he never stopped. Even Mother had to do this if it was necessary for her to report a telephone message to him.

When he was so busy as a stake president and serving in the Salt Lake City commission, and later, when he was heading up the new welfare program of the Church, I have definite memories of him moving quickly through the house, in and out, never wasting a moment. He would come home from work, greet Mother and us girls, then rush upstairs, where he would change his clothes in a miraculously short time. I've often told his grandsons how fast he moved, hoping they could learn to do as he did. He would don his yard-working clothes in seconds, it seemed, then out he would go to mow the lawn before supper, while Mother was still getting the food ready. Sometimes he would receive a phone call with a request to perform a priesthood administration or make some other unexpected visit. He would race back into the house, put on his suit again, and off he would go to take care of the request. (I asked him once, "Couldn't you just go without changing your clothes to administer to Brother Jensen? They would surely understand, wouldn't they?" He replied, "When I have an appointment with the Lord, I always want to look my very best.") When he would return he would change back into his work clothes, finish cutting the lawn, eat dinner, change again into his suit, and leave for a meeting that would last the remainder of the evening.

I have often reflected that most men wouldn't think they had time to do all that, and if they moved at a normal speed, they wouldn't. His formula for getting things done was simply to move fast.

In the mornings he would come in after he had worked in the yard and finished watering, shower or bathe very quickly, get dressed, eat breakfast, and leave in what seemed only a few minutes. It was unbelievable. I've realized since, that this work characteristic was unique to my father, but at the time I just assumed every man moved at this pace. Now I know that no one in my experience has matched his determination to use every moment available to serve others with all his strength. These qualities were singular to his personality and character.

AVOIDING THE APPEARANCE OF EVIL

This busy Church leader and father and his little family learned together many important lessons of life. Helen recalls that when the girls were perhaps five or six years old, she learned a lesson that lasted a lifetime concerning the example that was necessary for the family of a stake president, whose lives were on constant display and parade before the sometimes harsh judgment of fellow stake members. The internal life of such a family is open for inspection as people routinely come to the home of a stake president to be interviewed for temple recommends or to receive a priesthood blessing, and often these visitors arrive unannounced. It was so on a winter's Sunday night in the 1930s, as Helen remembers, that this learning experience took place:

> Just before bedtime we coaxed Daddy to play a game with us. We had received a deck of "Old Maid" cards for Christmas, and Daddy hadn't as yet had an opportunity to play the game with us. So, the four of us, Mother and Daddy and my sister and I, were sitting around a card table playing "Old Maid" when a young couple appeared at the door and wanted to be interviewed and have their temple recommends signed. We stopped playing while Dad took them into another room and interviewed them. In due time they left and we resumed our game.
>
> In the days that followed that experience we soon learned from various sources that this young couple had spread the word around the stake that if President Lee and his family could play cards on a Sunday night, it must be permissible for everyone to do so. Of course, the inference was that we were using face cards, which are used for a far different purpose than our "Old Maid" cards were. I recall thinking, as a little girl, how unfair that was for people to judge us so quickly when they didn't have the true facts. We felt we had done no harm in playing that simple game that night.
>
> From that experience my father taught us a powerful lesson. Through the years that followed he would remind us that it was not sufficient to just avoid evil and wrong-doing itself, but that we must avoid the very appearance of evil. I had many other occasions to appreciate that principle as I was growing up, and later too, as my husband and I reared our own family.

Throughout the dating years of the Lee girls, many situations brought teaching lessons from a father who consistently taught that commandments were to be lived without compromise, regardless of circumstances. One illustration occurred in Maurine's dating experience, the memory of which provided some good chuckles for the family for years to come. Helen recounts:

> It was a Sunday afternoon in early June, and Maurine had accepted a date earlier in the week from a young man she had not been dating for long. This fellow called her after our mid-day dinner to make final their plans. The conversation went something like this:
>
> "Hi! What would you like to do today?"
>
> "Well, what did you have in mind?"
>
> "Let's see . . . it's so warm and beautiful today, and since we haven't been out to Black Rock Beach on Great Salt Lake yet this year, how about going there to get some sun?"
>
> "Gee, I'm sorry, but I don't think my father would approve of that. Could we think of something else?"
>
> "Well, there's a new show at the Centre Theatre. Would you like to go there?"
>
> "I'm really sorry, but we've never been allowed to go to shows on Sunday. Maybe there's another possibility."
>
> "Hmmm . . . How would it be to go hiking up the canyon? Surely there's nothing wrong with that?"
>
> "I hate to tell you this, but I know Dad wouldn't think that hiking is an acceptable Sunday activity either. I hope you understand. Is there another alternative?"
>
> (With great disgust and sarcasm): "Oh, sure! Why don't you just ask your Dad if there's a good rousing funeral we could go to somewhere!"

Thus, it was humorous as well as stressful at times for the teenagers growing up in this home of an Apostle as social events came into conflict with family and Church mores, but the girls met with unyielding but comfortably consistent guidance from their parents. With his policy of no compromise between right and wrong, Harold B. Lee held the reins tightly but lovingly. His daughters knew that they had limits, and they tried to live within them.

SOCIAL INVOLVEMENTS OF DAUGHTERS

In the busy comings and goings in a family of two teenage daughters and a highly involved Church leader father there was little time for family talk except around the dinner table. There, questions were always asked about the events of the day. The girls could count on their Dad being sincerely interested in their friends and those with whom they were keeping company. Regarding this point Helen states:

Many of my girlfriends still recall experiences at parties or just coming to our home and having dinner with us. They remember how gracious and how unusually interested Dad was in what we did. Whenever we had a party, that was not a signal for Mother and Dad to leave. They were always very much a part of our entertaining, and we were glad they were.

Our home was always open at any time of the day or night to our friends. We came to appreciate parents who made that possible. Our home was never so fancy or so grand, nor was it in such a state of fine preservation but what we couldn't come in with our friends and feel welcome and wanted. We were never scolded when we came home late with friends and fixed snacks in the kitchen or played the piano while Mother and Dad were upstairs trying to sleep. Neither did they complain when there would be no milk for breakfast the following morning. Our friends knew that we could always go to our home after a date, or if we wanted to have a party we could always have it at our house. Our home and our yard were maintained for just that purpose. We had numerous parties in those years, always with our parents' complete approval and encouragement.

Now that I am a parent I probably realize fully for the first time that this type of involvement with friends frequently in our home could have been an inconvenience. I'm certain that many times we must have disturbed our parents when we'd sing round the piano and giggle and laugh and talk, but they never complained.

When the date was over, there was the matter of reporting in.

It was the practice of my sister and me after every date, before going to bed, to go into the bedroom of our parents and tell them goodnight so they would know we were safely home. But it never ended there. We'd perch on Mother's side of the bed and we'd whisper to her about all the events that had taken place that night. Sometimes we were excited and thrilled with the dates, and sometimes we were disappointed and miserable. Mother was always interested, so we'd talk and giggle and whisper, and I'm certain that it must have been terribly hard on my father, who would be trying to sleep over the conversation. But he good-naturedly tolerated all of it, for he always encouraged us to confide in Mother. He knew this would build a close relationship, which it most certainly did. In fact, he

would refer to us, through those teenage years, as "his three girls."
Mother indeed was our closest confidante. She was our very special
friend. It made every date much more fun to be able to come home
and tell Mother all about it.

TEENAGE DISCIPLINE

In most families who have teenagers engaged in social life,
conflicts arise over hours to return, use of the car, and quality of
friends chosen for companionship. However, the close bond
between these two sisters, reared almost as twins, formed a safe
and secure protection during those socially dangerous years. They
were taught in their earliest childhood that they must always go
together to their activities. They grew up playing with the same
groups of friends, and in later years double dating was not uncommon for the Lee sisters. But the girls, of course, were not perfect,
and there were those inevitable incidents, when they were older
and seeking social acceptance, that conflicts arose. Maurine,
apparently more independent than Helen, was described by her
father as "his little harness-fighter." Helen recalls:

> I believe this was on the occasion of a missionary farewell in our
> home ward, back in the days when they were held on week nights
> and there was always a dance following the program. At that time,
> we were in our early teens, interested now in boys and dances, but
> too young to date. Mother and Dad had left after the farewell
> program was over and had told us to be home at a certain time,
> allowing us to stay for a while to watch the dancing. Maurine and I
> agreed to those arrangements. When the hour came that we were
> supposed to be home I reminded Mar of the time, and she said,
> "Why don't you just run on home, and I'll be along in a little
> while?" She was still having a good time with her friends and
> wanted to stay longer. When I hesitated she said, "Just go and tell
> Mother and Dad I'll come home soon; it'll be okay!" Now, that was
> strictly against the rules of our home—we were never to go any-
> place alone. We were taught that when we went anywhere, we
> were to go together, two by two, for there was safety in that rule.
> But despite my misgivings I went on home alone, for there was no
> other choice, I thought. I just couldn't talk her into coming with
> me.
> I arrived home alone without Maurine, and I remember the
> sparks in Dad's eyes when I explained her absence: "Well, Daddy,
> she said that she didn't want to come right now, but that she'd
> come a little later." "How much later?" he demanded to know.

"Well, I don't really know, Daddy," I replied, "but she'll come soon, I think." This was the beginning of a new era in our lives, and none of us seemed to know quite how to handle the situation. I remember Dad speaking quite sharply to Mother, saying, "Well, I'll go and make sure she knows when to come home!" I thought it best not to get into that discussion! I can remember Mother saying very quietly, "Well now, dear, let's just wait a little bit longer and see if she will come on her own." So we waited a while longer. I tried to stay on the fringe of that issue, but was becoming anxious myself. When she didn't come, Dad said, "Well, I'm going to go and get her. She must learn that when we tell her to be home at a certain time, she must be here."

Mother, who always met issues quietly and with composure, suggested a better answer. She said to Dad, "Now, dear, don't go in an angry way and insist that she come home. Just think what that would do to her in front of her friends. It would embarrass her. If you feel you must go, then go on the pretense of accomplishing something else, like going to see someone about some unfinished business there at the ward. Make some other reason for going, but don't confront her with the idea that you have come for her." Well, I don't know what happened because I didn't go back with Daddy and I wasn't on the scene, but when he arrived at the dance and found her and brought her back, she apparently came willingly and happily. Mother and I were greatly relieved!

Through the wise handling of tense situations in this manner, discipline in our home never degenerated into the abrasive confrontations that are common today in too many homes.

HE MADE MOTHER OUR EXAMPLE

Fern Tanner Lee was an example of everything that a marvelous homemaker and mother ought to be. She taught her two daughters all the homemaking skills which she had perfected. She was an exceptional cook and a most gracious and lovely hostess, serving with charm and warmth the many groups invited to her home. For all these qualities, she was constantly praised and encouraged by her appreciative husband. Helen recalls how her father often called his daughter's attention to the excellence of their mother's skills and service:

All during my growing-up years, whatever Mother did, whether it was arranging furniture or flowers, making a bed or ironing a shirt, Daddy would always say to us, "Now, girls, when you can do that just like your mother, you'll be the best there is." I can remember when she hung her wash on the clothesline outside (this was long before we had heard of automatic dryers), he would watch her work as he was doing his jobs out in the yard, and would say to us as we played about, "Just look at that—your mother even makes the washing on the line look artistic."

It was true. She would hang the white clothes together and then the colored pieces and then the dark items, very carefully and in perfect order. The long pieces were all hung together and the short ones were alongside each other. He reinforced the wisdom of our learning from Mother by this oft-repeated admonition: "You will never find any better example of anything that you will do as women when you grow older than that which is provided by your own mother. She is the perfect example. You just watch the way Mother does it!"

FATHER ALWAYS AVAILABLE

Reference has been made already to the social conditions under which the Lee girls lived during their college days. Those were World War II years and dating was sporadic, made possible only as the boys would come home on leave from the military. This forced most young ladies to create their own entertainment; therefore, the girls would often gather at "hen parties." Many of these were held in the Lee's large and comfortable home, but others of their group also took their turns. Helen's memories illustrate how her faithful father supported his daughters under such conditions:

Because we didn't have escorts to take the girls home late at night after the parties it was my father who often got that detail. Many of the other girls were reluctant to call their dads that late at night, but Maurine and I knew that we would never be scolded if we asked our father to help us. He would never say, "I'm sorry, I'm too tired," or "I'm ready for bed, so you'll have to find another way home." Nor did he ever come begrudgingly to pick us up and sometimes deliver our friends to their homes, too. Many is the time he would get out of his bed during a snowstorm, get dressed, get out the car, and come for us. Not only would he bring us home, but he would deliver four or five others to their homes as well. We understood this willingness on his part and never questioned it, for it was ever so from the first days that we began to leave our home together for social purposes. He had always told us: "Girls, never hesitate to phone me when you need me, no matter the time, day or night. I will come whenever you need me, wherever you are." We knew he meant that, and I'm afraid there were times when we probably took advantage of his offer. What he really taught us, though, was that he loved us enough to serve our needs, even when it wasn't convenient. This gave us a wonderful sense of security in all our teenage years.

The busy life of a General Authority did not allow much time for the family to be together. A major exception to this was a period of time when Elder Lee was assigned to give a series of radio talks over KSL Radio on the "Sunday Evening from Temple Square" program. For a period of six months the Lee family enjoyed a unique season of togetherness, because Elder Lee's weekend stake conference travel assignments were cancelled while he prepared and delivered his radio talks. This brought about a collaboration which everyone in the family enjoyed, and all were made to feel a part of this stimulating challenge. Helen's memories of those months are choice. Regarding them she has said:

My sister and I were in our late teen years. I was probably about eighteen and Maurine was nineteen at the time. Since Dad had addressed himself to the subject of "Youth and the Church" during those war years, he was most interested in our reactions to every talk. He really was closer to youth than most men because of his involvement with us and our friends all through those years. He knew the problems which youth were facing at that particular time in the history of our country with its enlarged temptations when young people became displaced from home ties, so the subjects he proposed to talk about were discussed freely with the entire family. He always had three talks he was working on simultaneously. He was putting the finishing touches on the one he was about to give on the next Sunday; he was finishing his ideas on the one for the following week, which was in rough draft form; and at the same time was beginning to outline the third one farthest away from presentation. It required much study and work to keep the flow of presentations coming on a weekly basis.

He would bring home the scripts on which he was working, read them to us, and we would discuss them around the dinner table. They were free and open discussions. We would say, "Oh, no, Dad, you can't say that. It just isn't like that!" Or else, "You'll have to phrase that differently." As we would give him our realistic teenage views, he often would incorporate our ideas into his talks.

This series of talks therefore became for us a delightful family experience. Most importantly, it gave us the opportunity for those many months to have our father home with us on Sunday, a most singular blessing, for as a General Authority he had traveled every

Lee family portrait, 1941 (Helen standing)

weekend to stake conferences for years before that. The only exceptions for General Authorities in those years were a few weeks off in July when no stake conferences were scheduled.

We would all go to the broadcast together every Sunday night in the Salt Lake Tabernacle. Often he invited our favorite musicians to perform on the broadcast. We all felt a part of it with him. The association together and our interchange of ideas made it truly an experience which drew us closer together as a family. Those sermons became the basis of my father's first book, *Youth and the Church,* which later was republished under the title of *Decisions for Successful Living.*

HUSBAND-WIFE RELATIONSHIP

The partnership of highly spiritual and loving parents was a great blessing to the Lee girls. There was a spirit of peace and love in their home that they later found, much to their amazement, was not typical or even frequently equaled in other homes they visited. To achieve this, certainly there had to be a beautiful relationship between husband and wife, extending to their sacred roles as mother and father. Helen describes them as follows:

> Mother was small of stature, quiet and unassuming, but was always a source of great spiritual strength in our home. She sincerely felt that a man's home should be his castle, that it should be an oasis where he could return from the battles of the day and find there a tranquil, quiet atmosphere of peace to rebuild him for future struggles. That was the pattern of our home that Mother established.
>
> There is no doubt but what Mother had a most profound influence on my father's life. When one recalls that he grew up in a very small farming community in Idaho, it is easy to understand that he needed the refining influence of a loving companion to introduce him to gracious, genteel living. She incorporated those values, as well as spiritual dimensions, into their home.
>
> Though she was quiet and unassuming in personality, her inner strength was unquestioned as a powerful influence upon all who knew her. Her mind was filled with wisdom and her heart with empathy as she met my father's needs, as well as the needs of others around her. She had a remarkable sense of fairness. My father's personality was one of being very quick, moving ahead into a situation, making a decision and taking action promptly, regardless of whether the given situation was in Church work, employment, or in a family setting. He needed the influence of a wife who would say to him, as Mother would, "Now, dear, you need to think about this and you must not fail to look at the other side of the situation." She balanced him in this way.
>
> Mother also was his inspiration. My father has often said, "The loftiest thoughts for which I have been given credit were first expressed to me by my dear wife." That is true. I've heard him use phrases that were originally spoken by Mother, as he would deliver a sermon or counsel others. So, though she was quiet in manner, her influence extended to many lives, and was most keenly felt by my father. He worshipped her.
>
> Mother's health was always a source of concern to us. When my sister was born, Mother had a most difficult time. I was born fifteen months later. From then on she was never really healthy and strong. Although she was always able to carry on her duties as a wife and mother, she was frail in health most of the active years that I can remember. My father was always compensating for this limitation by being solicitous of her and her needs. He was careful to make certain that she had all of the modern, work-saving conveniences that would make life easier for her.
>
> There was a sweet relationship which existed between the two of them. He was always so kind and thoughtful of her needs, and

the limited strength she had was always extended for him first, as it should have been. He was at the top of her list of priorities.

That has been a great example to me, and I've passed it on to many other young wives and mothers. When women are pulled in so many different directions, as husbands and growing children and finally Church responsibilities make simultaneous demands upon their time and energies, many of us are in a dilemma about how to handle all those pressures. My mother solved the problem in a most exemplary way. Her husband came first, for he was most important to her, and then whatever else she could do after his needs were met, she was pleased to do also. The priority was never in doubt. My father was foremost in her life.

Our family has always been grateful for the refining influence that she had on this young farm boy, in whom she recognized such unlimited, unique qualities of leadership and greatness. Hers was a refining, polishing, and finishing touch which accelerated his growth and gave him the balance and dimension he needed to accomplish his destiny.

Because Mother was not in good health, there were periods of her life when she was dangerously ill. Gratefully, we would see her recover and we'd have her with us again for many years in fairly good health. On two or three occasions, however, when Mother was very ill, I can still remember the terrible loneliness and insecurity I felt as I thought about losing her in death. I could not imagine what life would be like without her! We were always reluctant to actually talk about that possibility, but one day when my sister and I were in our teen years, we were able to discuss it in a very natural way.

There had been a very fine man in our ward who had lost his wife and he had remarried quite soon after his first wife had died. I said to Mother: "I think that's just terrible! I think that's being so disrespectful to his first wife. He must not have loved her very much!" My mother then turned quietly to me and said: "Oh, my dear, you don't understand what it is to love someone. If I were to go before Daddy, and I think that we will have to face that probability, I could never rest until I knew that your father was happily married again. I just couldn't bear to think of him being alone." I replied, "Mother, how can you say that? Don't you love him enough so that you just couldn't stand to see another woman taking care of him and living with him and . . ." She answered, "It's because I *do* love him so much that I *can* think of it, and that's what I want for him. I cannot bear the thoughts of him being alone and lonesome and not having his needs cared for by someone who loves him as I do. I would want him to remarry, and I mean soon, after I go, so that he will not be lonely—don't you see?"

That was one of the most profound lessons of my life. Mother described to us that day what true love really is. My mother possessed it for my father, to a degree seldom achieved.

TRIBUTE TO PARENTS

These wise, inspired parents succeeded in building a near-perfect home life centered in the gospel of Jesus Christ and their love for one another, as is now abundantly certified by the results which have come from their lifetime of faithful service to God and to each other. The lives of their daughters and the thousands of other lives the parents have touched have been blessed by their exemplary models of how to rear a family in the gospel and win the happiness promised for the faithful. To this certification Helen adds her own personal witness and tribute to her spiritually powerful and loving father and her angelic mother:

> In retrospect, as I look back upon my childhood home from my present vantage point of maturity, I realize that I had the ideal combination of parents: a father who was gentle beneath his firmness, and a mother who was firm beneath her gentleness. They worked at rearing their two daughters as a team, equally yoked, as my father exercised his priesthood in our behalf, and Mother became a supplement and complement to that priesthood authority in our home. They provided for us an atmosphere of love and peace where we learned to know and to love the Lord and his holy words, and to recognize his supremacy in our lives. On this firm foundation was built an appreciation and acceptance of self, so essential as a stepping-stone to learning the more important and mature concept of loving and serving others, which then followed quite naturally.
>
> My eternal gratitude to these wonderful parents, and my resolve to live a life worthy of their efforts, is all I have to offer in return for their profound influence in my life, but this they shall surely have. (Neal A. Maxwell, *That My Children May Partake* [Salt Lake City: Deseret Book Company, 1974], pp. 56–57.)

1935–1936. The Works Progress Administration began to furnish jobs for artists, writers, and others. The Supreme Court declared the National Recovery Administration unconstitutional. John L. Lewis formed the Congress of Industrial Organizations to unionize workers on an industry basis. Congress passed the Social Security Act. The 1935 Plymouth car was the best seller during the Depression. The Spanish Civil War began, which was to take 611,000 lives.

CHAPTER 10

How the Welfare Plan Began

In 1935 Harold B. Lee was a young man of thirty-six, but seasoned beyond his years by having had burdens placed on his broadening shoulders that were far in advance of those placed on his peers. He was serving as the president of Pioneer Stake, located on the west side of Salt Lake City. He also represented those Saints, all other west-side citizens, and the public at large as a Salt Lake City commissioner, assigned to the Department of Streets and Public Improvements.

His ingenious leadership in providing the poor of his stake with the necessities of life—in the "Lord's way," teaching them to resist the dole of government handouts—had already attracted wide attention among Church leaders and government officials alike. He could not have realized it, but he was being prepared for the much larger, worldwide leadership roles he was yet to fulfill.

The true and complete story of how the welfare plan came into existence probably has never been told but it is contained partially in Harold B. Lee's personal journal, written at the time that the drama was being unfolded. From this record one can picture the historic beginnings of this fundamental Church program which since 1936 has been so influential in the lives of all active Latter-day Saints. That he knew in its earliest stages of development that he was inaugurating a lasting work is plainly evident in his inscription on the front page of his journal. Under his name and home address, Harold B. Lee wrote these memorable words:

This program will last as long as this Church exists as a Church.

Early Steps

The welfare story on a Churchwide scale begins in Harold B. Lee's journal history with his first meeting on this subject with the First Presidency of the Church. This meeting took place one year before the official announcement in the Salt Lake Tabernacle which started the welfare plan. The meeting was on a Saturday morning, April 20, 1935. There were no calls on the calendar, and for an entire half-day session they talked about a welfare movement to turn the tide from government, or direct, relief and about the means needed to put the Church into a position from which it could take care of its own needy. President Lee recorded the following impressions of that historic meeting:

On April 20, 1935, I was called into the office of the First Presidency, where with President Heber J. Grant and President David O. McKay (President Clark then being in the East, but they had had some communications with him so that all members of the Presidency were in agreement) I discussed the relief situation in the Church and various methods of handling the same. President Grant said he wanted to take a "leaf out of Pioneer Stake's book" in caring for the people of the Church. He expressed dissatisfaction with the then existent program of social service investigations. He said that there was nothing more important for the Church to do than to take care of its needy people and that so far as he was concerned, everything else must be sacrificed [so that] proper relief [could be] extended to our people. I was astounded to learn that for years there had been before them, as a result of their thinking and planning and as a result of the inspiration of Almighty God, the genius of the very plan that was waiting and in preparation for a time when, in their judgment, the faith of the Latter-day Saints was such that they were willing to follow the counsel of the men who lead and preside in this Church. My humble place in this program at that time was described.

At a later time, Harold B. Lee enlarged upon his feelings of inadequacy at that moment in these words:

There I was, just a young man in my thirties. My experience had been limited. I was born in a little country town in Idaho. I had hardly been outside the boundaries of the states of Utah, Idaho, and Colorado. And now, to put me in a position where I was to reach out to the entire membership of the Church was one of the most staggering contemplations that I could imagine. How could I do it with my limited understanding?

Returning to his journal entries of that historic day, we read further:

I left the First Presidency's Office about noontime with an assignment to work out a program of relief for the entire Church based upon my experience with the relief problem in the Pioneer Stake, where perhaps the greatest problem of unemployment in the entire Church was to be found.

Almost in a daze with the magnitude of this assignment overpowering me, I drove my car up to the head of City Creek Canyon into what was then called Rotary Park, where I could meditate and determine upon a course that would realize the objective that had been set for me by the Presidency. After I had driven my car as far as I could, I got out and walked up through the trees, seeking a secluded spot, where I knelt in prayer and sought the guidance of an all-wise God in this mighty undertaking. I told the Lord to guide me to conclusions dictated by his will, and that, for the safety and blessing of his people, I must have his direction. As I knelt down, my petition was: "What kind of an organization should be set up in order to accomplish what the Presidency has assigned?"

Having sought my Heavenly Father, I sat down to pore over this matter, wondering about an organization to be perfected to carry on this work. There came to me on that glorious spring afternoon one of the most heavenly realizations of the power of the priesthood of God, that God had already revealed the greatest organization that could ever be given to mankind and that all that was needed now was that that organization be set to work. It was as though something were saying to me: "There is no new organization necessary to take care of the needs of this people. All that is necessary is to put the priesthood of God to work. There is nothing else that you need as a substitute, and if you use it the temporal welfare of the Latter-day Saints will be safeguarded.''

And so, with much thought, prayer, and understanding born of practical experience, Harold B. Lee put the priesthood organization to work in directing the Church's newborn welfare labors. That he moved rapidly, energetically, and skillfully is attested by his journal history record of the subsequent events.

During the days that followed, I sought the counsel of a number of prominent men, including Brother Reed Smoot, John M. Knight, Stringham Stevens, Lester Hewlett, C. M. Brown, Jr., Paul C. Child, and others. Finally, after several weeks, I had prepared a report and a preliminary program together with a chart showing the various agencies to participate in a Churchwide relief program. This I submitted to the Presidency about June 1, 1935.

President Grant hesitated. He said he lacked faith in the Latter-day Saints and questioned whether or not they had sufficient integrity to carry forward under the leadership of the Church. Some members of the Church in high places demurred when approached with the thought of beginning such a plan. One General Authority questioned my counselor in the stake presidency, Charles S. Hyde, as to whether or not I was trying to get the Presidency to adopt Pioneer Stake's plan. Other specious reports were circulating.

In the face of this indecision and opposition, President McKay felt incapable of taking the initiative without the personal support and backing of at least one other member of the First Presidency. During that first six months President McKay talked with me frequently relative to the relief program, but nothing was done. President Grant had remarked to Joseph Anderson, his secretary, that he had asked the Lord for guidance in this matter, but had received no answer and that he was not going to move until he felt certain of what the Lord wanted.

During general conference in October 1935 a special meeting was called by the General Authorities requiring the attendance of all stake presidencies and ward bishoprics. The First Presidency announced a request for a Churchwide survey to determine the amount of relief extended to Church members by the Church and by each county from federal funds, the number of heads of families and single persons on relief, those who owned farms who received relief, those who didn't need the relief they received, and the physical conditions and family status of those assisted. Harold's journal reported:

The month of September 1935 was taken as an average month and the survey was based on that month. Talks by President J. Reuben Clark, Jr., and President David O. McKay revealed plainly their dissatisfaction with the present relief program and declared a God-given responsibility upon the Church to care for its own.

The results of the survey were compiled slowly, but were finally tabulated at the Presiding Bishop's Office and turned over to the First Presidency.

Specific data for the survey was not quoted by President Lee in his journal history, but from Leonard J. Arrington and Wayne K. Hinton ("Origin of the Welfare Plan of The Church of Jesus Christ of Latter-day Saints," *BYU Studies,* vol. 5, no. 2, Winter, 1964), the following detail is disclosed:

> A survey undertaken in September, 1935, which sought to determine relief conditions within the LDS Church, showed that 88,460, or 17.9 percent of the Church population were receiving some form of relief. Some 16.3 percent of the Church population (80,553) were receiving relief from public sources and another 1.6 percent (or 7,907) received relief from Church funds. Of members on relief, 13,455 were unemployed. Others were working on depression-inspired projects of the federal government. Reports also stated that between 11,500 and 16,500 of the Church members on relief "did not need" such assistance. The 13,455 unemployed Church members who received the "dole" were to be taken care of under the Church program at a cost estimated of $842,000 per year.

Returning to President Lee's journal history, we read of that moment when the time for action finally arrived:

> I was called to the office of the First Presidency in February, 1936, along with Campbell M. Brown, and we were instructed by President Clark and President McKay to study the results of the survey and, in light of its findings, submit a revised report for further consideration of the presiding Brethren. Working all the possible time, both day and night, it took about three weeks to study the survey statistics. I prepared a graph to show clearly the findings and, counseled by Brother Brown, revised, simplified, and extended my original report. On March 15, 1936, we read over the program carefully with President McKay. After the conclusion of the reading, he slapped the table with his hand and exclaimed: "Brethren, now we have a program to present to the Church. The Lord has inspired you in your work."
>
> On March 24, 1936, President McKay called to tell me that President Grant requested that I leave the next day for Fresno, California, to

Harold B. Lee, managing director of the Church welfare program, with secretary, Ted De Bry, 1937

attend the western conference of the Farm Chemurgic Council, for a discussion of the findings of scientists in the use of farm products for commercial uses. I attended the conference on March 26–27, where I was programmed to speak on the subject, "Finding Our Own Way Out." I returned home on March 28th.

At the general conference of April 6, 1936, another special meeting of stake presidencies and ward bishoprics was called and a statement was read from the First Presidency by President McKay, embodying the recommendations and results of our report following a study of the Churchwide survey. Filled with emotion, Presidents Clark and McKay pleaded with the local authorities to cooperate with a program they could expect shortly to be given to the Church, they declaring that the Church was under condemnation if it failed to take care of the Lord's people.

Following the general conference announcement, on April 15, 1936, I was called in by the First Presidency and told that I was to begin at once, together with such other help as necessary, to launch the Churchwide program. They thought it advisable that a member of the Council of the Twelve be named as chairman of the central committee to give the committee authority over any objections that might be raised. Accordingly, Elder Melvin J. Ballard was named and I was instructed to confer with him to arrange regional meetings throughout the Church to inaugurate the new program and to acquaint him with the details of the program.

A REVELATION

President Lee's account provides a clear case history of the development of a program resulting from a revelation from God to his prophet on the earth. It was not a revelation stimulated by a visitation of angels. The prophet of God had a strong feeling of need to correct a situation that was dangerous to the Saints. The government's attempts to help relieve suffering were proving to be spiritually debilitating to the Saints, sapping their integrity and self-will. An answer must be found.

The prophet prayed about it continually. He and his counselors studied intently all possible alternatives. They finally chose one, based upon the best success story available to them at the time. They didn't have to look far, for over on the west side of Salt Lake City were more people disadvantaged than anywhere else in the Church, and there an inspired stake leadership, under youthful President Harold B. Lee, had found their answers, also by revelation.

Even after early consultation with President Lee, the prayers continued, the opposition had to be weighed, the strength of the Church to endure the challenge must be measured, and the timing had to be right. Statistics were gathered to support the plan so it could be rationalized to those with lesser faith and to vindicate the proposed action. It was one year, lacking five days, from the time Stake President Lee was called to the office of the First Presidency and received the assignment to design a system of welfare relief for the entire Church, until he returned and appeared before the same prophets of God. This time he was asked to resign his political, elected position as a Salt Lake City commissioner and to set up a full-time office and begin implementing the revealed plan of "Church Security," as it was initially called.

Was the welfare plan the product of revelation from God to his prophets? The statements of those founding fathers who were on the scene at the time, and those who have advanced the work since, seem overwhelming to that effect.

With the inspiration of this movement attested to by such witnesses as coming from divine sources, any Latter-day Saint who believes in the principle of continuous revelation cannot fail to heed the call of the prophets "to set up a system where the evils of the dole will be abolished and where independence, thrift, industry, and self-respect can again be established among our people." (Heber J. Grant, October, 1936; "Church Security" by Harold B. Lee, as quoted in *The Church Welfare Plan,* by Henry D. Taylor, p. 37.)

I never heard President Grant say that he had seen the Master, that he had seen the Father, or that he had heard a voice about the welfare plan. But that does not mean that he did not have a revelation. . . .

But there is still another way in which revelation comes, and that way is through the ministrations of the Holy Ghost. . . . Now I say unto you, that that kind of revelation, revelation of the Holy Ghost, did come to President Grant. Not only in this case, but in others. And through that revelation, inspiration if you wish to call it, from the Holy Ghost, President Grant launched this great welfare plan. (J. Reuben Clark, Jr., in an address to the Central Utah Welfare Regional Meeting at Brigham Young University, August 3, 1951.)

That Church Security Plan has not come up as a mushroom overnight. It is the result of inspiration, and that inspiration has come from the Lord. . . . Those who have selfishness in their hearts would like to see it fail, but it is not going to fail. (David O. McKay at a meeting of the Salt Lake Region, February, 1937.)

I believe I have heard almost all the objections which have been raised against it, and also the labored arguments in justification for not living it. As I have listened to these objections and arguments, I have been painfully aware of the dull spirit in which they have been urged. . . . I believe I have made a rather complete study and I now testify to you that I do know beyond any doubt, by the same power that Peter knew that Jesus is the Christ, that the Church Welfare Plan in its inception was and now is inspired of the Lord; and that the great principles implemented by it are eternal truths, which the saints of God must abide if they are to purify and perfect themselves as the Lord has commanded. (Marion G. Romney, Conference Report, October 1945, p. 156.)

The Lord's will had been made known and he had raised up the man to help solve the oppressive problems of the Saints. That Harold B. Lee was a magnificent innovator, a spiritually directed master organizer, is abundantly attested by Church history. But it is especially well illustrated by his part in the development of the

Church welfare plan. It was of course at all times a program of the First Presidency, and their unflagging support was the key to its ultimate success.

PLAN IMPLEMENTED, WEST REGIONALIZED

Once the milestone decision of April 15, 1936, was made to move forward, no time was lost. Two remarkable features characterized this forward thrust. One was the speed with which it was done, and the other was the open support and powerful influence entrusted by the highest authority in the Church. President Heber J. Grant personally attended the first three regional meetings which launched the new program, and he later appeared also at another one as the stakes of Los Angeles were organized into a new region. He obviously was taking no chances that the plan would be lightly received.

Although the approval to proceed with the organization of the Church security program was only given on April 15, 1936, the plans must have been completed earlier and made ready for immediate implementation. Only six days later, on April 21, 1936, the first of many regional meetings was held to establish the organization and teach the principles by which stake leaders could begin to oversee and care for their own needy members. Following this initial meeting, which was held in Ogden, the pace was fast and furious.

Stake President Lee, Elder Melvin J. Ballard, and frequently Bishop Sylvester Q. Cannon, the Presiding Bishop of the Church, were on the road almost every night to hold meetings. This effort was the first regionalization of stakes in Church history, although undistributed writings of President Clark mention the concept as early as 1933. It was a new organizational development that was ultimately expanded in 1967 with the appointment of Regional Representatives of the Council of the Twelve. Such geographic division appears now to be firmly entrenched in Church government, but it had its start with the welfare program in 1936, when there were 115 stakes in the Church, 110 of which were in the United States.

A whirlwind tour around the Church in Utah (excluding Salt Lake City), Idaho, Arizona, and California was accomplished in an amazing fourteen-day period, these areas being organized into thirteen regions.* Accountable leadership was installed, record systems were initiated, and education about the new plan was commenced. Although this was not recorded in Harold B. Lee's welfare journal, the Salt Lake region was also organized in 1936. It consisted of the following stakes: Salt Lake, Ensign, Bonneville, Granite, Wells, Pioneer, Cottonwood, West Jordan, North Davis, South Davis, Tooele, Oquirrh, Liberty, Highland, Grant, and East Jordan.

In 1937, the second year, growth was apparent as three Idaho regions and the Cache Valley region were divided.

Regionalization continued unabated to match the growth of the Church through the years. The organizational structure was mainly used to manage welfare programs and properties, but it was also used in the Church Education System. By 1967 there were 72 regions of the Church. It was then that a major expansion movement took place as the Church expanded the regional territories from 72 to 111, at the same time creating a new Church leadership position: Regional Representatives of the Council of the Twelve. These changes went into effect on January 1, 1968. By February 10, 1972, there were 166 regions in the Church, and by 1984, there were 445.

After accounting for the organizational swing through the Church in 1936 when the first thirteen regions were created, Harold B. Lee's welfare journal contains references to his first return visits to selected regions. He first returned to the St. George region and made note of conditions in each stake:

> *Moapa Stake*—Each ward has a storehouse in the nature of a tithing office. The stake committee and executive council is organized. Ira J. Earl of Las Vegas has been chosen as work director. A planting program is contemplated. A surplus of clothing from Las Vegas is to supply the entire stake. There is little unemployment outside of WPA and regular employment. Appointments are: Robert Gibson, Chairman; Ira J. Earl, work director; Bishop Dan J. Ronnow, Panaca, chairman of the executive council; Lois E. Jones, Relief Society president, Overton; and Milton S. Earl, stake clerk. Their plan: Beet seed and increasing of acreage.
>
> *Kanab Stake*—Fred G. Carrol, Orderville, chairman. Committees are: Bishop Quimbly Roundy, chairman bishops' council; Vera

---

* For details, see Appendix.

L. Schuab, president of Relief Society; Franklin A. Heaton, stake work director; Ed Leo Chamberlain, stake clerk. There are seventeen on relief outside of WPA. In a coal mining venture, owners will share with miners. Storage facilities proferred to Presidents Rust and Odell Jelander, who plan to go into the storage business in the Church program. Hay, grain, and cattle expected from tithing in kind.

Parowan Stake—Lamont E. Tueller, Cedar; Bishop Henry L. Jones, Cedar; Barbara Adams; Bishop Frank B. Wood, work director; Glen Froid, stake clerk. A water shortage prevents farming projects. Clothing and canning will be done by sisters. Cooperative projects are plater making, sawmill, building of homes, brickmaking. Will the Church underwrite or provide loans on their projects?

Zion Park Stake—Ira Bradshaw and Sister Josephine Sandberg are leaders. Shall there be an affiliation with the stake cooperatives? Canning and preserving of food types such as apples, peaches, pears, and grapes, molasses. Building materials, bricks, lumber, cooperatives for sale or exchange are projects. Beet seed increase desired in this stake.

St. George Stake—Canning of fruits and vegetables surplus being done in seven wards. They want to know where cans can be purchased. A stake center for canning with labor from one ward taking care of produce elsewhere is planned. Ward buildings will be started. Molasses making, beet seed project for quorums and groups will be arranged on two acres each. Fuel projects, wood, adobe making, sawmill project, lumber in kind, flower culture, hatchery, are other projects. Potatoes from Enterprise are expected from tithing and fast offerings.

On May 14, 1936, only sixteen days after his first organizational regional meeting, Harold B. Lee returned to Richfield for a meeting starting at 9:00 A.M. Here he heard a stake-by-stake report, making the following notes on each:

Garfield Stake (Pres. Twitchell): The stake relief organization has been completed. Storehouse with manager and women's director is organized. Antimony—potato project; Boulder—no report; Circleville—canning project; Escalante—community coal mine to furnish coal for the entire stake along with canning, wood, and dairy projects; Widstoe ward is upset because of the resettlement program of the government. Very little direct relief cases exist.

Panguitch Stake (Pres. Hatch): Very little direct relief cases here either. Collection of fast offerings being stressed. The county agent is cooperating in urging every family in raising its own gardens with surplus to be sent to ward or stake depot. Henryville and Tropic wards are planning coal for stake assistance; Hatch Ward is raising seed potatoes under the direction of LeRoy Porter, also a sawmill project is taking all available labor in the ward and some from adjoining wards. There is not a very enthusiastic response from the people generally. A canning project is under the Relief Society in Panguitch wards and it will take care of all surplus fruits and vegetables. Organization is partially made.

North Sevier Stake (Pres. Williams): Bishops met with little response for obtaining land for beets. Redmond has no success since relief people are not willing to work in the Church program; Aurora has ten acres of beets under priesthood quorums; Salina Second Ward is canning and bottling fruits and vegetables. President Williams offered the stake brood sows on a fifty-fifty basis but no one at present has accepted the offer.

Beaver Stake (Pres. Farnsworth): Partial organization of relief program has been set up. Few relief clients are available. There are small gardening projects for those who will work. A potato project is planned if labor can be found. Canneries are planned by the Relief Society to take care of surplus commodities. Some people have preferred donations which may be stored rather than donate land for quorum use. Fast offerings are greatly increased already. On the alert to take up labor that might be available with the cessation of the WPA projects. They are centering their attention for the present on tithing and fast offerings. They will need cans for fall conservation. There is plenty of land here and water, but no labor.

South Sevier Stake (Pres. Ware): All land is under cultivation for this year, but they are planning now for next year. They have outlined three building projects following the counsel of Bishop Wells of the Presiding Bishopric. All available labor is now on WPA projects. They think they will be able to take care of their people. Fast offerings are increasing. They were urged in the planting of gardens.

Wayne Stake (Pres. Webster): The leaders of this stake are pledged to full payment of tithing and fast offerings. Teasdale Ward has little relief but twenty-five acres of produce donated for producing crops. Relief client in Bicknell refused proffer of an acre of garden. Lyman Ward is raising potatoes. Hanksville Ward can furnish tomatoes. They don't believe that relief clients can be depended upon.

Sevier Stake (Poulson): Organization is completed. Offers for land were made but no report of acceptance. Missionary farm owned by Richfield wards. How can men be found? Fertilizer project is pending. They are leasing a coal mine in Salina Canyon. Other projects are pending. Glendow Ward wants a recreational hall

Church Security (Welfare) Committee in April, 1938: (left to right) Ted De Bry, J. Frank Ward, Mark Austin, Stringham A. Stevens, Campbell M. Brown, Harold B. Lee, J. Reuben Clark, Jr., Heber J. Grant, David O. McKay, Melvin J. Ballard, John A. Widtsoe, Albert E. Bowen, Sylvester Q. Cannon, Henry D. Moyle, Robert L. Judd and their leaders have talked with Bishop Wells of the Presiding Bishopric about it.

OPPOSITION TO THE PLAN

No work of any true importance, seeking to blaze a new path over traditions and ruts of the past, seems to be free of harassment. The welfare program was no exception. From the beginning, and without cessation for years, opposition was everywhere, even in high places.

On April 29, 1936, Harold B. Lee returned home to Salt Lake City from St. George and was to leave the next day to effect the organization of the first California and Arizona regions. Letters were waiting from Ogden, Lyman, and Heber City asking for further instructions and announcing programs. While attending to this correspondence he was visited by Henry Smith, reporter of the *Deseret News,* who was checking out a critical story disparaging the storehouse program.

The story had been told that the Pioneer Stake storehouse operation had increased the cost of relief, stating that Pioneer Stake had cost $33,000 for 1935 compared with $20,000 for Salt Lake Stake in a similar locality. Stake President Lee called the reporter's attention to the fact that the September 1935 survey of stakes by the First Presidency showed that Salt Lake Stake had taken care of 106 families with an average of 3.6 persons per family, and 89 single persons, while the Pioneer Stake had taken care of 188 families with an average of 4.1 persons per family, and 59 single persons. The total for Salt Lake Stake was 471 persons, or an average cost per person per month of $4.40, while the total of Pioneer Stake was 830 persons, or $2.71 average cost per person per month. The entire Salt Lake area welfare statistics were then published to show the true facts:

Stake	Persons Assisted	Welfare Costs Average per person/per month
Salt Lake	471	$ 4.40
Pioneer	830	2.71
Wells	305	2.20
Bonneville	75	2.77
Ensign	276	4.66

Granite	146		3.42
Highland	64		3.22
Liberty	361		2.82
Grant	138		2.82
		City Average	2.71

Opposition had reached other places too. Arthur Winter had been told also the same fallacious story, and publication of the facts was needed to correct the errors. Some leaders were saying that Elder Ballard and Brother Lee were great proselyters, but that they needed the conservatism of some of the other Brethren.

ANOTHER REVELATION

Shortly after Elder Lee completed his first swing through the Church to organize the welfare work, he experienced a spiritual manifestation which he retold throughout the Church for many years thereafter. This account comes from his acceptance speech as a newly called member of the Council of the Twelve Apostles, in April 1941:

> It was in August of that same year [1936] that, with Brother Mark Austin of the General Committee, I had driven down to St. George and then back across the mountains to Richfield for an early morning meeting. At that time there was an upturn in business, so much so that some were questioning the wisdom of this kind of activity, and why hadn't the Church done it before now?
>
> There came to me, in that early morning hour, a distinct impression that was as real as though someone had spoken audibly, and this was the impression that came and has stayed with me through these years: There is no individual in the Church who knows the real purpose for which the program then launched had been intended, but hardly before the Church has made sufficient preparation, that reason will be made manifest; and when it comes, it will challenge every resource of the Church to meet it.
>
> I trembled at the feeling that came over me. Since that day that feeling has driven me on, night and day, hardly resting, knowing that this is God's will, this is his plan. The only thing necessary today is that the Latter-day Saints everywhere recognize these men who sit here on the stand as the fountainheads of truth, through whom God will reveal his will, that his Saints might be preserved through an evil day.

CHAPTER 11

Call to the Apostleship

"For five glorious, strenuous years I have labored, under a call from the First Presidency, with a group of select brethren, in the development of and the unfolding of what we have called the Church welfare plan." These were the words used by Harold B. Lee as he marked the end of that intense, struggling inception of the welfare plan and began his broadening labors in the Council of the Twelve.

He had traveled about the Church many times. He had helped to organize the Church into welfare regions. He had stimulated, begged, pleaded, inspired, and wanted to scold at times, the leadership of stakes, some of whom accepted the new program but many of whom were apathetic and skeptical and most of whom were slow to implement.

Harold B. Lee has often told of his stock answer to those who, having identified him so completely with the unfolding of the welfare plan, would casually ask: "Well, Brother Lee, how is the new welfare program going in the Church?" His standard reply was: "Just as good as the individual stake presidents and bishops want it to go!" This always sobered the more flippant inquirers and gave them deeper considerations to ponder.

He had learned from this experience that the innovator walks a rugged path where there are few immediate friends, and leaders who are mostly content with the status quo. As always, the greatest opposition seemed to come from within, where change would endanger status and vested interest. That the presiding Brethren were pleased with his labors, however, seems obvious by the events which were to occur in the general conference of April 1941. A vacancy in the Quorum of the Twelve Apostles had been occasioned by the death of Elder Reed Smoot on February 9, 1941.

Record of these milestone events is contained in the personal journal of President Lee. He became a daily-entry diarist coincident with his call to the Quorum of the Twelve. Never before had he maintained a journal accounting for every day's activities, but had written broad sketches of important phases of his life, undoubtedly having in mind the benefit they would be to his later posterity. Now, however, he knew he belonged to Church history and once more disciplined himself accordingly.

The first entry of over three decades of Harold B. Lee's personal daily history as a General Authority was written under the date of Thursday, March 17, 1941, ten days before he was called to the Quorum of the Twelve Apostles. It consisted of a brief note that he attended the General Church Welfare Committee meeting. The following day, on Friday, March 28, 1941, he merely reported that he attended the regular meeting of the First Presidency with the Church Welfare Committee and their advisors.

On Sunday, March 30, 1941, he fulfilled an assignment to attend the Lehi (Utah) Stake conference. He then returned to Salt Lake City and spoke at the Sunday evening MIA services in the Twentieth Ward at 6:30 P.M. that night. His entry under that date reads, "Sister J. Reuben Clark, Jr., and her daughter Marian were there and were very kind in their commendation of my humble efforts."

Then the life-changing events began to unfold. Under the date of Monday, March 31, 1941, he wrote:

> President Clark called to ask if I was trying to kill myself by carrying out the kind of schedule I had yesterday in attending the Lehi Stake Conference and then speaking at night in the Twentieth Ward. He commented on Sister Clark's commendation of my talk and said she was insistent that he go right down and urge my appointment as the new Apostle. I thought he was only joking, but I learned later that this was his way of preparing me for the shock that was coming to me the next Sunday at the April Conference.

The next three days were covered by mere mention of meetings attended: on Tuesday, April 1, 1941, he attended the Milk Processing Committee meeting, and on Thursday he met with President G. Chauncy Spilsbury of the Arizona Region and attended the regular weekly meeting of the General Church Welfare Committee.

GENERAL CONFERENCE BEGINS

General conference commenced on April 4, 1941, and featured an opening address by President Heber J. Grant. Elder Lee recorded his impression of that sermon in these words: "President Grant bore a most remarkable testimony that undoubtedly raised him to great heights in the affections of the people. He occasionally was overcome with emotion that moved the entire audience to tears."

The conference continued on Saturday, April 5, and Elder Lee made reference in his journal regarding the progress of the work he loved, noting that "the special welfare meeting was a remarkable success as a demonstration of the possibilities of the welfare plan."

As he was later to teach, many times priesthood leaders have a forewarning of their callings through the Holy Ghost prior to the issuance of the call. When Harold B. Lee awoke on Saturday, April 5, 1941, he experienced such a spiritual premonition of his calling to the apostleship. He described his feelings as follows: "Before I arose from my bed I received a definite impression that I would be named a member of the Quorum of the Twelve." His premonition was accurate and was fulfilled that very night:

> I was sitting in the audience attending the general priesthood meeting as the managing director of the Church Welfare Program. At the conclusion, President J. Reuben Clark, who was conducting the meeting, called my name out and asked that I come to the stand to meet Bishop Joseph L. Wirthlin. Bishop Wirthlin did have a matter of business to mention to me, but it was really a way to have me meet with President Heber J. Grant.
>
> When I arrived at the stand, Elder Joseph Anderson said that the President was waiting for me in the General Authorities' room. It amazed me, and I immediately sensed that there was something more than just a social visit that President Grant had in mind. It was then that he announced to me that I had been named to be elevated to the Quorum of the Twelve, to fill the vacancy which had been created by the death of Senator Reed Smoot.

Harold B. Lee often retold to his family the conversation of that precise moment. After learning of his appointment, he said: "Oh, President Grant, do you really think I am worthy of such an exalted calling?" The plain-spoken President replied simply, "If I didn't think so, my boy, you wouldn't be called!"

A RESTLESS NIGHT OF WORRY

Bowed down with the weight of this lofty calling, Elder Lee went home to share his burden with his little family, then living at 1208 South Eighth West Street in Salt Lake City. As was so typical in the Lee home, and particularly at conference time, their home was filled with house guests. Relatives visited often, as did young women whose parents Elder Lee had met in his travels through the Church and were invited to live with the Lee family while they were obtaining employment on moving to Salt Lake City. So at this time, when a chosen vessel of the Lord needed a moment of privacy with his family to gather spiritual strength from those he loved, Elder Lee found it necessary to seek that family solitude in improvised ways.

The guests in the home were the entire family of William H. Prince (Harold's cousin) of St. George, Utah, and Sister Mabel Hickman, one of two converted maiden sisters whom Elder Lee baptized on his mission in Denver, Colorado. These two sisters remained close to the Lee family and were accorded all the privileges of family membership. The large Lee home was arranged for accommodating these guests and all available extra space was made into sleeping quarters for the night.

Helen remembers well this general conference and the events of that particular Saturday night on April 5, 1941:

> My father returned from priesthood meeting quite late, an hour or so after the time when the meeting would have concluded. Mother and I were busy with dinner preparations for the next day, endeavoring to make our company comfortable and happy. My sister had gone to visit a friend for the evening.
>
> When Dad came home Mother explained to him that Maurine had called and that she needed someone to go and pick her up at her friend's house, and asked if he would do so. He agreed to go and then said: "Mother, you and Helen come with me." This seemed unusual for him to request that all three of us go to pick up my sister. It was late and Mother still had much work to do to prepare

for the Sunday dinner, but because of his serious manner and insistent voice, we didn't question his desires further. We left what we were doing and went with him in the car.

As soon as we got into the car with him he said, "There is something that I must tell you." Very quietly and obviously more subdued in manner than I ever remember my father being before, he explained to us that following the priesthood meeting, President Grant had detained him and in privacy had informed him that he was to be named the next morning as the new member of the Council of the Twelve. I was then fifteen years old and was fully capable of understanding the impact of this calling and what it would mean in his life, as well as in the life of our family. It was a very sobering but choice moment.

He then said, "Now, we'll go and pick up Maurine, and we'll tell her about it." As could be readily appreciated, with all the guests filling our home, he knew that this was the only place that he could share this momentous news with us without the possibility of interruption by others, and without arousing their curiosity. He then added: "When we return, you girls come up with us to our bedroom and we'll have our prayer together."

We did as he suggested, cherishing those sacred moments together. Of course, no explanations could be made to our house guests, so we tried to go on about our business as usual and make preparations for bed and for the following day. There was a message when we arrived home for Dad to phone President J. Reuben Clark, Jr., and after he made that phone call we had our prayer together.

The next day in conference, the newly appointed Apostle made reference to his sleeplessness of the night before:

Since nine o'clock last night I have lived an entire lifetime in retrospect and in prospect. I spent a sleepless night. I never closed my eyes one moment, and neither would you if you had been in my place. Throughout the night as I thought of this most appalling and soul-stirring assignment, there kept coming to me the words of the Apostle Paul. "Let us therefore come boldly unto the throne of grace, that we may obtain mercy, and find grace to help in time of need." (Hebrews 4:16.)

Helen continues with her recollection of that memorable day when her father was appointed as an Apostle:

We went to conference on Sunday morning, which we had not planned to do because of the crowds, the difficulty in finding seating, and the fact that Mother was not feeling well and was unable to attend the first two days of conference. But, of course, under the new circumstances of Dad's appointment we all went with our house guests, arriving very early to find seats. We sat almost to the rear of the tabernacle near the north wall. I remember still what a thrill it was to hear my father's name announced as the new Apostle.

As the meeting was about to begin, a few close friends found Elder Lee looking unusually pale and disquieted. On the stand of the Tabernacle sat the clerk of the conference, Elder Joseph Anderson, a close personal family friend of Elder and Sister Lee. Elder Anderson always had his son Bob sitting with him in those days; Bob turned to his father before the Sunday session of conference began and remarked: "Dad, Brother Lee looks so bad; is something going to happen to him?" Of course, Elder Anderson, who was President Grant's personal secretary, could only concur that Elder Lee did look ill that morning.

Harold B. Lee's diary entry for that most significant day in his life, Sunday, April 6, 1941, is as follows:

> I was sustained before the general conference at the ten o'clock session by President J. Reuben Clark, Jr., after which I was invited to a place on the stand "at the foot of the ladder," as he expressed it— "a member of the Twelve." In the afternoon session I was called to address the conference and enjoyed a remarkable peace that overcame all fright and fear that I had anticipated.

Meanwhile, in the Tabernacle congregation, the sustaining of Church officers was a moment to be cherished by the Lee family. According to Mabel Hickman, who sat next to her, as President Clark read the names of the General Authorities Sister Lee leaned forward "with both hands on the back of the bench in front of us, and the knuckles of her hands were white with tension."

A memorable scene was associated with Elder Lee's advancement to a seat as a new quorum member of the Council of the Twelve. His place at "the foot of the ladder" was next to his fellow stake member, Elder Sylvester Q. Cannon. Harold B. Lee was forty-two and didn't have a gray hair in his head at that time. The scene was indelibly impressed on Helen's mind. She recalls:

> It created a lasting picture when my father went up and sat by the side of Brother Cannon, who had snowy, white hair. When the audience stood up during the rest break midway in the two-hour session, I remember how startled I was to see all of the members of the Council of the Twelve standing in their places before us. The

Council of the Twelve at the installation of Harold B. Lee, 1941: (from left front, anti-clockwise) Rudger Clawson, George Albert Smith, George F. Richards, Joseph Fielding Smith, Stephen L Richards, Richard R. Lyman, John A. Widtsoe, Joseph F. Merrill, Charles A. Callis, Albert E. Bowen, Sylvester Q. Cannon, Harold B. Lee contrast was graphic. There stood Brother Cannon, tall and stately with his beautiful, white hair, and next to him was my father, who was much shorter, with his black hair, which gave him a youthful appearance. He almost looked like he didn't belong, for he was so much younger than the next youngest of the men who were then members of the Council of the Twelve. It came as a new and rather surprising realization to me to consider how much younger he was than the other Brethren.

Following Elder Lee in appointment to the Council of the Twelve in the next few years were others approximately his own age. It was the beginning of a new era in Church leadership, and Elder Harold B. Lee was the first of many of this new generation. He was followed by Elder Spencer W. Kimball, four years older than Elder Lee; Elder Ezra Taft Benson, who was forty-four years old at the time of his call, and was the same age and once a class-mate at the Oneida Academy with Elder Lee; Elder Mark E. Petersen, who was one year younger than Elder Lee and was ordained at age forty-four; and Elder Matthew Cowley, who was two years older than Elder Lee.

In an interview with the *Church News* when he was President of the Church, Harold B. Lee recalled his entry into the Council of the Twelve and his rapid rise in seniority, saying:

> I came to know what it meant to be at the "foot of the ladder," as President Clark called it, but I wasn't there for long. I heard Elder John A. Widtsoe tell about when he was called as a junior member. He sat there for fifteen years before there was a vacancy.
>
> Contrary to that, in thirteen years I had moved from that junior position until I was very near to the president of the Twelve. When called I was twenty years younger than the next youngest member of the quorum, Brother Stephen L Richards.
>
> I recall President Grant would look along the line, and noting my dark hair compared to the gray hair of those older brethren, would say that the color line was well marked. My hair, though, began to change pretty rapidly from that point on.

The days that followed immediately after general conference were filled with visits from well-wishers with their generous congratulations. Elder Lee's diary entry for the next day, Monday, April 7, 1941, explains the situation:

> In the days to follow I was able to do little else than to receive telephone calls and letters of congratulations from many friends on my appointment as a member of the Council of the Twelve. It was

pleasing that many of these were from those who were not members of the Church, with whom I had associated in politics or in business.

Helen recalls those busy days when telephone calls flooded their home after conference: "I remember that we had never been so busy with people coming to the house and calling on the phone. Those were beautiful, warm memories. It was a tremendous time in our lives. We heard from people that we hadn't heard from for years and years."

The house guest, Mabel Hickman, witnessed this joyful outpouring of love, and wrote of it in these words:

> That day was one to remember—the newspapers sent photographers, flowers arrived, telegrams came, with streams of callers, following the Sunday announcement of Elder Lee's appointment. His daughters were scheduled to play their musical instruments that evening, but this was one time when they wanted to "beg off." Their father told them that if they did not go to perform, their reason would be misunderstood, so they went obediently, but reluctantly, to keep their promise.

ORDAINED AN APOSTLE

President J. Reuben Clark, Jr., continued his watchful supervision over Elder Lee by thoughtful contacts to prepare him for the events leading up to his ordination. Elder Lee recorded in his diary on Tuesday, April 8, 1941:

> I went to lunch with President Clark, where he gave me careful and detailed explanation of the procedures on Thursday, where I was to be ordained an Apostle in the temple and accept a charge from the President of the Church as to my duties, obligations, and responsibilities as a member of the Quorum of the Twelve.

Even that contact was followed up with another phone call on Wednesday from President Clark, who wanted to make certain that Elder Lee was ready for the next day's meeting in the temple.

On Thursday, April 10, Elder Harold B. Lee was ordained an Apostle. He described the event as follows:

> I attended my first meeting in the Salt Lake Temple with the First Presidency and the Council of the Twelve. I was ordained an Apostle and set apart as a member of the Council of the Twelve by President Heber J. Grant, with his counselors and the eleven mem-

bers of the Council assisting. Before the ordination I was given a charge by each member of the Presidency in which they stressed important matters pertaining to activities of General Authorities.

The day ended with a dinner in honor of Elder and Sister Lee held in the home of Elder Stephen L Richards and attended by all the First Presidency, the Twelve, and their wives.

OTHER APPOINTEES

The April 1941 general conference was noteworthy and historic for additional reasons. At this conference President Grant announced a new category of General Authorities and named five brethren to the newly created position of Assistant to the Quorum of the Twelve Apostles: Elders Marion G. Romney, Thomas E. McKay, Clifford E. Young, Alma Sonne, and Nicholas G. Smith. Two of those named were close personal and social friends of Elder and Sister Lee. On the Friday night following general conference (April 11, 1941), the Lees' Church history study group met at the home of Roscoe E. and Irene Hammond in a social intended as a token of respect to the new appointees, Elders Marion G. Romney and Nicholas G. Smith and Elder Lee. Elder Lee's diary entry captures an interesting human relations slant on the talented brethren whom the Lord was priming for leadership in his kingdom:

> There was an excellent spirit in the gathering, in no small part due to the splendid attitude manifested by Hugh B. Brown [another member of the group], who had been prominently mentioned for appointment to fill the vacancy in the Quorum of the Twelve.

On this same day, April 11, Elder Lee performed his first temple marriage—for the son of Dr. John P. Gleave and his bride. On the weekend he attended his first stake conference since his ordination as an Apostle, accompanying Elder Charles A. Callis to the Riverside Stake.

ACCEPTANCE AS A GENERAL AUTHORITY

The appointment of Elder Lee to the Quorum of the Twelve pleased the membership of the Church. This feeling is revealed in a personal letter written by President Grant to Mrs. Glendora M. Allred of Burley, Idaho, on April 7, 1941, the day following the close of the general conference. President Grant, so very prompt in his correspondence, thanked her for her expressions of love and devotion and then wrote:

> I cannot recall the time since I became President of the Church when filling a vacancy in the Council of the Twelve has seemed to give such universal satisfaction as has been the case with the selection of Brother Harold B. Lee. (File #912, Letters of President Grant.)

Thus began the intensive labors of Elder Harold Bingham Lee as an Apostle of the Lord. It was a work that would take him to all corners of the earth and would cause him to be received and honored before royalty and the illustrious leaders of the world, as well as the poor and humble, of which he always considered himself to be a part. His sacred calling as a "special witness for Christ," which was never out of his mind and always fashioned his behavior, would end only at his death thirty-two years and eight months later.

First
Apostolic
Decade

———

1941–1950

1941–1943. The "Day of Infamy" at Pearl Harbor
—Japanese launched surprise attack on Hawaii.
Malaya, Hong Kong, and the Philippines. The next
day the United States and Britain declared war on
Japan. War came to West Coast as a Japanese
submarine fired on an oil refinery in Ellwood,
California. Rationing of food, clothing, gasoline in
the U.S.A. Glenn Miller, Betty Grable, Bob Hope,
and war bond rallies. Vaccine developed for
pertussis (whooping cough), and the world's first
operational atomic reactor was built in Oak Ridge,
Tennessee. FDR signed withholding tax law. Allies
landed at Naples, Italy. Bogart and Bergman won
1943 Oscars for *Casablanca*.

CHAPTER 12

A Seedling Among Giant Redwoods

As Harold B. Lee assumed his position in the twelfth
and last large oak chair in the semicircle surrounding the sacred
altar in the upper room of the Salt Lake Temple, a new era in
Church leadership commenced. It was 1941. Elder Lee was forty-
two years old, and there was not a man in the room who was less
than twenty years his senior. The next youngest was Stephen L
Richards, exactly twenty years older. Elder Lee was a seedling
among the giant redwoods.

Presiding over the Church in 1941 were President Heber J. Grant, President J. Reuben Clark, Jr., and President David O. McKay. Members of the Quorum of the Twelve were President Rudger Clawson, George Albert Smith, George F. Richards, Joseph Fielding Smith, Stephen L Richards, Richard R. Lyman, John A. Widtsoe, Joseph F. Merrill, Charles A. Callis, Albert E. Bowen, and Sylvester Q. Cannon. The last previously appointed Apostle, Elder Cannon, was also a product of Pioneer Stake and was twenty-two years older than Elder Lee.

The aging leadership of the Church concerned President Heber J. Grant, as his daily journal entries attest during the spring of that year. The need to fill the existing vacancy in the Quorum of the Twelve, and the possibility of creating a new cadre of leaders to assist the Quorum members, were brooding in the mind of the President. On March 10, 1941, President Grant wrote:

> I discussed with my counselors as to whether we should continue the discussion of a week ago, but we concluded to not have our secretary read the minutes of the week before at the meeting in the temple, but to wait for the return of Rudger Clawson, who is the President of the Apostles, before deciding on a man to fill the vacancy in the Quorum of the Twelve. It was quite remarkable the names that we had. I had asked the brethren for a first and second choice. There were ten of them and I am sure I had about twenty names. It is quite remarkable how many fine men there are in the estimation of the Brethren to fill the Quorum of the Twelve.

Five days later President Grant wrote:

> During the day I had quite a long talk with Brother Clark and Brother McKay regarding calling some men to help the Quorum of the Twelve, as so many of the quorum are in poor health. We are all getting along in years and not capable of doing the work we formerly did.

Within three weeks the decisions had been made concerning the vacancy in the Quorum and the creation of the new General Authority position of Assistants to the Twelve. Under the date of April 5, 1941, this entry tells in President Grant's words his invitation to Harold B. Lee to serve with the Quorum of the Twelve:

> After the priesthood meeting (at general conference), I had a little talk with Harold B. Lee and told him we had decided that he should fill the vacancy in the Quorum of the Twelve Apostles. He was over-

whelmed and shed tears. I feel sure that we shall be very happy with his work.

Five days later Harold B. Lee was ordained an Apostle under the hands of the members of the First Presidency and the Twelve, President Grant acting as voice. He was the sixty-first Apostle of this dispensation. Elder Lee obtained a copy of the blessing and referred to it often in subsequent years, concentrating on these words of President Grant:

> I say unto you, avoid the very appearance of evil, seek foremost and at all times for the advancement of the work of the Lord. Give your thoughts not to the ordinary things of life, but to things that are of great importance, and that are concerned with eternity. . . . We say unto you that above all other things, "obedience is better than sacrifice and to hearken, than the fat of rams." Humility is the key to the guidance of the Spirit of the Lord, and may that spirit of humility that you possess today, that spirit of humility when you had the impression that you might be called to be an Apostle, be ever with you, and the power and spirit of the priesthood of the apostleship shall be yours to withstand the temptations and allurements of life.

A new vision and an increased understanding of the kingdom began to unfold in the days that followed his ordination, but his life-style was unchanged. Harold B. Lee had given his life to the Lord long before he was ordained as an Apostle, by setting aside a promising political career at the call of the First Presidency. The previous five years had been spent in organizing the welfare program and traveling every weekend to the various stakes of the Church. His welfare assignment now seemed to have been an appropriate apprenticeship for his ministry as an Apostle among the Saints he had come to love.

First Experiences as an Apostle

Following the weekly Friday meeting of the Welfare Committee and the First Presidency on June 13, 1941, President Clark took Elder Lee to his office, commended him for his work with the welfare plan, and announced that the First Presidency had approved the appointment of Elder Marion G. Romney, sustained at the recent general conference as one of five new Assistants to the Twelve, to be the Assistant Director of the welfare program. Elder Lee, whose work as the Managing Director of the welfare program would continue to be his primary assignment in the Twelve, felt the appointment was "an excellent move." Until the day Harold B. Lee died, his bond of friendship with Marion G. Romney was among the most meaningful companionships men enjoy in mortality.

Along with the enjoyable assignment to serve as the organist for the weekly meetings in the temple came a weightier calling the following summer. The junior Apostle was given the assignment to prepare and deliver the "Church of the Air" nationwide radio broadcast over the CBS network. On July 6, 1941, he delivered his first major address, entitled "True Patriotism—an Expression of Faith," calling this speaking challenge "a thrilling one." Scarcely had he completed the sermon than the telephone rang in the broadcast booth. It was President Clark calling from his home to congratulate Elder Lee on the content and delivery of his message.

A few weeks later Elder Lee was assigned as the junior companion of Elder Stephen L Richards in the reorganization of the Idaho Stake. There he observed carefully the wise counsel and instruction given by Elder Richards.

Arriving home late one evening from a trip to Arizona with Elder Marion G. Romney to survey the extent of flood damage near Duncan, Elder Lee received a phone call from President Don B. Colton of the Salt Lake Mission Home requesting that he speak to the missionaries the next morning on the subject of the temple endowment. Elder Lee accepted, then spoke with President McKay about the subject, and spent most of the night in preparation. On October 16, 1941, he recorded the events of that day: "Enjoyed greatly my study and discussion with the missionaries in the temple on the significance of the temple endowment. It seems my presentation had the approval of the temple presidency and President Colton of the Missionary Home."

Over the years this subject was a focal point of Elder Lee's ministry as he met weekly with groups of new missionaries who came to the temple as they prepared to leave for their assigned fields of labor.

PROPHECIES

The trip into Arizona to inspect the flood damage brought him into contact with President Spencer W. Kimball, then serving as president of the afflicted Mount Graham Stake. During their visit

Elder Lee promised the Saints that if they would work together and apply the principles of the welfare plan, out of their crisis would come great missionary success with the nonmembers of the Church in that area, and their own prosperity would increase beyond what they had known before the flood.

One year later, traveling through the same region with President J. Reuben Clark, Elder Lee was delighted with their findings:

> We drove up to Duncan and Virden to visit with the Saints who had been damaged by the flood a year ago.
>
> They recalled our meeting with them when I promised them that as a result of the flood they would gain more than they lost. It was reported by Brother Payne, the work director, that with the exception of three, all the others were already better off than they were before the flood—also they had been counseled to stay with their farms instead of going to the mines and all had stayed but one, and he had returned after one month.

The gift of prophecy was in evidence early in Elder Lee's apostleship. On a trip to the Young Stake conference in Mancos, Colorado, in May 1941, Elder Lee described an unusual outpouring of the Spirit, as follows:

> At this conference I received a rather remarkable demonstration of the power of prophecy in the ordination and setting apart of Elmer Alphonso Taylor, former second counselor in the stake presidency, as the new bishop of the Farmington Ward. He received a blessing that his crippled foot and leg would not hinder his work as bishop and that because of his humility in accepting this new appointment he would be given such influence with his family that not one would go astray, and all would marry in the temple and all would be a credit to any community in which they lived. He had a family of six girls. A remarkable spirit was in the meetings, many people being in tears as they sang the closing song and bid us good-bye.

Seventeen years later this prophecy was literally fulfilled, although it required another miracle to do so when one divorced daughter finally was married in the temple.

Amid all these first and impressionable experiences with the Spirit in his new calling, Elder Lee remained a practical man who practiced in his daily life the counsel he gave to others. On August 19, 1941, he recorded that he worked late into the night preparing the fruit and storage room in his home. On a Saturday afternoon on September 6, 1941, he wrote, "I completed an extra storage bin for coal at home and unloaded a load of wood and coal."

Despite the impressionable experiences that were bursting upon this new Apostle, it was not until after the first summer in his calling had passed that he felt at peace in his stewardship. On August 21, 1941 he recorded:

> I met with the Twelve and the Assistants and later on with the Twelve and the First Presidency in the first meeting in the temple after the summer vacation. This was the first time I felt the close bond there should be toward these brethren. The spirit was wonderful and I was happy to be in tune.

In November, Elder Lee acknowledged President Grant's eighty-fifth birthday with a letter of love and appreciation. When he arrived home from California on November 20, 1941, a reply was waiting for him from President Grant. The prophet's sentiments of love and affection, as demonstrated in the following letter, were received by Elder Lee with a deep sense of gratitude:

> November 22, 1941
>
> Elder Harold B. Lee
> Building
>
> Dear Brother Lee:
>
> It is ten minutes to four o'clock, and I am sitting up talking to my dictaphone, sitting on the side of the bed. I have scores and scores of letters, telegrams, and cards containing birthday greetings.
>
> I appreciate your letter of the 19th as much as any I have received. From the first time I ever met you my heart went out to you with a feeling of love and respect, and I have been very happy indeed to see you grow in the work of the Lord from the day that I first met you.
>
> I pray that you and your good wife and family may be blessed with the substance of this world, so that you shall be comfortable and happy, but above all, may you ever have a love of the Gospel and a desire to work for the cause of Truth. God bless you and yours forever, I ask in the name of His son, Jesus Christ, our Redeemer.
>
> Affectionately, your brother in the Gospel.
>
> /s/ Heber J. Grant

In this first year of his calling to the apostleship, Elder and Sister Lee had been married eighteen years. In celebration of that anniversary, on November 14, which was also Sister Lee's birthday, Sister Lee went Relief Society block teaching, served as a guide at the Lion House in the afternoon, assisted the MIA with a ward road show act, and still had time to enjoy a ride through Parley's and Emigration canyons at the invitation of President and Sister Grant.

As he concluded his journal on December 31, 1941, Elder Lee wrote of the impact his first nine months as an Apostle had had on him:

> This page closes the greatest and most important year of my life. During the last twelve months, I have seen the prophecies of our present leaders fulfilled regarding war and economic trends, proving again their divine callings. In my call to apostleship I have experienced the most intensive schooling and preparation of any similar period. I have known the terrors of the evil tempter and in contrast the sublime joy of inspiration and the revelations of the Holy Spirit. My wife and family have been a constant source of encouragement and happiness and despite the terrors of World War, the peace of God seems to be with us.

Spiritual Manifestations

One of the signs of the true church is that the gifts of the Spirit will follow "them that believe" (see Mark 16:17). In few lives were these gifts more in evidence than in the life of Harold B. Lee. Many times he was the instrument through whom the Lord granted miraculous restoration of health to the Saints.

Following surgery on Elder Henry D. Moyle's wife, Elder Moyle reported to Elder Lee that her condition was remarkably improved after their administration. This account from his journal is typical of many similar entries:

> We had blessed her that her recovery would be so remarkable as to be astounding to the doctors. The next morning when her doctors, Dr. Ralph Richards and Dr. Earl Skidmore, came into her hospital room, one remarked that her condition was "phenomenal" and the other doctor said that it was "miraculous."

Many are the documented instances when not only was the Spirit of the Holy Ghost felt by those in Elder Lee's presence, but some bore witness of seeing visible manifestations. For example:

> Last night I spoke at the MIA services and following that to the "fireside" of the M-Men and Gleaners of Nampa, Idaho. Stewart Mason and his wife drove me in their car over to Boise, where I was to board the train for Salt Lake. Sister Mason told me she had witnessed

an "aura," as she called it, surrounding me as I spoke. Fern had previously seen the same manifestation about me in the First Ward.

A Brother George McLain came to see me at home. He told me of being at the sunset services at the state capitol last Sunday and of witnessing a spiritual manifestation of my being accompanied in my speaking by other personages who were near me.

I attended the meeting with the Saints at New Haven, Connecticut, where Yale University is located. There were a number of investigators who seemed greatly interested. One woman observed that the faces of the Elders seemed to glow as they discussed the gospel.

The attendance at April general conference in 1942 was reduced because of wartime conditions, so the participants were nearly all stake presidencies and represented virtually every stake in the Church. Elder Lee recorded in his journal yet another witness from an observer at the conference:

An excellent spirit was in each meeting. Brother Ray Haight, a police officer who was present to assist with the crowd, bore testimony to me that during the entire morning session an intense, white light flooded the First Presidency "as though from a huge spotlight above" and made President Grant's clothes to appear to be white. He felt it a testimony from heaven of their divine calling.

The Sunday session of that conference was held in the fourth-floor assembly room of the Salt Lake Temple. These were the impressions Elder Lee recorded:

Today in the upper room of the Salt Lake Temple was held one of the most spiritual meetings of this generation and certainly the most impressive meeting I have ever attended. The meeting commenced at 10:00 a.m. and ended at 4:30 p.m. The first part was the regular Tabernacle broadcast of the "Church of the Air" address by Stephen L Richards and radio addresses by President David O. McKay and Elder A. E. Bowen. At 12:30 p.m. the sacrament was administered to all those present by the Twelve Apostles. Many of the brethren wept as the sacrament was passed to them by the Twelve. Our joy was supreme in thus serving this people. In the next four hours, forty-five of the brethren bore testimonies, and in that time there was hardly a moment when tears were not in the eyes of the listeners. Testimonies of miraculous healing, raising the dead, divine guidance, power of cleanliness, and rewards for keeping the commandments of God were borne. President McKay testified that many of our loved ones were present in the meeting.

Following that memorable general conference, Elder Lee was attending stake conferences in Idaho and stopped at the hospital in Grace to administer to Bishop LeGrand Richards, then serving as Presiding Bishop, and recuperating from a heart attack which had occurred one week earlier. Speaking in the general conference at which Elder Richards was sustained as an Apostle ten years later, Elder Lee recalled the blessing he had pronounced on the man who would ultimately serve longer as a General Authority than any other in his day. Elder Lee bore this witness:

> In a brief moment, when my hands were on the head of Brother Richards, I knew that the Lord loved him and that he was going to live. The certainty of that was as sure to me then as it is today that he was spared for a great and glorious mission. (Conference Report, April 1952, p. 126.)

INFLUENCE OF PRESIDENT CLARK

From the moment Elder Lee assumed his calling as an Apostle, President J. Reuben Clark, Jr., took a special interest in him. He prepared the new Apostle for each step preceding his ordination and tutored him in advance of each upcoming experience. He then saw to it that Elder Lee performed the same important function for the other new Apostles who were called thereafter. President Clark became a father figure to Elder Lee, and their relationship was characterized by each of them in succeeding years as being as intimate as any father and son would share.

When Elder Lee's daughter Helen had an emergency appendectomy, it was President Clark who called first to see if there was anything he could do, and then he gently scolded Elder Lee for not having told him sooner. Elder Lee interpreted this loving concern in these words: "He has been a real father to me."

Word came to Elder Lee on August 2, 1944, that Sister Clark had passed away. This time it was Elder Lee who reached out to his mentor in a time of need. He wrote: "I went to see President Clark at his home and spent a few minutes with him. He had tried to call me to tell me of her passing. It is a wonderful experience to stand in the presence of a great man bowed in sorrow."

Soon after his wife's passing, President Clark took his turn in presenting the CBS "Church of the Air" address to a nationwide radio audience. Elder Lee, reciprocating President Clark's support

First Presidency from 1934 to 1945:
(left to right) J. Reuben Clark, Jr.,
Heber J. Grant, David O. McKay

of him for his first radio address in 1941, went to the Tabernacle to be with President Clark. "The next day President Clark called and expressed himself as being deeply touched that I had put myself out to go to the Tabernacle to hear his 'Church of the Air' address."

On one occasion, while visiting the Duncan flood area the year following the disaster, President Clark was in the company of Elder Lee, who recorded these memorable public comments about the future that President Clark envisioned for his adopted "son":

> President Clark related my experience in the welfare plan and in politics and told the people that he was confident that if I had remained in politics I would have been elected to the U. S. Senate. He said he loved me as his own son and that I had returned and reciprocated that love, as a son to a father. He said further that while he was not prophesying, that in the providence of the Lord, because of my age, I would one day be the President of the Church.

Another first experience as a member of the Council of the Twelve came in the fall of 1942 with the assignment to tour the Texas-Louisiana Mission, presided over by William L. Warner of Richfield, Utah. At Fort Worth, Texas, on November 21, Elder Lee held a conference meeting with 160 Saints present, some traveling from Dallas to attend. His journal entry for the night said, "The talks of three of the Elders were outstanding." Unbeknown then to Elder Lee, one of these missionaries, Elder L. Brent Goates, was to become his son-in-law.

A glimpse into the fascinating character and personality of President Heber J. Grant is seen in his interactions within a one-week period with Elder Lee. On November 30, 1942, Elder and Sister Lee met President Grant as he was leaving the Church Office Building; according to Brother Lee's journal, the President "told me how much he thought of me and that he thought the six members of the Twelve that he had appointed would compare favorably with the six others in the Quorum."

Three days later, after the Council of the Twelve had met in their regular meeting, Elder Lee wrote in his journal:

> I attempted to make a somewhat detailed report of my three-week visit to the Texas-Louisana Mission, but was stopped by President Grant, who said if everyone were to take as much time we would be here two days. President Clark and President McKay and Stephen L Richards all expressed regret that I had not been allowed to complete what to them had been a very proper and desired report. I was greatly humiliated.

Elder Lee never forgot that experience and, finally seeing the humor in it, enjoyed retelling the story.

FAMILY LIFE

The long conference weekends and extended travel away from home were difficult for Harold B. Lee, who longed for the company of his beloved companion and their two daughters, now both students at the University of Utah. He often told his family that the longest days of his life were the ones immediately preceding his return home from his far-flung travels on the Lord's errands.

Harold B. Lee was a gardener and a "do-it-yourselfer." He acquired his skills growing up on the farm where it was impossible to pick up the phone and hire a specialist for repairs. In fact, he actually preferred to do such work himself, and his gardening provided the one outlet he enjoyed from the constant demands of his calling. He describes his labors over the Memorial Day holiday in 1942:

This being declared a holiday I arose early and spent until the early afternoon gardening around the yard and cutting the lawns and trimming up the trees. The rains have made things very pleasant and the warm weather seems to induce a fine growth of shrubs. I did some studying and preparing for my conference tomorrow and rested, although I fancy my family were somewhat chagrined that I did not pay more heed to the celebration of the holiday. In the evening we drove to the cemetery and visited with my mother and sister Verda.

Holidays were always spent at home with the family, a welcome respite and retreat from his daily labors. His journal entry at Christmastime in 1942, reveals his feelings about the manner in which the holiday was being celebrated:

Father and Mother and Verda came down and spent Christmas Eve with us. Verda was lonely without Charlie, who is in the army, but that was largely banished by the many visitors who came throughout the day to bring Christmas cheer and goodwill. This was a lavish Christmas with money in evidence everywhere and the stores much depleted of their stocks, but all this seemed to promise a day when we must pay the penalty of reckless spending, so much needlessly, when sacrifice should be the order.

Soon after the holidays were over Elder Lee made the last payment on his home at 1208 South Eighth West Street in Salt Lake City. Together the family enjoyed the ceremonial burning of the mortgage. He then petitioned the Lord to consecrate and dedicate their home to the end that the Holy Ghost would always dwell therein.

Because January 1 was his mother's birthday, Harold always reserved that holiday for visiting with relatives. For years his home was the focal point for family celebrations on New Year's Day.

In 1945, the health of his family and the burden he always carried concerning the wayward members of his immediate family were of special concern to Elder Lee. His wife, Fern, showed signs of a heart strain that caused rapid beating, exciting an extreme nervousness. Because Sister Lee's health was always fragile at best, he often assisted his daughters with the housework. Many are the diary entries in early 1945, for example, that reflect his evening activities at home: "Spent the evening helping Fern with her house cleaning; . . . the girls and I went through the house and cleaned the living room rug and readjusted the furniture."

Two New Apostles Called

A tour of the Northwestern States Mission in June 1943 was interrupted with the news of the passing of President Rudger Clawson, President of the Quorum of the Twelve. Elder Lee immediately returned to be with his beloved Brethren in Salt Lake City.

President Grant sent word that he wanted to visit alone with Elder Lee, so he went to the Grant home and had a delightful hour with the President. They discussed two candidates to fill the vacancies in the Twelve occasioned by the deaths of President Clawson and Elder Sylvester Q. Cannon. Finding himself in complete accord with President Grant, and also having recommended a third possible candidate for appointment, Elder Lee turned to leave. He wrote that night of the tender scene that ensued. "When I started to leave, President Grant pulled me down and kissed me and commended me for the "wonderful work" he said I was doing. I told him that there was nothing more I desired than to please him and my Heavenly Father."

Not waiting for general conference to reorganize, on July 15 the Brethren made the announcement of Elder Spencer W. Kimball's calling to the Council of the Twelve. Many persons were pleased with the appointment of the president of Mount Graham Stake in Arizona. It was somewhat surprising since many had assumed that the automatic elevation of one of the new Assistants to the Twelve would take place. The second appointment in the Quorum of the Twelve was announced twelve days later when Elder Ezra Taft Benson was named.

It was not until the fall that plans were made to release Spencer W. Kimball as president of Mount Graham Stake, Elder Lee being the Apostle who reorganized that stake's presidency.

General conference in October 1943 was highlighted by the sustaining of the two new Apostles in the Quorum of the Twelve. Writing on October 7, Elder Lee made this entry about his two new companions in the Twelve:

Today marked a new chapter in Church history. The two new members of the Council of the Twelve, Spencer W. Kimball and Ezra Taft Benson, were ordained Apostles by President Grant in a special meeting of the Twelve and the First Presidency, held in the office of the First Presidency. President Grant was too weak to stand and had each of the brethren kneel while all the brethren of the

Twelve assisted in the ordination. A delightful meeting was held in the temple following the ordination, where the sacrament was administered and each of the new brethren was asked to speak briefly.

ASSIGNMENTS TO SERVE

President Clark called Elder Lee into his office on July 31, 1942, to inform him that he was being assigned with Elder Albert E. Bowen to accompany Hugh B. Brown, then a servicemen's coordinator, on a tour of all the military service camps along the West Coast. The purpose of their trip was to ascertain if anything might be done by the Church to promote the social and spiritual welfare of LDS servicemen. Elder Lee offered suggestions based on his observations during the three-week tour, and growing out of that experience came his assignment as chairman of the Servicemen's Committee.

Elder Lee's sermons reflected his concern for the young men of the Church who were away from home during the war years. His experiences in the war zones brought forth recurrent inspirational stories about the faith and courage of those who had been called to military duty away from home.

In mid-1943 Elder Lee and Elder Romney received another common assignment which further strengthened their bond of friendship when they commenced a long service as advisers to the general Primary board. The instructions on this calling came from President McKay and illustrate how tightly centralized the Church was in this early period. President McKay counseled at this interview on July 20, 1943, that the Primary officers would come to the Apostles for advice, but that they would take their problems directly to the First Presidency. A new presidency of the Primary Association was also announced, composed of Adele Cannon Howells, LaVern Parmley, and Dessie Grant Boyle.

By 1944, additional duties had been assigned to Elder Lee, including the chairmanship of a committee to study a proposed new hymnbook; and in July of that year he was named as a member of the newly formed publication committee, along with Elders Joseph Fielding Smith, John A. Widtsoe, and Marion G. Romney. This committee was charged with the mission to review and approve everything published by the Church. His major assignment in these years, however, was to serve as the chairman of the Melchizedek Priesthood Committee of the Council of the Twelve.

An Apostle Lost and Replaced

In November 1943 an event took place that deeply shocked and saddened many, particularly the First Presidency and the Quorum of the Twelve. Following a Church court that the Twelve held in the temple, Richard R. Lyman, one of their number, was excommunicated from the Church for violation of the Christian law of chastity. Elder Lee recorded, "It was a most saddening experience, with most of the Twelve in tears as Brother Lyman was asked to leave the meeting and shook hands with each brother in parting those sacred premises and that choice companionship for the last time."

The members of the Quorum of the Twelve slowly shuffled out of their council room, still dazed and bearing the deep hurt of the first excommunication of an Apostle in thirty-eight years. They left immediately thereafter to attend their various stake conferences, heavy of heart from their ordeal. Elders Lee and Kimball attended the Parowan Stake conference together, but their otherwise beautiful autumn drive to and from the conference was marred by their occasional conversation about the events of the trial.

It was not until the following general conference in April of 1944 that the vacancy was filled with the call of Mark E. Petersen. Elder Lee was delighted with this appointment and noted it in these words: "His choice was well received and, although he is not well known, the selection of one of his background and his age seemed appreciated by everyone. His initial sermon was delivered in a masterful fashion which left most of the congregation in tears."

1944–1946. Berlin bombed by eight hundred U.S. planes in daylight raids, beginning of round-the-clock bombings. Allies landed in Italy and entered Rome. "D-Day" launched by Gen. Dwight Eisenhower, the greatest amphibious military operation in history. American forces led by Gen. Douglas MacArthur recaptured the Philippines. Band leader Glenn Miller disappeared on routine flight from England to Paris. Germany surrendered, and war in Europe ended. President Harry S. Truman succeeded President Franklin D. Roosevelt, who died in Warm Springs, Georgia, age 63. Truman received Japanese surrender papers that formally ended World War II. He met with Churchill and Stalin at Potsdam to discuss peace plans. League of Nations formally went out of existence.

CHAPTER 13

Politician
or Apostle?

At the time of his appointment as director of the Church's welfare program, Elder Lee resigned his post as a Salt Lake City commissioner, closed the political chapter in his life, and never looked back. A little-known fact even to members of his immediate family, however, was the pressure that was exerted on Elder Lee to return to politics in 1944, three years after his call to the apostleship. He was sought after relentlessly by the Republican Party leadership to head their ticket, either as a candidate for governor of the state of Utah, or as a candidate for the United States Senate.

The interest in Elder Lee's possible candidacy first surfaced when he was told by President Clark on March 30, 1944, that a delegation of Republican legislators had urged him to request that the First Presidency give their consent for Elder Lee to run for governor. Elder Lee recalled the conversation with President Clark in these words:

> President Clark asked me as to my desires in the matter and I told him that the only terms on which I would even consider such a matter would be that the First Presidency were to call me on a mission to permit myself to become a candidate. President Clark said he had talked to President McKay and they had agreed that I should not run for office because of the need of my services in the Council of the Twelve and with the welfare program and that there was no certainty that I could be elected, due to the strong New Deal sentiment extant at the present time.

In the weeks following, however, a constant stream of visitors kept the speculation alive that perhaps Elder Lee was a potential candidate. George D. Keyser, a prominent Mason in Salt Lake City, offered his support as a taxpayer and citizen, but his advice as "a dear friend" to Elder Lee was to stay out of politics. The next day President Clark had a visit from J. Bracken Lee, then mayor of Price, Utah, urging the candidacy of Elder Lee for the U.S. Senate.

Soon therafter A. V. Watkins, chairman of the Utah County Republican Party, and Harry Clarke, a trusted friend, visited Elder Lee to inform him that a political draft committee, of which Bishop Hunt of the Catholic Church was a member, was proposing to call on President Grant to ask his consent for Elder Lee's candidacy for the Senate.

J. Bracken Lee (no relation) persisted in urging Elder Lee's candidacy a few days later, calling to ask if Elder Lee would consider a draft if an influential group of non-Mormon citizens of the state were to call upon the First Presidency and ask their consent. His response was consistent to all these requests: "The draft would have to come from the First Presidency themselves before I would consider it."

The question of his potential candidacy surfaced again in 1946, even after all the attempts to lure him back to politics had failed in

1944. On May 29, 1946, Elder Lee described the final attempt to engineer his political comeback:

> Following the weekly report meeting with the General Authorities, I was on the fifth floor of the Church Administration Building having my picture taken when I received an urgent message from President McKay's staff to come at once to the office of the First Presidency. When I arrived I found a delegation headed by W. W. Seegmiller who were insistent that I file my candidacy for U.S. Senator to run against Abe Murdock. He had told the Presidency that I would run if they gave consent. I told them that I would not run unless the First Presidency told me to do it. While the counselors seemed to be inclined, yet because President George Albert Smith was in Mexico, they refused to tell me to do it until he could be reached, and that would be too late for filing.

Thus ended forever the secret enticements that were offered to have Elder Lee include politics in his apostolic mission. His answer was always the same to those who sought him as their candidate, and his records suggest neither a preference for nor a disappointment about his aborted political career. After 1946, any possibility that Harold B. Lee would ever again be a political candidate was gone.

THE RADIO SERIES: 1945

In late 1944, plans were announced to have Elder Lee deliver the Sunday evening talks on KSL radio for the Church, a series of sermons scheduled to begin in January, 1945, and continue each week thereafter for six months. His concern over this assignment was registered in his journal comments of December 16, 1944:

> I spent the day [Saturday] entirely locked up in the office at the Church Office Building trying to get some inspiration to make some preparations for the beginning of the new series of radio talks to start on January 7, 1945. I prepared the first talk to the suggested title of "Choose You This Day," as a sort of preface to the talks that follow, endeavoring to prepare some gauge as to the proper length of each talk. I am certain that up until the present time I have had no assignment that has caused me, or that will cause me, any more excitement than this one, and except for the blessings of the Lord, my efforts will be futile.

Reaction was swift to his first presentation. Some thought he used too many scriptures, some said his applications of the scriptural lessons came too late in the talk, and some said it wasn't entertaining enough. One sentiment, however, was universal. Everyone seemed to feel that Elder Lee had issued a challenge that was going to be difficult for the youth to meet.

In January an incident occurred that briefly depressed Elder Lee: a high Church official asked him to delete a particular quotation from his sermon before it was published. The standard practice for these sermons was to correct the galley proofs following delivery on the radio, but prior to their publication in the following week's edition of the *Church News*. It was not actually deleting the quotation that bothered Elder Lee nearly as much as the unfriendly manner in which the demand was made.

For his ninth radio sermon, he addressed the topic, "Why the Church?" Later that night he wrote: "When I finished, President Clark called to commend me. He has been very kind and his constant encouragement has been a source of great strength."

Despite his careful preparations, errors did inadvertently occur. One night in March, he referred to the story of Joseph's experience with Potiphar's wife, inadvertently naming her as the wife of the pharaoh. President Clark, ever watchful of his young charge, called it to his attention after the broadcast and comforted him by relating a similar mistake he had made once in a "Church of the Air" address.

The intensity of his preparations and a measure of his devotion to this assignment is seen in this entry:

> I came back to the office and worked on a radio talk entitled, "In Holy Temples" until 7:00 p.m., and after supper at home, continued until I had completed it at 2:30 a.m. I enjoyed the spiritual experience of my preparation.

Given the broad spectrum of gospel doctrines the series contemplated, it is natural that there would be disagreement over some issues he raised. Before President Clark left for a trip to the East Coast, he came to Elder Lee's office to inquire about his health, seeking to determine if the radio assignment was weighing too heavily upon him. He told Brother Lee that some of the General Authorities thought he was speaking too plainly about some of the principles of the gospel, but he firmly told his young student Apostle, "If you pleased your critics, you wouldn't please me."

The pressures of the weekly deadlines for the radio sermons began taxing his strength emotionally, physically, and spiritually, resulting in the very conditions President Clark had sensed over a month earlier. In early May, Elder Lee received the results of a physical examination, and was told that he showed many signs of physical fatigue, evidenced by his rapid pulse and low blood pressure for a man his age. The doctor urged Elder Lee to abandon all Church work for a month, with a stern warning that if he did not heed that counsel he would likely suffer a heart attack. The pain in his neck and shoulders, the doctor explained, was a reflection of the strain on his heart.

As usual, President Clark was at Elder Lee's door the day following the medical report. He told Elder Lee to take his reference books home with him, and urged him to stay away from the office and all meetings except those with the First Presidency and the Twelve. The pressures continued to manifest themselves in his very next sermon as he found it difficult to read the script without several pronunciation errors. Despite these flaws, President Clark sustained him once again, calling to commend him on what he had said in his sermon.

PRESIDENT GRANT'S DEATH

Adjustments bringing abrupt and major changes were portending in the spring of 1945. First came word on April 12, 1945, of the sudden death of the President of the United States, Franklin D. Roosevelt, at Warm Springs, Georgia. Meanwhile, a reception was held in Provo, Utah, to introduce the new president of Brigham Young University, Howard S. McDonald.

The biggest adjustment of all, however, came on May 14, 1945, when at 7:00 P.M. it was announced that President Heber J. Grant had died. His death was not unexpected, for he had been in failing health since suffering a stroke on February 5, 1940, while attending to Church business in Southern California. Since that time his general conference sermons had been read by his private secretary, Joseph Anderson, and he had to be carried into the Tabernacle to attend general conference sessions.

Elder Lee, though not in good health at the time, went immediately with his wife to pay his respects to Sister Grant and the family. They invited the Lees to kneel in prayer with them as Elder Lee supplicated the Lord for his blessings upon the family.

Years later Elder Lee recalled these momentous events while teaching important lessons to an audience of youth leaders, asking:

Have you ever thought what a great experience it is to witness the calling home of a prophet of God? I have witnessed several. After the passing of President Heber J. Grant, each of us of the Twelve were called in the late afternoon by President George F. Richards, who was the senior member of the Council of the Twelve in the city. We were told that President Grant had just passed away and that there would be a very important meeting in the Church Office Building at nine o'clock the next morning at which we were all expected to be in attendance. With great expectations and with great heaviness of heart, we were all there. And as I looked around the circle, there was no one standing at the head of the table. President McKay had moved down, standing between President George F. Richards and Joseph Fielding Smith. President Clark had gone way down the row and was standing between Charles A. Callis and Albert E. Bowen. That was his place of seniority. There was no First Presidency, because the prophet had been called home.

We sat around the table and President Richards, with great feeling, said: "Now you understand that in the absence of President George Albert Smith, who is in the East and is now returning home, that we should get things underway for plans for the funeral service. I think none of you will suppose that I am presumptuous in taking the responsibility of calling this meeting. And I suppose that therefore I have the right to conduct it in any way that I see fit. Now it is rather awkward here with Brother McKay and Brother Clark sitting down here in our midst. President Clark and President McKay, get up and come here to the head of the table, and President Clark, you take charge of this meeting."

And as they stood up and walked to the head of the table, I could see the emotion of that moment. We recognized, as we saw a transition taking place, there was no politics after the passing to fill a vacancy. It was the Lord's way and his will, and the smoothness and the ease with which it was done brought about an amazing transformation. (From a tape recording of an unpublished talk at the Institute and Seminary Leadership Conference, 1969.)

Before relinquishing the meeting to President Clark, President Richards asked Elder Lee to prepare a tribute to President Grant from the Twelve, to be published in the *Deseret News*.

President Grant's body was taken to the foyer of the Church Office Building to lie in state until the time of the funeral services. Over twelve thousand people passed through the building to have their last glimpse of the beloved and respected prophet. Funeral services were held four days following his death, and Elder Lee carefully recorded the details in his diary as follows:

On Friday, May 18, 1945, the funeral for the President of the Church was held in the Salt Lake Tabernacle. The procession left the Church Office Building promptly at twelve noon, the General Authorities proceeding ahead of the hearse on foot with the Twelve leading and the counselors in the First Presidency immediately ahead of the hearse, and stake presidencies following the hearse. Thousands of people lined the streets and the temple grounds. The services started promptly at 12:15 p.m., with George Albert Smith presiding and President J. Reuben Clark, Jr., conducting the exercises.

Fourteen truckloads of flowers were taken to the cemetery and were distributed to the graves of each of the past presidents of the Church. The opening and closing prayers were offered by Patriarch Joseph F. Smith and Presiding Bishop LeGrand Richards, and the grave was dedicated by Elder Antoine R. Ivins.

And then Elder Lee added this final note: "I had at least twenty-five requests from bishops to speak at sacrament meetings which are to be in the nature of memorial services for President Grant. Because of my weakened condition, I thought it was wise to decline them all."

On the following Monday, May 21, 1945, the First Presidency was reorganized. Of this first experience with the succession process, Elder Lee wrote, "It was a day long to be remembered."

The Apostles, which then numbered fourteen, including Presidents McKay and Clark, met in the temple. All were requested to come fasting. After they had dressed in white temple clothing and had engaged in prayer, Brother George Albert Smith opened the meeting with a brief talk and then called upon each of the Brethren to speak, in the order of their seniority. Each declared his feeling that there should be no delay in organizing the First Presidency and the sentiment was unanimous that George Albert Smith, as senior member and President of the Council, should be named as the President of the Church. "There was a rich outpouring of spirit, and love was freely expressed," Elder Lee wrote.

The new Presidency was officially reorganized when George Albert Smith was ordained and set apart by George F. Richards, with all the Twelve assisting. President Smith then chose President Clark and President McKay as his counselors, and set them apart. George F. Richards was sustained and set apart as the new President of the Council of the Twelve. President Smith was seventy-five years of age when he was ordained, having served previously for forty-one years as an Apostle. He felt comfortable in retaining

President Grant's former counselors as his own, since they had been leading the Church for the past eleven years.

Because his nervous condition was aggravated by the events of the preceding days, Elder Lee spent a sleepless night following the reorganization of the First Presidency. He awoke the following morning weary and fatigued, and determined that he would stay at home to help Sister Lee with some housework. About three o'clock that afternoon, however, pressing servicemen's work forced him to go to the office, and once there he continued polishing his next radio address.

Elder Charles A. Callis came to visit him and stated that he had expressed to his wife the thought that he had hoped the two former counselors in the First Presidency would be chosen by Brother Smith, but that if there were to be any change he had also hoped Elder Lee would be chosen as a counselor so he could grow up with an inside knowledge of Church matters. Elder Lee quietly appreciated the vote of confidence from his friend who officed next door to him, but he never repeated the conversation.

TRIP TO HAWAIIAN ISLANDS

The First Presidency requested Elder Lee to attend meetings in Honolulu during July 1945. He was to be the first General Authority to visit the Islands since the Japanese attack on Pearl Harbor on December 7, 1941.

On Sunday, June 24, 1945, Elder Lee gave his last radio talk before going to dinner at his parents' home, located in the lower Avenues area of Salt Lake City. There he received a blessing from his sixty-eight-year-old ailing father in preparation for the journey.

What might seem like a luxurious vacation to us today was in fact an arduous one-week journey by sea in an ancient steam freighter filled with a cargo of milk cows, trucks, tractors, and produce. In addition to the cargo there were twenty-four passengers, comprising as motley an assembly of human beings as the mind could conceive. The accommodations were anything but comfortable, Elder Lee's cabin consisting of a 10x12-foot space he shared with five others. Each had a cot and a small wooden locker. Boxes served as chairs when they could be found, and the toilets and washroom were on the upper deck.

The old freighter *Maunawili,* built in 1921, lumbered out of the San Francisco harbor at eleven o'clock on the morning on July

First Presidency from 1945 to 1951: (left to right) J. Reuben Clark, Jr., George Albert Smith, David O. McKay

During visit to Hawaiian Islands, July, 1945

6, 1945. Engine trouble developed at about fifty miles out to sea, and the ship limped back to port at seven o'clock that night, thus wasting the entire day. After a two-day delay for repairs, the ship finally cleared the bay at 9:00 P.M. in a heavy fog, requiring the captain to sound the horn every few minutes as a safety precaution. Not surprisingly, Elder Lee recorded in his journal, "I had some peculiar feelings at the thought of the trip away from the Mainland for the first time in my life."

Elder Lee used the time at sea to review his recently completed radio sermons in preparation for their publication as a book. An impromptu Sunday service was arranged for nine of the passengers who accepted the invitation of the captain to use the mess hall for the meeting. Elder Lee's impression of the service described the diverse company he was keeping: "Seldom could one meet a less religious group than those who are on this ship. With vulgarity, profanity, and gambling, they, by every breath they draw, seem to defy the principles of truth, and it seems as though we are casting pearls before swine."

With one exception the voyage itself was uneventful and the seas calm, despite the war-time conditions. Strict rules governing war conditions were posted on the ship's bulletin board forbidding the passengers to write letters or keep diaries in which the movements of the ship were detailed. Sunday, after the Church services, those aboard were given a scare when the head of a steam turbine in the engine room was blown off with a great burst of steam. The ship was in the submarine danger zone, and the thought of lying adrift all night as a perfect target for the enemy gave no one any peace of mind. But within a half-hour the steam had been diverted through the use of an auxiliary turbine and the ship was again underway. War dangers were ever in mind, however. For two days the guns aboard the ship had been uncovered and oiled, ready for momentary combat.

At the Honolulu harbor, friendly faces were most happily recognized as President Ralph E. Wooley and his son-in-law, Jay Quealy, greeted Elder Lee. Afterwards, their travels through the Islands more than compensated for the inconvenience of the voyage.

On Maui Island Elder Lee recalled the early missionary incident of President Lorenzo Snow's miraculous restoration to life after having been underwater for thirty minutes. It was here, also, that

George Q. Cannon laid the foundation for missionary work in the Islands after others in his group had failed, when he received the gift of tongues sufficient for him to understand the native Hawaiian language.

Another historical visit was made to the monument erected at the place where the first branch of the Church in the Hawaiian Islands was established at Pulehu, in 1851. Here, also, in 1921, President David O. McKay and Elder Hugh J. Cannon, in company with E. Wesley Smith and David Kailemai, had a manifestation after a prayer offered by President McKay. Brother Kailemai saw clasped hands and remarked that the veil between them and the spirit world was very thin. Brother Cannon saw the same and said there was no veil.

Flying next to the island of Molokai, the group made a telephone call to President Waddoups at the leper colony. At Kalaupapa President Waddoups insisted the visitors come down to the colony to see them and the Latter-day Saints who were patients there. The trail on the end of this lonely island was covered on mules, three miles down a steep mountain path.

Fifty-two members of the Church were enrolled at the leper colony at Kalaupapa. A meeting was called by Brother Waddoups and twenty members attended. Elder Lee's journal described this not easily forgotten experience:

> All of them were in pitiable condition with eyes blinded, fingers eaten away, face and arms and legs mutilated. Yet they are carrying on faithfully every phase of the Church, including priesthood work, Sunday School, M.I.A., Relief Society, ward teaching, genealogical, and missionary work. The branch president made a brief report of their work, and Brother Kailemai, a counselor and chairman of the Genealogical Committee, bore testimony and in behalf of the Saints there expressed appreciation for our visit to them.
>
> When they sang to us, "Come, come ye Saints, no toil nor labor fear," and bore their testimony of what the Church meant to them, one of them turned to us, representing the visitors and the authorities and said: "If we had to choose between having the leprosy and being here with the gospel of Jesus Christ, or being well and whole, off the island, without the gospel of Jesus Christ, we would choose to be here as lepers so we could enjoy the blessings of The Church of Jesus Christ of Latter-day Saints."
>
> I then spoke to them briefly and extended the love of the presiding Brethren, and as an Apostle of the Lord I blessed them that they might remain true and faithful; and we closed with singing,

"We Thank Thee, O God, for a Prophet." The four girls in the colony under twenty years of age arrived just at that point from a picnic excursion to the north of the island. Their faces looked old and terribly disfigured.

After many meetings with the servicemen, Elder Lee came home with abundant evidence of the miracles produced by faithful adherence to the gospel which blessed and strengthened these brethren during their life-threatening experiences in the war-torn South Pacific.

Elder Lee's farewell at the conclusion of his tour prompted this note in his journal: "The genuine love and adoration of these people for a representative of the General Authorities is almost unbelievable."

OCTOBER CONFERENCE, 1945

With the dedication of the Idaho Falls Temple just completed, and the attendant blessings of a temple dedication still fresh in the minds of the members of the Church, it was time for another general conference. This was a significant time, because it marked the sustaining of the new First Presidency in a solemn assembly and the call of Elder Matthew Cowley to the Twelve to fill the vacancy created by the death of President Grant. Elder Lee recalled that "the weather was perfect and a splendid spirit seemed to be present. Someone characterized this as the greatest conference we had held."

The following Thursday morning Elder Cowley was ordained and set apart as a member of the Quorum of the Twelve. Elder Lee was impressed by Elder Cowley's remarks at the end of the meeting, stating, "when he was asked to speak he bore a remarkable testimony, and gave evidence that he will perform a splendid service as an Apostle."

Before the year was over other General Authorities had passed away. Walking arm in arm away from the cemetery after the services for one brother in which the speakers had waxed eloquent in the extreme, President Clark issued one firm and lasting instruction to Elder Lee about what should be said at his own funeral. He told Elder Lee that he wanted the speakers to be kind to his vices, but under no circumstances were they to make his vices his virtues. This instruction stuck vividly in the mind of Elder Lee, who later was a speaker at President Clark's funeral and carried out the counsel he had received.

THE GIFT OF HEALING

If there was a "routine" occurrence in Harold B. Lee's life, it may very well have been the frequency with which he was called upon to administer to the sick. The thickest folder in his file cabinet after many years as an Apostle was the one simply labeled "Miracles."

In addition to the growing administrative responsibilities that were accruing, Elder Lee's spiritual ministry among the Saints seemed to increase day by day. For example, the *Deseret News* published a story in 1946 of an eight-month-old baby named Levine, whose eyesight was miraculously restored through a cornea transplant, a new procedure in those days, by Dr. Castravejo of New York City. Elder Lee read the account more knowingly than anyone else, because he had assisted in giving the baby a blessing when he attended a conference in the area in September 1945.

Elder Henry D. Moyle, who shared many priesthood administrations with Elder Lee, testified that after Elder Lee had blessed him in the LDS Hospital the intense distress and pain he had suffered dissipated.

Following is another example of a typical night:

> Last night at the request of Sister Waters I went to the LDS Hospital to administer to Holman's baby, Ricky, and witnessed a wonderful calm come over him while my hands were on his head. I also went to the home of Gabriel Torres, whose little son is suffering from rheumatic fever.

Elder Lee understood the power was not his, but the Lord's, to give, and his to use as his faith increased. The blessing President Grant had given to him, reminding him that he must be humble to have the Spirit of the Holy Ghost with him, was the hallmark of his service. He seemed always to be most at home with the humble Saints, for he came from similar conditions, and his humble nature was a major source of his power. For example, after a stake conference in central Utah he paid tribute to the fine men leading the rural North Sanpete Stake:

> I held a very delightful meeting with the stake presidency of the North Sanpete Stake and with the welfare workers and later with the

priesthood leaders. These men impress one as being of the fine, old, pioneer stock and solid to the core. I feel I am a stronger and better man for having met with them.

WORK OF RESTORATION DEMEANED

Fawn Brodie and Maurine Whipple each had a book published in 1946 that drew concern from the General Authorities, sparking considerable attention. As Elder Lee traveled with Elder Spencer W. Kimball to a stake conference in Orangeville, Utah, Elder Kimball read aloud portions of Mrs. Brodie's book; Elder Lee labeled the book "another defilement of sacred things." Elder Lee also read the Whipple book while traveling to San Diego, California, thinking he could help others who might be concerned about its contents, and concluded that it was a "cleverly devised tool to strike at the divinity of the work of the Lord's Church."

In the years that followed, Harold B. Lee often cited statements that were made at the April 1946 general conference condemning those who had sought to gain fame and fortune by demeaning the Prophet Joseph Smith and the work of the Restoration. Elder Lee said the conference climaxed with Elder A. E. Bowen's biting denunciation of apostate writers who had maligned the Prophet Joseph Smith. Then President George Albert Smith furnished the capstone in prophetic words not written out in advance and not even contemplated. His words, thought Elder Lee, came with a crystal clear, glistening rhetoric that could only have been spoken by a prophet of God. Said President Smith:

> There have been some who have belittled him, but I would like to say that those who have done so will be forgotten and their remains will go back to mother earth, if they have not already gone, and the odor of their infamy will never die, while the glory and honor and majesty and courage and fidelity manifested by the Prophet Joseph Smith will attach to his name forever. (Conference Report, April 1946, pp. 181–82.)

ELDER BENSON'S EUROPEAN ASSIGNMENT

The four junior members of the Council of the Twelve enjoyed a close relationship with Elder Lee in many ways. They could relate better socially and administratively to him, their families were the same age, and they tended to look to him for guidance because

Farewell at the airport for Ezra Taft Benson as he departs for European assignment, 1946: (left to right) Fred Babbel, June Babbel, Matthew Cowley, Flora Benson, Ezra Taft Benson, Emma Marr Petersen, Harold B. Lee, Camilla Kimball, Elva Cowley, Mark E. Petersen, Fern Lee, Spencer W. Kimball of his experience. They also had some moments of relaxation together, one of which proved to be highly entertaining to all of the General Authorities and their wives at a Lion House social. Elder Kimball arranged a program of singing and stunts, and Elder Lee accompanied Elders Kimball, Benson, Petersen, and Cowley at the piano while they performed as a male quartet. Elder Lee pronounced the performance a success and said in his journal that their act "went over very well."

Now, as one of their members was leaving for an assignment abroad, the junior members of the Council of the Twelve and their wives were guests at a dinner in President Clark's home, in honor of Elder Benson. The next day, Elder Lee and the four junior members of the Twelve and their wives all went to the airport to bid farewell to Elder Benson, who was leaving for an indefinite period of time to preside over the European Mission.

Elder Benson's administration in Europe was backed up by the welfare plan through which post-war supplies were distributed to needy Saints. Elder Lee met with his welfare staff of Elder Romney and Brother Roscoe Eardley, first with President Clark and then with President George Albert Smith. They decided to accept a proposal worked out by the staff on the basis of a rough estimate of the amount of food necessary for each country according to the Church membership in each until the next harvest, which was seven months distant. They were therefore directed to send thirteen and one-fourth railway cars of food and five and one-fourth cars of clothing, in addition to that which had been sent previously to Europe.

Elder Benson's tour of duty on another continent kept him away from his family from January 29, 1946, until December 17 of that year.

Marriage of Daughters

Elder Lee was on a busy schedule in 1946, attempting to fulfill all the requests that came to have him officiate in temple sealings (live marriages). World War II had ended, the servicemen were home, and wedding bells were ringing wildly. He performed 196 sealings during that year, but none was as significant to him as the sealing of his younger daughter, Helen, to L. Brent Goates on June 24, 1946. He called it "one of the greatest experiences of my life."

After the honeymoon of the newlyweds, Elder and Sister Lee helped them move into a downtown apartment. The natural intimacy of the close family from which she had come produced very sentimental feelings in Helen, and emotions were near the surface. It wasn't easy for her dad, either. He wrote: "Helen was reluctant to leave us, but even though she is now a full-grown, married woman, she is still to me just my little girl and will always be so in my affections."

His travel assignments, taking him often away from home on birthdays and other holidays, prompted Elder Lee to write an affectionate letter to Helen on the occasion of her first birthday away from home after her marriage. She was then in Portland, Oregon, with her serviceman husband. The letter was handwritten on motel stationery from Mesa, Arizona, dated November 22, 1946. It has served as an oft-quoted teaching tool of Helen Goates.

> This is intended to be something of a birthday letter to my "youngest" from a sentimental old Dad who is lonesome for his lovely daughter. So far as I can recall this is the first time in your life that you will be spending your birthday and Thanksgiving away from us, and, with the exception of the year we were in Mexico, the first time away from your home on those days.
>
> As with every day of your life, you can never relive any part of it except in memory and if any day be wasted or misspent, that day becomes only one of regret or remorse. To live one's life to the fullest then becomes a daily responsibility for which you need the constant guidance of divine powers to avoid the pitfalls that make for long detours back onto the path of safety and truth. Too many adopt the philosophy of the old preacher "unless you are in desperate need, your prayers just ain't got no suction." One who has understanding realizes that we are always in great need of spiritual help. So it was that the Master taught:
>
> "Blessed are the poor in spirit who come unto
> me, for theirs is the Kingdom of Heaven."
>
> The "poor in spirit" are the spiritually needy who daily lean on and trust the arm of the Lord.
>
> To me your birthday, always on or about Thanksgiving Day, has always seemed most appropriate. I thanked God for my baby when you came twenty-one years ago and I have thanked him for you every day since. From babyhood you have possessed strong opinions and a will. Well do I remember your childhood efforts to make it an obedient will, and my prayer for you today is, as always in the past, that your will be made subservient to that which is right. As the depth of your thinking has been revealed on many occasions when

you have furnished us keepsakes of your thinking, I have gloried in the unfolding of the life of my own daughter. When you made the greatest decision of your life thus far, in choosing your life's companion, somehow I had complete assurance that you had chosen well. My own way would have been to have urged greater deliberation, but perhaps the times justified the means and I accepted your decision with thanksgiving.

There lies yet ahead greater joys and, yes, greater anxieties than you have yet known, for remember that great love is built on great sacrifice and that a daily determination in each other to please in things that are right will build a sure foundation for a happy home. That determination for the welfare of each other must be mutual and not one-sided or selfish. Husband and wife must feel equal responsibilities and obligations to each other. Two of the things that today strike at the security of modern homes is that young husbands have never sensed their full obligation in supporting a family and young wives have side-stepped the responsibility of settling down to the serious business of raising a family and making a home.

Your being with Brent now should prove a blessing to both of you. Together you can dream dreams and together you can work and sacrifice to make your dreams come true. With all my love to you and Brent and wishing you much joy on your birthday, I am, Your loving daddy, Harold B. Lee.

It is worth noting that Elder Lee's presence in Arizona was for the purpose of attending two stake conferences, taking "a complete rest" during the week separating the conferences, but as he explained in the following lines to Helen, there is seldom such rest for a General Authority:

I came to Mesa from Thatcher, Arizona, with instructions from the Brethren to hide out and take a complete rest before going on to Tucson next Saturday and Sunday. I fared pretty well until yesterday when I walked out to get something to eat and was "discovered" by President Wright. I escaped last night only after a Rotary Club luncheon, a visit to the welfare farm, to a house of death, to an MIA meeting, and to a welfare stake meeting, and after that a choir party. If all goes well, I should be home next Tuesday night.

By June of the following year, Maurine and her husband-to-be, Ernest J. Wilkins of Prescott, Arizona, were also making marriage plans following their simultaneous graduation from BYU. The date, set a week after graduation on June 11, 1947, excited prospects of another garden wedding reception like the one the family

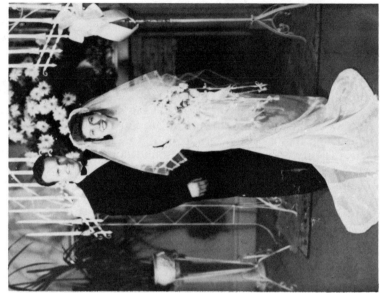

Maurine Lee and Ernest J. Wilkins wedding picture, June 11, 1947

Helen Lee and L. Brent Goates wedding picture, June 24, 1946

had enjoyed the year before. Two days before the wedding, however, a constant downpour of rain throughout the day and into the morning of the following day threatened their plans. When rain had come the year before on the day of the wedding, Elder Lee "laid the whole matter before the Lord and He tempered the elements and gave us a perfect day for our wedding reception." There was no reason to think the rain would spoil things this year either, but the deluge continued all through the day of the wedding.

That afternoon, following the sealing ceremony in the Salt Lake Temple, Elder Lee in customary fashion worked heroically the remainder of the day constructing a canopy to shelter the patio so that the reception could still be held outdoors. But alas, the weight of the heavy rains collapsed his improvised rescue creation, forcing the guests indoors. Maurine cried briefly in her disappointment, and Elder Lee pondered the Lord's judgment. When the elements needed to be tempered for the two June outdoor wedding receptions for the daughters he loved, he soberly contemplated the lesson that his prayers were granted as he requested, but only once.

With the wedding over, Elder Lee spent the remainder of his summer vacation painting his home. As always, he took delight in laboring with his hands, and frequently engaged in projects around the home. His tools were always neatly arranged in his workroom, and he knew the correct use for each one.

In the fall of 1947 Maurine's husband commenced his studies at Stanford University in Palo Alto, California, his course designed to lead to a doctorate degree in Romantic languages. Maurine's parents, always concerned and helpful, went to be with them as they settled into new housing. While in California, the parents learned of the birth of their first grandchild on September 9, 1947. Helen had given birth to a boy, later named David Brent Goates, but forever afterward known by his Grandfather Lee as "Skipper," meaning, the captain of Elder Lee's kingdom.

1947–1950. Truman and Marshall Plans presented. First microwave cooker went on sale in the United States. John Cobb set land speed record of 394.2 miles per hour. Cadillac started tailfin fad. First transistor developed at Bell Laboratories. Truman surprised Dewey. North Atlantic Treaty ratified. Beginning of Korea "police action." American military involvement in Vietnam started nation's longest war.

CHAPTER 14

The Passing of Elder Charles A. Callis

Elder Charles A. Callis had presided over the Southern States Mission for over twenty-five years prior to his being called to the Council of the Twelve and was virtually "sainted" in the hearts of Church members living there. The assignment to create the first stake of the Church in the South had been long contemplated in 1946, but was reserved for Elder Callis to perform when his failing health permitted him to travel. At the beginning of 1947 Elder Lee was assigned to accompany this mighty Apostle and on January 11 the Lees departed for Jacksonville, Florida.

Elder Callis arrived in Florida a day ahead of the Lees to clear up a personal matter with a dear friend. Once this was taken care of, Elder Callis told Elder Lee, his junior companion, that he was willing to leave the details of organizing the stake in his hands. In the course of the interviews, however, some difference of opinion arose concerning whether Orlando and some of the other mission branches should be included in the new stake. Differing from Elder Lee and some of the local priesthood leaders, Elder Callis was insisting that Orlando, Florida, ought to be included.

Eleven years later Elder Lee used this experience to teach an important characteristic of prayer to seminary teachers of the Church. He recalled:

> When Mission President Heber Meeks and President Douberly from the Orlando Florida Branch and I all disagreed, it worried President Callis. That was always a rather serious situation to me, too, to not be in agreement with Brother Callis. He was a man of strong, vigorous, and powerful thinking.
>
> He said finally, "I will have to sleep on this." With that statement he dismissed me. The next morning he called me into his room, and as he pulled his chair close alongside mine, he said to me with an impressiveness which I shall never forget, "Last night I talked with God, and he has given me to understand that you are right and I am wrong." (From an advanced course in theology at Brigham Young University, July 6, 1956.)

As they concluded their interviews they overheard the choir practicing in the chapel. When the choir began singing the hymn "O My Father," Elder Callis broke into tears, and said to the brethren, "Take care of your wives; I haven't and she's gone." His emotions were close to the surface, and it became apparent to those who were with him that he was preparing for the end of his life. He ordered a room in the church fitted up as a bedroom, and he insisted upon spending two nights alone in that room. He told the brethren that everywhere he went he saw Sister Callis. Elder Lee wrote:

> I had the impression, and so expressed myself to Sister Jenkins, that Brother Callis wanted to die and had wished it could take place in that room, by himself. He had us drive him to the old chapel and to the home where his twin sons were born and died. He seemed to be reliving these experiences for the last time.

Members of the Church came to Jacksonville, Florida, from as far away as Miami and Charleston, South Carolina, with 789 in attendance at the morning session and 1,043 present for the afternoon session of the history-making event. The spirit of prophecy

Speaking at creation of Florida stake, 1947 (Charles A. Callis seated to the right of the pulpit)

was upon Elder Callis as he presided at the conference, all the time very near his departed loved ones to whom he made frequent reference.

A PERFECT PARTING

After the announcement of the new stake presidency in the Sunday morning session, Elder Callis seemed to have suffered a mild heart attack, but grew stronger during the day. He spoke with great emotion to the Saints he loved and paid tribute to Sister Callis, declaring that she and others who had labored as missionaries in the South were in attendance at their meeting that day. He prophesied that there would be other stakes organized in the South, and that eventually a temple would be built there that the younger members of the stake would live to see. The fulfillment of his prophecy came on June 1–4, 1983, with the dedication of the first temple to be constructed in the South—in Atlanta, Georgia.

After setting apart sixty-four ward and stake officers, the visiting authorities were guests for dinner at the home of Brother and Sister O. H. Hawkins. The Lees left at 9:00 P.M. for St. Augustine, where they spent the night. Elder Callis, in excellent spirits that night, requested his host, Brother Hawkins, to retell a famous fight story. Later in the evening he asked Brother Hawkins to arrange for his return trip to Salt Lake City the next day.

The following day, driving toward Miami, Elder and Sister Lee were stopped by a highway patrolman who informed them that he had a death message for them. They learned then that Elder Callis had died suddenly the night before of a heart attack.

Elder Lee reported the death immediately to President David O. McKay in Salt Lake City, advising him that the Saints in the South were desirous of holding services in Jacksonville for their beloved leader, before the Lees left with his body for Utah. Elder Lee cleared the proposal with President George Albert Smith, and memorial services were delayed in Salt Lake City until after funeral services were concluded in Florida.

Twelve years later, while teaching a group of student leaders, Elder Lee drew on an experience he had at Elder Callis's funeral to illustrate the importance of praying for each other:

> I was the one to conduct Brother Callis's funeral service in Florida. It was a sorrowful trail that I had followed. I loved Brother Callis.

My heart was tender. In the quiet of my hotel room I shed some tears; I tried to prepare. Finally the day came. It was Thursday, January 23, 1947. The funeral was to start at 10:00 a.m. in the Jacksonville Ward Chapel.

Speakers were President D. Homer Yarn, president of the Georgia District; A. E. Jenkins, senior member of the high council and dear friend of Elder Callis; President Heber Meeks, president of the Southern States Mission; and myself.

As the first two speakers concluded it was now about a quarter to eleven, and as the song was being rendered, before the president of the mission and I then were to conclude the service, a Western Union messenger arrived with a telegram for me. When I opened it, it was a message from the First Presidency requesting that I read it at the service. I arose to read it and I suddenly found myself overwhelmed with some kind of a great feeling that I couldn't quite understand. It wasn't sorrow, because I had conquered that in those two days preceding. And then I began to think, "This is Thursday." What was it that I felt? Suddenly when that telegram came it was as though I was just as close to the Council of the Twelve and the Presidency as though they had walked in and taken their seats on the stand behind me. Up to that time I had felt so much alone, with such a heavy responsibility. Twelve o'clock in Florida meant it was 10:00 a.m. in Salt Lake City, and knowing the way the Council meeting is held, at 10:45 a.m. every member of the Twelve and the First Presidency would be dressed in temple clothing surrounding an altar in the place nearest to heaven on earth. And I said, "Now I know what is happening. They have offered a prayer for me, and this is the answer. I am receiving the answer of the prayers of the First Presidency and the Twelve."

When I returned home, my first question to President George F. Richards was: "Brother Richards, in your temple meeting last Thursday do you remember whether or not at the prayer at the altar there was a prayer offered for me particularly?" He thought a moment and said: "Yes, Brother McKay led us. And he prayed that the Lord would bless you down there all alone so that you would feel the strength of the Presidency and the Council of the Twelve to be with you." I said: "I received it in one of the most dramatic experiences of my life."

I was taught by that experience how important it is to receive the prayers of the faithful.

Elder Lee entered this final comment in his journal about a sacred moment at the conclusion of the services for Brother Callis in Jacksonville: "As the services ended and I went to Brother

Callis's room in the Church to get my hat, I seemed to hear him say to me, 'Well done, son, well done'—and I felt satisfied.''

On January 28, 1947, a funeral service was held in the Salt Lake Tabernacle for this powerful missionary-Apostle so revered in the South. Nearly four thousand persons attended, despite a snowstorm. At the following Thursday meeting with the Quorum of the Twelve, Elder Lee voiced Elder Callis's opinion that other stakes in the mission should be created, rather than further dividing the mission. He then repeated in the presence of the First Presidency the prophecy made by Elder Callis that other stakes, and one day a temple, would grace the Southern States.

At the meeting of the Twelve on April 24, 1947 it was decided to organize two new stakes from the missions, one centering at Columbia, South Carolina, which partially fulfilled the prophecy, and another one at Spokane, Washington.

1947: CONFERENCE AND CENTENNIAL

The highlight of the April 1947 general conference was the sustaining and installation of Elder Henry D. Moyle, longtime chairman of the General Welfare Committee, as the new Apostle. Once more President Clark asked Elder Lee to prepare the new appointee for the experiences and procedures he was about to undergo, as he had done when Elders Kimball, Benson, and Petersen were called. This Elder Lee did by going to the home of Elder Moyle on the Saturday night prior to his sustaining on Sunday. He repeated the preparation at the temple in advance of Elder Moyle's ordination on the following Thursday.

Other General Authorities appointed at this conference were Eldred G. Smith, Patriarch to the Church, and Joseph L. Wirthlin and Thorpe B. Isaacson, counselors to Presiding Bishop LeGrand Richards.

A special feature of this conference was a meeting on Monday, April 7, for all stake presidencies who came to the Salt Lake Temple for instruction from their priesthood leaders. Elder Lee later recorded: "A wonderful meeting was held in the Assembly Room of the Salt Lake Temple, where the General Authorities and two thousand members of stake presidencies and bishoprics partook of the sacrament and heard some plain, direct instructions on chastity, temple recommends, finances, ward teaching, and the welfare program."

One announcement changing mission field organization in the Church was made at this conference. President McKay attended the meeting of the mission presidents with all the General Authorities and announced a new plan of naming two counselors for each mission president, chosen from among the missionaries or from brethren living in the missions.

The year 1947 was observed as Utah's centennial year, and celebration events to last five and one-half months opened officially on May 1, 1947, with a meeting in the Salt Lake Tabernacle and with a special lighting of the Brigham Young Monument. The hoisting of a flag on Ensign Peak also began the celebration.

TOUR OF WESTERN STATES MISSION

Having served in the Western States Mission as a young missionary, Elder Lee was now filled with anticipation to return to his old territory as an Apostle, twenty-seven years later. It was summer, and the temperatures reached into the hundreds as his party passed by the famed White Sands of New Mexico en route to Alamogordo. High winds stirred up the famous pure white gypsum, which resembled banks of snow drifted into beautiful formations. At the Alamorgordo meeting the winds continued with a fury, bringing the choking desert dust into the hall and finally knocking out the electric lights. The congregation was obliged to hear the last ten or fifteen minutes of Elder Lee's sermon in darkness.

Natural disasters accompanied them wherever they went. For example, floods came as Elder Lee drove all day through devastated areas to meet with the Saints at North Platte, Nebraska.

At Colorado Springs a huge turnout came to hear the Apostle from Salt Lake City. Many investigators were in the congregation, and Elder Lee had these impressions of the meeting:

> Although we were very weary and hungry, the Spirit of the Lord picked us up and I felt the greatest freedom I have yet had on this tour in showing the value of a testimony and how, through faith, the work of the Lord has progressed, and bore testimony of it. I learned from the newspapers here that a tornado had visited Spearfish, South Dakota, just twenty-four hours after we had passed through there last Friday.

Elder Lee was classified by many as being a conservative or a fundamentalist. Certainly one manifestation of this was his contempt for card playing. Once while setting up a new mission in Billings, Montana, he was inspired to preach on this subject and put to flight a nest of bridge-playing sisters. He taught his daughters to totally avoid face cards, which sometimes were used for evil purposes, and to even avoid the appearance thereof. At the beginning of the New Year in 1947, he went with Sister Lee to a dinner party at the home of a dear friend, but left promptly after dinner when he learned that the entertainment for the evening was to play Rook, which he regarded as a substitute for regular playing cards and a complete waste of time.

In 1947 another important person was added to Elder Lee's life when Frances Cardall was recruited from the Welfare Office to become one of the secretaries in the Council of the Twelve Office. Ultimately, as the work grew, she became Elder Lee's private secretary and remained such for twenty-six years, until President Lee's death. She was a quiet, reserved, and efficient worker. Loyalty was her greatest asset, and she became trusted and loved by the entire Lee family.

SAMUEL MARION LEE DIES

While engaged in his usual calendar of meetings at the Church Office Building, Elder Lee one day learned that his father was seriously ill at home. Cancelling his remaining commitments at the office he went to his father's bedside and arranged for his transportation to the LDS Hospital so that accumulated fluids could be drained from his lungs. Elder Lee felt distressed that he was confronted simultaneously with the daily pressures of his increasing Church responsibilities and with the care of his aging parents. This conflict made it impossible for him to please everyone much of the time.

The strain and shock of the medical treatments proved too much for Harold's father and he began to fail rapidly. For three days and two nights the vigil went around the clock, until Samuel Marion Lee, father of an Apostle who would ultimately become the eleventh President of the Church, died on May 9, 1947. Memorial services were held in the North 20th Ward on May 12, with the prayer given by Elder Mark E. Petersen and the grave dedicated by Elder Henry D. Moyle. President Clark and Harold H. Bennett,

Samuel's employer at ZCMI, were the speakers at the services. Brother Bennett praised him for his loyalty and service as the supervisor of night employees at ZCMI. President Clark spoke of his valiant service in Church positions, and referred to a member of the Romney family who had told him that in forty years no ward teacher had visited them as effectively and faithfully as had Samuel Marion Lee. Many relatives from Clifton, Idaho, attended the services.

THE PRESSURES MOUNT

The strain and demands on Church leaders is heavy. That they live for the most part to such ripe old ages is ample testimony that the Lord sustains them. A typical stake conference schedule indicates the pressures of the weekends away from home. On October 26, 1947, Elder Lee recorded his experiences while attending the Spokane Stake conference: "I was kept constantly on the stand of the chapel from 9:00 A.M. until 7:15 P.M., interrupted only long enough for a sandwich and salad for lunch and supper. Caught the train for home at 7:40 P.M."

The rigors of his assignments began to take their toll on his health. The day following his forty-eighth birthday, he awoke with pains in his chest, reminding him that he was overworking his heart and that a slower pace was needed.

It is coincidental that he shared the same birthday with Elder Spencer W. Kimball, but Elder Kimball was then fifty-two years of age, four years older than Elder Lee. Harold B. Lee and many of his companions in the work of the kingdom experienced challenges to their health because of the demanding schedules required of them. Six weeks later when Elder Lee finally got to the doctor for an examination, he was happy to learn that his heart showed no weakening.

There seemed to be no rest, however, even on holidays, as this next entry attests. So confident were the Saints in the genuine concern that Elder Lee possessed for them that those in need of spiritual strength and the repentant unhesitantly sought him out. It is clear that he never refused them:

> Fortunately we were blessed with a clear day and the office was closed so I worked the entire holiday in the yard to get the leaves cleaned up and the water shut off before freezing weather. I had a call from a young Ryser couple whose baby had swallowed an open

safety pin and went with them to the hospital to administer to the baby before they took it by plane to Chicago for an operation. Also, I had a visit from a man who had been dishonest with his employers back in Indiana and a young man from Denver who thought he was under the influence of an evil power. I finished the day almost completely exhausted.

He often found relief from tension produced by the constant travel and office regimen by working in his garden at home, and used it as his therapy. He wrote on October 20, 1947, "I left the office early thinking some work in the yard at home would clear my head and quiet my nerves. Enjoyed my evening with the family."

TEMPER AND HUMBLE HEART

One of Elder Lee's most obvious flaws, behavior he said he observed in his ancestry, was his temper. An interesting anecdote illustrating this weakness comes from his journal. The day after a member of the Welfare Committee had referred to the early practices in the welfare program as the "dark ages," this entry appears:

> I met with the Welfare Committee in their weekly meetings, where in answer to a question of Brother Romney as to my discussion with the Welfare Committee member last night, I told him that my remarks were only a "burst of truth." He replied that he hoped that such would not "burst upon him," which suggested to me that I had been pretty severe with the brother.

Whenever he detected that same tendency in one of his own posterity, he attempted to "nip it in the bud." With one Little League grandson he entered into a pact that if Grandfather provided him with a new fielder's mitt, it could only be worn if he did not allow his temper to take control in the game. When his temper flared, the mitt was to be returned to Grandfather until there was evidence that control had returned. An understanding Elder Lee often had the mitt as much as did his grandson.

More typical of Elder Lee's ministry than his occasional "bursts of truth," however, was the humility that often caused him to doubt his effectiveness even at routine stake conferences. On Saturday, September 27, 1947, after holding the evening welfare and leadership meetings at the beginning of the Park Stake conference in Salt Lake City, Elder Lee wrote in his journal: "I came away from these preliminary meetings somewhat at a loss to know whether or not I had accomplished anything. Perhaps I was not close enough to the Lord.''

There were other occasions when there was no doubt, and the Lord worked in him mightily for the edification of the Saints. His former mission president, in attendance at the Hillside Stake conference in March 1946, told him that he had attended stake conferences for over fifty years, and had never witnessed a finer conference in his entire life. With such high praise, Elder Lee's evaluation is interesting:

> The high spiritual and emotional tension after Hillside Stake conference kept sleep from me until 3:00 a.m. when I arose to pray for rest and sleep. Bishop Denning of the Mountain View Ward came in Monday to express his appreciation for the instructions at the quarterly conference, and I received a letter from Merrill J. Brockbank speaking in superlative terms of the closing conference session.

DEVOTION TO DUTY

The crucible of service through which the General Authorities are called upon to pass daily is an indication of their keen reverence for the sacredness of their callings. The following incident illustrates the focus of duty that often supersedes consideration for their own personal safety.

On Saturday, February 7, 1948, Elder Lee received word that his conference appointment had been changed so that he could attend the funeral of a former stake president in Grace, Idaho. The night before he was to leave, snow and ice made the streets and highways extremely dangerous. The President of the Council of the Twelve, George F. Richards, had cancelled seven conference appointments so dangerous were the roads, and President Clark even cancelled Elder Lee's trip to Idaho. Later in the day, however, Elder Lee was called into President Richards's office, who reported on a visit with President George Albert Smith. President Smith, it seemed, had talked to the bishop in Grace, who informed him that they saw no reason why someone could not attend the funeral from Salt Lake City, representing the General Authorities. At that point it was clear that Elder Lee was going to Grace despite the road conditions, even when President Clark called later to say that he had done everything he could to discourage such an ill-advised journey.

Elder Lee left at 8:00 A.M. on Sunday with his wife to attend the funeral. Until he reached Preston, Idaho, he drove the icy roads, at one point narrowly avoiding a serious accident when the car skidded on a sharp turn and slid into a hill. Three men assisted Elder Lee by pushing the vehicle back onto the road. After all his effort to get to the funeral, there were five speakers and six musical numbers listed on the program, leaving him scant time for giving a meaningful sermon.

On Monday, after another harrowing return trip following the funeral, President Smith phoned to inquire of Elder Lee if he had gone to Grace the day before. By his comments he indicated that he thought bad road conditions was not a sufficiently valid reason to excuse filling an assignment.

This was not an isolated instance of such conflicting opinions. Later, in their last temple meeting before the summer vacation, President Clark urged the Brethren to take a concentrated rest and learn to say no to requests for speaking during that period. His comments were then followed by President Smith with a statement that the Brethren interpreted as meaning they should be constantly available throughout the vacation period for speaking engagements upon request.

Often bordering on nervous and physical exhaustion, the Brethren strove on with the never-ending demands of the callings they shared.

Elder Lee was called from his bed in the middle of the night on one occasion "to go to the home of a family threatened with the loss of their business due to a lack of capital and over-expenditures for equipment and buildings, etc." One week later he wrote: "The strenuous meetings all day drove out all possibilities of sleep until after 3:00 A.M." Five days later he recorded a similar entry: "Found myself on an extreme nervous tension last night that forbade several hours of sleep." During these times of stress, he found comfort in his family and often gathered them about him to refresh himself.

During this time, he was also concerned about the impending delivery of his second grandchild. Maurine, small in stature and thought by her doctors unable to have a child by normal delivery, was in his prayers after a long drive home from a conference:

> I found myself again very much worn out with the strain of conference and the long drive home from St. George. Because of Maurine's travail and the complications that have been found by the

doctors that might make the natural birth difficult, I have fasted throughout the day and went into the temple, where I had prayer for her.

The answer to his petition came at 2:30 A.M. the following day, when Sister Lee called from Orinda, California, to announce the birth of Alan Lee Wilkins, weighing 7 lbs. 12 oz. Maurine had not more than twelve hours of labor, and the baby had been delivered normally with no complications.

Working under pressure and fatigue seemed Harold B. Lee's lot throughout his ministry, almost as if there were not enough time to accomplish his life's mission. He described one Sunday as follows:

> I arrived in Los Angeles at 7:15 a.m. and was met by the stake presidency, who drove me to the Huntington Park Chapel, where I met with them until the high council came at 9:00 a.m., and through the general sessions, which were held at 10:00 a.m. and 6:30 p.m., with a priesthood leadership meeting in the afternoon and a fireside after the evening meeting. Ordinations and missionary interviews entirely filled up the day until 10:30 p.m., with hardly time for a sandwich.

Far from complaining about the long hours, constant fatigue, and excessive travel, he was often exhilarated by the Spirit of the Holy Ghost in the conferences. The fruits of his service were in evidence in the lives affected by his teachings. His joy was in his service, and many would say when he passed away at the "young" age of seventy-four that it was only because he had put the demands of his duties ahead of his own regard for his health.

Not the least of his physical problems were his chronic migraine headaches, accentuated by his difficult travel schedules, vastly different than they are today. On Friday, May 21, 1948, he wrote:

> I left at 8:30 a.m. on the Western Pacific train for Sacramento, California, to attend the regional meeting of the Northern California Region and the Sacramento Stake conference. I suffered from one of the worst headaches I have had for a long time, but I managed to make some preparation for my meetings and to study the reports. I arrived in Sacramento at 3:45 a.m.

The Church was expanding in 1948, and the travels of the Brethren to meet the needs reflected that fact.

In the midst of these pressures came the assignment to tour the New England States, where another General Authority, President S. Dilworth Young, and his wife were presiding at Cambridge, Massachusetts. It was unusual to see the ever-competent Elder Lee, the leader who always gave the impression of being in total control, rattled as he left for the mission tour with Sister Lee on May 29, 1948. He misplaced his train tickets and dashed to the office, only to find that they were in his briefcase all the time. Then, when they boarded the train, he discovered that he had left his briefcase at home, and wired from Evanston, Wyoming, to have it sent to him in New York by air express. By this time he was exhausted, and he took the opportunity to rest throughout the day.

The mission tour, however, provided a wonderful respite from pressures at home and gave the Lees their first opportunity to see at close hand the many historic sites of the American Revolutionary War period, as well as Plymouth Rock, where the Pilgrims landed in 1620. They also visited the birthplace monument of the Prophet Joseph Smith at Sharon County, Vermont, and on to Nova Scotia. At the end of this tour through quaint and beautiful New England, Elder Lee reported that the most impressive finding was that most of the investigators at each place he visited were located by missionaries while they were working in the country districts tracting without purse or scrip.

The growing church of 170 stakes had increasing financial requirements, and President Clark confided to Elder Lee his worries concerning the growth problems and finances. In 1948, the Church budget was the largest to that time.

Another concern was for the health of the Apostles, who now were traveling farther and longer than ever before. In February, six of the Twelve and President McKay were absent from the weekly temple meeting. President McKay was in Mexico, Stephen L Richards was in South America, John A. Widtsoe was in Canada, Albert E. Bowen and Mark E. Petersen were in the Northwestern States attending to business for the *Deseret News,* Ezra Taft Benson was attending agricultural meetings in Idaho, and Matthew Cowley was in the South Pacific.

They were all feeling the pressure, and a rash of illness came upon them. By April, three of the Apostles were sidelined because of heart ailments. At their weekly meeting, with only seven assembled, word came that Elder Benson had been diagnosed as having had a heart attack, though not serious. Then the Twelve learned only three weeks later that Spencer W. Kimball had suffered a heart attack in Arizona, and cardiograph tests revealed a marked weakness in his heart. One week later Elder Kimball had another heart attack, and Elder Lee went to bless him and to take a message to his son who was serving in the New England States Mission. President McKay was in the hospital with a heart attack when Elder Lee returned from the tour of the mission.

Travel was always a risk in those days, as Elder Lee learned when driving his dear friend Marion G. Romney's new DeSoto through Arizona en route to a stake conference. Elder Lee, taking a turn at the wheel, hit a farmer on a small tractor who had pulled into his driveway without any signal and had failed to see the approaching automobile as he crossed in front of them. Elder Lee records that he badly damaged the right front fender of Elder Romney's car, but doesn't comment on whether he was forgiven.

CALIFORNIA MISSION TOUR: 1949

It is clear from Elder Lee's journal that the spiritual highlights of his ministry often came when he was in the mission field. His visit to California in March 1949, accompanied by his host-companion President Oscar W. McConkie, is no exception, but he began the tour reluctantly: "I seem weary and hardly in the mood, but I'm hoping to feel better as the visit progresses." He described his traveling companion in these words two days after their first Sunday meeting:

> There was a remarkably fine spirit at the meeting, particularly at the dedicatory service at Blythe, where I enjoyed unusual freedom in offering the dedicatory prayer. President McConkie gave his usual forceful sermons in his strident, senatorial voice, but he displays a kindliness to the people and a marked deference to me that evidences a depth of humility.

At Hemet, en route from Palm Springs, he received a telegram informing him of the birth of Helen's second son, his third grandson, later named Harold Lee Goates after his grandfather.

President George Albert Smith was resting at a home in Laguna Beach, which the Church later purchased for such purposes, and Elder Lee was asked to administer to him, not realizing that he was yet far from them in the Arizona desert country. He had administered to the President three weeks earlier on his way to a conference in Snowflake, Arizona, but couldn't come to him this time.

The trip was filled with inspirational experiences, this one recorded after a meeting in Cottonwood, Arizona:

> I had an unusual experience of preaching on the Godhead and the difference between the Holy Ghost and the Light of Christ and afterwards I learned that only within the week they had here a spirited discussion on the subject, because of a sermon from a recent convert in which false doctrine had been taught.

At each stop inspiration accompanied them. In Lancaster they heard stories about visions that investigators had received concerning the coming of the missionaries to teach them and about incidents concerning healings. Again Elder Lee's sermons gave precise direction to the needs of the Saints, some assuming that the visiting General Authority had been instructed in advance about what he should discuss. In Mohave they were entertained at the home of a member for supper. After returning to the chapel the compassionate Elder Lee "had a heartache when [he] learned some of the Elders had had no supper and presumably no money with which to buy food." At Bakersfield a large audience of nearly four hundred people assembled to hear the Apostle speak. Three were baptized after the meeting, including one investigator who had reversed his feelings about the Church during the meeting.

The tour lasted sixteen days. Over 350 investigators had heard him speak, half the mission population of 7,090 had attended the meetings, and he had interviewed 179 missionaries, but the highlight of the entire experience came while traveling with President McConkie over the lonely desert road to Barstow, California. As they exchanged faith-promoting stories and spiritual experiences with each other, President McConkie related the details of a dream in which he had gone to the home of Satan, and later told of an experience when Satan had appeared to him and his son James. Elder Lee suggested a correct interpretation of the dream, and then related an experience with a member of the Pioneer Stake who had been possessed by an evil spirit. This experience, which he had recorded on July 3, 1943, is described in these words:

> I spent this Saturday afternoon cleaning up the yard, and while at work I had a visit from a man who came to tell me about the condition of his wife, who about six weeks ago gave birth to her sixth baby. During the last few days she had developed a peculiar attitude in quoting scriptures and repeating messages from spirits, etc. He requested that I go to their home and administer to her. I arrived

there and had a most unusual experience. As I sat beside her on the couch, she turned to me with a cynical smile and asked: "Do you know who you are?" I said: "Yes, I know; who do you think I am?" She replied: "You're the great physician; you're the head of the Church." When I tried to counsel with her she said: "Oh, no, you are not going to send me from this world." I had the distinct impression that she was in the power of an evil spirit and was impressed to rebuke the spirit and cast it out by the authority of the Priesthood. I trembled like a leaf and my hair seemed to almost be as pin pricks. I learned that a man who had been excommunicated for plural marriage had come to their home to sell insulation, and that she commenced to become irrational from the time he came to the home. He came to the home while I was there, and she immediately was greatly animated at his appearance. On Sunday evening I went to the home of a brother of the woman on Downington Avenue in Salt Lake City, and with her husband and two brothers I again administered to her as I had done yesterday, and found that she had greatly improved and at times was entirely rational, although she still spoke of her friend as a prophet who had been sent to her.

After Elder Lee had related this encounter, it was President McConkie's turn to provide the inspired interpretation. "President McConkie said he thought that the evil spirit in the woman had spoken of not that which now was, but of that which Satan knew I was ordained to become." Elder Lee pondered the statement of President McConkie, an inspired interpretation given by the Holy Ghost in 1949 of an event that would come to pass in 1972, as foretold in general terms by an evil spirit in 1943.

Inspired Blessings

In those days the departing missionaries were all set apart by the General Authorities, often requiring those who officiated to give upwards of twenty blessings in one afternoon. Many were the days that Elder Lee went home totally exhausted, but soaring in the Spirit. He recorded in January 1949 a singularly inspired blessing he gave to Alene Christenson of Hollywood, California. In the blessing she was told that her choice to serve a mission was the Lord's will, and that the call was a reward for her pure, chaste life. There was a sequel to the blessing he pronounced:

She came back later to tell me that she was a professional dancer with a Hollywood studio and that her choosing to go on a mission meant the giving up of a life's career, and furthermore, that constantly in her professional work she had been faced with temptations to become immoral. This blessing had been a testimony of divine guidance in her life.

A month later another Sister missionary was blessed under his hands, and she was told that out of some of her greatest disappointments would come the Lord's richest blessings. Afterwards she informed Elder Lee that she had just been told that day there was doubt as to whether her visa would be approved to permit her to enter Czechoslovakia, her assigned field of labor, and that she had been extremely distressed over the news.

STARTING OVER

Now that the nest was empty, offers were received and a sale finally consummated on the family home at 1208 South Eighth West, and 1949 began with the Lees moving to an apartment they subleased until they could arrange for more suitable housing. Their lives were somewhat topsy-turvy during this period, with meals frequently eaten with Helen and Brent's family. Most of their household belongings were in storage, but the inconveniences did not dampen this fifty-year-old grandfather's enthusiasm for his expanding role in the lives of his grandsons.

On March 27, 1949, Elder Lee had the joy of blessing his third grandson, naming him Harold Lee Goates. At the fast and testimony meeting in Helen and Brent's ward, Elder Lee requested that the bishop call on the paternal grandfather, Lesley Goates, to relate the events of his miraculous birth as a three-and-one-half-pound baby who survived and was then blessed in the language of Adam. His story added much inspiration and enjoyment to the meeting.

On one May day that year he tended David, his little "Skipper," at their apartment while Helen went shopping, then took him to ZCMI to buy him a small wheelbarrow. A few nights later he built a sandbox at Helen and Brent's home and had it filled with sand for his grandsons. David's first haircut was superintended by his grandfather on another day while Sister Lee and Helen were away shopping.

A favorite family story tells how Grandfather Harold B. Lee placed the highest priority upon the rearing of children. Helen has retold it many times to teach many lessons:

> While I was serving as the chorister in our ward Relief Society when our first two sons were about two and a half and four years of age, I

had arranged with Mother to come and tend my little boys while I attended a Friday afternoon stake leadership meeting. Mother called early that morning, however, to say that she had awakened with a bad cold and wouldn't be able to come. She felt badly to disappoint me but I assured her I could arrange with our pianist to excuse me and to bring me the information that would be given at the meeting. Sometime mid-morning, the phone rang again. This time it was my father, calling from his office in the Quorum of the Twelve. He said, "Dear, you plan to go to your meeting and I'll come tend the boys." I was appalled at such an idea and strongly protested. But he persisted and asked, teasingly, "Don't you think I'd be an acceptable babysitter?" "Of course," I replied, "but—well—I just couldn't have you do that! I'd feel like I was thwarting the work of the Lord to have you leave your important work at the office just to come and tend my babies!" His reply was sobering and taught me important lessons: "Why, my dear, who is to say which is the most important work of the Lord—to stay at my desk at the Church Office Building, or to tend two choice little grandsons while their mommy goes to her Relief Society meeting?" He came; I went to my meeting, and two little boys were blessed that day by the full attention of a loving, devoted grandfather.

Some order returned to the Lees' lives on July 4, 1949, when they moved to a new apartment at 107 First Avenue in Salt Lake City. They then shared a few days together as a family at a friend's summer cabin located on the Weber River, as they had done in many summers past.

Despite this improved order, the inconveniences at home began to tell in other areas of Elder Lee's life. Even in his close relationship with President Clark, there were evidences of strain. Words between these two strong-willed men had been misunderstood; these unintentional wounds were then enlarged as the two delayed their reconciliation. Indicative of the depth of President Clark's soul, he took the initiative to repair the damages by inviting Elder Lee to come to his office after a Thursday temple meeting. He pleaded that there be no coolness between them, and told Elder Lee again that he felt it would not be long before the younger members of the Twelve would rise to leadership in the Church, admonishing Elder Lee to see to it that the First Presidency members were always united and that they counseled together frequently. Elder Lee appreciated this additional counsel from his tutor, and reported in his journal: "He expressed his love for me, and I for him."

Reading to grandsons David and Hal

THE INSPIRATION IS THERE

Having just concluded another address at Brigham Young University, where the audiences continued to grow [this year 2,500 students], Elder Lee was assigned with Elder Kimball to create the California Glendale Stake on December 3, 1949, from a division of the San Fernando Stake. After a long weekend of calling and setting the new leaders apart, Elders Lee and Kimball were trying to relax in the home of Hugh C. Smith, who had been chosen to preside over the San Fernando Stake. After 10:00 P.M. President Smith was still asking questions, forestalling any respite the Apostles might have realized before their return trip to Salt Lake City. The answer to his inquiry, "To whom shall I take my questions after you brethren have gone home?" finally put an end to his interrogation of the two weary Apostles, for Elder Kimball replied with a deep and tired sigh, "Suppose, President Smith, you just ask the Lord." Elder Lee was fond of retelling that story for many years.

In mid-November of 1949, Elder Lee and Elder Clifford E. Young spent the Saturday in interviews with the leaders of Ensign Stake in Salt Lake City in preparation for a reorganization of that stake presidency the next day. At the conclusion of the Saturday evening priesthood meeting, they selected Bishop Alldridge N. Evans of the South Eighteenth Ward as the new stake president, with Bishop A. Palmer Holt and a young law student, Britton R. McConkie, as counselors. President Evans told the General Authorities of an unusual spiritual experience he had had earlier when he had been forewarned by an impression from the Holy Spirit that he might be asked to name the leading men of the stake for his counselors.

On January 4, 1950, only six weeks later, came word of the sudden death of President Alldridge N. Evans. The Saints of Ensign Stake were shocked and asked themselves the logical question: "Where is the inspiration in such a call, if the man is to be so soon taken in death?"

At the funeral on January 7, 1950, held in the Eighteenth Ward, so many friends and Saints came that scores were turned away, unable to enter the chapel. Elders Winslow Farr Smith, Henry D. Moyle, and Harold B. Lee were the speakers. Elder Lee came directly to the point and later used this episode to explain the principle—as years later he would do also in speaking at the funeral of President Joseph Fielding Smith, who served but a short time as President of the Church—that the positions a worthy priesthood leader achieves in mortality were often chosen in the premortal life and have a significant relationship to the callings, work, and blessings to be enjoyed in the world to come, regardless of the length of service in those positions.

President Joseph Fielding Smith sat on the stand with Elder Lee at the funeral that day and listened to his attempt to satisfy the Saints. He said to Elder Lee, "Don't you allow that to bother you.

If you have called a man to a position in this Church and he dies the next day, that position will have a bearing on what he will be called to do when he leaves this earth."

Elder Lee later returned to Ensign Stake and named Bishop David Edward Judd, an experienced Church leader, as the new president.

Elder Lee's influence in Utah politics was still felt; when the Republican Party came to him for advice on candidates for the U.S. Senate, he turned them around in their thinking as he suggested Wallace F. Bennett to head their ticket, stating that he was the most logical candidate with fewer political handicaps. His judgment was proven wise nine months later when, after a spirited election, Senator Elbert D. Thomas was defeated by Wallace F. Bennett by a margin of 20,000 votes. Elder Lee rejoiced in the general results of this election of 1950 because he felt dangerous legislative candidates of both tickets in the counties throughout Utah were eliminated by an alert people who apparently had followed wise counsel in being selective in their voting.

WELFARE PROGRAM PROGRESSES

The welfare program of the Church moved rapidly ahead despite several threats from the United States government, which at first seemed to be extremely adverse challenges. The following stories will illustrate.

In 1946 a presidential order designed to gather up excess grain storage in the nation produced a threat that the government might seize the Relief Society's wheat. Because this order would cripple the Church's wheat storage program, if obeyed, Elder Lee conferred with President George Albert Smith, who advised him to leave at once for the nation's capital with Elders Marion G. Romney and William L. Lawrence. The successful resolution of this question, after a surprising turn of events in Washington, D.C., was recorded in Elder Lee's journal:

> At 2:30 p.m., by appointment, together with Brother [Ernest L.] Wilkinson, we arrived at the office of Assistant Secretary J. B. Hutson, but he was detained for nearly an hour, during which time, Mr. J. B. King, the alternate administrator of the Wheat Order, waited with us. This gave us an opportunity to explain the entire welfare operation to him. We discovered that he had discussed this matter with our Earl Corey, head of the Commodity Credit Corpor-

With President George Albert Smith, 1946

ation at Portland, a former Salt Laker, of unfriendly background to the Church, and from him he had obtained the fixed opinion that our wheat must be sold to him. When we at last were given an audience with Mr. Hutson, Mr. King proceeded to explain our procedure and in answer to Mr. Hutson's questions as to what he thought about it, replied that he doubted if we were under the order. Hutson's remark was to the effect that in our program we apparently are doing now just exactly what the government is proposing to do under this order. He furthermore endeavored to help open the way for us to can our own meat for shipment to Europe by broadly interpreting the meaning of the word *form* in the present law.

Steps were taken after their return to Salt Lake City to ensure thereafter that the entire wheat production in the Church's budget was actually produced on welfare projects. Through the Lord's intervention, the storage program continued uninterrupted until 1978, when Relief Society President Barbara B. Smith, at the welfare session of general conference, presented the long-protected Relief Society wheat storage for consolidation with the grain stores of the welfare services of the Church. At the time of the transfer it amounted to 266,291 bushels of wheat.

Another trip to Washington, D.C., this time in May of 1950, was successful in winning for the Church a tax exemption for the Deseret Industries arm of the welfare program. After a brief consultation with Calder Mackay and Logan Morris, both attorneys, Elder Henry D. Moyle and Elder Lee met with the chief of the Bureau of Internal Revenue to press the Church's petition for an exemption from taxation in behalf of the Deseret Industries of California. The exemption was granted after only twenty minutes of discussion, and set the precedent for all other Deseret Industries and related projects.

The Church was growing in 1950. Elders Stephen L Richards and Harold B. Lee had organized in June of that year the 180th stake of the Church at Yakima, Washington. Now came a time for expansion of welfare properties, and large investments were made.

Land procurement began in earnest with the purchase of the Mayer Horse Ranch in Perris, California, which was tied to the expectation that reciprocal gifts would return to the Church every year from the Statler Trust. The farms consisted of 530 acres, and the purchase from Ellsworth Statler was for 504 acres.

A regional welfare farm project was organized on this beautiful property on July 1, 1950, when Elders Lee, Moyle, and Romney and Presiding Bishop LeGrand Richards arrived for a morning meeting with the ten stake presidencies of the region. The General Authorities outlined the broad guidelines governing the operation of the farm, the principal point being that each stake would be given some project on which to produce its budget, and any surplus would be placed in the common storehouse to be purchased by the General Welfare Committee, or disposed of through sales to build up other projects as required. Their immediate objective was to raise $100,000 in fifteen days for start-up costs, and the 807 people who attended the meeting in the Quonset hay barn went forward unitedly under the direction of their ten stake presidents.

A few months earlier Elder Lee had accompanied Elder Stephen L Richards on an assignment to divide the Pasadena California Stake and create the East Los Angeles Stake. They chose as stake president a man whose name was later to be known throughout the Church, Elder Howard W. Hunter. He distinguished himself in his first major assignment by raising the Pasadena Stake's assessment on the Perris Regional Welfare Project so quickly that the story was never forgotten. Through a series of inspirational circumstances arising out of the immense faith of the Saints, President Hunter wired the full amount of his stake's assessment so quickly that it was on Elder Moyle's desk when he returned to Salt Lake City two days later.

Other major expenditures included the Florida Ranch property. This bold venture envisioned the development of about 180,000 acres of the best ranch land in Florida, and was to be used for cattle raising and citrus production. It was while he was visiting the property in May 1950 that the oft-reprinted photograph was taken of Elder Lee while he was deep-sea fishing off the coast of West Palm Beach, Florida. He never tired of telling about the "one that got away from him" that day.

In the mid-1950s, with President Clark, Marion G. Romney, and Henry D. Moyle, Elder Lee spent two weekends at President Clark's Grantsville home rewriting and reducing the text of the *Welfare Handbook* until there was nothing left but sheer pearls and power. These Brethren often referred to these scholarly sessions when they sermonized on the basic principles of providing for the poor among us.

Then, as today, a popular stop for dignitaries visiting Salt Lake City was Welfare Square. At the request of President David O. McKay, Elder Lee escorted Mr. Guy Gabrielson, chairman of the National Republican Committee, through the facilities. The famous guest later gave a familiar summarization: "The attitude of those at the Square working for the aid they receive at the storehouse was to me the most impressive part of the tour."

PRESIDENT GEORGE F. RICHARDS DIES

Bessie Hollings was a special friend of Fern Lee's, and the two women had spent many enjoyable hours together as temple workers. Bessie had received a marriage proposal from the President of the Quorum of the Twelve, George F. Richards, following the death of his wife. For six months she pondered this proposal without coming to a decision. Finally, in July of 1947 she came to Elder Lee for counsel. Following a blessing from Elder Lee she received the spiritual guidance she had sought and gave her consent to President Richards, and one week later the Lees went to the temple to witness the sealing ceremony on July 20, 1947.

Brother Richards was a loved and admired Church leader and was uniformly respected and revered by the members of the Quorum over which he presided. His earliest pronouncements following the death of President Grant in 1945 were uncommonly wise and visionary. He recommended more ardent missionary effort throughout the nations of the earth, even if it meant reduced effort among the stakes by the Apostles. He advocated increased temple activity, and even though eighty-six years of age at the time of his marriage to Bessie Hollings, he was still seeking to broaden his celestial family.

Three years later Elder Lee had occasion to visit on an early August morning with President Richards, to see if his stake conference assignment could be changed to permit his attendance at the Southern California regional welfare meeting. He found President Richards complaining that he was so tired that all he wanted to do was rest. That night President Richards went to sleep for the last time. The Richards family asked Elder Lee to speak at his funeral.

The Salt Lake Tabernacle was filled to bid farewell to this inspiring Church leader with a gentle heart and the vision of a prophet of God. President J. Reuben Clark and Elder Joseph Fielding Smith joined Elder Lee as speakers. Elder Lee made preparations for his funeral sermon while erecting a picket fence around Helen and Brent's home. About this he wrote: "This work away from the office likewise gave me an opportunity to collect my thoughts in preparation for the funeral services tomorrow for President George F. Richards."

The death of President Richards occasioned the appointment of Elder Delbert L. Stapley during the October 1950 general conference to fill the vacancy in the Quorum of the Twelve. Elder Stapley had been serving as president of the Phoenix Stake. Since President McKay, the oldest of the Apostles in seniority among the Twelve, was already serving in the First Presidency, Joseph Fielding Smith was appointed Acting President of the Twelve. Elder Lee had introduced Brother Stapley to President Clark several years before, as he had written in his journal, "for future references."

In his sermon at that general conference Elder Lee was obliged to improvise his talk due to a shortage of time. He was the concluding speaker at the Sunday morning session, but the clock read 11:45 A.M. when he stood to speak. Elder Lee recorded his successful adjustment in these words:

> I made some improvisations and bore my testimony and the Spirit was wonderful. I found myself so much under its influence that I had difficulty controlling my feelings. The Brethren were very kind and I was again indebted to my Heavenly Father for sustaining me.

Ten Years as an Apostle

The events of the remaining months of 1950, concluding his first decade in the Quorum of the Twelve, continued to reaffirm the divine nature of his calling, while at the same time new medical disclosures threatened his effectiveness. He had developed a major digestive disorder, ultimately leading to severe ulcers in the years ahead. This problem forced him to cancel three speaking engagements during the Christmas holidays. Compounding his own physical problems were his wife's frailties. He had spent his fifty-first birthday in the hospital with her, she having suffered a bowel hemorrhage three days earlier.

The evidence that the Lord was with him, however, continued to surface as the Saints poured out their love for his service. Sister Nemelka, from a faithful German convert family in the Pioneer Stake, wrote to Elder Lee telling how her son, Nephi, has been reclaimed from inactivity. His first ray of hope had come, she said, when he read in Elder Lee's book *Youth and the Church* the chapter on repentance titled "The 'Successful' Sinners."

Elder Lee enjoyed an interview with F. L. Cook, formerly a Methodist minister and a recent convert from Cosmopolis, Washington, with whom he discussed the gospel while riding the train going east from Denver to Kansas City. Brother Cook bore a strong testimony of the power of the Holy Ghost, which had enlightened his soul with a certainty which before had been but a mere belief.

Elder Lee attended a stake conference in California in August of 1950, and wrote in his journal, "there is great evidence that conditions in this stake are not right and that the president will not take counsel." He didn't at the time know the cause, but the Holy Spirit told him there was disharmony. He returned to reorganize the stake in November and learned the day after the reorganization the cause that sustained his first impressions. This time he wrote: "Today I was told about the sad conditions in this stake, socially, involving the former stake president's wife, which had threatened a break between her and her husband. What I was told today confirmed my feelings after my conference three months ago."

A man who had protested his innocence for eighteen years since President Lee's high council in Pioneer Stake had excommunicated him, came to him in 1950 and confessed his sins. After being malicious and vindictive toward Elder Lee all these years, falsely blaming him, he came on this occasion and said that "he had the assurance at the last general conference of the Church that Elder Lee was an authorized servant of the Lord."

Elder Lee continued to use his unquenchable faith to bless his family. When his son-in-law Ernest Wilkins faced his Ph.D. examinations at Stanford University, Elder Lee fasted for his success. Visiting soon thereafter in Palo Alto, he learned that Ernest had faced his five professors with great composure and had correctly answered questions on subjects in which he was not well prepared.

Returning with Ernest and Maurine's family as they moved from California to Utah, they visited in Arizona while the Wilkins family celebrated Thanksgiving and Elder Lee was involved in releasing Elder Delbert L. Stapley at his local Phoenix Stake conference. En route home later, baby Alan, just one year of age, awoke from his sleep with a high fever. Maurine awakened her mother and father at 6:00 A.M. and Elder Lee administered to the baby. His fever immediately began to subside.

The character of this growing and blossoming prophet was becoming increasingly refined. Still asserting itself, however, was an occasional unruly temper. Like his mother, whom Elder Lee described as having a "fierce loyalty to her family," Elder Lee was known to defend his loved ones and his loyalties, sometimes to the extreme. Once in Elder Lee's earliest years as a member of the Council of Twelve, one of the senior Apostles minimized the Pioneer Stake's development of the religion classes organized when Elder Lee was stake president, attempting to show that the more affluent stakes on the East Bench of Salt Lake City had better statistics. This produced a swift and stirring defense by Elder Lee of his people and their faith.

This weakness appeared again as he defended his children in their attempts to locate their growing families in new homes in Utah. In 1949, Elder Lee vigorously protested the placement of telephone poles in front of Brent and Helen's new home. He tele-

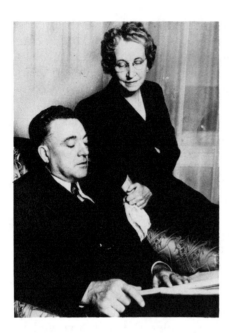

At home with Fern, 1950

phoned the developer and strongly urged eliminating the unsight-
liness and the hazard caused by the utility pole. The next week he
met with Brent's father, Brent, and the engineer from the telephone company, now insisting that the poles be moved to a spot
less objectionable. Under an embarrassing verbal barrage, the engineer yielded the point.

The following year, when the Wilkins family moved from California, Elder and Sister Lee were much concerned in finding a
house for them. The real estate agent had failed to hold out homes
for Elder Lee's family to inspect as he had promised. A sharp exchange followed when they met, and Elder Lee later wrote in his
journal, "My family thought my sharp rebukes to him had antagonized their cause, and in their eyes I think I had failed them."

He was forever a family man, and if any weakness might be
detected it was in defending and supporting his loved ones. While
touring the Northwestern States Mission in 1950, he tried to
telephone from Whitefish, Montana, to Maurine on her twenty-
sixth birthday; from Spokane he wrote his eldest grandson, David
Goates, a letter for his third birthday. On another occasion, he
proudly took this little grandson and Fern to Preston, Idaho,

where he participated in the ground-breaking ceremonies for the ward and stake building there.

Now it was Christmastime, the first in many years that his family were all together in reasonable proximity to one another. His digestive disorder and the complete rest ordered by his doctor conspired to make it a relaxing holiday season for him, basking as he did in the joy of having his family close to him once again. As they did nearly every year thereafter, he and Fern and the families of his two daughters spent Christmas day together, alternating between Provo and Salt Lake City. The highlight, wrote Elder Lee in his journal after one such lively afternoon and evening, "was the singing and musical playing of our girls with their husbands."

Second
Apostolic
Decade

———

1951–1960

1954. Texas Instruments invented the silicon transistor. First mass inoculation of children against polio with Salk vaccine began in Pittsburgh. First atomic-powered submarine launched. Communism looked to the West as a spreading menace. Soviets gripped Eastern Europe, China was lost to Mao Tse-tung, only "police action" saved the Korean peninsula, and Vietnamese were demolishing the French at Dien Bien Phu.

CHAPTER 15

New Era Begins for Church Growth

As Harold B. Lee's second decade of service as an Apostle began, it was once more time, in the provident wisdom of God, for another era of Church leadership.

On February 15, 1951, in the Council of the Twelve meeting in the temple, a letter was read from President George Albert Smith indicating that he felt his end was drawing near and that he was arranging his affairs accordingly. One week later he was a patient in the LDS Hospital. President Clark sent Harold B. Lee to visit with the President on some business matters.

By March 1, 1951, it was apparent that the President's health was now in precarious condition. Two of the Twelve took the sacrament to President Smith at his home, where he had relocated because he preferred to die in his own house. The Brethren returned pessimistic about his condition. By March 22, paralysis had set in, and by March 30, all hope for his recovery had been abandoned. On April 2, 1951, as final preparations were being made for general conference, President Smith's son Albert arrived from Boston to be with his father, now in critical condition.

PRESIDENT GEORGE ALBERT SMITH DIES

President Smith's actual passing was recorded in Elder Lee's diary as follows, under the date of Thursday, April 5, 1951: "Last night at 7:27 P.M. President George Albert Smith died at his home on 10th East and Yale Avenue. When word came I called Brother Albert Bowen and he and I went to the home to join others of the family and the General Authorities."

The regular temple meeting of the Brethren the next day was largely a discussion of details for the funeral services and a decision on how to integrate the honor to be given the President of the Church with the general conference soon to open. They decided to adjourn the conference only on Saturday, when the funeral would be held, and then hold a special session on Monday as the Solemn Assembly, in which the First Presidency would be reorganized. At this meeting the chairs of the First Presidency had been vacated, President McKay and President Clark taking their places in the Council of the Twelve in the order of their seniority.

Elder Lee wrote of his emotions at this time in these words:

> It is a great experience to witness the calling home of a prophet of God. My mind has reflected back at the mantle of leadership that was upon President George Albert Smith just a year previous, when he closed the April general conference of 1950 with this prophecy:
>
> "Brethren and Sisters: Let us go to our homes now. If our houses are not in order let us set them in order. Let us renew our determination to honor God and keep his commandments and love one another, to make our homes the abiding place of peace. Each of us can contribute to that in the homes in which we live. It will not be long until calamities will overtake the human family unless there is a speedy repentance. It will not be long before those who are scattered over the face of the Earth by millions will die like flies because of that which is to come. Our Heavenly Father has told us how it could be avoided, and that is our mission, in part, to go in to the world and explain to the world how it can be avoided."

Elder Lee called these words prophetic. Years later he still quoted them and noted some of the most horrifying stories of the devastations of whole peoples and nations, and stated that "the end is not yet."

The general conference of the Church opened on April 6, 1951, without a living President, but the senior Apostle, President David O. McKay, presided. He generously called President Clark from his place in the Twelve to occupy his usual seat on the stand of the Salt Lake Tabernacle.

On Saturday, the next day, the cortege for President Smith formed at the Church Office Building at 47 East South Temple Street at 1:25 P.M. and was led by the General Authorities, who walked ahead onto the Temple Square grounds for the services. Addresses were given by Elder Matthew Cowley, John F. Fitzpatrick, nonmember publisher of the Salt Lake *Tribune,* Elder Spencer W. Kimball, Elbert R. Curtis, and the former counselors in the First Presidency. The complete service rounded out the life of this "man of love" and each contribution was in remarkable harmony with the spirit of President Smith's life.

DAVID O. McKAY ADMINISTRATION BEGINS

General conference continued with the general priesthood meeting being held that night. On Sunday, April 8, 1951, following the conference sessions, the Council of the Twelve convened at 4:30 P.M. in a solemn and sacred meeting in their council room of the temple, at which time President David O. McKay was named as the new President of the Church. President McKay then startled the Twelve with his announcement that Elder Stephen L Richards would be his first counselor and that President J. Reuben Clark, Jr., would be his second counselor.

There was a numbing silence. The Brethren were unprepared for this announcement, although all recognized that nothing incorrect was being done, for the President always has the right to nominate counselors of his choice. There was just overwhelming sympathy for President Clark, who had served as first counselor to two previous Presidents for over sixteen years.

Elder Lee wrote:

Sunday night, after a dinner at the home of Elder Henry D. Moyle, Brother Moyle and I went to visit President Clark and found him humble, yet loyal to President McKay. He assured us that he would . . . try his best to be a good counselor, despite the humiliation that was inescapable, as his family and others would seek for an explanation as to why a change in the order of counselors.

Elder Lee's recital of events stated that the solemn assembly held on Monday, April 9, 1951, which concluded the conference, was just that for many—a very solemn assembly. Yet, wrote Elder Lee, "a wonderful spirit was in evidence, highlighted by the majestic conduct of President Clark who won love and honor to himself, and to the Lord's work, seldom equalled and perhaps never excelled," when he exemplified a classic lesson to the Saints regarding the subjection of the individual to the work of the Lord. In words now immortalized President Clark said:

> In the service of the Lord, it is not where you serve but how. In The Church of Jesus Christ of Latter-day Saints, one takes the place to which one is duly called, which place one neither seeks nor declines."

A DIFFERENT, LARGER CHURCH EMERGES

The beginning of the decade in 1951 saw a continuation of the same, small intimate church known for decades previous, but change was inevitable. The General Authorities went out every weekend to attend stake conferences and stayed in the homes of the local stake leaders. They knew the children in the homes by their first names and remembered them when they came to Church headquarters or went to college. Travel was to the outer perimeter in the East to attend conferences in Washington, D.C., and New York City, but predominately the weekend trips were to California and the Intermountain West, where the stakes of the Church were strong.

General conferences were also more intimate then in some respects than in more recent years. They are recalled now with some nostalgia. There were no television cameras to make the speakers feel they were "on stage." When the First Presidency spoke, their words were not beyond recall or correction, if later desired, before being distributed in Church publications. The informality of that day is gone now in today's different world and Church. Microphones and cameras follow the President of the Church wherever he goes. Conference has become a media spectacular along with all that it has ever been as an outlet of spiritual guidance for a wayward world.

While there is an obvious gain from the media coverage, which permits Saints in distant places to actually see their President address them, there is sometimes a loss in his opportunity to speak freely. When words once spoken are irretrievable he must now live in constant fear of a slip-of-tongue and be tempted at times to say no more than could be well put in a press release. The Brethren now read their sermons, in deference to permanency and split-second broadcast timing. This loss of freedom due to the media coverage may have produced a loss in effect to General Authorities, the Saints and perhaps ultimately to the world's listeners.

Much of this change was unavoidable. The sheer size of the Church today carries its own imperatives. Gone are the days when conversations with General Authorities could be held in your living room, or on the street at a chance meeting. Now, in this unstable world, the General Authorities must be more isolated. The type of intimacy between the Church leaders and the people known in the early 1950s seems forever lost. It is not possible to go backwards, to shrink the size of the Church and banish the microphones and cameras. The television era is here to stay. The earlier years of informal sociality with Church leaders have passed. The world and the Lord's Church were changing as the second decade of Harold B. Lee's apostleship began in 1951.

Membership of the Church in the United States was announced in 1950 as 926,700. In those days only 34,251 Saints were in all of Europe; 23,965 in the South Pacific; 2,089 in Australia; only 283 in Asia, with no Saints living in the Philippines, and only 1,936 in all of Latin America, not including the 5,915 Saints in Mexico. These figures show the infancy of the missionary effort outside the United States and Canada, where only 8.7 percent of the Church's population resided. Of course, migration to Zion helped to account for keeping these figures uncommonly low. (See *Church Almanac,* 1975, Section E.)

BEGINNINGS OF INTERNATIONAL CHURCH

President David O. McKay's administration ushered in a long, continuous growth period marked by the international expansion of the Church. President McKay, while serving as a counselor to President Heber J. Grant in the First Presidency, made a historic worldwide tour of the Church in 1922, accompanied by Elder Hugh J. Cannon. No doubt the experiences of that trip left indelible impressions on President McKay and influenced his interest in the international Church growth.

President McKay was again a world traveler after becoming the prophet of the Church. He went to Europe and chose two temple sites, and then returned there in 1955 to dedicate the Swiss Temple and in 1958 for the London Temple. In 1954 President McKay travelled 37,000 miles on a six-week trip to South Africa and South and Central America. In 1955 President McKay left in early January for a trip into the South Pacific, where for six weeks he visited the missions in those countries.

Fresh from his trip to the South Pacific, President McKay made a far-reaching policy announcement from the podium of the Salt Lake Tabernacle at general conference on April 5, 1955. He declared publicly that the First Presidency had decided to have all missions visited by a General Authority once each year, with the foreign missions to be visited by the members of the Quorum of the Twelve.

Even before this date visits to the foreign missions had been made, but the regularity had not been set previously by policy. In 1953 Elder LeGrand Richards toured the South Sea Islands and Elder Henry D. Moyle spent four and one-half months in Europe.

Apostles abroad in 1955 included Elder Joseph Fielding Smith in the Orient, Elder Spencer W. Kimball and Elder Henry D. Moyle in Europe, and Elder Marion G. Romney in Australia, where he had served his first mission.

By 1956 the population of the Church had reached 3.1 million. Elder Harold B. Lee had officiated at the creation of the 199th stake of the Church earlier in the decade. It took place on November 23, 1952, when the East Ogden Stake was created out of the Mt. Ogden Stake. By the end of the decade one hundred more stakes had been created. The first stake organized outside North America and Hawaii was the New Zealand Auckland Stake in May 1958, just as jet airplane travel was being introduced. Elder Lee divided the Washington Tacoma Stake, the 299th in the Church, on June 17, 1960.

The travel of Apostles abroad continued with Elder Adam S. Bennion touring Europe in 1957 and Elder Romney returning to Polynesia in 1958 and touring five missions in Europe in 1959. Elder Joseph Fielding Smith traveled to New Zealand in 1959. The First Presidency held tightly its control over Church units abroad and personally dictated every assignment of the Twelve to work with the Church leadership in these developing nations. In 1960 Joseph Fielding Smith, President of the Council of the Twelve, toured South America, and Elder Spencer W. Kimball visited New Zealand and Australia that same year.

Elder Harold B. Lee was among the Apostles traveling abroad to the fledgling missions of the world during the 1951–1960 decade. He had personally taken the stand that unless general board members were allowed to visit these overseas missions, to accelerate the training of new leaders, he felt the divisions and creations of new missions should be slowed down. Thus, the training of new leaders was even then a major concern.

Elder Lee's travel assignments from the First Presidency included a 1954 trip to the Orient, a 1956 assignment to divide the Mexican mission, a 1958 tour of South Africa with a return via the Holy Land and Europe, a three-month tour of South American and Central American missions in 1959 when he divided the Brazilian Mission and created the new Andes Mission, and in 1960 an assignment to create the Manchester England Stake, the first stake of the Church in that country.

These travels will be detailed on the following pages and serve to exemplify those taken by the Quorum of the Twelve during this decade to set in motion the Church's international expansion in the years to come.

Elder Lee Visits the Orient

Elder and Sister Lee arrived home from a long trip to the Orient on Saturday night, October 2, 1954, and attended their first session of general conference, then under way, the following morning. Elder Lee was assigned to be the closing speaker of the conference. There was some additional time left in that session, so in introducing Elder Lee, President McKay urged that he take time to include a report on his eventful journey to the Far East.

In his thirty-minute sermon he testified to the power of healing that has come to Fern, his dear wife, in being able to travel twenty thousand miles without a single day's illness within just six short months' time following a fractured hip. He also told of the unfolding of the Lord's work in the Orient and cited evidence of an awakening of those peoples following centuries of religious bondage and oppression. He also stressed the wonderful labors of military men who were members of the Church and explained that through them the way was paved for the reopening of the Japanese Mission.

The drama for this journey can only be understood by turning back the calendar six months. Shortly after Elder Lee's fifty-fifth birthday the Brethren came hurrying into his office one morning to inform him that Fern had suffered an accident at home. Elder Romney drove him home, where he found that his wife had fallen on the steps and had fractured her left hip bone. Surgery was performed later that day and the hip was pinned using a metal plate.

Four days later, while Elder Lee was sitting in the Tabernacle in the closing session of general conference on April 6, 1954, he felt as if he were bathed in a heavenly peace that assured him that the Lord would preserve his beloved Fern for him. He went immediately to the hospital after the meeting and found her in a much improved condition.

When Sister Lee was able to return from the hospital on April 17, 1954, Brother Lee brought in a single bed and placed it in the television room on the main floor of their home. Her spirits were lifted by the smell of spring in the yard and the feel of being in her home again. Tenderly, Elder Lee brought his mattress downstairs and placed it alongside her bed so he could attend to her during the nights.

Sister Lee's convalescence was speeded after an interview on May 21, 1954, which Elder Lee had with President McKay in which he announced that the Presidency had decided to have one of the Twelve visit the Orient, including Japan, Korea, and probably Hong Kong, as well as the Hawaiian Islands. They had decided, President McKay said, to send Elder Lee and he wanted Sister Lee to accompany him. He asked Elder Lee to obtain a medical opinion as to how long it would be before Sister Lee could walk without crutches. After additional X-ray studies, which proved that the bone was knitting properly and that the steel plate splicing the break was in proper place, they informed President McKay that Sister Lee could safely be off her crutches within two months or any time after June 15. Progress in Sister Lee's recovery came rapidly after this goal was set.

On July 26, President McKay gave blessings to Elder and Sister Lee for the visit they were assigned to make into the Orient. He blessed them with good health, with safety in their travels, with an awareness of the problems of their mission, with an ability to interpret the conditions in each country, and with the power to impress government officials as they met them. To Fern he gave a blessing and promise that she would return greatly strengthened in her body.

A glimpse into the tenderness of Elder Lee as a grandfather is seen in his diary note describing their departure from the Salt Lake railroad station on August 3, 1954: "Dr. LeRoy Kimball has been most considerate and attentive in providing us with medicines and our last 'shots.' Maurine prepared dinner for all our family but I didn't get to see Helen's little ones. They didn't seem to realize just how much I wanted to see all my little ones before I left. After family prayer we found many friends at the depot waiting to say 'good-bye' to us."

Just prior to his departure Elder Lee administered to Presiding Bishop Joseph B. Wirthlin, who had suffered a stroke, and paid his respects to his friend and tutor, President J. Reuben Clark, Jr. President Clark expressed concern at his being gone for so long. He said that while he had no premonition, he felt to remind him that his "four seniors" were all "old men" and that anything could happen in that length of time.

Before landing in Hawaii Sister Lee's general strength had already increased steadily, but she was troubled by a persistent pain in her left foot and her eyesight seemed greatly impaired. From that time forward, however, she gained strength consistently and the blessing given to her by President McKay became increasingly evident.

REPORT ON ORIENTAL VISIT

Elder Lee's general conference summary of his journey provides an immediate reaction and review, since it was delivered only one day after his arrival home. His text follows:

It seems incredible to me, as I think about it today, that six months ago yesterday my dear companion lay critically ill in the LDS Hospital, her body cruelly broken in an unfortunate accident. For someone to have told me and the doctors six months ago that before another six months should pass, that she would travel 20,000 miles and visit six countries and peoples, it would seem to me to have been such an impossibility as to have been wholly unthinkable.

But when our beloved leader, the President of the Church, took us into his office and gave us blessings for this mission, little did I realize how the Lord could even then, beyond the skill of doctors or human minds and skill, bless that dear companion and fulfill to the letter the words of the President when he said to her: "You will come back from this trip increased in strength and healed in body." It has been one of the greatest testimonies that has come to me, and I stand today humbly and bear witness to the effectiveness of the prayers and blessings of, not only our President, but also of the faithful Saints everywhere.

If I could take as something of a text, then, perhaps my feelings today could be best expressed in the words of the Master. John the Baptist had sent his disciples to Jesus, after John had received reports about the work of the Master, and they came asking him, "Art thou he that should come? or look we for another?" The answer that Jesus gave for them to carry back to John the Baptist was this:

"Go your way, and tell John what things ye have seen and heard; how that the blind see, the lame walk, the lepers are cleansed, the deaf hear, the dead are raised, to the poor the gospel is preached." (Luke 7:20, 22.)

To you, President McKay, before the body of the Church today, as a humble servant whom you sent out into the Far East to check on affairs there, to visit our boys in military service, our scattered Saints in that far-off land, I come back to you testifying, as the Master told the disciples to testify to John, the miraculous power of divine intervention is out there, which is one of the signs of the divinity of the work of the Lord.

We have seen one "nigh unto death" raised miraculously during this visit. We have seen the hand of the Almighty stay the storms and the winds, and overcome obstacles that otherwise would have made impossible the fulfillment of our mission. We have passed through danger-ridden country only a few hundred miles from where a war is brewing. We have seen the humble and the poor having the gospel preached to them. The signs of divinity are in the Far East. The work of the Almighty is increasing, with a tremendous surge.

I do not know whether it was just a coincidence, or whether President McKay had some thought about it, but one of the commanding generals, when I was introduced to him in Korea, said, "Well, you have a lot of relatives in this country." The five most prominent names in Korea are Yi, Chang, Kim, Pak, and Lee. I discovered that there were over 500,000 Chinese who have the surname of Li (Lee), and actually, some of the immigration authorities, when I signed my name on my passport, would ask: "Chinese?" And I answered, "No, American." Then the comment, "You look Chinese."

So, I was accepted, President McKay, as almost a native. My coloring as to hair and eyes and skin seem to fit the general terrain.

Fulfillment of Parley P. Pratt Prophecy

Some years ago I read a statement contained in Parley P. Pratt's *The Key to Theology*. I wondered then at the meaning of this statement, and I come back to you today testifying that it was a prophecy that is today being fulfilled. I read from that inspired statement:

"Physically speaking, there seems to need but the consummation of two great enterprises more, in order to complete the preparations necessary for the fulfillment of Isaiah and other prophets, in regard to the restoration of Israel to Palestine, from the four quarters of the Earth . . . under the auspices of that great, universal, and permanent theocracy which is to succeed the long reign of mystery."

Then he names those two great enterprises: one, the Europe-to-Asia railroad which was then in the process of being consummated, and the other, the Great Western Railway from the Atlantic to the Pacific in this country. Then he said this:

"Politically speaking, some barriers yet remain to be removed, and some conquests to be achieved, such as the subjugation of Japan, and the triumph of constitutional liberty among certain nations where mind, and thought, and religion are still prescribed by law." (*The Key to Theology,* pp. 75–76.)

Subjugation means conquering by force. I want to say to you that one of the most significant things that I have seen in the Far East is the fulfillment of what Elder Parley P. Pratt testified would be one of the significant developments necessary to the consummation of God's purposes, "the subjugation of Japan and the triumph of constitutional liberty among certain nations where mind, and thought, and religion are still prescribed by law."

High Caliber of LDS Servicemen

I traveled on this assignment with Sister Lee and President Hilton A. Robertson and Sister Robertson. We had visited our native Saints and servicemen in all the districts of the mainland of Japan, from Hokkaido on the north, to Kyushu on the south, and representatives from the great cities. I then went across with President Robertson to Korea and then to Okinawa, Hong Kong, the Philippines, and Guam. I want to say to the parents, who are anxiously inquiring about their boys, something that I hope will calm your feelings, and will encourage you in your faith.

From the time that the First Presidency announced this appointment our telephones were ringing at home and at the office from anxious parents, and the substance of their anxiety was summed up in what one father said: "Will you see my boy over there, and take him the love from a lonesome dad?"

We met with a total of 1,563 Latter-day Saint boys in military service, in our conferences in Japan, Korea, Okinawa, the Philippines, and Guam. They had arranged district conferences which simulated our stake conferences, and it was like holding a stake conference every other day all through this trip, because of the thoroughness with which they had organized their work.

I have never listened to better sermons that I heard preached by our five Latter-day Saint chaplains and our group leaders over there. They are studying the gospel. The excellence of their organization and the orderliness of their procedures under a mission committee comprising three lieutenant colonels, answerable of course to the mission president, and they, in turn, supervised by chaplains and by group leaders, is worthy of note. In every camp where we went, under military orders, we were accorded every privilege that could be accorded one going into those areas, and the first procedure was invariably an introduction to the commanding general of the camp, and a brief interview, during which he extended to us all the courtesies of the camp, and bade us welcome, and in a number of instances, came to our meeting.

They know our boys. They know of the work of the Latter-day Saints, and perhaps their attitude towards our boys is best summed up in what General Richard S. Whitcomb said to us down at Pusan, Korea, after we had been at the general's mess the night before, and he had indicated he would like to come to our meeting the next morning.

With 109 of our boys present, General Whitcomb rose to speak to them, and after a word of greeting, he said this, and I asked him if I might repeat it to you, President McKay, and to the fathers and mothers back home. (General Whitcomb is characterized by our boys there as one of the toughest disciplinarians in the United States Army.)

"I have always known the members of your Church to be a substantial people. Here in the Pusan area I have the largest court-martial responsibility of any command in the United States Army, but I never have had one of your faith brought before me for a court martial or disciplinary action, in this command. Wherever I have been, I have never known of a Latter-day Saint ever to be brought up for any disciplinary action."

On Guam I was furnished with a little paper from the camp which indicated that for the month of August one of our boys there, a Brother Douglas K. Eager, had been designated as the "Airman of the Month of August," and the citation read: "He won the award on the basis of his devotion to duty, character, appearance, industry, and military bearing."

One of the supervising chaplains, to take another example, from Clark Field in the Philippines, said this to me as we walked out of a meeting with the Protestant chaplains on the base: "I have never known any group of men in my military experience who have greater devotion to their country, and to their God, and to the

Greeting Brigadier General Richard S. Whitcomb, commanding general, at chapel in communications zone compound, Pusan, Korea, 1954

Church—no finer characters than are to be found among the boys of the Latter-day Saints.''

All through our visits, they had arranged their own programs—they sang three songs over and over again without anybody suggesting it. They sang first, "We Thank Thee, O God, for a Prophet," and in every district conference they sustained the General Authorities of the Church. It was one of the highlights of their conference.

The other that seems to have become their theme song while in military service is "Come, Come Ye Saints."

> Why should we mourn or think our lot is hard?
> 'Tis not so, all is right . . .
> And should we die before our journey's through
> Happy day, all is well.
> We then are free from toil and sorrow, too,
> With the just we shall dwell.

And then, finally, you must know what they were singing otherwise. They were singing about the hills of home: "O ye mountains high, where the clear blue sky arches over the vales of the free." And time and again I heard the wives of our few men, who are permitted to be with them in some places, and our boys everywhere, as they would shake hands, say, as tears would fill their eyes: "I wasn't homesick until I shook hands with you, Brother Lee." Someone from home!

Then they would say something like this: "Tell the folks back home not to worry about us. We are all right, but we worry sometimes about the folks back home."

I think my appraisal of what I saw among the boys there might be expressed in what Ralph Waldo Emerson is quoted as having said: "It is easy in the world to live after the world's opinion. It is easy in solitude to live after one's own, but the great man is he, who in the midst of the crowd, keeps with perfect sweetness the independence of solitude. . . ." Such is the way I found our boys, with the marks of true greatness upon their brows, keeping "with perfect sweetness the independence of solitude."

Servicemen's Missionary Efforts

From the contributions of our military men in the Far East, sufficient money is being raised each month to sustain 21 full-time missionaries from Japan, who otherwise could not fill missions as full-time missionaries in the Japanese Mission. That amounts to forty dollars a month for each missionary, or a total of between eight and nine hundred dollars each month. This is the second group of missionaries which, when completed, will mean that our boys over there have contributed from out of their meager military allowances a total of over forty thousand dollars for sending local missionaries to do the work that otherwise could not be done.

Directly as a result of the work of the Latter-day Saint servicemen there were 47 converts last year, while another 103 have been baptized so far this year by the missionaries of the Japanese Mission. It was on the first Sunday of last month at 6:30 in the morning, just at the break of the day, in Seoul, Korea, that we baptized a native Korean student and a young serviceman. At Clark Field last Sunday morning at 7:30 we baptized four, one a young native Filipino mother, who later bore her testimony in the conference session. What this means to servicemen as they come into the Church is perhaps best expressed in a humble testimony from a young seaman who came to Tokyo off the aircraft carrier, Hornet, which had docked at Yokohama. Later we met him down at Manila Bay. He came up at the close of the meeting in Tokyo, his arm in a sling, and explained that he had a badly infected arm. As he shook hands with me he said, "I am getting ready to be baptized a member of the Church, and if you are down at Manila and I meet you there, I hope to tell you I have been baptized."

At Manila he came, his arm now was perfectly healed, and said: "I was baptized on August 27. Something happened to me after I left that conference in Tokyo. My arm was swollen and was painful all through the meeting, but after I had shaken hands with you, I got on the train going back to the boat. Suddenly the pain ceased, my arm was healed, and now I am going back to that lovely wife who has been praying that I would straighten my life. I smoked, and I drank, and I did a lot of things to cause her sorrow, and I am going back to that sweetheart of mine, and I am going to spend the rest of my life trying to prove myself worthy of her love." His faith had brought healing to his body and his soul. That is what the gospel meant to this seaman, who became a convert to the gospel of Jesus Christ.

Over there we have boys who are homesick for home. How they are thinking about their mothers and their wives and sweethearts is suggested by the fact that when Sister Lee would speak, they would ofttimes come up at the close of services, and they would say to me some words of appreciation, but then they would say: "We really appreciated Sister Lee's talk," and they gathered around her because she was a touch of Mother. They would tell her how she reminded them of their mothers. She was the symbol of the home to which they one-time hoped to come, and I think they almost filled a notebook for her of the names and addresses and telephone numbers of the folks back home they wanted her to call and talk to.

The Church in Japan

Perhaps what our boys are doing over there can best be illustrated in what Elder Aki, a young Japanese missionary up at beautiful Nikko, a recipient of the missionary contributions of our servicemen, who is just completing a two-year mission, said as he bore his testimony in English: "As terrible as was war in Japan, it proved a great blessing, because as a result, it brought the Latter-day Saint servicemen back to Japan who paved the way for the reopening of the Japanese Mission."

President McKay, one of the things that is startling to me and significant pertains to the language there. Difficult as it is, because of the peculiar characters as well as the difficult language, the Lord is seemingly helping us even to solve that problem. Since the troops came in, every school in Japan and in Korea is teaching English, and most of those young students, who are being attracted by the gospel, can speak some English. They are helping to break down the language barrier and making easier the work of the missionaries.

Down at Osaka where we had 179 in attendance, as I looked over that audience and tried to estimate the ages of those in attendance, I would say that out of 179 in attendance, there were fewer

With Latter-day Saint children in Osaka, Japan, 1954

than 16 who were over 30 years of age. What these young people will do in aiding in that conversion is best illustrated by two incidents.

A year ago last April while I was in the Hawaiian Islands I interviewed and set apart under instructions from the First Presidency six lovely young girls to go over to Japan as missionaries. One of them, a young Japanese sister, was a bit hesitant to go because she had come of a Buddhist family. Her mother had opposed her going. Her brother had beaten her rather cruelly because of her insistence on Church activity. She was almost a nervous wreck, but she had the faith that somehow the Lord would help her through her problems, and we sent her on her way.

I met her at one of these conferences, and she whispered to me her story. She said: "Twenty-three people, Brother Lee, are being attracted to the gospel partly by my efforts," and then she introduced me to an elderly grandmother, whose husband is an Episcopal minister, and the little girl, the granddaughter of this elderly grandmother, was the one who played for our singing during the conference. This little girl came home after she had joined the Church and said to her grandmother: "Grandma, your church is not true because you do not understand God, and you do not understand about the Godhead,'' and then she proceeded to teach her the missionary lesson about the Godhead.

This elderly grandmother said, "Any Church that can teach a child like that must have something." Our young Japanese missionary sister from the Hawaiian Islands now reports: "That grandmother is now preparing to become baptized a member of the Church through the missionary efforts of her little granddaughter, perhaps not more than 11 or 12 years of age."

There is another evidence of an awakening in Japan. Representatives of some of the leading newspapers in Japan, many of them, interviewed us, and wrote articles, both in English and Japanese. Our Japanese Saints were a bit amused about one of these articles where the heading was "Mormon Polygamist Visits Japan." Fortunately the misleading statement was corrected in the body of the article. Following that announcement we received an invitation from a group who styled themselves, "The League of New Japan's Religious Organizations," who claim to have a following of 10 million people. For the first time Japan is enjoying religious freedom. They asked that I meet with 15 leaders of these 15 religious organizations, comprising the league, and there discuss with them Mormonism, and then submit to a discussion following that time. Their invitation is a bit interesting!

"Invitation to the friendly talk meeting with one of the leaders of the 'Mormon' Church. As Rev. Harold B. Lee, who is one of the highest leaders of 'Mormon Church' (The Church of Jesus Christ of Latter-day Saints) which is one of the most influential churches in America, is visiting Japan on his journey to fulfill his mission in the Pacific Ocean area. In order to promote goodwill we would like to hold a friendly talk meeting. . . . Also, paying respect to the laws of Mormonism no refreshment of tea or cake will be served at that meeting."

For that hour, with Brother Tatsui Sato from the mission office translating my words, they listened. Of these men, none claimed to be Christians, and yet in the discussion that followed I learned that they were in truth more Christian than many of the so-called Christians who neither accept the divinity of the mission of Jesus nor of his reality as the Son of the living God.

They recorded my talk on a tape recorder, and when the half-hour was finished for discussion, they were still asking questions, so that our interview extended into two hours and a half, and that recording they promised later would be presented in the quarterly paper where they proposed to give it publicity. I told them that if they were interested and would send me their names and addresses, I would see that each got a copy of the Book of Mormon for them to study.

A few days later I received a letter in Japanese, which Brother Sato translated and wherein the president in charge gave me the names and addresses. His letter reads: "We have no words to express our thanks for your very instructive address, which you gave us the other day. Although you were very busy and must have been tired on your way to preach the gospel in the Oriental area, yet you shared your very precious time for us, for which we have to be very grateful."

Then he said: "May we take advantage of your words that you would present us the Book of Mormon, that we may understand better? We send you the list of names who attended the meeting."

Copies of the Book of Mormon have been sent to these leaders.

In Korea and Hong Kong

There is one thing more I should like to tell you about. At Pusan we have only three members on record, but when we arrived at our meeting, it was something of a surprise party for us. We found to our astonishment that we had in attendance not just three members, but besides our more than 100 servicemen we had 103 Koreans, mostly all young people of about high school age. As a part of the proceedings they presented to me this scroll, written on silk parchment, both in Korean and in English, in which they had written these words—mind you, this was written and presented by a group most all of whom were nonmembers:

"We sincerely welcome Apostle Harold B. Lee who come to Korea. The mission of his visiting Korea is very important and we are thankful to our Father in Heaven from our heart deeply for the great support you have given us for the people of Korea.

"Here we would like to express our gratitude to the soldiers who stayed in Korea and preached the true gospel to us and also the chance we have had of gathering together with them under the name of our Heavenly Father; therefore we are under a vow to repay their kindness. With thanks with all of our eulogy to you for your distinguished service of the faithfulness which will perform your important mission to come to our Korea, and visiting our Korea in spite of its long distance. We humbly pray in the name of Jesus Christ, Amen.

"From: Korean Group in Pusan of The Church of Jesus Christ of Latter-day Saints."

Well, that is significant because for the first time they too are enjoying religious freedom.

I must tell you, President McKay, about the meeting with our lovely Chinese folks down in Hong Kong. We had no meeting place. They have not had much opportunity since they were baptized. It

Holding silk scroll presented by members in Pusan, 1954

has now been nearly a year since they received the sacrament. But in our hotel room overlooking the harbor from Kowloon to Hong Kong we held a sacrament meeting. We bore testimony to them. We had gone up to that high point overlooking Hong Kong, where Brother Cowley, in company with President Robertson, President Aki, and their wives, had dedicated that land to the opening of a mission, July 14, 1949. There, too, we bowed our heads and thanked the Lord for the degree of Brother Cowley's blessing that had been received, and asked the Lord for a further outpouring of his blessing. Then, after we had visited briefly with these young Chinese students, we talked with one of them, a young girl—little Yook Sin Yuen—they call her Nora, a beautiful little girl who speaks good English, as taught her by the missionaries. As our bus pulled out from the hotel the next day to take us to the airport, she reached up her hand through the window and said to me as a parting word: "Brother Lee, tell President McKay to send the Church back to China." I said to her, as the tears were in my eyes also, "My dear, sweet girl, as long as we have a faithful, devoted little girl like you who, without a shepherd, is remaining true, the Church is in China."

Well, I say, President McKay, as I commenced, I have gone now at your appointment to the Far East and I have seen the miracles of God's intervention. We have seen that the gospel has been preached to the nations as an evidence of its divinity. God grant that the time shall not be far distant until the death grip of Communism shall be unloosed, and those worthy shall be free to receive the fulness of the gospel of Jesus Christ, for I am convinced that there are hundreds of thousands of souls who are begging for the truth.

I bear you my solemn testimony that I know these things are true, that he lives, and that this is his work, and I bear it humbly in the name of Jesus Christ, amen.

Humor Amid War

There were, of course, some very human and even humorous circumstances on this memorable assignment, which Elder Lee didn't express in his conference report. One of these occurred on August 24, 1954, when his party was leaving to catch a plane from Tokyo to Sapporo on Hokkaido. Through Chaplain Gilmore, senior chaplain, a staff car had been provided for Elder Lee's transportation. The chaplain asked Captain Forsythe, the LDS Group Leader from Florida, how many stars they should show on the side of the staff car. He answered: "Sir, you don't have stars enough for this car!"

The Japanese Emperor and his party boarded a plane at Chitose that same day, within a two-block area of where the servicemen were having their meeting with Elder Lee, but not one of our boys left the meeting.

Another amusing journal entry appeared on September 3, 1954. The Lee party took a short thirty-minute flight to "Abel 2," the headquarters of the Ninth Corps, commanded by General Canham, with whom they had a brief visit and with whom they later had lunch, along with his entire staff. There were between 230 and 240 young men in attendance at the LDS servicemen's meeting and the spirit was excellent. Mission President Robertson became ill from something he ate at the lunch and through the night was challenged by the night guard each time he went from their tent to the rest room and was forced to give the secret password; ironically, the word was *ache,* after which the guard's salutation answer was *green.* Elder Lee thought that under the circumstances the military chose most appropriate passwords.

It was here that Elder Lee referred to coming within a few hundred miles of where war was brewing, as he flew within sight of enemy lines at the demilitarized zone on September 4, 1954. A large six-foot two-inch Captain Leives, whom Elder Lee had last seen as one of his fifth grade students at the Woodrow Wilson School in Salt Lake County, was his pilot. He requested permission of his commanding officer to fly Elder Lee over to "Abel 143" in an F19, a single-motor, four-passenger plane. The pilot took Elder Lee up the Chun Huan Valley where an entire division of ROK troops had been annihilated. Then they flew over the DMZ (Demilitarized Zone), where they could see the smoke from the Chinese camps and the PoppaSan Mountain, which marked the highly fortified area where the enemy set up their defenses.

LESSONS AND RECOMMENDATIONS

Many audiences have heard Elder Lee tell a famous servicemen's story which occurred on this trip, concerning the boast of a soldier concerning his virtue, which Elder Lee knew had been heard by Satan. At a meeting with the servicemen at Camp Crawford on August 25, 1954, a serviceman brother delivered a spirited talk on chastity and declared that he "would rather have his 'dog tags' sent home ahead of his body in a pine box," than lose his chastity. As he closed his talk he collapsed on the stand, and then fainted a second time after he was taken to his seat.

When Elder Lee spoke to the servicemen's audience he told this brother and the men that the devil, who had heard his pledge, would confront him with every possible evil temptation to force him to break that pledge. The next day, Captain Forsythe took Elder Lee aside to tell him of the struggle he and others had in keeping this soldier away from the bars in Chitose and had almost had to force him to break a date a few days before with a prostitute.

As an evidence of the temptations with which the servicemen were faced Elder Lee recorded in his diary this description:

> The town of Chitose, which reputedly has 4,000 prostitutes and purveyors of all kinds of vice to entice the servicemen, is known as the most wicked town in the world. One of our boys, Elder Thomas, however, shows how he resisted the evil. He makes only $70 per month and was sending $50 a month to keep a brother in the mission field. He saved $12 each month by laundering and

pressing his own uniforms, a fee which they would otherwise be charged.

The visit to Korea was the first ever made to that country by a General Authority, and Elder Lee felt he was well received because of the familiarity the people of that country had with his surname. His diary entry of September 2, 1954, emphasizes these points:

> Two general sessions were held in the Seoul Post Chapel at 10 a.m. and 2 p.m. at which we had an attendance of 325 and 338 from surrounding camps under the supervision of Chaplain Richard Henstrom. Two chaplains and two group leaders spoke at each session, along with Dr. H. J. Kim, a native Korean, who is a graduate of Cornell University. In their talks the brethren were impressed with the fact that my visit is the first of any General Authority to visit Korea. An interesting coincidence was that of the 298 family and over 2,000 Korean clan names, the four most predominating were Kim, Yi, Chang, and Lee. Dr. Kim said that Korea is greatly in need of spiritual rehabilitation and is hoping for a building (chapel) soon in which the Church here can be developed. The boys were loathe to leave for their camps and kept us for an hour having their pictures taken individually with us.

Elder Lee closed his Japanese tour with the concluding meeting at the all-missionary conference at Nikko, the beauty spot of all Japan in its mountain resort setting, where 103 baptisms were reported as of September 15, 1954, for the year. In the meeting lasting from 6:00 A.M. until 12:30 P.M., missionaries testified of many miracles. Elder Lee's thoughts were also of the one missionary absent. As he closed the meeting Elder Lee remembered Elder Ben Oniki, who was confined in a Tokyo hospital. Following his return to Tokyo the presidency of the mission and Elder Lee visited Elder Oniki at the hospital and gave him a blessing. Two days later his fever and blood count were normal and the scheduled operation was cancelled as unnecessary.

The vast lessons learned through personal experiences in the Orient were not forgotten by Elder Lee. He followed up on the impressions of the Spirit, but it was early in 1955 before his recommendations were being considered. Specifically, he recommended plans to divide the Japanese Mission and to get missionary work started in Korea to take advantage of the work done by the Latter-day Saint servicemen, Dr. Ho Jik Kim, and others.

The action on Elder Lee's recommendation came in the temple meeting of the First Presidency and Quorum of the Twelve on

Thursday, April 7, 1955, when it was decided to divide both the Australian and the Japanese missions. In this decision the Northern Far East Mission and the Southern Far East Mission were created from the former Japanese Mission. Korea, Japan, and Okinawa were placed in the Northern Far East Mission, with headquarters at Tokyo, Japan; and Hong Kong, Kowloon, Macao, the Philippines, and Guam were to comprise the Southern Far East Mission, with headquarters at Hong Kong.

This announcement was made public on May 5, 1955, and Elder Joseph Fielding Smith was assigned to visit the Japanese Mission and make the division as outlined. As this action was being taken, Chaplain Spencer Palmer, just home from Korea, reported to Elder Lee that there were then thirty-six members of the Church in Pusan, after the withdrawal of the servicemen.

1956–1958. Desk-top computer developed in the United States by Burroughs. Packard car, the last of the breed. Egyptians seized Suez Canal. Jack Kilby of Texas Instruments combined silicon transistors, resistors, and capacitors in a single chip. Thunderbird restyled from the 1955 T-Bird.

CHAPTER 16

To Mexico, South Africa, and the Holy Land

On June 7, 1956, Elder Lee, with Elder Spencer W. Kimball, his wife Camilla, and mission leaders, drove from El Paso, Texas, to Monterrey, Mexico, then left Monterrey at 6:15 A.M. for Mexico City the next day. Fully half of the more than six hundred miles of highway wound through rugged mountain passes. It was a delightful trip because of the magnificent scenery, but the party arrived exhausted after sixteen hours of mountain travel over incredibly poor roads.

MEXICAN MISSION DIVIDED

Sunday, June 10, 1956, saw the division of the Mexican Mission, which had been originally created from the Spanish-American Mission in 1936, and later was divided from the Central American Mission in 1952. Now the mission was ready again for division because in ten years the Church membership had grown from 3,400 Saints to a population of over 9,000.

The missionwide conference was held at Ermita on Sunday, with representation from as far away as Pugra Nugras and Tampico, and Puebla and Vera Cruz. Elders Lee and Kimball divided the Mexican Mission and officially created the new Northern Mexican Mission, the forty-fifth mission of the Church, with President Joseph T. Bentley as the mission president.

Elder Lee was pleased and thrilled to see many of the former "dissenters" now safely back in the fold. He renewed his acquaintance with these friends since his last visit to Mexico twelve years before, and rejoiced in meeting with many of the old faithfuls like Brothers Isaias, Juarey, Zarroga, and Parra.

After the division of the mission the two Apostles separated, with Elder Lee taking the Mexican Mission and Elder Kimball traveling through the new Northern Mission. Elder Lee's first meeting was a ten-and-a-half-hour testimony meeting with the seventy-nine missionaries remaining in the southern portion of the mission. With few exceptions all came fasting, and there was a rich outpouring of the Spirit. Elder Lee saw and appreciated the excellent manner in which President Bowman directed and inspired his young missionaries in the work.

The two mission presidents each coveted the services of one particularly outstanding potential leader, Elder Rex Edwin Lee, a great-grandson of famed pioneer, John D. Lee. President Bowman was fortunate to have Elder Lee become his counselor. He was later to distinguish himself as the first dean of the Brigham Young University law school, and went on to become Solicitor General for the United States.

At the several stops along the mission tour Elder Lee compared his impressions with those he remembered when he was last in Mexico, twelve years before. He was particularly impressed with the progress of the Mexican Saints in San Marcos, Puebla, and Cuernavaca. At the Hidalgo District of San Marcos the people were better dressed, now wore shoes, and their entertainment was much more polished. They also had a new chapel and a new school.

Travel difficulties were frequent. On their return trip from San Marcos they experienced a freak accident when a broken bolt fell into the carburetor of the president's car, causing it to stick and

With Elder Rex E. Lee (left) and Mexican Mission president, Claudius Bowman

Mexican Mission Home, 1956

damage the starter. Providentially, they were still able to drive the car home, arriving at 1:30 A.M.

The next day, June 16, 1956, the party left the mission home for Cuernavaca where Elder Lee dedicated a small chapel which had been neatly remodeled for the small congregation there. Here Elder Lee saw the most promising group yet in terms of intelligence and refinement. This was partly due to a young trained nurse who had been schooled at Brigham Young University. While there they met a Judge Gonzales, about sixty-five years of age, who seemed most interested in the Church and at his request was granted the privilege of speaking at the conference.

Early the next morning they left the mission home for Puebla, nearly one hundred miles over the mountains, for a Sunday conference. "Here," wrote Elder Lee,

> I was privileged to enjoy one of the biggest surprises yet to observe the impressive progress made here since my visit to this same group twelve years ago. They are housed in a fine, new meetinghouse. Approximately 50 percent (or 552) of their district membership attended. With but few exceptions they were well dressed. They sang well, the local speakers spoke well, the chapel was sumptuously decorated with flowers, and the leadership of the local brethren performed with confidence. All this is in marked contrast to the crude little groups we met on my last visit.

The next night a meeting was held at Vera Cruz on the Gulf of Mexico. Although only twenty-two members resided there, the attendance at the meeting reached ninety-two, all crowded into the two small rooms where the four Elders had living quarters. This, Elder Lee reported, "was one of the most promising groups we have yet met. They seem intelligent and enthusiastic and from all indications there should be a harvest here soon." At Tierra Blanca, twelve baptisms were reported that week.

The mission tour took Elder Lee's party to historic locations where they could view the archaeological ruins of Mexico's past. From Villahermosa they transferred to a single-engine Cessna airplane for Palenque, the place some Latter-day Saint archaeologists claim was the Land Bountiful and therefore near the alleged center where the Savior made his appearance to the Nephites. This was an interesting but most primitive area tucked away in the jungles, the ruins being about twenty kilometers (twelve to fifteen miles) from the town. The ruins here and at Chichen Itza were then regarded as the most famed yet discovered. Here Elder Lee found evidences of Christianity followed by pagan or mystic corruptions which all but obliterated the simple Christian doctrines or Mosaic observances which probably were once practiced here. As the party made their way back to Palenque and Villahermosa and thence to Merida, via Carmen and Comeche, Elder Lee was convinced the area possessed good possibilities for future missionary work and determined to encourage it as an expansion of the Mexican Mission.

Elder Lee was especially impressed with the possibilities at Merida, which he described as "a city of 160,000, which is to my thinking one of the cleanest-looking cities and its people the best dressed of any we have visited yet, including Mexico City." More archaeological ruins at Chichen Itza, eighty miles away, were also seen. This famous area showed but little of Christianity, but more of the superstitions of the Aztecs and the Toltecs, who followed the Mayans.

At Monte Alban, in the vicinity of Oaxaco, Elder Lee saw some of the most artistically decorated ruins he had yet observed. Monte Alban was apparently a burial ground for kings or priests of high station. In some of the tombs have been found fabulous wealth in ornaments with which the dead were buried. Here were found symbols of three and twelve, and Elder Lee noted that the cross was seen in the tombs and on the stelas. Some scholars told Elder Lee that this location is thought to have been the land of the Mulekites, who probably followed and overlapped the Jaredite civilization.

In his last day in Mexico, June 26, 1956, Elder Lee went shopping and bought some trinkets for his "little ones." He found himself, however, becoming very ill with chills and severe abdominal pains. He arrived home weak and most uncomfortable. He learned four days later that Elder Kimball had similar symptoms on his return. Both reported for physical examinations by Dr. LeRoy Kimball, who thought they might have picked up some infection at about the same time which had matured in both of them as they returned home.

TOUR OF SOUTH AFRICA

On Thursday, August 15, 1958, President McKay called Elder Lee to his office and announced that the First Presidency had assigned him, with Fern to accompany him, to tour the South African Mission as soon as arrangements could be made.

While Elder Lee was conducting the quarterly meeting of the Council of the Twelve in the absence of President Joseph Fielding Smith on September 11, 1958, he received the prayers and blessings of his Brethren for the South African Mission to which he was assigned.

On the night of September 15, 1958, Harold and Fern went to President Clark's home where their aging friend gave each of them a blessing for their assignment. In each blessing he counseled them to use wisdom in dealing with the racial questions and to avoid extravagance in any promise of temples and similar blessings. He also blessed them with protection, health, and discernment.

Before leaving the next day Elder Lee talked with President McKay by telephone. The latter had just returned the previous night from the dedication of the London Temple and his voice sounded very tired as he asked Elder Lee to give the Saints in South Africa his blessings. President Clark's final farewell was a somewhat pessimistic statement that he hoped to be around when the Lees returned, to which Elder Lee stated, "The Lord bless you, President." President Clark replied: "Well, he always has. My legs are shaky, but I'm glad I don't have to think with my legs."

Through friends and connections with Elder Lee's acquaintances in the banking, railroading, and insurance industries, and government officials in Washington, D.C., they were able to obtain many letters of introduction which secured them favors and opportunities for their travel abroad.

After a one-day visit to Rome, Italy, Elder and Sister Lee left on October 3, 1958, for South Africa, arriving in Johannesburg only one hour late the next day. The long trip plus immediate involvements in a Church social after their arrival completely exhausted Sister Lee, and she came down with a severe sinus infection. However, after being administered to by President Fisher, Brother Smith, and her husband, she showed a remarkable recovery.

At the first Sunday conference meeting, on October 5, 1958, Elder Lee dedicated a new chapel completed a year previous at a cost of about $100,000. The local architect, a Mr. Sayce, spoke at the services and made this astute and interesting comment: "I and my associates have given you a structure of brick and mortar, but you alone can make it a house of God." At this first meeting with leading African Saints, Elder Lee learned that much greater progress could be made if some literature might be printed in their native Afrikaans language. It was a recommendation he was to remember and act on.

Elder Lee went to Pretoria, the administrative capital of the Union of South Africa, where his attempt to increase the missionary quota for the Church was not accepted. From such contacts he learned how similar the early Dutch history resembled our Church pioneer story from Nauvoo to the Salt Lake Valley. The party made a memorable visit to Kruger Park, where the people, not the wild animals, are locked up for safety.

The visit to Durban was a particularly interesting and moving experience. The Lees were still tired from their hard ride of the day before but left early for Durban and their next conference. The trip took them through surprisingly fertile country and small but modernized villages, all of which seemed to have splendid missionary possibilities, most of it untouched, thought Elder Lee. The major problem was the great distances and inadequate transportation facilities for the missionaries. The mission president had therefore urged the moving of mission headquarters to Johannesburg from Capetown to provide for better administration and centralized supervision. Elder Lee could see evidence now to support that recommendation. The weather in Durban, which is located on the east coast, was unusually cool for October, contrasted with the 107 degrees the travelers experienced the previous Sunday. Under overcast skies they visited the "Indian Market," where imported goods from India and Malaya can be purchased.

The Saints in Durban expressed concern at the possibility of the black population, which far outnumbered the white people, one day becoming united under Communism and taking over the control of the country. Emigration to Canada and the United States was on their minds. They were also asking Elder Lee as to the possibility of patriarchal blessings and the obtaining of temple recommends to the far-distant London Temple. A lovely social was held in their fine seaport branch of the Natal District, of which Durban is the capital city.

The spiritual highlight of Elder Lee's visit to South Africa may have occurred on Sunday, October 12, 1958. That busy and memorable day is described in Elder Lee's diary as follows:

> I held meetings from 9:00 a.m. until 9:00 p.m. with from 200 to 250 in attendance, some coming from Bloomfintein over 300 miles away. Their new chapel, erected at a cost of $90,000, was dedicated

With Church leaders in Durban, South Africa, 1958

at the afternoon session. The Spirit seemed to direct our remarks, which were said to have been as well suited to the specific needs of those present as though we had known beforehand their problems. After I had finished speaking in the evening session and the meeting was closed, the people remained seated. Their branch president came forward and asked them what they were waiting for and if they wanted to hear more. There was a chorus reply of "Yes." I arose again and bore my testimony and gave them my blessing. It was a most impressive demonstration of a people seemingly overcome by the Spirit. Some came afterwards to confess their sins and to declare their determination to live more perfectly.

As Elder Lee traveled through this fascinating country he studied their racial ways of segregation. The native Bantu throughout the country were in great majority, numbering ten million to the three million whites in the Union who politically and socially dominate them. They lived literally on the ground, eating, sleeping, working, playing, and caring for personal needs in primitive ways. They performed most of the menial work for the Afrikaans and the English, and at a price which discouraged any other than the natives from performing the work.

Traveling toward East London on the southeast coast their fifty-mile trip took them through Basutoland, one of the three huge areas of South Africa where the native Bantus had been colonized. For hundreds of miles along the hillsides were seen their "rondovals," or adobe huts, all cone-shaped in appearance. The history of South Africa was further described to Elder Lee when a fellow automobile passenger, a Brother Helm who was a college professor at Rhodes University, detailed the past and present conditions in that interesting country.

At Capetown Elder Lee visited on a Saturday afternoon a diamond cutting and polishing plant. There they met Mr. Jacob Coopman, the foreman, who had become most friendly with our Saints. Through him Elder Lee arranged to purchase for his wife, Fern, a beautifully polished diamond in a new setting and had the small stone from her original engagement ring made into an earring, buying another stone to match for an earring set.

This was the story which became famous among family members and answered the question Fern often asked of her husband, "What ever happened to your slide trombone?" The trombone of his first married years had been sold to purchase the small stone, which Fern treasured far more than Elder Lee realized. She was visibly and emotionally moved with the new treasures from the South African diamond industry, but Elder Lee never knew how sentimental she had grown toward the ring she had worn all her life until it had almost become a part of her. How could she tell him now? She accepted her new gifts with the love intended from her sweetheart, and cried within at the loss of her irreplaceable engagement ring.

This same manager at the diamond company, Mr. Coopman, came to the missionaries at the close of the Sunday Capetown conference and said that although he was 99 percent converted before he talked with Elder Lee, he was now closer than ever. He said to Elder Lee when he shook his hand: "I was so filled when you spoke that I could hardly keep from crying." The Capetown conference drew 185 at the morning meeting and 263 in the evening, from a branch membership of 325.

The tour continued with a dedication of a meetinghouse in Port Elizabeth where the Saints again showered the Lee party with gifts. The young Church members sought the advice of this, the first Apostle to visit their land since President David O. McKay. Elder Lee turned to the Lord in counseling three girls who had mixed blood on what the Lord would have them do about marriage and having children. After giving them priesthood blessings he wrote in his journal: "The Spirit seemed to indicate that they should seek for a husband who likewise has mixed blood. I gave them assurances of their eternal blessings if they would live up to all they are permitted to do in their present state." This was typical of many members of mixed blood who came to discuss this problem with the touring General Authority.

Turning northward, the party moved into beautiful Rhodesia, which in October was a country ablaze with the brilliantly colored jacaranda and flamboyant bougainvillea vines, making this famed "copperbelt" a scene of splendor. While in this area Elder Lee witnessed and photographed the famed Victoria Falls, a spectacular sight as the mile-wide, powerful Zambezi River drops into a three-hundred-foot crevice. His rainbow photograph later was honored with placement on the cover of the Church's *Ensign* magazine.

On October 24, 1958, at Springs, Elder Lee held a concluding meeting with 261 persons in attendance. The following day he made his final interview of missionaries and the South African tour was closed with many unforgettable memories to ponder.

First Visit to the Holy Land

The highlight of the 35,000-mile trip came at the conclusion of their three-week mission to South Africa. Passing through Egypt, they came to the Holy Land for their first visit.

First, there were many evidences on this journey that God was with them, guarding them and opening doors for the accomplishment of the Lord's business. Upon his return home Elder Lee, as he spoke before an appreciative audience of Brigham Young University students, recounted in these words the blessings they had experienced:

> We had his healing powers from sinus infections, from head colds and congestion. He tempered the elements in places where extremes of heat and humidity could have hindered our travel and our work. He gave us a safe landing in Nairobi, the center of the great Kenya hunting area when one of the engines of the plane quit on us. He gave us a pleasant night and safe passage through Khartoum, the capitol of Sudan, a scant two weeks before a bloodless

revolution of the military took over the government of that unhappy African state. He helped us time our arrival in Arab countries of Lebanon and Jordan one day after the departure of the United States Marines from Beirut in answer to our prayers that somehow the way might be opened up for a visit to the Holy Land which we could not have had, had we been there a few days earlier. He raised up friends among American embassies, travel agents, and world news agencies, except for whom we could have been stranded in strange lands.

Surviving the airplane engine failure, Elder and Sister Lee visited Cairo, Egypt, and saw the famed pyramid and the Sphinx, located twelve kilometers out of the city.

Then, for three glorious days, on October 28–30, 1958, they "walked on sacred ground and felt the influence of the greatest character who ever lived upon this earth, Jesus the Christ, the very Son of the living God." Elder Lee entitled his recap of this unforgettable experience, "I Walked Today Where Jesus Walked," after the popular and lovely, sacred song.

Explaining the approach Elder and Sister Lee used in seeking truth in the Holy Land, Elder Lee wrote:

> As we approached the Holy Land we read together the harmony of the four gospel narratives so beautifully authored by President Clark and then, as we would leave our room each time, we prayed that the Lord would deafen our ears to what the guide said about historical places, but would make us keenly sensitive to the spiritual feeling so that we would know by impressions from the Holy Spirit, rather than by hearing, where the sacred spots were located. Although many changes have taken place in this sacred land since Jesus was there, we felt that in certain places there would still linger a spiritual essence that will last forever.

The Lees hired a car with an Arab guide, Hashem, who spoke excellent English and possessed a good knowledge of the Bible narrative and history. The first test of their spiritual discernment came as they rode with their guide along the seven miles from the walled city of Jerusalem to the town of Bethlehem. The words and strains of that sweet Christmas hymn, "O Little Town of Bethlehem," were on their minds and they presently were, as it seemed, with the shepherds at the mouth of the cave hewn out of rock now found in the basement of the Church of the Nativity. Elder Lee wrote of this visit: "There seemed to be in this place a kind of spiritual assurance that this was, indeed, a hallowed spot although marred by centuries of 'unhallowed embellishment.' It marks a sacred place."

Out beyond Jericho, the city of palms, the Lees again found a "wonderful spirit on the banks of the Jordan River, for here was the same river, the same locality, running as it had down through the centuries. It was here that the courageous John the Baptist had baptized the Son of Man, not . . . [by] pouring water on his head, as we saw pictured in the great painting in the St. Peter's Cathedral in Rome, but by immersion in the River Jordan 'because there was much water there.' "

The cottage of Martha and Mary and Lazarus, three miles out of the walled city of Jerusalem, and the Mount of Olives were also described as "sacred ground."

One of the most deeply spiritual places seen by Elder Lee and his companion was on the west slope of a mountain, near the Brook Cedron. Here in the Garden of Gethsemane are eight old gnarled olive trees showing evidence of great antiquity. They could have been just sprouts from trees that could have been there hundreds of years before, reasoned the Lees. It was here Jesus came after the Last Supper with his disciples, when he knew his hour of suffering was close at hand. He asked Peter, James, and John to stay with him in the Garden, and to watch for his enemies, lest he be disturbed while he was praying. Then Jesus prayed. When he returned to the disciples he found them sleeping and showed his disappointment in them. Elder Lee said of this powerful experience: "It was here where he kneeled, in the vicinity of the very spot where we were standing. We fancied we could hear again the agonized words of his intense suffering which he has given us in his revelations."

Time now was running out on the Lees' visit to Jerusalem. They had followed their guide through the traditional hall of judgment, where the Master was beaten and sentenced to death by a tribunal which made mockery of justice. They followed the way of the cross, supposedly to the place of crucifixion and the place of the holy sepulchre. Of this, however, Elder Lee wrote:

> But all of this, according to tradition, we felt is in the wrong place. We felt none of the spiritual significance which we had felt at other places, for had not the Apostle Paul said, speaking of the crucifixion: "Wherefore Jesus also, that he might sanctify the people with his own blood, *suffered without the gate.*" (Hebrews 13:12.) To us, we felt this meant he suffered to his death upon the cross for the sins of

mankind, not within the gates of Jerusalem, but outside the gates, and yet the guides were trying to make us think that his crucifixion took place inside the walls. Again, what we were seeing there did not square with John's description of the place where the crucifixion and burial took place, as John described it in John 19:41–42.

There was yet another place to visit where the Lees felt that they were on holy ground: the place called the Garden Tomb. It is owned by the Church of the United Brethren. Elder Lee remembered that moment in these words:

> Here our woman guide and her little son took us, as though it were an afterthought, through the garden to the hill outside the "gate" of the walled city of Jerusalem. It was just a short way from where the hall of judgment had been inside the city walls. The garden was right close by or "in the hill" as John had said, and in it was a sepulchre hewn out of a rock, evidently done by someone who could afford the expense of excellent workmanship. There was something that seemed to impress us as we stood there, that this was the holiest place of all, and we fancied we could have witnessed the dramatic scene which took place there. That tomb has a mouth which could be sealed by a rolling stone in the shape of a huge millstone and there was a channel at its mouth that had been built to guide the stone as it had been rolled across the opening to close the tomb. Although the rolling stone door had been taken away by those seeking sacred relics, the stone channel was still there. Within the tomb there is a room large enough to accommodate a half-dozen people; and across one end is a slab raised about a foot and a half from the floor beautifully carved out to fit a human body, with a place at the foot and the head where one might sit.
>
> In the beautiful garden, the holiest place of all, we looked at the hill nearby and gazed into the empty tomb. The sun was setting and the soft shadows fell around us, shutting out the whole world as it seemed. The peace of those few moments we shall never forget. Yes, at the Garden Tomb, outside the walls, we had the feeling that it, and the Mount of Golgotha, or the skull, seemed right. They were the holiest of all.

Following these days in Old Jerusalem on the Jordan side, the Lees passed through the Mandelbaum Gate, which in those days was the only means of communication between the Jordan side, where Old Jerusalem was located, and the Israel side, beleaguered by intense and bitter fighting. They were entertained that night in the King David Hotel in the New City of Jerusalem on the Israel side.

As we looked out that night from the veranda of our hotel room, there, silhouetted against the sky, was Mount Zion, and there was King David's tower, marking, as they told us, the place where they say the Last Supper was held just before He went down to the Brook Cedron and to His betrayal and judgment and finally to death. Here on this Mount Zion, or in America's New Jerusalem (our students of the scriptures are not in agreement as to which), is to be commenced the greatest drama of the whole history of the world to usher in the Second Coming of the Lord. (See D&C 133:18, 22.)

Then the Lees were taken the next morning in a car which government officials from Israel had graciously provided, and they went over the rocky slopes along the Jaffa Road to Tel Aviv and to the airport. They noted the back-breaking work of the returning Jews to make the "desert blossom as a rose," as the prophets had foretold. Fern summarized this never-to-be-forgotten experience as follows:

> Here closed our wonderful opportunity to come to this great land. As I have thought about it since that time, I know that our prayers had been answered and the glorious truths of the mission of our Lord and Savior were anchored deep in our hearts. My heart sings out with love and gratitude for him who has done so much for us; and the wonder and the glory of it all was beyond understanding.

Elder Lee's conclusion was a personal testimony:

> As we stood before the empty tomb in Jerusalem we too knew that because of this sacrifice, we too can have our sins remitted and be made worthy to stand in his holy presence in the days to come. I came away from these experiences never to feel the same again about the mission of the Lord and Savior and to have impressed upon me, as I have never had it impressed before, what it means to be a special witness. I say to you with all the conviction of my soul, I know that Jesus lives. I know that he was the very Son of God and I know that in this Church and in the Gospel of Jesus Christ entrusted to this Church is to be found the way to salvation.

THE HOMEWARD JOURNEY

The travel homeward was rich also in its experiences and opportunities. The Lees first visited Athens, Greece, for a brief tour of the Greek Parthenon, the Acropolis, Mars Hill, and the Market Place where the Apostle Paul preached. Elder Lee was discouraged about opening up missionary work in this country after a visit with the American ambassador.

A visit to Vatican City outside Rome came as the Catholics were making preparations for the coronation of their new pope. Although they marvelled at the works of art found at St. Peter's Cathedral, Elder Lee observed in his diary: "There was in all this not one semblance of the sacredness we experienced in the Garden near Golgotha where our Savior was laid."

Next the Lees saw for the first time the new Swiss Temple and were greatly impressed by the beauty of that sacred building, its decoration, and the dignity and spirituality evidenced by temple president Walter Trauffer. President Trauffer also took the Lees on a tour of the Swiss Alps, of which Elder Lee wrote: "Never have we seen more beautiful and picturesque scenery."

After meeting with and speaking to three hundred servicemen and their wives in the Heidelberg post chapel, the Lees moved on to Paris and finally to London via Edinburgh, Scotland, where they spent two days searching for Sister Lee's family connections with the famous Coats posterity.

A visit to the new London Temple closed out this memorable tour. After enjoying a three-hour drive through the beautiful Southern English countryside the party came to Southhampton, where they boarded the *Queen Elizabeth* for an ocean voyage to America. As they departed on November 15, 1958, they celebrated Sister Lee's birthday and their thirty-fifth wedding anniversary. To mark the occasion Elder Lee gave his wife the diamond earrings he had brought from South Africa, one of which was the precious stone taken from her old diamond engagement ring.

At sea Elder Lee complained at the forced idleness and wrote: "The hardest work I do, I have discovered, is to loaf for a few days with nothing to do." He did, however, busy himself the first day at sea, spending most of the afternoon and the next day writing: "I recorded our report of the South African Mission and the other countries where I inquired as to the possibilities of missionary work being established."

On November 19, 1958, the fog lifted as the massive *Queen Elizabeth* arrived in New York harbor, giving Elder and Sister Lee a thrilling view of the Statue of Liberty, the symbol "of all we hold dear so far as political freedom is concerned."

The safe arrival in Salt Lake City after a long, three-month, 35,000-mile journey provided a joyous reunion; all the family members, some of the Quorum of the Twelve, and a few other friends were on hand to greet the weary travelers. The family retreated to Helen's home for supper and a belated birthday celebration for Fern. The Lees' grandchildren were almost as excited as at Christmas as they opened presents of gidget knives for the boys, jewelry for the girls, and toys for the little ones, and sweaters and cuff links for the fathers.

1959. Sixteen dead as earthquakes smashed into West Yellowstone. Alaska and Hawaii joined the Union as new states.

CHAPTER 17

Tour of South America

On July 30, 1959, President McKay phoned Elder Lee to announce that the First Presidency had appointed Sister Lee and him to visit the South American missions, beginning the latter part of October, and to open two new missions in Brazil and Chile-Peru. J. Vernon Sharp had been named as the president of the new mission in the Andes, and Asael T. Sorenson, who recently had presided over the Brazilian Mission, was now being asked to return as the president of the new South Brazilian Mission.

When Elder Lee investigated with travel agents his tentative schedule, he found it would be impossible to leave in late October and be home by Christmas, and reservations by ship could not be obtained. As a result, President Moyle urged that they leave earlier to escape the intense heat which occurs in South American countries toward the last of the year, even though it would result in their absence from general conference.

In mid-August President Clark phoned Elder Lee several times to arrange for a private meeting before he left for South America. Urging that Elder Lee come alone, President Clark again reiterated counsel and conditions he had previously told him concerning matters he felt needed attention, apparently feeling that at his age he might not live long enough to see them carried out.

Having told his family farewell, Elder Lee arrived at the Salt Lake City airport for departure (Sister Lee was scheduled to join him later in New York City), and just before the plane left, President David O. McKay and his counselor, President Henry D. Moyle, arrived to see him off. In a few minutes of counsel together President McKay stated: "Your main mission is primarily to organize the two new missions—the Brazilian South Mission and the Andes Mission. The decision of where the headquarters for each new mission would be is left to your judgment, but I hope you get the inspiration of the Spirit to have Lima, Peru, as the headquarters for that mission." To this suggestion Elder Lee replied, "So far as I am concerned the Spirit has already spoken."

President McKay then instructed Elder Lee further as to the presentation of the new mission presidencies for each new mission. He asked that Elder Lee meet with all the missionaries, but that he not be concerned about a full mission tour to all branches. He then spoke with some emotion of his concern about Sister McKay's physical condition and expressed appreciation for Sister Lee's sweet note to his wife during her illness. It was an unexpected thrill, reported Elder Lee, to have the President of the Church come to the airport for the farewell instruction and blessing.

After a safe landing at Idlewild Airport in New York City, despite having the plane's number one engine quit and another one catch on fire, Elder Lee attended his monthly corporation board meetings in the East before leaving for South America. Gradually he was becoming better known to business tycoons in America, and he used his popularity to explain the gospel whenever possible at such meetings.

One such typical opportunity came at the August 20, 1959 meeting of the Equitable Life Assurance of America meeting when the directors met for dinner at a private club. Bob Hogg, vice chairman of the board, asked Elder Lee to tell the board about the welfare plan of the Church, which he did for about an hour. This provoked a number of questions from Judge John C. Knox about the Church's missionary work. Manley Fleishman asked about the effect of the Church's efforts on the public relief load of the state of Utah, and Grant Keehn asked about the efficiency of the Church's storage program, as against savings in a bank. The interest in the group was so high that Elder Lee was requested to repeat his discussion when all the board members were present.

Brent and Helen brought Sister Lee to New York City by airplane to join Elder Lee. It was a memorable time of family togetherness in joint rooms at the Waldorf Astoria Hotel. And Elder Lee delighted in showing the big city to his family. Brent had been invited to receive a recognition, about which Elder Lee recorded the following in his diary: "After the New York Stake conference on Sunday, August 23, 1959, in the afternoon we went to the Metropolitan Opera House where Brent was accepted as a fellow of the American College of Hospital Administrators, which is comparable professionally to a master's degree in that field." The following day they proudly watched the winning LDS Hospital's slide show sponsored by the Hospital Volunteer-Auxiliary at the American Hospital Association's national convention, which featured Helen and Brent's son Drew as a child actor.

Elder and Sister Lee sailed from New York for South America on the S.S. *Brazil* on the afternoon of Saturday, August 29, 1959. "The weather was very hot and muggy and we were grateful for the cool sea breezes as we cleared the port," wrote Elder Lee.

A glimpse into Fern's thoughtful kindness and sensitivity is found as she responded to the birthday celebration about to be observed by eleven-year-old Kristine Sorensen, a daughter of President Asael T. Sorensen, who with his wife and young family of six children was returning on the same ship to preside over the new Brazil South Mission. They had only been home from their first mission to Brazil eight months when they were called again.

When the ship dropped anchor in the bay off the town of Georgetown, in the Barbados, the most easterly of the West Indies, Sister Lee wrote her grandson David, who was celebrating his twelfth birthday, and also shopped for a gift for Kristine Sorensen. But Fern had the foresight to also bring small gifts for each of the Sorensen children, besides Kristine. This proved to be most satisfying to all, especially to little nine-year-old Colleen, who felt left out by all the big birthday celebration aboard ship as the crew sang "Happy Birthday" to Kristine.

At the special "tea" for grandmothers, Fern won the prize for the largest number of grandchildren and for the best saying of one of their grandchildren. She quoted twelve-year-old David's statement when his mother wanted him to bathe his younger brother Jonathan. David said, "Mom, I'd rather bulldog a steer."

President Sorensen, in recording his oral history at the Church Historical Department, recalled: "Elder Harold B. Lee, who at that time was one of the Twelve, was on the same boat, and he had been assigned to go to Brazil to divide the mission and to install us. So we enjoyed a wonderful trip down by boat and had many choice experiences with Brother and Sister Lee going to Brazil. Sister Lee endeared herself to our daughters and referred to them as her "little women.""

After a week at sea Brother and Sister Lee found their physical strength returning. Elder Lee wrote: "I'm feeling a return to normal health and vigor and hopefully believe that my physical difficulties are greatly lessened. Fern seems to have enjoyed this voyage."

The diary entry concerning their health had reference to the stressful conditions Elder Lee faced only two months previously. On July 7, 1959, Elder Lee was rushed to the LDS Hospital at 1:00 A.M., where doctors determined he had suffered from an internal hemorrhage. A bleeding ulcer in the duodenal canal detected one year previous had erupted and caused Elder Lee to faint at the end of a family dinner party at their home. Weeks of careful diet and rest had restored him sufficiently for this journey to South America.

In the same month he had the strain of his mother dying—on July 28—of a heart attack. As was so often the case, Elder Lee was traveling on Church business. He was paged to an emergency call at the Madison Square Garden in New York City and informed that his mother had been taken to the hospital with a coronary occlusion. Before he could leave New York by airplane to return home, he received notice of her death.

The funeral for Louisa Bingham Lee was held on July 30, 1959, in Salt Lake City. Speakers were President Henry D. Moyle and Lee Palmer, her home teacher. President Moyle quoted verbatim from Elder Lee's last testimony in the temple sacrament meeting, which talk he gave at the request of President McKay. Elder Lee summarized the life of his mother by the comment: "Everything seemed to be in perfect harmony with Mother's life, whose last days were, as the patriarch had promised years ago, 'her best days.' She was ready to go home. She had saved the entire cost of her burial and last illness."

These pressures were now in the past as Brother and Sister Lee were about to commence their tour of South America. In blessing

Elder Lee on July 7 during the ulcer bout, President Moyle had three times stated, "your ministry will not be interrupted." Elder Lee had recorded, "I had an immediate sense of strength come over me."

BRAZIL

Rested from the voyage, the Lees docked at Rio de Janeiro on September 7 and were met by President Wm. Grant Bangerter, his wife, the missionaries of the local district, and about fifty faithful members who were awaiting the arrival, Elder Lee thought, more particularly to welcome the return of President and Sister Sorensen, who still had the affections of the Brazilians.

When President Sorensen returned after one day's delay, due to a national holiday, to reclaim the large bags of the Lees, he told them that the customs official was very curt about their bags; however, after learning that Elder Lee was an Apostle of the Church of Jesus Christ, he came early to the boat to expedite the baggage clearance through customs and refused the usual tip, as did the porters who carried the bags. He said that he would accept no tip from an Apostle of the Church of Jesus Christ.

The first encounter with the Brazilian Saints was highly impressive and favorable. On September 9, a midweek meeting was held in a downtown Rio hotel lounge room and was a surprising delight. There were about 250 present from the district, including investigators and four of the five couples from the United States who lived in Rio. Elder Lee was pleased and wrote: "They were a brilliant and intelligent congregation and wholly responsive to all that was said. Here surely is the seed-bed for great future possibilities of the president if he will begin to give the leadership now in the branches and districts into local hands instead of the missionaries."

In 1959 the Church in São Paulo was in its infancy. There were fifty missionaries at the opening meeting. A total of six branches were located in the city of São Paulo, housed in rented buildings, ranging from 50 to 376 in membership. Seventeen new converts were baptized during the busy day of meetings held in the Center Branch building with 117 in attendance. Just previously, three Methodist ministers had joined the Church.

The mission tour moved on with visits to Campinar, Poracicabia, Rio Claro, and Bauru. Elder Lee's journal describes his initial impressions:

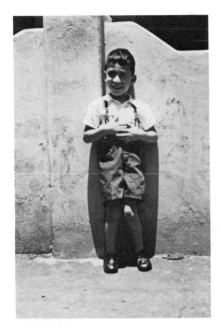

Young boy in Brazil who had never walked. Elder Lee wrote: "We administered to him, and after my return home [I received] this picture of him—now able to stand and to walk."

We went by "air-taxi" from Claro to Bauru in a small one-engine Stinson plane. The missionaries and Sister Bangerter came by train. Here we were to see one of the surprises, a black woman president of the branch Relief Society with her husband and children all members, and a young girl with black blood in charge of the Primary. Both, they tell me, are well received by the whites. We enjoyed here the most spiritual missionary meeting of any in our tour so far. The spirit of the Elders seemed characterized by one Elder who said: "We found ourselves by losing ourselves in the red dirt of Maringa." A pair of Elders told of traveling five hours in a hot, dusty bus to a new town and of bearing testimony to each other that entire distance.

At Curitiba, on Sunday, September 20, 1959, the conference was held where the official organization of the South Brazilian Mission was effected. The Saints from Curitiba and Joinville districts and some from Ponta Grossa, numbering 339 in attendance, accepted President Asael T. Sorensen and two full-time missionaries, Elders Ross Leroy Broadbent and Robert T. Owens as counselors. This mission thus became the forty-ninth in the Çhurch, with four districts, located at Curitiba, Joinville, Porto Alegre, and Londrina, and a population of four hundred members and about forty missionaries to serve them. Elder Lee's feelings were uplifted by the session in which a third of the total membership participated.

The Joinville Saints provided reminiscence that it was in that city that Elder Reinhold Stoof came in 1939 to commence missionary work in all of Brazil. When Elder Lee visited in 1959 the Saints were still largely German immigrants. Here again, without knowledge of their problems in this branch, Elder Lee addressed the membership on the importance of unity and willingness to accept their present leaders even though they may have held the same high positions in the past. He later learned that he had been inspired to touch on the very situations which this branch most needed to hear, a not uncommon experience in the ministry of Elder Lee. He needed no briefing by the mission president but discerned by the Holy Spirit the yearnings and needs of his audiences.

Spiritual experiences abounded as the tour moved on to Porto Alegre where the missionaries met in perhaps the most outstanding meeting in Brazil. A young Brazilian sister missionary was having her companion, Sister Gatenby, translate Elder Lee's English when suddenly she discovered she was understanding without the translation. This sister later told of a miraculous escape from the grasp of a man who accosted her and her companion in Curitiba.

At the same meeting a remarkable young missionary leader, Elder Ross Leroy Broadbent, who was called as the first counselor to the mission president a week earlier, related an inspiring experience of when he was hopelessly lost in Petropolis, unable to speak the native language and with no address for the chapel or the missionaries. After a fervent prayer in which he pleaded with the Lord that he must have help to fill his mission, he heard a voice which told him twice to follow the man on the corner. Obediently he followed the man as directed and was led directly to the chapel without further difficulty.

PARAGUAY AND URUGUAY

The tour through a small portion of Brazil was now ended, and the Lees boarded a plane for Fiz de Eqyaocym and a meeting with their next hosts, President and Sister Arthur Jensen from Asunción, Paraguay. After arriving at Iguaçu there was yet an hour's ride over extremely rough unimproved roads. When the Lees settled into their hotel room, Fern suffered a hemorrhage in her eyes. Elder Lee blessed her and implored the Lord to be mindful of their immense need of his healing power, even to a miraculous intervention if needed. Fern stayed in her room while Elder Lee left with the group to photograph the famed Iguaçu Falls. When he returned to the hotel he found his wife greatly improved. The Lord had once more answered their prayers with a miracle.

The visit to Uruguay was notable because of a blessing given by Elder Lee to the head of the government and a continuation of spiritual gifts on the travelers. After explaining the gospel for an hour to the ambassador, and after conducting a huge press conference, Elder Lee went to meet the president of the government council of nine, the man who directed the affairs of Uruguay. President Echogoyen was in his late sixties. Elder Lee recorded in his diary this interesting account of their visit:

> President Echogoyen took about 10 minutes to welcome me as a representative of the North Americans and the Church, which he said was not merely a Sunday religion, and then spoke of my humble beginnings as an educator, as he had been, and added that he felt we were kindred spirits. I then had a strong feeling to give him and his country my blessing as an Apostle of the Lord Jesus Christ. He seemed to have been spiritually moved by the incident.

At Montevideo, the gift of tongues continued to help the local Saints understand Elder Lee's message in English. The meeting held on Sunday, October 4, 1959, was the first conference session of the Capitol District of Montevideo held in their newly constructed chapel, and over six hundred persons attended. Elder Lee recorded this unusual experience in his diary, recalling this meeting:

> In the morning session it was evident that as I spoke the audience was understanding and reacting to what I said before the interpreter had repeated it, even though they knew no English. It was a veritable evidence of the gift of tongues to many there. The music was excellent, the talks by native brethren were remarkable, and the spirit was superb. The audience seemed loathe to leave. They presented us with many gifts as a token of their love to the leaders of the Church.

Throughout their travels the Lees often experienced situations in which the elements were tempered to provide safe passage through storms so that they might keep their appointments with the Church leaders and Saints. Examples come from Elder Lee's diary:

> At Salto, after a four-hour missionary meeting yesterday, a sudden thunderstorm came up about 7:30 a.m. and made questionable whether or not our plane would leave as scheduled for Artigas and Rivera. We again sought the power of the Lord to intervene in tempering the elements, and before our breakfast was finished we had word that the plane would fly on schedule. While it was still raining, the plane would fly despite the lightning and wind, and we took off from the grassy runway at Salto. At Artigas we were scheduled to have four or five hours delay, but found that a previously disabled plane was just being readied to leave and that it would likely be the only flight, so we had a hurried meeting with 25 of our humble Saints, including a former rough-looking gaucho who is now a faithful refined Elder in the Church. Word came that the plane was leaving immediately and there was doubt that we could make it to the airport. To add to our woes our taxi had a flat tire, which required my helping the driver change, while the president went for our bags. We arrived to find one of the two planes had tried to take off, but was delayed by a strong cross-wind and slippery grass, so that our plane was still waiting as though being prevented from leaving with our four Elders from Artigas. That "Someone" is He in whose service we are laboring. By the time we were all together, the rain ceased and the wind stopped, and both planes took off, including ours which took us to Rivera where we arrived hours ahead of schedule with the skies almost entirely cleared. How gratefully we give our thanks to a watchful Heavenly Father.

From Montevideo the tour moved to Paraguay, over extremely rough roads entailing a six- to seven-hour ride in a bus without shock absorbers. Yet at the three-hour meeting Elder Lee found the Spirit richly directing his concluding remarks.

On Sunday, October 11, 1959, members from Melo and Triente y Tres and one from the nearby Isla Petrulla, where a new chapel has been built, came to the conference. In this meeting three faithful sisters came up excitedly at the close of the meeting to declare that they had understood what Elder Lee had said before it had been translated, although they knew no English.

ARGENTINA

Next the tour moved to Buenos Aires, where a meeting was held with one hundred members of the Caseros Branch, which would be the site for the first Church building to be constructed in Argentina and was just getting underway. The next Sunday conference was at Rosario, the second largest city in Argentina, with a population in 1959 at 800,000. It was located some six or seven driving hours from Buenos Aires. Here Elder Lee noted that the district leadership was in the hands of local members who were growing rapidly in ability and numbers. President Lorin Pace said that eighteen months earlier there had been a total attendance in these two branches of only 76, but at the conference on October 18, 1959, a record attendance of 331 in the morning and 371 in the evening came to hear Elder Lee. "This was a most satisfying experience," Elder Lee wrote.

Elder Lee met with forty-three missionaries in an all-day missionary conference at Buenos Aires and again heard of the miracles of the latter-day work in Argentina. Elder Ravsten told of obtaining a working knowledge of Spanish in forty-five days by reading the Spanish edition of the Book of Mormon, most of which he could only pronounce the words without knowing their meaning. Some bore testimonies of individuals becoming converts after they had given to them their first memorized lessons, even though the missionaries didn't understand all they were saying. The power of the devil had tested some missionaries; others reported their missions had brought unity and even some conversions to their family members at home. The meeting brought a spirit of repentance, too, as several missionaries confessed to certain previously undisclosed transgressions. The long, strenuous, but satisfying day ended at 8:00 P.M. when Elder Lee finally finished interviewing the missionaries.

The largest attendance in Argentina came at the concluding Sunday conference in Buenos Aires with five hundred present for the morning meeting and over six hundred in attendance in the evening.

CHILE AND PERU

Next came a visit to Concepción, Chile, the southernmost branch in Chile, where in two years Church population had gone from zero to a membership of ninety in 1959. About 130 persons came to the meeting to hear Elder Lee, and he noted that the members here were distinctly of Indian extraction, "faithful, but not demonstrative."

Elder Lee organized the new Andes Mission at Santiago on

October 30, 1959, at a conference held on the grounds of the Providencia Branch. Members came from all seven branches in Chile and the audience totalled 318 persons or 63 percent of the membership. Here it was announced that Lima, Peru, would be the headquarters of the mission, a motion which drew a few negative votes, despite reference to Santiago, Chile, as the "southern headquarters of the mission." President J. Vernon Sharp was presented as the president of the mission, with Joseph Robert Quayle as his first counselor and Elder Wallace Baker as the second counselor.

There were, on this historic occasion, seven branches in Chile with a total membership of about five hundred, and five branches in Peru with a total of about three hundred, making a grand total of eight hundred members in twelve branches. With such a modest Church membership the population of the mission increased by 10 percent when forty-five converts were baptized the day following the conference. Elder Lee met for eight hours with the thirty-five missionaries serving in Santiago.

The organization of the new Andes Mission was repeated on Sunday, November 1, 1959, at Lima, Peru, when Elder Lee declared the mission officially in existence. Two sessions of conference were held with about two hundred persons attending, over 60 percent of the total Church membership at that time.

Through communications with the First Presidency, Elder Lee's recommendations had been approved to have President Jensen, who had had considerable construction experience, consult with the two Brazilian mission presidents incident to the building of chapels in Latin America. Also, some mission boundary changes were made so that cities on the Brazilian side could be worked from the Uruguay Mission.

The route homeward took the Lees to Cuzco, Peru, and a visit to the famed ruins of Machu Picchu. Flying over the Andes at a height of 20,000 feet Elder and Sister Lee landed at Cuzco, which has an elevation of 11,600 feet. This was the capital city, Elder Lee was told, of the great Inca Empire, one of the greatest socialistic empires ever known, and which was destroyed by the Spaniards in 1535 and years following under Pizzaro and others in their greedy search for gold. Visiting with a Mr. Cohen, a wealthy cotton producer, the Lees saw a magnificent array of gold ornaments and even gold children's playthings, and wondered if the plentiful supply of gold even then meant that the early settlers probably had

Among the Incan ruins of Machu Picchu, 1959

abundant access to gold for plates or sheets of gold materials on which to write the records of the people of Lehi and Nephi. They regarded it as another evidence that this land was probably the first Nephite center in the Western Hemisphere.

In company with about twenty other visitors the Lees went to Machu Picchu, where the last Inca stronghold was discovered by Dr. Hiram Bingham in 1911. They were told that from here the high Inca lord probably fled with his "chosen" women, personal attendants, and guards. Elder and Sister Lee enjoyed this learning experience at one of the most famed archaeological finds in the Americas.

TWO PRESIDENTS' IMPRESSIONS

In retrospect both President Wm. Grant Bangerter, of the divided Brazilian Mission, and President J. Vernon Sharp, newly installed as the first president of the Andes Mission in Chile and Peru, wrote into their personal histories and the oral histories they prepared with the Church Historical Department their vivid impressions of being with President and Sister Lee in this mission tour. President Bangerter's account follows:

Brother and Sister Harold B. Lee . . . came (to Brazil) with the purpose of effecting the division [of the mission]. In the process Brother Lee and his wife toured the mission, and we were with them for . . . a period of nearly three weeks, which was about the term of a mission tour by a General Authority in those days. Those occasions with . . . [our touring General Authorities] . . . were outstanding in their personal effect upon us. To be able to associate from day to day for that prolonged period with these men and their wives was an unusual and very treasured opportunity.

President Lee, of course, in his visit did similar [work] to what President Kimball [had done the year before], in that he strengthened the missionary work and encouraged us. He taught us constantly about the spirit with which we should work, gave instructions about leadership and Church government, and projected us to move in the organization of districts with local leadership and branches under local presidencies.

As we would walk along the street with President Lee he told us many stories [and I appreciated so much my association with him]. Brother Lee had a habit, I think, with his companions, whoever they happened to be, of tending to confide in them. And many of the things that he talked about were personal stories of an inspirational nature. One of the things we did discuss that is vivid with me was his relationship with President J. Reuben Clark, Jr. President Lee had been trained as a member of the Twelve under the tutelage of President Clark, working with him closely in the welfare program. As I commented to him about this relationship, he said, "I suppose that no father was ever closer to a son than President Clark has been to me."

Other incidents—and they were too numerous to mention in full or even to recall—would include some like his personal stories of the testimony of various members of the General Authorities. One that is vivid was his recounting of the time when Heber J. Grant was supposedly on his death bed . . . [and the concern that was registered about his successor]. President Lee told us that story as an indication of how the Lord is in complete control and directs the succession to the Presidency of the Church. I think this subject was always of great importance to President Lee. He was assured as to the manner in which the Lord selects the Presidents of the Church.

President Lee made no particular reference to a readjustment in Church order at that time, but of course he had, years before, fixed his mind on attitudes that indicated that the Church already had the structure to give it proper leadership and that we should not expect to form new patterns of leadership and organization. He always understood that the priesthood was the proper organization and governing agency and that the structure was established by the Lord. I heard him say that in those days and before and since.

But I would like to say that to have experiences of this kind, walking and living personally by the side of men of this nature, was an opportunity very rare to people on earth. We prized it very much.

We had another experience that I recall of having family home evening with Brother and Sister Lee in our home. To have them sit and visit with our children and talk with them and to hear him bear his testimony about how he knew that he had been called of God when he was named one of the Twelve Apostles was a very inspiring experience.

President J. Vernon Sharp recapped his visit with Elder and Sister Lee in these words, taken from his oral history with the Church Historical Department:

In Santiago, Chile, . . . we proceeded with the details for the formation of the Andes Mission. In the Hotel Carrera on the mezzanine floor, toward the front, we had a huge flag of Chile and a huge flag of Peru. Under the two flags with the masts crossed, we held our planning meeting for the formation of the mission and took care of the details. Later on we met at the rear of the property at El Bosque and held the organization meeting under the direction of President Harold B. Lee.

At that time he announced that the Andes Mission was to be formed, or was being formed, that there would be two cities that would hold the offices for the mission, but that the main records of the mission were to be kept in Lima, Peru, under the direction of President David O. McKay. We held a very inspirational meeting. We toured with President and Sister Lee the branches of the Church that were at that time in Santiago. When we went down to Concepcion, we took them out to a whaling station and President and Sister Lee watched them process some whales.

We gave advance publicity to the newspaper, and this is not in the mission history so I think I should tell it to you. There were good press releases—and some not so good—and in an article that came out in the leading paper in Santiago was a picture of a man on a burro surrounded by many women. It said, "Mormon leader arrives in Chile to organize missionary work in Chile. We asked where his other wives were, but he said he only brought one." When we showed that to Brother Lee, he laughed. I still have it in my possession. But, it wasn't very long until we received very good publicity there.

Now when the mission was organized President Lee told the audience before Sister Sharp and I had even heard of it, that the mission was to include Bolivia as well as Peru and Chile, and at our discretion, as we got the work moving in the other countries, we were to proceed in Bolivia. So towards the end of this year, 1959, we began making plans for that which we should do in the coming year. Going to Bolivia in January 1960 had a great bearing on the activities of the Andes Mission.

Northward and Home

Saying farewell to South America the Lee tour moved northward to visit the Panama Canal Zone. On November 9, 1959, the Lees were guests on a government boat trip through the canal channel into the Pacific Ocean and then to the Miraflores Locks, where they saw larger vessels taken up over an eighty-five-foot elevation and then lowered again down to sea level. After speaking at a priesthood and Relief Society conference Elder Lee wrote, "My talk seemed to the mission president to have especially been well-timed for the solution of internal problems of the Saints here."

Continuing on, Elder Lee observed the failure of early attempts at local leadership in San Jose, Costa Rica, and tried to meet the situation by speaking of the power of the devil which overtakes those who fail in keeping the Lord's commandments. In Honduras an American educator who served as branch president was challenged by Elder Lee to make substantial contributions and to raise funds for a branch chapel at Tegucigalpa, and then Elder Lee blessed President Nathan J. and Allie Rogers Barlow so that their unselfish plans would succeed.

Elder Lee heard a report in San Salvador that the Coffee Growers Association was protesting against the Church because our missionaries were preaching against coffee drinking, thus opposing their financial interests. It was a signal that caution must be observed to avoid statements against political governments, as President McKay had warned, and although Elder Lee taught him the Church President's counsel, the mission president found it difficult to accept.

Some of the greatest spiritual experiences of the entire trip came in Guatemala, a country which greatly impressed Elder Lee. He wrote in his diary on Sunday, November 15, 1959, these significant words:

Today we had a most thrilling experience in meeting with over 1600 members of the Church from the five districts of Guatemala. This is among the most distinctive Lamanite people I have yet been among. Somehow I had a strong feeling that this place is without question the Lamanite capital of North America and that a temple for the Latin American people should be built here. President Alfredo Mosso Amada told of the town of Kumen in Northern Guatemala which has the same name as one of the twelve disciples Jesus chose on the western continent, and there were other remarkable indicators.

Brother Daniel Mich, a full-blooded Indian of the Patzicia Branch, told of a dream where seven men were beckoning him to follow, each one taking a different road. He had just been visited by the missionaries and despite the vicious stories being told, he was praying to know the truth of their message. In his dream he saw a tall, stately, white-headed man who introduced himself as David O. McKay, a prophet of God, who told him the way to the right road. When later his Elders showed him a photograph of President McKay, he immediately recognized him as the prophet of his dream. He has now been a member for the last three years.

The spiritual stories continued as the Lees moved northward, arriving by plane in Mexico City on November 17, 1959. There they were met by President Harvey H. Taylor, his wife, and the mission staff. President Taylor told this interesting story to Elder Lee, which came from Elder Hall, who was a member of the mission office staff. Elder Hall's words were recorded in Elder Lee's journal:

> When I was working in Southern Mexico, I met a 75-year-old woman, who, when the first missionaries came to that area, told them she knew that their message was true because three elderly men had come to their community some time before, and had taught these same doctrines and had gone from there south into Central America. This story agrees with the report of natives in Guatemala, when the first Elders opened the work there.

The inspirational direction of a divine providence in choosing the right areas for the missionaries to work was demonstrated in a story told to Elder Lee by President Taylor. Elder Lee's diary recorded it as follows:

> President Taylor related the experience he and Jose Davila and four Elders had in opening the work in Yucatan. They drove to the town of Motul and parked in front of a hotel, where they planned to stay while they started the work. He had a very depressed feeling, and

Exchanging hugs with Marion G. Romney upon return from South America, 1959

when he consulted Elder Carter, who was in another car, he found that Elder Carter likewise had a depressed feeling. The president then decided to leave immediately and go to another town, where they stayed for the night. The next morning again he and Elder Carter conferred and both had an exultant feeling and they knew they should start the missionary work there. Two or three months later Motul had a revolution during which several were killed and many wounded, thus attesting to the providential warning which came to him.

A midweek conference at the Industrial Branch was hastily arranged by President Taylor so that the Saints could meet Elder and Sister Lee; 425 members were in attendance. Elder Lee again reflected about his favorable impression of the progress of the Saints in Mexico in these words: "The remarkable improvement in the appearance and performance of our Mexican Saints never ceases to amaze me."

The long, three-month journey on the Lord's errand finally came to a close when the Lees' plane landed in Salt Lake City on November 18, 1959. Sister Lee, whose health was always frail, came home fatigued and suffering from a cold and sinus infection, but rejoiced greatly to be reunited with the family and General Authorities who gathered at the airport to welcome them home. They went immediately to the home of their daughter Helen for a joyous visit with the family.

The next day was Thursday, November 19, 1959, and Elder Lee joined his Brethren in the customary meeting of the First Presidency and Council of the Twelve in the temple. There President McKay requested that he report on a number of spiritual experiences connected with his three-month tour of the missions in Latin America, and on hearing many of the stories mentioned above, the President seemed to be most pleased with the report.

Following the counsel of President J. Reuben Clark, given in his pretour blessing, Elder Lee had made no public mention of his prophetic insight that a temple was someday to be built for the Latin American Saints in Guatemala, "Lamanite capital of North America." That nonpublished prophecy was fulfilled in 1981 when President Spencer W. Kimball announced temple construction plans in Guatemala on the day prior to the opening of the April general conference.

1960. The United States and Japan signed a mutual
cooperation and security treaty. John F. Kennedy
was elected president after engaging in four
nationally televised debates with Richard Nixon.
The USSR sentenced American U2 pilot Gary
Powers to ten years in prison.

CHAPTER 18

Saving the Voice
of a Prophet

On February 12, 1960, Elder Harold B. Lee received
an assignment from President McKay to join with Alvin R. Dyer,
president of the European Mission, and President Bowring T.
Woodbury, president of the British Mission, to organize a new
stake of the Church centering at Manchester, England, the first
stake in Great Britain. The assignment also entailed creating the
new North British Mission.

At the temple meeting on Thursday, March 3, 1960, Bernard T.
Brockbank, president of the Salt Lake Cottonwood Stake, was
approved to become the president of the new mission in Great
Britain, and he immediately reported to Elder Lee with the assurance that he would be ready to fly from New York to London with
him on March 17. In those two short weeks President Brockbank
arranged for his final preparations and the transfer of his business
to other hands.

ORGANIZING THE FIRST BRITISH STAKE

Elder Lee fulfilled this assignment and returned home just in time to participate in the April 1960 general conference of the Church. He learned from President Henry D. Moyle the night before Elder Lee was to speak at general conference that President McKay would be disappointed if he didn't report on his assignment in Great Britain, so he prepared notes to do as President Moyle had suggested. He explained this at conference the next day:

> Because of the desire expressed by the Brethren that I say something about the history-making events of the past week in the British Mission, I have put aside the text of that which I might have prepared otherwise to say on this occasion. I have determined long since that the expressed desire of my presiding Brethren is to me as a command. Therefore, I trust that I might in some measure give you a picture of some of the events which have transpired of a momentous nature in Great Britain.

It was on March 18, 1960, that Elder and Sister Lee flew for the first time in a jet aircraft. Leaving from the Idlewild Airport in New York for London with President Brockbank, they soared at a height of 37,000 feet and traveled at an air speed of six hundred miles per hour. They described the sensation aboard as hearing "a noise like rushing wind, but experiencing practically no vibration."

The assignment from the First Presidency took the Lees to the scenes of some of the most soul-stirring incidents and experiences in the history of missionary work in this dispensation. After arriving at Manchester the Church leaders drove to Liverpool, thirty-seven miles distant, where they searched for a suitable building for the headquarters of the new North British Mission. Elder Lee later recorded other visits to historic sites: "We went from here to Preston, where our first missionaries started their work in 1837. We went to the Pier Head, where their ship docked, to their living quarters on Wil-Vauxhal, Temperance Hall, the Cockpit, where they preached, the Obelisk on the market place, and the River Ribble, where the first baptisms were performed."

Recalling the miracles of the first missionary work in the midlands of Great Britain near Preston, Elder Lee rehearsed in brief the tremendous manifestation of the power of evil spirits to those early missionaries, and the almost incredible harvest of over 1800 baptisms in just eight months by Elder Wilford Woodruff about three years later.

Elder Lee quoted from the *Documentary History of the Church* to describe the early days of missionary work in England, and stated that times were not much different now in opposition and disinterest. The early record stated: "It seemed that it almost required a horn to be blown from the highest heavens in order to awaken the attention of the people."

The parallel came in the 1960 press notice from the *Manchester Guardian* newspaper, which announced the creation of this stake and the organization of the new mission with this tiny story hidden in an obscure place:

Mormons Hold a Mass Meeting

British Mormons formed their first diocese in Europe yesterday at a mass meeting of more than 2,000 members of the Church of the Latter-day Saints in Manchester, the new center to be built without delay at Wythenshawe, Manchester, at a cost of about 100,000 pounds. The diocese, or stake, covers Manchester, Halifax, Huddersfield, Dewsbury and Leeds.

In his diary Elder Lee recorded the events accompanying the organization of the Manchester Stake and the new North British Mission as follows:

Today (March 26, 1960) we spent the day interviewing those called to various positions. I had an unusual experience, when after consenting to the ordination of the three members of the district presidency in the new Preston District, I was impressed to instruct the priesthood not to be ambitious to have offices in the priesthood after that of elder, explaining that these other offices come after being called to positions required by further ordinations. I found only one or two men unworthy to hold the positions to which they had been called.

The conference sessions were held in the Manchester Hippodrome Theatre, on Sunday, March 27, 1960. There were nearly 1,700 in the morning session and 2,026 attending in the afternoon. In the morning session we presented the organization of the new Manchester Stake, with nine wards and two branches, and a total population of 2,400. Our new presidency of Robert G. Larsen, Dennis Livesy, and William Bates gave a good account of themselves and were well accepted. The organization of the North British Mission was presented also at this meeting, with President Bernard P. Brockbank as president and Fredrick W. Oates and Elder John Evans as his counselors. We also announced the organization of the Preston District of the North British Mission. After the closing session we went to the Manchester Ward chapel and set apart 65 new stake and ward officers. Following this we met until 9:30 p.m. with Presidents Woodbury and Brockbank and over 200 missionaries.

Elder Lee described his mission of organization in England, as well as his observations and feelings, in his public general conference address:

> It was interesting to discover that the leadership of the stake and wards and the branches had to be largely composed of brethren who were baptized converts to the Church of less than five years. Fortunately, and it seemed as though almost by the hand of Providence, we found a few "anchor" men who had been trained in the stakes here at home, who will become the trainers of these new able but inexperienced leaders. This stake becomes now a training ground for leaders of organizations yet to come.
>
> This new stake brings the full Church program into action, so that such an organization will be a demonstration to the world "to shine forth as a standard unto the nations," showing the work of the Church at full flower. Zion, which the Lord declared is "the pure in heart," in that land now will "increase in holiness and beauty." Zion will now begin "to arise and put on her beautiful garments." (See D&C 82:14, 97, 21.) This first stake will provide a pattern for stakes yet to come from these great missions. We think we have set it up in such a way that new leaders, so trained, will shortly be able to take over still other stakes in that same vicinity, and become a pattern for leaders of stakes in that and the other European missions.
>
> In truth, then, it now begins to build "a defense, a refuge from the storm, and wrath when it is poured out without mixture, upon the whole earth" (see D&C 115:6), which, as the Lord declared, was the purpose of a stake being organized.
>
> We now have organized in the North British Mission eight missionary districts, with nine missionary districts still remaining in the British Mission, which will continue to have headquarters in London. The new mission will have headquarters at Manchester, England.
>
> The power of God is resting again in the missions of Europe today, as in the century which has passed. During the month of March alone, the British Mission has baptized 360 converts. In the French Mission there were another 114 new converts baptized, which seems for the first time in our day to give evidence that the work is beginning to take root in France, after a shocking demon-

stration of the power of evil in that mission only two short years ago. And from the North German Mission, to use another example, which we have usually thought of as being behind the Iron Curtain in part, they baptized in the month of March alone 85 new converts.

So it was, likewise, during the three months of last fall, when we toured the Latin American missions of South America and in Mexico, we saw evidences of the giant of God's eternal power, if I might speak of it that way, awakening among those wonderful people, where in some of those missions they are having 600 to 700 convert baptisms each year, as compared with only 50 to 75 in previous years.

Indeed, in the language of Mark's testimony of the early missionaries of the apostolic period, who received the divine commission of the Lord: "Go ye into all the world, and preach the gospel to every creature. He that believeth and is baptized shall be saved; but he that believeth not shall be damned. And these signs shall follow them that believe; In my name shall they cast out devils; they shall speak with new tongues; They shall take up serpents; and if they drink any deadly thing, it shall not hurt them: they shall lay hands on the sick, and they shall recover." (Mark 16:15–18.)

And then Mark records this significant fulfillment: "And they went forth, and preached every where, the Lord working with them, and confirming the word with signs following" (Mark 16:20).

President McKay, I have been a personal witness in these last six months that, as the Apostles of old found, we are finding today that the servants of the living God are going forth, the Lord is working with them confirming the work, with the same signs following.

I bear personal witness that the gift of tongues to a whole congregation, which I witnessed, as in the day of Pentecost, was observed down in one of the Latin American missions, by which this congregation understood what I said although what was being spoken to them was in a strange tongue. I have witnessed the healing of an impotent and crippled child from birth in the Brazilian Mission. I have witnessed the healing of a blind child in the Central American Mission.

And so, enumerating all of these, more important than any of these signs, I have witnessed the reformation in the personal lives of individuals who accept the gospel and are true to its principles, which results from a true conversion to the gospel of Jesus Christ. I bear you my solemn witness to the onrolling of the work of the Lord. The work is awakening everywhere.

Elder Lee seemed pleased with his report in general conference of his historic organizational trip to England; he also felt President

McKay was pleased with his summary: "The President seemed pleased with what I had to say, and as he closed the conference he was very emotional and declared this conference to have been the greatest, and an evidence of the apostolic power resting upon the Twelve."

The organization of the first stake in Great Britain accompanied by the first division of the British Mission was indeed a milestone which signaled a rapid Church expansion in the British Isles. By the time Elder Lee became President of the Church in 1973, twelve other stakes had been organized and all were operating under local leadership. The Church membership in Great Britain in 1972 was 74,000, with membership in the nine stakes reaching 32,000 and membership in the seven missions recorded as another 42,000. There were at that time 300 wards and branches of the Church in Great Britain. Of these, about 120 were then in chapels that the Church had constructed and dedicated for worship services and instruction. Indeed, the British Isles, to which President Joseph Smith sent missionaries when the Church was but seven years old, produced for a second time a rich harvest of dedicated new converts.

A PROPHET'S VOICE PRESERVED

One of the most inspiring and significant experiences in terms of its long-range ramifications was Elder Lee's close involvement with the cancer throat surgery that threatened the life of Elder Spencer W. Kimball in 1957. Had not the Lord been kind to the Brethren in their fervent appeals for guidance and healing, the magnificent leadership of President Spencer W. Kimball, as Elder Lee's successor as prophet, seer, and revelator, might have been lost.

Elder Kimball first suspected difficulty with his voice in 1950. For many years he had feared that cancer might be developing, but it was not until Christmastime of 1956 that a renewed threat became apparent. After awakening one morning with blood in the back of his throat and a weakened voice, he sought medical assistance. Dr. Leland Cowan, a cancer specialist in Salt Lake City, urged consultation in New York City with the world's leading medical specialists.

After attending a stake conference in New York City in February 1957, Elder Kimball submitted himself to examination by Dr. Hayes Martin. He performed an immediate biopsy of the throat, but the results proved inconclusive. Elder Kimball was sent back home to be watched by Dr. Cowan and to rest his voice in silence for thirty days.

Elder Lee's involvement first came one month later, on March 16, 1957, when he and Sister Lee went to the train depot to welcome Spencer and Camilla Kimball back home from New York City, where, according to Elder Lee's records, "Spencer had undergone a serious operation on his throat, supposedly for a cancerous growth which, if it was fully removed, could destroy his voice permanently."

Five days later Elder Kimball attended the temple meeting with the Brethren; he had dutifully written out his reports but asked Elder Lee to read them for him. Of his medical treatment in New York he said that his surgeon called his throat growth "benign" and yet had written on his medical report "in situe carcinoma," indicating a malignant tumor. The contradiction gave no peace of mind to anyone.

In early April Elder Kimball's throat was mending from the surgery, and he reported to Elder and Sister Lee at a social that "after you and the Brethren blessed me last night, this morning my voice was strong enough to seem almost nearing normal." Yet in early May it was still necessary for Elder Kimball to use Elder Lee as his spokesman in their weekly temple meeting as he whispered or wrote notes to his seat companion. Elder Lee noted it in his journal because he felt President McKay had thought him to be too active in the meeting speaking for both Spencer and himself.

In July of 1957 Elder Lee was in New York City attending some corporate board meetings when he received a letter from Elder Kimball. He and Camilla would be arriving the next day to be reexamined by the cancer specialist at the Cancer Memorial Hospital to determine whether further surgery would be needed.

This course had been recommended by President McKay after Elder Kimball had placed his future in the hands of the prophet. President McKay was emotional about his responsibility of giving advice and asked for time to ponder and pray overnight concerning the problem. The next day he advised Elder Kimball to go to New York and follow the advice of his physicians; he also advised him to consult with Elder Lee in New York City in making the final decision. With uncertainty as to what the future would hold, Brother and Sister Kimball left for New York City.

On July 26, 1957, Brother and Sister Lee went to Grand Central Station early in the morning to meet the Kimballs on their arrival. Elder Lee suggested that the Kimballs accept President Theodore Jacobsen's invitation to stay at the Eastern States Mission home, which they did.

At Elder Kimball's request, Elder Lee accompanied him to the interview with Dr. Hayes Martin, the cancer surgery specialist who had stripped his vocal cords of the growth on them four and one-half months earlier. After a careful examination, Dr. Martin told Elder Kimball that further surgery was imperative immediately to check the cancerous growth, which had advanced considerably since the previous stage.

This was a crucial moment of decision and persuasion. The entire effectiveness in useful service of a future prophet of God swayed in the balance.

Deliberately and forcefully Elder Lee implored: "Dr. Martin, this patient of yours is no ordinary man!" Then, both Elder Lee and Elder Kimball impressed on him the necessity of preserving the Apostle's voice, if at all possible, because his voice, in his present position, was his very life. Dr. Martin responded with a quotation to indicate that he understood the importance of his delicate decision. Quoting from Justice Oliver Wendell Holmes, who was answering the inquiry as to when he would retire, he said: "There is not time to retire; to live is to serve."

Then Dr. Martin said that it seemed to him likely that by an immediate operation he might be able to save one vocal cord, although he insisted on an understanding that he be left free to make that decision when he operated, and by actual examination determine how much the entire voice box was involved. He was hopeful that he might be able to perform a partial laryngectomy, which would leave Elder Kimball with some voice, but probably not even as good as he presently possessed.

With such a grim outlook, at best, but fearing the even more ominous alternative, the two Apostles concluded that the only course open was to go forward with the surgery. Arrangements were made to admit Elder Kimball to the Cancer Memorial Hospital on Sunday afternoon. The Lees took the Kimballs to lunch and suggested that they take an excursion boat ride around the island of Manhattan to relieve their anxieties. Elder Kimball took the surgeon's decision calmly, according to Elder Lee, but Camilla was considerably shaken by the conclusion to operate again.

After Elder Lee had concluded his Sunday sermon at the famed Cathedral of the Pines in Ringde, New Hampshire, he returned to New York City by automobile, thinking as he rode down the beautiful Merritt Parkway through Connecticut of the spiritual challenge that awaited his return to the bedside of his beloved associate. With Elder Roy Fugal, his driver, he went directly to the Memorial Hospital, where they administered to Elder Kimball before he went to the operating room. After Elder Lee's blessing, Elder Kimball found peace and relief from fear. Elder Lee returned shortly thereafter to stay at Camilla's side until she had word of the extent to which the surgeons had to go in removing the malignant tissues from Spencer's throat.

Courtesy service was extended to Sister Kimball and Elder Lee by Dr. Rulon Rawson, a member of the Church and chief of the Department of Medicine at Memorial Hospital, who came twice during the operation to report results and answer questions regarding the extent of the operation. Finally the doctors reported that they were required to remove completely the left vocal cord and to trim the right one, taking off a portion on the right side where the two join. They also removed an afflicted portion of the larynx that was determined to be malignant. They explained that there would necessarily be a "significant" change in his voice, but with sufficient mechanics Elder Kimball would be able to converse and speak audibly. They also opened his throat from the front and inserted a silver tube through which he could breathe.

The day after surgery, on July 30, 1957, Elder Lee returned to the hospital and found Elder Kimball fully recovered from the anesthetic and able to take nourishment by mouth and to move about. Elder Kimball asked Elder Lee to phone President McKay and report all that had happened. President McKay was greatly relieved at the report. On the following day Elder Kimball was able to breathe freely, so they removed the silver tube from his windpipe and changed his dressings, telling him he could leave the hospital in two days and could return to his home in Utah after ten more. Actually it became four weeks before they arrived home.

Before the Lees left their vigil for their return home, they went late Wednesday night to see Spencer and Camilla at the hospital, presenting them with a bouquet of beautiful flowers and extending their love and faith that all would go well during Elder Kimball's convalescence.

Three weeks after leaving Elder Kimball in New York City, Elder Lee and the Quorum of the Twelve devoted their quarterly meeting in the temple to a special fast for Spencer Kimball's return to health, and specifically that he would regain the use of his voice to continue his work. Elder Lee read to the Brethren, after they had prayed, an optimistic progress report from President Jacobsen of the Eastern States Mission where Elder Kimball was convalescing, stating that he now had possession of a "working" voice.

Working with the New Voice

Finally, in December, Spencer declared himself healed. The doctors at first had not released him to fulfill appointments with the stakes and missions, but before the end of the year he was told to use his voice in public speaking and the First Presidency consented to his plaintive appeals to return to routine travel assignments.

These renewed travel appointments included an assignment with Elder Harold B. Lee to divide the Dallas Texas Stake and to organize a new stake at Shreveport, Louisiana. These brethren left on January 15, 1958, by train for a strenuous two weeks. Concerning that trip Elder Lee wrote in his journal: "It is remarkable how diligently Brother Kimball struggles to use his remaining voice, which effort is greatly hampered by noise interference on the train."

After the hard work of reorganizing the Houston Stake was taken care of on Saturday, the Brethren tried to sleep, but Elder Kimball twisted and turned and was in such pain that sleep was impossible. Finally he revealed to Elder Lee his suffering, announcing that he had a severe pain in his back and was coughing greatly. He did so reluctantly for fear that Elder Lee might curtail his activities at the conference. Elder Lee gave him some medicinals and then administered to him. At last Spencer slept, and on the next morning he declared that he had had no return of the pain from which he had suffered. Gratefully, he thanked the Lord for his goodness to him.

At the Sunday morning session of stake conference, after the reorganization had been accomplished, Elder Lee called Elder Kimball to speak. Twice he tried but was quite unintelligible. About to quit in despair, the courageous Elder Kimball made a final

With Spencer W. Kimball in Dallas, 1958

attempt to speak and this time succeeded. He ended up doing his share of the preaching, although his voice, according to Elder Lee's description, was "little more than a hoarse whisper. He was helped, however, by a sensitive microphone fastened around his neck, which device gave him the needed volume for all to hear."

The two companions pressed on through Texas, holding a meeting on January 29, 1958, at Many, Louisiana, with the Saints of the surrounding branches which were being brought into the new stake at Shreveport. Here Brother Kimball excused himself from speaking because of a soreness in his throat, which gave him some anxiety lest it be the result of overtaxing his voice so soon after his operation. However, in Texarkana, one week later, where the Brethren had a four-hour layover between trains, a meeting was held in a huge, long and narrow Methodist chapel. Earlier Elder Kimball had asked to be excused from speaking, but responded when called on by Elder Lee. Although there was no loudspeaker available, Brother Kimball addressed for thirty minutes the 184 rapidly assembled Saints. Every person present had heard him and was uplifted by his message. Elder Lee comforted his companion and assured him that he was finding favor with God.

From this appointment in Louisiana, Elder Lee was traveling on to New York City for corporate board meetings. Elder Kimball, after checking with his office and finding he had no assignment for the next Sunday, decided to go to New York City with Elder Lee. He felt that if he could obtain some clinical voice training he might be able to avoid some bad habits which he felt were developing. After arriving in New York City, Elder Lee stayed at the side of his worried companion, accompanying him to the speech clinic and making certain that arrangements were made for a series of lessons or training periods.

This was the beginning of better days for Elder Spencer W. Kimball. He gained control over his new voice and passed through the medical and emotional trials that could have rendered him impotent of communicative skills for his later ministry as the prophet of God. What was the measured value of this victory? Millions of people on all continents of the earth were later to hear him speak as the mouthpiece of God, using a unique, damaged, but mended voice.

As one young sister, Carmen Nunez of Cebu City, Philippines, expressed it for millions of others at the 1980 Far East Area Conference of the Church in that land, "I'll never forget this conference and the words of the prophet. It's such a blessing to see the prophet and to *hear his voice.*"

ELDER LEE'S RISE IN SENIORITY AND INFLUENCE

Elder Lee became an Apostle on April 6, 1941, as the newest and by far the youngest member of the Quorum of the Twelve. After ten years, he had moved from being twelfth in seniority to fourth.

When Elder LeGrand Richards was sustained as a new member of the Quorum of the Twelve on April 6, 1952, Elder Lee welcomed him into the ranks of the Apostles and recounted in these words his own movement in seniority in the Quorum: "Eleven years ago this morning, I climbed the steps and took my place on the stand where Brother Richards is today. In eleven years to the day, I have moved from the arm rest to my left, to the arm rest to my right. That call was an overpowering experience, as only these, my brethren, know."

The ordination of Elder Richards to the apostleship was the eighth such experience Elder Lee had witnessed since his arrival in that circle in 1941.

Two of his initial fellow quorum members, George Albert Smith and Joseph Fielding Smith, rose to preside over the Church as its President. Two became President of the Council of Twelve Apostles, Elders Rudger A. Clawson and George F. Richards. Another member served in the First Presidency (Stephen L Richards). Death took Elders John A. Widtsoe, Joseph F. Merrill, Charles A. Callis, Albert E. Bowen, and Sylvester Q. Cannon, and tragically, excommunication claimed another, Richard R. Lyman. Most of these changes occurred during the first ten years of Elder Lee's apostleship.

The second decade of Elder Lee's service as an Apostle saw him advance from being fourth in seniority to being second only to Elder Joseph Fielding Smith.

The first Apostle to pass away in that second decade was Elder Joseph F. Merrill. He died in his sleep early on Sunday morning, February 3, 1952, while on a stake conference visit.

Elder A. E. Bowen had a stroke while attending a temple meeting of the Council of the Twelve on June 25, 1952. The Apostles were gathered in their quarterly meeting; while Elder Henry Moyle was speaking, Elder Bowen became ill. When his brethren rushed to his aid they found him unable to stand on his feet and surmised that he had suffered a stroke, crippling his left hand and impairing his speech. They laid him on a couch and after administering to him called for his physician and then for his son, Albert. He was rushed to the hospital. One year later, on July 15, 1953, Elder Albert E. Bowen, Elder Lee's esteemed friend, died.

Elder Lee wrote in his journal on October 7, 1952, that he was grieved by a discouraging report on the health of Elder Widtsoe. The entry read: "I was saddened by the report that a Dr. Crowley, who had waited on Brother Widtsoe in California, had reported to friends that Brother Widtsoe's intestines were 'filled with cancer.' I am hoping the report is exaggerated." The report, however, was accurate, and on November 29, 1952, Elder John A. Widtsoe died. When the funeral was held on December 2, 1952, a terrific snowstorm prevented thousands from attending the memorial services in the Tabernacle on Temple Square, and the hearse had to be pushed up the hill to the cemetery.

By 1960, at the end of the second apostolic decade of Elder Lee's service, he stood next in seniority to his revered friend and much more senior associate Elder Joseph Fielding Smith, whom he was destined to follow into the First Presidency after the death of President David O. McKay. Not only had he risen quickly due to the passing of the older Brethren, but also his talents were being increasingly called on and his leadership abilities increasingly expanded with new and larger responsibilities.

1951–1960. This was the "Space Age." Peace brought moon flights and McCarthy extremism. Bomb shelters were built and paradise was sought in the suburbs. Elvis Presley and television rocked the country.

CHAPTER 19

Vignettes from the Second Apostolic Decade

A period of restless nervousness came over Elder Lee as he faced unusual pressures in the fall of 1951. He returned home late on a Sunday night from a conference in Smithfield, Utah, highly nervous and tense. He considered that this may have been "induced by a combination of Maurine's illness, the pending purchase of a home, and a general feeling of unrest that runs as an undercurrent among the Brethren."

The first week of October saw another restless period with the worries of plans for completing the transaction for their new home weighing on his mind. With Fern, he cashed bonds and savings deposits to obtain sufficient money to purchase their new home at 849 Connor Street in Salt Lake City. His attorney friends were most accommodating in examining the necessary papers. "For some reason," he wrote, "I find myself in a highly nervous state of mind with extreme difficulty in concentrating upon a subject which I could prepare for general conference."

In front of home at 849 Connor Street, Salt Lake City

A week later the condition still prevailed; he wrote on October 7, 1951, "I am still oppressed by feelings I seem unable to overcome or explain."

Moving day came on October 19, 1951, compounding his worries. Describing his pressures Elder Lee wrote: "This was one of the most hectic days of my life as we moved from the apartment at 107 First Avenue to our new home at 849 Connor Street. Ralph and Beth Davey brought our dinner over and served it to us last night, as a neighborly gesture, the first night we had slept in our home."

MARION G. ROMNEY ORDAINED AN APOSTLE

The general conference of October 1951 brought with it significant changes. With Elder Stephen L Richards now serving in the First Presidency a vacancy in the Twelve was to be filled. The Brethren were growing older, with President J. Reuben Clark, Jr., now age eighty and Joseph Fielding Smith, the President of the Quorum of the Twelve, age seventy-five.

Earlier, Elder Lee had a delightful visit with President Clark en route to Cedar City where he was a guest at the Cedar City Centennial. As they traveled, President Clark told Elder Lee about some of the financial problems confronting succeeding Church administrations and said that he wanted to explain some of these problems to Elder Lee, in the event he should succeed as a member of the Twelve to some greater responsibility. President Clark said that he was not saying this because he thought his own life was coming to an end, because the doctor had assured him that his health was excellent, but he had to admit that he was over eighty years old and anything could happen to him or to others now in authority.

Just prior to the opening of general conference President McKay invited all the General Authorities to the temple for a prayer circle and to partake of the sacrament, following which there was a brief testimony meeting and short remarks from each member of the First Presidency. For the first time in Church history, President McKay told the Brethren in advance at which session each would be expected to speak. Also at this meeting Marion G. Romney was sustained as the new Apostle and the following were named as new Assistants to the Twelve: George Q. Morris, Stayner Richards, ElRay L. Christiansen, and John Longden. Elder Lee wrote in his diary that after the meeting "President Clark came to my office to share with me my joy in Brother Romney's appointment."

The opening of general conference on Friday, October 5, 1951, brought the usual conference rains but this did not diminish the size of the audiences which crowded the Tabernacle and adjacent buildings to overflowing. Elder Lee spoke in the Friday afternoon session. Still suffering from his nervous condition, Elder Lee wrote in his diary: "I was able to shake off the weariness and nervous tension under which I have been laboring, although it returned after the session. Apparently I have been suffering a sort of nervous exhaustion. Brother Moyle and Brother Stapley administered to me in the evening."

At the Saturday morning session the names of Marion Romney and the other Brethren were presented publicly. "Everyone seemed delighted with Brother Romney's call," Elder Lee wrote. "Needless to say, my joy is unbounded at his coming into the Council of the Twelve."

This call further solidified a relationship begun in 1941 when Brother Romney was appointed as Elder Lee's assistant in the welfare work, at the time Elder Lee was appointed to the Council of the Twelve. Elder Lee thought it significant that President McKay's first appointment to the apostleship was drawn from the ranks of the pioneers of Church welfare administration.

After general conference, Elder Lee turned to a function that had been routine with almost every new appointee to the Quorum of the Twelve since President Clark performed the service for him —orientation of the new Apostle in advance of his ordination. This time he was the teacher for Marion G. Romney, preparing him for his first meeting with the Twelve on the following Thursday, and explaining the procedure that was generally followed in those meetings.

When his restlessness returned, just prior to moving to his new residence, Elder Lee found seclusion in the temple for prayer and meditation. His diary entry states: "After performing a temple marriage I went to an upper room of the temple for some spiritual strength, which I sorely need."

The final chapter in Marion G. Romney's call to the Quorum of the Twelve was to tell the entire Church of his superb qualifications. This Elder Lee did in an article requested by the *Relief Society Magazine*. His diary reference tells of Elder Romney's approval: "Marion Romney seemed pleased with the article I had written about him and his new appointment."

A Rescue Mission Brings Elder Lee Almost Within the Veil—1952

In 1952 Elder Lee was fifty-three years of age and his wife, Fern, was fifty-six. They had celebrated their twenty-ninth wedding anniversary, and their youngest daughter, Helen, was by this time age twenty-seven and raising a wonderful family in the shadow of illustrious parents.

The dominant influence in Elder Lee's life continued to be his tutor, friend and "foster father," President J. Reuben Clark, Jr. An incident which occurred on the last weekend of January 1952 indicates the closeness of their relationship, when Elder Lee was assigned to conduct a stake conference in Grantsville, Utah, where President Clark maintained a second family home as a rural retreat and ranch.

President Clark phoned, as did his daughter Louise, also, to invite Elder and Sister Lee to stay with them at President Clark's home during this conference weekend. On Saturday, after the welfare and leadership sessions were held, they had an enjoyable visit until near midnight with President Clark, his daughter, Louise, and his son, Reuben, and his wife, Emily.

Early on Sunday morning Elder Lee arose to accompany President Clark on an inspection of his barnyard and fine Hereford animals. Then they went to stake conference, where nearly 25 percent, or 588 attended, and in the afternoon 539 Saints returned, the largest attendance in their stake history of six years. President Clark attended and spoke in the afternoon session. Then the Lee diary records a statement which describes the uniquely close bond between these two magnificent Church leaders. Concerning his comments at the stake conference, Elder Lee wrote: "President Clark thought my public remark, 'that I esteemed him above any other man,' might have some repercussions, as well it might, if repeated by those wishing to make trouble." Between the two of them, the statesman-like mentor and the now maturing, most apt protegé, there was a complete understanding that most resembled an ideal father-son relationship, which was quite uncommon for Church leadership circles.

Totally unassociated with his Church relationships came a sudden, severe challenge. In August 1952 Elder Lee received a telephone call which greatly surprised him and his wife. The call concerned a close friend who had committed a tragic mistake and, in the aftermath, lost his job. Elder Lee and his wife sat up until midnight talking about these serious matters, and then Elder Lee spent most of the remainder of the night praying and pondering the proper course to take to help out in this regrettable situation which had devastated the family of his friend. Going to the aid of the stricken family the next day, at his destination Elder Lee met and talked with a number of people to obtain all the available facts. After almost an entire day and night of fasting and prayer he was prompted to seek the aid of two Latter-day Saint attorneys. He reviewed the case at length with his attorney friends, and as evening came on he had a feeling of peace and assurance for which he could find no rational reason.

Although the next day was Sunday, Elder Lee awoke with everything as dark and forbidding as if his task were "the most impossible thing in the world," as he described his circumstances.

He contacted the bishop of the family, who promised every aid in extending love and sympathy under this trying situation. Elder Lee spent the remainder of the Sabbath afternoon in prayerful meditation and fasting to find the best method of resolving this crisis.

Then the miracle of a heaven-provided solution broke through the gloomy maze. In the middle of the night, after Elder Lee had prayed several times, a direct communication from God enlightened his mind and soul. Elder Lee's own words in his diary describe this powerful spiritual event: "I was startled by a realization that I was being shown from a divine source the procedure to be followed . . . , which completely changed what I had planned yesterday."

The next day Elder Lee met with the attorneys and proceeded to present the case as he had been shown the night before. With this information in hand, the attorneys were able to bring the matter to an immediate and favorable conclusion. Elder Lee records that the family "was overjoyed when we reported our results, and felt they had been participants in a human experience which was a miracle." The cloud of doubt and suspicion which had surrounded the friend dissipated, and he was rehired.

Later that week Elder Lee wrote from Salt Lake City to the two attorneys who had assisted him in his remarkable rescue of his close friend. Elder Lee wrote:

> Since leaving you . . . , I have pondered over and over again in my mind the resulting actions in which you two brethren have played such a vital part with such soul-stirring and unusual results. . . . I have learned as never before the power by which the Almighty opened the prison door to Peter and by which the angel of God stood by Paul when shipwreck threatened. So He stood by me and us, and I knew the power by which we moved. So thin was the veil that I knew the nearness of powers of divine direction, even as I know now that Joseph knew as he made his moves which protected and directed him in his early service towards the setting up of the kingdom.
>
> May the Lord bless you always and bring you to me if I likewise might on another occasion . . . [assist] you as you [assisted] me. As ever your brother, Harold B. Lee.

Two days later Elder Lee met his long-time friend and former counselor in the Pioneer Stake presidency, a most spiritual man, Paul C. Child. He told Elder Lee that he had had some terrible dreams concerning his safety. Elder Lee's reply was: "Your dreams were describing actual dangers, Paul, and I have been through hell during the last few days."

Years later Elder Lee made statements from the Tabernacle podium concerning a moment of pure revelation, following wrestling with the powers of Satan. His words were: "And had I prevailed for a moment longer, there would have been no veil." He likely was describing this remarkable experience when he dropped everything and rushed to the aid of a stricken family, using his unmatched spiritual powers to overcome the evil one and rescue a grateful family from disaster.

MANY-SIDED SERVICE—1953

In 1953, Elder Lee's aging mother reached her seventy-fourth birthday, President Clark became eighty-two, and Elder Lee's younger brother Clyde suffered a heart attack and died.

Despite all else occurring in his life, Elder Lee never forgot his grandfather role, a relationship he dearly loved. On June 11, 1953, he took "Skipper" (David), age five, and "Hal" (Harold Lee), age four, to attend the Mutual Improvement Association Dance Festival in the University of Utah stadium. His official diary entry stated that "they were tired boys, but seemingly very happy."

The inside story, however, was a contest of wills from which this General Authority grandfather learned a lesson he often used in his sermons. As the long evening wore on, it became obvious that four-year-old Hal was not able to sit still that long, nor have his interest sustained in the panorama going on some distance away on the stadium floor. Grandfather Lee, not wishing to disturb his General Authority friends who surrounded him, tried in vain to quietly direct him to sit still as Hal taxed his patience by running up and down the aisle. Finally, in exasperation he caught the restless youngster with a firm grasp, sat him down very hard on his own lap, and held him tightly. A second later he felt the impact of a little doubled-up fist against his cheek, accompanied by Hal's indignant response, audible to all, "Grandfather, don't shove me!"

Embarrassed and realizing too late his mistake in handling the matter, he relaxed his hold on his young grandson, and reassuringly and lovingly cuddled him in his arms. It was not long until Hal submitted to the warmth and security of Grandfather's arms and drifted off into a contented sleep.

Receiving honorary doctorate from University of Utah, with President A. Ray Olpin (left) and Dr. Henry Eyring (right)

The title of Elder Lee's next sermon to Primary leaders? "Love—Don't Shove!"

The first of Harold B. Lee's honorary degrees from Utah colleges came on June 1, 1953, when he traveled to Logan to participate in the graduation exercises at Utah State University. He was awarded an honorary doctor's degree in Humanities; also receiving honorary degrees were Mrs. Ella V. Reeder and the former chief of the United States Forestry Service, Lyle Watts.

On the previous day Elder Lee delivered the Baccalaureate sermon, which he entitled "I Dare You to Believe." In this address he discussed the fundamental concepts of true religion. Evidently it was a successful mental and spiritual probe because the next day Elder Lee overheard a Dr. Farrell of Kansas State College telling President Emeritus E. C. Peterson that the services on Sunday were "the finest he had attended."

Elder Lee carried a huge load as an officiator at temple marriages, a service to the Saints which he enjoyed but which represented a relentless drain on his time and energies. Despite his efforts to please, sometimes he failed. There was one such instance in June of 1953.

At the regular Thursday meeting in the temple a letter addressed to the Council of the Twelve was read. In this letter a mother attacked an unnamed member of the Twelve who had been asked to perform a marriage for her son at 8:00 A.M. one morning. After changing the hour to suit his convenience, and after waiting for this Apostle until 10:30 A.M., the family were told that he could not come. The writer bitterly assailed such discourtesy.

When Elder Lee returned to his office, he checked his calendar and found that he was the guilty party. He immediately sent for the young couple to come to the office to make amends for his forgetfulness, although it was his understanding that all such appointments made by his secretary were tentative and subject to cancellation at the last minute.

To put this rare communications breakdown in proper perspective and to understand the immense volume involved, it is well to note that Elder Lee performed 122 temple marriages in 1952, and was maintaining that pace with 42 performed up to June 18 in 1953. A more careful appointment procedure was thereafter instituted, but Elder Lee's personal service to the families of the Church continued unabated.

A Fundamental Doctrine Taught at BYU Institute Course—1954

The year 1954 found Elder Lee concerned by many family illnesses. On January he recorded: "Fern is down with a very distressing cold, as is also our baby Marlee [his first granddaughter] in Provo. Helen is also sick. We need the blessings of health. I went to my quarterly meeting with the Twelve, fasting and praying for improved health."

Elder Lee celebrated his fifty-fifth birthday this year. Three days before this anniversary he was honored, along with all other former Pioneer Stake presidents, at the Golden Jubilee of Pioneer Stake, where they presented him with a scroll. In it was the notification that from that time forward the name of the Pioneer Stake gymnasium would be changed to Harold B. Lee Hall, and that a plaque would soon be placed on the building documenting this fact.

Through the years much inspiration had come to Elder Lee in dreams. On February 24, 1954, he recorded in his journal a dream which predicted President David O. McKay's physical condition during his last years as President of the Church. The entry stated, "I had an ugly dream last night about President McKay, whom I saw very thin and emaciated, so much so that I carried him in my arms."

This became fact as President McKay was unable to walk in his last years of life. Many times Elder Lee and the other General Authorities carried him into the Tabernacle at general conference and other meetings which he desired to attend.

In April 1954, Elder Lee conferred with President Joseph Fielding Smith after he had thought through his teaching assignment at Brigham Young University, which was a summer course designed for seminary and institute instructors. Together they decided that other members of the Executive Committee of BYU and President Clark should be invited to deliver some of the lectures to enrich the course.

The course was fraught with some anxiety because Elder Lee had already been labeled an extreme conservative by some of the more liberal BYU faculty members. These members knew Brother Lee for his "narrow-minded" attitude on fundamental Church doctrine.

On June 15, 1954, Elder Lee commenced teaching his morning classes at BYU for seminary teachers of the Church. He began his doctrinal discussion on the Godhead and attempted to feel out his audience. The first negative reaction soon came as Roy A. West told him some senior faculty members of the Religion Department were objecting to giving credit for the class, because Elder Lee didn't have a Ph.D. degree.

His final lecture was on "The Church and Divine Revelation," in which he discussed by whom in the Church the gift of prophecy might be exercised.

Brother Lee brought his work at BYU to a close with a final examination. His diary entry reveals appreciation for his efforts, both in jest and in earnest: "My final examination was termed by President Clark and Brother Moyle, before a banquet of the seminary and institute teachers and their wives, as 'unconstitutional and inhumane.' At the banquet the teachers presented me with a German 'Retina' camera as a token of their esteem and appreciation for my work with them this summer."

As assigned by Elder Lee, Elder Moyle gave the closing address and lecture to the teachers on "The Value of Witnesses." According to Elder Lee, Elder Moyle made a masterful presentation of this subject, evaluating, as a lawyer might do, the witnesses who have testified of the divinity of the latter-day work of the gospel, and closing with a powerful, personal testimony. After a hymn, the teachers bore testimony to each other for three hours in a glorious spiritual experience.

Elder Lee's final summation of his five-week effort among the student-teachers was recorded in his journal in these words:

> The testimonies of those enrolled in the course were inspirational. They bore testimony of a seventeen-year-old boy who asked for a blessing to help him in the experience of death, which came only moments thereafter, and of the value of the gospel in combating error, etc. The testimonies of the teachers also concerned their struggles to overcome the false teaching of so-called "higher" education. If I have made any enemies by my teaching this summer, I have not known it. All seemed to have been impressed by little things that evidence my sincere interest in my assignment, such as coming with the Brethren who came to give special lectures and to come, personally, to administer the final test. Even Brother Moyle confessed that he thought I was unduly attentive in my regularity in following this assignment.

The highlight story of this interesting summer experience was an incident which went into Elder Lee's famous "miracle" file.

He frequently shared it with youth leaders whom he was attempting to inspire. It illustrates a true Harold B. Lee characteristic—he always sought first the miracle and believed with a pure heart, never doubting. To youthful seminary leaders assembled on campus at BYU in 1979 and 1980 he related this story:

> In 1954 I came on this campus each day for five or six weeks for a class with all the seminary and some of the institute teachers. It was a grueling summer, but I learned, along with them. We had a glorious time together.
>
> At the conclusion we had a banquet, something like the one we had tonight, only President Clark and Brother Moyle had come down to be with us. We were seated at the front and the tables before us were fixed so that all of them could get a side view of the speaker's stand. At the conclusion of the banquet one of these seminary teachers took me aside. He came with glistening tears in his eyes and was almost trembling. He said: "Come over here in this corner, Brother Lee. I have got to tell you something. My wife and I were sitting over there at that table. We were looking over into this corner. Suddenly there appeared the faces of the Prophet Joseph Smith and Brigham Young. I thought, Isn't that marvelous to see the pictures of those two men together? As I watched, that picture faded; it wasn't there anymore. I turned to my wife and said, 'Did you see that picture?' She replied, 'I didn't see anything.' But, even though there is no picture there now, Brother Lee, it was there. I saw it. I wasn't dreaming."
>
> "I'm not surprised," I said. "Aren't you aware of the fact that all through our summer course we have been quoting from the words of the Prophet Joseph Smith and President Brigham Young? Why wouldn't they want to be here? Where else would they rather be on such an occasion than to be permitted to come here at the conclusion of this great seminar where you are going out to influence 150,000 youth from all over this Church? I wouldn't be surprised that they are very close, to let their spirits attend such a gathering. Perhaps most haven't seen them, but have no doubt that they were here. Heaven isn't a million miles away. It's here."

Then Elder Lee concluded with a larger lesson from this seminar story for the benefit of the young student leaders in his audience. His moral was:

> Yes, the Savior, too, is in our midst. His eyes are upon us, but we can't always see him. But the day can come when we could see him. It isn't the Lord who withholds himself from us; it is we who withhold ourselves from him. And if we were living completely worthy,

we could see him and have a personal visitation and we would have the assurance, even though we couldn't see him, that he was there, walking, talking, listening, aiding, directing. Make no mistake—this is his work.

INSPIRATIONAL WELFARE STORIES—1955

In 1955, at age fifty-six, thirty-six years had passed since Elder Harold B. Lee was serving as young missionary in the Western States Mission. His oldest daughter, Maurine, was now thirty-one and expecting her fourth child. Sister Lee spent some time during this year with Maurine while her husband, Ernest, conducted a travel tour of South American countries. And the family received its first baptized grandchild as David Goates turned eight.

It was a time of trial still for the family. Some were ill and others were beset with personal problems. In May, Elder Lee was so intent on seeking a blessing from the Lord that he remained in the Salt Lake Temple after performing a marriage there. Dressed in his temple clothes, and at the altar in the Council of Twelve Room Elder Lee pleaded for the Lord to protect his family from any unfortunate circumstances. This prayer was answered in part within five months.

While touring the Central States Mission in April 1955, Elder Lee returned to Independence, Missouri and there found a letter from Fern telling of a providential safeguarding of her eyesight. When he arrived back home, however, on the first day of May, he was much disturbed at his wife's condition and wrote in his journal:

> Returning from my tour of the Central States Mission, I found Fern in rather precarious health with her blood pressure out of control somewhere between 200 and 300. She had suffered a hemorrhage in one of her eyes that made a red blotch before her vision. As usual, her faith and courage were great, but my heart almost melted as I contemplated the possibility of her failing health. I stayed home with her all day Sunday as she decided against making any calls.

President McKay was then eighty-two years of age, serving, as were all members of the First Presidency, under some limitations of health. President Stephen L Richards missed many meetings because of his periodic low blood pressure and President J. Reuben Clark had a nerve ailment in his back.

Through the years Harold B. Lee's relationship with Walter Stover was intimate and prized. Elder Lee never failed to praise highly the sweet spirit of Brother Stover, a most valued member of the Church General Welfare committee. At stake conferences Brother Stover always stimulated a high spiritual atmosphere and never failed to inspire Church members with his sermons of faith. He often illustrated his appeals for welfare preparation by referring to his personal experiences in Europe. The following notes from Elder Lee's journal entry of April 10, 1955, record a few of these inspirational stories and illustrate how welfare commodities from the storehouses in Utah, Church headquarters, and the gardens of European Saints were used to save the starving German Saints during the Berlin blockade:

> I held the welfare and leadership meetings where Brother Stover related an experience in Germany where a little twelve-year-old girl was possessed of an evil spirit (or spirits). She had counted one hundred of them. He told how he first prayed for a forgiveness of his sins and waited for peace to come so that he could rebuke the spirits.
>
> In the Sunday sessions, Sister Matis from the Finnish Mission told of an experience in making a quilt in the Chicago Ward Relief Society, which she brightened by a patching from her little daughter's pink, plaid skirt. Then, later in Finland, she unpacked a box of quilts sent from the General Welfare Committee of the Church to warm the freezing Saints, only to find on the top of the box the same quilt she had helped to make in Chicago.
>
> Brother Stover told also of President Zappey, who at this time was suffering a slow death from cancer, by whose cooperation the Saints in Holland planted potatoes in their flower beds for the German Saints threatened by starvation because of the Russian blockade in Berlin. In donated amounts from five pounds to a half a sack, the total amount came to nine truckloads. He obtained permits to get them out of Holland and into Germany by calling them the "Lord's Potatoes," and explaining the welfare program to the authorities and the Saints. He told me of getting eighty barrels of herring from Holland also via Switzerland and Czechoslovakia and East Germany. Because of his military permit from the Russian government, he was able to haul these barrels, two at a time, all through the night, across the line into West Berlin to deliver to the starving Saints. He had women riding with him as a blind, suggesting to the police that he was just another man "out with his women."

DREAM-REVELATION PRECEDES LOS ANGELES TEMPLE DEDICATION

Harold B. Lee was fifty-seven in 1956, his mother was seventy-seven, and he and Fern had been married thirty-three years.

The travels of General Authorities, often thought by many Saints to be glamorous and exciting, are frequently both physically and emotionally exhausting. These long and tiring separations from family and loved ones mark one of the greatest sacrifices made by the Lord's anointed. In 1956 Elder Lee returned sick from both major trips he took. On May 2, 1956, he went to his physician for an examination. A congestion in his lower left lung was discovered, which apparently stemmed from his early childhood bout with pneumonia. This current infection was an aftermath from an illness suffered while Elder Lee was touring the Hawaiian Islands. The physician gave him immediate treatment to overcome the infection and cautioned him against too much activity until the infection was under control.

Another examination on June 30, 1956, after Elder Lee had returned from a trip to Mexico, disclosed that both he and Elder Spencer W. Kimball, his traveling companion, had acquired infections which had matured in both Apostles after they had returned home.

Continuous sacrifice for the sake of their daughters' young growing families marked these years as the Lees proved to be ideal grandparents to the young children and ideal parents to the men who had married their daughters.

In July 1956, Elder Lee donated his car to his son-in-law Ernest to increase safety on a Brigham Young University–sponsored travel tour he was conducting through Mexico and Central America. Then the Lees and Helen took care of the Wilkins children while their parents were out of the country.

Elder Lee's journal entry of July 23, 1956, explains how Maurine's boys came to stay with their grandparents:

> Maurine's boys, Alan and Larry, came up to stay with us until Ernie and Maurine return. They seem to have gotten somewhat out of hand with the young couple assigned to watch over them in Provo. Possibly we won't fare much better, but at least our minds will be at ease and they will feel of the genuine love and care of a devoted grandmother. We hear from Maurine, but each card or letter indicates she is lonesome for her babies and is having a pretty rugged time of it.

Helen's husband, Brent, tried to help out by arranging an outing for their two families of boys at the summer cabin home of Lewis Farr on the south fork of the Weber Canyon. There Grandfather Lee took his exuberant young grandsons to play: "I left early with Brent and our five boys to take them to the Farr mountain cabin where they have a large outdoor swimming pool with plenty of playground. They came back tired and sunburned, but hardly less than their grandfather. Helen had prepared a fine lunch, so with eating and baseball and swimming, the boys were happy."

After another week of tending, Grandfather and "Nana" Lee were glad to welcome home the parents. On the final, grand effort on July 30, 1956, Elder Lee wrote in his diary of giving his all to the boy-caring project: "I took Helen's and Maurine's older boys with me to a cowboy show, which took much of the afternoon. That was preceded by some shopping and was followed by some refreshments at Keeley's, and it was about all the energy and patience I had. Ernie and Maurine arrived home at about 7:30 p.m. It was a joyous reunion with their children and a pleasant evening relating travel experiences."

The dedication of the splendorous Los Angeles Temple in 1956 was a highlight for the Church and also the labors of Elder Lee. He was asked by President David O. McKay to serve as the chairman of arrangements for that grand event, and as such was busily engaged in all the details for the transportation, housing, feeding, invitations, and similar arrangements.

On Saturday, March 11, the entire party of General Authorities, their wives and families, after lunch were taken through the temple to view the paintings and the facilities. They, like the thousands of visitors before them at the open house, were impressed by the spaciousness and beauty of the building.

The opening dedicatory service was a memorable event with nearly six thousand Saints in attendance. The First Presidency spoke, as did President Noble Waite, chairman of the temple committee, under whose direction a total of $1.6 million had been contributed by the Saints in Southern California. The music was furnished by the Mormon Choir of Southern California under the direction of Frederick Davis. Sister Ewan Harbrecht sang the beautiful hymn "Bless This House" preceding the dedicatory prayer by President McKay. After that, the Hosanna Shout was led by President Richards.

Some persons have heard of an alleged dream or revelation which Elder Lee was supposed to have received during the Los Angeles Temple dedicatory services. The truth of this story is told simply in Elder Lee's diary entry of Sunday, March 11, 1956: "I was deeply moved as the dedicatory prayer was read because of a dream I had two weeks ago, in which President McKay was impressing me with the meaning of the love of God, as it relates to the love of our fellow men and of His service. The dedicatory prayer closed with similar instructions to those I had heard in my dream two weeks before."

After the dedicatory service, Elder Lee was taken Sunday night to the Adams Ward of Los Angeles; following that he spoke at the Institute building on the University of Southern California campus where about five hundred persons had assembled. He recorded this spiritual experience in his diary on March 13:

> There was a wonderful spirit present at the fireside and seldom have I talked to a group who gave more rapt attention. When I returned home I received a letter from a young girl from Redondo Beach, who had been present, who told how, as a convert of three months, she had begun to doubt that there were prophets and that this Church was true. She testified that as I spoke (and I will use her own language)—"I wish I could explain to you how I felt at that moment. I seemed to glow inside and had no trouble in praying to my Father in Heaven. . . . I thought that this must all be my imagination, but I know that it couldn't be just that. Elder Lee, I want to thank you so much for helping me so very much in that thirty minutes last night. I know now that this is the true Church and I'm so proud to be a part of it."

Appointments to National Corporation Boards—1957

On a flight (unusual for him) home from New York City, Elder Lee wrote, "I note my fifty-eighth birthday with a realization that advancing years bring increased problems and anxieties." His mother was now seventy-eight years of age, and changes were inevitable for the Lee family. This year, 1957, however, brought the bigger changes in Elder Lee's professional life, rather than in his service as an Apostle, for in this year he was introduced to the inside operation of large national business corporations.

The year opened with notification from E. Roland Harriman, chairman of the Union Pacific Railroad Board of Directors, that Elder Lee had been accepted in their meeting on December 27 and that he would be officially elected to membership on the board at the January 24 meeting in New York City. Elder Lee immediately wrote his acceptance of the appointment and inquired as to the first meeting he would be expected to attend.

The president of the Union Pacific, A. E. Stoddard, phoned nine days later inviting Elder Lee to the January meeting of the Union Pacific Board of Directors in New York City. He was most gracious in urging that Elder Lee attend that first meeting. Already Elder Lee was thinking of and planning a reception and luncheon with a number of the leading Church Brethren, including the First Presidency, when Mr. Harriman and other Union Pacific officials would next be in Salt Lake City.

Reaction to Elder Lee's appointment among the Brethren was mixed. At the temple meeting on January 17, Elder Lee told Joseph Fielding Smith, President of the Quorum of the Twelve, about his forthcoming appointment to the Union Pacific Board of Directors, and he seemed most pleased. However, when he mentioned to President McKay that he had been invited to be in New York City on the next Thursday and would miss the temple meeting if he went, he offered no congratulations and brushed aside the conversation quite impatiently. President McKay earlier had given a reluctant and slow approval for Elder Lee to serve on the Union Pacific Board of Directors.

En route to New York, Elder Lee stopped for a layover in Chicago during the severe cold and stormy January weather. He visited with David Kennedy, who as the new president of the Continental Illinois Bank, was learning quickly about the problems of serving in that executive capacity. After Brother Kennedy left for a meeting, Brother Lee stayed in his office to learn about the men with whom he would be associating on the Union Pacific board, finding abundant information from a directory of corporations and a volume of *Who's Who in America.*

A pattern of hospitality by the management of the famous Waldorf-Astoria Hotel commenced with Elder Lee's first business trip. Frank Wangeman, son-in-law of Henry D. Moyle and executive of the Waldorf-Astoria Hotel, made his reservations in New York. Because of this connection, the assistant manager, Mr. Murphy, and the manager, Mr. Wallace Lee, graciously greeted Elder Lee on his arrival. For years later the hotel's "VIP" treatment was accorded Elder Lee each month as he returned for corporation meetings.

Upon arrival in New York, Elder Lee was suffering from severe distress in his digestive system and had little sleep the first night. He therefore rested for the first day in his hotel room.

A glimpse into the humility with which Elder Lee approached his new association with the Union Pacific Railroad is contained in his diary entry of January 24, 1957:

> I came to the experiences of this day with a humble feeling that in my appointment to the U.P. Railroad I was there as a representative of the Church, and for no other reason. I decided to fast in preparation for my first meeting at 10:30 a.m., to which I had been invited by E. Roland Harriman. I arrived a few minutes early at the railroad headquarters, at 120 Broadway, where I was met by Mr. Harriman and was introduced to the other members of the board. Four new board members were elected, including George S. Eccles of Salt Lake, Elbridge Geary of New York, and Oscar J. Lawler of Los Angeles. Following the board meeting we and other members of the board were guests of Mr. Harriman at a lunch served in his office at 59 Wall Street. After the lunch President Ted Jacobsen of the Eastern States Mission met me and we visited briefly at the New York Stock Exchange and the Federal Court Building, observing a tax evasion trial.

At the temple meeting the next week Elder Lee intentionally avoided reporting his election to the Union Pacific Railroad Board of Directors, since he had not received a very enthusiastic response earlier. However, President Stephen L Richards commented on the subject and said he thought the minutes should show that Elder Lee had been elected to the leadership of one of the great corporations of the world.

Elder Lee's second appointment to high station in the national business world came through an apparent unintentional introduction by President J. Reuben Clark to the officers of the Equitable Life Assurance Society of New York. Elder Lee had accompanied President Clark to his Equitable meeting, going early to his own Union Pacific meetings to ensure President Clark's safety and convenience. On June 20, 1957, President Clark took Elder Lee with him to the executive offices of Equitable Life for an appointment he had made so that Elder Lee could meet Ray D. Murphy, chairman of the board, and Mr. James F. Oates, Jr., the new president of the company. Elder Lee recorded his impressions of this first meeting in these words: "It was a pleasant meeting and for a purpose which at the present does not seem clear, but may later have meaning. Later, after President Clark had met in their board meeting, he told me that I have made a 'wonderful' impression on these two men."

The next day, June 21, he wrote:

> Today, before we left New York City, President Clark was invited to meet with the new president of the Equitable and with Ray D. Murphy, chairman of the board. When he came back he said they wanted to talk with him about his retirement as a member of the board of directors, a subject which he had mentioned to the two presidents. They told him that they thought he should stay on until the annual meeting near the first of the year, and then tender his resignation shortly thereafter. Then they surprised him by saying that they wanted to appoint me to fill the vacancy at that time. President Clark declared that he had never mentioned to them the idea of my becoming a member of the board. He wondered what the reaction of the President of the Church would be. Before this he had talked about coming back to the December meeting, but with this decision, he thought he would reconsider the whole question and requested that I keep the matter confidential until Equitable announced it.

According to the plan, President Clark and Elder Lee did attend their respective board meetings in New York in December, 1957, at which time President Clark announced that it was his intention to return to the New York meetings of Equitable Life in February and resign at that time. It was the intention, President Clark said, for the president of Equitable to nominate Elder Lee to fill his vacancy at that time.

This schedule actually was delayed some at the request of President Clark, so that it was July of 1958 when Elder Lee was notified by a long-distance telephone call from President James F. Oates, Jr., that he had been elected at a meeting of the board as a director to fill a vacancy caused by the resignation of President Clark. Elder Lee attended his first Equitable board meeting on August 20, 1958, when plans were made for a testimonial dinner honoring President Clark. This formal dinner was delayed until December of 1958 to allow Elder Lee time to return from a trip to South Africa.

WELFARE PLAN MODIFICATIONS

The concern over the acceptance and weakening support for the welfare program's founding principles began as early as 1952, when a feeling of stiffening opposition was felt. As individual proposals were brought to the First Presidency for welfare project investment, it often seemed as though the entire welfare program was undergoing testing and was on trial. In 1953 President Clark was urging a slow, cautious path by the leaders of the welfare program, for fear of losing past gains.

As 1957 arrived the climate was tense. At the first meeting of the Brethren in the temple, two references to welfare brought critical responses from the First Presidency. By March of that year it was learned that a complete investigation was being launched at the request of the First Presidency. When Elder Lee saw the report it was evident to him that it contained "the same antagonisms against the program which were common back in 1936 when the program began."

It was while this debate was going on over the welfare program that general conference convened. President McKay opened the conference on April 3, and Elder Lee captured the dramatic situation in his diary:

> President McKay's opening address on the text "Be Ye Doers of the Word, and Not Hearers Only" was a remarkable keynote sermon. In his talk he told of the hours of prayer in preparation for his address. For the first time during his presidency, he made reference to the welfare program, extolling its leaders and declaring that "its methods had been tested and proved sound." I told him afterwards I felt as though the welfare program had gained a reprieve and that I had relived the feelings I had in the beginning when I was almost daily in his office as he directed me.

Thus, probably the most severe testing the welfare program had undergone had come and passed, but while the plan was saved, it was not to remain unchanged by President McKay and his colleagues. Elder Lee was grateful the program was retained, but he groaned inwardly at what he saw as modernization and liberalization of its original concepts.

By August the growing issue of Federal Social Security Insurance coverage for Church employees was being raised. At the Welfare Finance Committee meeting, Brother Lee refused to go along with a motion to provide Social Security for the Deseret Clothing Factory employees. He thought it was moving a step away from original welfare program principles.

His opposition soon became ineffective, however, because in September 1957 the First Presidency instructed the Presiding

Keeping up with his heavy load of office appointments, 1957
(Courtesy of Ensign *Magazine)*

Bishopric to inaugurate government Social Security for all Church employees, in addition to the Church's own insurance program. This step caused sober reflection by the welfare plan pioneers.

The pressures to conform were mounting in those days, but even after Elder Henry D. Moyle lined up and supported having the regional welfare coordinators and storehouse employees covered by government Social Security, Elder Lee wouldn't yield. This attitude is disclosed in a reference in his diary made on December 11, 1957:

> This morning Henry Moyle chided me because I was unwilling to join with him in recommending that our welfare workers be covered by government Social Security. He said he considered that we would be "in rebellion should we refrain from doing so." I took sharp disagreement with him and further information confirmed my feelings as being correct.

Elder Lee persisted in his conservative views, and late in the year, when he was inspecting the welfare farm of the New Jersey

Stake, the stake president argued the necessity of putting their farm manager under government Social Security. Elder Lee, being very consistent and determined, suggested to President Mortimer that they instead consider increasing the salary of the farm manager so that he could buy his own insurance.

The ups and downs of the debate during 1957 regarding welfare plan principles ended with President Clark urging on the last day of the year that his associates not press for important decisions at that time for fear such action would bring an impasse and perhaps threaten gains already achieved.

One welfare-related issue on which the presiding Brethren did not at that time see eye-to-eye was that of the federal social security program. Among both leaders and other members of the Church there were those who argued that as individuals they were paying out of their income the same tax dollars as other citizens, but were receiving less benefits. Just as the federal government's action had forced a change on the Church in the early days of plural marriage, now the movement of government to adopt a more liberal social philosophy brought its powerful influences into Church leadership circles. Modification of conservative welfare practices was inevitable, but it was nonetheless painful.

ELDER ADAM S. BENNION PASSES—1958

Many valuable and historic experiences filled the life of Elder Harold B. Lee during 1958. His mentor, President J. Reuben Clark, Jr., had reached eighty-seven years of age. Elder Lee's family also was growing older: his eldest daughter, Maurine, became thirty-four and his eldest grandson, David Goates, reached eleven years old.

Elder and Sister Lee celebrated their thirty-fifth wedding anniversary as they left England to return to the United States aboard the giant ocean liner, the *Queen Elizabeth*.

Discovery of an ulcer in Elder Lee's duodenal canal didn't prevent his usual arduous travel schedule; in fact, this is the year he completed a memorable trip to South Africa.

One interesting sidelight on the sensitive nature of Elder Lee is seen in Elder Lee's decision not to accompany Elder and Sister Moyle on a trip to Europe. Henry and Alberta Moyle had generously extended an invitation for Fern and Harold to accompany them to Europe during the summer of 1958, with all expenses being paid by the Moyles. After thinking it over Elder Lee declined because as a part of the itinerary the Moyles wanted to attend the dedication of the temple in England during the first part of September. Elder Lee explained his position in his diary: "I felt certain that my going uninvited would be construed as my trying to become something I was not. I told Brother Moyle that some other time would be appreciated, but urged that they make their plans and go anyway."

A footnote is offered regarding the previously mentioned election of Elder Lee to serve on the board of directors of the Equitable Life Assurance Society. One week after the announcement, on July 23, 1958, Elder and Sister Lee were guests at the home of President Clark along with Mark and Emma Petersen and their good friends from Heber City, the Cummings and the Probsts, who brought the dinner. Still showing his weakness from a recent illness, President Clark took occasion this night to explain how it happened that Elder Lee was appointed to the Equitable Life board of directors by the request of Ray D. Murphy, former chairman, and Mr. James Oates, Jr., president, and not by President Clark's nomination.

Typical of Elder Lee's spiritual experiences of this period was an incident in the Salt Lake Temple on April 10, 1958. On this day he performed a temple marriage for David James Thomas and Betty Joan Holt, daughter of Harry Holt, deceased. When Elder Lee walked into the sealing room he felt an overpowering influence that made it difficult for him to control his emotions. "I felt certain the father of the bride was not far away," he wrote later.

Elder Adam S. Bennion had been appointed a member of the Quorum of the Twelve in 1953. His choice might have been more expected some fifteen years previous, so popular was he as a teacher of the gospel when he was Commissioner of Education for the Church. Nonetheless, on April 5, 1953, he was sustained to fill the vacancy occasioned by the death of Elder John A. Widtsoe. President Clark told Elder Lee that some twenty-eight names had been recommended as worthy of the calling, but stressed that the right of nominational selection always rests with the President of the Church.

At the request of Elder Bennion, Elder Lee went with him to an upper room of the Salt Lake Temple and spent a delightful hour reviewing temple ordinances and acquainting him with the procedures that would follow the next Thursday morning when he would be ordained. When the hour came Elder Bennion was perfect in performance and was "magnificent" in answering the charge, according to Elder Lee's proud diary entries.

Thus began a close and rewarding relationship between these two mighty men of God, both of whom were among the Church's greatest teachers. In 1955 Elder Lee characterized Elder Bennion: "He is so enthusiastic and so able in meeting human problems that it is always refreshing and stimulating to be with him." Tragically, however, it was to last but five short years, for on February 6, 1958, Elder Lee had a phone call from Dick Bennion, who informed him that his father had suffered a stroke and was hospitalized. He asked that Elder Lee come to give him a blessing. Elder Bennion was paralyzed on the left side and the physicians reported that the right side was involved also. While the situation didn't look good, the Brethren were hopeful as they united in pleading with the Lord for Elder Bennion's life in their weekly temple meeting.

At 2:00 A.M. on Sunday, February 9, 1958, Elder Lee received word from the hospital that Elder Bennion was dying. He dressed, went to the hospital, and stayed until 4:00 A.M., when Elder Bennion's condition improved. At the hospital Elder Lee blessed both Elder Bennion and his wife, Minerva.

After a busy stake conference and a weekend with little sleep, Elder Lee went to the hospital early on Monday and found his friend in a deep coma. With the family now resigned to his passing, and at his son Dick's request, Elder Lee blessed him that he might be released soon if he were not to recover to normal health.

Very weary from lack of sleep Elder Lee went to Provo to speak at a Brigham Young University assembly; before the meeting was adjourned, word came that Elder Adam S. Bennion had died at 8:35 A.M. President Joseph Fielding Smith informed Elder Lee that the Bennion family had requested that President McKay and he speak at the funeral on Friday.

The Council of the Twelve met the day before the funeral, saddened by the untimely death of their beloved brother. President McKay had felt encouraged when he had last seen him, and thought that his life might be extended.

The funeral service was held in the Salt Lake Tabernacle; President Clark conducted and President McKay and Elder Lee served as speakers. Elder Lee's journal tells of the most remarkable aspect of this funeral in these words:

There was a wonderful, peaceful spirit at this service. I was amazed by the number of people who afterwards told me that at times during my speaking, my voice sounded as though it were Adam, himself, speaking. Possibly this was because I had taken lessons from his sermons, or because his influence was very near. Adam's wife, Minerva, said: "Strangely, yesterday, at the services, was the greatest experience of my life." Ned, Adam's son, stated, "I wouldn't have missed this experience for all the world."

Having been asked to write an article on the deceased Apostle, Elder Lee summarized Adam S. Bennion's superb life and labors while traveling on a Union Pacific train through a wet snowstorm. He was able to finish writing his tribute in memoriam to Elder Bennion's life by the time the train arrived at Cheyenne, Wyoming, and from there mailed it back to Salt Lake City in time to meet the printing deadline of the *Relief Society Magazine* in which the article was published.

HENRY D. MOYLE APPOINTED TO FIRST PRESIDENCY—1959

When Elder Harold B. Lee reached his sixtieth year in life, others in his family were passing from mortality. A grand open house was given by Elder and Sister Lee in honor of his mother on her eightieth birthday, but six months later she was taken in death while Elder Lee was in New York City. He was also in New York City when word came that his younger brother Waldo died from a ruptured appendix on February 25, 1959.

An interesting phenomenon with respect to the passing of time is noted in Elder Lee's journal on November 28, 1959. Apparently unaware of the inroads time was making on himself, he wrote concerning his visit to his old Pioneer Stake: "I marvel at the way many of our faithful Saints in my old stake have aged considerably since I left them."

Nostalgia not only set in when returning to Pioneer Stake, but every visit to Cache Valley also brought back memories of his youth. When assigned to a conference in Logan in December 1959, Elder Lee wrote in his journal, "It always seems like going back home for me to go to Logan." When he was called to speak at the funeral of John J. Croshaw, one of his loyal friends at Oxford, he had reason to recall his days at Oxford and Clifton, Idaho, and his first job as a seventeen-year-old principal of the school there.

Remarkable spiritual experiences, so consistent in Elder Lee's life, continued in 1959. One of the most significant occurred in April after Elder Lee had conducted interviews with men of the New York Stake to select a patriarch. On Saturday, April 25, 1959, Elder Lee interviewed Brother DeWitt Paul and described the experience in his journal as a "comforting, spiritual experience." The sequel setting apart, however, is where the miracle occurred. In his own words he retold the story to the LDSSA Youth Conference on Leadership held on December 5, 1969, when he said:

Let me bring the lesson [of conveying holy authority] to a modern day and read you the testimony of Sister Mortimer, the wife of the president of the New York Stake.

"I went into the room where Brother DeWitt Paul was to be ordained a patriarch of the Church. There were Brother and Sister Paul, some new bishoprics and their wives, and the stake presidency of the New York Stake. A chair was set in the center of the bishop's office in the Manhattan Ward building. It is not a large room—very full with eighteen to twenty people in it. It is situated in the basement floor of the building. It has no windows, the only ventilation for the room coming from a ventilator fan. The door is the only opening in the room. The chapel is on the floor above.

"Brother Paul sat in the chair in the center of the room with his back toward the door. The door was closed. You, Elder Lee, stood behind Brother Paul and gave him the ordination and blessing.

"Just as Elder Lee lifted his hands to place them on Brother Paul's head, a shaft of bright light came onto the back and top of Elder Lee's head. It was like bright sunshine suddenly coming through a square window—eight to ten inches square—and shining down on a forty-five-degree angle on the back and top of his head. It was as if a shade had suddenly been drawn to let in the bright sun. I saw the light just before I bowed my head. I thought what a coincidence that that shaft of light should shine on Elder Lee just at this particular instant—as he was putting his hands on Brother Paul's head.

"Just as quickly as I thought this I realized that there were no windows, therefore this was not sunlight. I knew in the same instant that it was a stream of light from Heaven that needed no physical window to come through. I opened my eyes and looked up to see and again the shaft of light was visible. Finally, my eyes could no longer see the light, but I knew it was still there for Brother Paul was receiving information and advice that could only come from the Lord, and then I knew the source from which Brother Paul could declare lineage and project blessings that would come to the individuals he would bless in the years that lie ahead."

Elder Lee concluded the lesson to the youth conference leaders by summarizing:

> In other words, I was laying my hands upon the head of Brother DeWitt Paul and the Lord was laying his hands upon Brother Paul's head by a humble servant who bore the Holy Priesthood. So it is with you who exercise your priestly responsibility in whatever you do—when you baptize, when you administer the sacrament, when you bless the sick, or when you confirm membership. Whatever priesthood rites—it is as though the Lord was putting his hands upon you or upon that one whom you bless by your own act. That's priesthood power.

On May 19, 1959, President Stephen L Richards was stricken early in the morning with a heart attack and died shortly after arriving at the hospital. Again Elder Lee was in New York City attending his Equitable meetings. He was advised to return home immediately and did so despite great difficulty with plane connections, arriving home at 2:00 A.M.

The funeral was held on Friday, May 22, 1959, with President Clark, President Joseph Fielding Smith, and Elder Gordon B. Hinckley serving as the speakers. President McKay conducted and wisely refrained from speaking, except briefly, because of the genuinely deep sorrow he felt at the loss of his companion and counselor.

In early June President McKay spent a week in seclusion in California contemplating issues, communing with heaven, and planning for the Church. He returned to announce the reorganization of the First Presidency with President Clark to serve as first counselor and Elder Henry D. Moyle as second counselor. Under date of June 12, Elder Lee confided to his diary his reaction to the reorganization and related issues. Included in that entry was this remark: "It seemed to me almost too good to be true. President McKay announced that he wanted to discuss with me the reorganization of the General Welfare Committee and indicated that he might call me later in the day."

In the temple meeting of June 18, President McKay set apart President Clark and President Moyle as his counselors and reiterated again the evidence of divine direction in the reorganization of the First Presidency. Again Elder Lee wrote in his diary: "There seemed to be a remarkable spirit of acceptance although only six of the Twelve were present. At about 10:30 p.m. Henry and Alberta Moyle came to see us and visited until near midnight. They wanted to share the joy of their new appointment in the First Presidency."

Elder Lee's intimate friendship with Elder Moyle permitted Elder Lee to have an added insight on activities as they would unfold in the newly structured First Presidency. After watching President Moyle assume his new role, he wrote of these developments as follows on July 14, 1959: "Henry Moyle has indicated some pending changes in mission presidents and has adopted a suggestion that the Brethren visiting the European Missions call all the presidents of those missions together for some roundtable discussions. It is becoming increasingly clear that Brother Moyle is going to become an aggressive mover of plans representing the First Presidency."

The relationship between Elder Lee and Elder Moyle is a fascinating history of dear, trusting friends, whose bonds became strained at times over the years as power and responsibility moved upon these two strong-willed, but extremely talented leaders. Elder Henry D. Taylor was closely associated with both Elder Lee and President Moyle in the welfare work of the Church. His observations about their relationship are revealing.

> Elder Henry D. Moyle, who was the chairman of the Church Welfare Committee, and Elder Harold B. Lee, who was the managing director, worked well together. They were both vigorous, forceful, and progressive, but extremely considerate of one another's feelings.
>
> Their offices were adjacent on the second floor, in the northeast corner of the Church Administration Building at 47 East South Temple Street. They had a sincere love and appreciation for each other, although they often differed in their opinion of a problem.
>
> When Brother Moyle had a sensitive matter to discuss with Brother Lee, he would inquire of Frances Cardall, Brother Lee's secretary, as to his mood; and vice versa, Brother Lee would ask the same question of Liliu Peery, Brother Moyle's secretary, and if the climate seemed right, he would then present his problem. (The Church Welfare Plan, p. 97.)

Early in October 1951, these two dynamic leaders were sent to Washington, D.C., to confer with John L. Lewis of the United Mine Workers Union regarding the Church's welfare coal operations. They were a powerful negotiating team and could dissolve any opposition, it seemed. Elder Lee spoke of working on this trip with Elder Moyle in these words: "I enjoyed visiting through the day with Brother Moyle, who with his great faith and loyalty is a constant support and strength."

An interesting observation on the constant safeguarding of the General Authorities while "on the Lord's errand" was seen in two diary entries within a four-month period of 1960.

On June 14, 1960, Elder Lee and President Franklin Richards of the Northwestern States Mission arrived in Seattle after a tour into Alaska. The next day they learned that on the same airline, a plane exactly like the one they had flown on had crashed between Cardova and Anchorage; all fourteen passengers and crew were killed. "We thanked the Lord again for our safe journey," wrote Elder Lee.

Just four months later, on Sunday, October 30, 1960, Elder Richard L. Evans told Elder Lee that he was waiting to board a Northwest Airlines plane at Missoula on the previous Friday night when word came that it was lost; he heard later that it had crashed twenty-two miles from the landing airfield at Missoula, Montana.

With the Brethren of the General Authorities so frequently traveling in the air to and from their weekend assignments and mission tours, it is indeed faith-promoting and inspirational to observe that not one life has been lost in an airplane mishap. The prayers of the Saints for their Church leaders and the love of the Lord for his chosen ones is abundantly manifest in their safety during their arduous travel schedules.

As the second decade of apostolic service drew to an end, Elder Lee's youngest daughter, Helen, was now thirty-five years of age. On Christmas of 1960, Elder Lee was worried about his wife's health and began to make plans to do what he could to help Fern improve in strength and enjoyment of life. He summarized his Christmas holidays in this way:

> This was a delightful Christmas with all our family together, and well and happy. We have facing us Fern's operation, and her hearing is becoming increasingly more difficult. If the Lord is willing, we hope with the coming year to correct some of these difficulties.

Third
Apostolic
Decade
———

1961 – 1970

1961–1970. A turbulent decade of challenges with social and cultural changes. The British retaliated with an invasion of their own, introducing to America, Twiggy, miniskirts, and the Beatles. Woodstock, communes brought people together . . . Riots, Vietnam, and assassinations tore the nation apart.

CHAPTER 20

Death's Dark Angel Strikes

On Friday, October 6, 1961, President J. Reuben Clark, Jr., Elder Lee's tutor and the father-figure in his life as a General Authority, died after an extended illness. President Clark, who toward the end of his life had preached about the importance of "enduring to the end," found it a difficult challenge for him when he approached his demise. Thus it was a welcome release for this scholarly and statesman-like leader, whose First Presidency service spread through three presidential administrations of the Church.

Elder Lee had just returned from the airport—where he had said his farewell to President Henry D. Moyle, then en route to Europe—when word of President Clark's passing reached him at his office. He went to the Clark home, where he met with President McKay and urged the President to recall President Moyle for the funeral. Much to the satisfaction of President Moyle and the

Clark family, they located President Moyle at the Denver airport and invited him to return.

The funeral was held on October 10, with a general conference-sized audience in attendance at the Salt Lake Tabernacle. President McKay conducted the service and made brief opening and closing remarks. Elders Mark E. Petersen and Hugh B. Brown gave the prayers. The speakers were President Henry D. Moyle, Elder Joseph Fielding Smith, Elder Harold B. Lee, and Elder Marion G. Romney. Elder Lee's diary indicated that he had many persons comment about the more personal references he made in his farewell eulogy to the most influential man in his life, and that he had remembered President Clark's instructions to "not make my vices my virtues."

THE REFINING FIRE

God has always exacted the highest price of personal sacrifice from those whom he would trust to become his prophets, the spokesmen-leaders over his children here on earth. They must go through the fiery furnace and have their mettle proven beyond question and doubt.

He asked Abraham to choose between the life of his only son and obedience to Jehovah. The faith of prophets must be great enough to disregard their own safety and confidently walk into lions' dens, as did Daniel. Alma and Amulek were imprisoned for many days, where they suffered mockery, hunger, thirst, nakedness, and being bound by strong cords, but when their faith had been tested sufficiently, the cords fell off them, the earth shook, the prison crumbled, and they alone walked out alive (see Alma 14:22–28).

President Spencer W. Kimball's entire public ministry, since his call to the apostleship in 1943, was conducted against a backdrop of constant physical threats to his life. His chances for extended longevity never seemed to himself, family members, physicians, or Church leaders to offer much hope for prolonged service. Yet, overcoming all, he endured and matured. Having been fully tested, President Kimball rose to preside over the kingdom.

In the case of Job, the classical biblical lesson in enduring hardships, even his family was taken from him. Such was the crucible through which Harold B. Lee was asked to pass to prove his worthiness to stand, in his time, as the singular prophet, seer, and revelator of God's church on earth.

The most severe of his refining tests commenced in the autumn of 1961. Because of her mother's failing health, Helen felt that she should be nearer to her and that they needed a one-level home to avoid stressing her heart. The search culminated in the purchase of a beautiful home at 1436 Penrose Drive in the Federal Heights area of Salt Lake City. Elder and Sister Lee moved into this home on October 29, 1961: "We started at 4:30 a.m. with early car loads for our new home, and we were ready for the movers at 8:00 a.m. Movers worked nine and one-half hours to conclude our move, which was made without mishap. We were 'dog-tired' at the end of the day, but Fern said she was so happy she couldn't sleep, so I'm happy, too."

At the beginning of 1962, just barely settled into her newly redecorated home, Sister Fern T. Lee's deteriorating condition manifested itself. On the first Saturday of 1962, she blacked out three times during the night; Elder Lee cancelled his stake conference trip to San Bernardino, California, to stay with her.

A similar episode occurred in April, 1962, while Elder Lee was in New York City; she was hospitalized after becoming unconscious twice during the night and suffering a slight concussion from a fall. After ten days she had improved, but the neurosurgeon consultant attending her warned that more such attacks might be expected because of her long history of high blood pressure.

Sister Lee improved sufficiently to accompany Elder Lee to the Oakland Temple groundbreaking service on May 27, 1962, where she was honored with a seat at lunch next to President David O. McKay. This lifted her spirits measurably. She entertained her family on the patio of her new home on the July Fourth holiday, and hosted a dinner in honor of President Jay and Virginia Quealy, who were leaving to preside over the Southern Far East Mission. But the fainting spells continued intermittently.

THE PASSING OF FERN TANNER LEE

A lengthy hospitalization in September 1962 led to the more precise diagnosis that beyond the serious hypertension condition, Sister Lee was suffering from periodic brain clots. The final chapter of her fatal illness began on September 14, 1962, while Elder Lee, with Elder Delbert L. Stapley, went to the Logan Temple for his customary teaching session with newly called missionaries. Elder Lee's diary records this tragic series of events:

> I called home and found that Fern had been desperately ill for the entire day with intense nausea and vomiting. I immediately called her doctor, who ordered some medicine which didn't seem to help lessen the nausea. I called the substitute doctor for her own attending physician, who came and gave her an injection which didn't prove effective. Two hours later, at about 10:30 p.m., I called him back to relieve her pain. This time he gave her two injections for pain and to help her sleep. About 3:00 a.m. she called for me to take her to the bathroom. She blacked out, with her head becoming cold and clammy, as also her feet and hands. For thirty minutes her sister Emily and I worked over her with all the faith and prayer we could muster. Her body gradually became warm again. For a time we wondered if we would bring her back. She went to sleep until about 6:00 a.m. As she awakened the entire nausea returned. I called Dr. James F. Orme, her doctor, and he advised that we take her immediately to the hospital. To give her a feeling of greater security I urged Dr. Orme to also involve her former physicians, Dr. J. LeRoy Kimball and Dr. L. H. Viko. He thought this would be well. Special-duty nurses were engaged around the clock. She said to me: "You won't let them leave me alone will you?"
>
> The doctors advised me to cancel my assignment to meet with the BYU student leaders at the Jackson Lodge on the weekend. I had Frances [his secretary] wire Jackson, Wyoming, following the advice of Dr. Orme, and advise that I would not be there with their leadership students from the BYU.
>
> After the first day her condition improved markedly. The neurosurgeon told Helen and me that he was convinced her nausea was still caused by minor arterial "accidents" in her brain, which might be classed as mild strokes. This reasoning argued the necessity of keeping her pressure to a minimum to prevent reoccurrences. She seems to be worrying about my cancelling of trips to the East, as evidence of a more serious condition than we had told her. President McKay has advised that I attend my Equitable and Union Pacific meetings, which I probably will do if Fern remains the same or improves. I will make plans to further her sense of security. I have had a strong feeling that I should not go East this week, but probably next week. (I assisted in setting apart nearly 200 missionaries).

On Thursday, September 20, 1962, Elder Lee wrote this comment in his journal: "For the first time since Fern has been in the hospital, this time she said she felt better and she looked like she did. With the aid of the nurse she had walked to the end of the hall and back. President McKay was very solicitous about Fern and sent a box of large peaches to us."

By Saturday, Sister Lee seemed so much better that Doctor Orme thought it would be safe if Elder Lee kept his appointment for a stake conference at the Lake Mead Stake in Nevada. Elder Lee discussed the proposition with his wife Saturday morning, at which time they also arranged plans for her homecoming from the hospital.

Such plans were useless, however, for before that night was over Sister Lee suffered a massive cerebral hemorrhage. Her spinal fluid indicated that her condition was near fatal, and from that moment her life was sustained only by an artificial, mechanical resuscitator. Helen's husband, Brent, notified Elder Lee in Nevada by a phone call at 12:30 A.M., and told him to rush home immediately. The airline contacted would not hold their scheduled flight, then preparing to leave the airport, so Elder Lee was forced to charter a small, two-engine plane which flew him to the Salt Lake Airport, arriving at 4:00 A.M.

Elder Lee then began a long vigil at the bedside of his beloved wife, praying mightily for the preservation of her life. With profound grief, he watched his dear companion slipping, responding less and less to the artificial means of sustaining life. Finally he was urged to go home to bathe and rest. At home, reflecting on having watched her frail unconscious body suffer for thirty hours, he realized what he must do. Only then could he kneel down and ask the Lord to take her quickly if she couldn't be returned to a normal life. After he was resigned to placing her in the hands of a loving God, the end came quickly.

Shortly after his prayer of resignation, while Elder Lee was at Helen's home for breakfast, at 9:00 A.M. that Monday, September 24, 1962, he received a call from his other daughter, Maurine, at the hospital. She urged them to come quickly, as her Mother was failing rapidly.

Arriving in the hospital room Elder Lee felt her presence so strongly that he began quietly talking to her as though she could hear what he was saying. With his fingers lovingly stroking her forehead, the minutes ticked on while he whispered to her . . . ten, fifteen, thirty . . . until the nurse attending her suddenly stepped out of the room to summon the doctor. The doctor came,

Fern Tanner Lee

checked her in that final moment, and said gently, "She's gone, Brother Lee."

Harold B. Lee straightened up, left her bedside with a departing kiss, and said to his family waiting close by, "Mother always said, after each funeral sermon she heard me deliver, that I would have to speak at her funeral someday because I said all the words that were important to her." He continued, "But of course we both knew I could never do that, so I've just been reminding her of those precious truths which I thought she would like to hear as she embarks on this great new experience."

She had passed away peacefully, and no doubt, contentedly, upon hearing her dear husband recite as only he could the message of hope which will link them eternally as loving companions.

The family returned to the Lee home and planned the funeral services, which were held three days later in the chapel of the Monument Park Ward where the Lees formerly lived. Bishop George R. Hill, of the Federal Heights Ward, conducted. Speakers were President David O. McKay and President Henry D. Moyle of the First Presidency; Dr. Richard S. Tanner, a nephew; and Luacine Clark Fox, a daughter of the late President J. Reuben Clark, Jr., and a dear friend of Sister Lee. Richard Condie led a double mixed quartet from the Tabernacle Choir in singing "O My Father" and "I Know That My Redeemer Lives"; Blanche M. Christensen sang "How Beautiful upon the Mountains"; and Jessie Evans Smith sang the Lee couple's love song, "The Link Divine." Prayers at the service were given by the sons-in-law, L. Brent Goates and Ernest J. Wilkins. Elder Lee's elder brother, Perry, dedicated the grave at the Salt Lake City Cemetery.

The diary of Elder Lee tells of his special sensitivity to his wife's parting: "I had the feeling that Fern would want to say her farewell in her beautiful home which she loved so much. So, after a public viewing where about 1,000 or more persons came to the mortuary, we had her casket brought and placed before the living room mantel in our home at 1436 Penrose Drive at 10:00 a.m. the next morning."

There Elder Lee met with his family for one hour. As patriarch of his family and fulfilling his grandfatherly role, he appealed especially to the little ones of his "kingdom" as he tenderly showed them how beautiful death could be to one so nearly perfect as their "Nana." As he had taught his family members to live the gospel and merit happiness and blessings, he now taught them the important lesson on death. He captured the teaching moment, despite an aching heart, and that lesson vividly lives on today in the lives of his family.

At 11:00 a.m. the General Authorities and their wives joined the family to offer their condolences to their friend and beloved associate in his greatest sorrow. The cortege left from the home at 12:30 p.m. in time for the services to begin at the Monument Park Stake Center at 1:00 p.m.

The emptiness of home and heart was immediately manifest. Elder Lee's sister, Verda, testified that on the day of Fern's death she had a strong impression, which she felt came from both her mother and Fern, that it was her responsibility to look after her brother now that his wife was gone. This comforting and loving arrangement was agreed on the night of the funeral. Verda and her husband, Charles J. Ross, then moved in and lived with him in his home. They also kept their apartment on Third Avenue, to which they returned occasionally when Elder Lee was away so that Charles could continue to serve as the stake clerk in the Ensign

Stake. Elder Lee often expressed his appreciation for them, both publicly and privately. In his journal he wrote:

> Such love and selflessness on the part of both Charlie and Verda surely will be blessed by an all-wise Heavenly Father, who knows my great need now that Fern has been taken from me. No man could have more loyal and devoted daughters and sons, or a sister and brother. How grateful I am that I can keep our home together and give time for wounds to heal which at the present are too painful to permit even clear thinking as to the future. I am finding true what President J. Reuben Clark once told me years after Sister Clark had passed away: "It's something you never get over, but which you can get used to."

The demands of his Church leadership forced him to begin immediately to prepare for his assignment of explaining developments of the correlation program at the forthcoming October 1962 general conference of the Church. He gave two major addresses at the conference under great tension and was totally exhausted by the effort.

He excused himself from attendance at the customary dinner of the General Authorities and their wives during the week following conference. He confided in his journal, "Without my sweetheart, I felt I had no place and certainly no desire to be there."

In late October Elder Lee took a Friday off and drove with Verda and Charlie to Provo through American Fork Canyon to spend a few hours visiting with Maurine and her family. Verda, who had prepared most of the dinner that they took with them, said that she never was so eager to get out of a car in her life, because her brother Harold had driven like a madman, his mind completely absent from his driving. His suffering continued as he tried desperately to restore some order to his life.

Recognizing the heavy burden in Elder Lee's heart President McKay intervened with an assignment to attend some European conferences to be held in November. After a sleepless night Elder Lee replied to President McKay that he could go if he could take Elder Walter Stover with him to represent the Priesthood Welfare Committee. With Elder Stover's knowledge of German and other languages, he felt that he could be more independent and secure while he was in Europe. He was authorized to make the arrangements with Brother Stover.

On November 9, 1962, Elder Lee, with a heavy heart, and Brother Stover left from the Salt Lake Airport for Europe. Elders

Spencer W. Kimball, Mark E. Petersen, and Richard L. Evans were there with family members to see him off and give him the encouragement he so much needed.

No sooner did they arrive in Europe than memories began to hamper Elder Lee's slight grasp on emotional control. November 14 was his wedding anniversary and Fern's birthday. He called it "a most difficult day of memories." Two nights later he wrote, "Nervous tensions and depression turned last night into a nightmare."

On Saturday, November 17, he received his first letters from home and suffered another emotional setback. After a full day of conference meetings on Sunday in Berlin, Elder Lee had such a severe nervous reaction that he remained away from the Monday evening meetings which were highly advertised and attended by over seven hundred persons.

While only briefly mentioned in his own journal, his despair and grief is better described by his traveling companion, Elder Walter Stover. Recalls Brother Stover:

> When his beloved wife, Fern, passed away President Lee and I were assigned to go to Germany, Austria, and Switzerland for four weeks. We held many conferences. At that time he was in deep sorrow for the loss of his beloved eternal companion, and I have seen him weep on many occasions, and it was very difficult for me to cheer him up. We held many meetings with our missionaries and members in the armed forces in different cities in Germany. On many occasions, I was his translator. In Berlin he was so depressed he had to go to his hotel room and turn the conference over to me.

At the close of the European trip Elder Lee wrote in his journal while in Stuttgart, Germany, on November 26, 1962: "I had a strong impression to go back to Frankfurt today, instead of waiting until tomorrow, as scheduled, for our return flight to the United States." The next day he better understood this spiritual direction he had received and wrote this journal entry: "Had we waited at Stuttgart until this morning instead of coming on to Frankfurt as prompted, we would have missed our plane for New York. Stuttgart was 'fogged-in' and the plane on which we were to have come to make connections had not yet arrived when we left for home. Frankfurt seemed to be the one major airport clear. Amsterdam also had to be by-passed because of the fog."

Walter Stover's recollections of this experience, twenty years later, was: "When we were at the airport in Frankfurt it was announced over the loudspeaker that the flight from Stuttgart to

Frankfurt, which we were to have taken, had been cancelled. I didn't say a word, but President Lee just looked at me, knowingly. I knew that he was a prophet of God."

While courageously carrying on his routine Church assignments, the despair and loneliness in Elder Lee's life was only intensified with the arrival of the Christmas season. In early December his thought was to clean up the yard at their new home for the winter season and trim the shrubs "as he knew Fern would have it done to look as beautiful as possible for Christmas." He wrote in his journal another tribute to his sister Verda "who is not well, but is fully devoted to her 'mission' of making our home as beautiful and lovely at Christmas as she feels Fern would have had it."

Elder Lee installed an artificial gas log in the living room fireplace "to add a bit of cheer which seems lacking now." He found it necessary to leave the community-sponsored testimonial dinner honoring President McKay and watched the remainder of the program on television, because "something seems to be increasing in my nervous system when I am too long confined and in an idle mood."

On Saturday, three days before Christmas, Elder Lee spent some time at the office and then, at the depths of his despair, felt an extreme loneliness as he did some last-minute Christmas shopping. On Sunday morning he thought he would go to his ward chapel in Federal Heights where President McKay was scheduled to speak, but after walking there and encountering the crowd which had assembled, he changed his mind and returned home again to study and pray. Only then did he find a measure of peace. Later on that Sabbath day he was a speaker at the nearby East 27th Ward but wrote of his frustrations in these words: "The spirit was not with me in my sermon at the East 27th Ward, although my family was in attendance. I felt keenly Fern's absence, which on similar occasions in the past has been such a strength and support."

The emptiness in his life and grieving continued as this schooling and testing worked its inexorable way to the innermost chambers of Harold B. Lee's soul.

With the abundance of the spiritually chosen ones around him, it is interesting to note that the most effective counsel to the grieving Harold B. Lee came not from his Church-leader friends but from an associate on the Board of Directors of The Equitable Life Assurance Society on January 17, 1963:

I attended the Insurance Committee meeting of Equitable, followed by the regular board meeting and then lunch with the directors and staff officers. It was good to be with these great men again. Following our board meeting, John A. Sibley, one of our older and most respected directors, a banker from Atlanta, took me aside and related to me his experience in losing his first wife in 1934 in a tragic auto accident. When word of the accident came, his first reaction was that of wishing that he might have died with her. As he later philosophized, he began to see the possible values to himself which he now wanted to pass on to me in the loss of my beloved Fern. This was his reasoning: "This is the most severe test you will ever be confronted with in your life. If you can meet and surmount this test, there will be nothing else in life you cannot meet and surmount." Strangely this bit of wisdom from this fine man gave me comfort as I thought of the days ahead.

Harold B. Lee was beginning now to see a light at the end of a very long and dark tunnel and dared for the first time to think of the future.

A Second Personal Tragedy

Elder Lee was blessed greatly in July 1963 when he married Freda Joan Jensen. This story will be unfolded later. Here we concentrate on the necessity for Elder Lee to encounter heartbreaking sorrow once more. Coupled with his many triumphs, he was again brought low through personal tragedy.

This next trial commenced with an assignment to travel abroad in August 1965. In July, Elder Lee met with Elder Paul H. Dunn to plan for conferences in Samoa and Australia, a trip that was to last from August 21 until September 19, culminating with a new stake to be organized at Adelaide, in New South Wales, Australia.

Shortly before his departure, however, Elder and Sister Lee drove to Provo to see the Wilkins family; while there he gave Maurine a blessing for her forthcoming motherhood.

After only six days in Hawaii, Elder Lee was awakened at 5:45 A.M. on Friday, August 27, by a shocking telephone call from his wife giving him the shattering news that Maurine was in critical condition at the Utah Valley Hospital in Provo, Utah. Elder Lee immediately phoned the hospital where his son-in-law, Ernest J. Wilkins, told him through his sobs that the doctors were fighting for her life, but that they were giving him no hope. Elder Lee immediately obtained reservations for a flight back home. Minutes later, Ernie called again to say that Maurine was gone, dead at age forty from a lung embolus, while expecting her fifth child.

Elder Paul H. Dunn, a then newly called General Authority on his first lengthy trip with a senior Apostle, has vivid recollections of sharing this tumultuous event in the life of Elder Lee. He had witnessed Elder Lee giving encouragement and faith to the grieving family of a Hawaiian stake president just the day before. The deceased wife, Sister Moody, was a dear friend of Sister Fern Lee and the counsel Elder Lee had imparted in his funeral address, he would have to follow himself the very next day. Elder Dunn's memory of this experience follows:

> In sharing the traumatic experience of the sudden loss of one's cherished daughter in this way, I saw the tender, father side of President Harold B. Lee. We knelt in prayer, and while it was one of the most heart-tugging experiences I have ever had, it was also one of my most spiritual blessings. I learned from this experience how a man reacts who is really under fire with his apostolic calling. I saw there the making of a prophet; I saw how a man destined to be a prophet truly acts under pressure.
>
> I'm not implying that that's why his daughter died, but certainly the Lord permitted it to happen. President Lee was struck down by this blow, as any father would be in the loss of a loved one, a precious daughter. But to witness that even in that terrible moment the adversary still didn't have control, I thought, was one of the greatest lessons of my life.

Elder Lee's journal captures his immediate sorrow. He wrote: "My heart is broken as I contemplate the passing of my darling 'Sunshine' and the great need that Ernie and her family of four little ones have for her."

Elder Lee's plane was delayed forty-five minutes in leaving Honolulu and to his already abundant worries came the additional concern that he might not make a tight connection at Los Angeles. Elder Lee called this plane trip "the longest and most tortuous ride I have ever taken. It seemed like an eternity."

At the end of the flight in Salt Lake City was awaiting the most sad and shattering scene of his life:

> I found all my little families at the airport. I was completely overwhelmed and could hardly control myself physically or emotionally when I saw the little motherless family with Ernie. I went to our home to lay plans for the days ahead. All of us seemed to be in a

Maurine Lee Wilkins

daze from the shock and the strain of my darling Maurine's passing. This seemed to compound my sorrow in losing Fern three years ago next month.

Four years later Elder Lee preached about this never-to-be-forgotten scene, at a stake conference in the Brigham Young University Sixth Stake. At that time his recollection was:

Suddenly, and without warning, that little mother was snatched away in a moment. The pleadings of Grandfather over in the Hawaiian Islands and the piteous cries for the mercies of the Almighty to spare her were unavailing. And in the hospital, surrounded by doctors with all the medical skill that they could summon, she slipped away. The children were called, and around the lonely table in the family room they sat with bowed heads sobbing their hearts out. The grandfather was summoned to come and that night flew home, and all the family were at the plane to meet him, hoping that surely he could do something to lift the burden. And with arms surrounding that little family the grandfather said: "I do not know how you can be so brave. Grandfather is crying his heart out and you stand here with your arms around each other, seemingly with no tears." And one of them said: "Grandfather, we have no more tears to shed. We have cried our tears away all day long."

That drama was enacted right here in your community. I was the recipient of that phone call; I was the grandfather who pleaded at five o'clock in the morning, "Please, God, don't let her die." But it was as though our Heavenly Father was saying, "I have other plans," and all the faith that could be mustered was unavailing.

Life had to go on and the shocked family in Provo needed loving administration. Aunt Helen never left the family those first two weeks. The bags she had packed for a two-week vacation, which was aborted at the news of Maurine's death, served Helen well as she stayed to take care of her sister's grief-stricken family. That first night she slept with Maurine's daughter, twelve-year-old Marlee, to comfort her. This little flaxen-haired girl had a dream so vivid that she awakened, gripped her aunt by the arm, and said: "Aunt Helen, I've had such a funny dream! I dreamed we were sitting in the family room with Mother—you and me and Jane [her cousin]. Mother was sewing a button on Jay's shirt. [Jay was her younger brother.] We were all talking while Mother sewed. Jay came in and said he was sad because Mother was gone, and I said, 'No she's not gone—see, she's right here—can't you see her?' Jay couldn't understand what I was saying, and I asked you and Jane if you could see her, and you just smiled. None of you could see her, but I could—I knew she was there. Isn't that funny, Aunt Helen?"

Aunt Helen, conditioned by the wise teachings received in her childhood home, replied: "No, Martsy dear, that's not just a funny dream. I think it's Heavenly Father's way of letting you know that even though your mommy has been taken from you, she can still be with you when you need her. You won't always be able to see her as you did in your dream, but she'll be close by and you'll feel her presence. Remember your dream, Martsy, when you're sad and lonesome for her, and it will help to make you feel better." Reassured, Marlee went back to sleep.

The passing of Maurine Lee Wilkins was not just a family tragedy. It sent an entire community into grief. As her friends and acquaintances gathered at the Berg Mortuary in Provo, Utah, visiting stretched beyond the announced hours of 6:00 P.M. to 8:00 P.M., extending from 5:30 P.M. until 10:30 P.M. It was one of the most amazing expressions of genuine sorrow ever displayed in the passing of a young LDS community leader, who had been active in church, Parent-Teachers Association, politics, faculty wives groups of Brigham Young University, and the Chamber of Commerce.

The funeral services were held at noon on August 30, 1965, in the East Sharon Stake Center. Elder Lee recorded his impressions of the funeral in these words: "Elder Marion G. Romney's closing sermon was a masterpiece, full of faith and hope and sound of doctrine. He was right when he said "the veil was very thin." We brought Maurine to Salt Lake to be buried in our family plot, opposite her mother. This gave us much comfort."

Five days later the grieving Elder Lee began to feel some hope, yet he couldn't find full relief from his sorrow. He wrote: "Our heartbreaking experience in losing our darling Maurine seems to bear promise of binding our families together as we all seek to share in the heavy burdens of sorrow in our loss. Somehow I seem unable to shake off this latest shattering blow. Only God can help me!"

In mid-September, 1965 Elder and Sister Lee took their heavy-hearted families to a cafeteria dinner, but the Church leader observed, "Ernie is still having a struggle with his emotions, as am I." When friends came to visit him, any recall of the harrowing events of Maurine's passing left Elder Lee upset, resulting in journal entries such as this: "My nerves were so disturbed that it took me until 1:30 A.M. before I could get to sleep." On September 28, 1965, he wrote: "It seems as though I was experiencing some reaction following the strains of the past months. I find it difficult to sleep."

During the October general conference of that year Elder Lee was a speaker at the special missionary session on Friday night and the first speaker at the Sunday afternoon session. His subject related closely to his own experiences and feelings and severely taxed him. Of this he wrote: "I discovered this talk and the one on the subject of trials and tribulations were almost more than I could do." He had said to the capacity crowd in the Tabernacle: "As I advance in years, I begin to understand in some small measure how the Master must have felt [in the Garden of Gethsemane]. In the loneliness of a distant hotel room, 2,500 miles away, you too may one day cry out from the depths of your soul, as was my experience: 'O dear God, don't let her die! I need her; her family needs her.'"

As always, holidays and anniversaries brought back memories and were the hardest days to emotionally surmount. November 13, 1965, was such an uneasy day. It was the eve of Fern's birthday and their wedding anniversary. But when Elder Lee arrived home late that night from attending a conference in the Klamath Stake near Portland, Oregon, tired and emotionally weary, his daughter Helen had a beautiful letter waiting for him to lift him over his depression. Despite this comfort, it was after 2:00 A.M. before Elder Lee could quiet his nerves and fall asleep.

Christmas 1965 offered another such emotional hurdle. Helen visited her father in early December and shared her ideas for spending the holidays together in a different way than ever before. She felt this would help them all to feel less keenly the loss of both Fern and Maurine.

Accordingly, the entire Lee family spent two days before Christmas and the three days following in a comfortable cabin home owned by kind friends in Kamas, Utah. All went well with little outward evidence of sorrow and sad remembrances of past Christmases. When they came down from their mountain cabin retreat after the holidays, Elder Lee left immediately for a trip to New York City. Upon his return he again recorded that he "had a sleepless night, perhaps due to a combination of a heavy heart and travel weariness."

The grieving continued sporadically for another year or more as Elder Lee struggled to gain an emotional foothold and make a new life after the family deaths had registered their tremendous effect on him. On the first anniversary of Maurine's passing, with the memories of his losses poignantly on him, and analyzing the event one year later, he wrote this commentary in his journal: "This is the anniversary of Maurine's sudden passing while I was in Hawaii. . . . I returned home that night to the saddest experience of my life, as I saw her shocked little family, hoping that Grandfather's return would somehow lift them above their tragic loss. Somehow my emotions and nervous tensions seem to have been intensified as the memories of Fern and Maurine come back to me now."

Undoubtedly Maurine's unexpected death did produce the "saddest experience of [his] life." She was in her prime, her family needed her so desperately, and she had always produced a never-ending source of sunshine and happiness for all who knew her. Her passing compounded his grief in losing Fern.

With one-half of his small family of four now taken away from him, Elder Lee's challenge was to courageously overcome his profound grief, which undoubtedly strengthened him for his future role as the Church's prophet. Certainly it filled his heart with empathy for all other sufferers. His funeral sermons and generous efforts at comforting the grieving souls about him, always a personal strength, now reached new heights of inspiration, in part because he had become acquainted with the bitter depths of despair. This experience was forever afterward a key to his spiritual power and compassionate service, and he learned to more fully appreciate the lesson taught in Hebrews 5:8–9: "Though he were a Son, yet learned he obedience by the things which he suffered; And being made perfect, he became the author of eternal salvation unto all them that obey him." The refining formula used by a loving Heavenly Father to season and prepare his son, the Savior Jesus Christ, while in the flesh, was also being applied for producing a mighty prophet of the last dispensation, Harold B. Lee.

A HEAVEN-PROVIDED SECOND COMPANION

When Harold B. Lee was but a lad of eighteen in the farm community of Clifton, Idaho, Patriarch James Reid McNeil gave him a patriarchal blessing. It was prophetic in many respects, but particularly in reference to his future family. The blessing promised him "sons and daughters who will labor jointly with thee in the work of the Lord," and "wives and children who would be caught up in the clouds of heaven to meet thy Redeemer."

Thus Harold B. Lee knew that there would be more than one female companion for him. Even more impressive is to know that his dear first wife and mother of his children, Fern, taught her daughters throughout their lives that their daddy should marry again promptly after her death. She made what first seemed to them a cruel jolt, become in time a logical culmination in the building of an eternal family.

The Christmas season of 1962 was a mournful period for Harold B. Lee, since he had just buried his dear Fern two months earlier. Among the friends calling to lift Elder Lee's spirits during the Christmas holidays was one whose impact was to be forever felt in his life. Elder Lee's diary captures this meeting on the last Sunday of 1962:

> Freda Jensen came by pre-arrangement to visit us. This seemed to have been a mutually satisfying experience for both of us. She wrote later her feelings that at times Fern seemed so near that she wanted

to only whisper, or at times, just sit and reflect. There was such a strange and wonderful peace from her visit that we both seemed to desire that such visits might be repeated. I had referred to our home as "Fern's masterpiece," to which she later wrote: "It is truly beautiful, a symphony of color—a beauty that lies in the accumulation of memories which nothing can wholly displace." She closed her letter by saying: "And you sitting there in that lovely, big chair, reminiscing—words spoken and listened to. Many thanks for a glimpse into Paradise. [Signed] Always, Freda."

Freda Jensen had been a friend to the Lees for many years. They first became acquainted before Harold and Fern were married. They had associated with each other through the years in joint Church circles. Freda was the veteran supervisor of primary education in the Jordan School District of Salt Lake County and was renowned as a prominent educator. She had served in the Church as a member of the Church Music Committee and on the general boards of both the Young Women's Improvement Association and the Primary Association. Through all those years, whenever Freda and Fern would meet, there seemed to be an unmistakable bond between them.

Following Fern's death both Freda and Harold seemed to recognize early that their feelings and desires for each other must have been inspired and right. Perhaps in preparation for this time, Freda had a special experience once when she had taken ill years earlier while in Canada on a YWMIA general board assignment. She sought a priesthood blessing from President Edward James Wood, president of the Alberta Canada Temple. In this blessing President Wood told her that one day she would be called to a position of such magnitude that at present she would not be able to contemplate it.

The story has a further fulfillment. At one point in her life Freda was engaged to marry Ray Beck, but the groom-to-be was taken in death two weeks before the wedding day. Ray was a widower and had three lovely children, one of whom chose to live with Freda Jensen after the death of her father. Freda raised Geniel Beck Rasmussen from early childhood, never again considering marriage, but no doubt pondering through the years the unique calling predicted for her by President Wood.

Freda Joan Jensen's story began in Provo, Utah, where she was born in the Church to stalwart parents, Julius and Christine H. Thuesen Jensen. Her father, a retired sea captain, taught her world geography in her childhood. After retiring from the sea, he became an excellent jeweler, bringing his skills to America from Denmark.

She grew up in Provo taking piano lessons from the time she was age seven. She had an older sister, Mrs. Gerald (Edna) Cazier, and a brother, Franklin J. D. Jensen.

In early January 1963, Elder Lee stopped at Freda Jensen's home in Sandy to leave her a copy of the latest book by President J. Reuben Clark. Elder Lee had written the foreword of this book at the request of the Clark family. That night was sacred to the couple, because it was then that they first confessed their deep feelings for each other which led ultimately to marriage.

After that night, letters from Joan, as she preferred him to call her, were always on hand to greet Elder Lee on his semimonthly trips to board meetings in New York. These trips gave Elder Lee some time to think through his plans for the future, a task he found most difficult. It was then he received the valuable counsel from his Atlanta banker friend, John A. Sibley, and he gained the courage and comfort to think of the days ahead and plan what he must do to fulfill his dedicated career for the Lord.

As his meetings with Joan continued, he wrote in his journal: "I'm praying fervently for the wisdom and guidance and the assurances of the nearness of my lovely Fern. How I want her to approve of what I may do!"

Elder Lee created an occasion to discuss his developing plans of marriage with his two daughters. He took Helen and two of her little boys to Provo to see Maurine and used this occasion to discuss frankly with them the question of a possible future marriage. It was most important, he stressed, that such plans be made with their knowledge and acceptance.

At that time he outlined unique criteria he had formulated of three characteristics he would like to find in a candidate for marriage: (1) someone near his age; (2) preferably someone known and admired by his first wife; (3) preferably someone who had never been married, so that she could become part of his eternal family. He pointed out to his daughters that Freda Joan Jensen personified these ideals, and then shared with them his feelings for her. When he gained supportive, positive response from his daughters, Elder Lee's marriage plans began moving forward.

Elder Lee used the seclusion for a necessary hernia operation to draw his family into his plans. Meditating about the two women in his life while convalescing in the hospital Elder Lee wrote in his journal, after having intimate visits with his family members: "This was a rare opportunity for intimate and satisfying talks about events ahead for us as a family and our lovely Joan, without detracting from our wonderful mother and my darling, Fern."

Elder Lee wanted President McKay to be aware of his planning. Following the temple meeting on June 6, 1963, Elder Lee was impressed to tell him of his marriage plans, now only eleven days distant. He was pleased when President McKay said he was taking the right action. The President advised, "It is not good for a man to be alone," and gave Elder Lee his blessing on the plans. He asked to meet Joan and to have Sister McKay meet her, too. On June 12 they went to President McKay's Hotel Utah apartment. At that time President McKay agreed to perform the wedding ceremony and again assured them of his blessing. He praised Elder Lee's choice and judgment, and the next day he told Sister McKay that "Joan is a wonderful girl." Sister McKay added in reporting it later, "and when he says that it means something!"

Elder Lee shared his marriage plans with only two other intimate friends of the Council of the Twelve. His journal reveals this conversation: "After the Sunday concluding session of June MIA conference I told Marion Romney of my plans to be married Monday. He was very emotional. Henry Moyle came and asked if he could be at the marriage. I asked if he would like to be a witness. With emotion he replied, 'Would you permit me to?' Marion Romney asked also. I told them if President McKay would perform our marriage ceremony and they two would be witnesses it would be perfect."

The wedding in the Salt Lake Temple on Monday, June 17, 1963, was ideal. According to Elder Lee, President McKay "was magnificent in his counsel to us before and after the ceremony was performed." A wedding breakfast for fifty-one guests followed at the Hotel Utah.

Afterwards the newlyweds left immediately for New York City. Their honeymoon was to be conducted from coast to coast and included a trip from Omaha, Nebraska, to Los Angeles and Salt Lake City aboard the luxurious, private railway car of the president of the Union Pacific Railroad.

After six weeks of travel and subsequently resuming leadership pressures and adjusting to a new life, some of the former anxieties and depression returned to Elder Lee. He described his feelings in his journal as follows: "I went through another wave of intense

With Freda Joan Jensen Lee shortly after their marriage

loneliness such as I have experienced frequently throughout the past year. I'm almost afraid to reveal how I long for my loved one who is gone, an emptiness which is only eased when my lovely Joan is near me."

Freda Joan Jensen Lee took her place at the side of Elder Lee as his eternal companion and filled her role admirably. Frequently Elder Lee would praise her. He said of her extraordinary teaching ability: "She has the key that unlocks many a child's heart. She has the ability to teach the teacher this secret. Her conversation with a child is a beautiful thing to hear. Her skill and understanding are born of a lifetime of knowledge and application of child psychology. She is constantly reaching out to the child that is not understood."

After living with his wife Joan for just six months, and observing her characteristic conduct on trips, relating so well to the people wherever they went, Elder Lee opened his private diary of January 1964 with these observations: "I went with Joan and her sister, Edna, to Midvale and Sandy, Utah, to visit some of their close friends and to deliver some belated gifts. It is amazing to note the unusual talent Joan has in extending herself to maintain old friendships and to make new friends. Always she maintains as well a feeling of intimate relationship with Fern, with beautiful holly wreaths and evergreen sprays for Fern's grave and headstone."

Joan Lee became well known throughout the Church as she traveled with Elder Lee, especially after he became President of the Church. They crossed almost every part of the globe in meeting with the Saints. She often spoke and inspired Saints, missionaries, and leaders everywhere they went.

She was the wife and companion of Elder Lee for ten and one-half years. She was the widow of the President of the Church for another eight years before her passing, which she welcomed, on July 1, 1981, one day before her eighty-fourth birthday.

CHAPTER 21

The Correlation Program

Some historians may well argue that President Harold B. Lee's most significant lifetime work for the Church, though not generally understood by the membership, was the reorganization of the kingdom under the direction of President David O. McKay during the 1960s. What is little comprehended about that magnificent achievement was that it resembled so many of his other accomplishments in that it was born out of heartbreaking failures in the 1940s and 1950s. Undoubtedly the Church could have profited by a correlated program even then, but although the principles were right, the timing was not.

In reference to those frustrating years, Elder Lee would often reflect on how he was obliged to learn patience. The decade of the forties was a time of valiant striving and waiting. Close friends and family members have heard Elder Lee remark often that in those years he found it necessary to fold away his charts of reorganization, changing job descriptions, and dreams of an integrated Church program led by the priesthood, and wait out the delay. He filed his papers in his rolltop desk where they remained for twenty years, awaiting a more propitious and receptive time.

Simply stated, the correlation program is the placement of the priesthood of God where the Lord by revelation has set it—at the center and core of the Church organizations, with all auxiliary organizations affixed appropriately as a support to the priesthood. Also, correlation emphasizes priesthood in the home, through the father (or parents), by priesthood home teaching and the family home evening program to encourage the teaching of children in the home.

The title "correlation" came from an official letter from the First Presidency which defined areas of responsibility that must be aligned if every part of the kingdom of God was to fit into its proper place. The heart of the priesthood correlation program was the home and family.

The 1960s mark what might well be considered the most significant development in this century pertaining to the responsibilities of the priesthood, especially as they relate to the home. Procedures were redefined and intensified and some new approaches were inaugurated. To accomplish the fundamental objective of the Church, which is the saving of the living and the dead, a priesthood correlation program was established, with emphasis on four basic thrusts: the priesthood missionary program, the priesthood welfare program, the priesthood genealogical program, and the all-encompassing priesthood home teaching program. All Church auxiliaries were then related to these four functions as directed through priesthood correlation.

The key statement of instruction to Elder Lee and his associates in developing the correlation program came in a letter from the First Presidency in which they called attention to the fact that

> the home was the basis of a righteous life and that no other instrumentality can take its place or fulfill its essential functions, and that the utmost the auxiliaries can do is to aid the home in its problems, giving special aid and succor where such is necessary; that in aiding the home the auxiliaries may well consider thinking of home-life of the people as having three periods—the first, from birth to twelve years of age or the childhood period; then the youth period from twelve years up to the early twenties; and then adulthood, from the early twenties on to the end of life.

These were the developmental objectives of the correlation program seen clearly now from hindsight vision. Yet in the earliest years the concepts were blurred and needed the refining development of intensive, prayerful, arduous work by scores of dedicated pioneers to produce the current definitions which now are commonly accepted.

The roots of the priesthood correlation program certainly began early in the 1940s, but no fruits came then. The true genesis of the priesthood correlation program in the 1960s may have come much earlier from the personal, visionary philosophy of President J. Reuben Clark, Jr. After only three months of service as a new member of the Quorum of the Twelve, Elder Lee, Elder Marion G. Romney, and their wives were invited to the home of President and Sister Clark. That evening, on July 10, 1941, President Clark unfolded some of his ideas relative to what he called then a simplification of the present Church programs. The concepts sunk deep into the fertile mind of Harold B. Lee, whose destiny it was to persevere and to finally see them implemented twenty years later.

In order to attend a quarterly meeting of the Council of the Twelve in 1948, Elder Lee returned from a weekend conference and went directly from the train to the meeting, where as a special order of business the subject of ward teaching was to be discussed. Elder Lee again presented some of his ideas which had emerged from his studies of priesthood responsibility and simplification, made in association with Elders Stephen L Richards and Albert E. Bowen. No decisions were made and no action taken on this presentation. (It wasn't until fourteen years later that these basic concepts were finally adopted as the home teaching program of the Church.) Elder Lee ended his journal for 1948 with this doleful note: "Not much progress has been made."

The quarterly meeting of the Council of the Twelve in March 1949 was another scene of discussion on redesigning the ward teaching program of the Church. On this occasion, Elder Lee spent four hours in an "outstanding" temple meeting. Most of the time was spent in a discussion of a new approach to ward teaching, where the responsibility for laboring with inactive members would be placed on priesthood quorum officers. When it came time to report these deliberations the next day to the First Presidency at the weekly temple meeting, the proposed plan was taken under advisement.

The correlation of Aaronic Priesthood work, then directed by the Presiding Bishopric, and the Melchizedek Priesthood activities, as supervised by the General Priesthood Committee headed by Elder Lee, from the Council of the Twelve, was itself a monumental task.

The first apostolic decade of Harold B. Lee thus passed, with his ideas of priesthood correlation, then known as "simplification of Church programs," just beginning to germinate in the minds of future senior leaders.

With the appointment of Elder Stephen L Richards to the First Presidency in 1951, after President George Albert Smith had died during the April 1951 general conference, Elder Lee hoped that a renewed interest could be taken in the long-awaited revisions elevating priesthood work to its rightful place. Elder Richards had served with Elder Lee in the preparation of earlier plans which were presented to the First Presidency.

Elder Richards began his service in the First Presidency by attending for the last time the quarterly meeting of the Council of the Twelve on April 11, 1951, for the purpose of having brought to his mind the various communications and recommendations of the Twelve which had not yet been moved forward by the First Presidency. It was recalled for him that the Twelve had recommended a simplification program to give more emphasis to the priesthood, a revised priesthood-ward teaching program, recommendations relative to the ordaining and setting apart of high councilors and bishoprics by local stake presidents, and a priesthood insurance plan. In his new role in the First Presidency, President Richards promised to expedite these matters and obtain decisions. Again Elder Lee was asked to review for the Twelve the proposals on the priesthood simplification program submitted in January 1948.

After four months had passed, however, it was apparent that Elder Lee could not yet achieve the correlation needed with the Aaronic Priesthood and the Presiding Bishopric-controlled ward teaching program. A second decade of personal frustration on this issue passed by for Elder Lee.

The concept of a comprehensive study of Churchwide curriculum first surfaced in 1951, but it was several long years before positive action was taken. The first directive for the study of the entire Church curriculum came in May of 1960. Elder Lee captured this important breakthrough in these words: "I conducted a lengthy meeting of the General Priesthood Committee, whose membership is now instructed to undertake a study of the whole curriculum of the Church organizations and to recommend some correlation."

As the 1951–60 decade closed there was renewed hope that the time was approaching when the First Presidency would decide to proceed with the reorganization of priesthood and auxiliary organization functions, since it now appeared that the proposals were gaining the support of President David O. McKay. In November 1960, the Presiding Bishopric was directed to involve the Council of the Twelve in developing a vigorous ward teaching program. Gratefully, Elder Lee wrote in his journal on November 3, 1960: "In our temple meeting with six of the Twelve present, there was a very pointed discussion of the advisability of the Twelve having more to do in working with the Presiding Bishopric in directing the ward teaching, as well as other programs, which have been withheld from the Twelve."

This time it appeared that the forward movement would be sustained. Two weeks later Elder Lee wrote these hopeful words: "We had two lengthy sessions with the General Authorities in a discussion of two important matters, one of which was reviewing proposals to upgrade ward teaching to make it more effective in meeting our growing problems, which require constant 'watching over the Church' in the way the Lord has directed."

In 1960, the climate finally turned favorable for the sweeping reorganization. It appeared now that all of Elder Lee's painful labor and careful preparation would not be wasted. He could act now, instead of merely recommending and planning. The first actual movement came on March 22, 1961. On that day Elder Lee wrote in his journal: "I conducted a meeting of the Priesthood Committee where the principal item of business was to consider the final draft of a proposed overhauling of the ward teaching program of the past, under the new title of 'Priesthood Correlation Program,' with those participating as 'Priesthood Watchmen.' Twelve or 14 stakes will be selected for the experiment before launching as a Church-wide operation."

During that first year fourteen stakes did pilot the upgraded ward teaching program, with Elder Marion G. Romney prominent in the experiment's leadership, which involved redefining priesthood-auxiliary relationships. Elder Lee discussed the inspiration of the correlation program with President McKay as the plan moved to the First Presidency for approval. President McKay told Elder Lee that he had awakened one morning at 6:30 A.M. with a clear impression as to the proper theme for the general priesthood meeting of general conference in October 1961. He was impressed that the newly approved correlation program should be that theme and asked Elder Lee and Elder Richard L. Evans to speak on this subject.

It was then that Elder Lee first explained publicly the function of the proposed All-Church Coordinating Council, with associated

correlation committees for adults, youth, and children age group-
ings, each headed by a member of the Twelve Apostles. This
group, composed of Elders Marion G. Romney, Richard L. Evans,
and Gordon B. Hinckley, was led by Elder Lee as the chairman.
They first met on October 4, 1961.

From this organization came the impetus to reach out over the
next ten years to almost every program and organization in the
Church for refining and restructuring. At the October 1971 general
conference President Lee provided the Regional Representatives of
the Twelve with a partial list of accomplishments and change,
saying:

> Even as I repeat them now it seems unbelievable that we have been
> able to do what we have done in this time: priesthood home teach-
> ing; family home evening; unified social services; the expansion and
> clarification of the missionary responsibilities of the seventies quor-
> ums; expansion of the home-study seminary course; bishops' train-
> ing course; priesthood teacher development; libraries and how to
> use them; definition of a closer relationship between the Aaronic
> Priesthood and the MIA; improving and making more effective
> preparation, editing, translating, and distributing of teaching
> materials, and the distribution to meet the deadlines at seasonal
> beginnings; introduction of a Church-wide library program; the
> experimental study of the Church membership all over the world to
> achieve a feeling of closer relationship with the full Church pro-
> gram; the correlation and clarification of the LDS Student Associ-
> ation role to meet the unmet youth needs using the existing struc-
> ture rather than a separate professional staff; and the correlation of
> military relations programs using existing Church structure instead
> of professionals. So we go on and on, and all of this under the
> direction of the Twelve, as I have already explained, acting under
> the responsibility given by the First Presidency; and you, their
> brethren, are to carry this to the ends of the earth so that these
> things might be implemented in every part of the world—a tremen-
> dous responsibility.

His list also might well have included such programs as Church
athletics and a correlated music program. Basic ward and stake
leadership meetings were changed, with the high council meetings
becoming the stake priesthood correlation committee meeting,
and, on the ward level, a priesthood executive committee meeting
was introduced, along with a ward council meeting. A new executive secretary position was created to support ward and stake presiding officers. Work with the inactive male members was changed

to the prospective elder program. Church magazines were consolidated and the Relief Society was included for the first time in the general Church budget.

Those changes took many years to develop and implement. It was in June of 1962 that the correlation program first approved a Church curriculum for each age level, thus achieving a spirit of acceptance for the general principles of correlation. Even then some leaders whose organizations were squeezed by change mounted opposition to the new movement.

On August 3, 1962, President David O. McKay called President Joseph Fielding Smith and Elder Lee, the two senior Apostles in the Quorum of the Twelve, to confer with him and to "consider some matters which are giving me much concern." The discussion developed into an assignment from President McKay to find an alternative to the General Authorities going into stakes and missions as assigned teaching visitors. They were given also a specific charge to eliminate the area supervision plan set up by the Missionary Department. They were also assigned to find an alternative to the general auxiliary board's annual conventions with the stakes, which then were scheduled during vacation months and involved midweek meetings.

Elder Lee worked day and night on this assignment; four days later he presented to President McKay an outline that called for General Authorities to cover quarterly stake conferences two of the four times during the year, with teams from the auxiliary organizations alternating on the other two occasions. A worldwide missionary responsibility program under the direction of the Quorum of the Twelve was recommended to replace the old program then being led by the First Presidency and the Missionary Department.

President McKay was pleased with the report, but at the same time he recognized how sensitive were the feelings of those Brethren responsible for the programs being replaced, and chose to wait for a season before implementation. The stake conference schedule was adopted and inaugurated during 1963. The missionary program was deferred for another six months to give President McKay more time to work out the details.

The place of the auxiliaries in the Church in relationship to the priesthood was finally being defined. Elder Lee's organization chart showed the proposed relationship between the correlation program and the general boards of the auxiliaries. The auxiliaries

In the Tabernacle with President David O. McKay prior to general conference session, October, 1963

would now attend two of the four stake quarterly conferences of all stakes to conduct leadership training, but the correlation program assumed their former responsibilities of preparing the courses of study.

Regarding his correlation associates and the progress of their work, Elder Lee reported:

> They were all certain that the Lord had now given us the "light" we had all been seeking to see the place of the general boards. Now we were shown how we could present the old traditions of the auxiliaries and at the same time give the much-needed correlation to courses of study and activities. We thought it prudent to preview our presentation with President McKay privately before giving it to the Twelve. We found him intensely interested. We received the approval of the Presidency and the Twelve in our Thursday meeting on August 30, 1962.

> When this correlation plan, thus far developed, was finally presented, President McKay made this statement: "This is not only a wonderful step forward but a bound forward. My soul rejoices! I think the whole thing is glorious! We can all see opportunities for the priesthood to become active and as quorums also: I think this is growth. It warms my soul!" (*Improvement Era*, June 1963, p. 505.)

Organizational changes are always painful for those persons involved, and implementation of innovations is never easy. As late as November 9, 1962, Elder Lee called general auxiliary organization executives to his office to deal with their unwillingness to accept the program adjustments.

On February 8, 1963, Elder Lee asked his associate, Elder Marion G. Romney, to present to the Council of the Twelve the complete priesthood correlation program which was to be introduced at the April 1963 general conference and thereafter taught at all stake conferences, and finally to be put into operation on January 1, 1964. These recommendations proposed a General Priesthood Board consisting of four subcommittees of about twenty-five members each, including the Missionary Committee, with President Joseph Fielding Smith then nominated as chairman, and incorporating most of the former missionary field representatives. Also proposed was a Priesthood Correlation Committee (later to be called the Home Teaching Committee), headed by Elder Romney, with field representatives yet to be chosen; the Genealogical Committee, with newly appointed Apostle N. Eldon Tanner as chairman, with staff and part-time field representatives to teach at stake conferences; and finally, the Welfare Committee, with Presiding Bishop John H. Vandenberg as chairman, replacing Elder Romney. This marked the first time that the welfare program had not been headed by a member of the Council of the Twelve, and fulfilled a thirty-year-old vision by welfare pioneers that the Presiding Bishop should direct that program.

These one hundred men were to be part-time, unpaid, full-Church-service representatives, subject to appointment and releases as were members of the auxiliary general boards.

Although the plan had been unanimously approved by the Council of the Twelve and the First Presidency, it was under constant questioning and review as the April 1963 general conference approached. Two days before the conference convened Elder Lee was called to the office of the First Presidency to explain what he was going to say in his sermon at the general priesthood meeting, where President McKay had requested him to speak on correlation-organizational subjects. Elder Lee, sensing the difficulty, suggested that the entire plan be presented again to the Council of the Twelve and the First Presidency to see if they wished to rescind their former action of approval. Elder Romney made the presentation to review the entire correlation plan. Only one change was made when Elder Lee agreed to show on his charts that the General Authorities be constituted as the General Priesthood Board, with the four subcommittees under them.

With unity established, Elder Lee presented an outline of priesthood correlation at the general priesthood session of the April 1963 general conference. It was a major forty-five-minute address. He introduced the concept of the new General Priesthood Board with the four priesthood committees (welfare, genealogical, missionary, and home teaching). He used eight charts to clarify his message and introduced the new home teaching program to the Church for the first time.

Although the correlation program now had been launched, the changes in the missionary program proved to be the most difficult to execute. These changes, although requested by President McKay, gained acceptance slowly. A system of worldwide area supervision was finally adopted with Elder Gordon B. Hinckley as the chairman of the Priesthood Missionary Committee, and Elder Boyd K. Packer serving as the managing director. Several times, even as late as September 1965, it was necessary for President McKay to clarify that the entire Council of the Twelve were in reality the Church Missionary Committee and not just the few Quorum members who served as the Missionary Executive Committee.

From 1963 through 1966 the Church membership received a thorough education with respect to priesthood dominance and the new focus of correlation centering on the importance of the home. The four priesthood subcommittees traveled throughout the Church on stake conference assignments to teach fundamental correlation principles. With this foundation established, Elder Lee could look for a more basic organizational change which would take the Church into its future of unprecedented growth.

Still recovering from stomach surgery, Elder Lee spent Sunday, May 7, 1967, at home and took advantage of the opportunity to think through the many problems confronting a growing Church numbering 2.5 million members, most of them living in 434 stakes. Elder Lee focused on the seventy already constituted regions of the Church. He wrote his musings in his journal:

> If we could have in each region three "Church-service-time" assistants to the Twelve, answerable to the Twelve, to conduct the regional meetings twice a year, and between times work with individual stakes needing their attention in all phases of priesthood activities, in correlation with Church auxiliaries within each such region to which such part-time assistants are assigned, then the Church could meet the growth now taking place.

On May 16 Elder Lee spent some time at his office dictating a memorandum relative to the future role of priesthood committee representatives and the desirability of vesting them with a designated priesthood authority by naming "regional coordinators" in the seventy regions of the Church. He began to envision the auxiliaries coming to the regional meetings, two at each semiannual meeting, to hold training sessions with their stake and ward auxiliary leaders. This would mean that only General Authorities would attend stake quarterly conferences in 1968. The plan was jelling in his mind.

Rapid progress followed. After approval of the First Presidency and the Council of the Twelve was obtained at a special meeting

called on May 30, 1967, the details were quickly added and presented to other leadership groups. The entry in Elder Lee's journal
for June 1, 1967, describes the activity:

> In the afternoon we met with all our correlation "team" and out-
> lined the new procedure in supervising the priesthood of the
> Church by "Regional Priesthood Representatives of the Twelve,"
> the new 1968 plan to have general board auxiliary representatives
> go only to regional meetings to be presided over by the Regional
> Priesthood Representatives of the Twelve, also the new plan to hold
> stake quarterly conferences. This was repeated and in more detail
> given to the General Authorities, priesthood heads, and auxiliary
> general board leaders. Almost all seemed favorable and some were
> very enthusiastic. One was not.

Now it was time to consider manpower to breathe life into the
new priesthood leadership plan, which would have the inherent
hazard of introducing an entirely new level of leaders above the
stake presidents and below the General Authorities of the Church.
Quite naturally, that would be unpopular with both existing levels
of leadership because of widening the space between them.

Elder Lee spent the entire day of July 7, 1967, at home studying
the proposed assignments of the brethren nominated by the
Apostles of the Church for consideration as Regional Representatives of the Twelve. Though it was a laborious task, Elder Lee was
delighted as he became aware of the splendid nonpaid leadership
available for pioneering this work. He felt it was vitally important
to see that only the most qualified men be placed in these positions.

In the meantime, under the direction of Elder Thomas S.
Monson, the leadership team of Neal A. Maxwell and Wendell J.
Ashton was busy preparing the leadership training program for
General Authorities and for the first seminar for newly appointed
Regional Representatives of the Twelve, which was to be held in
conjunction with the forthcoming October 1967 general confer-
ence of the Church.

Finally all was in readiness for this historic action of installing a
new level of Church leadership. Elder Lee arrived home late on
Sunday, September 24, having just created at Fort Worth, Texas,
the 443rd stake in the Church. He immediately began to make
preparations for an intensive week preceding and during the
October general conference of the Church. With his responsibility
to supervise the first two-day seminar for the newly called
Regional Representatives, there were many last-minute details to

attend to and many questions to answer. Elder Lee praised the outstanding preparations made by the Leadership Committee, composed of Elder Monson, Neal Maxwell, and Wendell Ashton.

Elder Lee's journal entry for Thursday, September 28, 1967, provides a summary of the first seminar:

> We began the day with an hour's devotional in the Salt Lake Temple with the General Authorities and the Regional Representatives of the Twelve. The meeting was held under the direction of the First Presidency and lasted one hour. With the exception of President McKay and Elder Antoine Ivins, all were in attendance. Our meetings in the Seventeenth Ward were wonderfully developed according to an outlined plan. I was particularly blessed in a closing instruction on the subject, "How to Use the Scriptures in Our Teaching." In the evening, all the General Authorities, Regional Representatives of the Twelve, and their wives, with all our correlation workers, attended a dinner in the Lafayette Ballroom of the Hotel Utah.

The new strata of Church leadership had been prepared. As yet, however, they did not know where they would be called to serve. On Friday night, September 29, 1967, all stake presidents in the Church were invited to attend a special meeting in the Assembly Hall on Temple Square with the Regional Representatives of the Twelve. There the entire new regionalized program for 1968 was presented by the Correlation Executive Committee, composed of members of the Council of the Twelve.

Then came the climax. The historic, long-awaited moment arrived for assigning priesthood leadership to the entire world. The breathless silence was broken as President N. Eldon Tanner began reading the assignments of Regional Representatives to stakes and regions across the globe. Following this two-hour meeting the stake presidents went to the Church Office Building to meet in small designated rooms with their new Regional Representatives.

At the Saturday night general priesthood meeting Elder Lee again was assigned to present the new regionalized program to an estimated audience of 100,000 priesthood holders who were gathered in the Tabernacle on Temple Square and in 475 different chapels throughout the world. His expansive explanation required forty-five minutes of prime time, but with history unfolding it was justified and it fulfilled the request of President McKay.

At subsequent annual conferences of the Church, the seminars for Regional Representatives of the Twelve were held for two days preceding the conferences. Beginning with the first seminar in

October 1967 a tradition was established which lasted many years: as chairman of the Correlation Committee and encouraged by President McKay, Elder Lee set the stage and the spirit with a major address at the beginning of each seminar.

As Elder Lee ripened in leadership and spoke for the First Presidency, and finally as President of the Church, he presented the confidential "State of the Church" addresses as the keynote speaker at each seminar. Because of the exclusive audience and the absence of pressures brought on by reporters, television cameras, and time limitations—which characterize the general sessions of conference in the Tabernacle—these sermons have emerged as being among the most significant addresses to the priesthood leaders attending general conferences since 1967.

EVALUATION OF RESULTS

How well was the fundamental lesson of priesthood correlation taught and learned? One measurement might be demonstrated by focusing on what members and nonmembers alike have come to recognize as the hallmark of the Church—the importance of families.

In the early 1970s, ten years after the correlation program was introduced to the Church, a major survey was conducted for the Church by an outside consulting firm. In this study Frank N. Magid Associates, Inc., reported what nonmembers first thought about when the "Mormon" religion was mentioned. In this image association series the nonmembers reported that after obvious geographical links with the state of Utah and Salt Lake City, as well as the strictness of our code of living, they thought that Mormons were "closely united," and "help one another." These were family-related traits inaugurated as the heart of the correlation program in 1962.

Ten years later, in 1981, this same professional research group studied nonmember attitudes and opinions specifically in the cities of Phoenix, Arizona, and Denver, Colorado, with abundant interviews in many other American cities. These findings were reported under the title of "Comparative Evaluations" as follows:

> Without question, the strong, close family relationships among LDS Church members is its strongest selling point. It is with this criterion that the Church is most associated—and that is significant since it also is considered the most important of the five criteria tested.

Scores given the Mormon Church, in general, increase with socio-economic standing, as well as with knowledge of the Church. Although the Mormons are best rated on this criterion, they are not the only religion to score well. Baptists, Catholics, and Jews also get high grades on this trait, although none of them do quite as well as the Mormons. *

This emphasis on strengthening the family, which came into prominence in the early 1960s before today's extreme challenges were obvious, is one of the most powerful evidences that modern revelation flows from true prophets to prepare the Saints of God for the adversary's attacks. Certainly none too soon were the Saints warned to get their houses in order before the true concept of family life was attacked anew and became one of the most bitter battlegrounds between the forces of good and evil. The correlation pioneers were prophetic in their warnings and the Church gained a lasting trademark of family strength, internally and in the world, through the reorganizations of the 1960s led by Elder Harold B. Lee.

---

* A Study of the Denver and Phoenix Markets'' (May, 1980, Message Dissemination Phase II Study, Frank N. Magid Associates, Inc.).

CHAPTER 22

Racial and Financial Challenges to the Church

The United States underwent severe racial disruption during the 1960s, and the Church was pointedly singled out for charges of discrimination against blacks. This caused many tense moments, tremendous debate, and unrest among the membership, particularly in the Church leadership ranks.

The most memorable events to typify this stressful period were the racial riots at Los Angeles in 1965. On August 14 there were massive black riots in South Los Angeles: four hundred or more fires were started, scores of stores were looted, and numerous whites were attacked.

Elder Lee had been scheduled to hold a conference in Los Angeles that weekend, but after the explosive situation was explained he conferred with President Hugh B. Brown of the First Presidency and they decided to adjourn the conference after only the leadership meeting had been conducted. The days that followed showed the wisdom of that decision as rioting continued and the situation remained tense. The National Guard was in "ready combat" at every block within a forty-two-mile radius.

Before that, on Sunday, March 7, a group of three hundred protesters marched to the Church Office Building in Salt Lake City, demanding that the Church speak out in favor of civil rights for blacks. The march was repeated also the next day.

There were rumors of blacks invading Salt Lake City to take vengeance upon the Saints and the Church. In 1962 the Salt Lake Temple east doors were bombed. The vandalism was never totally ascribed to racial problems, although it appeared a possible act of racism.

The peak of the challenge on racial issues came in 1969. Late in October Elder Gordon B. Hinckley came to Elder Lee to express his concerns about current issues and struggles. Prominent among his worries were the difficulties facing Brigham Young University because of the protests blacks made against their athletic teams. Of course, the problem had its roots in the long-standing doctrine relative to restricting the priesthood from those of black descent. Now there were strong pressures being placed on the Church Board of Education to permit the recruiting of black athletes to appease those who were protesting against the university.

Three days later the Brethren assembled for their weekly meeting in the Salt Lake Temple. Elder Lee described this temple meeting as characterized by an unusually deep spiritual atmosphere. Elder Lee was called on to pronounce the opening prayer at the temple altar. He was strongly impressed to pray for a oneness such as the Master prayed for with his disciples long ago in Jerusalem. He prayed that God would safeguard the portals of the temple and, if necessary, send the protective agency of those personages translated, but not yet resurrected, who were reserved to protect the Lord's work on earth. He pleaded for direct intervention to give the leadership of the Church divine guidance in decisions that must be made within the week and would determine the course of action the Church would take to meet the racial issue. The ramifications of such an important decision could stay with them as long as they lived.

In the first week of November a spirited Church Board of Education meeting was held. The Brethren met under the backdrop of a recent meeting of the athletic directors of the Western Athletic Conference universities, which ended in a brawl when a delegation of blacks forced themselves into the meeting. At that meeting, the BYU representative had read a policy statement rebutting the charge of racial discrimination at the Church school. Now at the Church Board of Education meeting the subject of prime concern was the adoption of a policy permitting recruiting of black athletes at BYU. Obviously, only the Church Board of Education could discuss the real issue, the long-standing prohibition of black male members from holding the priesthood.

Knowing that a policy statement would be necessary from Church headquarters, Elder Lee had spent several days documenting his own thinking on this weighty subject. He then asked G.

Homer Durham and Neal A. Maxwell, prominent educators, to do likewise. Placing their texts with his own he delivered the three approaches to Elder Gordon B. Hinckley and asked him to formulate out of their combined thinking the most satisfactory statement that could be read by the critics of the Church, as well as the Church members, to make the Church's position clear.

The background to that position, which President McKay had always reaffirmed, was that the priesthood restriction was not merely a practice or a policy but was based upon a principle handed down by divine order; and that therefore a change could be made only by a revelation from the Lord through his prophet. After two or three drafts and revisions, the statement on the Church and the blacks was ready.

Although misleading announcements in the media caused much confusion during the Christmas holidays of 1969, the statement, which earlier had been circulated to Church leaders in missions, stakes, and wards, was released nationally. It appeared in print for the Latter-day Saints to read in the *Church News,* on Saturday, January 10, 1970, signed by all members of the First Presidency.

The Church tried to take some positive steps to give black baptized members an improved status in the Church as a social organization. Under date of June 10, 1971, President Lee recorded in his diary his concerns and action: "I spent considerable time in the temple meeting of the First Presidency and the Quorum of the Twelve considering what could be done with our black members locally who want to be more fully fellowshipped. More meetings will be held with these members."

A study was made by three members of the Quorum of the Twelve, Elders Howard W. Hunter, Thomas S. Monson, and Boyd K. Packer, which resulted in the organization of a social group of black members known as Genesis. In deciding how to implement this organization, which met in addition to the customary involvement in local wards, where they participated in Primary Association, Relief Society and social activities, President Lee, according to the recollection of Elder Monson, gave this counsel, after deep and solemn pondering and prayer: "I can see where we should not have Sunday School included in the program, but my feelings are, however, that we should extend to our black brethren every blessing up to the holding of the priesthood, and then the Lord will show us the next step."

The subject was not easily put to rest, however. But when it was finally handled and resolved, eight years later, it was done so as a divine principle requiring a revelation from God to his prophet on earth. President Spencer W. Kimball's historic announcement* on June 8, 1978, declaring that all worthy male members of the Church, regardless of race, may be ordained to the priesthood brought joy and happiness to almost everyone and ended a social issue which had been a divisive and burdensome trial to many people in and outside the Church.

OPPOSING DEFICIT FINANCING IN THE CHURCH

Elder Harold B. Lee was an avowed conservative in his political and social programming and organizational perspectives, which bias probably derived from the molding influence of his tutor, President J. Reuben Clark, Jr.

The political philosophy of the 1960s encouraged deficit financing, and some of this thinking infiltrated into the Church. Perhaps this was the reason for Elder Lee's calling to return on July 11, 1961, for a second term of service on the Church Expenditure Committee. This committee became the scene of many situations in which Elder Lee cast his vote in favor of avoiding debt, as he had taught so long in shaping the welfare program.

As 1961 ended, the 1962 budget was being prepared in the Committee on the Disposition of Tithes. Elder Lee's account indicates his opposition to deficit spending as based upon the financial facts available to him at the time.

> I led the discussion in what proved to be a debate when there was proposed a budget of 11 percent more than the anticipated revenues for 1962. My stubborn resistance to the principle of "deficit spending," supposedly justified in the hope of increasing the tithing of the Church to cover the deficit, . . . resulted in the meeting ending with a call for the Twelve to come up with suggestions a week hence as to where cuts should be made to stay within the anticipated income for 1962.

The propensity for spending persisted into 1962, however, and by May of that year there was considerable apprehension

* Official Declaration—2, Doctrine and Covenants, pp. 293–94.

caused by a suggestion to finance such spending by selling Church securities for the next fifty years.

On May 17, Elder Lee received a telegram while in New York City asking him to accompany President Henry D. Moyle and Leland Flint, the president of Zions First National Bank, on a visit to the First National City Bank of New York City to seek counsel on the proposed multi-million-dollar bonding of the Church, for what Elder Lee called the "lavish" building expenditures now anticipated. They were strongly advised against a long-term bond issue and encouraged instead to engage in long-term mortgage borrowings at more favorable rates. The counsel was helpful because when Leland Flint presented his proposals for the financing of huge buildings then being planned (the Kennecott Copper Building, the ZCMI building, the Hotel Utah expansion and underground garage on the Church Office grounds), at an estimated total cost of $30 million, it pleased Elder Lee to note that his proposal had changed. Now it was proposed to proceed to build these projects until completion, when a long-time mortgage at the most favorable rates could be obtained, and to build the tax-exempt buildings on the Administration block in stages to make possible the financing out of current income.

Typical of the routine business before the Expenditures Committee was a discussion on May 23, 1962, to purchase a building lot in a small Peruvian city for $24,000 where only fifteen members of the Church were located. During the discussion period Elder Lee vigorously opposed the purchase plan. He was not afraid or uncomfortable in standing alone. Courage of his convictions was always a Harold B. Lee character trademark.

Elder Lee noted that a movement toward conservatism was coming into the Church financial planning, but he saw a strange paradox in the thinking of some leaders. While all vigorously gave voice to resisting a Church "indebtedness," they felt these projects were exempt because the borrowing was in the name of Zions Securities Corporation, and therefore it was still possible to say "the Church is out of debt." Elder Lee felt his banking associates would surely construe such borrowings as a lien against the Church.

Elder Lee's conservative spending campaign continued through June 1962 as he blocked attempts to give more generous percentages of Church participation on new buildings to which institutes of religion were attached. A rental program was substituted instead. At Expenditures Committee meetings Elder Lee always impressed the idea of economy and staying within the budget. In one instance this led to a decision to deny a recommendation to build a new three-stake tabernacle in Arizona and to air-condition their present three-stake center, which was already owned and free from debt.

The Expenditure Committee meetings continued to be the focal point of conflicting views during this period. One particular issue in August of 1962 was the question, which was hotly debated, as to whether or not the new Genealogical Building should be built, as publicized, on 2100 South and Redwood Road or on the northeast corner of Main Street and North Temple Street. Each location had its strong and vocal advocates. When the Genealogical Society leaders, in arguing for the North Temple site, indicated they were happy in their present quarters in the old Montgomery Ward Building at First South and Main Street, Elder Lee moved that that location become their permanent quarters and save the cost of a new building. After the debate on the new, costly building, President McKay seemed much impressed with the Harold B. Lee idea that could save $6 million.

Sometimes the spending pressures called for a tactical retreat by Elder Lee, however. In August 1962, he intentionally stayed away from a missionary meeting because of the proposed discussion on the budget for missionary automobiles, which was already overspent. "I have already voiced my opposition to deficit spending," said Elder Lee.

On the other hand, in that same month Elder Lee stayed home from his New York directorship meetings because of the importance of some business with the Building Committee's overspending its budget. The same arguments for free spending were heard, that the First Presidency would take care of the "non-budget" items beyond spending limits, that there had been a "lag" of some fifty years of deferred building and neglect in keeping pace with growth, that with the appreciation of Church holdings such as its ranches in Florida and Georgia there were more reserves now than ever before, and that borrowing by wholly owned subsidiaries of the Church did not constitute an indebtedness against the Church, etc. Elder Lee argued strongly against all arguments for free spending, and later described his feelings in his journal:

> I was very blunt in challenging these assertions and brought forth a very blunt and frank discussion which resulted in an action to post-

pone all future buildings beyond the budget, with the exception of the anticipated increase of tithing for this year. Several in the meeting continued to display the fallacious reasoning used by the federal government with reference to deficit spending to "increase the economy," and urged also that we should overspend the budget to "keep faith with the people."

One year later, in December of 1963, the annual budget again was presented to the Committee on the Disposition of Tithes, composed of the First Presidency, the Council of the Twelve, and the Presiding Bishopric. Elder Lee called this a "tame meeting" in comparison with the vigorous sessions of the past. Yet, he recorded in his journal: "There is still some cloudiness as to where the money is to come from to finance so-called 'non-budget' items, which we have come gradually to know means 'deficit-spending,' with a philosophy of spending ourselves into prosperity."

Elder Lee remained always the fiscal conservative, whose energies and counsel were always directed towards safeguarding the Lord's sacred tithes.

NEW YORK WORLD'S FAIR MORMON PAVILION

When the exhibitry planned for the Mormon Pavilion at the New York World's Fair seemed to lack budgetary controls, Elder Lee was made chairman of the committee preparing for the Church's full-scale public relations involvement. During the 1964 – 65 project he became a moving influence, mainly in the area of making the pavilion an effective missionary project.

Two themes were originally considered for presentation. One was to portray the history and growth of the Church from its humble origin in New York state to its worldwide importance. The other was to teach the message of the restored gospel. Elder Lee pointed out that the result of the first theme would be to make friends for the Church. The second theme would bring converts into the Church.

The gospel theme was chosen. Exhibits and displays centered around the message of the restored gospel. Bertel Thorvaldsen's magnificent marble sculpture of the *Christus* became the focal point, signifying that Mormons are Christians and follow the Savior's teachings. The motion picture film *Man's Search for Happiness* was created to depict the Latter-day Saint belief in the Resurrection and our eternal family relationships.

During the two-summer-month World's Fair period, 360 full-time missionaries, working under Eastern States Mission President Wilburn C. West, and more than a hundred volunteers presented the restored gospel message to 5,767,835 visitors. They sold 97,385 copies of the Book of Mormon and distributed more than five million tracts and pamphlets. Thousands of visitors investigated the Church, and many were baptized as a result. Said Elder Lee at the conclusion of the Fair: "The impact of our success at the Mormon Pavilion will be felt in missionary work from this time forward."

THREATS TO HEALTH

Under the seniority system the health of a future prophet of God is always of major concern to all the Church membership. Survival to the years of leadership is necessary, yet the path is strewn with trials and many potential dangers.

As Elder Lee matured into greater leadership responsibility during the 1961–70 decade, aging began to take its toll along with the unrelenting pressures from his work as an Apostle.

Early in the decade Elder Lee underwent minor surgery for a hernia repair. On the fourth postoperative day he wrote in his journal, dated March 10, 1963: "After the intensive visiting of the Brethren and their wives for the last three days, I found myself becoming very nervous inside and decided that since there was no need for treatments or medications that I would be better off at home, although it has been but four days since my surgery. Many came with problems and anxieties until I felt like I was swimming against an impossible current."

One year later, just before his sixty-fifth birthday, Elder Lee contracted a serious virus infection while on a trip to Washington, D.C., New York City, and Cincinnati. He barely made it through the Cincinnati Stake conference, and then only after receiving a priesthood blessing from the stake presidency, but he was hospitalized immediately upon his return home. After a thorough physical examination, doctors concluded that he had a touch of pneumonia. Tests also discovered some loss of blood from two ulcers, only one of which had healed. Elders Marion G. Romney and Spencer W. Kimball came to the hospital to administer to Elder Lee, at his request. There they received instructions for carrying on the Priesthood Correlation Committee's two-day seminar, which now Elder Lee was forced to miss. On March 6,

1964, Elder Lee wrote: "I had reports from Richard Evans, Harry Brooks and Brent [Goates] as to the success of the priesthood representatives seminar. They were all certain that much good had resulted, but were kind to me in the thought that I might have added something to it."

The year 1966 commenced with Elder Lee undergoing another complete physical examination, which revealed that his blood level was only 56 percent of normal. A series of blood transfusions eliminated his pallid coloring and gave him renewed energy. While still wobbly and not completely back to full strength, Elder Lee underwent other tests to determine the possible causes of his persistent headaches, a malady he suffered all of his adult life. No help was found.

In March 1967, Joan Lee again observed that her husband's face was unusually pale. Subsequent blood tests indicated that Elder Lee's blood count was dangerously low and he was taken to the LDS Hospital for blood transfusions and iron shots, hoping to build him up before his departure to tour the Florida Mission.

After an exhausting pace including three chapel dedications, many interviews, studies on chapels, and much travel through Florida, the Lees went north where Elder Lee was scheduled to divide the New Jersey Stake. With Elder Franklin D. Richards they interviewed throughout Saturday, March 26, but on Sunday morning Elder Lee became so faint that he was forced to lie down to clear his head. Sister Lee called President W. Jay Eldredge of the Eastern States Mission, who came with two missionaries and administered to the Apostle. Elder Lee was then able to limp through the remaining conference schedule.

When he awoke on Monday morning, after a full ten hours of sleep, he became conscious that he should leave immediately for home although he had planned to stay in New York for other meetings. His weakness of Sunday morning was returning, and he was certain that he was again losing blood and should reach his physician, Dr. James F. Orme, as quickly as possible. Concerning this trip, President Lee related the following incident in the Salt Lake Tabernacle at the general conference on April 8, 1973:

> On the way across the country, we were sitting in the forward section of the airplane. Some of our Church members were in the next section. As we approached a certain point en route, someone laid his hand upon my head. I looked up; I could see no one. That

happened again before we arrived home, again with the same experience. Who it was, by what means or what medium, I may never know, except I knew that I was receiving a blessing that I came a few hours later to know I needed most desperately.

As soon as we arrived home, my wife very anxiously called the doctor. It was now about eleven o'clock at night. He called me to come to the telephone, and he asked me how I was. I said, "Well, I am very tired; I think I will be all right." But shortly thereafter, there came massive hemorrhages, which had they occurred while we were in flight, I wouldn't be here today talking about it.

I know that there are powers divine that reach out when all other help is not available. . . . Yes, I know that there are such powers.

Elder Lee was hospitalized immediately on his return to Salt Lake City. Extensive testing finally concluded that the outlet from his stomach was so nearly closed that foods and liquids could not pass through properly, causing the severe pain and nausea which he had been experiencing. Scar tissue from previous bleedings had further aggravated the problem. All agreed that stomach surgery was required following conference. Dr. V. L. Rees was chosen as the surgeon. Physicians also ruled out Elder Lee's participation in the April 1967 general conference; his ordeal in the hospital already had dropped his weight seven pounds down to 158 pounds.

Harold B. Lee became a spectator watching general conference from home over television. He noted in his private journal the names of the Brethren who came to see him, but more especially, the names of some who did not come nor even telephone their interest. For his own purposes, in his journal he wrote his impressions of the sermons: "I spent the day of Sunday conference listening and watching the proceedings by television. Outstanding addresses were given by Hugh B. Brown, Mark E. Petersen, and Marion G. Romney. Boyd Packer did an unusual job in speaking to sectarian ministers as to why we cannot accept ecumenical Christian unity as the solutions of the problems of the Church. Ezra Taft Benson gave his usual eloquent oration on an old theme."

On April 12, 1967, Harold B. Lee survived a three-and-one-half-hour operation during which over half of his stomach was removed because of a large perforated ulcer. The resident surgeon on his case told Elder Lee after the surgery that the same surgical team had operated on another man with almost an identical problem, but that this other case proved to be cancerous. A sobered

Elder Lee wrote in his journal his innermost thoughts: "One can only suppose that the Almighty has it in his hand to give or to take and he alone keeps the timetable. To the thoroughness and the skill of the doctors I owe much, but I'm not unmindful of the spiritual power which has been in evidence in the events leading up to the operation as well as circumstances resulting therefrom. When I was released to come home I found I weighed but 150 pounds, a loss of 15 pounds."

The parting injunction of Dr. Orme to his patient, as Elder Lee left the hospital, was to now do only half a man's work rather than the work of ten men as in the past. He told Elder Lee that over the years as he had been treating him, he had known that the Apostle had stamina and courage, but since discovering the true conditions found at surgery, the medical team was astounded that he had been able to endure the pain which he must have experienced.

One year later an old chronic weakness which had started in boyhood, lung difficulties, arose again. A lung infection called pleuropneumonia forced Elder Lee to cancel his involvement in dividing the Boston Stake on April 13, 1968. He missed several weekend appointments before returning to the circuit again.

In October 1969, Elder Lee again was forced to the sidelines and was unable to participate in the general conference of the Church. Unexplained exhaustion started on September 7, 1969, when Elder Lee was told by his doctors, after they had studied a blood sample, that he must cancel his conference appointment in California. Instead of traveling he was hospitalized for tests and then ordered home for a rest. He met the Leadership Committee at his home as they planned for the forthcoming seminar for Regional Representatives to be held two days preceding general conference. After this planning meeting, his secretary, D. Arthur Haycock, anointed and Elder Thomas S. Monson sealed a priesthood blessing on Elder Lee.

Quietly awaiting the diagnosis while studying for sermons he was assigned to give at conference, Elder Lee wrote in his journal on September 10, 1969, concerning his attitude toward this illness: "I spent considerable time working on talks I am to give at the seminar, to the Relief Society conference, and for the general conference. My mind seems to be clearing and I awoke in the early morning hours feeling that somehow I was being 'cleansed,' as nearly as I could describe the feeling."

When the medical reports were summarized after an intensive day of hospital tests and X-ray studies, doctors concluded that Elder Lee's left kidney was not functioning properly because of a large kidney stone blockage. Surgery was planned immediately. The pre-surgical diagnostic testing was the most vigorous he had ever experienced.

After Elder Lee entered the hospital he wrote in his journal: "Despite it all there was a peaceful feeling come over me, especially after a blessing by President N. Eldon Tanner and Gordon B. Hinckley, assisted by my family members, Perry, Brent, David, and Charlie. My faithful Joan was a great comfort as I prepared for what seemed a fateful experience."

A large kidney stone was removed in surgery at the LDS Hospital on September 22, 1969. After two days in the intensive care ward, Elder Lee's convalescence was uneventful. He was, however, again ruled out of general conference activity.

Elder Lee's operation transferred an additional sudden burden to President Tanner and Elders Spencer Kimball and Thomas Monson, all of whom came to the hospital as soon as Elder Lee was in a private room to obtain instructions for carrying on without him. Elder Lee did his best in his weakened condition to give them counsel and direction. Others, too, sought counsel. Elder Marion D. Hanks asked about the LDS student organizations now moving under priesthood correlation. Elder Marion G. Romney, substituting for Elder Lee in counseling patriarchs at the conference, wanted advice. President Tanner asked for suggestions about sustaining the new Unified Social Services organization at general conference.

One important decision made concerned who should take charge of the Regional Representatives seminar meetings which would be held for the first time without Elder Lee. Brother Lee asked Elder Kimball to conduct the meetings, thereby deciding that seniority should prevail over the Leadership Committee, which had made all the preparations. Following the morning session of the seminar, President Tanner, Richard Evans, Neal Maxwell, and Brent Goates were among those who called to commend Elder Lee on his message, which was read to the Regional Representatives by Neal Maxwell, using several charts Elder Lee had prepared based upon recent surveys of the Church membership. Many gifts and flowers arrived and all indicated they had missed Elder Lee's participation.

As if this latest surgery weren't enough, Elder Lee's convalescence was complicated by a new ailment, a sciatic nerve pain in his right leg.

Elder Lee patiently and philosophically accepted these various physical ailments. His viewpoint, as always, was that he was ready to leave this earthly existence whenever his Heavenly Father wanted or needed him, and his future role in the Church was entirely in the hands of Almighty God. His concern only was to live worthy of the Holy Spirit in the conduct of his sacred calling and to eventually await divine judgment from an all-wise Providence, which he was convinced ever was watching over the Church and his personal career of service.

TEACHING IN THE TEMPLE

Early in the 1960s Elder Lee had commenced a routine teaching role that became precious to him and all whom he taught. He was asked to meet in the Salt Lake Temple with all departing missionaries for a ninety-minute question-and-answer period between two endowment sessions. This represented the first exposure to the temple for such missionaries and this person-to-person education by a senior theologian of the Church was a highly valued experience. Thousands of young ambassadors of the Lord thus came under Elder Lee's profound spiritual wisdom.

In August 1962, while the Salt Lake Temple was closed for vacation, Elder Lee drove to the Logan Temple for a session with a company of missionaries. He wrote of this occasion: "This was an unusually alert and well-schooled group and the discussions raised by their questions were most interesting and challenging."

Elder Lee considered these experiences a personal challenge to his own encyclopedic knowledge of the scriptures and Church doctrine. He always welcomed this opportunity to search for more and more knowledge through the scriptures.

Elder Lee had one standard rule in meeting the onslaught of questions from these eager minds. He went to the temple with only the standard works under his arm and told his attentive audience that if their questions could not be answered from the approved scriptures of the Church, he would give no answer. His personal copies of the scriptures, however, were slightly augmented with choice quotations from the Presidents of the Church which he had inserted into the binding of his standard works.

Many of his General Authority colleagues came to the temple to monitor what this master teacher was giving in these unusual teaching moments under such sublime spiritual conditions.

Whenever Elder Lee couldn't attend the teaching sessions he would ask Elder ElRay L. Christiansen, head of the Church's Temple Department, to take his place. In October 1962, when Elder Lee was grieving over the passing of his wife, Fern, he thought it best that he not go to the temple with the missionaries and asked Elder Christiansen to substitute for him. He noted quizzically in his journal, "for some reason he seems to be somewhat reluctant to go." A logical question might be, "Who wouldn't be reluctant to take his place?"

He always approached such an assignment with reverence for the sacred subjects under discussion. On August 11, 1967, he noted in his journal: "This temple session of outgoing missionaries was large, about three hundred in the group, and the communication was not too easy. This is always a soul-searching assignment, to answer their questions on the temple ceremonies and the doctrines underlying each."

On rare occasions Elder Lee made note of unusual questions that were asked in his temple sessions. He wrote of one such case in his diary entry of Tuesday, February 11, 1969: "I found again that I must be very careful not to leave answers not fully explained, so as to avoid false conclusions. This was apparent in my first answer to the question today: 'Is Satan the god of this world?' The Master called him the prince of this world. In its most precise sense, Jesus is the 'God' of this world."

Elder Lee felt that by 1969 he could see that the questions from the missionaries were showing evidence of greater maturity. In March he wrote, "On today's temple session with about 250 outgoing missionaries the questions were unusually well thought-out and meaningful."

Reflecting on this interesting assignment while speaking to youth leaders in 1969 Elder Lee stated:

> I have an interesting session with every missionary company in the temple on the fifth floor, in the big assembly room, where they are invited to ask any questions they may wish to ask about the temple ordinances. If you would like to have an interesting experience sometime, you try to stand and be bombarded by 350 missionaries, and accept the responsibility of covering the whole gamut of the gospel from the creation to exaltation.

In one of these missionary sessions a missionary asked the other day, "Can you tell us a place in this temple where the Lord has appeared?" I suppose he was referring to a testimony that some have born about someone who had appeared in the temple.

I said, "Now don't look for *a* [single] place. This is the House of the Lord. This is where the Lord comes when he comes to see us on the earth. I imagine he has walked all the halls and every room. He is looking at us; maybe he is here today. I can't imagine a place where he would rather be than right here. Here are 300 or so of you going out on missions to preach his gospel. Maybe he is here with you."

"Behold," the Lord said, "verily, verily, I say unto you that mine eyes are upon you. I am in your midst and ye cannot see me; But the day soon cometh that ye shall see me, and know that I am; for the veil of darkness shall soon be rent, and he that is not purified shall not abide the day." (D&C 38:7–8.)

While the value of these temple sessions with the missionaries was obvious to those young men leaving for service throughout the world as teachers of the gospel, it is interesting to note the personal reward that returned to Elder Lee for such service. He wrote in 1969, "It is always a great spiritual uplift to be in the temple with the missionaries."

Even after Harold B. Lee became President of the Church he continued to teach the missionaries in the temple. It seemed to bring him immense challenge and increased spirituality, and the thrill of being personally instructed by the prophet of God in the temple fortified the missionaries as no other experience could.

Thousands of missionaries treasure their personal experiences in the temple with this man of God, and they will likely always remember Elder Lee standing before them dressed in his white temple suit and unfolding the hidden meanings of the ordinances and the scriptures, teaching "as one having authority."

A Pentecostal Outpouring of the Spirit

Spiritual experiences were often interspersed into crowded historical happenings during the expanding 1961–70 decade of Harold B. Lee's apostolic ministry. Characteristically, Elder Lee's high spiritual moments came amid some of the greatest stress periods; the following example occurred during the major controversy regarding blacks and the priesthood in 1969.

On December 5, 1969, a large body of young people and their leaders gathered expectantly for a most unique meeting in the

Speaking at the Institute of Religion, University of Utah

Institute of Religion building on the University of Utah campus. The occasion was the LDS Student Association's International Convention. Every one of the three hundred invited attendees was hand-picked from college campuses in the United States and Canada.

It was a time of intense college unrest and these campuses were not like the Brigham Young University, with its steadying influence from a dominant church orientation. Church leaders had determined that these young students needed spiritual strength to become the beacon lights that many could follow to safety and peace in a darkened world.

After a banquet in the East Institute Building the congregation filled to overflowing the large institute chapel and cultural hall areas, including the stage. There was a special air of excitement and expectation permeating the building. Elder Marion D. Hanks, then responsible for the Student Association program of the Church, conducted the meeting. Harold B. Lee of the Quorum of the Twelve was to be the featured speaker. The early part of the meeting laid an appropriate foundation for that which was to follow.

Prior to the meeting, in two separate conversations, Elder Lee had received suggestions for his sermon text from Elder Hanks and from Sister Elaine A. Cannon, founder and adviser for Women's Affairs for the Lambda Delta Sigma, the Church sorority. He was told that the youth of the Church needed to know that God indeed was not dead. They explained to Elder Lee that the young people were generally grateful to belong to the Church with its fine programs, but they were searching for a defense of its truthfulness, its leaders, its system, and its practices. He had been urged to bear testimony of personal experiences in an effort to spiritualize these student leaders who had been brought from many distant places for this week-long seminar.

Elder Lee responded to these suggestions with a powerful sermon in a defense of the kingdom, taking his text from Doctrine and Covenants 115:4–5, "Shine forth, that thy light may be a standard for the nations." He related personal experiences of true modern miracles which had occurred to him, attesting to the power of the priesthood; illustrating inspired callings, relevant practices, and eternal principles; and exemplifying the effectiveness of prayer in the lives of the Saints. He supported this with scriptural references throughout. His counsel was good, and the personal experiences were interesting.

Then, considerably more than midway in his sermon of one hour and fifteen minutes, the mood changed. Elder Lee paused. His voice became quiet. He bowed his head over the pulpit, grasping it tightly with both hands. He took a step back and then looked up.

Then it happened! The spirit of the meeting suddenly changed as Elder Lee concluded his sermon with considerable emotion, firmly and fervently witnessing to the truth of his convictions as they had been expressed, and bearing personal, heartfelt testimony that God lives. He told of how he had come to know this truth as one of His special witnesses on the earth. Everyone there knew that he knew! The windows of heaven seemed to open, and the Savior's spirit flowed over the entire congregation.

The concluding song was sung by Brother Marvin Higbee, then a professional worker with the Student Association and employed by the Church Education Department. He later became president of both Snow College at Ephraim, Utah, and the Utah Technical

College at Orem, Utah. Brother Higbee sang in his beautiful tenor voice the well-known song, "I Walked Today Where Jesus Walked." Sung with simple and stirring beauty, it was inspiring. Many in the audience wept.

Then Tom Schwartz gave the benediction. This gifted young man, a bright, converted atheist, an intellectual trained in journalism in the Midwest, was battling for his own faith as he made his way through what Elder Hanks called the "academic catacombs."

His prayer was similar to Elder Lee's talk in that it was divided into two parts. The first was sincere and fervent, but not unusual. In the second part, Tom abandoned the formal language of prayer as the intensity of his feelings mounted. In spiritual anguish he pleaded with the Lord to allow President David O. McKay, who was listening by direct wire in his Hotel Utah apartment, to feel the fervor, sincerity, and faith of the youth gathered in that building, to feel the love they felt for him, and to know that they yearned to have him lifted up as their prophet to lead them back into God's presence. He then made an earnest, powerful, and compelling appeal to the congregation to live worthy of such a spiritual adventure. It was an uncommon prayer in phrasing, feeling, and subject, but was most appropriate for this rare spiritual atmosphere.

This remarkable and unusual prayer had followed a remarkable and unusual song, and a remarkable and unusual sermon. Now the meeting was over. Over? How could it end so abruptly?

No one moved after the prayer. Elder Hanks went back to the pulpit and stood there in silence as waves of spiritual power swept through the audience. Still no one stirred to leave. There was no sound or movement of any kind. Elder Hanks stood with head bowed and silently permitted the spiritual cleansing of that vast congregation. These were long, full minutes of quiet meditation, wet with tears. Elaine Cannon described this unforgettable moment in these words:

> A sense of being one of God's own and being known to him came over us. It was as if all those you've loved and worshipped, or owe something to, were hovering about in a marvelous spiritual reunion. Brother Hanks stook there in his special poised way, allowing the moment to happen. Someone less sensitive might have just dismissed the meeting. Still no one moved. Elder Hanks stood for long minutes, alone, up front, head bowed. Finally he turned to look at Elder Lee, eyes brimming with tears, who then stood with his wife, as did Elder and Sister Richard L. Evans. Along with Elder Hanks,

they, too, were silent, weeping. No one moved as we drank in the precious reality that this was "An Experience!" It was a silent communion and a flooding witness. I covered my tears and was alone with God. Each person there must have felt the same.

Elder Hanks recalls what happened next:

After a long period of utter motionless silence, I nodded to the audience, turned and invited Elder and Sister Lee to walk with me, and led them to the front foyer area of the institute building, where Elder and Sister Lee shook hands with an absolutely mute and generally tearful group of young people as they filed by. Interestingly, during the long silence, which lasted about twenty minutes or even longer, punctuated only by sobs and sniffling, someone started to sing "The Spirit of God Like a Fire Is Burning." Only a few joined in. After one verse they quit, and the silence continued. Even that sacred song was an intrusion on the sublime Spirit.

With great reluctance the other leaders on the stand moved from their seats to congregate by the sacrament table, where they stood as the young people filed out two at a time in the most reverent exit ever witnessed from a Church building.

An unprecedented decision then was made by the students following that amazing experience. Although an orchestra had been hired for the dance which was to end the week-long schedule, they chose to cancel the social, which to them now seemed entirely inappropriate.

Meanwhile, Elder and Sister Lee left the building and did not speak until they knelt in prayer at home in thanksgiving for a most remarkable witness of God's presence. Later, Elder Lee described it as one of the most spiritual experiences he had ever enjoyed outside of the temple.

When Elder Lee wrote of the event in his journal he quoted a comment made to him by Elder Marion D. Hanks concerning that night: "Marion D. Hanks expressed what many of those present felt. He said: 'This is a night those present will never forget, nor will I. It has been the greatest spiritual experience I have ever had, also.' "

Asked to recall and reflect on this spiritual experience thirteen years later, Elder Hanks reiterated his previous appraisal in these words: "The total effect was not like any other experience of my lifetime. It is still the most powerful spiritual experience of my life."

Greeting members of the audience following one of his many talks to youth, this one to seminary students at the Assembly Hall on Temple Square

Over the years Church leaders have had many wonderful, enriching experiences. All can recall meetings where the Spirit was present. Only rarely there is an occasion where it is evident in such power. Sister Cannon remembers three such glorious events in her experience, but reflects: "As I review these three, none compare with the Friday night, December 5, 1969, meeting at the East Institute Building with Elders Harold B. Lee, Richard L. Evans, and Marion D. Hanks, who were so moved they were weeping and unable to stir from their places. We all knew, even felt, the presence of the Lord. We were incapable of resisting it."

As in the original day of Pentecost where "many wonders and signs were done by the apostles" of Jesus, spiritual outpourings come as a gift from God. They are not easily staged, no matter how diligently one prays or prepares. The way to obtain such an experience, Elder Lee once explained, is to look to your "spiritual housekeeping" and leave the rest to the Lord's will. As the Master said, "The wind bloweth where it listeth, and thou hearest the sound thereof, but canst not tell whence it cometh, and whither it goeth; so is every one that is born of the Spirit" (John 3:8).

First
Presidency
Years

———

1970–1972

1970–1972. GNP reached $1 trillion and voting
age was lowered to eighteen years. Microprocessor
computer chip introduced by Intel of California.
Church construction under way with new twenty-
eight-story general office building on same Salt
Lake City block as the Administration Building;
and two new temples—in Ogden and Provo,
Utah.

CHAPTER 23

First Presidency Years with President Smith

In the wisdom of God and by precedent throughout most of this last dispensation of the Church, the President and prophet has been by design a venerable and most often an aged, proven leader. In the seniority system we may always expect that the Church President will be an older man whose stability and wisdom, born of years of experience, qualifies him uniquely for his role to commune with God in behalf of his Saints on earth.

A review of Church history since the restoration of the gospel sustains this observation. The Presidents of the Church from John Taylor to David O. McKay became President at ages ranging from sixty-two (Joseph F. Smith), to eighty-four (Lorenzo Snow). They died at ages ranging from John Taylor at seventy-eight to David O.

McKay's ninety-six years of age. On the average, these eight Church Presidents were seventy-three years of age in assuming the Presidency, and at death averaged eighty-six years of age, having served slightly less than twelve years each in office.

In such a system it is not unlikely that the President of the Church will grow old in office, and such has been the actual fact more often than not. How does the Church function so well with aged leadership? Much of the resiliency of the Church's leadership lies in the support system that the Quorum of the Twelve Apostles provides. The Apostles are usually younger men with tremendous leadership skills and energies, and their ordinations carry with them the latent powers to preside over the Church when called to do so by proper authority and sustained before the membership.

Still, questions of succession arise and provide interesting and necessary study, especially under unusual but predictable circumstances. Such was the case in the last days of President David O. McKay, who was again unable to attend general conference—in this case October 1969—because of illness.

In this situation of the President's disabilities and the evident nearness of his death—at which time the Quorum of the Twelve would immediately assume the governance of the Church—the Quorum of the Twelve asked Harold B. Lee to represent them in meeting regularly with President McKay's counselors in all First Presidency meetings. It is interesting that this call came to Elder Lee even though President Joseph Fielding Smith, the President of the Quorum of the Twelve, was already a counselor to President McKay in the First Presidency. But President Smith was then ninety-three, just three years younger than President McKay.

At 6:00 A.M. on Sunday, January 18, 1970, Elder Lee received a telephone call from Joseph Fielding Smith's wife informing him that the President had just passed away and that President Smith wanted to meet Elder Lee immediately at President McKay's Hotel Utah apartment. When Elder Lee arrived, he found all the McKay family present except a son, Llewelyn, who had suffered a stroke, and a daughter, Jean, who lived in Chicago. There they developed preliminary family plans for funeral arrangements.

After further consultation with a committee consisting of the three senior members of the Quorum of the Twelve, other than President Smith and President Tanner, it was decided that the services would be conducted by President Hugh B. Brown, with

President Smith giving a tribute and President Tanner and Elder Lee serving as additional speakers. President Alvin R. Dyer and Elders Ezra Taft Benson and Richard L. Evans would offer the prayers at the service and at the graveside.

On the day prior to President McKay's funeral, President and Sister Joseph Fielding Smith came to Elder Lee's office and seemed most nervous about the rumors which were abounding that an effort might be made to bypass the traditional appointment of the senior Apostle to be the next President, due to his age and poor health. The Smiths indicated that if Joseph Fielding Smith were sustained as President, he wanted Elder Lee to be "by his side," which Elder Lee interpreted to mean that he wanted him to serve as a counselor in the First Presidency. Elder Lee sensed then that if this were to happen he would likely be simultaneously both a counselor and the President of the Twelve for a period of time.

These speculations before the decisions induced in Elder Lee an overwhelming sense of obligation and responsibility. He wrote, "I could not assume such burdens without the Lord's help." He pondered the portending responsibility and his immense need for guidance as he looked out of his Church Office Building window to see thousands of people lined up on Main Street, moving slowly towards North Temple and all the way around the block for a final glimpse of President McKay's body lying in state in the foyer of the Church Office Building. It was natural that this outpouring of grief would be extreme: more than a million members of the Church had never known any other President in their lifetime than President McKay.

Early on the morning following the funeral, Friday, January 23, the Twelve, and including Presidents Brown and Tanner, met in the temple to consider the question of reorganizing the Church's leadership. According to the Prophet Joseph Smith's teachings, there was now no First Presidency in the absence of the President. This meant that the counselors who had been members of the Quorum of the Twelve took their places in the order of their seniority among the Twelve. Before this meeting, President Smith had confirmed his desire to Elder Lee that he serve as his First Counselor, assuming he was appointed. He also chose N. Eldon Tanner to continue in the First Presidency as Second Counselor.

There was an air of expectancy and some tension as the meeting in the temple began. Each Apostle, starting with the junior member of the Twelve, spoke his true convictions. When it was Elder Lee's turn, he read a letter written by President Wilford Woodruff to Elder Heber J. Grant, then a member of the Twelve, in which he answered the question as to whether an Apostle other than the President of the Twelve could become the President of the Church. Elder Lee later quoted this same letter, dated March 28, 1887, in his general conference address on April 6, 1970:

> "When the President of the Church dies, who then is the Presiding Authority of the Church? It is the Quorum of the Twelve Apostles (ordained and organized by the revelations of God and none else). Then while these Twelve Apostles preside over the Church, who is the President of the Church? It is the President of the Twelve Apostles. And he is virtually as much the President of the Church while presiding over twelve men as he is when organized as the Presidency of the Church, and presiding over two men."

Elder Lee commented: "This principle has been carried out now for 140 years—ever since the organization of the Church. Then President Woodruff's words continued":

> "As far as I am concerned it would require . . . a revelation from the same God who had organized the Church and guided it by inspiration in the channel in which it has traveled for 57 years, before I could give my vote or influence to depart from the paths followed by the Apostles, since the organization of the Church and followed by inspiration of Almighty God, for the past 57 years by the Apostles, as recorded in the history of the Church."

With President Woodruff's convincing testimony setting forth God's order to have the current President of the Twelve automatically ascend as the "Acting President" of the Church until a new President has been duly called and ordained by the Twelve, the Church had its leader. Now it remained only to decide if the First Presidency should be reorganized.

Following Elder Lee's remarks in the temple, he made the motion that the Church leadership be reorganized and that President Joseph Fielding Smith be named President of the Church. Elder Spencer W. Kimball seconded the motion, which was unanimously sustained. This action put to flight the rumors that President Smith would not be named as the President because of his age and poor health.

President Smith then took the chair of the President at the head of the altar in the temple council room. He proposed that Harold

First Presidency from 1970 to 1972: President Joseph Fielding Smith, Harold B. Lee, N. Eldon Tanner

B. Lee and N. Eldon Tanner become his first and second counselors, respectively; that Elder Lee be designated as the President of the Twelve because of his seniority in the Twelve; and that Spencer W. Kimball be named as Acting President of the Twelve.

Then came the confirming of priesthood authority, the ordination and setting apart by the laying on of hands by the Apostles, who held that authority. President Smith requested that Elder Lee be voice in setting apart and ordaining him the President of The Church of Jesus Christ of Latter-day Saints and confirming on him all the powers of leadership earlier received, which are inherent in this awesome calling. He then set apart his two counselors, and President Lee also as President of the Twelve. At President Smith's request, Elder Lee then set apart Spencer W. Kimball to become the Acting President of the Twelve.

Immediately thereafter, Elder Mark E. Petersen was directed to release this information to the press and the electronic media so that the waiting world, and the members of the Church in particular, would no longer be in suspense and would know that the Lord's usual and orderly manner for reorganizing his earthly kingdom had once more been followed. Elder Lee wrote of the inspired protocol: "This procedure thereby nullifies any political lobbying which, if we didn't follow precedent, could be a very dangerous threat to the unity of the Church."

On Saturday, January 24, 1970, a press conference was conducted at the Church Office Building. About twenty men and one woman, representing all the news-gathering agencies, including national radio and television networks, were permitted to record the answers to written questions which had been submitted to the new First Presidency. The questioning barrage lasted for over an hour.

Despite his new role as a member of the First Presidency, President Lee kept an earlier appointment on this momentous weekend to divide the South Davis Stake and create the new Val Verda Stake in Bountiful, Utah. Accompanied by Regional Representatives L. Brent Goates and D. Arthur Haycock, President Lee went to the last such assignment in his lifetime to appoint new stake leaders. That day Robert J. Martin was named the new president of the South Davis Stake, and Milton W. Russon became the president of the new stake, the 501st stake in the Church.

NEW FIRST PRESIDENCY COMMENCES WORK

The first meeting of the new First Presidency was held on the morning of Tuesday, January 27, 1970. There a division of responsibilities was discussed. Of necessity President Tanner had been carrying most of the load himself in the former First Presidency. Now Elder Lee, at age seventy-one, dynamic, energetic, capable, and with thirty years of apostolic experience behind him, could assume much of the burden.

They decided to give to Elder Lee the leadership of the temple work knowing that President Smith must be kept close to the conferring of the sealing powers. Genealogical work is a close companion to temple work, so it too was assigned to President Lee. Elder Lee also asked that he be kept as close as possible to the finances of the Church, long managed by President Tanner. The new Presidency further decided to defer the appointment of a new member of the Quorum of the Twelve until the April 1970 general conference.

Elder Lee commenced his seemingly endless meetings of corporations owned by the Church, which duty now claimed much of his daily schedule. He divested himself of assignments long held as chairman of the Executive Committee of the Church Board of Education and the BYU Board of Trustees (to Elder Kimball); the chairman of the Military Relations Committee (to Elder Petersen); and chairman of the Beehive Clothing Mills (to Elder Stapley). After thirty years as a substitute, Elder Kimball succeeded Elder Lee as the regular organist to accompany the singing in the temple meetings of the Quorum of the Twelve and the First Presidency.

Elder Lee also was faced with the serious consideration of how to move forward the entire correlation program to which he had been giving his utmost attention and energy since 1962. Now that he could no longer devote daily effort to this responsibility, he became engaged in prayerful thought to redesign his involvement in the program.

The answer came, and subsequently he proposed that the first Thursday of each month, when at his urging all the General Authorities had been meeting together in the temple with the First Presidency, be hereafter used to discuss Correlation Executive Committee business, thus allowing the work to be directed and controlled by the First Presidency. This would permit the continuation of all correlation subcommittees as before, with their work peaking to this monthly report meeting to the General Authorities. As a result the First Presidency and all other General Authorities would have a full knowledge of continuing efforts to bring all Church activities into complete correlation under the priesthood. Elder Lee saw this procedure as strengthening the other General Authorities in their role as area supervisors under the direction of the Twelve, so that they would be as well prepared at stake conferences and in the supervision of missions to teach more effectively the priesthood-led programs as were the seventy-five Regional Representatives who benefited from their continual training program. This arrangement was discussed with Elder Thomas S. Monson and Antone Romney, on whom President Lee would continue to depend for the many details of the total correlation effort.

With his mind relieved of this major workload, President Lee felt that he should next tackle challenges in the field of communications, an area in which he felt the Church was only loosely organized and in much need of correlation.

EFFECT OF NEW LEADERSHIP ROLE

Following the first general conference of the new First Presidency, in April 1970, Elder Lee found that he was buried with speaking invitations. His emergence as the new member of the First Presidency undoubtedly stimulated this avalanche of speaking requests. He found it necessary to work late into the nights to prepare for these appointments. Requests had come from the University of Utah, Ricks College, Dixie College, College of Southern Utah, a Denver convocation, an organization of LDS students at Harvard University, and others. Of necessity, he was forced to decline many such invitations to preserve his strength for the "must" requirements of his new office.

Another curtailment came in the number of temple marriages he could perform. He was now being asked to perform marriages for the children of couples he had married twenty or more years previously. Had he not drastically cut back his marriage ordinance work in the temple, he would have had time for little else. Thereafter, only family, relatives, and close friends could expect to enjoy his personal service for weddings in the temple.

Shortly after the April 1970 general conference, President Lee was approached for his cooperation in preparing a documentary film, for use when and if there would come another change in the First Presidency. His reply demonstrates his consistent reserve and humility, forbidding him to ever assume any ambitions for the future. He abruptly brushed aside the suggestion by saying: "No one but the Lord knows what the next change will be, and I will have no part in such a documentary, as though I were anticipating any changes in the future, as it might involve me personally."

After almost a year in his new assignment in the First Presidency, President Lee closed out his 1970 personal journal with these significant words: "This past year has been, of course, the most demanding of any year of my life because of my call to the First Presidency, bringing never-ending responsibilities and problems. Through it all there has been a continual awareness of the influence of spiritual guidance and heavenly direction."

The quickened pace and unceasing responsibilities in the First Presidency are demonstrated by this brief profile of a typical, meeting-filled and demanding day in July 1971, as recorded in President Lee's diary:

> Besides meeting with President Smith and the Expenditures Committee, I was kept fully occupied with many problems. A complaint

came relative to the proposed demolition of the mission home in Hong Kong; the decision to go forward with plans for the new 18th Ward and the demolition of the old historical building on that site; complaints about the proposed water fountain on the plaza of the new Church Office Building; the lack of security at the temple. Then word came that President By Woodbury, famous mission president, had been told by his doctor that he didn't have long to live.

The next day's schedule was similarly packed with business. According to President Lee's notes it included "a special meeting to consider some matters needing attention, principally to approve nine members of the Executive Committee for the new General Sunday School Board. We also made plans for the solemn assembly at the St. George Temple on November 13, 1971, and the opening of the Ogden and Provo temples."

With such a relentless schedule, President Lee found he had little time except on weekends to prepare his general conference talks or perform any matters of personal business.

On a Saturday in September 1971, he wrote of this problem: "The continual round of meetings and interviews left me no time to tend to my personal affairs, much less to give some thought to my preparation for the forthcoming conference sessions. I came to the office and spent the entire day so that I could be undisturbed in trying to get the needed spiritual direction for a conference address."

AGED PRESIDENT SMITH MAKES HIS UNIQUE CONTRIBUTION

At ninety-three years of age President Joseph Fielding Smith assumed the mantle of leadership over the kingdom of God on the earth. For sixty years he had worked incessantly to build up the Church. He had been sustained as a prophet for six decades. Now that he was the singular prophet, venerable and bowed with age, he needed the help of strong, loyal counselors, which he received when the First Presidency was reorganized at the solemn assembly, April 6, 1970. On that occasion President Smith described his counselors with these tributes of gratitude:

President Harold B. Lee is a pillar of truth and righteousness, a true seer, who has great spiritual strength and insight and wisdom, and whose knowledge and understanding of the Church and its needs is not surpassed by any man.

President N. Eldon Tanner is a man of like caliber, of perfect integrity, of devotion to the truth, who is endowed with that admin-

A tender moment with the prophet

istrative ability and spiritual capacity which enables him to lead and counsel and direct aright.

At times the aged President was unable to perform duties that he would have liked to do, such as officiating at the marriage of his granddaughter, Susan Smith. President Lee performed this marriage in May 1970.

On other occasions, however, his contributions were invaluable. He was a bridge to the bygone generations, a link to still hold the Church close to the Prophet Joseph Smith and his brother Hyrum, who was Joseph Fielding Smith's grandfather. For decades he had served as Church historian and had sequestered priceless articles dating back to the beginning of the Church which now he alone knew about and whose invaluable information he could pass on to the new generation of leadership through his counselors.

President Smith courageously carried out his duties despite his age limitations. He spoke with difficulty at the funeral of Sister David O. McKay on November 18, 1970.

Whenever the opportunity presented itself President Lee never failed to build up and magnify the venerable President. At a memorable meeting of all the General Authorities in the temple, just prior to the October 1970 general conference, President Smith asked President Lee to take the lead and conduct the testimony and sacrament service. As he introduced President Smith to speak, President Lee took the occasion to commend his ability to rise to the challenge when the need required his decision, and cited in particular the calling of a new Apostle (Boyd K. Packer) as an example. As President Smith arose to speak, he was emotionally moved by President Lee's introduction and he spoke well for fifteen minutes.

At the October general conference in 1970 President Lee again upheld the ninety-four-year-old President Smith before the Saints. He introduced President Smith as the concluding speaker of the conference and, at the urging of President Tanner, took this occasion to parallel the role of President Smith's counselors with the service rendered by Hur and Aaron as they upheld Moses' hands so that Israel would triumph over its enemies.

On Sunday, November 8, 1970, President and Sister Smith were driven to St. George, Utah, in a snowstorm by his personal secretary, D. Arthur Haycock, for the purpose of installing a new temple presidency. What was thought would be a small reception following the meeting turned out to be a massive congregation of three thousand Saints gathered from the entire temple district. At first Sister Smith advised the President not to attempt to speak at this meeting, but President Lee urged that he at least leave his blessing with the large congregation. This he did, requesting that President Lee stand at his side while he spoke. The President stated, "I don't know how I could get along without Brother Lee, my strong right arm, who supports and defends me."

President Smith's administration suffered a severe setback in July 1971, when his wife, Jessie Evans Smith, was hospitalized for a fatal illness. She died on August 3, 1971, from heart failure.

Her funeral was held on August 5, 1971, in the Salt Lake Tabernacle and featured the Tabernacle Choir, with which she had sung for over fifty years. The choir sang many of Sister Smith's favorite hymns that she had performed as a Tabernacle Choir soloist. Elders Richard L. Evans and President Lee were the funeral speakers, with President Tanner conducting. Prayers were offered by Elder Robert L. Simpson, a relative, and by Elder Sterling W. Sill, the Smiths' former bishop.

Elder Lee had made some hasty notes for his funeral address, but when he came to the office early on the day of the funeral he had a distinct impression to refer to the words spoken by President Smith's father, President Joseph F. Smith, at the services for Aunt Rachel Grant, mother of President Heber J. Grant. These words, which were forcibly impressed upon him, were added to his other notes. The quotations of his father immediately caught President Smith's attention; he nodded approval as President Lee spoke and then uttered a strong, audible "Amen," as President Lee concluded his sermon.

President Smith continued to attend the weekly temple meetings but was still in a state of shock over the passing of his dear wife, Jessie. After conferring with President Lee, he decided that he should now accept the invitation to live in the home of his daughter, Amelia, wife of Elder Bruce R. McConkie, where his future and care could be made more certain.

Following the general conference of October 1971, the Quorum of the Twelve and the First Presidency sat in their weekly temple meeting reflecting on the events of the recently concluded conference. In identifying the salient features of the conference the Brethren recalled President Smith's complimentary remarks about his counselors. President Smith had told the stake presidencies and ward bishoprics present that he would wish for them the same choice unity he felt with his own counselors in the First Presidency. He then described his first counselor, President Lee, as a "spiritual giant, with the faith of Enoch and one magnifying his calling as a prophet, seer, and revelator." His second counselor, President Tanner, was described as "one of those chosen before he was born and possessing surpassing integrity and ability."

When 1972 came, the year of President Smith's passing, there were times when he was not able to function well, but there were other moments when the Lord permitted him to give uncommonly clear direction. President Lee recorded one such occasion on January 8, 1972: "I had an interesting experience in our First Presidency meeting when I brought to President Smith a number of policy questions involving genealogical and temple sealings. His mind was very alert and he was able to respond with decisiveness and clarity."

GENERAL CONFERENCES AND THE SOLEMN ASSEMBLY

President Smith's formal installation as President of the Church came at the general conference and solemn assembly of April 1970. A beautiful, calm spirit marked the pre-conference meeting for all General Authorities in the Salt Lake Temple for the fast and sacrament meeting which was followed by a special prayer. After this spiritual meeting, Bishop Victor L. Brown briefed the Brethren on the security measures which had been taken to safeguard the Saints during the forthcoming conference sessions. It was a time of racial unrest and frequent civil rioting, especially on college campuses.

General conference opened on Saturday, April 4, 1970, amid frightening threats of bombings on Temple Square. President Lee started the day with a 7:30 A.M. Welfare Agricultural meeting, where he spoke briefly. Earlier in the week he had spoken to the Regional Representatives and both sessions of Primary Conference. Now he turned to the general sessions of conference, where there was tension and apprehension because of two bomb scares on the nights preceding the conference. On Thursday night the Tabernacle Choir rehearsal was threatened with a bombing and the next night the Utah Symphony Orchestra had evacuated the Tabernacle for fear of bombing consequences.

The Sunday morning session was covered nationwide by radio and television as was also the Saturday morning session. All went well, with President Lee conducting at the request of the President of the Church, and with President Joseph Fielding Smith, President N. Eldon Tanner, and Elder Hugh B. Brown as the speakers.

The far-reaching and potentially disastrous climax came as feared in the Sunday afternoon conference session, when another bomb threat occurred as Elder A. Theodore Tuttle was at the pulpit preaching on the theme "If ye are prepared, ye shall not fear." A telephoned message was delivered to President Lee on the stand of the Tabernacle stating that a bomb would go off during that session. According to Salt Lake City Public Safety Commissioner

James Barker, President Lee emphatically said to the policeman delivering the note in the Tabernacle: "There is no bomb in here; relax." The session continued uninterrupted.

The responsibility for that instantaneous decision and the assurance of that conviction are mind-boggling. It is one of the most significant illustrations of the seer-like qualities of President Lee. It was his gift to be guided by an intuitive inspiration, which quality his associates of the General Authorities understood and deeply admired in him.

Following this tense but spiritually rewarding Sunday afternoon session, the First Presidency and the Twelve met in the temple for prayer and began a twenty-four-hour fasting for divine protection. On this occasion they presented the names of new General Authorities to be announced the following day at the concluding session of conference. After approval by the Twelve, Elder Boyd K. Packer, the newly called apostle, and Elders Joseph Anderson, David B. Haight and William H. Bennett, nominees to be added to the Assistants to the Twelve, were called in, interviewed and given time to spiritually prepare themselves and their families for this historic happening scheduled the next day.

On Monday, April 6, 1970, the solemn assembly became the highlight of general conference. President Tanner conducted the session in the morning and President Lee was assigned to present the same formal voting procedures which have been followed without deviation during the last century, whenever there was a reorganization of the First Presidency. Despite continued threats of demonstrations in this session there was a tremendous evidence of unity and power of faith, as everyone in the Tabernacle, the Assembly Hall on Temple Square, and in the Salt Palace, and all the unseen audience tuned in by radio and television, were invited to stand and, when requested, witness with uplifted hands their sustaining vote of confidence and loyalty. In the three buildings mentioned not a single hand was raised in opposition.

President Lee's address concluded this solemn assembly after President Smith and Elder Spencer W. Kimball, newly sustained as Acting President of the Quorum of the Twelve, had spoken. President Lee felt a great spiritual uplift in carrying out his key role in this impressive service. There was a marvelous spirit of acceptance and joy as President Lee, at President Smith's direction, presented the charge to Elder Packer (formerly an Assistant to the Twelve) and the three new General Authorities before they were ordained and set apart at the next Thursday temple meeting.

At the general conference one year later, in April 1971, the emphasis was on the growth of the Church, especially international expansion. At the concluding session of that conference, the Church membership was announced as having reached 2,930,000, with the 3 million mark expected to be achieved by July. President Lee reflected that on this same date, April 6, thirty years previous, when he was called to the Council of the Twelve, the Church population was a mere 600,000.

President Lee felt now a greater satisfaction than on other occasions when he addressed the Regional Representatives Seminar two days earlier on the theme "The Challenge of Simultaneous Growth with International Problems." He took particular pride in the announcement and introduction of Brother Angel Abrea from Buenos Aires, Argentina, as a new Regional Representative. With the addition now of South America all the major continents where the Church was strong were represented in this powerful body of leaders.

The messages of the general conferences in 1971 concentrated upon meeting the pertinent needs of the Saints. In April there was a sharp warning against the inroads of immorality and drugs, the importance of instruction and training in the home, leader and teacher training and the need for love and understanding in holding fast to the iron rod when the buffetings of sin and temptation threaten the stability of the home and family.

Six months later the theme had shifted as the First Presidency stressed the imperative necessity of a sustained effort to reclaim the many inactive members of the Church and to give them opportunities of service.

A New Presiding Bishopric

In early 1972, an investigation into the reorganization of several business departments of the Church led to a recommendation by the Building Advisory Committee that a new Department of Physical Facilities be created. This move would unify the Real Estate, Church Building, and Maintenance departments under a single head for greater efficiency and economy.

As the recommendations unfolded, both President Lee and President Tanner had the simultaneous impression that Presiding Bishop John H. Vandenberg was the ideal choice to become the first managing director of this important new department. He was called to this new assignment. He was also made an Assistant to the

Twelve, as was his counselor, Bishop Robert L. Simpson, who was now appointed managing director of the Unified Social Services Department.

Early in April the call had gone to Bishop Victor L. Brown, formerly second counselor to Bishop Vandenberg, to succeed him as the tenth Presiding Bishop since the restoration of the gospel. High praise was given to Bishop Brown's prayerfully chosen counselors, H. Burke Peterson, Regional Representative and former president of the Arizona Phoenix Stake, and President Vaughn J. Featherstone, president of the Idaho Boise North Stake. President Joseph Fielding Smith stood in the circle to give his support as President Lee gave the charge and set apart this new Presiding Bishopric of the Church following April 1972 general conference.

President Lee's own sermon at this general conference came as a result of much prayerful searching and study. On Sunday, March 19, 1972, he wrote:

> During the past two days or more, and really for the week in particular, I have spent many "lonesome hours," but hopefully not alone spiritually, pondering what the Lord would have me say at the forthcoming general conference. My decision was to undertake the subject heading "Time of Decision," the caution in controversies, political and otherwise, and to offer five guidelines suggesting how all might be guided to wise decisions in their personal and public life. I feel content after my diligent search.

In reference to controversies that would accompany the intense political campaign in the fall of 1972, President Lee outlined five certainties by which one could detect and know the path to safety in the search for truth. These were: (1) Follow the Light of Christ within us. (2) Follow the positive teachings of the gospel of Jesus Christ. (3) Do your business by the voice of the people. (4) Seek for statesmanlike men. (5) Judge by the light of gospel truths.

NEW THREATS TO PRESIDENT KIMBALL'S LIFE

While President Lee was in New York City in February 1970, he joined Spencer and Camilla Kimball in their visit to Dr. Martin, the cancer specialist who had operated on Spencer's vocal organs thirteen years previously. Dr. Martin gave the patient a surprising but welcome appraisal of his condition by saying that because of this man's position in the Church he would advise no further surgery or cobalt treatments at this time, but recommended careful observation continuously to see if the wart-like tumor on his vocal cord was growing. He allowed that it was possible that Spencer could live out his years without any further surgery. He admitted, however, that this decision defied all the rules of medical practice, but after considering all aspects of his case, he was modifying his previous diagnosis and recommendations.

Increasing hoarseness in his voice, however, caused Elder Kimball concern and he asked to be excused from speaking at general conference in October 1970, because he thought he might be an embarrassment to the Church.

One year later, immediately after October 1971 general conference, Elder Kimball was now faced with another potentially fatal threat to his life. His weakness and fatigue had led to heart studies, and now operations to both his heart and his throat were being investigated.

President Lee urged Elder Kimball, following the temple meeting of October 14, 1971, to rest for a week at the Laguna Beach, California home owned by the Church, with the hope that it would give him and his wife a respite from the tensions they had been under during the last month.

Physicians decided that the heart operation could not be performed for Elder Kimball unless some attempt was made to arrest the growth of the cancer in his throat. Accordingly, Elder Kimball submitted to a long series of cobalt treatments. Again in December 1971 President Lee urged Elder Kimball to recuperate at the Laguna Beach home.

On March 13, 1972, Elder and Sister Kimball requested that President Lee and President Tanner attend a meeting with them and Spencer's physicians, Dr. Ernest L. Wilkinson and Dr. Russell M. Nelson, to consider the alternatives relative to his heart condition. His choice was to go on without an operation, with progressive weakness and loss of effectiveness (he gave himself just two months to live, and Dr. Wilkinson said death would come in the not-too-distant future), or to undergo open-heart bypass surgery to correct a valve leakage in his heart pump and to submit to a second procedure calling for bypass surgery to correct an obstruction in the main arterial supply line to the cardiac muscle, which would increase the blood supply to his heart.

Elder Kimball and his presiding authorities heard the medical report of this high-risk surgery. He wearily stated that he was an old man and perhaps a new, more vigorous replacement should be sought to do the work he could no longer do. President Lee and President Tanner were surprised that Elder Kimball should question whether they thought his continued service was important enough to seek an extension of his life.

Aroused by Elder Kimball's plaintive doubts, President Lee, speaking for the First Presidency, rose to his feet, pounded his fist to the desk, and said, according to Dr. Nelson's written summary of that crucial moment: "Spencer, you have been called! You are not to die! You are to do everything that you need to do in order to care for yourself and continue to live."

This positive declaration seemed to settle the issue. President Kimball said he would submit to surgery. Sister Kimball wept at the thought and Dr. Nelson sunk under the weight of the newly transferred burden which passed to him. The momentous decision, which was to shape the history of the Church, was not made by the physicians, Dr. Nelson reported, but was based solely on the desire of an Apostle of the Lord to follow the inspired direction of the First Presidency. It was decided that the surgery would be performed following the April 1972 general conference, provided that Elder Kimball would allow himself complete rest beforehand.

On April 6, 1972, Elder Kimball spoke in the general conference and did "very well," according to President Lee.

Following general conference the Presiding Bishopric and Assistants to the Twelve were taken with their wives to the council room of the Salt Lake Temple. There, before setting apart the new General Authorities, the First Presidency gave Elder Spencer W. Kimball and his wife, Camilla, and Sister Lois Brown, wife of the new Presiding Bishop, special priesthood blessings. With President Joseph Fielding Smith consenting, President Tanner anointed Elder Kimball and President Lee sealed the priesthood blessing. To some present, it was the most spiritual experience of their entire lives. On the eve of the operation President Lee also gave a blessing to Dr. Russell Nelson in which he told the surgeon that the operation would be performed without error.

The surgery day came on Wednesday, April 12, 1972. Because President Tanner was leaving the next day for a trip and Elder Kimball was being operated on this day, the Council of the Twelve's normal Thursday meeting advanced to Wednesday. During that meeting, a telephone call came from Dr. Nelson reporting that Elder Kimball had come through four and one-half hours of surgery without mishap and "his heart was prepared" for a perfect operation. Dr. Nelson said that he felt like a baseball pitcher who had just thrown a perfect game. He and his surgical team at the LDS Hospital had completed the entire procedure without loss of a blood vessel or a broken stitch. The long and difficult operation had been performed exactly in accordance with the blessings invoked by the priesthood. The Brethren in the temple sighed in grateful relief. The Lord had answered their prayers.

Eight days later President and Sister Lee went to the hospital at Sister Kimball's request and found Spencer in a highly nervous state, the aftermath of his extensive heart operation. President Lee gave him a priesthood blessing and he was quieted.

Just prior to Elder Kimball's release from the hospital on April 24, 1972, President Lee was back at the hospital blessing Elder Alvin R. Dyer, who had suffered a slight stroke that had impaired his speech. After the administration his speech improved and he was able to talk much more clearly. With President Smith also suffering recurrent impairments, some felt that the leadership circles of the Church were weakening.

Throughout Elder Kimball's long and discouraging convalescence, President Lee always encouraged and supported his future successor. On June 18, 1972, President and Sister Lee arranged a special visit to meet Spencer and Camilla Kimball at Laguna Beach, California, where Spencer was again recuperating. President Lee briefed him on many matters, hoping that he might be able to bring Elder Kimball a feeling of belonging and involvement after his three-month absence. Sister Kimball thought the Lees had produced a marvelous transformation by lifting her husband out of his depression and making him feel that he was wanted and needed.

Now Elder Kimball was ready to begin his return to physical and mental health and start his advancement toward vigorous leadership activity.

1971. The United States and the Soviet Union
signed pacts designed to avoid accidental nuclear
war. It took only eight and one-half years for the
Church to reach its third million in membership in
July 1971.

CHAPTER 24

The First
Area Conference

The first glimpse of a plan to have the leadership of
the Church travel to distant areas of the world to take a general
conference – sized program on the road came in November 1970—
another product of President Lee's imagination and inspiration.
On November 19 that year he confided with his associates plans
for a possible regional conference for members of the Church in
Great Britain. From this early probe it was decided to have the
advisers of the auxiliary organizations consider the type of program which might be carried out for a three-day conference in
England.

A fortuitous opportunity for consulting the women's auxiliary
executives came on October 30, 1970, while the sisters were in
New York City for the farewell testimonial of Sister Belle Spafford, who was retiring as the president of the National Women's
Council. President Lee was in New York also for his business meetings, so he took the occasion to meet with the sisters regarding a
proposal to have regional conferences in ten or twelve areas

throughout the world where the members of the Church could attend in large numbers not possible in the semi-annual worldwide conferences in Salt Lake City.

When the announcement was made in Great Britain of the All-British area conference to be held in Manchester in August 1971, a public media excitement was triggered. The British Broadcasting Corporation sent a television team of four men and a young woman interviewer, Esther Ramtzen, to Salt Lake City for two weeks to make a documentary film on the Church.

With all their electronic equipment the BBC team came to President Lee's office and explored for one and one-half hours his thinking on his family background, positions most enjoyed in his Church service, the nature of revelation in the Church, the place of blacks in Mormon doctrine, the relationship between Church and state, how the Church retains its contact with Church members, the secret of Mormon longevity, and other similar topics.

Later Esther Ramtzen came back to see President Lee for a brief personal visit, and he gave her a copy of his book *Youth and the Church*. She informed him that her team would attend the Manchester conference. Elder Richard L. Evans was present for the entire interview and pronounced it "magnificent."

This was by no means the sum of the media curiosity sparked by the announcement of the first area conference of the Church. On August 9, 1971, Brother Henry A. Smith of the Church's Information Service brought a reporter from *The London Times,* Philip Norman, for another interview with President Lee. He asked that he might tape record the conversation, with a photographer sitting across the table snapping pictures. The interview was nearly an hour in length.

Then Elder Lee briefly interviewed Mr. Norman, asking him what had impressed him the most during his careful research at Church headquarters in Salt Lake City. He answered: "The efficiency I find in each phase of the Church I have studied is most impressive. I attended the funeral services in the Salt Lake Tabernacle for Jessie Evans Smith and I am much impressed with the great promise of hope in the life after death which your gospel teaches."

President and Sister Lee left Salt Lake City for the Manchester conference, just prior to the August 21, 1971 weekend, making a stop on the way to dedicate a new stake center at the Mid-Michigan Stake conference. (President Lee had organized this new stake in

December 1968.) In the process of changing planes from Midland to Detroit, President Lee lost his briefcase containing his English conference papers, his sermons, and their passports.

With great anxiety he retraced his steps through the different terminals. After looking in vain in each place, he went out to board the shuttle back to the American Airlines terminal, thinking he possibly had left the case on the bus. Before boarding the shuttle bus he suddenly spotted his briefcase on the ground, intact and unmolested. Relieved, he later wrote in his journal: "Why I hadn't seen it before, I'll never know, and why it was safeguarded for nearly an hour, I'll never know. Only the good Lord could explain this experience. It was a miracle!"

First Area Conference—Great Britain

The assigned General Authorities began assembling in Manchester, England, on August 25, 1971. President Joseph Fielding Smith arrived with his son, Douglas; his secretary, D. Arthur Haycock; and his nephew and physician, Dr. Donald Smith. The President was still grieving over the recent passing of his wife, but seemed to adjust somewhat through the loving attention of his son.

Preliminary youth sessions for the student leaders from Great Britain and the Laurel girls were successfully conducted by Sister Florence Jacobsen and Elders Marion D. Hanks, Joe Christensen, and W. Jay Eldredge. The first separate sessions for the adults as well as the youth, in King's Hall at the Bellevue Sports Center, were both addressed by President Smith and President Lee.

On Thursday, August 26, President Lee was impressed to call a special meeting of the General Authorities who were in England for the conference. The party was led by seven members of the Council of the Twelve. After briefing them on the details of the conference, he asked each of the Brethren to report his labors since they had last met. Dr. Russell M. Nelson, General Superintendent of the Sunday School, and his wife had come from Moscow, Russia, where he was lecturing. President Joseph Fielding Smith responded at President Lee's invitation and spoke with a clarity and freedom which his associates had not observed in a long time, just as so many were praying he could do when the conference started.

The meeting continued as each bore strong testimony at the end of his report. President Lee then closed the meeting with the Brethren all kneeling in prayer around a long table. It was a meeting long to be remembered by those in attendance.

On Saturday evening four thousand sisters met in one session while about two thousand priesthood holders met in the Trade Hall in downtown Manchester. The earlier public relations effort in Salt Lake City paid dividends, because both the *Manchester Guardian* and *The London Times* contained very satisfactory newspaper articles and the BBC aired its fifty-minute documentary on the Church prior to the conference. In the main the coverage was quite fair and positive, President Lee thought.

Approximately ten thousand persons attended the general sessions of the conference on Sunday. At a special entertainment for youth the night before, five thousand were in attendance.

President Lee gave high praise for the planning and management of the conference. He said that the excellent preparation was made possible by the splendid cooperation of the English Regional Representative, Elder Derek Cuthbert, and the stake and mission presidents under the chairmanship of Thomas Fyans, with Jim Conkling and Ray Loveless checking the public address and television systems.

The conference closed on a tremendously high spiritual note with President Smith's testimony and blessing on the English Saints. President Smith seemed stronger at the closing session. President Lee had also spoken well earlier at the Sunday morning session and at the Saturday night priesthood session. Lyrics of a special song had been composed by President Ernest Hewett of the Leicester Stake to go with original music. The entire audience joined with the excellent choir in singing the theme message in the last verse:

> This is our place, here will we stay.
> To build, to strengthen ward and stake,
> Until the Lord supreme shall reign.
> This is our place, here we will serve.

The audience seemed loathe to leave, President Lee noted, as they all sang "God Be with You till We Meet Again" and lined the driveways to wave their farewells to the visiting authorities of the Church.

President and Sister Lee returned home after a visit to Switzerland, where they found missionary work moving very slowly. At the Swiss Temple President Lee also urged the possibility of having the endowment translations on two or more sound tracks for simultaneous transmission for patrons of different languages.

As they left Zurich for Frankfurt, where they were to have taken a plane to New York City, they found that their plane was delayed in Vienna. Shifting to another airline they arrived at Kennedy Airport only thirty-five minutes before their plane was to leave for Salt Lake City. President Lee always gave credit to the Lord for watching over them in successfully managing these tight travel arrangements. He wrote: "With the Lord's intervention with airline officials and customs and immigration authorities, we were rushed with our luggage and bags to the courtesy car which took us directly to our airline, where passenger agents were waiting to move us with our bags directly to our plane, with fourteen minutes to spare. Another miracle!"

President Lee arrived home on September 4, 1971, just in time to meet with the three astronauts of Apollo 15, who were on a nationwide tour and came to pay a courtesy visit to the First Presidency. They were accompanied by Church member Dr. James Fletcher, then the administrative director of the National Aeronautics Space Agency. President Lee invited all the General Authorities to share this joyful moment with these national heroes. Speaking for President Smith, President Lee told these courageous men of space: "We stood in awe and wonder at your phenomenal feat. We watched, we listened, we prayed, and we're glad to see you back on earth, safely home."

RETURN VISIT TO THE ORIENT

The day following the close of the April 1971 general conference, President and Sister Lee left Salt Lake City for another trip to the Orient. In Hawaii they were joined by Brother and Sister Adney Komatsu; after a flight of eight and one-half hours, they arrived in Tokyo, where a large number of Japanese Saints were at the airport to greet them. The heartwarming welcome signs throughout the airport expressed well the love of the Oriental Saints.

President Lee summarized the effects of their first event there, the Mt. Fuji servicemen's conference: "This conference was characterized by a young serviceman who said that in the past there had been more of fun and entertainment, but this conference was marked by deep spirituality. Never have I felt a finer spiritual uplift than in the closing session of the general priesthood meeting followed by a conference for the sisters. We left for Korea, our next stop.''

Welcome signs also greeted the Lees when they arrived in Seoul, with many Korean members of the Church assembled at the airport. President Lee noted that in addition to the Choseen Hotel where they stayed—a fine, modern structure—many new buildings had arisen in the great city of Seoul, in contrast to the devastation he had witnessed when there seventeen years earlier on a mission tour with President Hilton A. Robertson of the Japanese Mission.

After listening intently to reports of the presidents of the four mission zones, comprising nineteen branches, President Lee was delighted to note the understanding each had of his leadership role. He observed also the many men of prominence, professors and businessmen, who now were joining the Church. On April 14, he dedicated a newly constructed chapel and spoke to an audience of about five hundred persons.

President Lee participated in the ground-breaking ceremonies for two more new chapels in Seoul the next day. He praised the guidance of President and Sister Slover for their work in developing local leadership and in promoting a solid and stabilized growth in the Korean membership, now numbering five thousand Saints. With 107 missionaries serving in Korea, the Church membership was increasing at the rate of one thousand per year. Praising the growth and spirit of the Korean members, President Lee said, ''Bringing the gospel to the Korean people is like sowing good seed on fertile ground.''

The next stop was Taipei on the island of Taiwan, where again a large company of Saints welcomed them with signs and roses. The meeting was held in a beautiful, new chapel, where an estimated audience of six hundred was in attendance. Total membership then was 5,100. They came from all parts of the country to be with and see a member of the First Presidency. President Lee wrote of his impressions here: ''It was a sight to behold to see these interesting and faithful Saints attend in such numbers. Possibly this country is not too far away from achieving an organized stake. This country is surprisingly clean and colorful and measurably prosperous. A new mission home is to be constructed on the chapel property."

Next the Lee party went by plane to Hong Kong for a brief visit to this great international city of four million people. President Lee reflected that when he first visited here with Fern in 1954, seventeen years earlier, the Church had but ten members in Hong Kong. They had met in a hotel room with twenty persons present. Now the membership had increased to over five thousand. Again an enthusiastic and heartwarming reception came from the Saints. Over four hundred members attended the meeting before the Lees hurried back to Osaka, Japan, where despite a heavy rain more Saints were there to greet them at the airport. These Church members had waited patiently for President Lee's arrival, and it was after 9:00 P.M. when he dedicated their chapel before a capacity audience of about two hundred Saints.

It was still raining on Sunday, April 18, 1971, when President Lee began the Tokyo Stake conference. He was delighted to see the large attendance of over seven hundred at the morning session, and a similar number gathered for the Tokyo Mission conference. After an intensive day of conference and leadership meetings they finished their schedule at the mission home with a fireside meeting, attended by stake and mission leaders and their wives.

President Lee observed that the family home evening and home teaching programs were barely getting underway in Japan. He challenged the Japanese Church leadership to attain the level of at least 30 percent of families holding family home evenings and at least 50 percent home teaching visits by their next General Authority conference visitor. At the time of his visit these figures were a minuscule 3 ½ percent and 15 percent, respectively, with less than 20 percent of membership attending sacrament meetings. By a show of hands President Lee discovered that a tremendous number of those in the congregation had been members of the Church less than two years.

The Japanese Saints were reluctant to see President and Sister Lee leave Tokyo on April 21, 1971. President Lee thought that this was partly due to the remarkable empathy Sister Lee had developed for these wonderful Oriental people. They seemed to go to the extreme to shower the Lees and Elder and Sister Komatsu with gifts of genuine love.

The Church in the Far East, President Lee believed, was a sleeping giant, just awakening to the immense possibilities available through the influence of the gospel. He wrote, after returning home:

> The growth of the Church in the Orient is most exciting, not only in numbers but also in strength of organization and leadership. We went to be with the people and we were certainly made welcome. It was heartwarming. A piece of your heart is left when you visit the Far East members. I have nothing but admiration for the spirit of the people and the growth of the Church. Greater days certainly are in store for the Saints in the Far East, if we can continue to teach and train them to hold those who are newly found members.

En route home President Lee addressed a special assembly of students, faculty, and many others at the Church College of Hawaii. He counseled the students against interracial marriages and urged the students from other countries to return to their homelands, rather than to remain in Hawaii. He also stressed the importance of problems and so-called "defeats" as a means of finding oneself through the aid of adversity. Discovering the reasons for setbacks and then solving those problems could be the very device to help people keep their priorities straight in reaching eternal goals with an eye single to the glory of God, President Lee taught.

TEMPLE WORK EXPANDED AND PERFECTED

Even before President Lee entered the office of the First Presidency he vigorously led a pursuit of studies on temple ordinances to ensure that they were in exact compliance with original texts. This was a consuming four-year campaign which was not culminated until May of 1972.

President Lee approached the investigation with characteristic humility and deep spirituality. On Sunday, January 31, 1971, he went alone to the temple and spent the entire day in prayerful meditation while studying the instructions and procedures prepared for temple presidents. He declared in his journal at the end of the day: "It was a glorious experience. I was fasting and did not return home until 4:00 p.m."

The spiritual probe continued into the next week. The following Saturday he wrote: "I went alone to an upper room in the temple and there prayerfully reviewed in full all the instructions and policies in temple procedures in the light of the revelations and the oldest documentation of ceremonies. I came to some very definite feelings about these vital matters."

Having received the spiritual direction he had sought, President Lee then launched a penetrating search for all records dating back to President Brigham Young's administration. The activity took him to the Oakland Temple and to Brigham Young University's motion picture studio, where efforts to produce foreign language sound tracks led to a decision to move forward into many languages for temple films.

President Lee continued to assist President Smith with his singular responsibilities in controlling the sealing powers for administration of temple work. On May 13, 1971, the First Presidency made a decision to go forward with the construction of the Washington Temple, after agreeing at a negotiated price with Temple Contractors Associates, comprising the Jacobsen Construction Company, the Okland Construction Company and the Sidney Foulger Company. An impressive building program at a prime location in Manhattan, New York City, was approved also.

On May 21, 1971, President Lee, under President Smith's direction, officiated at the laying of the Provo Temple's cornerstone, while a crowd nearing six thousand attended. Ben E. Lewis, chairman of the fund-raising campaign, announced that the suggested contribution goal of $1 million had been exceeded by $831,000, with more donations still arriving.

A solemn assembly at the St. George Temple, on November 13, 1971, commemorated the one hundredth anniversary of the breaking of ground for that sacred edifice, the first temple completed in Utah under the direction of President Brigham Young. The meeting was attended by 1,250 stake, ward, and quorum leaders.

After the sacrament was administered by the General Authorities, addresses on assigned topics were delivered by the members of the First Presidency and Elders Gordon B. Hinckley and Mark E. Petersen. The Brethren spoke with a clarity which made misunderstanding impossible. The three-hour meeting was described by President Lee in his journal as a "never-to-be-forgotten occasion. Undoubtedly, instructions given under such sacred circumstances are bound to be vital, which they most certainly were."

During early 1972, two new temples in Utah were dedicated. During the Ogden Temple dedication, approximately five thousand Saints from the twenty-eight stakes of the temple district were accommodated in each of six sessions beginning on January

First Presidency at cornerstone laying for Provo Temple (above) and at dedication of Ogden Temple (below)

20, 1972. They were seated in twenty-seven different rooms of the temple and in the nearby Ogden Tabernacle.

Though weakened from the heavy demands of the occasion, President Smith still spoke at the dedication, as did others in the First Presidency, the Council of the Twelve, and additional General Authorities.

Many spiritual experiences were reported at the Ogden Temple dedication. Following the closing session President Lee's eldest grandson, David Goates, telephoned his grandfather to tell him of his unusual experience. David, his wife, Patsy, and his mother, Helen, all reported having seen a brilliant light at the pulpit whenever the First Presidency members stood to speak in the celestial room of the temple. The light, however, did not envelop the other speakers.

Three weeks later the companion temple in Provo, Utah, was dedicated. Because of more Church buildings on the campus of nearby Brigham Young University, linked by closed circuit television, an estimated thirty-five thousand or more were in attendance for each of the sessions.

As at the Ogden Temple dedication, President Lee was the concluding speaker, after which he gave the dedicatory prayer and led the Hosanna Shout. In his sermon, President Lee was impressed to speak of some personal spiritual experiences which unmistakably indicated the nearness to those on the other side of the veil. Elder Alvin R. Dyer testified later that he had seen the deceased President David O. McKay there, along with others whom he couldn't identify. Sister Norma Anderson, wife of Elder Joseph Anderson, Assistant to the Twelve and long-time faithful secretary to the First Presidency, also saw her own mother. President Lee noted in his journal that he was watching the strange look on Sister Anderson's face as she was probably witnessing this visitation.

Two BYU students seated in one of the large campus buildings told President Lee that many of the Saints were shedding tears when the prayer and the Hosanna Shout were delivered and also during the concluding anthem sung by the choir. The Holy Spirit visited these television-linked buildings with the same power as in the temple proper.

PASSING OF ELDER RICHARD L. EVANS

Shortly after the conclusion of the October 1971 general conference Elder Richard L. Evans became ill with what was at first thought to be influenza. President Lee was much concerned and went immediately to his home bedside, giving him a priesthood blessing at the request of Sister Alice Evans. Already Elder Evans's speech was becoming incoherent.

Elder Evans's brother, David W. Evans, wrote to President Lee concerning this noon visit in these words: "Richard told me with great feeling and affection of your visit and the comforting blessing you had given him. He had always known of your affection, but it was especially pleasing that he had this reassurance in his last hours of reflection."

On Sunday, the next day, the Evans family telephoned President Lee to report that Elder Evans was hospitalized after he became completely disoriented. After performing a spinal tap, physicians reported that their patient was suffering from a severe attack of encephalitis, a disease affecting the brain. Again President Lee rushed to his beloved associate's bedside and offered to Alice and her four sons the possibility of having a special prayer with the available members of the Quorum of the Twelve and others, along with the family.

This select and distinguished group of Church leaders and relatives surrounded the bed of Elder Evans in the intensive care unit of the LDS Hospital. There President Joseph Fielding Smith asked President Lee to proceed. He called on Elder Ezra Taft Benson to offer a prayer, following which Elder Marion D. Hanks anointed him and Elder Marion G. Romney was voice in sealing the anointing and blessing him as all men participated. Despite the combined prayers of such faithful men, the condition of Elder Evans remained critical.

By the following Sunday, physicians were reporting that, with Elder Evans in a deep coma, all signs were pointing to the end of his life. The family asked President Lee to sit with them in an adjoining room and talk of spiritual themes. Providing the comfort requested, President Lee said to the family: "I stand ready, as always, should you feel the need to draw close to me for any purpose. I love you and your dear mother, and I want to assure you that I will do anything that lies within my power to help to take the place of one whom I loved as my dear brother, or perhaps more so, because of the bond of fellowship that we have as Apostles of the Lord Jesus Christ."

Late on Sunday, October 31, 1971, Elder Richard L. Evans died. At President Smith's request, President Lee then directed that the Twelve and President Tanner be gathered back home from their traveling assignments around the world. The growing internationalization of the Church is indicated by the distant lands from which they were called home. President Lee telephoned President Tanner in Tiberias, Israel; Marion G. Romney was in Hong Kong; Gordon B. Hinckley in Munich, Germany; and Thomas S. Monson in Guatemala.

The Evans family requested that President Lee speak at the memorial service, along with President Smith and Elders Mark E. Petersen and Marion D. Hanks. They requested that prayers be offered by Jim Conkling and Ike Terry, associates from the Public Communications Department, with music to be furnished by the Tabernacle Choir, which organization Brother Evans had been intimately associated with for many decades. Everywhere there was the feeling of great loss, many saying that Elder Evans belonged not to just the Church, but to the world.

The Salt Lake Tabernacle was crowded to capacity as many nonmembers of the Church joined a sorrowing membership at the funeral service. President Lee thought the service was so harmonious and skillfully programmed and carried out with such finesse that it appeared that Richard himself must have masterminded it. The overwhelming sentiment was the tremendous loss felt by the leadership of the Church and the loyalty which existed among the Brethren. Fifteen top officials from Rotary International, including Dr. Walk, their immediate past president, came across the country to attend this funeral and to honor Elder Evans, who some years earlier had served this distinguished civic organization as its international president.

Because of the daily pressures of Church administration, President Lee was obliged to spend most of the previous night collecting his thoughts and making some notes for his part in the service honoring Elder Evans. His summarization for his diary indicated he felt that the effort had been blessed: "Perhaps as never before, as many expressed, there was a spiritual uplift and deep sense of spirituality if ever such were realized at a funeral service. For my part in the funeral it seemed that I had as much 'freedom' [direction from the Holy Spirit] in speaking as I had ever before experienced."

CHAPTER 25

First Church
Public Relations Department

The loss of Elder Richard L. Evans was particularly felt in the developing movement to create the first public relations department in Church history. President Lee had moved him into the forefront of this planning in January 1971. Reporting to President Lee on the promotion of the public relations and communications activities, Elder Evans had expressed himself as being "overwhelmed" with the remarkable advances which had been made in the last two years.

President Lee wrote in a letter: "I suppose there are few who have passed from the circle of the General Authorities whose passing had touched me more deeply than the death of Richard Evans. I had him working close to me on some very important communication matters."

This public relations effort was born out of the earlier militant harassment of Brigham Young University athletic teams and the possibilities that such persecution could snowball at the hands of those who had developed a hostility toward the Church, basically over the prohibition preventing blacks from holding the priesthood. President Lee found that little had been done to safeguard the offices of the Church and to protect the sacred buildings on Temple Square and the homes of the Church leaders, in the event of a riot or a militant demonstration—and rumors that such would happen flowed freely.

In February 1970, when President Lee was in New York City to attend Equitable Assurance Society meetings, he convened a two-and-one-half-hour meeting at the Waldorf Hotel with other Church leaders also in New York, for the purpose of exploring how the Church could move to the offensive, rather than always being defensive in its public relations. The priesthood-black issue had brought the Church to probably its lowest public image since the persecutions of the late 1890s.

A combination of General Authorities and Church leaders in the eastern United States were assembled at this pioneering study of Church public relations. Elders Richard L. Evans and Gordon B. Hinckley of the Church Information Service were present, along with Elders Ezra Taft Benson and Spencer W. Kimball, who were in New York City on other business. These Brethren were joined by eastern Church leaders—Robert Barker of Washington, D.C., Lee Bickmore, George Mortimer, G. Stanley McAllister, Bob Sears, DeWitt Paul, President Harold Wilkinson of the Eastern States Mission, and George Watkins. Together they counseled on how the Church could improve its dwindling public image.

Lee Bickmore, chief executive officer of the National Biscuit Company, emerged from that early meeting as the man in President Lee's mind whom the Church could recruit to coordinate the public relations, communications, publications, and translation and distribution activities. Seeking his leadership, President Lee set up an appointment to meet further with Brother Bickmore.

Brother Bickmore came to Salt Lake City in March 1970 and met with Elder Mark E. Petersen and the Church Information Service Committee, under President Lee's direction; for one and one-half hours the issues were discussed again. This meeting led to the hope that Brother Bickmore might take the lead in the restructuring period.

By November 1971 a committee headed by Lee Bickmore and consisting of such industrial giants as Lorenzo N. (Ren) Hoopes of Safeway Stores, G. Roy Fugal of General Electric, and Jim Conkling, formerly of Columbia Records, was making recommendations to divide the communications work into two departments: (1) internal, for functions within the Church Office Building, and (2) external, the Church's public relations challenge with the public. This committee screened seven leading candidates and made recommendations for the top executive for the internal communications work. J. Thomas Fyans emerged as the chosen leader in this new position.

On January 4, 1972, President Lee and President Tanner called Thomas Fyans, newly appointed director of Internal Communications, to consider with them the men he would choose to head the divisions of Internal Communications – Distribution. He named, without any prior coaching, the same four men the First Presidency desired. They were: James Paramore, administrative services; Dan Ludlow, instructional materials; Doyle Green, editorial; and John Carr, translation. The organization was immediately set in motion, with Lee Bickmore and Ren Hoopes providing consultative direction.

Exactly six months later the Bickmore committee was ready to give the First Presidency their recommendations for organizing the External Communications Department. President Tanner and Elder Gordon B. Hinckley met with President Lee as Lee Bickmore gave his committee's report, which included candidates for the director of External Communications.

President Lee indicated that the director of this new department must be a man in whom Church leaders could place complete confidence and loyalty, and who had the organizational ability to make his place, along with natural abilities to greatly improve public relations and to communicate appropriately for the Church whenever the occasion required. A search commenced to find the man with such qualifications. On June 4, 1972, President Lee and President Tanner concluded that Wendell J. Ashton was that man, and offered him the position as the director for External Communications.

In two weeks Elder Mark E. Petersen was named an adviser to the External Communications Department and Elder Gordon B. Hinckley was released from the Internal Communications leadership to also aid in the new public relations work.

Meanwhile, Brother Ashton moved vigorously to launch the new program. President Lee found him full of ideas and plans. For example, he proposed that a dinner be planned for Lord Thomson of British broadcasting and publishing fame, that a national release be prepared on the appointment of Lee Bickmore as a special consultant to the First Presidency, that an announcement of the new mission representatives appointments be made to obtain greater publicity, and that a release be made announcing the forthcoming Mexico City regional conference. After observing this burst of energy and the helpful ideas from Wendell J. Ashton, President Lee wrote in his journal, "It is delightful to see how quickly he is moving into his new responsibilities."

Thus the correction of one of the Church's most glaring weaknesses that had worried President Lee as he joined in the new First

Presidency in January 1970 was finally brought to fruition two and one-half years later, with the hope that the Church could reverse its negative public image and become better known for its worthy accomplishments.

RESTRUCTURING DUTIES OF COUNCIL OF THE TWELVE

The introduction of Lee Bickmore as a business management consultant to the First Presidency opened the door to a much more extensive reexamination of the ecclesiastical assignments of the General Authorities. Soon after the April 1971 general conference, Bickmore recommended expanding the consulting function through a firm in the Eastern United States with which he was very familiar. Accordingly, the First Presidency authorized the management consulting firm of Cresap, McCormick, and Paget, Inc., to begin a comprehensive study of Church operations to establish more objective administration guidelines.

President Lee used an interesting approach in making this assignment. He gave the nonmember consultants copies of the Doctrine and Covenants with sections marked pertaining to Church priesthood government operation and told them to read how the Lord had directed the Prophet Joseph to set up the kingdom of God. He then asked the consultants to translate this information into the best management organizational theory for the business world. In this approach President Lee capitalized on his exposure to big corporate management. His fertile and ever-searching mind permitted him to use his background in industry to challenge old concepts and introduce the best of his new learning experiences from all reliable sources.

By August 1971, the investigations were beginning to bring results. Through the efforts of Ren Hoopes, an industrial engineer from the Safeway Stores organization presented a thorough analysis of the Church's distribution problems and suggested solutions for the Church's system. Lee Bickmore also participated. Another two-hour meeting followed as Mr. Fredericks, one of the senior account executives of Cresap, McCormick, and Paget, Inc., made his first report on the internal operations of the Church, pointing out specifically that the Twelve Apostles were doing "staff" work assignments, rather than centering their efforts in broader policy-making functions. President Lee wrote of his impressions regarding this report:

This we have been aware of before. These studies will now be placed in the hands of Lee Bickmore and his committee to study further, with the assignment to come back with recommendations. Hopefully these studies will point us to a clearer look at our problems and the most effective solutions. The transition, I foresee, may be "painful," but necessary, if we are to keep pace with the mounting problems of rapid expansion of the Church throughout the world.

President Lee spent the 1971 Thanksgiving Day weekend at the country home of relatives. Although he had little time to himself, he put together an outline of proposals for strengthening the missions of the Church and for restructuring the work of the Twelve. He defined the staff and administrative roles of the Assistants to the Twelve and the First Council of Seventy, who would be asked to assume the direct administrative load of supervising the departments of the Church. This rough draft, completed during vacation hours, was the beginning of major changes in the administrative functions of the General Authorities. The content of these proposals was a composite of ideas and suggestions from some of the Brethren and from the Cresap, McCormick, and Paget consultant's recommendations. Arriving home from the holiday weekend, he continued his studies and prepared to present his draft to the First Presidency at their next meeting.

Application of these delegation principles began to take place in early 1972 as members of the Council of the Twelve Apostles were taken from daily supervision over departments and other managerial advocacy roles so that they could fulfill their primary roles as special witnesses of Jesus Christ and of watching over the affairs of the Church generally. Accordingly, Elder Howard W. Hunter was released as the Church historian and Elder Alvin R. Dyer was installed as the managing director of the Historical Department, with Dr. Leonard J. Arrington as Church historian and Earl Olson as archivist. The new managing director then began reporting through two of the Twelve, Spencer W. Kimball and Howard W. Hunter.

The Genealogical Society was the next department to be so streamlined to relieve the Council of Twelve leader of day-to-day management responsibility. On April 13, 1972, Elder Theodore M. Burton became the president and managing director of the Genealogical Society, with Elder Howard W. Hunter of the Council of the Twelve being relieved of those duties to become the adviser to that organization.

A new pattern was being established. On May 31, 1972, the First Presidency held a two-hour meeting with the Twelve. In this special session, President Lee sought to impress on the Twelve their newly focused responsibilities in planning, policy-making, and exercising strict control of the funds being budgeted by the departments over which they were assigned as advisers, but not managers. The Presidency stressed that as much work as possible should be turned back to volunteers and regularly appointed priesthood and auxiliary leaders, rather than hiring specialists to do it.

This major restructuring effort of the highest echelons of Church government continued to serve well the quickly growing kingdom and make possible the administrative efficiency required as the Church expanded its worldwide borders.

Steady Stream of Programs Passes Through Correlation Review

The plan to keep the correlation review program moving, designed by President Lee when he entered the First Presidency, proved to be an effective one. On June 4, 1970, he commented in his journal:

> The temple meeting for all General Authorities is now becoming more and more meaningful to everyone as the total development of the Church programs are presented for the consideration of all the General Authorities. This meeting today featured the newly proposed Churchwide teacher training program under the priesthood, and was ably presented by Rex Skidmore and his associates. The plan was approved. The Presiding Bishopric presented the Bishop's Youth Committee proposals, revised more appropriately to fit into priesthood correlation. Elder Howard Hunter presented the Unified Magazines Committee's proposal for personnel organization to move this plan forward.

One of the most satisfying developments came to President Lee at the temple meeting for all General Authorities on the first Thursday of July 1970. The Brethren came fasting and were spiritually bolstered by partaking of the sacrament and engaging in a prayer circle, as was their usual procedure for their first meeting of each month. The policy decisions were again discussed in the business meeting that followed. The outline for the Presiding Bishopric to become the Church Committee for Scouting, along with the correlation advisors to the Primary and the MIA, was most enthusiastically received. President Lee wrote of his satisfaction by saying: "This is a phase of correlation I have been seeking since the correlation program was begun years ago." Actually, it fulfilled dreams and goals discussed with President J. Reuben Clark in the earliest days of the "simplification program" in 1941.

MIA June Conference in 1970 became the platform for announcing these and other changes to the public. The high point of the conference was the music festival in the University of Utah Special Events Center, in which four thousand young singers and musicians from throughout the Church participated in a most creditable performance. The announcements were made on Sunday, June 28, during the final session in the Salt Lake Tabernacle under the direction of the First Presidency, and included the new Scouting program and information regarding the three new magazines: the *Friend* for children, *New Era* for youth, and the *Ensign* for adults. All other Church magazines would thereafter cease publication.

The Saturday night general priesthood meeting on October 3, 1970, was hailed by many as one of the most spiritual ever held. It included announcements concerning the three magazines, the teacher development program, and the new bishop's training course. Neal A. Maxwell also was introduced as the new commissioner of education for the Church. One of the first changes in the educational organization was the merger of the Institute of Religion coordinators under Joe J. Christensen and the Latter-day Saint Student Association under Elder Marion D. Hanks to promote a greater harmony and closer cooperation.

The 1971 thrust of correlation review worked to the goal of bringing auxiliary teaching materials under budgetary controls for the first time. Early in the year the problem was outlined by the Presiding Bishopric and John Carr of the Distribution Department. They demonstrated how the various auxiliaries had continued to multiply materials without any control. A decision was made to place all units under Church budgeting procedures.

Meeting with President Tanner, President Lee called into counsel Elders Gordon B. Hinckley, Thomas S. Monson, and Boyd K. Packer, advisers to the auxiliaries and correlation chairmen, along with Doyle Green of the editorial department, in an endeavor to control the exorbitant demands of the several Church organizations to create teaching materials, which added up to an impossible load for the editorial department. Each was asked to work with his respective organization to establish guidelines and limitations to reduce the workload to reasonable levels. After this meeting the Brethren counseled together and submitted proposals which later were approved by the Council of the Twelve and the First Presidency.

The goal of gaining control over mounting Church expenditures elsewhere was a major campaign for President Lee in 1972. It may have been triggered by the request of the forty Church departments for increased employees, which if approved, would increase the personnel budget by over $3 million. This President Lee called a "staggering proposal."

Control measures were instituted in the Building Department and close scrutiny was made of the Financial Department's handling of the vast details of the Church's finances throughout the world.

Next President Lee urged a restructuring of the missionary program, which was presented and approved in the temple meeting of March 16, 1972. One significant feature established the First Council of Seventy into three committees: one with Elders S. Dilworth Young and Milton R. Hunter to give attention to organizational details at Church headquarters; another with Elders Bruce R. McConkie, A. Theodore Tuttle, and Loren C. Dunn to train and supervise a newly appointed body of missionary-minded brethren to be known as Mission Representatives of the Council of the Twelve and of the First Council of Seventy; and a third with Elders Paul H. Dunn and Hartman Rector, Jr., to develop more adequately the stake missions. It was decided that this newly organized Mission Representatives program would be set up and begin to function following the Mission Presidents Seminar during the last week of June 1972. Elder Lee felt deeply the importance of these innovations.

Two weeks later the First Council of Seventy approved their new assignments. There was excitement and challenge as the Seventies' leaders adjourned from their meeting with the First Presidency and the Twelve, and began to finalize their plans to implement the program with the mission seminar in June.

The correlation program now was also becoming a lesson in conservation of resources. When auxiliary leaders came to President Lee to complain about the Correlation Committee's handling of lesson materials, President Lee impressed the necessity of keeping costs to a minimum by presenting lessons for each class prepared in rotating series, rather than to introduce new lessons for every class every year as had been the past practice. Better planning now permitted the reduction of the translating, printing, and distributing costs which otherwise would cause continued delays in having new texts in the field on time at the beginning of each new year. It was a painful transition period and a learning experience for everyone involved.

President Lee advised a "leveling-off" period with new programs in the Correlation Executive Committee meeting of February 3, 1971, to give leaders and teachers in the Church an opportunity to thoroughly digest and to implement what they had already been given.

Emphasis continued on teaching earlier concepts not fully understood. The Presiding Bishopric, for example, needed time to comprehend that the general Young Men's Mutual Improvement Association leadership was in reality their staff. Such lessons needed constant reinforcement.

The only major new programs to be announced in mid-1972 came from the temple meeting of June 1. Here the entire plan of mission supervision by appointing Mission Representatives was reviewed, along with a revision in the lesson plans used by proselyting missionaries throughout the world. A control committee for automobiles and houses owned by the Church was proposed. President Lee was impressed that the business was timely and orderly managed. He summarized the feelings of his Brethren with this comment: "After a lengthy discussion all of the General Authorities approved and seemed to sense the fact that here was another evidence of the power of the Almighty guiding the leaders of the Church."

A change in titles also was approved on the suggestion of Russell M. Nelson, newly called Superintendent of the Sunday Schools of the Church. In June of 1972, President Lee announced that hereafter the titles of superintendencies and assistants of the Sunday School and the YMMIA would become presidencies and counselors.

SPIRITUAL EXPERIENCES CONTINUE

The demanding and even harried pressures of administering the far-flung business of the Church during this period did not block the steady flow of inspiration in President Lee's life.

Always attuned to the spiritual, though writing in his diary more of the historical business of the Church than of his own feelings, President Lee recorded this significant observation in his entry for Thursday, May 27, 1971: "In the temple meeting today the two prayers by Elders Hugh B. Brown and Richard L. Evans were among the most inspirational we have ever heard there. We knew we were brought near to heavenly things. The Spirit lingered on throughout the meeting and afterwards."

On May 19, 1971, he was a speaker at the funeral services for Sister Pearl Lambert in the Hawthorne Ward of Salt Lake City. Of this event he wrote in his journal of a most singular experience: "There was a remarkable spirit at the funeral and I was uplifted thereby. As I was seated on the stand, I seemed to see a congregation facing me which included Fern in a black dress. Over her shoulder was someone whom I surmised might have been Maurine."

While time probably didn't permit further comment on such an unusual experience, his family members were aware of how he had prayed mightily for such reassurance after these two loved ones had passed away. None came then for him, but this experience is one of the only two instances where his beloved family members were permitted to be with and comfort him.

It is not unexpected that many of the spiritual events of President Lee's life came in association with his service as a funeral speaker. Such a setting seemed to bring President Lee into contact with another, more spiritual realm. One most interesting experience, demonstrating his spiritual perception, came on Saturday, July 3, 1971. His personal diary account describes this spiritual moment:

> Today I was at the office waiting for Joan to call me when suddenly someone seemed to say to me: "You should be at a funeral." Suddenly it dawned on me that several days before, Charles Perschon had asked Frances [his secretary] if I would speak at his father's funeral honoring Bishop William F. Perschon. She had failed to put it on my calendar. I immediately looked in the morning paper and found that it was at 2:00 p.m., which was the exact time when I had been reminded. I was about twenty-five minutes late, but arrived in time to speak at the services for as fine a bishop as I have known.

President Lee rendered continuous service in using his gift of healing for the blessing of the sick. Elder Neal A. Maxwell often has remarked that President Lee bore the burden of administering to his Brethren with great patience and love, but not without personal anxiety. His service to the sick and the bereaved included relatives, countless friends, and often even strangers. One miraculous experience is recounted here to represent such unforgettable memories.

On April 27, 1972, Dr. O. Preston Robinson, general manager and editor of the Deseret News Publishing Company, suddenly became ill with flu-like symptoms. After his condition worsened, with a fever of 104 degrees, he was admitted to the LDS Hospital on May 1, 1972.

When the Robinson's son, Bruce, a prominent neurosurgeon, arrived from Michigan to tend his father, he broke down and cried bitterly to find his father so desperately ill. As he was taken into the intensive care unit Pres's wife, Christine, remained in his former room to pray on her knees for many hours. She stated that she felt there was someone actually in the room with her, although she was alone, and that this personage had come to take Pres away.

In the four or five days of terrific struggle for life, many of the Apostles of the Church came to express concern and to bless Pres. Included was his brother-in-law, Elder Gordon B. Hinckley, who prayed long and fervently. His prayer especially had great force, profound meaning, and also conveyed a spirit of humility and genuine love for his sister's husband.

Christine writes of the ordeal in these words:

> I could not rest, sleep, or eat during this period of time and early Saturday morning, when I was on my knees, I felt a great need to call President Harold B. Lee. I waited until I thought that Brother Lee would be awake and I called him about 7:30 in the morning. He said that he and his wife, Joan, had just arisen from their knees where they had been imploring our Father in Heaven to help Pres, and he said that he felt a great urgency, and that he would come to the hospital and be there in about fifteen minutes.

Christie, daughter of Pres and Christine, met President Lee when he arrived. Later she wrote her impressions, saying: "I was so impressed with the spirituality and humility of this man. We walked together down the corridor of the hospital, our arms entwined, to see Mother. I felt the great power of his presence and his great love."

Christine continued:

> When President Lee arrived, he; my doctor son, Bruce; and I entered the intensive care section where Pres was lying in a coma. I

had not previously been in that room, because the doctors had asked me not to look at Pres for fear I would get upset when I saw him connected with all the different medical equipment, looking so very ill. It did seem that every part of Pres' body was connected to some type of medical equipment.

Pres, of course, was unconscious, but when President Lee put his hand on Pres's shoulder and said, "Pres, look at me," my husband briefly opened his eyes. I took one of Pres's very swollen hands in mine, and as President Lee prayed, it seemed in reality as if there was a shaft of light which went up from Pres in his bed to our Father in Heaven.

President Lee's prayer was long and I have never had such a feeling of spirituality and closeness to my Father in Heaven as I had at this time. Brother Lee said that he was speaking for the prophet himself, the only living prophet of our Father in Heaven on earth at this time. He requested that his prayers go past the angels and to the very foot of the throne of our Father in Heaven himself. President Lee pled for Pres's life. He did not say that his life would be spared in any way. He said that we were to bide by the will of our Father in Heaven. He spoke of our Father in Heaven giving his own son's life that we might have eternal life. He put Pres's life directly in the hands of our Father in Heaven and prayed that whatever would be done for him in any way whatsoever would be directly in accord with the wishes of our Father in Heaven. President Lee prayed that our Heavenly Father would personally take over Pres's care and direct it. Our son, Dr. Bruce Robinson, was then blessed that he would have unusual powers to know what to do at exactly the right time for his father.

After the prayer, not any of us moved for some time because we were all so very affected by this tremendous spiritual outpouring to which we had been witnesses. Then, President Lee took hold of Pres's hand and said to him: "Fight! Fight with everything you have to the last rampart!" He instructed Bruce that if he had any feelings whatsoever that anything should be done for his father, to do it immediately and not delay even a second. The doctors had been debating whether or not Pres's condition could stand a tracheotomy. It was at this time that Bruce said: "I feel strongly that we should perform this operation." President Lee then pushed Bruce and said: "Go, have it done immediately." This operation took place an hour later. Following this operation, his grave illness began to improve gradually.

Some time later that morning, when I went to Pres's bedside and took hold of his hand again, I stood there looking at him. I was all alone, the curtains were pulled, and I felt like a tremendous mantle then came down out of heaven and completely covered me. I could actually feel this mantle start with my head and cover every bit of my body down to the very tips of my toes. I have never had such a feeling. I felt that it was actually a piece of cloth, or something I could reach out my hand and feel. As it covered me, I had a tremendous peace which entered my soul and a great conviction that I knew, beyond a shadow of a doubt, that Pres's life was going to be spared, that he would have all his faculties, and that he would live and yet do a great work here upon the earth.

Many times after this, I was told by the doctors that Pres would not live, but this did not affect me in any way, because I knew that he would live. The personage, or whoever it was that had been at my side all the time, disappeared and no one could convince me that Pres was not going to live and have his full faculties, despite the fever which reached 106.6, the highest ever seen by this doctor, who said if it were not lowered it would have burned out Pres's brain cells.

We were told that President Lee and President Tanner, both of whom had visited Pres, had announced in the Council of the Twelve meeting on May 11, my birthday, that a miracle had taken place in Pres's recovery, and it had been recorded in the "modern Acts of the Apostles." President Lee visited Pres twice after he had administered to him, once to give him another blessing.

After his remarkable, rapid, and complete recovery, Pres Robinson wrote to President Harold B. Lee and conveyed his heartfelt appreciation for his "great expression of pure love in action," stating:

Although I did not hear the marvelous administration and blessing that you gave me, both Christine and Bruce have filled me in on a few of the details. They have said that it was the most humble yet the most powerful and beautiful blessing that either of them had ever heard. We are all convinced that it went straight to the throne of our Father in Heaven, who, through the special keys and gifts you possess, heard and answered positively.

When President Lee recorded in his journal this experience it was in his usual terse and humble words: "On the following day Pres rallied, talked coherently, seemingly has passed the crisis, and was on his way up—no doubt another miracle of healing, in the Lord's way."

Pres Robinson lived a happy and fully productive life for well over a decade after his near escape from death.

New President of BYU Chosen

At the request of the search committee seeking to screen candidates for a new president of Brigham Young University, Dr. Dallin Oaks, a law professor at the University of Chicago, made arrangements to travel to Salt Lake City for an interview. When Dr. Oaks arrived at the airport in Chicago to board his plane, a powerful foreboding came over him. So strong was that oppressive feeling that he called another airline, and after learning that he could take a later flight to Salt Lake, he changed his reservations and walked with his bags to the other terminal building.

When he arrived at the ticket counter at the departure gate, he saw among the waiting passengers President Harold B. Lee of the First Presidency. He greeted him only briefly, for they didn't know one another well at that time. Later, however, aboard the plane there was a fifteen-minute delay in departure, which gave Dr. Oaks an opportunity to make himself better acquainted with President Lee. President Lee invited him to sit next to him and they talked until the plane was ready for takeoff. That visit, which might also be construed to have served as an interview, was to have profound significance in the days ahead. Now Dr. Oaks had reason to understand his feelings which led to a switch in airlines that day.

The search committee completed their work and nominated Dr. Oaks as the prime candidate to become the next president of the university. President Marion G. Romney made a long report of the committee's search to the First Presidency, but before he could announce their decision, President Lee interrupted impatiently, saying, "We all know who the next president is going to be." Apparently President Lee knew before the search committee had even begun its work, although the impromptu interview aboard the plane in Chicago had never been mentioned to anyone.

When the selection committee completed their assignment and referred the business to President Lee, he felt impressed to telephone Dr. Oaks and invite him to come with his wife for a final meeting to clarify certain statements made before the search committee. That visit with President Lee on March 30, 1971, proved to be very satisfactory. President Lee recorded in his diary his delight with the experience, saying: "Dr. Oaks's attitude was right, his humility impressive, yet he had a vision of the work which would be entailed. All this left us with a complete unified feeling that he was our man."

The inauguration of President Oaks occurred on November 12, 1971. President Lee felt that the inaugural address of President Oaks, and his own speech on that occasion, were well coordinated and on a distinctly spiritual plane.

This significant career move was destined to affect forever the life of the Oaks family, as well as the Church at large. After serving nine years as President of Brigham Young University, Dallin H. Oaks returned to his first love, the law profession. He was soon thereafter appointed a justice of the Utah Supreme Court. Not long thereafter he was named and sustained as a member of the Quorum of the Twelve Apostles, at the general conference of the Church on April 7, 1984.

INTIMATE GLIMPSES OF PRESIDENT LEE

The demanding, quickened pace associated with President Lee's rise to direct the affairs of the Church as First Counselor in the First Presidency caused many adjustments in his personal life. He recorded in November 1970 the confession that for the first time since his calling as an Apostle in 1941, he had not kept pace with his daily entries in his personal diary: "I spent some hours at the office on Saturday trying to catch up on personal matters and was startled to discover that I hadn't had time to keep my financial records for the whole month of October, nor my diary."

Through all his adult years President Lee suffered from migraine headaches. His heavier administrative pressures didn't help this malady and it continually plagued his efforts. He wrote on January 13, 1972: "Following the temple meeting today I became ill with an intensely severe headache and nausea. I was unable to come to the office, as I had promised, to set apart and ordain my Dr. Hal Bourne a bishop, for which I was very sorry."

Advancing travel technology during these years made it possible for the Lord's servants to be more places faster and return home quicker than ever before. President Lee noted on November 23, 1970, as though he were recording history, the fastest air trip he had taken to New York City: "I left by American Airlines nonstop to New York at 1:00 p.m., arriving three hours and forty-five minutes later, the fastest trip by plane I have taken across the country. I was in the hotel room by 8:00 p.m., Eastern time."

For thirteen years President Lee had made monthly round trips from Salt Lake City to New York City to attend the board of directors' meetings for the Union Pacific Railroad Company and the Equitable Life Assurance Society of the USA. On March 17, 1971, he made the trip for the last time to attend a formal black tie dinner of the Equitable Board, held at the University Club in New York City, given as a farewell testimonial to Robert Blum, Grant Keehn, and himself. All three had reached retirement age. There were fifty directors and officers in attendance. Each of the retirees were asked to speak. President Lee had accompanied President J. Reuben Clark, Jr., to give his farewell address under these circumstances and noted with pride how President Clark chose to testify of Jesus Christ despite the mixed backgrounds of the audience. Now, in his turn, President Lee didn't hesitate to do the same. His own journal summary of the event follows:

> There was a warm, friendly attitude manifested towards me with a letter from James F. Oates, Jr., former president of The Equitable, containing most laudatory comments. I spoke to them of the educational opportunities I had while a director for nearly thirteen years, since 1958. I spoke of the fact that they were all active members of their respective churches, that insurance company activities had a definite relationship to the welfare work of the Church with which I have been identified for forty years, and closed by a recital of the incident of Peter and John blessing the crippled man at the temple gate . . . "Peter took him by the right hand and lifted him up," significant of the greatest need in the world today. In the final Equitable board meeting they presented me with an embossed resolution of commendation.

The passing years were adding to President Lee's beloved progeny. While President and Sister Lee were in Oakland investigating the plan for filming temple work in January 1971, their first great-grandchild was born. David and Patricia Goates were the proud parents of a robust baby boy named Jeffrey Hewlett Goates. Impressed with this new extension of "his kingdom," President Lee wrote: "This now advances us to the third generation of our lives with much to remember and more to contemplate in the future."

President Lee was never one to allow the pressures of his Church leadership to cause him to forget his patriarchal relationships, although time for family contacts became increasingly more constricted. He encouraged the visits of his maturing grandchildren. On Sunday, November 29, 1970, President Lee's five oldest grandsons, in company with their wives and dating partners, had

Visiting with grandsons (left to right) David Goates, Alan Wilkins, Larry Wilkins, Hal Goates, Drew Goates

dinner together at David and Patsy Goates's home, and then came to President Lee's home about 9:30 P.M. for a visit which lasted until midnight. At the suggestion of grandson Alan Wilkins, the group knelt in prayer before returning home.

President Lee's second wife, Joan, had repeatedly urged that he take her to see his childhood home in Clifton, Idaho. While vacationing in Wellsville, Utah, on August 13, 1971, President Lee fulfilled his wife's longings. Concerning his reflections about "going home," President Lee wrote:

> The old saying: "You can never come back home again," came back forcibly as I saw the sad deterioration of the old homes where the pioneer families had with pride kept their lands in a respectable condition. These people have now passed on, and those who have come along to inherit or purchase from the former owners have built newer homes, but have left the old homes to fall to pieces and present a shocking spectacle of a dying generation. I was comforted

somewhat when I found that our old home had been torn down and a fine new home had replaced it.

After returning home, President Lee dictated on a tape recorder some of the events of his boyhood and growing-up years. The following Sunday, with his entire family gathered at his daughter Helen's home for a monthly fireside, President Lee played the tape for his grandchildren. It became a cherished possession, an authentic recitation of his most inspiring childhood stories, told in his own voice.

During these years in the First Presidency, President Lee found that one of his most effective service roles was to accept invitations to speak at weekend youth conferences. He involved his wife, a most able and inspirational speaker. It was a conscious decision to devote his energies as an investment in the future generations. He loved the youth of Zion. Typical of such regular exposures to youthful audiences was one he wrote about on Sunday, April 16, 1972: "I spent a day at home resting from the extreme exertions of the past week, but after a few hours of rest, I went with Joan to an M-Men and Gleaner Girl Fireside at the Mt. Ogden Stake Center, where approximately two hundred were in attendance. We had considerable satisfaction and I was actually refreshed and revived after returning from Ogden about 11:00 p.m."

The following weekend President and Sister Lee were on the road again, this time attending an early morning all-girls fireside group numbering one thousand, which he addressed in Provo, Utah, in the Joseph Smith Building on Brigham Young University campus.

Even after becoming President of the Church, he continued his commitment to youth conferences, but with much larger audiences and increasing effectiveness in building the faith of future Church leaders.

These experiences seemed to be moving President Harold B. Lee inexorably toward his ultimate destiny as President of the Church. He undoubtedly would have been content to remain as he was, but such was not to be. He was born to be a prophet, and he was prepared. Soon he was only a quick heartbeat away from becoming the eleventh President of The Church of Jesus Christ of Latter-day Saints.

*President
of the
Church*

———

1972–1973

1972–1973. President Nixon visited Peking. A
freeze on retail prices was declared to curb
inflation. A period of controversial intervention in
Vietnam ended, having taken 58,014 American
lives and wounded 303,000 more.

CHAPTER 26

538-Day Ministry
as President Begins

For two and one-half years, lacking twenty-one days,
President Joseph Fielding Smith presided over the Church. In that
First Presidency, Harold B. Lee served as a strong leader, carrying a
heavy load with wisdom, aggressiveness, and yet with a humility
which always gave respectful deference to the aged President, who
would die just prior to his ninety-sixth birthday.

July 2, 1972, dawned as any other Sabbath day for these two
Church leaders. President Joseph Fielding Smith spent most of the
day attending his local ward church meetings and in reading the
scriptures in his favorite chair at the home of his daughter, Amelia
McConkie, located on the high bench area just below Ensign Peak
in Salt Lake City.

In the Lee family a celebration of Sister Freda Joan Lee's
seventy-fourth birthday had taken place with a dinner at the home
of President Lee's daughter, Helen. As was often necessary, President and Sister Lee left hurriedly following the dinner for another
meeting.

In the early evening Helen decided to deliver the remainder of the birthday cake to "Aunt Joan." As her father greeted her, Helen thought he looked very weary. She said to him: "Oh, Daddy dear, you look so worn out. I'll just leave these things and run on. You don't need to visit tonight; you look like you're all visited out."

But President Lee protested: "No, you wait a minute. Aunt Joan is just changing her dress. She'll want to see you."

PASSING OF PRESIDENT JOSEPH FIELDING SMITH

They stood and talked for a few minutes in the kitchen, with Helen still remonstrating, feeling that they needed their rest and thinking she should leave. But as President Lee asked about his grandchildren living in Provo, for whom he was always concerned, the telephone interrupted their conversation. It was 9:30 P.M. Sister Lee answered the phone and recognized the urgency of this call. She announced: "Harold, this is President Smith's son Joseph Fielding Smith, Jr. on the phone. He seems to be very agitated."

Quickly, President Lee took the phone. Helen remembers:

I'll never forget the look on his face. He kept repeating: "Oh, no. No. Oh, no." (Apparently Joseph was rehearsing the details of President Smith's passing.) He covered the phone receiver and looked as though all the cares in the world had suddenly settled upon him. He said to us, so gravely, "President Smith is gone." He finished his conversation with Joseph, but was left visibly shaken by the sad news.

He hung up the phone after having given instructions as to whom should be notified. He slumped against the door frame close by and put his head in his arms. He just kept shaking his head . . . over and over.

Aunt Joan and I went over to him, and I put my hand on his arm and said: "Daddy dear, I guess the day has finally come that you must have thought through the years you would never be prepared for." He answered: "Oh, I'm afraid I'm not, I'm afraid I'm not." Aunt Joan quickly assured him that he was prepared.

I had never seen him look so weak and so completely at a loss. All through the years, except for the circumstances of my mother's passing, Daddy was a "Rock of Gibraltar" to all of us-the very epitome of strength and goodness. But at that moment he was completely devastated.

It was only a moment, however, until he straightened up, squared his shoulders, and began to take charge. He said to Aunt

Joan: "Now, dearie, you must go change your dress again while I make some phone calls, and then we must quickly go to Bruce's [McConkie] home." The moment of weakness was gone. It seemed as though he had reached back into his thirty-one years of apostolic preparation and found there the resources at his command to meet the challenge of this inevitable moment.

Helen left President and Sister Lee and returned home to find her husband, Brent, working at his desk. Quickly conveying the news, Helen said:

"Let's hurry and gather the children together. We must pray for Dad. I think he needs the strength of our prayers—he looked so tired and so ill. You could read the pressure of the situation on his face. Let's all assemble now in family prayer for him."

It was a choice experience to unite our faith under such grave circumstances. We knelt around our bed. My husband prayed, and then called on me to pray. Then he asked each of the children to add whatever they wanted to our prayers. That was a sweet, lovely experience as they poured out their hearts to their Heavenly Father in behalf of their grandfather.

Even at that point we weren't allowing our minds to jump ahead to what might occur after the Council of the Twelve would meet to select a new president. Our only concern at this moment was that this father and grandfather needed the Lord to give him strength to face extreme pressures and circumstances in the next week, including the funeral service and all else which would follow. We wanted to give him our united faith and help.

Soon President N. Eldon Tanner and his wife, Sara, arrived at the Lee home and took President and Sister Lee to the McConkie home to meet with President Smith's grieving family. President Lee went immediately to the couch, where the body of this venerable, faithful servant of the Lord rested. For a long time he held the lifeless hand, reluctant to part with his longtime associate in Church leadership. After prayer with the family he arranged for them to meet with a committee of the Twelve at the Church Office Building on Monday morning.

Earlier on that memorable day at the birthday dinner for Sister Lee, President Lee had requested that his granddaughter Jane come with her family to the Lee home for a family home evening on Monday to play her violin. Jane had played at a ward sacrament meeting a few weeks before when her grandparents were away and unable to hear her perform. Her selection was a number the two daughters of President Lee played when they were young girls

—a family favorite. Realizing the pressures now on President Lee a phone call was made to him the next day to change or confirm the appointment. President Lee emphatically said: "By all means I want you to come. It is all the more important now than it was when we talked about it yesterday."

Thus, by invitation and appointment, all the family came to be with President and Sister Lee for Monday family home evening, including his son-in-law Ernest J. Wilkins and his children from Provo. It was one of those enchanted moments when all family members wanted to draw close to their beloved grandfather at this special time.

President Lee greeted his progeny as they arrived, but soon a rather uncomfortable pall hung over the group. All were reluctant to speak of the events that would shortly come to pass. President Lee asked Jane to play her violin. At the conclusion of the performance he expressed his pleasure and asked for a second number to be played. Jane explained that she had brought no other music with her, so she agreed to play some hymns while the rest of the family sang. Jane asked her grandfather to choose the hymns he wanted to sing. He immediately requested two, "Love at Home" and "I Need Thee Every Hour." Then President Lee said he would like to finish with "How Firm a Foundation," reciting these words from the third verse, which at that moment were particularly significant to him:

> Fear not, I am with thee, O be not dismayed,
> For I am thy God and will still give thee aid;
> I'll strengthen thee, help thee, and cause thee to stand,
> Upheld by my righteous, omnipotent hand.

Recognizing that all of his grandchildren would have in their minds many questions about that which would shortly unfold in the history of the Church as it related to their grandfather, President Lee then explained the events in the coming week. He told them about making the arrangements with President Smith's family for the funeral and about their requesting him to be one of the speakers. Then he told them that the day after the funeral all the members of the Council of the Twelve and the counselors to President Smith would meet by appointment in the council room of the First Presidency and Council of the Twelve in the Salt Lake Temple. He explained that it was the order of the Church that following the death of its President, the keys of leadership are immediately transferred to the Council of the Twelve, and that as the President of that quorum, he would have the responsibility to take the lead in governing the Church until such a time as that body would direct that the First Presidency would be reorganized.

President Lee carefully explained, in words that even the little children would understand, that three options were open to the Council of the Twelve: (1) the First Presidency could be reorganized and, if that were done, the senior member of the Council, himself, would likely be chosen as the new President of the Church, if precedent were followed; (2) they could take no action and allow the Quorum of the Twelve to govern the Church as was happening at that moment; or (3) by revelation they could choose any member of the Twelve, if so directed by the Lord, to preside over a new First Presidency.

The children asked many questions and a good discussion followed the words of President Lee, who was always the teacher to his family when the teaching moment arose. A phone call interrupted the discussion and soon President Lee announced that he must leave. Before the family meeting was adjourned, however, Brent Goates asked: "Before you go, Dad, would you just tell us what you want us to do as your family to help you the most, not only during this week as you move through these historic and emotional experiences, but in the years ahead? What is it that we can do to support you most as your family?"

Hesitating only a moment, President Lee responded with this challenge: "Be true to the faith—just live the gospel as I've taught you to do, as you know it to be right. That is all I want my family to do for me. Be undeviating in the path of righteousness. That's all I could ask of my loved ones, you who are dearest to me. There is nothing you could do that could help me more or make this grandfather happier than that."

His message was clear. None of the family members looking back on this experience could have any doubt as to his expectations. He was acting in the role of a true patriarch, emulating the Heavenly Father of us all in repeating the simplest yet most important message of the ages in a clarion call to keep the commandments. Family members still remember him most for the gospel truths he taught and the powerful direction he provided throughout their lives, but especially for that family home evening where all their hearts were united and intimately entwined through his leadership.

Picture taken for film *Strengthening the Home,* 1972

IMMEDIATE THREAT TO HEALTH

With history in the making, and pressures for spiritual communion never greater, opposition was the immediate companion. It came now in the form of a serious attack on President Lee's health. He had been experiencing pain in his lower left side, like a pleurisy irritation. It gradually worsened, and the phone call which interrupted and ended the family home evening just described was from the physician, whom Sister Lee had phoned.

Early on the July 4, 1972 holiday, Dr. James Orme came to the home and examined President Lee. He requested that President Lee go to the LDS Hospital for X-ray and heart studies. There physicians examined carefully his chest area. By means of sophisticated nuclear machines, after injecting radioactive iodine, they were able to discover that blood clots were forming in President Lee's lungs. Physicians insisted that despite all the worries and burdens of Church reorganization on his mind, he be isolated in a room for an entire day and night while a series of injections of heparin were administered to dissolve any clots and to thin his blood. These treatments were spaced four hours apart at first, and then six hours apart, necessitating a young medical intern coming to the Lee home at 1:30 A.M. Even moments before leaving his office to attend the funeral of President Joseph Fielding Smith he was required to receive these injections.

Faced with the responsibility of conducting the funeral services and speaking his tribute to the late President, and also appearing at a testimonial honoring the later Elder Richard L. Evans, amid never-ceasing medical treatments, President Lee spent a hectic day and night with this tumultuous schedule. Observing the turmoil, Sister Lee suggested a priesthood administration. In the most humbling experience of their lives the healing ordinance upon the head of the soon-to-be-chosen President of the Church was performed by son-in-law Brent Goates and brother-in-law Charles J. Ross.

President Lee had to give early consideration to the choice of counselors, in the likely event that he would be selected as the next President. He knew whom he had in mind, but he had to obtain the confirmation of the Lord. To do so President Lee spent an hour or more in the temple and then continued through the night in prayer. When Thursday morning came there was no doubt in his mind that N. Eldon Tanner should be named as the First Counselor. President Tanner, when approached, graciously assured President Lee that he would willingly remain as Second Counselor, unless President Lee directed otherwise.

It also was clearly manifest to President Lee that Elder Marion G. Romney should be his other counselor. This proposition was pleasing to President Tanner and was then again spiritually confirmed to President Lee's satisfaction. President Lee testified concerning the revelation to appoint Elder Marion G. Romney to the First Presidency in a letter to John K. Edmunds, president of the California Los Angeles Mission, dated July 10, 1972. President Lee wrote: "I am sure if there was ever a man in the world the Lord loved and wanted to be honored in such a call, it was Marion G. Romney."

Both President Lee and President Tanner agreed that the filling of the vacancy in the Twelve should be delayed until the next general conference and that a solemn assembly should be planned in the same manner as when President Smith was installed as President of the Church at the October 1972 general conference.

TRIBUTES TO PRESIDENT SMITH

But now it was time to pay a proper homage to their dear, late President Joseph Fielding Smith. The Salt Lake Tabernacle was filled to capacity, including most of President Smith's 169 direct descendants. The music was furnished by the Salt Lake Tabernacle Choir. President Tanner eulogized the family. Elder Bruce R. McConkie, a son-in-law, "provided a superb portrayal of the President's life," according to President Lee's diary notes. President Lee's sermon spoke more particularly to the spiritual phases of President Smith's life. He stated:

> As we have been associated, particularly in the last two years as the counselors of President Smith, we have marveled at the clarity of his mind, the health of his body, the fact that he could speak well, and could walk without difficulty when most men at his age could have done neither. . . .
>
> This we have witnessed time and again, as we were engaged in discussing very serious matters—decisions that should only be made by the President of the Church. It was then that we saw this sparkling wisdom come to light as he recounted, undoubtedly beyond his own present understanding, things that he called up from the depths of his soul.

The innermost feelings and thoughts of the soon-to-be President surfaced as President Lee closed his eulogy for President Smith:

> Since the shock of his passing came, and realizing now that the Twelve would have the responsibility to take up the labors and determine what path to take in order to reorganize the Presidency of the Church, and serving as I do as the senior member of the Council, I have been concerned. I have wanted to know what the Lord's will would be. I wanted to do nothing except I knew it was of the Lord. I have sought most earnestly to know, to be guided, so that this Church could go on and be worthy of those who have sacrificed, who have given their lives that this Church might grow.
>
> I have received a special witness these last few days. I had a comfort from one who wrote, "Men who are called to these leading positions in the Church were foreordained to that mission before they came to this earth." If I didn't believe that, I wouldn't dare stand in the place where I am today; believing that, I have no fear,

anxiety, and concern, because I know the Lord is at the helm in guiding the work of the Church.

If the Lord knew me before I came here, as my friend reminded me, and he knows me now and has accepted of me, the Lord being my strength, we will attempt to follow in the footsteps of this beloved leader of ours. Brother Tanner and I have loved this man these last two and one-half years. It hasn't been pretended. He begat love. Because he loved us, we have stood by him, as he stood by and trusted us. We have mourned his passing with you, his dear family; and we want to express to you our feeling that now he has gone, you may not feel that you are alone. You still belong to us. We want you to know that the arms of our love are about each and every one of you here in this great family of President Smith.

Earlier in the week President Lee, along with other Church officials, paid tribute to the late President in the *Deseret News* of Monday, July 3, 1972. Part of President Lee's praise follows: "We who have been his closest associates knew of his kindness, his gentleness, and his concern for others. He sought no honors of men. His purpose in life could well be penned in one sentence— his was an 'eye single to the glory of God in bringing to pass the immortality and eternal life of man.' His death closes a chapter of history when the leadership of the Church has been in the hands of great men who were acquainted with the earliest leaders of this dispensation."

The days between the death of President Smith and the reorganization of the First Presidency were once more a time of speculation and curiosity, not only for members of the Church but also for the media and the public at large. Brent Goates was approached by Jack Goodman, a veteran Salt Lake City journalist, free-lance writer, and correspondent of *The New York Times.* Jack explained that the *Times* wanted him to file a story on the reorganization of the First Presidency, but to have it ready in New York City on the day of the reorganization required him to file an advance story. Knowing President Lee wouldn't allow such a presumptuous, premature interview, Mr. Goodman asked Brent, whom he had known in newspapering circles in earlier years: "What type of leadership may be expected when Harold B. Lee becomes the President of the Church? What are his dominant leadership characteristics?"

The penetrating questions forced serious reflection on the part of Brent, who knew his father-in-law well as a person and as a Church leader. The analysis required was not difficult, but the communication of those conclusions to the unbelieving readers was extremely complicated. Brent's answer by necessity eliminated the prime characteristic of the next President of the Church. How could he explain that Harold B. Lee's primary virtue was his spirituality, his intimacy with the God who directed his thoughts and footsteps, his totally uncommon ability to obtain flashes of inspiration and illuminating light in answer to his ponderings and prayers? He was a revelator and a seer and he possessed the miraculous powers of his office and calling in unusual abundance. But how could this be explained, and if explained, comprehended by those not understanding continuous revelation to the leaders of the Church?

The spiritual depths of President Lee's leadership simply had to go unspoken, Brent concluded. And so the interview emphasized other salient qualities of President Lee, which also were impressive. His amazing organizational ability was cited, as attested by the development of the welfare plan of the Church, and recently proven anew through the correlation reorganization of all phases of the Church. His ability to instill confidence in Church members, develop discipleship among the leaders, and thrill the young people with a sense of their importance were among other characteristics mentioned. Yes, greatness could be expected of this man of God in many aspects of leadership, but the greatest quality of all, his spirituality, would not find its way into print on the pages of *The New York Times* or any other public media.

First Presidency Reorganized

The day of President Smith's funeral, which was also the day before the reorganization meeting of the Council of the Twelve, was a time for final meditation and prayer on President Lee's earlier conclusions. He wrote of his activities in his personal journal in these words:

> I have talked with President Tanner after making certain that my choice of counselors is in accord with the Lord's desire. I have had no one in my mind but President Tanner and Marion G. Romney, and in that order. Even though Eldon agreed heartily with the suggestion of Brother Romney and left the way open to continue him as second counselor if I desired to do so, I felt the order was correct.
>
> I felt certain that despite the difference in seniority, President Tanner had earned the right for this advancement in recognition [as

First Presidency from 1972 to 1973: President Harold B. Lee, N. Eldon Tanner, Marion G. Romney

first counselor] in my judgment, and I feel with the Lord's sanction, after having spent an hour or more in the temple in prayerful meditation.

I sat for a moment where I was joined in marriage to my darling Fern in 1923 by President George F. Richards and again in the sealing room where my lovely Joan was sealed to me by President David O. McKay. I poured out my soul in gratitude for these, two of the greatest women who have ever walked the earth, who have been brought to me through circumstances which attested to the divine guidance of the Almighty, who knew my need.

Friday, July 7, 1972, is entered on records of the history of the Church as one of its most important dates in modern times. At 8:00 A.M. on that clear, warm, summer day, the entire Council of the Twelve and ordained Apostles in the former First Presidency met in the sacred council room of the Salt Lake Temple to consider the reorganization of the First Presidency of the Church. Following an opening prayer by Elder Hugh B. Brown and a prayer at the altar by Elder LeGrand Richards, each member of the Twelve expressed his own thoughts on the subject. Finally it was time for Elder

Spencer W. Kimball to speak, and he made the motion that Harold B. Lee become the President of the Church; when this motion was unanimously approved, President Lee assumed his seat as the prophet.

With all of the Twelve participating, Spencer W. Kimball was voice in ordaining Harold B. Lee and setting him apart as the eleventh President of The Church of Jesus Christ of Latter-day Saints, as prophet, seer, and revelator, and as Trustee-in-Trust of all Church properties. Then President Lee set apart and blessed President Tanner as first counselor and Marion G. Romney as second counselor in the new First Presidency, and also Spencer W. Kimball as President of the Quorum of the Twelve Apostles.

Elder Kimball had been suffering from Bell's palsy, which affliction had cut short his recuperation in California from heart surgery and caused his face to sag noticeably. At first it was believed that he had suffered a stroke, but the later examination after he returned home confirmed the palsy diagnosis. While much relieved, still Elder Kimball felt embarrassed by his weakened condition and poor physical appearance. After the blessing by President Lee, however, there was a marked change in his appearance. It was an indication that he had received a special spiritual blessing, wrote President Lee.

In a letter of appreciation ten days later, Elder Kimball wrote to President Lee to thank him for the great honors and blessings conferred on him. He said that he knew beforehand by the Spirit the counselors President Lee would choose and said that his sentiments paralleled that of the President. With regard to his physical condition Elder Kimball wrote:

> I felt somewhat ill prepared for such a responsibility. It has been some nine months since I could fully immerse myself in the spiritual, and I fear I failed in measuring up to the great opportunity and privilege. I am getting back to normal. My face has improved and I am stronger. I expect to be back part-time very soon. I asked my doctor if an hour or two a day would hurt me now and he said it would be good for me. I think he wanted me to ease into the work the next two or three weeks.
>
> You and your sweet wife have been so kind and good to us—so far beyond our deserts—that I wish there was something I could say or do that would adequately express proper gratitude and affection. I shall try to do so by just serving more efficiently.

Immediately following President Lee's setting apart in the temple, a press conference was requested where fifty or more representatives of wire services, television and radio stations, and newspapers were permitted to ask questions of the new President. When asked what his first message would be to Church members and the world, President Lee replied: "The greatest message that one in this position could give to the membership of the Church is to keep the commandments of God, for therein lies the safety of the Church and the safety of the individual. Keep the commandments. There could be nothing that I could say that would be a more powerful or important message today."

In response to a question about conditions of the world at that time President Lee noted that the Prophet Joseph Smith was informed by the Lord 140 years earlier that peace would be taken from the earth and Satan would have power over his own dominion. He then added: "After 140 years, is there anyone here who doubts that that time is here? But the Lord said he would reign among his people, and the most powerful weapon that can ever be forged against the wickedness of the world is the powerful teachings of the principles of the gospel of Jesus Christ. That's what he gave them to us for, to combat fear and untruth and wickedness in the world."

Commenting about the challenges ahead, President Lee called the task of leading more than three million members of the Church "ominous." He also said that the greatest challenge facing the Church was to keep pace with the growth in the membership:

> We approach this task knowing that the Church is growing, which is our greatest challenge today. To keep pace with the growth and to see that the members everywhere are properly shepherded, taught, and led becomes now our greatest responsibility. Through the graces of the Almighty we have been directed to lay some cornerstones, and we hope to build on that foundation in the years ahead. We approach the future like the prophets of old . . . like Nephi, when he said: "I, Nephi, went forth not knowing beforehand the things which I should do." We will lean on the spiritual guidance of the Lord.

When asked why blacks could not hold the priesthood, President Lee answered: "For those who don't believe in modern revelation there is no adequate explanation. Those who do understand revelation stand by and wait until the Lord speaks."

As President Lee introduced his counselors, he testified of their call by revelation, saying:

> May I say that it is my responsibility to name counselors. We have some of the great men of the earth who form the membership of the

General Authorities of the Church. Any one of them is just as qualified as any of us, or others; but to know which ones were to receive the sanction of the Lord required some soul-searching, and to that task I devoted myself. I have had the witness as to the men who should be called to be my counselors. They've been called not by the will of men or the choice of men. They've been called by the direction and guidance of the Spirit of the Lord, and they are the men who are acceptable to the Lord. We know that. We have received a witness of it.

Thus was launched into that service the eleventh President of the Church, President Harold B. Lee. He was the first native of Idaho to be called to the highest position in the Church. The average age of the eight Presidents of the Church from John Taylor through David O. McKay was seventy-three years of age when assuming that office. President Lee was exactly seventy-three years old, the youngest President of the Church in nearly forty years.

The new First Presidency were a unique international blend, since President Lee was born and reared in the United States; President Tanner, although born in the United States, lived most of his life in Canada; and President Romney was born and reared in Mexico.

Press conferences and interviews, as President Lee was soon to discover, were frequent events. The Church itself encouraged and sponsored many through its new Public Communications Department. It had been a long time since the Church had had such a vigorous President who could perform so well before cameras and photographers. A series of remarkable, unusual interviews followed. In content and tone they were masterful.

On July 19, 1972, Mr. Dan L. Thrapp, religion editor for *The Los Angeles Times,* sought an appointment. During this one-hour interview, many searching questions were asked, including the inevitable query concerning the blacks and the priesthood.

Mr. Thrapp wrote of President Lee's physical appearance: "Although his unlined face makes it scarcely credible that he is seventy-three, he is relatively young, compared to recent presidents who died at ninety-six and ninety-five years of age."

Mr. Thrapp asked how President Lee could explain the phenomenal growth of the Church, doubling within twelve years at a time when many other churches were stagnating or losing membership. His answer: "The basic reason is that this Church alone holds the truth among many great churches." President Lee wrote in his diary how he welcomed with pleasure answering this question: "This gave me the opportunity to impress the fact that the great strength of the Church is the individual testimony of each member, communicated by faithful missionaries and received after soul-searching by those who are honest seekers for truth. The report of this lengthy interview is to appear in an issue of the *Times,* which also syndicates to a large number of newspapers throughout the country."

The almost-adoration of people toward the new President caused the mantle of leadership to rest uncomfortably on his shoulders. The first evidence of this came on July 14, 1972, when President Lee met alone with the Presiding Bishopric, who requested to have his photograph and message to the Aaronic Priesthood of the Church, as a part of the leadership program, replace a similar one from the recently deceased President Smith. President Lee hesitated, not wanting to discontinue President Smith's work, but when the Presiding Bishopric persisted in showing its necessity, President Lee finally reluctantly consented.

Further efforts to diffuse attention from himself came as Utah's Twenty-Fourth of July holiday approached. The Days of '47 parade committee had repeatedly urged him to follow the usual practice of having the President of the Church ride at the head of the parade on its long march. President Lee countered with the suggestion that it would better demonstrate the unity of the new First Presidency by having all three ride with their wives, while his secretary, D. Arthur Haycock, would drive the open limousine. President Lee recorded his pleasure at this arrangement as follows: "This proved to be a very satisfying change, both to the counselors, who had previously never been included, and to the spectators, who lined both sides of the parade route, ten deep, even beyond the final stop into Liberty Park. As we passed it was heartwarming and humbling to have many stand and applaud out of their respect for their new leaders."

FIRST PUBLIC SERMON OF THE PRESIDENT

A long-planned return vacation to the Grand Teton National Park near Jackson Lake, Wyoming, seemed all the more inviting now that the new burdens of worldwide Church leadership had settled on President Lee. He welcomed the opportunity to rest, think, and write in the beautiful mountain setting of the Grand

Tetons, where twice before he had vacationed with his wife and Helen and Brent. But somehow it was different this time. President Lee rode uneasily in the back seat of the automobile, while this time, Brent never relaxed a moment as he drove his precious passengers to Jackson, Wyoming. The earlier events of the month had changed the easy family relationship to a keen awareness that now President Lee belonged to the world, which exacted an accounting of his safety every minute.

Everywhere along the way, whenever Brent stopped the car for gasoline or refreshments, many well-wishers, recognizing the new President of the Church, paused to express their commendation, faith, and loyalty. Young people especially, working at summer jobs on the ranches and inns, passed the word faster than telegraph that the President of the Church was coming to Jackson Lake. They were more than ready when the word came later that President Lee would hold a meeting which they were invited to attend.

The impromptu speaking invitation came officially from Brother Stone, a faithful Church leader and the manager of the Jackson Lake Lodge. He set the time at 9:45 P.M. so that the employees, numbering several hundred, could be off work and assemble in the spacious ballroom of the lodge. They came from all the nearby tourist spots, park locations, and ranches, and when the meeting commenced a crowd of 637 was eagerly awaiting the first public sermon from the new President of the Church.

President Lee sensed the missionary opportunities which existed at this tourist center where many members of the Church were employed. He chose to speak to this challenge and did so by using a missionary dialogue which these faithful youth could use with their fellow workers or the never ending visitors they served. It was an excellent lesson on how to do missionary work, followed by his fervent testimony, sharpened by his new prophetic calling. Long into the night, President Lee shook hands with the young, admiring members of his audience. He recalled this experience in his diary with these comments: "These young people had come from many distant places. There was a good spirit present. This being my first major speaking appointment since becoming President, I suppose some came out of curiosity, but mostly our faithful Saints came seeking and hungering for the truth."

A few weeks later he received a letter from a member of his home ward, John W. Jay, who arranged the Lee party reservations in the Grand Teton National Park in connection with his work with the National Park Service. In this letter Brother Jay told about a visit he had had with Bishop Wilde of the Jackson Ward, who related an interesting story of seventeen-year-old Steve Rogers. Steve was not a member of the Church, but had attended the meeting at the Jackson Lake Lodge. He was so impressed with that meeting that he also attended the sacrament meeting at the Jackson Ward, where President Lee spoke again. Brother Jay's letter gave further details:

> Bishop Wilde returned to his home after the church meeting on Sunday evening and about 7:30 p.m. he received a telephone call from this boy. He told the bishop that, after hearing your two talks, he was so convinced that there was no other way—that ours was the only true church. He was very anxious to be baptized and confirmed a member of the Church by Bishop Wilde that evening.
>
> Bishop Wilde stated that several of the young people who are not now members of our church, but who were in attendance both at the lodge and at the church, have expressed an interest in learning more—but Steve Rogers was so convinced after hearing your messages that he wanted the baptism performed as soon as possible.

President Lee rejoiced in this splendid result from his sermonizing at Jackson Lake and thanked his host, Brother Jay, for such a "restful and joyous experience." He then testified to Brother Jay that he knew that the Spirit was powerful for that first presidential address, saying: "I was interested in the story of the conversion of this young man. I was not surprised because the Spirit that was in our meeting at the lodge was the kind that could have brought joy to the hearts of all who were there. I felt it and I suppose this young man did likewise."

Even though he was now inundated with the constant demands of presiding over the Church, President Lee still chose not to delegate to others the privilege of meeting with the departing missionaries in the temple. He always loved this teaching experience and no doubt reasoned that he seldom could be of more ultimate influence than to persuade the ambassadors of the Lord, going to all parts of the world, concerning the vitality of the true gospel they would teach. President Lee's diary entry of August 11, 1972, contains these thoughts: "I had my first session in the temple with the missionaries since my present call was received. This fact seemed to intensify both in me and in the missionaries an unusual depth of spirituality. One young missionary, representing the group, and with the fervor of the occasion, pledged loyalty, love, and support to me in my new calling."

CONVERSION OF A LAMANITE

On August 18, 1972, President Lee had an interesting meeting with a group of about thirty Indians from the Cheyenne and Arapaho tribes of Oklahoma, who were brought to Salt Lake City on a bus by Rodney N. Dotson, an Oklahoma Stake high councilor. The purpose of the trip was to teach these largely nonmember Lamanites more about the Church.

President Melvin Longhorn of the Watonga-Canton Seiling Branch, Oklahoma Stake, told President Lee that there are more Indians in Oklahoma than in any other state: "We have 97,000 Indians from sixty-four tribes there. Missionary discussions are being taught to the Indians by full-time Elders who have met our bus along the way. They ride with the Indians for a few miles, teach them a lesson, and then get off the bus."

President Lee welcomed the touring Indians to Salt Lake City as he met with them in the First Presidency council room of the Church Office Building. In his remarks, he said: "As you have been told, we have a feeling of brotherhood with you because of our knowledge of your history and people."

He then explained the relationship of the Indians and Church members through the blood of Israel. He related a story which illustrated the parallels between the tradition of the Indian people and the history of the Lamanites as found in the Book of Mormon. Only three of the Indians in the group were Church members when they arrived, but Elder Dotson hoped for baptisms before the end of the trip.

President Lee bore his testimony to the group in a characteristically familiar manner, saying: "When you feel something as you read the Book of Mormon, it is your heart telling you things that your mind doesn't tell you. That is the Spirit of the Lord speaking to you, bearing witness to your soul that it is true."

President Lee then gave each Indian a copy of the Book of Mormon. Two chiefs, one representing the Cheyenne nation and the other, the Arapaho tribe, presented President Lee with beautiful feathered headdresses and two shawls for Sister Lee made by the Indian women.

There was a much deeper significance to this meeting, however. Among the group, like the righteous Alma in the court of the wicked King Noah of Book of Mormon fame, there was at least one believing Indian who listened with his heart. President Lee's appearance touched him deeply; fourteen months later, Robert Allen Fletcher wrote a letter telling President Lee of his part in his conversion. Robert had come with his grandfather to learn of the Church's program for the Lamanites. He wrote of the meeting with the prophet:

> I was so impressed by the surroundings I was in, and especially your presence. I knew that there was something different about you, but I didn't know what it was. I developed a love for you, as if you were a very close friend. I have a great respect for my prophet of my Lord. I will always cherish that day, for you gave me a paperback Book of Mormon that has been with me all this time.
>
> Back home, I was asked to attend the institute at my college. I did so, and my institute teacher, who was one of the men who was on our trip, asked if I would like to speak to the missionaries. By this time I couldn't wait. I had to find out more about the Church. After they gave me my discussions I was baptized on October 17, 1972.
>
> I love you and respect you and would ask for your blessings and your counsel. I can't stop writing this letter. I feel you close to me as if you were one of my own relatives or even one of my immediate family.

MEXICO CITY AREA CONFERENCE

Exactly one year after the British Saints enjoyed in Manchester, England, the first area conference of the Church, a second area conference was held in Mexico City, August 26–28, 1972.

At this time Mexico was the home of the largest number of Church members in any country in the world except the United States. Statistics read at the conference showed that there were more than 82,000 Latter-day Saints in Mexico. In addition, 33,000 Saints then resided in the republics of Central America. Membership of the Church in these areas since 1960 had increased more than 500 percent. At the time of the conference there were 256 wards and branches in Mexico and 90 in Central America.

President Harold B. Lee explained in his opening address one purpose of the area conference in Mexico City: "Many have wondered why this particular conference was held in Mexico City for the Saints residing in Mexico and Central America. One of the reasons is to give recognition and to commend the wonderful labors of the many, who over the years have been instrumental in bringing about the tremendous growth of the Church in these countries."

Many history-making and unusual accomplishments came about at this conference. It was the largest gathering of Saints ever to meet under one roof at a general or area conference. It was the largest gathering of Spanish-speaking Saints and the largest gathering of the Latter-day Saint descendants of Lehi. The Mexican and Central American members also had the privilege at this conference to be the first to sustain President Lee and his counselors in the new First Presidency. (They had been set apart just two months earlier on July 7.) It was also the first time a separate Aaronic Priesthood session was held in connection with an area conference.

The participation by the Tabernacle Choir also set some new records. For example, it was the first Tabernacle Choir Sunday morning broadcast over CBS to emanate from a non-English-speaking nation. This occurred at the Sunday morning choir broadcast, which also marked the 125th anniversary of the choir, and its 2,245th traditional nationwide broadcast.

X The scene was a far cry from the choir's first appearance at the old bowery on Temple Square. The historic broadcast from Mexico was presented from the 17,500-seat amphitheater at the National Auditorium Chapultepec Park in Mexico City. By 7:30 A.M. on Sunday, two hours before its broadcast, there were seven thousand persons in the mammoth hall, about twice as many as ever attended the broadcast in the choir's Salt Lake Tabernacle home during summer months. Yet by air time, there were in excess of sixteen thousand persons present in what may have been the largest audience ever to attend a live broadcast.

The principal motivation for the attendance of this large audience was to see and hear the prophet, seer, and revelator of the Lord for the first time in their lives. Traveling from as far away as Panama, Honduras, and Costa Rica—as well as from Tijuana, Mexico on the north, a fifty-three-hour bus ride—these faithful Saints came and sacrificed much to see the living prophet, President Harold B. Lee. Said one member of the Church from Guatemala: "We did everything we could to come see the prophet of the Lord, the representative of our Savior on earth."

Another member stated: "To be able to sit and listen to his

words and to know and feel in your heart that you are listening to a prophet of God is one of the most beautiful experiences in my life."

The conference began on Saturday night with four simultaneous meetings at four different locations to which President Lee rotated in a whirlwind visit.

The first of these four separate but simultaneous meetings began at 7:00 P.M. and the last one ended at 9:30 P.M. Harold Brown and D. Arthur Haycock drove President Lee to each meeting, where he spoke briefly. It was an evening never to be forgotten.

The first stop was at the Mexico City Stake center at Churusbusco, where over five hundred Aaronic Priesthood youths, immaculately groomed and polished, stood up the instant they learned of the President's arrival. Not a whisper could be heard as all of these young eyes focused on one man. President Lee spoke to them of prayer. As he left, the President turned to his companions and repeated several times: "Did you see those faces? Did you see those faces?"

After next visiting Teatro del Bosque, where 450 young women of Aaronic Priesthood age heard the President, the drivers whisked him on to the women's session in the nearby National Auditorium, where over three thousand sisters were gathered. At the conclusion of his visit there, not a whisper, not a sound, could be heard except muffled sobs and the footsteps of the departing President.

The final stop was at the priesthood session held in the Mexico City North Stake Center at Camarones. On his arrival all stood as if in one army of priesthood while President Lee walked to the front of the hall. As in the other three meetings nearly all present had never before seen a President of the Church in person. Tears were rolling down the cheeks of many men, who wiped them away with white handkerchiefs or the back of weathered fists. After President Lee had impressively taught important lessons about the priesthood, many present wanted to shake his hand, and if they could have done so, would have pressed themselves on him.

The emotions at every meeting had been high. President Lee, at his first opportunity, had gone to these Latin-American Saints and taught them in a close and intimate way. They had heard his voice. They had looked into his eyes. They had personally felt his spirit. "We shall never forget this experience," one man said, as if for all.

A new method of translation was introduced at this conference. It was a system of direct, simultaneous translation similar to the one used at the United Nations. President Lee, however, preferred to use Brother Eduardo Balderas from Salt Lake City as his translator.

In his major Sunday morning address President Lee noted that the amazing growth of the Church in Latin America would not have taken place without the conviction of the truth in the hearts of the faithful members of the Church. Stating that the strength of the Church is not to be measured by tithing contributions or membership, President Lee said:

> The real strength of the Church is to be measured by the individual testimonies to be found in the total membership in The Church of Jesus Christ of Latter-day Saints. The evidence of the hastening of which the Lord spoke in the Doctrine and Covenants can be found in no greater measure than in this land of Mexico and in the countries of Central America, as witnessed by the overwhelming, superabundance of the blood of Israel to be found here. Now there is a grand total of 115,132 in Mexico and Central America in eight stakes and seven missions.

The closing session of the area conference on Sunday afternoon permitted President Lee to again teach the Saints, to express his love for them, to commend their growth and progress, and to share his intimate feelings concerning his new presiding position in the Church. Among his teachings were these memorable statements:

> It would be my prayer that we might have restored your confidence and love for the work of the Lord, and for the General Authorities who preside over this church. It is hoped that you have received the guidance necessary to enable you to feel the divine spirit which has flowed from our Heavenly Father through all which has been done during this conference.
>
> And now in my place as the President of the Church, and with my heart full of love toward all of you people, I extend my blessing to you and pray that your lives will become symbols of your faith and your love for your Heavenly Father.
>
> May you have a renewal of your desires to serve him more fully and to keep his commandments in order that you might feel his nearness and be persuaded to be more faithful and diligent in all your performance in the Church.
>
> I bear you my testimony to the divinity of this work. I know with more certainty than I have ever known before that we are engaged in the work of the Lord.

Remember that the head of this Church is our Lord and Master. During the experiences of these last few weeks, I have come to know more certainly than ever before in my life that the Savior of this world is a living personality.

To him should we give our loyalty, our faith, and our love. I will endeavor to serve you and lend all the strength I have to see to it that the work of the Lord can be projected to the fullest extent as you faithful Saints will prepare yourselves to receive all that our Heavenly Father has in store for his faithful servants.

On Monday morning, August 28, 1972, a press conference was conducted by President Agricol Lozano of the Mexico City East Stake presidency. There were about ten representatives of the leading newspapers and radio stations in attendance. They requested that President Lee respond to questions about the war in Vietnam, abortion, use of drugs, and many other current issues of the day. President Lee started off the conference with this superb statement: "Every time I come to this republic I am touched by the deep faith, the dedication, and the warm friendliness of the Mexican people. They are a choice people. There is in Mexico and Central America a superabundance of the blood of Israel."

Burton F. Howard, legal counsel for the Church in Mexico, was among those attending and listening most intently to all that transpired. He later told President N. Eldon Tanner that he had never been more spiritually uplifted than at this press conference.

The native Spanish-speaking Saints felt the inspiration of the conference deeply, too. The stories and faith-promoting sermons lived on to bless their lives for many years and proved to be a fresh affirmation that indeed "sacrifice brings forth the blessings of heaven."

A Prophet in Hiding

President Lee returned from Mexico City to face conditions that must have given him a glimpse into the persecutions and physical dangers which constantly surrounded the first prophet of this dispensation, Joseph Smith. He was learning that prophets are hated as well as loved, and their lives at times are endangered. It is a risky occupation to dare to be called God's spokesman on earth, for the enemies of righteousness can be vicious and murderous.

According to a *New York Times* story out of San Diego in 1974, under the byline of Everett R. Holles, an apostate church faction was involved in a frightening intrigue. The newspaper article said, in part:

> More than twenty members of various branches of the LeBaron family migrated to Mexico from Utah beginning in 1956 after their expulsion from the Mormon Church in Salt Lake City for apostasy and refusal to renounce polygamy.
>
> Under leadership of Joel LeBaron, the dissidents set up their first splinter sect in the Mexican state of Chihuahua, where a venture in turkey-raising collapsed in 1962. Having increased the cult's membership by bringing in more excommunicated U.S. Mormons and Mexican converts, the sect moved to Las Molinos on the Baja, California peninsula.

The leader of the Church of the Firstborn of the Fullness of Times, Joel LeBaron, was beaten and shot to death, leaving his brother Verlan as his successor. Verlan also became a new target for an ambitious brother, Ervil LeBaron, who was later convicted and imprisoned for murder. Verlan, fearing for his life, kept on the move and traveled thousands of miles shortly after Joel's funeral, providing the Federal Bureau of Investigation and the leaders of the LDS Church with details of the fugitive Ervil's history and threats.

During a visit to Salt Lake City in the late summer of 1972, Verlan LeBaron had learned through another polygamist leader, Rulon Allred, that Ervil had said two weeks before Joel's death, that both Joel and the prophet of The Church of Jesus Christ of Latter-day Saints, President Harold B. Lee, would be killed. It was later found that the report was a misinterpretation, that the "hit list" referred only to the "false prophet," Verlan, as the prophet marked for death.

This distinction not being recognized, a tight blanket of Church security was thrown about President Lee. He wrote of this unusual circumstance in his diary in these words, under date of September 4, 1972:

> Because of the security that has been thrown around me due to the threats and possible dangers from the fugitives of the so-called Church of the Firstborn, Joan and I thought it prudent to stay home. This was providential inasmuch as it gave me much needed time to begin some preparations for the forthcoming solemn assembly and the October general conference.
>
> As the pressures from the Police Department and Church Security continue to mount and are now so visible to everyone, thus

arousing doubts and speculations, it was thought advisable for us to obtain an apartment on the tenth floor of the Hotel Utah where we could stay at night. This has some convenience, but only served to intensify the number of officers who were surrounding us wherever we moved.

Now any appearance of President Lee was accompanied by a large personal security force. Neighbors had wondered about the "stake-out" on the streets near the Lees' home in the Federal Heights area of Salt Lake City. On the second Sunday of September, 1972, President Lee attended the Olympus Stake conference at the request of President Jack H. Goaslind, Jr. Although he had urged that the police protection be as inconspicuous as possible, all precautions had to be taken, including an inspection of the chapel the day before the conference and three or four automobiles traveling ahead of, behind, and by the side of the President's car, which was driven by his secretary, D. Arthur Haycock.

Additional protection was provided at the executive offices of the President of the Church, and electronic door safety devices were installed which could be used to control any undesirable visitors whose purposes in calling might be questionable.

Despite the harassment of accompanying security officers President Lee was grateful for his police protection. Just before leaving for Europe he wrote to Salt Lake City police chief Earl Jones concerning his appreciation for their services, saying:

> Before leaving the city for the next two weeks I want to express to you my personal thanks and appreciation for the protective service that you and your department have so freely and so graciously extended to me.
>
> While I have felt no fear, I realize full well that when vicious men are on the loose, and especially when they are of a cult, an offspring of the true Church, that the devil could stir them up to enmity, therefore precautions were thought to be important.
>
> In order to show my appreciation for what you have done in a tangible way, I am attaching hereto a modest check as a contribution to the Police Mutual Aid Fund, in the hope that thereby you will know that I have not been unmindful of the time and concern you and your men have extended in my behalf.

The next day when President and Sister Lee left for the Salt Lake City airport, they were driven by Brother Haycock and flanked by three police cars. A member of the Church employed at the airport told President Lee that he had thought he would never live to see the day when a President of the Church would be obliged to come to the airport guarded by police. Soon thereafter the clarification of the death threat was made and the extreme protective measures were relaxed.

One year from the day of Joel LeBaron's murder, which occurred on August 20, 1972, the successor president of the Church of the Firstborn of the Fullness of Times, Verlan M. LeBaron, wrote to President Lee and apologized for the threats of violence to the Mormon prophet. He said: "I regret that you were inconvenienced at all by these terrible happenings and sincerely trust that you will have no further problems as a result of these dangerous fanatics."

The tense precautions passed, but brought impressively more awareness and experience to this new prophet, not yet even sustained by the general membership of the Church, on some unique and surprisingly dangerous aspects of his sacred calling.

CHAPTER 27

First Church President Visit to Holy Land in 2,000 Years

When the General Authorities held their monthly meeting in the Salt Lake Temple on September 7, 1972, the meeting turned into a summary of the magnificent Mexico City area conference. Then President Lee requested that Elder Gordon B. Hinckley explain some of the purposes for their proposed trip to Europe and the Middle East.

After President Lee concluded the meeting, there was such a spiritual outpouring that some present were in tears, particularly Elder Hinckley, who was much concerned about the responsibility he was to bear soon in escorting the President of the Church over many miles of possible dangers and evil influences. There were some reservations about going to Israel as planned because of the bitterness engendered by the massacre by Arab terrorists of eleven members of the Israeli Olympic Games delegation at Munich, Germany, earlier that week. This violence had triggered reprisals from Israel's military; the crisis could have escalated and exploded into armed conflict at any time.

The first meeting on the European trip was held on September 14 in London. It was a luncheon appointment with Lord Thomson of Fleet, a wealthy and influential British newspaper owner who on this occasion entertained about twenty-two guests representing some of the most influential men from various fields of endeavor in England, some being lords who had received that honor from the king or queen for distinguished service outside of Parliament.

Lord Thomson, followed by Lord Netherthorpe, who had been to Salt Lake City, spoke in most complimentary language about their honored visitors and about the Church, which they represented. In concluding his compliments Lord Thomson, who owned the *London Times* and the *Sunday Times,* said: "But there is one thing about these people—if you join them, you have to give one-tenth of your income to the Church, and I don't think I could do that."

The day was completed with a visit to the London Temple, where President Lee gave the sealing powers to seven brethren, and with an impromptu meeting requested by the presidents of the North London and East Anglia stakes in the Hyde Park Chapel, where Elder Hinckley and President Lee spoke. Over six hundred Saints attended this memorable occasion with the President of the Church. At the end of the first day, Elder Hinckley wrote in his journal: "President Lee appears extremely tired and even sick. He says he is all right, but I am concerned. He has been the victim of too much 'police security' at home, in addition to the very heavy demands of his office."

The next day President Lee, Elder Hinckley, and their wives, along with mission president Milan Smith and his wife, Jessica, were again guests of Lord Thomson at a luncheon at Thomson House, especially arranged for the Church leaders. He invited some of the leading religious leaders of the Jewish, Catholic, and Protestant churches, in addition to the top officials of his own editorial executive staff, about twenty persons in total. This event proved to be one of the most delightful experiences of the entire tour, as again Lord Thomson spoke in highly complimentary terms concerning the Church. Questions about the Church and world problems were discussed around the table. Lord Thomson asked about the Church's missionary program and Elder Hinckley responded in considerable detail. All attending seemed to be most interested.

Indicative of the influence of those present at this luncheon was a Mr. G. C. Brunton, managing director and chief executive of the Thomson organization, a man second in command to Lord Thomson, and who was seated on Elder Hinckley's left. On the right side of Elder Hinckley was Sir Isaac Wolfson, a most impressive person and a leading benefactor to the nation of Israel. "Surely the Lord was with us and prompted us in that which was said and done at this luncheon," wrote Elder Hinckley.

Following the Lord Thomson luncheon, a press conference was arranged at Connaught House, where President Lee and Elder

Hinckley were to meet the British journalists and media. Nine reporters from the leading papers in London and the Thomson newsmen attended, and the conference went extremely well. Providentially, the discussions were on various topics of a high level, with no mention of the usual controversial issues which are typically encountered at such occasions.

In the evening President Lee and Elder Hinckley and their wives met with four hundred missionaries of the England East and England South missions, where Presidents Milan Smith and Wallace G. Bennett presided. President and Sister John Madsen of the England South Mission also attended. Elder Hinckley summarized the day with this journal entry: "I am sure this was an occasion the missionaries will never forget. It was worth all the effort that it took. Tonight we were on our knees thanking the Lord for his marvelous blessings upon us, and asking that he will give the President strength for the long journey ahead of him."

On Saturday morning, September 16, Lord Thomson sent his private car, a beautiful new Rolls Royce which had been delivered from the showroom only a week earlier, along with a courteous driver, to take the Church leaders to the British Museum, where they saw the famed Rosetta Stone and the artifact relics from Egypt's King Tutankhamen exhibition. That night and on Sunday morning, Elder Hinckley reorganized the London Stake presidency; thirty-one-year-old John Henry Cox, bishop of the Kingston-upon-Thames Ward, was sustained as the new president. When Elder Hinckley told President Lee his only concern was Cox's youthful age, President Lee passed a note to Elder Hinckley which read, "I was thirty-one when I became stake president."

Sunday night the Lees and Hinckleys flew to Athens, Greece, arriving in time to go to the military base, where they held a meeting with fifty Latter-day Saints, most of whom also had been at the airport to greet them. The next day was spent in meeting officials of the Greek government to learn the procedures necessary to legally establish the identity of the Church as "a house of prayer." The project was left in the care of President and Sister Edwin Q. Cannon of the Swiss Mission, which also had stewardship for both Greece and Israel in those days.

After completing the business of the day the six Americans went to the famed Acropolis just as the sun was setting over the Mediterranean Sea. There the Parthenon again displayed its glorious past in culture, wisdom, and ancient architecture. It was a thrilling sight to these leaders to stand on this mountain with the

At the Parthenon with Gordon B. Hinckley, 1972

city on all sides. Since it was about closing time at the Acropolis, Elder Hinckley suggested that the party return to Mars Hill at 7:00 A.M. the next morning and have President Lee speak in commemoration of the famed address given there by the Apostle Paul to the learned citizens of Greece.

Ominously, that night President Lee recorded in his journal that he was experiencing a somewhat severe distress in his lower right back, similar to the pain he had felt before the funeral of President Smith in early July.

In accordance with the plan, President Lee, Elder Hinckley, President Cannon, and their wives came early to Mars Hill where centuries ago Paul had preached his famous sermon on the "unknown God." Together they climbed the rocky hill. Elder Hinckley spoke first, and thoughtfully recorded all that was said on this glorious occasion on his cassette tape recorder so that this event could become a part of documented Church history.

After President Lee had recounted the New Testament account of Paul's sermon on Mars Hill (Acts 17), he concluded his sermon with these words:

> Here then was the opening of the work among the Grecian people. As Paul began to expound the doctrine, he gave us a key as to how we all could know that Jesus was the Christ. He said to the Corinthians, "No man speaking by the Spirit of God calleth Jesus accursed: and no man can say [the Prophet Joseph Smith said that should have been translated 'and no man can *know*'] that Jesus is the Lord, but by the Holy Ghost." So we who have been baptized and received the gift of the Holy Ghost, we too can know by the witness of the Spirit that he is the Christ, to know which is to gain eternal life.

At this point a number of the local brethren and sisters had joined the meeting, so President Lee continued to speak for their benefit. He added his own current feelings about the trials and testing to which Presidents of the Church are subjected:

> As we come to positions of trust and responsibility centuries later, bearing the same message, teaching the same gospel, worshipping the same God, faced with the same opposition, we must not hesitate or slacken our zeal to project the work of the Lord. The work of the Lord never was presented with ease. It had to be brought forth out of blood and sweat and tears and sacrifice. So it may require that in our day, too, more than we know. As I read back over the history of the Presidents of the Church in our dispensation, I have become

aware that all of these men went through periods of trial and testing before they came to their position in the Church. So, today, may this kind of a meeting make each one of us have a feeling of dedication.

After President Lee bore powerful testimony to this handful of faithful Saints on Mars Hill, Elder Hinckley offered the closing prayer. It was so eloquent and sweeping yet so humble that President Lee summarized with a powerful statement: "We shall let that prayer become a prayer of rededication of this land."

The remainder of the day was spent visiting various officials of the Greek government and the Greek Orthodox Church. The Lees and the Hinckleys then flew by plane to Tel Aviv, arriving after dark. Just to set foot on the Holy Land seemed inspirational and filled them with anticipation for the experiences that awaited.

The first of three days in the land where Jesus walked began with visits to various government and Church leaders, all of whom received President Lee graciously. After a visit to the famed Israel Museum, President Lee had a delightful interview with Jerusalem Mayor Teddy Kollek. Concerning this historic visit President Lee recorded in his journal: "We talked about the possibility of a monument on the Mount of Olives containing the Orson Hyde Dedicatory Prayer, which is well known to the mayor and all Jewish officials. We also discussed the possibility of a visitors' center."

The mayor said that the city was trying to acquire property on the Mount of Olives to create a park for meditation. He indicated that it might be possible to have a monument with a reproduction of the Hyde prayer in the park. He promised to write to President Lee on the proposed project as progress developed.

There were additional fascinating visits to high officials and some beginning stops to see the sacred shrines of Jesus' ministry. In early evening they came to the Garden Tomb, where about thirty Saints who live in Israel gathered to be with the prophet. The light from a bright, September moon filtered through the olive trees, spreading a soft glow over the Garden Tomb area in Jerusalem. Ordinarily at this hour the spot would have been deserted, but on this occasion a special meeting was about to take place on this night of September 30, 1972.

Elder Hinckley's dictated journal captures the feelings of the Church authorities as they met in this sacred place, embroidered with such deep significance.

As we stood in the tomb cut from stone, we could imagine Joseph of Arimathea, Mary, and others bringing the body of Jesus and laying it there in a hurry to have this done before the Jewish Sabbath. We could then imagine the first day of the week, when the burial clothes were left in the tomb, but the body was gone, the stone being rolled away. We could imagine the two angels sitting at either end of the tomb, and Peter and others of the Apostles coming and looking in consternation at the empty burial place. And then we could see in our mind's eye the risen Lord with Mary, and hear again the conversation which took place.

It seemed to us that this was in very deed the place of the burial and resurrection of the Master, the place where occurred the greatest event in human history, when the Master of life broke the bands of death.

President Harold B. Lee, the prophet of God, who only recently had been ordained to that calling, was now presiding at a meeting in those holy surroundings. Hymns were sung and prayers were spoken. Organizing a Jerusalem branch of the Church was an idea which came unpremeditated as inspiration of the moment. David B. Galbraith was sustained as the president of the first branch of the Church of Jesus Christ to be organized in the Holy Land in nearly two thousand years. A children's chorus sang "I Am a Child of God." Then, Elder Gordon B. Hinckley spoke movingly, recounting from the book of John some of the events of the death, burial, and resurrection of the Savior. President Lee's sermon was then delivered. Elder Hinckley recorded these statements in his journal:

President Lee said that when he and his wife Fern came to the Garden Tomb in 1958 there was a feeling about this place that was different from all other places. He read the scripture: "In the place where he was crucified there was a garden." "That is," President Lee went on, "in the hill where he was crucified there was a garden." He had concluded that Golgatha was right up on the top of the hill above here and that this was indeed the very garden where Joseph of Arimathea brought the body of the crucified Lord.

He told the group assembled, "Though you are few in number, you are laying the foundation of something that will be great." He indicated that in the visits we had made to various officials during the day, there had been a respect of us greater than we could have hoped for.

We sang "Now Let Us Rejoice," after which Brother Brandly offered a prayer. We set apart Brother Galbraith and Brother

Tvedtnes and then we sang "God Be with You till We Meet Again." No one present will ever forget this occasion.

The fast and long pace of the day had fatigued President Lee, whose body was weakened by his lung disease. Back at the hotel President Lee wrote of his concern over his physical condition and pain: "These are exhausting days. My physical strength is at a seriously low ebb. I know something is seriously wrong. There is a severe pain in my lower back and a weariness that was emphasized by a constant effort to expel mucus. Joan insisted that I have Brother Hinckley and President Cannon administer to me."

Just as the Hinckleys, next door in the hotel, were about to retire, Sister Lee knocked on their door and asked if Elder Hinckley would give President Lee a blessing. President Cannon anointed him and Elder Hinckley sealed the anointing. Concerning the blessing Elder Hinckley wrote: "I felt the power of the Spirit of the Lord as I spoke the blessing. I felt confident that the Lord would heal his servant."

The journal account of President Lee reveals the fulfillment of the blessing:

> The next morning, after a severe coughing spell, I expelled two clots which seemed to be blood—one, about the size of a dime, was like dried blood, and the other one was red, as a fresh clot. Immediately my shortness of breath ceased, the weariness was diminished, and the back pains began to subside, and twenty-four hours later they were entirely gone.
>
> I now realize I was skirting on the brink of eternity and a miracle, in this land of even greater miracles, was extended by a merciful God who obviously was prolonging my ministry for a longer time, to give to him in whose service I am all the strength of my heart, mind, and soul, to indicate in some measure my gratitude for his never-failing consideration to me and my loved ones.

The next morning Elder Hinckley said President Lee appeared stronger, but he said only that he felt better. It wasn't until one day later when they were finishing breakfast that President Lee shared with his companions his testimony that the Lord had brought to pass a miracle in his behalf in response to the blessing given to him. By this time Elder Hinckley observed that his health was remarkably improved. Undoubtedly the expelled material had nearly blocked off one of the lobes in his lungs. Divine intervention had rescued him from a most serious extremity.

For the next two days, under the leadership of "our faithful David B. Galbraith, about whom I cannot say enough of good as our driver and guide," said President Lee, the Lees and the Hinckleys toured the Holy Land, seeing again the sacred places and walking where Jesus had walked. It was a tiring and wonderful two days in which they saw much, completely enjoyed the experiences, and had their faith renewed.

From Israel the touring General Authorities flew to Rome, where, on the weekend of September 23 – 24, they attended youth conferences and other church meetings, with visits between meetings to religious shrines and art galleries. President Lee's journal gives his impressions of both the general meetings and group sessions which he and Elder Hinckley and their wives attended:

> About 250 of fine appearing young people and their chaperones participated at a three-day conference which proved to be a great success. The youth of both the Italy South and North missions participated. In the evening we met first with the missionaries and following that, a meeting with the branch members and the missionaries, with about 200 to 275 persons in attendance. It was again an amazing indication as to how the work has taken root in Italy.

Elder Hinckley's journal speaks more of the blessings these young and new members of the Church felt as they saw for the first time the President of the Church:

> We drove to Santa Severa, a distance of about sixty kilometers, where the young people of the two Italy missions were having a youth conference. They were overwhelmed with joy at the sight of President Lee, of whom they spoke as "the Prophet." We came into their testimony meeting and listened to quite a number of their testimonies before I spoke. Then President Lee spoke briefly. They surrounded him and besieged him as he tried to get a bite to eat. We returned to Rome, a drive of about one hour and a half, and to our rooms in the Ambassador Hotel, weary but gratified with the opportunity of participating in the Lord's work in so wonderful a manner.

Again the next day, Sunday, the Lees and the Hinckleys were up early to return to the youth conference. Elder Hinckley explained his excitement on this occasion in his journal: "It was a stirring thing to look into the faces of some 250 Italian Saints. These are pioneers of what will become a great future for the Church in this land. I explained how the President of the Church is chosen and how meaningful this is to have him present in this meeting. We all bore testimony, and it was an inspirational occasion."

Next some three hundred more fine-looking Italian Saints assembled for a special meeting in Milano, having gathered from over a wide geographical area. These long and tiring days found President Lee looking extremely fatigued. "The President was under terrible strain before we came, and there is no rest on a trip of this kind," wrote Elder Hinckley. Yet they were up at 5:00 A.M. the next morning to meet with 180 missionaries from the Italy North Mission.

The European phase of the long journey came to a close with a visit to the Swiss Temple in Zollikofen, not far from Bern. There President Lee presided over a change in the leadership of the temple by releasing President and Sister Charles Grob and installing President and Sister Immo Luschin on September 26, 1972.

The final European sermons were delivered at the chapel in Lausanne, Switzerland, where people began to gather at 9:30 A.M. for an 11:00 A.M. meeting. Some had traveled more than four hundred miles, and 318 were on hand as the meeting began. Elder Hinckley wrote of this occasion: "They had come to see the President of the Church. It was a tremendous treat for them to hear President Lee and, for many of them, to shake his hand. They were a wonderful looking congregation—intelligent, refined people."

Back in the United States President Lee's party was met at the New York City airport by President and Sister David Lawrence McKay and missionaries of the New York City Mission. The immediate pressures continued, for en route from the airport to the hotel, Wendell J. Ashton, Director of the Public Communications Department, briefed President Lee and Elder Hinckley on the details of a luncheon and press conference planned at the Waldorf Astoria Hotel the next day.

On September 28, President Lee and Elder Hinckley enjoyed lunch in the hotel with a small but important group of men, including such luminaries as Lowell Thomas, the famous radio commentator; Norman Vincent Peale, well-known Protestant preacher; Frank N. Milligan, president of Kennecott Copper Corporation; George Scott, executive vice president, First National City Bank of New York; Lee Bickmore, chairman of the board of National Biscuit Company; Frank Wangeman, president of the

Waldorf Astoria Hotel; and various Church officials. Elder Hinckley called it a "delightful occasion."

Following the luncheon President Lee, Elder Hinckley, and their staff went to the third floor of the hotel to conduct a press conference in which President Lee met twenty-two of the most sophisticated news reporters he had ever faced. Staffing the interview were representatives of United Press International, Associated Press, *Time, The Washington Post, The New York Times,* Religious News Service, Hunter College, *New York Daily News,* and others, including three from WRFM in New York.

President Lee's recollection of the press encounter is as follows:

> I announced the appointment of Lee S. Bickmore as a special consultant to the First Presidency after Brother Ashton had introduced him and explained our need for his services. For an hour I fielded searching questions about the Church's finances, welfare program, the reasons for the rapid Church growth, etc. The only question relative to the black question came after the press conference from a Jewish reporter, while a *New York Times* woman reporter questioned me further. George Cornell, religious editor of the Associated Press, characterized my responses as more honest and forthright than are usually given at such interviews. Frank Wangeman of the Waldorf Hotel management, said it was his most inspirational hour. The results seemed favorable.

That assessment seemed to be supported by Elder Hinckley's appraisal, for he wrote in his journal that "President Lee handled himself remarkably well."

The long journey came to a close as the weary travelers arrived at the Salt Lake City airport on Thursday, September 28, after a five-hour, nonstop flight from New York.

President Lee recorded his impressions on being home that night in these words: "We returned home somewhat weary, but of necessity must plunge into the problems awaiting me—general conference and the solemn assembly, where I will be sustained, the transgressions of trusted men in high places requiring disciplinary action, and the call of a new Apostle. Joan has returned home with a cold, but is recovering. It's great to be home. I found all is well, and America is beautiful."

Elder Gordon B. Hinckley, President Lee's loyal, faithful companion whose experience at world travel and skill at special events management is unsurpassed, summarized this portion of his personal journal under the title "A Journey to Be Remembered." He wrote:

> All four of us came home feeling well. I have never taken a trip for so long a period and felt better than I have on this trip. I have not had a single sick day and have felt well. We have witnessed a miracle in the restoration of the President's health. Moreover, the respite from the pressures of his office has been a wonderful relief for him. The good he has done in getting out among the people can never be estimated. They will never forget the occasions of meetings when he bore testimony, and personal interviews when they listened to him and shook hands with the Lord's chosen prophet.
>
> And for Marge and me it has been an incomparable experience, one we shall never forget. The unfailing kindness of President Lee and his delightful companion made traveling with them a joy and a privilege.
>
> We thank our Heavenly Father for his blessings. His watchful care has been over us. We have been preserved from accident and evil. His Spirit has gone before us to touch the hearts of those on whom we have called. Nature has favored us and men have respected us and honored us. We have given encouragement to a thousand missionaries, have enjoyed them, and have been enriched by their expressions of faith. We have borne testimony to the Saints in England, Greece, Israel, Italy, and Switzerland. We have walked where Jesus walked and testified of his divinity as the Son of the Living God. We have declared our knowledge of these things where Paul declared his knowledge centuries ago. We have proclaimed the prophetic calling of Joseph Smith and affirmed the prophetic calling of his successor in office, Harold B. Lee.
>
> This has been a journey to remember. This has been an experience to cherish.

SIGNIFICANCE OF PRESIDENT LEE'S VISIT TO JERUSALEM

Over the years, many General Authorities had come and gone, visiting in the Holy Land. Each time the handful of Saints who lived in Tel Aviv and Jerusalem would eagerly inquire whether their coming was an official visit, to organize the Saints or start the work moving forward. Each time the Brethren would answer that they were there to vacation, or tour, or were just visiting while passing through on other assignments. This continued until President Lee visited the Holy Land in 1972.

David B. Galbraith, the first president of the Jerusalem Branch, had lived in the Holy Land since 1969. His perspective is important in assessing when the Church began to move forward in that sacred territory. In delivering the 1979 Mediterranean pre-Cruise lecture at Brigham Young University to those who were traveling to Jerusalem for the dedication of the Orson Hyde Monument on the Mount of Olives, Elder Galbraith said:

> And now, as we look back on President Lee's visit, it stands out as a landmark. It may even be so important that it will be regarded as a landmark of the restoration of the Gospel.
>
> It was most importantly the first visit made by a living prophet of the Lord in two thousand years. Never before had the prophet, seer, and revelator of the Church of Jesus Christ come to the Holy Land. For this reason, it was a very special occasion.

While in Jerusalem, President Lee repeatedly said that this was a time of preparation. He said it was a time to win friends and bring the name of the Church before the Jewish people and keep it prominently before them.

Elder Galbraith remembers the first major breakthrough accomplished at the time of the organization of the Jerusalem Branch.

> During the prophet's visit we asked if we could meet on Saturday to worship instead of Sunday, explaining that in Israel everyone works a six-day week and Saturday is the Jewish Sabbath, the only day when school and work are closed. We were shocked when President Lee said that there was no precedent for this, that the scriptures were clear and that Sunday was the Lord's day. But just before he left he said: "I feel your request is too important to answer on the spur of the moment. Write me a letter directed to the First Presidency and the Council of the Twelve and explain your reasons for such a request." Just a few months later we received authorization to meet on Saturday instead of Sunday.
>
> That Sabbath day decision was especially significant because it accommodated the local Saints and allowed them to meet their personal obligations on Sunday and to worship on Saturday.

President Lee's decision to authorize Saturday worship was an important change in direction and offered new thinking to the handful of Saints in the Holy Land. But Elder Galbraith also cited other important milestones:

> While in Jerusalem President Lee suggested that we find a parcel of land on the Mount of Olives on which we might honor Orson Hyde. This wasn't the first time this suggestion had been made, but it came to us very strongly when made by the prophet. Well, we looked,

and I can assure you that there is probably not a more sensitive piece of real estate on earth than the Mount of Olives, unless it is the Temple Mount across the way. There was nothing for sale, or at least nothing that would meet our needs.

But one day the mayor of Jerusalem, Teddy Kollek, called me on the phone and said: "Do you think your church would be interested in developing a five-acre tract of land right in the heart of the Mount of Olives and naming it after your Orson Hyde?" "Would we ever!" I exclaimed. Months of negotiation brought a fulfillment of mutual goals of the Church and the city of Jerusalem. I always felt that this was a very positive step in demonstrating our interest in a beautiful meditation park which could be enjoyed by Moslem, Christian, and Jew alike.

Why was this such a significant event in Church history?

Elder Orson Hyde was an original member of the first Council of the Twelve chosen by the Three Witnesses in 1835. He served with Joseph Smith in the leadership of the newly restored Church in this last dispensation. He left Commerce, Illinois (Nauvoo), on April 15, 1840, in response to a prediction by the Prophet that he should do a work among the Jews. He journeyed to Europe, calling upon Jewish leaders in England and Germany. Later, on this same mission, he traveled on to Constantinople, Cairo, Alexandria, and finally to Jerusalem. Eighteen months after departure, on Sunday, October 24, 1841, he ascended the Mount of Olives in Jerusalem and pronounced an eloquent prayer dedicating the land of Palestine for the gathering of the Jews. This was long before the Zionist movement under Thedor Herzle was flowering.

The Prophet Joseph Smith had blessed Orson Hyde, assuring him that inasmuch as he was interested in the Lord's people, the God of their fathers would bless him. His blessing stated: "In due time thou shalt go to Jerusalem, the land of thy fathers, and be a watchman unto the House of Israel; and by thy hands shall the Most High do a great work, which shall prepare the way and greatly facilitate the gathering together of that people" (*History of the Church,* 4:375).

His name is now being blessed by peoples of many lands. A monument to this Latter-day Saint Apostle stands on the very hill where he, and Jesus, spoke and taught. He is honored by Jews and Mormons as the symbolic reminder of a common belief in the gathering of the Jews back to their native land.

Additionally, while President Lee was in Jerusalem in 1972, he authorized also the local leaders of the Church to start searching for land which could be purchased. It was a most exciting idea to contemplate that after nearly two thousand years there might someday be a meetinghouse in Jerusalem.

The search for land was started and it continued through almost a decade of discouraging years. Yet the mere thought of the ultimate millennial world rule, after the second coming of the Savior, when there will be two world capitals ("for out of Zion [United States] shall go forth the law, and the word of the Lord from Jerusalem"—Isaiah 2:3), gave the local Saints a feeling of being a part of historic destiny.

Citing still another breakthrough springing from President Lee's visit, Elder Galbraith said:

> Now you can better appreciate why we consider President Lee's 1972 visit such an important landmark. Prior to his visit none of these movements were happening, and now, one event after another, meant that we were really moving forward.
>
> He authorized the translation of the Book of Mormon into Hebrew and Aramaic.

Elder Galbraith continued in his 1979 presentation to emphasize later developments since President Lee's visit in Jerusalem:

> In August 1975 the First Presidency announced that Israel would be administered by the International Mission. It was only about a year after that that the Brethren decided to call Special Representatives to serve nonproselyting friendshipping missions.
>
> Also, in April 1977, the Church was first recognized as a legal association in Israel and became a legal entity in that country. We are no longer there by sufferance, but we are there by right.
>
> Since then there have been other developments in education growing out of the decisions of the First Presidency. They approved sending the seminary and institute teachers of the Church to the Holy Land. The program is called the Scriptures Workshop, and in my opinion it is one of the most important accomplishments we have made.
>
> Another important development was the Study Abroad Program, under which Church youth are brought to Israel, not for six days or for six weeks but for six months. This provides an in-depth exposure so that in this extended period our young people can get an understanding and appreciation of the culture, the tradition, the

language, and the religion of the Jewish people and get a real feel for them and an appreciation for their way of life.

Elder Galbraith concluded his presentation with this summary:

> I hope through this explanation you can see the progress we have made in this land since President Lee's visit. Please note the stepping-stones, and you can see what President Lee meant when he said: "First we have to do all we can as a people and as a Church, and only then can we expect the Lord to remove the obstacles."

Thus was commenced a mighty movement which, while slow in starting, will not conclude until the windup of the great millennial events, which will be of interest to all Christendom. The Lord's church will be there, and perhaps historians looking backward will trace the commencement of preparation for these climactic experiences to a visit of the prophet of God, President Harold B. Lee, to Jerusalem in 1972, after an absence of such priesthood influence for nearly two thousand years.

BRUCE R. MCCONKIE CHOSEN NEW APOSTLE

One of the most urgent of the pressing problems President Lee found at home awaiting his attention was the necessity to make a selection of a new member of the Quorum of the Twelve Apostles, filling the vacancy created when President Marion G. Romney was taken from those ranks to become the Second Counselor in the First Presidency. Now with the October 1972 general conference near at hand, President Lee pondered over the names earlier nominated by the Quorum of the Twelve at President Lee's request. While he didn't know it at the time, President Lee would make only this one appointment to the apostleship.

President Lee recorded in his personal journal on Sunday, October 1, 1972, the details of how he received the revelation to make this appointment:

> Today while fasting, I went to the most sacred room in the temple. There for an hour I prayerfully considered the appointment of a new Apostle. All seemed clear that Bruce R. McConkie should be the man. When I told my counselors they both said that from the first they seemed to know also it was to be Elder McConkie.
>
> When I talked with Brother McConkie he related an experience he had at the recent Mexico City area conference. When the General Authorities were sustained, following the reading of Elder Marvin J.

Quorum of the Twelve sustaining Bruce R. McConkie (foreground) as an Apostle at solemn assembly, October 6, 1972

Ashton's name (the eleventh Apostle in seniority), he heard his own name spoken. Since that time he had wrestled with this forewarning in the temple for a long time, and seemed to feel, as President Grant had expressed himself when he was called, that he "seemed to see" a council of the Brethren on the other side, where they were advocating his name.

The reference to President Grant's call to the apostleship was not an unfamiliar story. Nine months later it was to resurface in the form of a personal letter from President Grant to Don Carlos Young, whose son, George Cannon Young, brought it to President Lee to read. In the letter President Grant related his testimony of his being called to be an Apostle, when he "seemed to see and hear" a council meeting beyond the veil in which his father and Joseph Smith were consulting together relative to the filling of two vacancies in the Quorum of the Twelve. The Prophet Joseph said to Jedediah M. Grant, Heber's father: "Here is Heber who is my son and bears your name. If he were to be called he would represent both of us," an obvious reference to the fact that Heber's mother had been sealed in a temple marriage to the Prophet Joseph Smith.

With the choice of a new Apostle made, the General Authorities were stirred to a spiritual pinnacle by the preparatory meeting of the Brethren in anticipation of conference, where Elder Gordon B. Hinckley and President Lee reported on their travels to the Middle East. All now was in readiness for the commencement of the 142d Semiannual General Conference of the Church.

CHAPTER 28

"The Greatest Moment of My Life"

On only ten previous occasions since the Church was organized in 1830 had the Saints voted to sustain a new President. Such a moment in eternity came again on October 6, 1972, when Harold B. Lee was sustained in a solemn assembly as the prophet and President of The Church of Jesus Christ of Latter-day Saints.

Following the voting, which was done in quorums of the priesthood, after the Saints in general had raised their hands to sustain the new prophet, President Lee spoke:

> Today at the greatest moment of my life, I find myself without words to express my deep and innermost feelings. What I say, therefore, must be actuated by the Spirit of the Lord, that you, my beloved Saints of the Most High God, may feel the depths of my soul-searching on this momentous and historic occasion.

President Lee spoke openly of his inner feelings and the bonds of brotherhood he felt with the Saints, as he continued:

> Again, in the mighty demonstration of this solemn assembly, I am moved with emotions beyond expression as I have felt the true love and bonds of brotherhood. There has been here an overwhelming spiritual endowment, attesting, no doubt, that in all likelihood we are in the presence of personages, seen and unseen, who are in attendance. Who knows but that even our Lord and Master would be near us on such an occasion as this, for we, and the world, must never forget that this is his church, and under his almighty direction we are to serve! Indeed, I would remind you what he declared in a

similar conference of the Saints in Fayette, New York, and undoubtedly would remind us again today. The Lord said: "Behold, verily,
verily, I say unto you that mine eyes are upon you. I am in your
midst and ye cannot see me. (D&C 38:7.)"

After paying tribute to his ten predecessors in the office of
President of the Church, President Lee returned to his soul-searching thoughts to allow his audience to look into his heart:

> To him who sought no earthly honors, but whose soul delighted in
> the things of the Spirit, President Joseph Fielding Smith was there
> with his smiling face, my beloved prophet-leader who made no
> compromise with truth. As the "finger of God touched him and he
> slept," he seemed in that brief moment to be passing to me, as it
> were, a sceptre of righteousness, as though to say to me, "Go thou
> and do likewise."
>
> Now I stood alone with my thoughts. Somehow the impressions
> that came to me were, simply, that . . . when an individual is
> ordained and appointed to lead the people, he has passed through
> tribulations and trials, and has proven himself before God, and
> before his people, that he is worthy of the situation which he
> holds . . . , and that when a person, as Elder Orson Hyde said in
> 1853, has not proved himself before God, and before his people and
> before the councils of the Most High, to be worthy, he is not going
> to step in and lead the Church and the people of God.

Comparing his tempering and molding to the shaping by
adversity of the Prophet Joseph Smith, President Lee added:

> At times it seemed as though I too was like a rough stone rolling
> down from a high mountainside, being buffeted and polished, I
> suppose, by experiences, that I too might overcome and become a
> polished shaft in the quiver of the Almighty.
>
> Maybe it was necessary that I too must learn obedience by the
> things that I might have suffered—to give me experiences that were
> for my good, to see if I could pass some of the various tests of mor-
> tality.

The refining, purifying Spirit of the Lord had attested to his
acceptance and pronounced a spiritual blessing upon him, which
was described in self-analysis by the new President in these words:

> The morning after my call came, as I knelt with my dear companion
> in prayer, my heart and soul seemed to reach out to the total mem-
> bership of the Church with a special kind of fellowship and love
> which was like the windows of heaven, to give me a brief feeling of

First Presidency gives sustaining vote at solemn assembly, October 6, 1972

belonging to the more than three million members of the Church in all parts of the world.

I repeat what I have said on other occasions, that I most fervently seek to be upheld by the confidence, faith, and prayers of all the faithful Saints everywhere, and I pledge to you that as you pray for me, I will earnestly try to so live that the Lord can answer your prayers through me.

From President Lee's journal comes his personal reflections on "the greatest moment of his life":

The solemn assembly, as was expected, was a tremendous spiritual experience, especially for me, and from all that has been observed and said, it lifted the people heavenward. I conducted the session and President Tanner directed the voting, which was done with no dissent. My acceptance had to have been heaven-inspired, for without that my humble offering would not have had the impact which was in evidence.

In expressing his support of the First Presidency, the newly called Apostle, Elder Bruce R. McConkie, described President Lee as "a seer, a man filled with the spirit of revelation and of wisdom, who is on intimate terms with that Lord whose we are."

Speaking at the world broadcast of general conference from the Salt Lake Tabernacle on Saturday, October 7, President Lee again declared the principles and doctrines of the Church to provide the solution to the problems that afflict the world. President Lee observed in his diary after two days of general conference: "All the talks at each session were so harmonized as to make one think that each speaker had been assigned his topic, which was not true."

At the general conference priesthood meeting, President Lee bluntly denounced the actions of certain members of the Church who in defiance of the law were refusing to pay their income taxes to the government.

President Lee told those assembled at the general priesthood meeting more concerning his calling to preside over the Church.

Never had I thought of myself as one day becoming the President of the Church. As a boy in my rural community, I used to hear the Brethren talk about a "pillar" in the Church. I wondered what in the world it meant. It must be something great to be a pillar in the Church. Well, now, maybe I am beginning to realize something about what that means.

When he bore his testimony at this general priesthood meeting, President Lee firmly taught the constancy of modern revelations:

I bear you my solemn witness that it is true, that the Lord is in his heavens; he is closer to us than you have any idea. You ask when the Lord gave the last revelation to this Church? The Lord is giving revelations day by day, and you will witness and look back on this period and see some of the mighty revelations the Lord has given in your day and time. To that I bear you my witness.

In the closing sermon of the conference President Lee conceded that the experiences of the conference and his installation as President of the Church had made him a different man. He said:

I come now to the closing moments of this session when I have time for some sobered reflections. Somehow I have had the feeling that during the expressions here, whenever my name has been mentioned, they were talking of somebody other than myself. And I really think that is so, because one cannot go through the experience that I have gone through these last three days and be the same as before. I am different than I was before Friday morning.

I cannot go back to where I was because of the love and faith and confidence that you, the people of the Lord, have reposed in me. So you have been talking of somebody else. You have been talking of somebody that you want me to become, which I hopefully pray God I may, with his help, become.

His last words to his beloved Saints on that occasion were:

My love goes out to my own family, to my associates, to all within the sound of my voice, even the sinners; I would wish that we would reach out to them and those who are inactive, and bring them into the fold before it is too late.

God be with you. I have the same feeling as perhaps the Master had when he bid good-bye to the Nephites. He said he perceived that they were weak, but if they would go to their homes and ponder what he said, he would come again and instruct them on other occasions. So, likewise, you cannot absorb all that you have heard and that we have talked about, but go to your homes now and remember what you can, and get the spirit of what has been done and said, and when you come again, or we come to you, we will try to help you further with your problems.

Thus ended the 142d Semiannual General Conference of the Church with its historic solemn assembly. The summary commentary in the diary of President Lee included these interesting reflections from the person most affected by the conference:

> I gave the closing remarks of the conference and opened my heart to all my people and gave them my blessing as they were to now leave for their homes. Never has there been ever a greater spiritual experience when it seemed as though the Lord was indeed in our conference. There began an avalanche of letters, not only from our faithful leaders and members, but from those not in the Church. One of the choicest was a letter from my dear old friend, John A. Sibley, a great Southerner and a former director of the Equitable Life Assurance Society of the U.S.A. with whom I worked.
>
> I was particularly impressed by a letter from my second cousin, Sterling McMurrin of the University of Utah, who has seemed to withdraw from any contact with me. He extended the prayers and blessings of the McMurrin family and warmly commended my efforts. One sentence was somewhat significant: "Your uncommon strength as a leader and your personal talents and abilities and broad experience will be of inestimable worth to the Church in the crucial years ahead."

The public acceptance of President Lee was overwhelming. The spiritual momentum had built from session to session. Few if any in the congregation could remember a time when a President of the Church dominated the conference scene so completely. President Lee's complete visibility seemed to add to the spiritual excitement of the Saints.

He opened his heart to the Saints, allowing everyone in the international television audience to look for the first time within memory into the heart of a prophet. The Saints loved it and loved him for it. During the interlude before the morning session on Sunday, the last day of the conference, the Saints began to sing spontaneously, "We Thank Thee, O God, for a Prophet," as they caught the first glimpse of their President. It was an expression of love for him who had been so magnificent in his leadership of the conference, lifting the congregation to the highest spiritual peaks and yet remaining ever so humble.

Rarely had a President of the Church talked so freely about his feelings as he ascended to the highest position on earth. This seemed to allow Church members to relate in a personal way with him, establishing an immediate, tremendous rapport. Obviously he was the youngest President after several aged prophets. The sermon style of the past, however, while always inducing respect, seemed seldom to place the prophet on a level which permitted his followers to empathize with him on a human relationship basis. President Lee did this and was loved for it.

President Lee's capacity to influence others was magnified by the fact that he conducted every session of conference himself, thus controlling the tempo and the spirit of the meetings. It had been a long time since the Church had had a President who was physically able to work that hard during general conference. Too, President Lee was so at ease as the Church's presiding authority that he also felt free to make little editorial comments and admonitions between the speakers, providing a welcome break from the all-too-familiar television script. It was a delightful change of pace which conference listeners found refreshing.

So at ease and so much in command was President Lee at this conference that, despite a huge television audience, he paused at one point to teach a lesson on light-mindedness and avoidance of laughter in sacred assemblies.

This conference also saw the appointment of five Brethren who were given new general Church leadership assignments. Elder Bruce R. McConkie was sustained as the new member of the Quorum of the Twelve Apostles; Elders O. Leslie Stone, James E. Faust, and L. Tom Perry were added as Assistants to the Twelve; and Elder Rex D. Pinegar, president of the North Carolina-Virginia Mission, was called to fill the position vacated by Elder McConkie as a member of the First Council of Seventy.

Elder Faust came to President Lee's office thirteen days after his conference appointment was announced to inform him of a remarkable personal revelation by which he knew ten days before the conference through spiritual communication of his call to be an Assistant to the Twelve.

Having thus been installed and sustained, President Lee settled more firmly into his work of presiding over a fast-growing Church with 3,200,000 members. The time and challenge ahead was verbalized by President Lee in his address at the final session of the conference when he said: "We now come to the closing moments of a momentous conference, history making and in many ways a conference that has great significance because of the time in which we live. Perhaps never have we turned a page of the history of the Church with greater challenge, with greater problems, or with greater promise for the future."

Dr. Sterling McMurrin, in his family's letter of support to President Lee, saw the challenge of the Church in this manner: "It is a time when the Church itself is moving toward a fulfillment of its own universality and the cultivation of an authentic world-mindedness."

Faced with the unrelenting demands of his worldwide ministry, President Lee underwent a physical examination by his physician, who, when he heard about his narrow escape from death in the Holy Land, concurred that his life had been spared by the spiritual aid he had received through the priesthood blessing administration. For three hours President Lee again submitted to X-ray studies at the LDS Hospital to see if there were further need of steps to reduce the threat of blood clots to his lungs. Despite all this President Lee wrote: "I feel exceptionally well, considering the pressures and experiences of the last month."

REVEALED CHANGES IN THE MIA

The next major developmental change in the Church concerned the restructuring of the Mutual Improvement Association to make it conform to the Aaronic Priesthood program, and the establishment of a Department of Melchizedek Priesthood designed to help Young Adults and Special Interest groups, so that they too could receive their activity program under the direction of priesthood quorums. On October 27, 1972, President Lee interviewed Robert L. Backman and Ruth Funk, and extended calls to them to preside over the newly aligned Aaronic Priesthood MIA programs for youths ages twelve to eighteen years. Both accepted their calls with humility and showed much promise for providing splendid leadership in the future.

Elder Backman will remember forever the counsel and significance of his interview with President Lee. He has written of that experience:

> When I was called by President Harold B. Lee to be president of the Aaronic Priesthood-MIA, I had a most interesting conversation with him. He talked about the young people of the Church and about the challenges they face in growing up in this world in which we live. He expressed his deep concern about the fact that some of them could go through Primary, Sunday School, Mutual, priesthood quorums, and seminary and come out the other end without testimonies.
>
> He said: "Do you know why I think it is? Because our young people have grown up spectators." Then he gave me a challenge that I've never forgotten and one which I have passed on to the

youth of the Church on many occasions. He said: "Bob, I challenge you to provide a program that will prepare this generation to meet the Savior when he comes."

At a meeting on November 7, there was an unusually fine response from newly called leaders and commendation for the past work of those being released. The need for this new organizational structure was again stressed, which in part was a move to outline a program for the older single persons, including widows, because in the future the married couples would find their activity programs with the priesthood quorums where their husbands belonged.

After receiving the unanimous endorsement of the new MIA program from all the General Authorities in their monthly temple meeting, the changes were announced by the First Presidency in a circular letter on November 10, 1972. The *Deseret News* carried the announcement in its daily papers. Some, including some friends and relatives close to President Lee, thought this history-making move might be considered radical and revolutionary, especially in terminating the long prominence of the Mutual Improvement Association general boards. The answer by President Lee indicates the depths to which he felt these moves were not only justified, but inspired. He wrote in his journal: "I sought as kindly yet as forcibly as I could to tell these dear people that these were moves long studied, prayed over, and heaven inspired, and that they must accept without question the divine nature of these changes. Only God knows how I must stand alone ofttimes in making final decisions, and then must leave the results with the Lord."

President Lee was always concerned with strengthening the youth of the Church. A trip to San Diego, California, and Mesa, Arizona, by President and Sister Lee underscored his intense desire to build the youth of the Church whenever his time and energies permitted. A spiritually charged audience of two thousand young adults—eager, clean, and choice people, seemingly seeking earnestly to know what their role in the Church and world might be—heard the Lees speak in San Diego. After dedicating the San Diego Mormon Battalion Visitors' Center with Elder Mark E. Petersen, the Lees moved on to Mesa, Arizona, where over thirty-two hundred young people flocked to hear sermons from the President and from Bishop Vaughn J. Featherstone. President Lee's modesty concerning his appointment as President of the Church is clearly evident in his journal as he wrestled uneasily to defuse the adoration heaped on him by these admiring youthful audiences: "The spiritual fervor generated in such a gathering as the Mesa youth conference was almost frightening in its intensity, as they adopt in some cases an almost worshipful attitude, which I am trying earnestly to play down to a respectful and appropriate loyalty to their Church leaders."

President and Sister Lee came home by plane on Sunday, November 5, with this issue still on his mind as he attended, with Sister Lee, the Emigration Stake conference, his home stake. Following a talk by a priest who spoke of his spiritual commitment at the solemn assembly, President Lee was asked to speak. His comments included the same admonition he made in Mesa the day previously: "I took occasion to urge that they respect the position and not the person, in order for my next door neighbors to 'comfortably' accept me in my calling as the President of the Church."

Back home in Salt Lake City President Lee consented to another interview by a newspaper reporter, representing the United Press International. Meeting in his small, conservatively furnished office in the administration building of the Church, President Lee, at seventy-three years of age, was described by the reporter as a man who looked and acted like a man in his fifties or sixties.

Inevitably the most piercing question of the day emerged in the interview as the reporter asked why the Mormon Church prohibited blacks from holding the priesthood—a practice that brought protest and criticism to the Church throughout the world. In answer President Lee gave the most positive reply yet announced to this vexing question, predicting that the Church would some day grant that privilege to blacks. His statement, published on November 16, 1972 by the UPI, was: "It's only a matter of time before the black achieves full status in the Church. We must believe in the justice of God. The black will achieve full status, we're just waiting for that time."

The article went on to clearly indicate that any change in the policy of the Church toward the black must come in the form of revelation, or divine communication from God to the President of the Church. President Lee ended this discussion with this classic statement: "Our doctrine towards blacks cannot be explained in abstract terms. If one believes in revelation, then the reason is clear; if he doesn't, then there is no adequate explanation."

The business of the over 3-million-member Church rolled on under the watchful stewardship of this dynamic prophet, seer, and revelator. This included giving tentative approval for a chapel and commercial building in Tokyo, Japan, to be constructed on a most expensive piece of property purchased earlier by the Church.

In the monthly temple meeting President Lee took occasion to ask the new leadership of the Melchizedek Priesthood-MIA to speak. The result was most pleasing and inspirational, as he recorded it:

> In the temple meeting with all the General Authorities present with the exception of those ill, we enjoyed one of the most unusual spiritual experiences that seemed to have radiated into the souls of everyone. A most unusual testimony was borne by Bishop Vaughn J. Featherstone, whose early family life provided little to uplift him, and yet he, through great personal effort and determination, became one of the chief executives of the Albertson food chain, and now a General Authority of the Church. All of us had difficulty restraining our tears as we listened to this great man as he laid his soul bare to us.

When President Lee was shown the finished movie film of his admonition to the Saints regarding the subject of home and family, which had been filmed in the living room of his own home, his mind began to probe other forms of effectively teaching the Saints. Already this film, intended for all stake conferences in early 1973, was programmed for use in all stakes and missions with translations in seventeen different languages. These experiences impressed on President Lee at this early date the possibilities of using videotape communications in regional meetings and instructional programs, thereby avoiding the mounting burden of travel throughout the world by general board members from the auxiliary organizations. While the equipment costs would be great, they would be offset by immense savings on travel, reasoned President Lee, and its application in seminary and institute classrooms would be unlimited. His active mind was ever pioneering new ideas.

One adaptation President Lee made with the traditional Christmas observance for Church employees remained thereafter as the practice for many years. He changed the plan for the usual Christmas dinner for Church employees to a devotional meeting in the Salt Lake Tabernacle. On this first event, in 1972, three thousand persons were in attendance to hear the First Presidency speak. This was followed by a two-night reception in the foyer of the then new Church Office Building, where five thousand employees and partners came to personally shake hands with members of the First Presidency. The innovation was declared a success in President Lee's words: "While it was a strain on us, as the Presidency and our wives, the great feeling of unity and fellowship were ample compensation."

UNUSUAL PRIESTHOOD BLESSINGS

As with all other periods of his life, President Lee continued to exercise his seemingly unlimited faith for the purpose of bringing peace, happiness, and health to those who were suffering. Several interesting incidents occurred at the close of 1972.

A widow of a deceased Apostle came to the President to ask if he would give a blessing to her son-in-law who was out of work. Another somewhat "different" request came from a sister in Wyoming who sent a handkerchief and requested President Lee to bless it and return it to her so that she could place it over her husband's eyes. She had faith that his failing eyesight could be thus corrected and that through faith he would be made well. President Lee told her that he knew of no such ordinance, but with that kind of faith they would certainly be rewarded.

On December 19, President Lee received a letter from Mrs. Leora Johnson of Burley, Idaho, a faithful mother of a seventeen-year-old daughter, her seventh child, who had just been operated on for what was believed to be Hodgkin's disease, a form of fatal cancer. The daughter, Norma, was then facing a further abdominal spleen operation and cobalt radiation treatments. In this letter the mother explained that her daughter felt that if she could just shake the hand of the President of the Church (not even asking for a blessing), or receive a letter from the prophet, that her faith was sufficient that further surgery would be unnecessary.

President Lee responded by inviting the Johnson family to come to his office. He recorded in his journal the circumstances of their coming on December 27:

> A lovely family by the name of Johnson drove all the way from Burley, Idaho, to bring their seventeen-year-old daughter with the faith that this beautiful child, if she could but shake hands with the President of the Church, could be made well. She is suffering from Hodgkin's disease in its advanced stages. The roads were hazardous

from the ice and snow. Surely such faith will be rewarded. I gave
her a blessing.

In a follow-up letter to President Lee, received on January 17,
1973, Norma Johnson explained the results of that blessing.

> I would like to tell you something which happened to me after we
> left your office. You see, I was very tired after traveling all morning
> and all, so after we had eaten, we went to a motel. I lay down in the
> bed and took a nap. Then I awakened and wasn't awake enough to
> think clearly. I pushed myself up into a sitting position with my
> right hand. That may not sound unusual, but when I had my
> operation they cut through all the muscles to my shoulder, and not
> only was it painful to try to move and use it, but it just wouldn't
> work. As I sat there I realized I hadn't been able to do that before.
> Then I started moving it around to see how much movement I had.
> I found I could move it any way I could move my other shoulder.
> And it didn't hurt, either!
>
> It was really hard to believe at first and I just sat and thought
> about it for a minute. Then, I remembered a phrase in the blessing
> you gave to me. It said something like all my nerves and muscles
> would be connected and returned to their normal functions.
>
> I really felt wonderful. I really do love you and the Lord. You're
> both so wonderful to those of us who are weak and need help.

President Lee answered the glorious news in the above letter
with a reply to Norma's parents, which demonstrates how he typically extended himself to see that those receiving blessings continue to find favor with the merciful God, who watches over the
faithful.

> I was so pleased to receive your letter. I had concern about the
> travel conditions following the hazardous trip you made to Salt Lake
> City, knowing that the roads could be worse upon your return. I
> assure you that I joined with you in praying that the Lord would see
> you safely home. Apparently he heard our prayers.
>
> It was so reassuring to hear your testimony about Norma's
> returning strength. Surely the faith of that sweet, little girl will be
> rewarded in the Lord's own way and in his own time. Tell her to
> keep up her faith and her prayers and they will avail her much in
> support of the blessings of the priesthood which she has received.
>
> You may tell her that we had her name on our prayer roll in the
> temple this last Thursday, where the First Presidency and the
> Twelve have their regular meeting in the council room of the
> temple. Here, around the altar, we offered a special prayer for her.

To Norma, President Lee directed a personal letter:

Yes, my dear girl, the day of miracles is not past. The same kind Heavenly Father sends through his priesthood the powers of healing to those who have faith in him and in the sacred ordinances by which he has granted special favors to those who are worthy, like yourself.

I am not surprised at your testimony. I had a good feeling after you left here and as I told you I was confident your faith would be rewarded. Yes, I will await with interest further word from you, but I want you to know that we have you in our prayers constantly as your name is now on our prayer roll in the council room where we have a special prayer circle when the Presidency and the Twelve meet each Thursday.

YEAR-END MEDITATIONS

The musings and ponderings of the President of the Church on the last day of 1972 were recorded in his private journal:

Without doubt this year has been the most momentous year of my life, with the death of President Joseph Fielding Smith and the reorganization of the First Presidency. Already I am looking ahead and seeking for solutions and answers from spiritual sources. The Lord will point the way to give direction and instruction to our Saints in all the world, without the necessity of having our general auxiliary boards continuing to make their worldwide travel, which has about reached a point that we must now begin to utilize the modern techniques which have been developed by industrial concerns. We must devise other ways to do the work of training by eliminating the extreme travel, about which some of our leaders are beginning to raise a warning flag. I am certain I have received, in some measure, a partial answer, and with the aid of the great leaders, and under divine guidance, a way will be found.

Thus, 1972 was closed, completing the first six months of the ministry of Harold B. Lee as President of the Lord's church on earth.

1973. Seeds were sown for the Watergate scandal, which would topple President Nixon from office. Overextension of credit and debt financing brought promise of fiscal problems ahead for New York and other big cities. The price of oil quadrupled, and Syria and other Arab states put pressure on Saudi Arabia to use its new wealth against Israel. Millions of Americans were bound together watching Archie Bunker and "All in the Family," the top-rated television show.

CHAPTER 29

Another "Brief but Shining Moment"

Interesting projects continued to develop and concerns mounted as President Lee moved further into his leadership role as the prophet, seer, and revelator of the Lord's church.

He was pleased with the recognition of the Church as one of the world's major religions as indicated by a request made by the Columbia Broadcasting System to record a statement for television relative to the ending of the United States' participation in the Vietnam War, and also about the position of the Church on the decision of the United States Supreme Court to nullify all anti-abortion laws in the individual states. The commentary was released on a Sunday morning world religion broadcast and featured similar statements from the Catholic Church, the Jewish religion, and the Lutheran churches, as well as a spokesman from a national women's organization. President Lee's answers placed the LDS Church closest to the Catholics on the abortion question.

Negotiations were pursued leading to the development of new visitors' centers on Temple Square, in Salt Lake City, at the Washington Temple, and at a project in Jerusalem. A representative of the Council of Churches came in January 1973 to discuss the proposals for a "meditation park" on the Mount of Olives in Jerusalem, which project was being promoted by Mayor Teddy Kollek of Jerusalem.

By February 1, President Lee also was moving toward the solution to the problem of excessive travel required to teach new leaders in the expanding Church. He learned from Jim Conkling and Elder Thomas S. Monson that some new recording developments were just coming on the market which held promise of providing the answers to the Church's communication needs, and which would be marketed at lesser expense than videotapes. He immediately dispatched Elders Monson, Neal A. Maxwell, and Thomas Fyans to see a demonstration of the products in Los Angeles, California.

President Lee's confident administrative style permitted him to trust his associates. It was not necessary for him to build a rigid dictatorship to maintain control of the decision-making processes within Church administration. Instead, he favored placing responsibility on leaders and then holding them accountable for their stewardship.

This openness of trust is illustrated by a situation which came to his attention in early 1973, when a department managing director came to discuss some business with him. From this interview President Lee discerned that this director's immediate superiors were holding the supervisory reins so firmly that he and others felt restricted in their assignments. They did not feel free to act as their titles indicated that they should perform. President Lee determined that he would interview those leaders to help loosen the controls and allow more independence for men in managerial roles at the Church headquarters.

One month later President Lee dealt with the problem of overreaching managing directors. When all the General Authorities were assembled for their monthly meeting, President Lee took occasion to repeat again the role of General Authorities in working with those who were not General Authorities. He urged them to remain in the role of a "coach" (his favorite and familiar simile for comparison), and not become the "quarterback on the field." As he was speaking, a flash of inspiration prompted him to quote from Doctrine and Covenants 107:99, "Now let every man learn his duty, and to act in the office in which he is appointed, in all diligence." President Lee emphasized the meaning of the word *let* in his inspired, uncommon interpretation. To impress his point he defined it to mean to allow each man the freedom to act in his office and calling, and to restrain from meddling or interfering in his performance of duty. President Lee advocated instead that the leaders teach "correct principles," as the Prophet Joseph urged, so that those who follow can learn to govern themselves. This philosophy of management became another hallmark of President Lee's leadership.

At this same February temple meeting, preliminary reports from the Melchizedek Priesthood MIA management team were given by Elders James E. Faust, Marion D. Hanks, and L. Tom Perry. Their plans relative to the beginning of the activities among the eighteen- to twenty-five-year-old age group and the proposals for those persons twenty-six years of age and over were enthusiastically endorsed. President Lee described this meeting as one in which "we had a great outpouring of spiritual refreshment."

On February 7, 1973, a multi-million-dollar addition to the library at Brigham Young University was approved with student and private contributions promised to augment general Church funds. This library was later to bear the official name of the Harold B. Lee Brigham Young University Library.

An unusual dinner meeting in the Lion House became a memorable event, when 225 young adults of the Olympus Stake came to honor their outgoing stake president, Jack H. Goaslind, Jr., who then was called to be a counselor in the presidency of the Young Men's Mutual Improvement Association. Sister Lee spoke first at this meeting, and before President Lee began his address the stake leaders presented him with a replica of the famed Michelangelo sculptured figure of Moses. This gave President Lee a theme text for his remarks, and he later wrote that it "led me to some spiritual expressions that were beyond anything I had contemplated. There seemed to be an unusual spiritual outpouring." For President Lee, however, this was not such an uncommon circumstance; he often was led by the Holy Spirit while he was sermonizing.

No amount of business or problems at home seemed to keep President Lee away from his favorite practice of teaching the departing missionaries in the temple. Even on a holiday in

Dedication of the Harold B. Lee Library at Brigham Young University, 1974: (left to right) Freda Joan Lee, Helen Lee Goates, Marion G. Romney, Dallin H. Oaks

February 1973, when the Church offices were officially closed, President Lee went to the temple for the usual question-and-answer session with the missionaries leaving for their missions.

The monthly meeting in the temple, which President Lee had inaugurated to keep all General Authorities informed, now had become an established, regular meeting. At that meeting on the first day of March 1973, President Lee learned that Elder Gordon B. Hinckley was assigned to a youth conference to be held in Johannesburg, South Africa. This gave him the idea that following such a conference they both might go to Brazil and explore the possibility of locating a temple site there. This was the initial development of the small temple concept for distant places, South America being the first desired site, which would look to the future pressing need for bringing temples closer to the increasing membership of the Church. This dream culminated with the dedication of the São Paulo, Brazil, Temple on October 30, 1978.

President Lee received something of a hero's welcome when he, his wife, and his secretary, Arthur Haycock, returned "back home" to Idaho on March 9, 1973. The occasion was a speaking request from the president of the Idaho State University student stake. At the ramp of the plane he was met by city, county, and state officials who presented him with an inscribed medal from the governor of Idaho. It was presented by one of the Idaho State Supreme Court justices. In the afternoon he spoke to a standing-room-only audience in a stake center, from which the address was broadcast by television and radio into two other buildings. President Lee summarized this event by saying: "While it was a pressure-packed experience, it was something of a homecoming for me, an Idaho native, now 'coming home' again."

During the month of March 1973, President Lee underwent extensive treatment to cure a chronic lung infection. He had suffered from a lingering cough and the presence of dark-colored mucus. A bronchoscopy was performed in the hospital. An intensive physical therapy program continued for a week in the hospital and after he returned home. It was conducted three times a day, from morning until late evening. Heavy medicinal support augmented the physical therapy. Through it all President Lee good-naturedly endeavored to maintain contact with his Brethren at the Church Office Building, though the hectic period of treatment made it most difficult. He wrote, "With the aid of my faithful Arthur Haycock, my son-in-law Brent, and plus Joan's untiring help, I have managed to keep meeting my responsibilities."

President Lee's seventy-fourth birthday, on March 28, 1973, which was to be his last, found him almost smothered by gifts, cards, letters, and bundles of Primary children's personalized expressions of love. The latter was no doubt stimulated by a calendar picturing a montage of President Lee's life, which appeared in the *Friend* magazine. He also took time on his birthday to perform a marriage for Kent Wirthlin Parker—a grandson of his dear friend, the late Bishop Joseph L. Wirthlin—and his bride, Pat Cracroft.

On the Sunday before the birthday, his daughter Helen invited all of President Lee's entire family for a home night to honor their grandfather. On this occasion each family member expressed his feelings about the contributions Harold B. Lee had made to him or her during the growing-up years. "It was a delightful occasion," wrote President Lee in his journal that night.

In April it was time for another general conference and the General Authorities assembled again in their pre-conference temple meeting where, as President Lee described it, "a wonderful outpouring of the Spirit was in great abundance." Following this meeting, President Lee recorded an Easter message on the Resurrection to be released on April 22 during the Tabernacle Choir broadcast.

The pre-conference events started with President Lee delivering the keynote addess as the Regional Representatives and Mission Representatives of the Twelve and the Seventies met in their seminar, which was held for the first time in the auditorium of the new Church Office Building.

On April 6, 1973, the first general session of the 143d Annual General Conference of the Church began. Explaining the inspiration that had come to him to counsel the Saints at this time, President Lee said in his opening address in the Salt Lake Tabernacle: "Today we are witnessing the demonstration of the Lord's hand even in the midst of his Saints, the members of the Church. Never in this dispensation, and perhaps never before in any single period, has there been such a feeling of urgency among the members of this church as today. Her boundaries are being enlarged; her stakes are being strengthened."

President Lee noted that in the early days of the Church the Lord had appointed specific gathering places, but now, in concurrence with the teachings of Elder Bruce R. McConkie at the Mexico City area conference, President Lee instructed that, with the Church membership distributed over the earth in seventy-eight countries and the gospel being taught in seventeen different languages, the gathering place for the Saints was in their own native countries. Rather than move to a "Utah Zion," they must make their homes and local stakes the places of refuge and strength by keeping the commandments of God. The Church would reach out to stakes throughout the world.

On Sunday afternoon, April 8, 1973, President Lee rose to give his concluding remarks after a marvelous and inspirational general conference:

> I believe I have never known when the General Authorities have so completely covered the various areas where we have had great concern.
>
> If you want to know what the Lord has for this people at the present time, I would admonish you to get and read the discourses

that have been delivered at this conference, for what these Brethren have spoken by the power of the Holy Ghost is the mind of the Lord, the will of the Lord, the voice of the Lord, and the power of God unto salvation. I am sure all who have listened, if they have been in tune, have felt the sincerity and the deep conviction from those who have spoken so appropriately and so effectively.

President Lee concluded his teachings at this conference with his powerful testimony and blessing:

And so I come to you today with no shadow of doubting in my mind that I know the reality of the person who is presiding over this church, our Lord and Master, Jesus Christ. I know that he is. I know that he is closer to us than many times we have any idea. They are not an absentee Father and Lord. They are concerned about us, helping to prepare us for the advent of the Savior, whose coming certainly isn't too far away because of the signs that are becoming apparent.

All you need to do is to read the scriptures, particularly the inspired translation of Matthew, the 24th chapter, found in the writings of Joseph Smith in the Pearl of Great Price, where the Lord told his disciples to stand in holy places and be not moved, for he comes quickly, but no man knows that hour nor the day. That is the preparation.

Go home now to your people, I pray you, and say as did Joshua of old: "as for me and my house, we will serve the Lord" (Joshua 24:15). Teach your families in your family home evening, teach them to keep the commandments of God, for therein is our only safety in these days. If they will do that, the powers of the Almighty will descend upon them as the dews from heaven, and the Holy Ghost will be theirs. That can be our guide, and that kind of Spirit shall guide us and direct us to his holy home.

And so, as it is my privilege to do, I give you faithful members of the Church everywhere my blessing. God bless you, take care of you, preserve you as you travel home so that there may be no accident or no untoward experience. Take to your people out in the far reaches the feeling of love that we have for all of them; and indeed, as the missionaries go out, that love extends not only to those of our Father's children who are already members of the Church, but those who are our Father's children to whom he would have us bring the gospel of truth; make them also to enjoy all the blessings that we now have.

May the Lord help us so to understand and do, and fill our stations, and not be found wanting in the day of judgment that we have not done all we know how to do to advance his work in righteousness, I humbly pray in the name of the Lord Jesus Christ. Amen.

President Lee sensed that this testimony and blessing had been directed by the Spirit, for he wrote in his journal "that it seemed to have lifted me spiritually beyond my natural self and made me know that that which I felt was heaven sent."

The Tabernacle Choir closed the conference with a song which held enormous sentiment for President Lee, titled "The Link Divine." It was sung at the funerals of both his wife Fern and his daughter Maurine. He confided in his diary: "I was so emotionally moved by the music, as well as by the spiritual experience of my remarks, that I had difficulty controlling my emotions."

The weekend after general conference found President and Sister Lee and Arthur Haycock in New York City to participate in a press conference held at the famous Lincoln Center to announce the official commencement of construction on a new stake and two-ward facility in a thirty-six-story apartment house building complex which the Church was erecting on Manhattan Island.

Their first day in New York, April 13, began with a breakfast interview with Edward B. Fiske, religion editor of *The New York Times*. It was hoped that this visit would result in a more favorable reporting by the *Times*. After that President Lee met with two hundred missionaries in the Manhattan Ward chapel, and later in the evening, with the members of the New York Stake to explain the details of the new building plans as they affected those Saints.

The press conference was held in the Chorus Room of the Philharmonic Hall, across the street from the site of the new Church construction. In attendance were sixty-two representatives of radio and television stations, newspapers, magazines, and wire services. Emil Fetzer, Church architect, and Fred A. Baker, manager of the Church's Department of Physical Facilities spoke and unveiled an architect's rendering, in color, of the proposed building. President Lee explained to the journalists the significance of the Church coming to the largest city of the world with a major building program. At the end of the conference Wendell J. Ashton declared: "This was really a historic day for the Church in New York City."

The New York City weekend concluded with President Lee dedicating a newly completed stake and ward building for the New Jersey Central Stake. He returned home somewhat weary, but was not deterred from meeting the next day with 195 outgoing missionaries in the Salt Lake Temple for the usual question-and-answer session.

The next weekend was spent at home attending his own Emigration Stake conference. The Lees were entertained for Sunday dinner at his daughter Helen's home. He wrote true words in his journal respecting this family time when he stated, "This seems to be the only time we get to see much of our family anymore because of the varied activities and our intense schedule."

A most significant new idea was germinating in the mind of President Lee as he called Neal A. Maxwell, Church Commissioner of Education, to consult with him on Monday, April 23, 1973. The topic of conversation was the suggestion that there should be a "single voice" in the preparation and the production of teaching and training materials if the Church was to properly correlate its efforts in achieving desired educational objectives. The idea was favorably accepted. President Lee wrote: "This seems to be, in light of experience, much needed to avoid the overlapping and confusion now in existence." From this conceptual beginning came later the powerful, controlling Correlation Department of the Church.

On Sunday, April 29, 1973, President and Sister Lee were again away for a Young Adult area conference, this time in Long Beach, California. More than fourteen thousand young members of the Church from Southern California assembled within two hundred yards of the Pacific Ocean in the Pacific Terrace Center, the largest indoor auditorium in the area. So great was the interest in this conference that each attendee had to be admitted by ticket, and it was surmised by the sponsoring seminaries and institutes of religion and the stakes of Southern California that fifty thousand could have been assembled under similar circumstances in the Rose Bowl at Pasadena, California.

President Lee spoke of sanctification, which produces the right to "see Him, for He will unveil His face unto you," and said that the laws and ordinances of the Lord are the way by which we are purified and made holy. Continuing this thought he added: "Keeping every law that the Lord has given us is one step closer to receiving the right to enter one day into the presence of the Lord. The most important of all the commandments of God is that one that you're having the most difficulty keeping today."

The sermon was an intensive scriptural study. President Lee believed that the youth of the Church were hungering for the gospel truths. He taught them how to find Christ and gave them his powerful witness that here was the sure ground on which they could build happiness. His final admonition was: "You keep your eye on him whom the Lord calls, and I say to you now, knowing that I stand in that position, that you don't need to worry about the President of the Church ever leading people astray, because the Lord would remove him out of his place before he'd allow the President to lead his children astray."

Reaction from the young people attending the conference was most positive. They felt inspired, uplifted and blessed to have been able to hear President and Sister Lee, according to a letter of gratitude from Karl S. Farnsworth, Coordinator of the Church Educational System.

A glimpse into how President Lee's mind approached his opportunities to teach the youth of the Church is disclosed in a letter written May 15, 1973, to Bishop Gaylen R. Jackson, bishop of the Lompoc Ward, Santa Maria Stake, California. Bishop Jackson had praised President Lee's address and spirit at the Long Beach conference. In reply President Lee wrote: "I am always hopeful that when young people come needing and wanting so much, that I am able to respond to their needs. Your kind letter and comments have given me encouragement that our efforts have been fruitful."

Varied Concerns and Activities

President and Sister Lee, and Arthur Haycock and his wife, Maurine, then spent a few days vacationing at the Church's Laguna Beach, California, home. President Lee wrote in his journal, "This provided me a much needed rest from the pressures, and a time to catch up on matters long delayed at the office." He spent most of the day Monday dictating correspondence to his secretary and just trying to relax and to be free from the "worries which had troubled me."

President Lee's pleasant hiatus was disturbed, however, when he turned on the television that historic day of May 1, 1973, and became aware of the broad coverage given the Watergate scandal, which involved the president of the United States. He was greatly distressed by the continuing investigation of the "bugging" of the Democratic headquarters by overzealous Republican campaign managers. He heard President Richard Nixon give a lengthy national radio and television broadcast denying any personal involvement "by knowledge of or any effort to cover up" such activities. It was obvious, however, that every effort would be made to prove otherwise, and rumors of threatened impeachment were lurking should the stories be proven true. President Lee noted that ten of President Nixon's aides were summarily dismissed or had voluntarily resigned, and one, John H. Dean, was prepared to make new charges if granted personal immunity by the Senate Investigating Committee.

The worries on the mind of President Lee were not confined to Church and national affairs. Returning home for a quiet weekend President Lee spent much of his Sunday dictating letters to some of his grandsons, about whom he was concerned.

On Friday, May 4, 1973, all the General Authorities were again called to meet with the First Presidency in their monthly temple meeting. Of this session President Lee wrote: "As usual, there was a great spiritual outpouring, with a highlight being a testimony of Marion D. Hanks concerning his new work in the Melchizedek Priesthood-MIA."

President Lee called on Elder Gordon B. Hinckley to explain to all the Brethren the plan of the First Presidency to go forward with an "experimental" model of a small, stake-center-sized type of building which would serve as a temple in the Latin-American countries, nearer to the people than the larger, existing temples. He then assigned Elder Hinckley and Elder O. Leslie Stone to go to Europe and to South Africa, instructing Elder Hinckley to return home by way of Brazil, where a search could be made near the São Paulo area for a site where one of these new temples might be constructed.

Later this same day President Lee was surprised by a request for an immediate television interview with a team of reporters from the National Broadcasting Company, who had come to Salt Lake City for the purpose of preparing a documentary on the Church to be released in the fall of 1973. For an hour and a half President Lee sat before the brightly lighted cameras and responded to numerous questions from Tom Pettit, the interviewer, and head of the seven-member news team. The penetrating questions covered many Church doctrines. Without the aid of his scriptures or notes, President Lee was forced to depend on his memory of doctrine and history, but his performance brought praise and sincere admiration for his remarkable ability to perform so well without notice or preparation.

On the weekend President Lee spent all day Saturday reviewing an avalanche of divorce clearances, restorations, and cancellations of sealings, which duty he thought was indicative of the times and showed a weakening of morals and an acceleration of sin and transgressions moving in upon the Latter-day Saints, who must live in this wicked world. This exercise was repeated on many weekends and always brought the President depression and occasionally even physical distress as he bore the burdens of the Saints.

The press interviews with this gifted and articulate President of the Church continued, the next being with James Reston, columnist and vice-president of *The New York Times,* who was in Salt Lake City to deliver the commencement address at the graduation exercises of the University of Utah on June 2, 1973. Mr. Reston very adroitly asked questions relating to how the Church was meeting various problems—with youth, missionary methods, welfare program, and finances—and President Lee, just as adroitly, moderated the discussion around the table to include President Marion G. Romney, Elder Mark E. Petersen, and Wendell Ashton, who had arranged the interview.

While President Lee was most interested in worldwide progress and growth in the Church, he was not willing that this expansion occur until it was totally justifiable. The questionable availability of leaders to support a major expansion in Brazil, and political ramifications of a too rapid expansion in Korea, caused President Lee to hold up these ambitious developments in early June 1973.

The same caution was exercised by President Lee when one week later he turned around proposals which would place two of each stake's four quarterly conferences in 1974 under the direction of Regional Representatives of the Twelve. President Lee's reasoning was expressed in his diary as follows:

> I called attention to the fact that this was wrong because of the time these volunteer, unpaid brethren would be called away from their families and their businesses, and also that they were not "line officers" in the priesthood line of authority. This brought out the fact that where the General Authorities could not go, then stake presidents must be assigned to conduct their own conferences. Therefore, no stakes should be created until there are presidents competent enough for such a responsibility. This seemed to bring some realistic thinking into the minds of some Brethren who seem-

ingly are bent upon speeding new stakes without thorough consideration of their readiness to take over full responsibility in the event of fewer visits from General Authorities due to political restrictions or war conditions.

On June 20, 1973, the First Presidency commenced their three-day open house celebrating the completion of the new Church Office Building, which dominated the downtown skyline of Salt Lake City. At twenty-eight stories it was the tallest office building in Utah. Business and community leaders were invited on the first night, and all three members of the first Presidency and their wives were in the reception line, along with other General Authorities of the Church. President Lee's comments on this experience were: "While these nights were very tiring they seemed to provide a gesture of goodwill to our non-Church fraternities. We have received many expressions of appreciation and commendation."

Lord Thomson of Fleet (London, England), who had so graciously hosted President Lee in March 1972 on that historic trip, came to visit Salt Lake City and the leadership of the Church. On June 23, 1973, the General Authorities and their wives were hosts to him and his son, Kenneth. They were guests at a mountain restaurant, as Church officials tried to reciprocate for the gracious hospitality extended to President Lee in London, when they were privileged to meet a number of the top political, business, and religious leaders of England.

The Thomsons attended the MIA June conference general sessions and the Church's dance festival at the University of Utah stadium. On the following day, Elders Gordon B. Hinckley and Marvin J. Ashton took their guests to Lake Powell for a boating day, hosted by Bishop Robert Rice. There, under the evening stars, they held a "family home evening." Lord Thomson's son, Kenneth, greatly impressed the Brethren. He indicated that he wanted to return next year with his wife and sixteen-year-old daughter, whom he hoped would enroll at Brigham Young University.

CHAPTER 30

A Historical Reorganization from the Lord

At the MIA June Conference of 1973, nearly thirteen thousand leaders and officers of the Melchizedek and Aaronic Priesthood MIAs from throughout the Church met in Salt Lake City to learn their new assignments and responsibilities. Announcements had been made by the First Presidency during the previous November regarding the MIAs' planned merger into the existing priesthood leadership structure, and the time had come to put those plans into action.

This reorganization was actually another in a series of changes in the Church's youth program which, under President Lee's direction, gradually moved the priesthood into the major leadership role previously held by auxiliary management. For example, in December 1970 the Aaronic Priesthood and the YMMIA teachers were instructed to serve simultaneously in both organizations, which began the unification between priesthood and auxiliaries.

This conference became a history-making event as the newly constituted Aaronic Priesthood and the Melchizedek Priesthood MIA was presented to the leaders, thus launching a new stage of priesthood leadership over the youth and the older single membership of the Church.

The June conference address of Ruth Hardy Funk, general president of the Aaronic Priesthood MIA Young Women, outlined the process by which this new adaptation came into being:

> I recall a unique experience that was granted the general presidencies of the Aaronic Priesthood MIA when, on Thursday, March

29, we were invited to share a celestial hour with the Brethren in their weekly temple meeting at which all of the General Authorities were in attendance. At the time we were called, President Lee referred to the direction and change of the MIA program, as it now would become the Aaronic Priesthood MIA, as the most significant change I would see in my lifetime as far as the organization of the Church is concerned. After days and months, I am beginning to know in just a small way this enormous significance, which I am sure will grow and grow and encompass all the priesthood programs of the Church.

After weeks of prayerful pondering with our Presiding Bishopric, appraising considered suggestions by our board, after deep deliberation by the Correlation Committee, and exact scrutiny by members of the Twelve Apostles acting as advisers for the curriculum of the Aaronic Priesthood MIA, and finally after careful review by the First Presidency, the proposed organization was refined and made ready by this divine process to be presented in the temple. Our joy was great.

The day prior to this appointed hour, President Lee extended through the Presiding Bishop an invitation to the joint presidencies to be in attendance at the temple meeting when the proposal would be presented to the governing body of the Church. This would include us as women. The significance of this occasion was reinforced when President Lee said that according to his knowledge this was the first time in the history of the Church that any women had been invited to be in attendance at this special meeting.

The formality, the order, the spirit, the tremendous feeling of power, the strength of the priesthood manifest, and the sacredness of the entire setting were almost overwhelming. President Lee commented on the historical nature of our being there and then asked us to stand and be introduced individually.

Following Bishop Victor L. Brown's presentation and the discussion that followed, at which he initiated a response from the women present, a vote was called for, after which President Lee assured us of the support of everyone in the room. Official approval was thus made for the Aaronic Priesthood MIA.

In this holy setting in the company of these Brethren, prompted by President Lee's great consideration for the young women of the Church in allowing us to come, we were allowed to witness the process whereby all matters and all programs of the Church become official.

A simultaneous program to reach out to the single adults in the Church who are eighteen years of age and older was announced as the Melchizedek Priesthood MIA. This organization was to correlate Church activities that would meet the needs and bless the lives of these sometimes forgotten individuals in a couple-oriented society. President Lee expressed his immense concern for these single members and had earlier said to them:

> Some of you do not now have a companion in your home. Some of you have lost your wife or husband, or you may not yet have found a companion. In your ranks are some of the noblest members of the Church—faithful, valiant, striving to live the Lord's commandments, to help build the kingdom on earth, and to serve your fellowmen.
>
> Life holds so much for you. . . . The Church offers so much opportunity for you to help souls, beginning with your own, to find the joy of eternal life. (*Strengthening the Home* [pamphlet].)

In words of absolute certainty President Lee made public his positive declaration that these revised programs were the product of revelation from the Lord. Speaking at the June Conference in the Salt Lake Tabernacle, President Lee said: "During the year that has passed, we have pondered, we have prayed, we have searched, and now we come with a declaration to all of you that you may know with a certainty that defies all doubts that this which you have witnessed, this which you have heard, has been divinely inspired."

Quoting from Doctrine and Covenants 59:21–23, which states that nothing offends God so much as to confess not his hand in all things, and noting the promise that the worker of righteousness will receive God's reward, President Lee stated his position:

> I choose not to offend God by claiming that all of this has come by the will of men. I confess with all my soul that these things are of the Lord, and they have come through righteousness, through prayer, and through great needs.
>
> What is that great need? During the last year I have tried to reach out to the youth at several youth conferences. From one of those youth conferences I received from a member of the stake presidency a note that suggests something that the world needs greatly.
>
> He said: "One recently reactivated young man of about fifteen years said in our fast and testimony meeting, 'President Lee must have known that there was lots of wickedness and evil in this area and that the kids here were in trouble, and just to think that he loves us enough to come all this way just to help us.' "
>
> If it means nothing more to the youth, to the children, to those who are young adults, and those who are over those ages, that all of this is to evidence a love for them that comes from the General Authorities and from your Heavenly Father, then we have yet accomplished much.

President Lee concluded his address with this reaffirmation: "You have had unraveled before your eyes an evidence of the revelations of the Almighty God in your day as he has poured out his blessings in this great step forward in building the kingdom of God."

The trend toward shifting the responsibility for youth programs to give more priesthood direction continued into the June conference one year later, in 1974, when the dissolution of the Mutual Improvement Association was announced. The Aaronic Priesthood MIA then became simply the Aaronic Priesthood and the organization for young women ages twelve to eighteen became known as Young Women; these functioned under the direct supervision of the Presiding Bishopric of the Church and under the bishop of each ward. This action released the APMIA Young Men's Presidency under Robert L. Backman, and the APMIA Presidency of Young Women, although President Ruth H. Funk, with her counselors Hortense H. Child and Ardeth G. Kapp, were resustained as the general presidency of the new Young Women's organization.

Thus ended the MIA of the Church, which traced its beginning to 1869 when President Brigham Young organized his daughters into what he called the Cooperative Retrenchment Association. An activity program for young men was organized also by Brigham Young in 1875 and named the Young Men's Mutual Improvement Association. The Cooperative Retrenchment Association became the Young Ladies Mutual Improvement Association in 1878 and the Young Women's MIA in 1934. The two auxiliaries became the Aaronic Priesthood MIA for Young Women and Young Men, under President Lee's reorganization, in 1972. The Melchizedek Priesthood program for LDS singles over the age of eighteen continued unaffected by the 1974 announcements.

The growing membership of the Church was announced at the 1973 June Conference as being contained in 244 regions, 935 total units made up of 624 stakes and 311 districts. At that time there were 44 non-English speaking stakes.

MISSION PRESIDENTS SEMINAR

Three days later at a two-day seminar for new mission presidents and their wives at the new general Church office building, it was announced that there were a total of 107 Church missions, including six new ones opening on July 1, 1973.

At the new mission presidents' seminar, President Lee was asked to provide the usual keynote address to guide the thirty-five new presidents and their wives. This he did, speaking, as he recorded in his diary, "freely, without notes, to impress matters that I felt were 'heaven-inspired.' "

President Lee's remarks centered on the spiritual guidance needed by every individual associated with missionary work, at any level. He illustrated by explaining how he applied revelation in his missionary work, declaring:

> When I ponder the lists of names submitted to me, I realize that these are not just names; they are real people, individuals, and I want to know something about them. I want to fulfill my responsibility with that same spirit of prophecy. No callings in the Church are given more careful consideration than are those for the mission field.
>
> A prospective mission president once asked me, "Do you have a department to help me get my affairs in order?" I replied, "Yes, we do. It is the Lord. If you will go to him prayerfully, and humbly, he will help you get your affairs in order." That mission president returned to tell me that I was right.

President Lee further admonished the mission presidents:

> Your work will not be judged by how many baptisms you put on the records of the Church, but by how many converts you have— how many are still active after a few years. No one is thoroughly converted until he sees the power of God resting upon this church, until he knows that Joseph Smith was a prophet of God, and that the present leadership of the Church is directed by the Lord. The new member must do his spiritual housekeeping and be prepared to receive the witness of the Spirit. After that he must work to keep his testimony alive, because it is as fragile as an orchid: it will die if he departs from gospel principles and activity in the Church.
>
> You are being sent out to teach your missionaries to convert the world. Teach them the simple principles of the gospel. And what is the gospel? The answer is found in the scriptures:
>
> "And this is my gospel—repentance and baptism by water, and then cometh the baptism of fire and the Holy Ghost, even the Comforter, which showeth all things, and teacheth the peaceable things of the kingdom. (D&C 39:6.)"

On June 27, 1973, after speaking for an hour at the mission presidents' seminar, President Lee left by plane for New York. He wanted to attend his Union Pacific Railroad director's meeting there; but first he visited with Lee Bickmore, who was convalescing from a severe illness at his home in Short Hills, New Jersey.

At the Union Pacific meeting which he felt was so important to him, he heard an oil expert from a Union Pacific subsidiary give a clear picture of conditions then confronting this country and the world, a time when the need for oil and gasoline supplies was at an all-time high.

Having been briefed on the economic and business conditions then existent, which information President Lee prized and felt important to his data bank for decision making in administering a worldwide Church, he then tried to return hastily to Salt Lake City in the hope that he could arrive before the mission presidents' seminar had adjourned. On his return flight he failed to make connections in Chicago for Salt Lake City because he received no personal courtesy from the booking airlines company. The airline was apologetic, but that didn't erase the need for seventy-four-year-old President Lee to make the long walk from one airline terminal to another without assistance. President Lee noted in his journal "that if this experience had been taking place a week earlier I could not have physically been able to carry my bag that distance." No doubt that this was the last time that the President of the Church ever traveled across country alone, and the airline companies were thereafter much more attentive.

Back in his office on July 3, 1973, President Lee found the usual accumulation of correspondence awaiting his attention, but he also had time to think back on the events of the previous year. It was on July 2, 1972, that President Joseph Fielding Smith died suddenly. President Lee wrote of his feelings after having served one year as the President of the Church: "The tremendous responsibilities that were to be then thrust upon me were little realized, but as the time passed, in retrospect now, I could never have contemplated the magnitude of problems that we were confronted with. One of the major challenges was the challenge of what to do to meet the problems of our young people who were needing guidance and direction, as young adults in a changing world."

WITH FRIENDS AND FAMILY

Amid an intense heat wave that sent Salt Lake City temperatures soaring as high as 104 degrees, the first anniversary of the current First Presidency's installation did not pass by unnoticed by other members of the Presidency. President Tanner and his wife, Sara, invited the First Presidency, along with the President of the Twelve, Spencer W. Kimball, and their wives to a dinner at their apartment. In President Lee's personal commentary describing that event there is contained a goal statement which had dominated his administration. Wrote President Lee: "It was a most delightful experience to review the unity which had developed a warm, spiritual feeling of brotherhood to bind us together with bonds more sacred than blood relationships, as we together had sought the blessings of the Lord upon his work. We have strived to unite our brethren and the Church, with the priesthood to predominate as the center and core of the Church and kingdom of God, as set forth in the revelations."

During the second week of July, there was a brief respite from duties as President and Sister Lee, with his secretary and his wife, Arthur and Maurine Haycock, took several days of rest at Laguna Beach in California. While there they again listened to the Watergate hearing, in which testimony was being given that involved the president of the United States in compromising situations.

The Lees returned on July 14 for a Lee family reunion, held in Tooele, Utah, the town where two Lee brothers first settled on arriving in the West in 1850. The Church position of President Lee had been maximally exploited to produce a crowd numbering over a thousand, resembling a stake conference assemblage in filling the Tooele Stake Center to capacity. For years previous the Lee family reunions had struggled with only modest numbers attending.

The program was carried out in such a manner as to give the Lee family a great thrust in genealogical research and temple work. A huge chart reaching around the cultural hall gave all present a chance to identify themselves with their ancestral lines. Many of those present stayed until after President Lee had spoken so that he could shake hands with them and their children. Some even handed their small children to President Lee and then snapped photographs of their progeny with the prophet. In all, President Lee was delighted with the new enthusiasm being generated in the family reunion, for he wrote, "I felt it was the most successful reunion we had ever had and that much good will result from it."

NEW YORK AND BACK

Following the late July meeting of the Union Pacific Railroad

Board in New York City, President and Sister Lee went to Rochester, New York, where Wendell J. Ashton had arranged for news media representatives to photograph and question the President at the Hill Cumorah, just prior to the opening of the annual pageant. The President and his party saw the pageant two nights from different points each night. President Lee noted great improvement in the continuity of the "New Witness for Christ in America" and likewise in the music, composed and arranged by Crawford Gates. A heavy rain fell an hour before the performance one night, but none fell during the pageant.

Personal appearances at the pageant were demanding. One day before the pageant President Lee met in the Sacred Grove, where the Prophet Joseph's first vision took place, with about one thousand participants in the pageant and with the missionaries. On the Sunday morning of July 29, President Lee spoke to about ten thousand persons assembled on improvised seats at the base of the Hill Cumorah. Again that evening at a sacrament meeting in the Rochester Second Ward chapel, seven hundred members of the pageant cast and the area missionaries came to hear the President of the Church. By now, and with the constant greeting of the crowds who surrounded him as he moved from place to place, President Lee's voice had begun to show the strain, and a hoarseness developed that made his speech difficult. After a restless night he was the guest of the Eastman Kodak Company on a tour of their facilities before returning home to Salt Lake City.

The first Sunday of August found President Lee at home in Salt Lake City and responding to an invitation from President Francis M. Gibbons, the president of the Bonneville Stake and "our faithful secretary and administrative assistant to the First Presidency." The setting was the annual Bonneville Stake's sunset services on the grounds of the Garden Park Ward. There was such a large crowd, estimated at 2,100 people, that many were standing; young people were on the adjoining rooftops, and some were even perched in surrounding trees. Music was furnished by the Bonneville Stake Symphony Orchestra and Chorus under the direction of Harold Gottfredson, and was superb, according to President Lee, who also praised the audience by reporting, "never was there better attention."

The message was one of patriotism, as President Lee explained how the Saints might save the Constitution of the United States, if that tragic day was to come. President Lee's summary in his diary follows:

I concluded by calling attention to the prophecy of Joseph Smith that "the constitution would hang as by a thread." I then pointed out that the basic principles of the three separate and independent branches of government were being threatened in the demands of the present Senate investigation. I then read a statement of President J. Reuben Clark, Jr., pointing this out that if either the executive, the legislative, or the judicial were to presume to make the law, enforce it, and then pass judgment, we would approach tyranny. At least the audience heard and listened to this last statement. I finally said that if the basic principles laid down in the Constitution were to be threatened, as is now a possibility, that we might come to [such] a time as when Abraham bargained with the Lord to save Sodom and Gomorrah from destruction, if he could find some righteous souls. Similarly, if such a downfall of the Constitution were imminent, the righteousness of this people might again importune the Almighty to save it because of their pleadings.

Into this busy mixture of business, development of the Church's administration, pressures from family, and the constant demands of the Saints, President Lee never overlooked the opportunities to do his personal missionary work. An interesting experience developed out of the regular monthly board meeting of the Bonneville International Corporation on August 10, 1973. President Lee recorded the event in his diary as follows:

Following the meeting Lloyd Cooney, station manager of our KIRO radio and television station [Seattle], and I continued a discussion we have been having on religion in an effort to get him baptized. His wife, daughter, and two sons are members, but he has delayed until he received a testimony of the truths of the gospel. During our interview I reviewed the process by which one may know when, beyond his reasoning, he feels in his heart that it is true. Then, I said, the Spirit is conveying that witness. He then told me he was ready and his first thought was to have me baptize him, and to have Tony Eyring confirm him a member of the Church. I readily agreed, but then related the experience of the Grimm family of Tooele, Utah, when Pete was baptized by his son. This put into his mind the thought that this would be a great experience to share with his family, also. A few days after his return home he called to say that one of his sons was to baptize him and the other confirm him that same evening. He seemed to have a tone of great joy in his voice. I told him that when he had been in the Church a year that I would be delighted to perform the sealing in the temple for him and his family, perhaps at the time one of his sons was to be married.

Memories of his boyhood missionary days in Denver, Colorado, later resurfaced when President Lee spoke at the funeral services for Willis J. Woodbury on August 13, 1973. Elder Woodbury was Harold B. Lee's first missionary companion in the Western States Mission in 1920. Being a cello player, Elder Woodbury would often offer to play music as an entry into the homes so the two Elders could then teach the gospel. While they were companions Elder Lee provided piano accompaniment many times for Elder Woodbury as they performed for Church and civic groups, in addition to the homes they had tracted out.

Area Conference in Munich, Germany

On the weekend of August 18–19, 1973, President Lee spent many hours preparing his sermons for the Munich area conference, timing each talk to be certain he was within prescribed bounds. This was difficult to do because approximately half of the time would be allotted to a translator. In addition, President Lee recorded a taped message for the servicemen in Europe which was to be released from Munich. President Lee wrote of his concerns during these pressure-packed days: "These are the last-minute pressures that seem never ending as I try to meet the demands that come repeatedly from various departments and elsewhere. Only with the Lord's help can I begin to encompass all that is expected of me."

In that humble spirit President and Sister Lee and Arthur Haycock and his wife left by plane to travel to Munich, via New York and London. They arrived in Munich, Germany, for the area conference to begin on Saturday, August 25, in the spacious Olympic Auditorium, where the 1972 Olympic Games were held.

It was the largest group of Latter-day Saints ever assembled in continental Europe for a conference of the Church. Some fourteen thousand members from many areas of Europe—Germany, Spain, France, Holland, Belgium, Switzerland, Austria, and Italy—had gathered eagerly to hear messages from the General Authorities and their own Regional Representatives of the Twelve and stake presidents. The conference included the participation of the Salt Lake Tabernacle Choir, along with other fine local choirs. Roadshows, folksinging, and folkdancing provided color and interest during the Friday night preconference activities, which included entertainment from many nationalities.

With Spencer W. Kimball in expression of love at area conference in Munich, Germany, 1973

This conference was an experience in love and brotherhood. The Saints came from varied cultures and backgrounds. They came from nations that had been enemies and had previously been engaged in mortal combat. There were tremendous language barriers to be overcome. It was finally decided to broadcast the proceedings in German over the loudspeaking system and provide simultaneous translation into five other languages through cordless headsets.

XThe Saints came by bus, by car, and by train. Crossing at country borders was not easy. They were housed in public campgrounds, in temporary dormitories, such as schoolhouses, in small guest houses and hostels; the seven hundred members of two Munich branches invited some seven hundred visiting Saints into their homes. These housing arrangements had been made six months in advance.

Munich was chosen as the conference city not only because it is centrally located but also because facilities were available there that would accommodate the expected crowds. Olympic Hall was none too large. For some meetings every seat in the fourteen-thousand-seat capacity building was taken, necessitating the setting up of extra chairs.

All three members of the First Presidency were in attendance, as were ten other General Authorities, many of whom spoke in languages other than English. In his opening conference address President Harold B. Lee said:

> My beloved brothers and sisters: It gives me genuine delight to stand before a congregation of Latter-day Saints in this city of Munich.
>
> In this congregation there are those who speak at least six different languages, including the Germans, the Italians, the French, the Spanish, the Dutch, and the English. Although we are of different nationalities, I am reminded of the remarks of the Apostle Paul as he wrote to the Galatians in his day when he said: "There is neither Jew nor Greek, there is neither bond nor free, there is neither male nor female: for ye are all one in Christ Jesus." [See Galatians 3:26–29.]
>
> As I paraphrase that statement and apply it to this congregation, I might say, using a part of the Apostle Paul's language: "We are neither English nor German, nor French, nor Dutch, nor Spanish, nor Italian, but we are all one as baptized members of The Church of Jesus Christ of Latter-day Saints, and also we are Abraham's seed."

President Lee then explained why area conferences were held:

We have planned to go out to many of the far reaches of the Church because of the great worldwide increase of Church membership that has grown in 143 years. From 1840 to 1973, we have gone from that mere handful of members who were organized on April 6, 1830, to over three million members, who live in seventy-eight countries throughout the world, speaking seventeen different languages.

One of our purposes in coming to these various areas is that many more of our people can assemble than could come to the semiannual conferences held in Salt Lake City. Our first desire is to evidence to our members everywhere, even in the most remote areas from the headquarters of the Church, that they are not forgotten and that the General Authorities of the Church have their interests at heart. They are working for your interests no matter where you are, just as they are doing for members who are nearer to the headquarters of the Church.

Another reason we have come is to feel the spirit of our members everywhere, to become acquainted with the conditions under which you live, to meet the local leaders of the Church, and to communicate with them in such a way that they may feel the unity of the purpose for which they have been called to preside in the stakes, missions, and branches of the Church.

And finally we have come together in a more intimate way to strengthen the members of the Church to stand true to the covenants that they made in the waters of baptism at the time they came in as converts to the Church. The nature of this covenant was explained by the ancient prophet, who before the baptism of some new converts, spoke these words that have great meaning: "that ye have entered into a covenant with him, that ye will serve him and keep his commandments, that he may pour out his Spirit more abundantly upon you. [Mosiah 18:10.]"

Then President Lee spoke of the immense contributions that the peoples of the countries involved in the conference had made and were then making to the building up of the kingdom of God, followed by a strong plea to the Church members to follow the current leadership. He then bore this personal testimony:

Now, my dear brothers and sisters, as one whom you have sustained in the high position as the President of the Church, I declare unto you in all soberness and sincerity, with all the humility of my soul, that I know that The Church of Jesus Christ of Latter-day Saints is indeed the kingdom of God on earth. The priesthood of God is here and has been handed down since the restoration of the Church through messengers who were sent to restore that authority that the ordinances of salvation might be administered to all the faithful on the earth. The priesthood of God holds the keys of salvation; it is our responsibility to discharge our obligation to the Lord in carrying the message of the gospel to all our neighbors and friends in every way we can to assist in the spread of the gospel so that the time may come when the prophecies of ancient days might be realized, when truth will cover the earth as waters cover the mighty deep. So I bear my witness as to these things and leave my blessing with you this day as we now go into the proceedings of this great conference, in the name of the Lord Jesus Christ, amen.

In his closing remarks President Lee referred to the youth activities held on the Friday night prior to the general sessions. In his personal journal he recapped his thoughts on this subject:

We are sure that bringing together these young people at this first attempt was a beginning that will bear fruit for the future. Many of these young people saw for the first time how many youth there are in the European area. Before this many of these have been in small branches where there are just a handful of young people. Now suddenly their vision has been enlarged. Their pride in performance will be improved.

President Lee gave reassurance to the European Saints by saying:

Don't be afraid of the testing and trials of life. Sometimes when you are going through the most severe tests, you will be nearer to God than before.

I say to you faithful Saints, be true and faithful in keeping the commandments of God. Then the power of Satan cannot touch you. You will feel peace in your heart as you live the commandments and you will know that the Father is in heaven, that all is right in the world, and even though you may at times be forced to suffer persecution, if you will be true to your faith, the Lord will reward you far beyond the value of money.

This testimony closed his public address: "I know that Jesus is the Savior of the world. I received this special witness at the time I was called to be an Apostle of the Lord Jesus Christ. Before I was worthy to accept a position in the Council of the Twelve Apostles, I knew I must love everyone who walks the earth."

The final song of the conference was sung, the benediction offered, and the conference was closed. But the people could not leave. Spontaneously they joined with the choir in singing "God

Be with You" as President Lee stood smiling and waving. When he left the building to get into his car to return to the hotel, he was all but overrun, mostly by the young people who desired one more look, one more word, one more smile, one more picture, one more wave and a possible handshake.

The editor of the *Ensign* wrote of the conference: "They knew they may never see their prophet again. Once more they burst forth into song and nearly everyone was crying, singing, and waving as the car pulled away. The experiment in love and brotherhood was complete. Blessings from the meeting in Munich will flow from the Alps to the Pyrenees, from the North Sea to the Mediterranean for years to come."

The results of the conference were most gratifying to President Lee. He recorded in his journal on Sunday, August 26, 1973 this summary statement: "Never have I experienced such a response from an audience as I have had here, where all animosity of past wars were forgotten in a brotherhood which made everyone a 'kin' in The Church of Jesus Christ of Latter-day Saints. The choirs provided a marvelous harmony of appropriate music for the conference."

The route homeward after the Munich area conference took President and Sister Lee to visits with missionaries in Vienna, Austria, and on to London, England, where President Lee reorganized the London Temple presidency. While in England the President spoke to all the missionaries in the England Central and England Southeast missions, and also to the British Isles Young Adult conference. Here they shared the spotlight with Elder and Sister Gordon B. Hinckley.

On the last day of August, President Lee was taken to the Loughborough Stake center, where nearby a college facility was utilized for housing representatives of the young adults from the British Isles and some parts of Ireland. As he spoke to a general session of this conference President Lee was impressed by the quality and appearance of these wonderful young people. To take further advantage of the presence of the President of the Church, a joint session was held in a stake building which would accommodate a crowd of fifteen hundred. Tickets were issued to members and leaders of the Birmingham, Bristol, and Loughborough stakes.

On the final day of the youth conference, a theater provided seating for an even greater audience to hear President and Sister Lee and Elder and Sister Hinckley. President Lee wrote in his journal that "the spiritual response was overwhelming and many tears were shed as we bade farewell to those in attendance after giving our testimonies and our blessings upon those assembled."

President Lee arrived home in Salt Lake City on September 3, 1973 and the next day at the office was greeted by the concern over a governmental revolt in Chile, where the Communist regime under President Salvadore Allende Gossens was ousted. The safety of the mission president and missionaries was assured by a telephone call which miraculously brought contact with the mission president after repeated failures.

LAST CONFERENCE PREPARATIONS

On September 11, President and Sister Lee went to Brigham Young University, where, at the first devotional assembly he had attended since becoming President of the Church, he was presented with the Exemplary Manhood Award from the Associated Men Students of BYU. ASBYU President Mark Reynolds presented the award to President Lee "for his brilliant and dynamic leadership" and his sterling qualities as a man.

For the occasion a record-setting attendance of 23,304 students and visitors filled the Marriott Special Events Center on campus. The crowd was said to be the largest worshipping congregation ever held in one place in the Church, so far as was then known.

President Lee seized the opportunity to again counsel his young friends: "Keep your eye on those who preside over the Church today and look to them. Jesus Christ stands at the head of the Church today and thus current revelation is the strength of the Church.

"The measure of your true conversion is whether or not you see the power of God resting on the leaders of this Church and thus gain a testimony that goes down into your heart like fire."

President Lee also had specific advice for students. He said: "Learning by faith is no task for a lazy man. Someone has said, in effect, that such a process requires the bending of the whole soul —the calling up from the depths of the human mind and linking them with God. It makes those who follow this course great in the sight of the Lord."

The President also reinforced the statement of President Dallin Oaks, made the week before in his opening address to BYU students when he noted that the main reason for establishing BYU was for students to perfect their education. President Lee added that the need to develop the whole person while at college, and not just the intellect, is vital.

The small temple concept was much on President Lee's mind when offers to purchase Church-owned property in Tokyo, Japan, appeared to present sufficient earnings to finance such a project. The First Presidency sent a team of attorneys and building and financial advisers to Japan to make further studies.

With the October 1973 semiannual general conference looming ahead, the meeting in the Salt Lake Temple on Thursday, September 27, summoned the attendance of all General Authorities of the Church. There President Lee had the new Melchizedek Priesthood-MIA leaders, Elders James E. Faust and Marion D. Hanks, present reports, and Bishop Vaughn J. Featherstone did likewise for the new Aaronic Priesthood-MIA. President Lee was pleased with the reports and wrote: "There was a delightful spirit and harmony which has laid the stage for a most spiritual general conference."

He also chose this occasion to more broadly introduce the latest administrative development in his ever fertile mind. Having just called Dee Anderson to become the full-time auditor of the Church budgets and also the executive secretary of the Budget Committee, with the hope to gain a constant watch over the expenditures of the Church and thereby achieve long-needed control, he then explained in the temple meeting that the First Presidency was now considering a similar move to "audit" the teaching materials of the Church. This move would be for the purpose of making certain that the end result would be like assuring that the "water would go to the end of the furrow" —meaning that these materials attained the goals for which all the Church teaching efforts were intended. President Lee later wrote his impressions of that day, saying, "This will be one of our next moves to improve and to give us a 'security' in spiritual as well as in financial matters."

This early insight was the forerunner of the Church Correlation Department. Already he had in mind the one man who had the vision and the ability to do what was needed in this venture, Elder Neal A. Maxwell, then serving as the Church Commissioner of Education and as a Regional Representative of the Twelve.

CHAPTER 31

Last Conference Messages

The October 1973 general conference began as usual with the Regional Representatives of the Twelve Seminar, attended also by all General Authorities. As was customary, President Lee set the theme for the seminar at the opening session. He tried again to impress the Regional Representatives with their role as "staff" officers, as contrasted with "line" officers, and to re-emphasize the importance of the training and teaching they did to prepare stake and mission leaders.

Balmy autumn weather allowed thousands who could not find seating in the historic Salt Lake Tabernacle and other buildings to sit on the lawns and flower boxes around Temple Square as the 143d Semiannual General Conference opened. Favored with such beautiful weather the Saints came expectantly in great numbers to obtain counsel and instruction from their Church leaders on meeting the challenging evil influences of the world.

Speaking in the opening session President Lee used the text, "Who Am I?" stating that the answer to this question was desperately needed if the Saints were to cope with the lack of self-respect evident among the people of the world, especially in their manner of dress and personal behavior, which in many cases seemed to lack the basic principles of decency. The message was a timely one and deeply struck a responsive chord with his listeners. President Lee declared:

Self-respect and the behavior that flows from it grows out of an understanding of who we are, where we come from, and our relationship to God, our Heavenly Father. . . . When one has departed from the path which would have given him peace, he is like the troubled sea, casting up mire and dirt (Isaiah 57:19–21). It seems to me that it all results from the failure of the individual to have self-respect.

Who are you? You are all the sons and daughters of God. Your spirits were created and lived as organized intelligences before the world was. You have been blessed to have a physical body because of your obedience to certain commandments in that premortal state. You are now born into a family to which you have come, into the nations through which you have come, as a reward for the kind of lives you lived before you came here and at a time in the world's history, as the Apostle Paul taught the men of Athens, and as the Lord revealed to Moses, determined by the faithfulness of each of those who lived before this world was created.

At the general priesthood meeting, more than 185,000 men and boys, listening in person or by closed-circuit radio and television, heard President Lee give instructions regarding marriage, divorce, the programs for single persons in the Church, and a summation of area conferences. President Lee wrote in his journal brief comments about this meeting in these words:

I spoke plainly to men who are over the usual marriageable age and have neglected finding a wife. I also urged the local brethren to give sanction and leadership to the new Melchizedek Priesthood-MIA. Some of them have not yet done so, and expressed their conviction that this work should be carried from now on. I hope that from the present emphasis much more good will be realized, rather than to lag behind and then miss the thrust of enthusiasm which has been engendered.

President Lee began his general priesthood meeting sermon by reference to the recent area conference in Munich, Germany:

As we witnessed the feeling that was there, we have felt that we should continue these area conferences. The first such conference was held in Manchester, England, where we had about fourteen thousand there. We were in Mexico City next, where we had representatives from all the Central American countries and from Mexico. We came away with a feeling that if . . . we all realized that we were the children of one father, we would stop shouting at each other as much as we do. We are all of one great family. And that should apply not only in political matters, but it should apply in our dealings with each other.

As politicians, or as those who are engaged in competitive temporal activities, we must say: "Because I am a holder of the priesthood of the living God, I am a representative of our Heavenly Father and hold the priesthood by which he can work through me; I can't stoop to do some of the things that I might have done otherwise, because of my fellowship with the priesthood of God."

We can't be holders of the priesthood and be like other men. We must be different, because priesthood means a fellowship in the royal household of the kingdom of God.

President Lee spoke plainly about the Melchizedek Priesthood-MIA program—which dealt with single persons eighteen years and over—encouraging priesthood leaders to assume their responsibilities and to see that the program functioned in the wards and stakes, saying:

Now brethren of the priesthood, if you knew the processes by which these new programs came into being, you would know that this just didn't come out of somebody's imagination; this was done after some of the most soulful praying and discussing that I believe I have ever experienced. We know, and we announced when it was given, that this came from the Lord. This was an evidence of a thing that the Lord was giving us to do to meet a special need.

But it troubles me when I read some of these things where sisters are pleading with us to try to do something to stimulate the activities where the bishops or stake presidents have not caught on to what it is all about.

In the early days of the welfare program, everywhere I went people were saying to me, "Brother Lee, how is the welfare program going?" And I would answer, "Just as well as the individual bishop of each ward makes it go. In some wards it is an absolute failure. In other wards it is going great guns." And that is exactly what is happening with what we are now launching.

He also spoke directly to the single priesthood holders over twenty-five years of age and still unmarried, warning them: "There are some examples that point up an area of need which applies directly to young men in the past-twenty-five age, who for some reason, and hard to understand, as holders of the priesthood are shirking their responsibilities as husbands and fathers."

President Lee quoted President Joseph F. Smith, who also spoke as a prophet on this same subject, saying: "Marriage is not a man-made institution. It is of God. It is honorable, and no man who is of marriageable age is living his religion who remains single."

President Lee also warned about the growing tendency of married people seeking new companions, which had become then a growing problem in the world. In urging all married brethren to avoid being caught up in the fearful wave of marriage dissolutions, President Lee cautioned:

> One of the painful things that I have as a responsibility is to have to work through the flood of recommendations for cancellations of sealings of those who have been married in the temple. It is frightening, brethren, and much of it stems from one of the greatest of all sins, next to murder, the sin of adultery, that is running rampant throughout the Church. Brethren, we must ourselves resolve anew that we are going to keep the law of chastity; and if we have made mistakes, let's begin now to rectify these mistakes. Let's walk toward the light; and for goodness sake, brethren, don't prostitute the wonderful opportunity you have as men, as those who may link hands with the Creator in the procreation of human souls, by engaging in an unlawful relationship that will only go down to disgrace and break the hearts of your wives and your children. Brethren, we plead with you to keep yourselves morally clean and to walk the path of truth and righteousness, and thereby gain the plaudits of a Heavenly Father, whose sons you are.

The sunny, autumn weather lasted uncharacteristically throughout the entire conference, to the delight of the thousands of Saints who came from throughout the free world. Finally, on Sunday, October 7, 1973 the time arrived for President Harold B. Lee's closing address. No one suspected these would be the last words he would speak in general conference from the podium of the Salt Lake Tabernacle.

Listeners paid close attention as President Lee began his last conference sermon by discussing the conditions of the world and current events. He announced the safety of two hundred missionaries and the members of the Church caught in the political uprising in Chile, and also the students and members of the branch of the Church in Israel, which nation was then involved in the three-week war initiated by Egypt and Syria.

Then President Lee mentioned those who would persecute the Church, saying: "Some of the greatest of our enemies are those within our own ranks. . . . When we see some of our own today doing similar things as was done to betray the Master in his day, some who have been recognized and honored in the past as teachers and leaders who later fall by the wayside, our hearts are made sore and tender. But sometimes we have to say just like the Master said, 'The devil must have entered into them.' "

President Lee used a favorite quotation from President George Albert Smith regarding those who have disgraced the honors that the Church had given them in times past and who were trying to join the forces of the enemy against the work of the Lord, and then added: "So, you Saints of the Most High God, when these things come, and they will come—this has been prophesied—you just say: 'No weapon formed against the work of the Lord will ever prosper, but all glory and majesty of this work that the Lord gave will long be remembered after those who have tried to befoul the name of the Church and those of its leaders will be forgotten, and their works will follow after them.' "

President Lee gave personal witness concerning the direction given at this conference:

> Now, you Latter-day Saints, I think you have never attended a conference where in these three days you have heard more inspired declarations on most every subject and problem about which you have been worrying. If you want to know what the Lord would have the Saints know and to have his guidance and direction for the next six months, get a copy of the proceedings of this conference and you will have the latest word of the Lord as far as the Saints are concerned.
>
> As I say, realizing that is a very bold statement to make, I have thought of a great revelation where the Lord said something about the creation of the universe. . . . (D&C 88.)
>
> May I paraphrase what the Lord has said in this great revelation. Any man who has seen any of the least of these happenings among us today, has seen God today moving in his majesty and in his power. Let us make no mistake about that. . . .
>
> Likewise I say to you, as I stand with you and see the moving hand of the Lord in the affairs of the nations of the world today, we are seeing the signs of our times as foretold by the prophets and by the Master himself, and we see what is happening and the things transpiring before us in our day. In the Church, we have been witnessing some of the most dramatic things, and I can testify that you are seeing what the Lord is revealing for the needs of this people today.

Referring again to world conditions, President Lee asked the question:

Where is there safety in the world today? Safety can't be won by tanks and guns and airplanes and atomic bombs. There is only one place of safety and that is within the realm of the power of Almighty God that he gives to those who keep his commandments and listen to his voice, as he speaks through the channels that he has ordained for that purpose.

President Lee then quoted extensively from Matthew, chapter 24, but said that the message could be better understood from the Inspired Version, which is found in the Pearl of Great Price, telling of the signs and wonders preceding the Savior's coming. He indicated that Church members should be familiar with those signs, and stated:

> Brothers and Sisters, this is the day the Lord is speaking of. You see the signs are here. Be ye therefore ready. The Brethren have told you in this conference how to prepare to be ready. We have never had a conference where there has been so much direction, instruction, so much admonition; when the problems have been defined and also the solution to the problem has been suggested.
>
> Let us not turn a deaf ear now, but listen to these as the words that have come from the Lord, inspired of him, and we will be safe on Zion's hill, until all that the Lord has for his children shall have been accomplished.

President Lee then paused. For a moment he collected his thoughts. As he concluded, there was a certain intimacy in his manner as well as in his voice:

> And so in the closing moments of this conference, I have been moved as I think I have never been moved before in all my life. If it were not for the assurance that I have that the Lord is near to us, guiding, directing, the burden would be almost beyond my strength, but I know that he is there, and that he can be appealed to, and if we have ears to hear attuned to him, we will never be left alone.
>
> I am grateful for strong men like President Tanner and President Romney and the Twelve and all the General Authorities, who are united more so than I have ever experienced before during my lifetime. The General Authorities are united and working together and are speaking with one voice to the world.
>
> Follow the Brethren; listen to the Brethren. I bear you my witness as one whom the Lord has brought to this place, as Brother Gordon B. Hinckley has said. I thank the Lord that I may have passed some of the tests, but maybe there will have to be more

before I shall have been polished to do all that the Lord would have me do.

Sometimes when the veil has been very thin, I have thought that if the struggle had been still greater that maybe then there would have been no veil. I stand by, not asking for anything more than the Lord wants to give me, but I know that he is up there and he is guiding and directing.

Peace be with you, not the peace that comes from the legislation in the halls of congress, but the peace that comes in the way that the Master said, by overcoming all the things of the world. That God may help us so to understand and may you know that I know, with a certainty that defies all doubt, that this is his work, that he is guiding us and directing us today, as he has done in every dispensation of the gospel, and I say that with all the humility of my soul, in the name of the Lord, Jesus Christ. Amen.

And so it was finished. Over sixty times Harold B. Lee had stood before the Saints in the Salt Lake Tabernacle during general conference, and now he had declared his last message, powerfully and humbly. He had witnessed, as it was his divine commission to do, to the Lord Jesus Christ's impact on His modern Church. Emotion filled the Tabernacle as he sat down. He had opened his prophetic heart to the visibility of all. He had conducted all the sessions of the conference and had once again interjected praise, recognition, and commendation for each speaker. He had personalized the meetings and provided additional warmth seldom seen in the televised, script-bound proceedings.

Elder Wilford W. Kirton, Jr., the Church attorney, offered the benediction, his voice wavering, visibly touched by the spiritual force of the meeting.

Following conference President Lee received numerous commendations and personal testimonies from many who had received a spiritual resurgence from President Lee's leadership and counsel. For example, the Church historian, Leonard J. Arrington, wrote to President Lee: "The staff of the Historical Department was particularly inspired with your Saturday night talk in priesthood meeting, in which you were willing, as was characteristic of Brigham Young, to share your own personal experiences and thoughts in an informal way for the edification of the Saints."

Sister Olga C. Brown of Salt Lake City, a former member of the Primary Association General Board, wrote: "I admire your ability and efficiency in conducting the sessions, and your thoughtfulness

Delivering last conference address, October, 1973

in making little remarks of praise and encouragement to many of the speakers.''

Paul H. Evans, director of Broadcast Relations for Bonneville International Corporation, wrote to report to President Lee that the coverage was successfully given through 250 television and radio stations broadcasting from within fourteen countries and forty-eight states in the United States to a total of forty-one countries in five languages. Then he added his own appreciation for President Lee's conduct of the conference:

> Our great admiration for you continues to grow as proudly we have observed the effective and gracious manner in which you most prestigiously direct the carefully programmed segments of the various proceedings. Your warm and thoughtfully placed comments, spoken within each of the sessions, to us were offerings of such appropriateness as to significantly strengthen the inspirational tone of the entire conference. Also, how beautifully your major

addresses completed totally the inspirational flow of those meaningful gatherings.

Even nonmembers were moved to write. Mr. and Mrs. John C. Matheny from Richmond, Virginia, wrote:

> Gentlemen: We have had a problem in our family that we just did not know how to solve and had been praying for inspiration for two weeks as to how best to handle it. Today, we turned to your station and the "Mormon Conference"—and there was the answer to our prayers!
>
> The messages carried on this program concerned so many of the general family problems of today that it was unbelievable that so many could be on the same program. We realize that just listening to the program will not solve our problem in itself, but at least we know what to do in trying to solve it ourselves. Keep these messages coming!

One week later, President Lee wrote in his journal:

> From everywhere, and including the Council of the Twelve, the unanimous expression came that there was something unusual in this conference. The Brethren were inspired to define the problems confronting us today, and then suggested the application of gospel teachings to supply the solution. There seemed to have been something in my closing remarks which came spontaneously that seemed to many to be prophetic of the times, and to outline the need for our people to "stand in holy places and be not moved" as the Master has counseled, when the signs of his second coming were drawing near.

AND A LITTLE CHILD SHALL LEAD THEM

There was one more grand postlude to the general conference. As was traditional, the General Authorities and their wives met for dinner the week following general conference. The committee in charge chose to reenact a meeting of the pioneer Polysophical Society, which President Lorenzo Snow founded in 1852 and featured every two weeks a varied program of talent in music, literature, and dramatics to broaden the cultural and intellectual edification of the membership. (This organization became the forerunner of the Mutual Improvement Association of the Church.)

At the conclusion of this program, held on the twenty-sixth floor social hall of the new Church Office Building, little seven-year-old Michael Van Harris, grandson of the master of ceremonies, Francis Urry, brought a note to President Lee. Michael had taken similar notes to each of the performers throughout the evening. The note asked President Lee to "leave his blessing" upon the gathering. Led to the stage before the assemblage by little Michael, President Lee picked the young boy up in his arms, turned his back to the audience, and spoke quietly with him. Then he faced the audience and said:

> This is about the greatest honor that I've ever had, to be led by Michael's hand. The Savior said, "and a little child shall lead them and . . . he that would be the greatest among you must be the servant of all." Michael says I am supposed to give you our blessing. I asked him what that meant, and he said, "I guess it means to pray."
>
> This has been a most delightful occasion. And not the least of the performers has been this sweet, lovely child. I'm sure we've been impressed by Michael. You must have a wonderful mother and father, and you must have a sweet family life. We're proud of you, Michael.

The innocent little lad answered politely, "Thank you." President Lee went on, saying to Michael:

> And so if you'll stand by my side now. . . . We've just come, Michael, from a great conference—our Heavenly Father's conference. We've felt a great spirit that our Heavenly Father wanted to pour out upon his Saints and we were there, and as we bowed our heads in prayer, and lifted our eyes to heaven, we knew he was up there. You know he is up there, don't you? You've talked to him, haven't you Michael? You know that he answers prayers. So now, you and I, you silently and I will speak a prayer tonight. . . ; you close your eyes and just whisper to yourself your prayer, and I'll pray out loud.
>
> "Heavenly Father . . . we present ourselves in this glorious company where have been assembled some of the most choice Saints in all the world. We have felt the joys of thy attending influence, our Father. We've known what it has meant to hear Thy voice, through thy servants. We've heard thy words, as thou hast spoken into our minds, and impressed upon our hearts, and the Saints have felt that, Father, for this is a day when thy people need so much, realizing as we do, that we have the keys for the salvation of all mankind. In a day of great troubles, when waters are heaving over their banks, great earthquakes occur, wars and rumors of war, bloodshed, horrors, oh, if it please thee, our Father, that in the tops of the mountains thou hast builded a throne to which thou could come, even a Holy Temple, that we've tried to keep clean and worthy. We remember the lament that thy Son did make. It saddens our hearts

when He said, 'the foxes have holes, the birds have nests, but the Son of Man has no place to lay his head.' Holy Father, we trust that that may never come in our time, where there shall not be a place where thou canst come and where thou canst lay thy head. We'll try our best to keep these sacred places for thine abode. Keep us under thy watchful eye, our Father. As never before, we need thee.

So, tonight with united hearts, we thank thee our Father, for the privilege of being in thy service. We know what it means to humble ourselves realizing that in order for us to win thy favor, we must, like thy Son, be willing to kneel at the feet of those who need their feet bathed in cooling water and lifted up above the sordid trials and miseries of today. Give us the grace, Father, to be that humble, and follow the pattern that was laid down by Thy Son.

With these humble words of prayer, led to this point by this dear, sweet pure child, take us home in safety. Let our homes be filled with thy love, and to thee we will ascribe the honor the praise and glory, forevermore.''

The social was ended, but President Lee's acquaintance with Michael Harris was not. They seemed to have a special kinship with each other, as though they had met before in another sphere. President Lee called for Michael to come and visit him in his office. When his parents brought him, the prophet had him occupy the chair of the President of the Church, saying, "One day, Michael, you just might be sitting there." When it was time for him to leave, President Lee put his arms around Michael's parents and said: "I have never been so impressed with a child's spirit in my life. He has a very special mission to perform. If you will guide him in the paths of righteousness, you will stand back and marvel at the things that this boy will accomplish."

In subsequent correspondence Michael received a beautiful letter from President Lee and an autographed photograph. Michael wrote back and sent his photograph, saying to his mother, "President Lee is my very best friend, and Mom, President Lee really loves me." Subsequent events in the lives of these two special friends were to confirm Michael's declaration.

When President Lee passed away, just two and one-half months later, Michael felt as though one of his immediate family had died. His parents comforted him with the thought that if he would always choose to do right, as President Lee would want him to do, he could see him and be with him again.

In the spring of 1976, two and one-half years later, a sudden unprecedented foreboding came on nine-year-old Michael and his family. Their thoughts turned to death and dying, for no apparent

Michael Van Harris visits the President in the Church Office Building, October, 1973

reason. Within two weeks Michael became ill and was treated at the hospital to clear his lungs from congestion. The congestive attack occurred again when his father was at work, and his mother, Jane Urry Harris, hurriedly prepared to make another emergency trip to the hospital. After arranging for the other children, Sister Harris came out of the house to find Michael sitting on the step of the porch with a beautiful, peaceful look on his face. He had an almost transparent, ethereal appearance and was not struggling or fighting for breath as before. When his mother called for him to come, he stood up immediately, then fell backwards, unconscious. From this attack he was not to recover, and he died a few days later. He lingered only long enough for his mother to learn that she must not oppose a divine will that was calling back home her oldest son. The peace and warmth that followed her acquiescence gave her the assurance that Michael's passing was the Lord's will.

Elder Boyd K. Packer, who had selected Michael from among many other young boys for his role as messenger for the Polysophical Society program, wrote to Michael's parents that, in his opinion, Michael's death was not untimely and that he felt that President Lee had played a part in his passing, because they had such an unusual relationship.

Sister Harris later spoke of this heart-wrenching experience and offered this testimony: "I also believe, with every fiber of my being, that President Lee did come to again take Michael by the hand and lead him, for I will never forget the look on Michael's face before he became unconscious. It was the same look of peace and love that he had the day we spent with Michael's 'very best friend,' President Harold B. Lee."

CAREFUL USE OF AUTHORITY

Now it again was business as usual at the President's office in the stately old Church Administration Building on South Temple Street in Salt Lake City, Utah. The routines found President Lee slowing down the appetite of the External Communications Department for establishing new, staffed centers throughout the world. Instead, President Lee again turned the effort inward and urged the leaders to work through the regular priesthood channels with volunteers to obtain better results.

A favorite, oft-repeated teaching lesson, which had its origin in President Lee's early welfare experiences, found renewed application immediately following the October 1973 general conference.

President Lee found it necessary at this time to counsel with a Church-appointed administrator whom he had sustained in a stressful personnel controversy but whom he later privately counseled with love so he would become more compassionate with his workers. President Lee wrote to this leader of "lessons that I had to learn the hard way," recalling this experience:

> On one occasion, just before I was called to the Council of the Twelve, a certain matter was referred by the Welfare Committee to the new Presiding Bishopric, the President of the Relief Society and myself, for a study and a recommendation. I waited to be invited to a discussion of that subject, but I received no invitation. Shortly there came a letter signed by all three members of the Presiding Bishopric announcing a decision. This, of course, was construed by the Welfare Committee as a slight and an affront to the Welfare Committee.
>
> Brothers Henry D. Moyle and Robert L. Judd of the Committee went over to see President J. Reuben Clark, Jr., and voiced their disappointed feelings. President Clark, being a good diplomat, sidestepped any head-on controversy between these brethren and the Presiding Bishopric.
>
> Within six weeks of that incident I was called to the Council of the Twelve. President Clark invited me one day to ride with him to his ranch in Grantsville so that he could have the opportunity of talking with me about some matters, and during the course of our visit together I made mention of the incident with reference to the Presiding Bishopric refusing to meet with me, representing the General Welfare Committee, and then I made some such remark as, "I suppose that now the Presiding Bishopric would be willing to sit down with me and discuss the problem."
>
> President Clark saw in this remark a continued feeling of resentment on my part. He said to me, rather sharply, but with a fatherly look: "Yes, my boy, now you do have the whip hand, but in your position, you must never use it."
>
> As additional responsibilities have come up to the present time I have found that President Clark's counsel was very wise and timely. The greater my responsibilities the more careful I must be in using that authority in a way that would be not inconsistent with my position. The greater authority one has the more careful he has to be to not use his whip hand.

Then, after assuring his leader-student of his personal love for him and confidence in his operation of one of the Church's largest corporations, he summarized: "I would have you think, as I have been taught to think over the years, that the greater my responsibility the more careful I must be in using my authority to the hurt of individuals whose feelings might be more tender because of my position.''

President Lee again turned his love and energy to the young people when on October 13, 1973, he was a speaker at the University of Utah Institute. About three thousand students crowded into three buildings to hear the President, but through telephone connections with twenty other institutes throughout the West, the total audience was estimated at ten thousand persons. His subject was "In Whom Can You Trust?" a topic chosen in the wake of the betrayals of trust by national political leaders and some, as well, in the Church.

Prominent visitors continued to pay their respects to the President of the Church. On October 16, 1973, Mr. McKinley—president of the Texaco Oil Company, one of the world's largest producers of oil—and his wife visited with President Lee. His guest expressed his concern about the acute dangers of the Arab nations cutting off their oil supply to the United States because the Americans were supporting their enemy country, Israel, in the growing Middle East crisis. President Lee told his visitors of scriptural statements as to the "signs of the times" which were to precede the second coming of the Lord and that this conflict could be related to such predictions. In retrospect, both men were right. An Arab oil embargo did leave America in short supply, and President Lee's warnings were prophetic.

The next day eleven of the leaders of the Pentecostal Church, who were among those attending a ten-day world conference revival in Salt Lake City, were received by President Lee in the First Presidency's room of the Church administration building. He described his visitors of the clergy as well appearing and respectful in every way, with the exception of one young man. President Lee was intrigued by the doctrinal aspects of their conversation and wrote in his journal concerning this exchange:

> They opened up avenues for a dialogue on points of doctrine to pinpoint the differences in their beliefs as well as to call attention to their teachings as to abstinence of liquor and tobacco, which if we were to exclude the use of tea and coffee, would be close to our Word of Wisdom. When it came to the importance of baptism of the Spirit, as being essential to salvation, they had difficulty in their lack of understanding. Also, vicarious work for those who had no opportunity while in mortality to accept the gospel was new to

them. They seemed very interested and yet amazed as we called attention to the promise of the Master that they would hear the voice of the Son of God and would come forth out of their graves. The whole concept of salvation for the dead was unfamiliar doctrine which they apparently had overlooked. They asked why this doctrine wasn't taught in the Book of Mormon, since we declared that therein was the fulness of the gospel. This called for a definition as to what constituted "the gospel," and that where the power to confer the Holy Ghost was to be found, therein was the source of all that pertained to the gospel.

HIS BOOKS

Apart from the initial book *Youth in the Church* (later republished in 1973 as *Decisions for Successful Living*), which had been offered for public sale twenty years previously, the first reference President Lee made in his journal to the publication of his sermons and writings appears under date of October 22, 1973. On that date he learned that Doyle Green, managing director of Church Magazines, with President Lee's knowledge was working on a compilation of his sermons for a proposed book that would be published soon. Besides the *Decisions* book, President Lee authored *Ye Are the Light of the World,* the book just mentioned, and *Stand Ye in Holy Places,* which was published in 1974 after his death.

CHAPTER 32

Final Spiritual Crescendo

On October 26, 1973, President and Sister Lee went to Ricks College in Rexburg, Idaho, where, after a luncheon with faculty and Church leaders, both were speakers at a devotional assembly before a student body and homecoming audience of over five thousand persons assembled in the Hart Auditorium and two other buildings. Before speaking, President Lee was presented with a painting of the Teton Mountains and a plaque containing a beautifully inscribed tribute. An originally composed song entitled "Listen to the Wondrous Voice" and other music dedicated to President Lee was sung by the combined Ricks College choruses.

At Ricks College—A Spiritual Peak

President Lee recognized a spiritual peak on this occasion and was prompted to say to his audience: "There is a wonderful spirit here today. There is something unusual about this meeting today. I don't know what it is. Maybe it is one of those occasions when we could feel and hear and see remarkable things happen. You have brought with you a tremendous spirit, and I feel it."

President Lee's entire message hit a pinnacle of patriotic spiritualism and has been quoted often in defining the Church's attitude toward its elected officials and the destiny of America as a chosen land. President Lee's call for optimism, even in the gloom of the Watergate scandal, which shortly would bring about the resignation of President Richard M. Nixon, became a rallying banner for the Saints to follow. He firmly stated that this country would survive against all its enemies, whether from within or without.

President Lee told his listeners that the United States is a great nation:

> We are living in a time of great crisis. The country is torn with scandal and with criticism, with faultfinding and condemnation. It is an easy thing to climb on the bandwagon and join the hotheads in condemnation, little realizing that when they do, they are not just tearing down a man, they are tearing down a nation, and they are striking at the underpinnings of one of the greatest of all nations of all the world—a nation that was founded upon an inspired declaration we call the Constitution of the United States. The Lord said it was written by men whom he raised up for that very purpose, and that Constitution stands today as a model to all nations to pattern their lives.

President Lee then pointed out why the United States is such a favored land: "This is the cradle of humanity, where life on this earth began in the Garden of Eden. This is the place where the New Jerusalem is. This is the place which the Lord said is favored above all other nations in the world. This is the place where the Savior will come to his temple."

Stressing again that the United States will never fail, he said: "Men may fail in this country. Earthquakes may come, seas may heave themselves beyond their bounds, there may be great drought and disaster and hardship, as we may call it, but this nation, founded as it was on a foundation of principles laid down by men whom God raised up, will never fail."

President Lee then shared with his collegiate audience a portion of his remarks made recently in a meeting of the First Presidency and the Council of the Twelve:

> While it is true there are dangers and difficulties that lie ahead of us, we must not assume that we are going to lie down and watch the country go to ruin. We should not be heard to predict ills and calamities for the nation. On the contrary, we should be providing optimistic support of the nation. You must remember, brethren, that this Church is one of the most powerful agencies for the progress of the world, and we should all bear our testimonies [so] that we . . . all sound with one voice. We must tell the world how we feel about this land and this nation and bear our testimonies about the great mission and destiny that it has.

It is the negative, pessimistic comments about the nation that do as much harm as anything to the country today. Brethren, we must tell them in a positive way what they should be doing. We should not be so concerned about finding out what is wrong with America, but we should be finding what is right about America and should be speaking optimistically and enthusiastically about America.

His classic statement of trust in the destiny of America was also made during this sermon: "Yes, men may fail, but this nation won't fail. I have faith in America, and you and I must have faith in America if we understand the teachings of the gospel of Jesus Christ."

Another spiritual event took place prior to the devotional assembly. A committee of college students was assigned to prepare a tribute to President Lee by an instructor, Mrs. Dora R. Jenkins, teacher of creative writing at Ricks College. All were busy with homecoming activities and were overwhelmed with the assignment. But even the selection of these eight students seemed to be inspired, as were their individual contributions.

The students sat with their instructor, who had received a priesthood blessing as her personal preparation, awed with the job that faced them. They sought inspiration in prayer and committed themselves to a twenty-four-hour fast. When the fasting started, so did the mini-miracles. The group met at 4:00 P.M. and wrote until 1:00 A.M., struggling for the right words. The next day they met again, thinking they had only to finish up the text. Instead, they found they were not in tune and spent the next six hours in futility. After they had sufficiently humbled themselves, the Spirit returned and they concluded their work at 4:00 A.M. the next morning. Many hours and much prayer was spent before the Spirit had directed one particular word, *chastened,* which seemed to strike a deep chord in President Lee's heart when he read it.

The tribute, presented to President Lee by Steven Flint, student body president, reads as follows:

As sons and daughters of the living God, we stand united in tribute to the living prophet. Since Eden, God has called his chosen servants—men of faith and wisdom who rise above the sins of the world by mastering themselves, their lives perfected in virtue by earthly trial; so are prophets raised up in the necessity of time to join this line of inspired men.

People of all nations cry for leadership—not leadership of oppression or bondage, but the divine leadership of Christ's church, where men are foreordained to lead God's children from sin into celestial glory.

That leadership requires years of preparation and celestial refinement. For possession of those keys of peace in this last dispensation of time, the keys that unlock modern miracles and usher in Christ's millennial reign, a man must be chastened of God.

> given life in a small world
> where the things of man
> were smaller still
>
> raised up at first by candlelight
> and always by gospel light
> to be a man while still a child of God
>
> made strong by a loving father's design
> tempered and mellowed by youth
> and placed before mountains
> on which to strengthen his feet
>
> then given a burden to bear alone
> with the light of an earlier life
> to show the way
>
> encircled again
> given future light
> and a call from an earlier home

Called from the simplicity of farms and fields to stand in the upper rooms of the temple, where the veil is thinnest, comes such a man, whose life is a testimony that speaks the praises of God. This is a man who is more than a man, a man bearing Israel's prophetic inheritance, one of God's choicest sons.

Thanks be to God that we live in a prophet's time, when his inspired leadership draws us close to standing in those holy places where we prayerfully await Christ's second coming.

President Lee wrote of his appreciation to the Ricks student tribute committee in these words: "I think never before have I been so moved by the outpouring of love and genuine loyalty which was in evidence at the devotional we had recently at the Ricks College. My wife, Joan, and I came away uplifted and perhaps more benefitted than the students because of this demonstration and faith in us. You gave us the courage and strength to try to carry on and to be worthy of the commendation which you so generously extended towards us."

A week after his experience at Ricks College, as President Lee was having lunch at the Lion House next door to the Church

Receiving tribute at Ricks College from student body president, Steven Flint, October, 1973

Administration Building, he walked over to the table of Dr. Truman G. Madsen, director of the Institute of Mormon Studies at Brigham Young University, and after a cordial greeting made this startling statement: "A translator who was assigned my closing address at the general priesthood meeting of general conference had an experience which was most remarkable. It helps me understand how the Prophet Joseph Smith could translate the Book of Mormon. I would like you to have a copy of his story."

Without further explanation President Lee excused himself, leaving his hearers breathless and wondering. Brother Madsen wrote for the promised story, but first it appeared publicly in President Lee's words in this press account of the memorable Ricks College address:

> We had something happen at the last conference that I am going to tell you about to indicate something that will give you a key to how the Lord can open the mind of a man and give him spiritual understanding beyond what his natural self could do.
>
> We had eleven translators or interpreters who were down in the basement of the Tabernacle, translating in eleven different languages. One of these brethren was translating for the Swedish breth-

ren, and for most of the talks they had the script so they could study it, and as the speakers spoke in English, they would repeat it for the benefit of those who were listening. This man, who was translating from my English into Swedish at the priesthood meeting, where he had no script (I was talking from an extemporaneous standpoint in my closing address), said something happened, and I want you to hear what he said:

"The whole conference was a spiritual experience, but at the general priesthood meeting I had an experience which I have never had before. I knew that there were some Swedish brethren attending the conference who had never been here before and perhaps would never come again. Therefore, I had a great desire that they receive everything that the prophet had to deliver. Not having a script, I commended myself into the hands of the Lord, and as you began to speak, I was startled by the fact that I knew one or two words and even three ahead of the time you would say them. At first, I was so startled that I did not dare to pronounce them as they were given. Usually I close my eyes and listen and then interpret as I hear the speakers deliver, but this time I was prompted to look at your face on the television screen. In this very unusual situation, I looked at you and began to translate the words as they came, but to my amazement I did not receive just the words in my mind, but with my inner eyes, I saw them emanating from the vicinity of the temple of your head and coming toward me. I did not see them actually as written on something, and yet, I saw them and how they were spelled and experienced the power of the Spirit as I received them.

"One of the things that made it even more dramatic was that when a complex sentence was about to be delivered, I received more words so that I could reconstruct the grammar into good Swedish and deliver it at the very moment you pronounced the words. Never have I experienced the great force with which the interpretive message was flowing as I did at that time.

"The same experience happened during your closing remarks on Sunday afternoon, except that I did not see the words coming to me. I have talked with the Swedish members in attendance who have expressed an awesome amazement of what they experienced. They said they heard the interpretation and understood the interpreted message delivered at the same moment as you delivered the words in English. But the interpretation was all they heard, that the message came directly from you to them. They have all expressed that their attendance at the conference was a fantastic experience, never to be forgotten."

President Lee provided his interpretation of the experience for his Ricks College audience, saying:

Latter-day Saints, don't you think for a moment that the Lord does not have means of communicating with us, sending us messages that are beyond our understanding, even to translating an unknown language into our understandable language. He did it with the Prophet Joseph. He did it with King Mosiah. He has done it with others. He will do it today, as we have need. I have no doubt.

My whole soul pleads that I may so live that if the Lord has any communication that he would wish me to receive for my beloved people that I could be a pure vessel through which that message could come. I do not ask for anything. I do not want anything more than the Lord is willing to send, but I trust that I may live worthy so that I won't be a lame vessel or a broken reed that the Lord cannot use in times when he wants to communicate with his people.

PLANS HE WOULD NOT FINISH

With apparently no hint of his imminent death, President Lee moved vigorously into planning the next area conference. His diary entry of November 22, 1973, stated: "I met with the committee of the Twelve and J. Thomas Fyans relative to the next year's area conference for the Scandinavian countries in Stockholm, Sweden, in August 1974." This was a meeting President Lee would plan but would not live to carry out.

A significant management study was on his desk which also would remain as unfinished business. Lee S. Bickmore, whom President Lee looked forward to involving soon on a full-time business consulting staff position at Church headquarters, conferred with President Lee on December 4, 1973 regarding a comprehensive study of the Health Services Corporation. At that time the entire First Presidency discussed with Brother Bickmore the problems of the former Church Hospital System. They decided to engage the consultation firm of Cresp-McCormick-Paget to make a formal study of these problems.

A FINAL TESTIMONY OF SATAN'S REALITY

On the first Sunday of November 1973, President Lee spent the early morning hours, as was his practice, at the Salt Lake Temple considering problems on which he alone, as President of the Church, could decide. With these matters weighing heavily on his mind, along with a personal problem on which he had consulted with one of his family members, he came to rejoin Sister Lee at their Federal Heights Ward fast and testimony meeting. He arrived late, quietly sat down, and received the sacrament. Just prior to the close of the meeting, President Lee's familiar voice came from the back of the chapel, asking permission of bishopric counselor E. Douglas Sorensen to delay closing the meeting, for he "thought the Lord had been so mindful of me in a special way, a few days before, that he would think me an ingrate if I failed to express myself." According to ward member, Sister Elaine A. Cannon, who recorded his statements in her journal, he spoke these unforgettable words as he remained standing at the rear of the chapel:

> Brothers and Sisters, beloved friends and neighbors, members of my ward family, and those in my own little flock over whom I have stewardship: I'm sorry to disturb you, but I know that it would be disturbing to my Father in Heaven if I don't say something to you at this time.
>
> By way of testimony I want you to know that I know that God lives, that Jesus is the Christ and our Redeemer, and he is at the head of this Church; I am not. I *know* that he operates in all the affairs of this church and I say this by way of testimony that you may know that I know he lives.

And then, after a long pause, he uttered these remarkable words:

> I say this to you by way of a serious warning, that I also know that the adversary lives and operates in the affairs of man. And he is determined to cause a downfall of men. If he can't get to us, he will try to get to those closest to us, for he is in a mighty battle with the work of the Savior. And I must tell you these words of warning. So keep close to the Lord. Don't be discouraged. The Lord will take care of his own. If you are prepared, you need not fear, if you are on the Lord's side."

This was a powerful, most unusual testimony, not alone because it came from the prophet of God to his own neighbors, friends, and relatives who had often heard him bear witness to the reality of the Savior Jesus Christ, but also because he had never before borne such a fervent witness to the reality of Satan. It was his last message to the members of his ward, for seven weeks later he was taken in death.

EARLY TEACHINGS REAPPEAR IN HIS LAST SERMONS

During the Christmas season in early December 1973, President Lee was sought after constantly to attend innumerable

Among the many December engagements was that of grandson
Drew's wedding

Christmas socials for the many Church departments and business
organizations with which he was affiliated. While enjoyable, the
incessant demands, every day and every night, did drain his physical and emotional strength. President Lee's grandson, Alan Lee
Wilkins, reflected:

> We were visiting during the Christmas season when I became aware
> of the tremendous schedule and the manner in which Grandfather
> drove himself. As we visited, we remarked that Grandfather looked
> tired and asked if he couldn't take some time to rest.
>
> He had Grandmother Joan bring out his schedule calendar, and
> she showed us that they had two and three appointments, starting at
> six o'clock every evening during every day of the week through
> that whole month and into the next month.
>
> I was amazed—a man of his age keeping that kind of a schedule.
> He put in a full day at the office and then had this kind of a schedule
> to go home to, plus his travels throughout the Church and the
> demands that brought. He told us of staying awake most of several
> evenings during area conference trips. He said to us: "Now you see
> what my schedule is like. I can't rest. I know the Lord will sustain
> me as long as he wants me to be here, but I can't rest."

So with characteristic courage and dedication he plunged into his December schedule. Still President Lee engaged in some of his most rewarding activities, such as the sessions in the temple teaching the outgoing missionaries, in which he welcomed the challenge of answering new questions that stimulated his resourceful gospel compendium.

It was uniquely appropriate that the last days of President Lee would include a brief focus on his earliest and most enduring labors in developing the welfare plan of the Church. On December 5, 1973, President and Sister Lee were guests of the Deseret Industries in their new branch located at Murray, suburban Salt Lake City. The occasion was their annual Christmas dinner. As usual, the two visitors were requested to speak to these choice workers, including many handicapped persons, following a dinner which was served to four or five hundred employees and their guests.

In his remarks President Lee paid tribute to the Deseret Industries workers, whom he described as "those who are willing to give so much for others. Deseret Industries is a place where people can come and work and feel that they are needed. There is nothing more important than knowing that there is someone who cares."

He then recalled for his attentive audience the early years of the welfare work when the Deseret Industries program was developed, patterned after the Goodwill Industries but adapted to the Church plan of compensating the workers mainly with commodities, plus some cash to meet their financial needs. President Lee paid tribute to the lifelong accomplishments of this endeavor when he wrote in his journal, "This has now become one of our greatest, truly welfare developments." The pages of his journal beyond December 12, 1973, remained blank.

For many years President Lee had stated that he would rather spend his Christmas season with the poor and handicapped personnel at the Deseret Industries than anywhere else. They were his kind of people. He loved them and understood them, for he considered himself one of them "by the things which he had suffered." Quoting from his old schoolbook, he once described his life as "but the simple annals of the poor."

Another return to nostalgia came on Sunday, December 9, when President and Sister Lee were invited to speak before a conference-sized audience composed mainly of high priests and their wives of the Cannon Stake, where his elder brother, Perry, presided as stake president. At age seventy-eight Perry Lee was the oldest stake president in the Church. Cannon Stake was once a part of the Pioneer Stake, where Harold B. Lee presided at age thirty-one as the youngest stake president in the Church at that time. In returning to the scenes of his Pioneer Stake roots, President Lee described it as "a most satisfying experience to recall the years gone by when I served as their stake president."

President Lee prefaced his remarks with comments on the theme of personal revelation that had been chosen for the Cannon Stake ward conferences. He illustrated the theme by telling of his experiences in Florida, South America, and at the most recent general conference, when incidents of spiritual interpretation of languages were manifest. Yet, when concluding his address, the lifetime impress of the welfare plan was still on his mind and he returned to his early philosophical moorings and urged his listeners to store food, clothing, and fuel against shortages that were occurring throughout the country. President Lee warned, "Some have not listened, and even now it may be too late."

Last Major Public Address

On December 13, 1973, President Harold B. Lee spoke plainly of the needs of the day in his last major address. His audience was some seven thousand Church employees and their partners at their annual Christmas gathering in the Salt Lake Tabernacle. It was, he noted, a throng as large as the original number of Saints who had gathered in that edifice in the early days.

After drawing parallels between the martyrdom of the Prophet Joseph Smith and the crucifixion of the Savior, with particular references to the mourning mothers of both prophets, President Lee again harked back to the Depression days of the 1930s when he helped inaugurate the Church welfare program. He wondered whether the present evidences of food and fuel shortages might not represent the tip of the iceberg of deprivation predicted almost forty years previously. Pressing the point, President Lee asked: "Do all of you who are close to us here as employees and their families listen to the Brethren who said that to you, and have been trying to urge you to put aside in storage for at least a year, food, fuel, clothing? Have you done that today?"

Noting that he was speaking to the young fathers and mothers as though they were his own family, he expressed a humble, heartfelt wish that he could do more, saying: "I wish I could be a thousand times more understanding, to deal a thousand times more kindly, and with a thousand times more wisdom and foresight. Please, God, I only want what he wants me to have. And I only want to be what you, the faithful members of the Church, would wish me to be."

Fittingly, the final entry in President Lee's personal diary, dated December 12, 1973, also referred to a long-sought welfare achievement. When power failures and possible sabotage had halted work at the Church's Deseret Clothing Mills some years before, President Lee insisted that preventive measures be adopted. After attending a Christmas dinner at the plant where 437 women were employed, he proudly wrote of the accomplishment in his last journal entry: "They have now, at my urging, a second auxiliary plant and a diesel unit for emergency electrical power if they had a power failure."

President Lee believed in self-sufficiency and preparation. That was his "theme song" from his earliest days in the welfare plan leadership to the last note written on the pages of his journal.

No Sermon—Just a Prayer

As the Christmas parties peaked, so did the fatigue of the President of the Church. On December 18 he arrived about fifteen minutes late at the Lafayette Ballroom of the Hotel Utah where the annual Christmas party of the Beneficial Life Insurance Company was held. President Lee apologized to the company president, Douglas H. Smith, for his tardiness, saying: "I would not have come out tonight for anyone else except you. I am so weary that I would have stayed home, but I felt strongly compelled to be here in support of you and Beneficial Life."

After the dinner and presentations, the time came for President Lee to give his annual Christmas address. The company employees were eagerly awaiting his message, because they knew that on this occasion the previous year a miracle had resulted after the President urged prayers in behalf of a blind girl performer, and later she was blessed with improved vision. Now, as he stood again before them, every eye in the large ballroom was focused on him. After arriving at the podium he stood silent and motionless for what seemed like a long time but was probably only forty seconds. Then he began speaking.

He said that the world was on the brink of another war; Egypt and Israel were in severe military combat. The United States' Secretary of State, Dr. Henry Kissinger, had been dispatched to the Middle East to attempt to resolve the crisis. Acknowledging Mr. Kissinger's unique aptitude as an international negotiator, he then said, "I would ask that all of you join with me in a prayer of petition to our Heavenly Father."

This unforgettable moment was captured through the poetic words of Elder S. Dilworth Young:

> Here, gathered in the City of the Saints,
> At this happy Christmas time,
> Well fed—
> Well clothed—
> Sheltered from the cold,
> We sit waiting,
> Waiting to be told, the often
> Spoken tale
> Of angels, and of shepherds,
> Of wise men come to worship.
>
> The prophet of the Lord
> Begins to speak.
>
> He speaks not of a birth
> But of his feelings at the
> Place of crucifixion,
> Of suffering.
> Then suddenly
> We are reminded—
> Reminded of the hate
> And hold of Satan
> On the world—
> The stern reality of men
> Dying for what to them
> Is sacred land.
> He prays that men
> Who hold the fate of
> Palestine will remember
> Who it is they represent—
> And call for peace,
> Christ's peace,
> To be until he comes again.
>
> And asks our faith
> Be exercised that
> It be so.

> The party ends.
> He stands aloof, alone,
> The tragedy and sorrow of the world
> Etched in his face.
> His drooping shoulders
> Mutely witness his great sorrow.
>
> Can't we understand?
> The love of Christ is
> Love of fellowmen
> And charity!*

Douglas Smith described the effect of President Lee's supplication:

> The feeling of direct communication of the prophet and the Father in this emotional appeal was intensely felt by all. There was no question that he, as a prophet of the Lord, was talking with the Father in Heaven, and was sharing this most intimate experience with each of us.
> After he finished, there was total silence. Most of us were extremely hesitant to open our eyes, because we knew he was talking with the Lord. His deep compassionate love for all of the children of the Lord—Arab, Jew, and Gentile—was appealingly expressed.

The party ended on this quiet, reverential, subdued mood. As President Ezra Taft Benson was leaving, he asked Douglas Smith if President Lee's prayer had been recorded, to which he explained that no message at any of their parties had ever been recorded. President Benson then expressed his keen disappointment, adding, "In all my experience I have never been more deeply touched by such a happening."

This appraisal, coming from one who had prayed with Apostles and prophets in the temple for decades, accentuated all the more the singularity of the event they had just witnessed—the night when several hundred were allowed to listen in as the President of the Church talked with God on a person-to-person basis.

Eight days later President Lee was taken in death.

* © S. Dilworth Young 1976. Used by permission.

CHAPTER 33

Death of
a Prophet

There are moments in the life of every person which are locked forever in the heart, and defy all contrivances to call them back, except as precious memories. Such an enchanted moment is remembered by Jane Goates Reiser, President Lee's granddaughter, recalling such a time in her life—the early hours in the Goates home on Christmas Day, 1973.

> I remember how my heart was singing with the joy only Christmas Day can bring. Everyone was bustling to prepare an enormous meal, and I loved the companionship of working together with other kind hands—my special Mom and my sweet sisters-in-law.
>
> All was ready at last and we looked around the table at so many happy faces of loved ones. As I gazed upon the beautiful meal laid before me, a warmth and joy filled my heart and I gave thanks to my loving Heavenly Father for his outpouring of blessings upon my head. Soon our beloved Grandfather and Grandmother Joan would be joining the family throng—no one suspecting it would be for the last family gathering.

At 2:00 P.M. the sumptuous turkey feast was declared ready to be served. Helen telephoned to see if President and Sister Lee were ready to join the remainder of the family and learned that a "five-minute visit" from one of the local Federal Heights Ward families was stretching out and delaying them. Reluctantly the family proceeded with the dinner, but all were disappointed that Grandfather Lee was not present to pronounce the blessing and family prayer.

The delay at his home presents an example of the sacrifice so typical in the life of President Lee. A young mother dying with cancer had come with her husband and three little boys for President Lee's advice. Now that the doctors had given no hope for preserving her life, they wanted to know whether they should return to their home in California or stay in Utah with their families, with whom they were visiting during the holidays.

President Lee's advice follows: "There is a time of testing ahead. When you are a 'golden nugget' you must prepare for a fire. Go back home and live each day, and when the Lord wants us he'll take us, and it will be all right."

He was unaware that this advice might have personal application to him on the next day of his own life. The little family returned to California, comforted by the prophet. In departure, they took the last photograph of President and Sister Lee. They reported later that he had confided that he was not feeling well. They described his cheeks as puffy and his color ashen. He had told them that he was fatigued and that in recent days he had felt the presence of his deceased wife, Fern.

It was past 3:00 P.M. when President and Sister Lee joined the family for Christmas dinner. They took their places and were soon busy eating the turkey and his sister Verda's traditional holiday ham. During the meal President Lee suggested to his grandson namesake, Harold Lee Goates, that he bring in the tape recorder from the other room so the family could listen to a tape recording of the Tabernacle Choir's Christmas gift to him, a special broadcast rendition of his favorite hymns. Included on the tape were: "O Link Divine"; "How Beautiful upon the Mountains"; "I Need Thee Every Hour"; "I Know That My Redeemer Lives"; and "One Sweetly Solemn Thought." When the batteries in the tape recorder failed, President Lee seemed disappointed that he couldn't share his pleasure with his loved ones.

After dinner the happy family moved into the living room, where gifts were exchanged. President Lee's sisters, Stella and Verda, and Verda's husband, Charles, were there. A convert from President Lee's long-ago missionary days in Denver, Mary Dean, who was visiting from California, was also part of the group. All the Brent Goates family were present, including President Lee's eldest grandson, David, with his wife, Patsy, and their two children, who represented two of the three great-grandchildren of President Lee. Another grandson, Lesley Drew Goates, brought his bride of only twelve days, Jane Stephenson Goates.

As had been customary for many years, President Lee had come prepared with little envelopes containing cash gifts for every member of his "kingdom," but this time he seemed tired and spent as he proffered his generosity. Although entering into the events with appreciation and interest, he showed no effort to project himself.

Helen had prepared a Christmas program based on an article written by her mother, Fern, and published in the *Friend* after she and President Lee had toured the Holy Land in 1958. Fern had made reference to several Christmas songs which took on new meaning to her as she "walked where Jesus walked." Her beautiful words describing the sacred scenes of the Holy Land were to be interspersed with the music referred to in the text, using talent from the family. The violinists and vocalists were ready to perform, but her father's fatigue prompted Helen to suggest canceling the program. He quickly objected, however, and urged her to proceed. President Lee listened and made comments, but much of the time his eyes were closed. Afterwards, he said to Helen: "Thank you so much, dearie. That was just beautiful and gives us the real Christmas spirit, to reflect upon the land where Jesus lived and taught."

It was after 6:00 P.M. when President and Sister Lee stood up to retrieve their coats. Surprisingly, however, it was evident that President Lee was in no real hurry to depart. With hat in hand and overcoat over his arm, he lingered for almost an hour, uncharacteristic of his usually rapid departure. He moved slowly from room to room as he made his way to the back door, pausing frequently to share his feelings and thoughts with those around him. He seemed to be in good spirits, though his manner was quiet and reflective.

PARTING WORDS TO FAMILY

What subjects were on the prophets' mind on the day before his death? The topics discussed at his extended departure on Christmas Day reveal some of his thinking. He reiterated the faith-promoting stories he had told earlier at his brother Perry's stake high priests meeting regarding translation experiences with the gift of tongues. One such story occurred in Italy, where a young lad named Filipo was his interpreter. Sister Lee reminded him that he was to perform Filipo's marriage in the temple on the following Friday morning. The President replied, "Yes, that's right, if I just have the strength." Sister Lee quickly added, "Of course you will, dear. You must be there." He also told of the miraculous finding of some sacred temple manuscripts earlier thought to be lost, which relieved his mind immensely.

To Brent he spoke privately for the first time of the development of plans for the new, small temple in São Paulo, Brazil, not yet publicly announced. Of particular interest was his optimism concerning improving relationships with the leaders of the Reorganized Church of Jesus Christ of Latter Day Saints. This reconciliation he was quietly promoting through an intermediary, Buddy Youngreen, and the President was most pleased with the promising possibilities ahead.

Finally, for each of the three younger grandchildren, he had special messages of encouragement, praise, and kindly admonition. To Jane he gave counsel about choosing a companion in marriage. To Jonathan, almost sixteen years old and already taller than his grandfather, he said, noting the maturing changes that had taken place in him the past year, physically and spiritually, "I'm proud of you, big boy!" He lingered long in praise of his youngest grandson, Timothy, saying, "You are indeed special to all of us, our sweet Tim." Those benedictory and loving words, now emblazoned as with fire on their hearts and minds, were his last to his family.

President Lee paused just long enough before going out of the door and down the back steps to kiss his daughter Helen and thank her for the lovely day and for providing the opportunity for the family to be together. The door closed behind him and he was gone.

About an hour later, Helen received a telephone call from the daughter of Clyde Edmunds, one of the original members of the Church Welfare Committee, announcing that her father had passed away that morning after a lingering illness. She asked for President Lee's phone number so she could give him this information, but Helen hesitated to oblige, remembering how weary her father had been as he left her home. She offered, instead, to relay the message to him, thinking she could call the following morning after he was more rested. Helen felt impressed later, however, to phone him that evening.

She gave her father the message and President Lee readily agreed that he would by all means call the Edmunds family, though he said: "I almost hesitate to do so since they will probably ask me to speak at the funeral and I just don't know if I have the strength." Helen replied, "I know, Daddy dear, you looked so tired tonight! I felt guilty about keeping you long enough for our little program. Perhaps we should have let you go home sooner."

"Oh no, no, dear," answered President Lee, "that was lovely! We needed that spiritual touch to our day. It was wonderful to hear Mother's beautiful words about the Savior once more and to listen to the girls sing and play. I enjoyed the spirit in your home all through the afternoon and evening."

Then, responding like a true patriarch to his family, never content until each and every child was accounted for, he expressed his concerns for those who had not been there, and spoke of his desire to keep all his family close together. The last wishes of Helen's mother on the same subject were then recalled, and resolves were renewed as Helen urged her weary father to put his mind at ease about all the family and try to get some rest. Unknown to either of them, this was to be their final conversation. It is significant that though he had the burdens of the world on his mind, he never lost his deep love and concern for each one of his precious family.

The day after Christmas was spent in the Goates family leisurely exchanging gifts and running errands. At 5:00 P.M. on December 26 a phone call from Sister Lee announced to Helen the surprising news that President Lee had been admitted to the hospital two hours earlier. Brent, former administrator of the Latter-day Saints Hospital, rushed immediately to see what had occasioned the admission of President Lee and to check on his privacy and the adequacy of his accommodations.

Sister Lee explained on the phone to Helen that the President had gone to bed on Christmas night soon after returning home. He had slept longer than usual—a full ten hours, and yet on awakening the next morning, he still felt fatigued. Concerned, Sister Lee called his physician, Doctor James Orme.

Doctor Orme arrived promptly at the home and carefully conducted a physical examination. He found railes in his lungs; this, in addition to his marked fatigue, prompted Doctor Orme to recommend hospitalization. They agreed that President Lee would enter the hospital, where tests could be conducted to narrow the diagnosis. The President declined the immediate ambulance service urged by Doctor Orme.

President Lee then phoned his private secretary, D. Arthur Haycock, and requested that he come to his home and bring some work that was pending and some letters to be signed. After they had worked together at the Lee home for some time, Brother Haycock drove President and Sister Lee to the hospital at 3:00 P.M., and he was admitted to Room 819.

AT THE HOSPITAL

When Brent arrived at 5:00 P.M. he found the room darkened, with President Lee facing the wall, trying to obtain rest and relief. In a whispered conversation President Lee requested that Brent and Arthur Haycock give to him a priesthood blessing. Arthur answered that President Marion G. Romney had been notified of his hospitalization and was then on his way. With this news President Lee decided to wait for President Romney to arrive.

President Romney was the Second Counselor in the First Presidency and a dear friend of forty-three years in the Lord's work. When he came into the room President Lee directed that Brent anoint him with consecrated oil and President Romney seal the blessing, with Arthur Haycock joining in the circle. President Romney pronounced a tender and beautiful blessing, reminding our Father in Heaven how invaluable was President Lee's leadership to His work on the earth, and then blessing him with the faith to be healed, and those participating with the faith to heal—true gifts of the Holy Spirit. After the blessing all were comforted, and President Lee said: "I feel much better now. There are not three men of greater faith in the world than you three and I am grateful for that blessing."

President Romney leaned over the bed, kissed President Lee, and exchanged with him words of love and confidence and even a bit of humor.

While Brent attended to many administrative details, President Lee now tried, as often as possible, to turn his face to the wall and to rest in the darkened room. He was often interrupted, however, by professional technicians serving their important patient. One of these was Nola Hunt, R.N., Administrative Assistant Director of Nursing. Her recollections of first seeing President Lee are as follows:

> President and Sister Lee were in the room. The President, who was lying in bed, reached out and shook hands with me and said, "I thought you might be a little lonesome for me so I came back to see you."

I thought to myself, "He is so weary and tired." His color was ashen, and I seemed to detect a slight cyanosis [discoloration] about his lips. I spoke briefly with his wife and then left to evaluate other patients.

Between these medical visits President and Sister Lee had prayed together and enjoyed an "intimate conversation" in which President Lee told his wife, "God is very near."

Nurse Hunt ordered additional nursing help for the division, and with Brent Goates and Arthur Haycock reviewed the President's chart and physician's orders. There were no emergency orders and a chest X-ray had been ordered, but no special time was set. No urgency was indicated.

Now the doctors, consultants, and house physicians began to assemble. Brent was relieved to find Doctor Alan H. Morris was on the job. He was a brilliant lung specialist recently recruited to become the assistant director of the hospital's pulmonary function laboratory. He took his two residents to the bedside and thoroughly checked President Lee's lungs. He then carefully briefed the resident doctors, quizzing them as he proceeded, and prepared them with instructions for proper treatment to meet every eventuality.

After that examination Brent sought a private interview with Doctor Morris, who revealed that President Lee was anemic, probably due in part to the blood loss from coughing that morning; his lungs were in poor condition, which was not surprising, since he was known to be suffering from chronic bronchitis; and he was in heart failure.

This latter conclusion came as a great surprise and Brent reminded Dr. Morris that never before had that diagnosis been made, and that his medical history would prove that fact. Doctor Morris firmly, but quietly replied: "That may be true, but I am certain he is in heart distress now. The blood gas studies confirm this. Perhaps if we get him oxygenated properly these symptoms will disappear." Immediate steps were taken to introduce more quantities of oxygen through an oxygen mask.

About this time President Lee inquired about his dinner. When his supper tray came, Mrs. Hunt wanted to put it across his bed but President Lee wanted instead to sit on the side of the bed. The nursing supervisor slipped his robe on him and put on his house slippers. She remembers thinking that "his feet were cyanotic and slightly swollen, but the shoes went on without difficulty. He looked so ill. I thought to myself, 'What is really going on?' "

It was 6:00 P.M. when Mrs. Hunt brought a food tray for Sister Lee as well. President Lee ate only a little of his chicken and rice dinner, but then finished with his favorite—bread and milk.

When Mrs. Hunt returned she noted that he had carefully covered his tray with his napkin and was lying in bed with the oxygen going. He had slipped down in bed, so Mrs. Hunt asked Sister Lee to help her get him up in the bed. Mrs. Hunt recalls:

> We took hold of his arms, and I asked him to bring his knees up and push with the bottom of his feet. This was a great effort for the President and seemed to take all the energy he had. I looked at his face and the thought crossed my mind, "This man could arrest any moment." He turned to his left side. I took a pillow and placed his hands and arms on it, saying, "I'm a pillow girl and I know that this will help you rest better." His usual response would have been, "Thank you," but he seemed too weary to say that.
>
> He appeared asleep, so I talked with Sister Lee and told her how I felt about his being so very tired and that we must do all we could to save his strength. She concurred with this and mentioned the beautiful blessing given to him by President Romney. I stepped out of that quiet and peaceful room and told Brother Haycock that I felt the President was very ill and I had never seen anyone more weary.

She then attempted to persuade Sister Lee that it was best for her to return home for the night. In a few minutes Sister Lee agreed, although she hesitated until Mrs. Hunt promised her she would stay with him and take good care of her husband. Arthur Haycock agreed to wait at the hospital until Brent returned from taking Sister Lee home. There was a tender exchange of love between Sister Lee and the President as she bade him goodnight.

Brent drove Sister Lee home. Before returning to the hospital, he stopped at his nearby home to tell Helen what was happening. He also told Helen to save his dinner, for he would be home as soon as her father was settled for the night.

In the meantime, Arthur Haycock took up his vigil on a chair facing President Lee's bedside, reading the newspaper while the President rested. Suddenly President Lee sat up in the bed, took off the oxygen mask, cleared his throat, and produced a specimen in a tissue, saying to Arthur, "Here, they'll want that."

That precise moment is remembered forever by Arthur. He later reported:

He acted as though he wanted to get out of bed. His face was ashen, covered with perspiration, and his eyes were glazed and bulging. He was staring at me. He didn't respond to my comments. I think he may at that moment have suffered a fatal atack. I laid him back down in his bed.

I didn't like what I saw, so I went immediately to get the doctor. It was only fifteen feet from Room #819 to the nurses' station. I motioned to the nurse to come, and said to her, "He tried to get up out of bed."

"Good," replied the nurse, not sensing the gravity of the situation. "If he's awake we'll take him to X-ray."

It was approximately 7:50 P.M. when Nurse Hunt took a wheelchair to President Lee's room in preparation for his trip to the X-ray department. As she passed the nurses' desk she said to the clerk, "Have someone from Inhalation Therapy come up and accompany us to X-ray." The comment even surprised herself. She mused:

I had never made such a request before. Why did I say it then? I took the wheelchair into the room. At that brief moment I was alone with President Lee. With super effort and strength I saw him raise himself up in bed so he was resting on both elbows. His eyes were open wide, and he was looking straight up. He appeared to be in a trance, and I took hold of his right arm and said—

"President Lee, can you hear me?" There was no response that he did. His eyes closed slowly and he slipped back onto the bed pillow. I knew his spirit was gone from his body. I knew, too, what my training had taught me. I needed to sound the cardiac arrest alarm.

CALLED HOME

At that precise second Arthur Haycock brought the resident doctor to the room. Arriving at the doorway, the doctor took one look at the patient and shouted down the hall, "Cardiac Arrest!" The nurse adjusted President Lee's oxygen mask and lowered his head, and help was there from many doctors immediately.

Just as Brent returned, he saw Arthur Haycock motioning him to hurry to the room. He announced that a cardiac arrest had been called. Without entering the room, Brent rushed to the nursing station for help. He was passed by nurses running to the room, but he remained to get Doctor Morris, who was speaking on the telephone. He was ignoring Brent's motions until the latter shouted

"Cardiac Arrest!" At that Doctor Morris slammed down the phone and raced to the room. Everyone knew then that an intensive care expert was at work. Brent then tried to phone Doctor Orme. Much later the doctor was reached and told to rush to the hospital because his patient was in heart arrest.

In the meantime, Arthur Haycock had phoned President Romney to return to the hospital, and also had reached President Tanner in Arizona and President Spencer W. Kimball, who was at home.

Brent phoned Helen and informed her of the disaster which had struck, and told her to notify Sister Lee. Helen and Jane drove to Sister Lee's home and brought her back to the hospital, where they met Brent down the hall in a room to which President Lee was to be transferred.

Shortly afterward President Kimball came through the door. He was stunned, almost in shock. The family asked him to lead them in a pleading prayer to Heavenly Father, but he was hardly able to speak. Next, President Romney arrived. The family could only ask him to help them pray again, to add his faith to the urgent, broken-hearted petitions. There was nothing else to be done.

Doctor Douglas Ridges, director of the cardiology department at the hospital, came in to explain that attempts were being made to install an electric pacemaker, because at that moment President Lee had no heartbeat of his own and artificial respiration was still required.

About ten to twelve persons, plus much equipment, jammed the room as the doctors asked for more and more specialized drugs and equipment, and runners were meeting every demand. Doctor Morris, fortunately, was directing the emergency care. Dr. Orme arrived and gravely explained to the family that the prognosis was very poor and that a new complication had developed.

Brent's account of the agonizing vigil written a short time later, states:

> Still, despite the obvious bleak medical reports, as President Romney and I paced the floor neither of us felt that the end could come to our prophet-loved one. I still waited for the miracle. He had been saved through three other hospitalizations. He was at the pinnacle of his performance in Church leadership. The kingdom needed him. No one could take his place. We knew the Lord knew that, and we had exercised our faith and priesthood. Now when was

the Lord going to come to our rescue? He could send angels to help. I knew it must come soon, but I waited, expectantly. It could come any moment now. But . . . it never came.

I was back in the room with Helen and the family when Doctor Orme came down the hall and announced that they had ceased treatment and that at 8:58 p.m. he had passed away. No one can describe the emptiness and awfulness of that announcement. It just couldn't be! Yes, he was sick, but certainly in possession of his faculties. Our greatest concern at that time was how we were going to forestall his giving a talk the next Sunday night to the Special Interest members in the Salt Lake Tabernacle. That was then the extent of our worries. Now, he was gone and we were lost in grief, and soon the entire Church membership would be devastated. How could it be? How could the Lord allow this tragedy to happen?

Such were the human, very mortal, protestations of loved ones. But the protests changed nothing. The Lord's will had been announced, and from this verdict there was no appeal.

The necessary nursing care was tenderly and reverently attended to after the room in which President Lee's body lay was cleared and had become suddenly silent once more.

Mrs. Hunt closed her record of this poignant experience with these reflective comments:

> The room was then made clean and tidy. Before I left, I stood at his bedside and felt within me that this was according to God's plan. I saw him changed in the twinkling of an eye. All the knowledge and wisdom of medicine or the most skilled physicians could not bring him back. It was simply not to be. Peace and tranquility filled his room. I quietly closed the door.

CHAPTER 34

Shock, Tributes, Funeral, and Burial

When the door closed on the life of President Harold B. Lee, President Romney, President Kimball, and Brent Goates stood together in stunned silence. No one could speak. Finally Brent became aware that he was witnessing a transference of power and authority to a new prophet. He described that historic moment in his journal:

> The three of us, President Romney, President Kimball, and I, stood with our arms about one another, bowed in grief and sick beyond words. After the longest time my administrative training finally overcame the blanket of grief enough for me to realize that some action had to be taken.
>
> Courageously I ventured into the sacred, grief-laden silence and whispered to the new leader of the Church: "Do you want me to phone Wendell Ashton with the news of the President's passing?" Two heads nodded mute approval as the others, too, broke momentarily back into reality. Then President Kimball, senior Apostle and President of the Quorum of the Twelve, in his first executive order as the leader of the Church, said: "I think you'd better tell him to prepare a news release.'
>
> I fumbled in the directory for the phone number and obtained the line, then listened as President Romney, who now had stepped aside because there was no First Presidency, told Wendell the sad, shocking news. I then gave Wendell the details—death came at 8:58 p.m. from lung and cardiac arrest. The cause of death I gave was my own conclusion, but I felt that my medical-hospital background and

intimacy with the medical treatment of President Lee was sufficient to provide accuracy under the stress of the moment.

How quickly the transformation had occurred! It was automatic. With the last heartbeat of President Lee, President Kimball assumed the mantle of leadership over the kingdom of God on earth. Arthur Haycock, sitting at the side in abject sorrow, suddenly found himself responding to the crisis and working now for the successor to President Lee. He went to the hospital board room and commenced notifying members of the Council of the Twelve, while Brent handled arrangements for the family with the mortuary and the hospital.

In the room down at the end of the hall feeble efforts commenced to comfort the loved ones and President Kimball, who stood in unbelieving anguish. This family could empathize with President Kimball because they remembered just seventeen months before when a phone call had brought word to President and Sister Lee of the passing of President Smith, and then it was President Lee who was in that same bewildered state of wishing it had never happened.

Helen's immediate task was to comfort and give support to Sister Lee. But all of these principals to the tragedy were just going through the motions with a numb and automatic response.

The day-after-Christmas drama, which seemingly had not taken on any significance until the 5:00 P.M. phone call from the hospital, had resulted in an unbelievable crisis at about 7:15 P.M., and ended when Brent drove Sister Lee back to a husbandless home at 11:00 P.M., where her family awaited her arrival.

Brent returned to his home to find Helen and Jane back from the hospital, and a housefull of their broken-hearted children, who couldn't comprehend yet that they never again on this earth would be with their beloved grandfather. It was many hours past midnight before this gathering of mourners adjourned.

Thus ended an unfathomable, heart-breaking ten-hour period on a day never to be forgotten by the Church. That day was December 26, 1973, his last in mortality.

THE SHOCK SPREADS

When the announcement of President Harold B. Lee's sudden passing reached the public there was an immediate reaction of disbelief, shock, and despair. Four years later Elder W. Grant Bangerter, speaking in the Salt Lake Tabernacle at the October 1977 general conference of the Church, recreated this historic situation:

> President Lee's death was completely unexpected. It is necessary to remember that over a period of twenty-five years members of the Church had awaited the time when Harold B. Lee would become the President. There had been every reason to think that this would eventually happen, due to his relative youthfulness and because he occupied a position in seniority following Joseph Fielding Smith and David O. McKay, both of whom were of advanced age.
>
> In addition, Harold B. Lee had gained more than average prominence. His leadership in the welfare and priesthood programs of the Church, his forceful nature, and his sound judgment had made him one of the Apostles most listened to and one whose influence and advice were most respected. He had an evident spiritual stature which commended him to the members of the Church as one of the great men of our time. He possessed an unusual ability to relate as a personal friend to countless people. It was expected that when he became President he would preside for twenty years or more.
>
> Suddenly he was gone!—called elsewhere after only one and one-half years. It was the first time since the death of the Prophet Joseph Smith when the President had died before it was time for him to die.
>
> In deep sorrow and concern the surging questions arose in the minds of the people, much as they did at the time when Joseph Smith was killed in Carthage, Illinois. "What will we do now? How can we carry on without the prophet? Our great leader has gone. Can the Church survive this emergency?"
>
> Of course we knew that the Church would survive, but it could not possibly be the same. We had never expected Spencer W. Kimball to become the President, and we had not looked to him for the same leadership evident in the life of Harold B. Lee.

Elder Bangerter then followed with a magnificent tribute to the new President, Spencer W. Kimball.

The news was indeed a stunning shock to members of the Church who for the past century had grown accustomed to watching Presidents of the Church grow old and live unusually long lives. President Lee, at seventy-four years of age, was the youngest Church President to die since the martyrdom of Joseph Smith. When he assumed the world leadership of the Church on July 7, 1972, at age seventy-three he became the youngest man to head the Church in the thirty years since World War II. Now, unbelievably, he had served the shortest tenure of any of the eleven Presidents, just less than eighteen months.

It is not surprising that the simple facts of his death seemed unbelievable, even to journalists and the media reporters, who accused the Church and family of withholding information from them. Shock and stunned reaction was universal among those who loved and appreciated President Lee. President N. Eldon Tanner wrote of his feelings, typical of many other responses: "President Lee's passing is a great shock to all of us, the greatest shock I've experienced in my life, and our sadness cannot be adequately expressed."

TRIBUTES ARRIVE

Immediately following the announcement of President Harold B. Lee's death, tributes and messages of sympathy and appreciation began to pour into Church headquarters by telegram and by letter. Only a small sample, beginning with President Spencer W. Kimball's first published reaction, is included here:

President Harold B. Lee and I have been associated in the Council of the Twelve from 1943 until he was called into the First Presidency by President Joseph Fielding Smith in 1970. Even before that time we had established a friendship. He was my ideal. He had a tremendous understanding of the doctrines of the restored gospel of Jesus Christ, and of the organization and functioning of the Church.

President Lee was a great friend of the downtrodden and sorrowing. While he was an outstanding administrator and tireless worker, frequently he found time to visit the sick and those heavy of heart. When President Lee prayed, he really talked with his Heavenly Father.

He truly measured up as a prophet of God in every way—in leadership, perception, activity, and in his responses. He was a man of superior courage. Many times I have seen him stand alone for a principle. He would give his unshakable witness of the divinity of the restored gospel without hesitation, to the mighty of the earth as well as to the lowly.

President Lee was loyal to his family, friends, and brethren. Only a few days ago, in a meeting of the First Presidency and the Twelve, he spoke of his esteem and affection for his associates in the leadership of the Church.

The Resolution of the Council of the Twelve read as follows:

The world needed President Harold B. Lee when his time came to be the Lord's leader among mankind.

He was a prophet continually in tune with heaven, who spoke and acted with unswerving courage and boldness in applying the teachings of the Savior to the challenges and problems of these turbulent times. Indeed it could be said of him, as it had been said of his predecessor, Brigham Young: "He was a lion of the Lord". . . .

President Lee lived the words of his Master. Harold B. Lee believed and taught with all the fiber of his soul the divinity of the Lord's mission, the reality of the resurrection for all mankind, and the restoration of the fulness of the gospel of Jesus Christ through the Prophet Joseph Smith.

President Lee stood tall as a leader among men, both within and without the Church.

To all Church members as well as to all people everywhere, we reaffirm to the world the words of Harold B. Lee on the day he was ordained and set apart as President of the Church: "Keep the commandments."

From the President of the United States, Richard M. Nixon:

Mrs. Nixon and I were deeply saddened to learn of the sudden death of Harold B. Lee. All Americans mourn the loss of this dedicated President of The Church of Jesus Christ of Latter-day Saints, and we send our heartfelt sympathy to the members of the Church and to President Lee's family.

As President of the Church, and as an educator, missionary, businessman, and public official, President Lee's influence for good has been deeply felt. The Church's successful welfare program that began in the 1930s gives just one example of how President Lee's administrative and organizational skills combined with his faith and courage to bring hope and inspiration to millions in our nation and in our world. For my part, I knew him as a warm and generous friend whose counsel and prayers I valued greatly.

From Lord Thomson of Fleet, London, England, owner of the *Times* of London as well as some two hundred other newspapers:

I have lost a warm friend and the world has lost one of its great leaders in the passing of President Harold B. Lee. He was an inspiration to all who came in contact with him. The work he has accomplished has been a great blessing not only to members of The Church of Jesus Christ of Latter-day Saints, but to all mankind. His passing leaves a great void in my life.

From corporate executives of American industry, including Frank E. Barnett, chairman of the board, Union Pacific Corporation, Union Pacific Railroad Company:

It was with profound sorrow that we learned this morning of the passing of Harold B. Lee. On behalf of the entire board of directors and officers of Union Pacific, I convey our deepest condolences on his passing. His influence for good extended throughout the world, and I am confident there were few men more loved and respected. He was a tremendous inspiration to those of us at Union Pacific who had the privilege of knowing and associating with him for almost twenty years. I know that the inspiration and teaching of this great leader will be a force for good for time immemorial.

From James F. Oates, Jr., retired chairman of the board, Equitable Life Assurance Society, and a personal friend of President Lee, wrote:

No one that I have known has ever lived a more useful life of service than President Harold B. Lee. He was enormously effective, not only in the business aspects of his great enterprise, but also as a spiritual leader. The country will miss him very much indeed.

From Dr. Norman Vincent Peale, famed author and pastor of Marble Collegiate Reformed Church, New York City:

I was shocked at the news of the passing of my good friend, President Harold B. Lee. I admired him tremendously. He was one of the most enlightened and creative religious leaders in the world. A giant has fallen.

From Elder Ezra Taft Benson, the Council of the Twelve:

President Harold B. Lee was a man of faith, vision, and a warm and compassionate heart toward all people. He has been an international leader without a peer. Programs he has initiated will bless people in many nations for generations.

His distinguished leadership has shown a grasp of Church and world needs which has revealed his prophetic insight as a prophet of God.

From Neal A. Maxwell, Commissioner of Education, The Church of Jesus Christ of Latter-day Saints:

The suddenness of his passing is such a shock, and yet so much was accomplished under his leadership that his presidency made up in height what it lacked in length of time.

From Rabbi Abner Bergman, Congregation Kol Ami, Salt Lake City:

> I knew President Lee both in an official capacity as well as personally, and always found him to be a paragon of warmth, kindness, and personal integrity. . . . I will miss him. Many will miss him.

From the Presiding Bishopric of the Church:

> President Harold B. Lee's untimely death was a great emotional shock to us. We will sorely miss this noble, Christ-like Latter-day prophet. He truly was a man of God. His short tenure as President of the Church was packed with decisions and spiritual guidance that will have a far-reaching impact not only on Church members but on the whole world.
>
> He had an understanding of business like few men. His knowledge of doctrine of the Church and kingdom was unmatched. His life was one of total integrity and unwavering loyalty to the Master. He had empathy and compassion for every living soul.
>
> Surely in his passing we lose one of the sweet, noble souls in all humanity.

From Belle S. Spafford, General President, Relief Society:

> For thirty years members of the Relief Society General Presidency have had close and rewarding association with President Lee. We have benefited therefrom. We have felt the warmth of his personal friendship. We have marveled at his tender concern for the "one," and his selflessness in giving of himself. We revere him as prophet, seer, and revelator, chosen of the Lord to lead His earthly kingdom in a precarious period of time.

From D. Arthur Haycock, personal secretary to President Lee:

> In the sudden passing of President Harold B. Lee, I have lost a long-time and cherished friend. President Lee was my seminary teacher over forty years ago. That association has continued ever since. While I was in my early twenties, he ordained me a bishop. Whenever there was a serious problem or a special event in our family, President Lee was close by to comfort and cheer or to encourage and commend, depending upon the circumstances. During the thirty-five years since I first began employment at the Church headquarters, I've had close personal association with President Lee. He's always been so kind and gentle, wise and strong—virtues which he shared freely with others. To know him was to respect and love him. To be in his presence was to know for a surety that he was a prophet of God.

Scores of other tributes, too many to list, came from respected leaders from all walks of life.

A Period of Mourning

On Friday, December 29, 1973, the first handful among thousands of mourners began arriving before dawn on the steps of the Church Administration Building, 47 East South Temple Street, headquarters of the Church in Salt Lake City, where the body of Harold B. Lee would lie in state. The *Deseret News* told of three teenage boys in shirtsleeves who were the first to arrive and shivered in the predawn chill as they waited for the viewing to begin. "We wanted to be here first," one of them said. It was 7:25 A.M. and there was a faint light in the east behind overcast skies as the hearse arrived and the coffin bearing President Lee's body was carried to an inner foyer.

Flowers began arriving at 7:55 A.M. and the line awaiting admittance to the building stretched east halfway up the street by the time the first mourners entered the building. A drizzling rain began about 8:00 A.M., with many umbrellas being raised above the waiting crowd.

By 11:00 A.M. an estimated 2,575 persons had passed the open coffin. The mourners came from all walks of life, the poor and the rich, and included government leaders, older couples, businessmen, young girls, and entire families including small children clasping their parents' hands. Many had tears in their eyes as they left the building through the northeast door.

A silence broken only by whispers prevailed in the inner foyer, but many of the mourners stopped in a corridor near the exit door to examine memorabilia on display, including a greeting sent to President Lee by Korean members of the Church. He was the first General Authority to ever travel and teach in Korea.

President Lee's body lay in state for one and one-half days. Even though it snowed and rained almost continually, the lines of mourners showing their esteem never diminished. President Lee's grandsons took turns standing at both ends of the casket in a reverent honor guard, sometimes in three-hour shifts. Though many who passed by were their friends and acquaintances, there was no acknowledgment or conversation now, as mutual grief bowed everyone in silent sorrow.

One poignant moment to be remembered was when the line

Mourners standing in line outside Church Administration Building

Line files past casket, where grandson Drew stands as honor guard

temporarily came to a halt as a young woman, with five small children, quietly lifted each child up to the casket's edge.

Counting the last visitors on the day of the funeral, more than fifteen thousand persons came to view President Lee for the last time in this lifetime.

MEMORIAL SERVICES

In the beautiful marble rotunda of the Church Administration Building, the public viewing ended as nearly 250 persons remained for the family prayer, which was led by President Lee's elder brother, Perry, who then was serving as the president of the Cannon Stake in Salt Lake City. Following the prayer, the General Authorities left the foyer and formed two lines on the steps of the building.

President Lee's body was then brought from the inner foyer of the office building to a hearse waiting at curbside by seven grandsons of President Lee, along with Richard Callister, a grandnephew of Sister Lee. The grandsons serving as pallbearers were: David Brent Goates, Harold Lee Goates, Lesley Drew Goates, Jonathan Lee Goates, Timothy Lee Goates, Alan Lee Wilkins, and Jay Earl Wilkins. Honorary pallbearers were all the General Authorities of the Church.

Because of the inclement weather, most persons accompanying the casket moved to Temple Square in the nearly one hundred automobiles which had been parked along the street to carry the family and General Authorities and their wives to the Tabernacle.

With bowed head, President Lee's wife entered the Salt Lake Tabernacle, which was filled with five thousand friends, relatives, and leaders from all walks of life. She was accompanied by family members.

President Spencer W. Kimball conducted the service and was also a speaker. Other speakers were President Lee's two counselors in the First Presidency—President N. Eldon Tanner and President Marion G. Romney, along with Elder Gordon B. Hinckley of the Council of the Twelve.

The invocation for the service was offered by Elder Marvin J. Ashton of the Council of the Twelve and the benediction was given by D. Arthur Haycock, President Lee's private secretary and a Regional Representative of the Twelve.

Leaving Church Administration Building for the Tabernacle

The rostrum was filled with flowers. Members of the Salt Lake Tabernacle Choir were in their seats, and Dr. Alexander Schreiner was at the organ filling the giant, oval-shaped hall with solemn organ chords and quiet melodies. During the service the choir sang some of President Lee's favorite music, the same selections they had recorded a few days before as a Christmas present to him: "I Know That My Redeemer Lives," "Lead Kindly Light," "I Need Thee Every Hour," and "How Firm a Foundation."

PRESIDENT KIMBALL SPEAKS

In his fifteen-minute address President Spencer W. Kimball, borrowing a phrase used by the late President at a funeral for a stake president, characterized Harold B. Lee as a "giant of a man." He bore strong testimony of the Savior's divine leadership over his church and President Lee's mission as a "great, noble and good man who became one of the Lord's rulers here upon the earth," after the manner of Abraham (see Abraham 3:22–23).

Saying "a giant redwood has fallen and left a great space in the forest," President Kimball further characterized President Lee as follows:

A giant of a man he was. A man endowed with a rare native intelligence, he recalls a thousand experiences over the terrain of time, having a unique gift to quickly get to the heart of matters under consideration and quickened by a capacity to discard extraneous information, thus freeing the mind for decisive action.

A giant whose shadow fell across the world, bringing under it the influence of the gospel to millions of members and friends of the Church.

A giant, who, while carrying the challenges of the apostleship and the First Presidency under divine influence, anxiously still took time to share his thoughts and his counsel with countless thousands on an individual basis.

A great giant, who, with inspiration, made the experiences, stories, and the counsel of the scriptures find a place in the hearts and minds of men the world over.

A giant who reached into the inner recesses of his listeners' hearts to plant understanding, vision, direction, and comfort.

A great giant who represented our Father in Heaven to all of his children and bore them comfort, strength, and godly influence.

A master teacher, who much like the Savior, took the ordinary experiences of today to teach the will of the Lord.

At the funeral in the Tabernacle

Yes, among our generations has walked one of God's most noble, powerful, committed, and foreordained giant redwoods— President Harold B. Lee.

Comparing him also to the ancient prophets Samuel and Saul, President Kimball said: "President Lee was a mighty prince among us. He was a dynamic leader, one easy to follow. Everybody knew that President Harold B. Lee was a prophet, as did Israel concerning Samuel. 'And all Israel from Dan to Beersheba knew that Samuel was established to be a prophet of the Lord' (1 Samuel 3:19–21.)" President Lee's similarity to Saul, said President Kimball, was "that with the mantle of authority upon him, he came soon to be another man with a new heart and the revelations continued to illuminate him and the people through him. President Lee has thus given leadership to the Apostles. He has stood high, taller than any pine."

President Kimball, speaking in his hushed, husky voice, then made reference to his role as President Lee's successor. Referring to his fervent prayers for President Lee's welfare, President Kimball continued:

President Lee has gone. I never thought it could happen. I sincerely wanted it never to happen. I doubt if anyone in the Church has prayed harder and more consistently for a long life and the general welfare of President Lee than my Camilla and myself.

I have not been ambitious. I am four years older than Brother Lee (to the exact day, March 28). I have expected that I would go long before he would go. My heart cries out to him and for him. How we loved him!

President Tanner's Tribute

President Tanner showed an uncharacteristic emotional edge as he approached his task of paying tribute to President Lee. He had to pause briefly amid his tearful remarks, his voice cracking with emotion, explaining "it's the third time I've stood here on such an occasion," meaning the deaths of three prophets to whom he was serving as a counselor.

President Tanner described President Lee as "a true servant of God," citing the relationship which brought them together in the leading councils of the Church as the basis of that conclusion.

When I was called by President McKay to be his Second Counselor in the First Presidency, though President Lee had been a member of the Council of the Twelve for approximately thirty years, he, a senior member, supported me in that position and worked with me, showing me every respect and courtesy a junior member could have shown to a senior member in such a position. I always admired him for this, and loved him, realizing again more fully than ever before that he was a true servant of the Lord.

He had only one thing in his mind, and that was to serve the Lord, do his will and keep his commandments, and help build the kingdom of God here upon the earth.

President Tanner's unique experience provided a basis for appraising President Lee's work:

It has been a real opportunity, privilege, and blessing to be able to work so closely with these three prophets of God, to sit at their feet and see how the Lord works through them, and I bear testimony without reservation that these men were prophets of God.

There has never been any question in my mind about President Lee as a prophet, and I was so pleased that members of the Church as a whole accepted him so quickly and so completely, and were prepared to follow him as one speaking for the Lord.

Concerning President Lee's missionary zeal, President Tanner noted: "His whole desire was to spread the gospel and to help the people understand the mission of Jesus Christ, which he did so ably. He never missed an opportunity to bear his testimony and answer questions and explain the principles of the gospel."

He also described a meeting between the First Presidency and the Ambassador of Iran, in which world conditions, particularly those in the Middle East, were discussed, and President Lee said with conviction and humility: "We think the only solution to this difficult problem is for all of us to belong to the one true church of Christ. When that happens, we will realize that we are all children of the same God, and that we ought not to quarrel with each other, but that we should love one another."

President Tanner said President Lee concluded with this remark: "Why is it that they are shouting at one another in the Middle East? It is because they don't really believe in the one and true living God, and they are not members of the true church of Jesus Christ. If they would accept this, we would have peace, and the same would be true throughout the world."

President Tanner observed that President Lee was always very careful not to criticize or belittle any individual or any church, but was emphatic in his beliefs and convictions.

Presidents Spencer W. Kimball, N. Eldon Tanner, and Marion G. Romney (sustained the following day as the First Presidency) lead Apostles from Tabernacle after funeral service

Continuing, President Tanner said:

His influence was felt for good wherever he went, and with whomever he was associated. As we came out of our December meeting of the First Presidency and the Quorum of the Twelve, to which all of the General Authorities had been invited, and where President Lee had counseled and instructed the Brethren and had borne his testimony, I said to President Romney, "There is no greater evidence that we have been listening to a prophet of God than what we have heard this day." President Romney replied: "I agree fully. There is no question about it. The Spirit of the Lord has borne witness unto my soul that he is a prophet."

Describing his untiring service, President Tanner said of President Lee:

Our beloved President was always working as though he had a deadline to meet, and that he must meet it while running at high speed. He never thought of his own comfort or convenience. We urged him on many occasions to take a little respite, to relax and rest, but he seemed never to be concerned about himself. He wanted to be of service to his fellowmen, and . . . he was determined to do all in his power to further the work of the Lord and to build people. He loved and showed an interest in everyone, and was loved by them.

TRIBUTE FROM AN OLD FRIEND

President Marion G. Romney, who was at President Lee's bedside the night of his death, composed for the newspapers this tribute to President Lee:

> He was not only a prophet but also a great seer and revelator. I have never been associated with a man who drew more heavily upon the powers of heaven than Harold B. Lee.
>
> He had an unshakable assurance that God lives, that Jesus is the Christ, and that His gospel in all its purity and fulness was restored to the earth through the Prophet Joseph Smith. He never flinched before anyone in giving that testimony.
>
> Long before he became President of the Church, he made inspired contributions to the upbuilding of the kingdom of God on earth which will strengthen the Church for decades to come. He was a pioneering leader in the establishment of the great welfare program, and he was the leader who, under the First Presidency and the Twelve, organized and molded the correlation program of the Church. Never in my experience has the Church been better organized and better administered than under his great leadership. He truly was one of the greatest prophets who have walked the earth.

Now at the funeral, President Romney, his voice quavering with emotion, described his first meeting with President Lee some forty years earlier:

> The operator of a neighboring grocery store introduced me to his brother-in-law, Harold B. Lee. He was dressed in striped coveralls. His left hand was on his breast, and he reached out his right to shake my hand. Captivated by his magnetic presence, I felt I had found a friend. The experiences of forty years and his last words to me, spoken as he lay on his deathbed last Wednesday afternoon, confirmed that first impression.

The theme of President Romney's tribute was that Harold B. Lee was in the shadow of the Almighty:

The source of his greatness was his knowledge that he lived in the shadow of the Almighty. God was his partner and his guide. With Him, he was in constant communication. He accepted the gospel of Jesus Christ for what it is—the eternal truth. In it he found the key to the solution of every human need. His convictions were conceived and fortified by his experiences.

In his tribute of love and respect to a "mighty man of God, my long-time friend, President Harold B. Lee," President Romney gave this eloquent description:

> Humility before God and fearlessness before men were the essence of his character. His ministry has been characterized by an uncommon originality and daring. He was neither circumscribed nor restricted by the learning of the world nor by the wisdom of men. We who sat with him daily were frequently amazed at the breadth of his vision and the depth of his understanding.

President Romney outlined the development of the Church welfare program as guided by President Lee and said:

> Many there were in the midst of the great depression of the 1930s, who having faltered, turned to state and federal governments for help. Harold B. Lee was not among them. Taking the Lord at his word that man should earn his bread in the sweat of his face and convinced that all things are possible to him that believeth, he struck out boldly with the fearless ingenuity and courage of a Brigham Young to pioneer a way whereby his people (he was the President of Pioneer Stake at the time) could, by their own efforts and the help of their brethren, be supplied the necessities of life.
>
> Those who were close to him in those dark days know that he wept over the suffering of his people, but more than that, he did something for them.
>
> With all his heart he loved and served his fellowmen. He loved the poor, for he had been one of them. "I have loved you," he said. "I have come to know you intimately. Your problems, thank the Lord, have been my problems, because I know, as you know, what it means to walk when you have not the money to ride. I know what it means to go without meals to buy a book to go to the university. I thank God now for those experiences. I have loved you because of your devotion and faith. God bless you that you won't fail."

The development of the welfare program seemed to President Romney to be a preparation for greater works to come, particularly the correlation program as directed and guided by President Lee. President Romney explained:

> During the last fifteen or so years, his has been the predominating influence in organizing, developing, and correlating the organizations and functions of the Church. That the Church is today well on the way to being so structured that it can efficiently administer to the spiritual, temporal, and educational needs of its rapidly expanding membership, is, in large measure, due to his genius.

In closing, President Romney recalled an article he had written about President Lee many years earlier, in which he had predicted, "The future must reckon with Harold B. Lee."

> Since then, we have been reckoning with him for twenty years, and he has not once faltered. We mourn his passing, but there is no need to mourn for him. . . . There is laid up for him a crown of glory. He will dwell in exaltation and eternal life with the prophets of ancient and latter-day times.

Tribute from a Traveling Companion

Elder Hinckley said "President Lee's was a magnificent heritage" and pointed out how his ancestry and early life had combined to mold him into a superb instrument to carry out God's will on earth.

> As I look over this vast congregation, as I see this veritable garden of floral tributes, as I have noted the hundreds of telegrams and other expressions of love and sympathy, there have crowded across my mind the images of a hundred contrasting scenes of his earlier life—of days of struggle and poverty and anonymity; and I have marveled at the manner in which the Lord has magnified his chosen servant.

Elder Hinckley told of family deprivation, sorrow, and tragedy in the Lee ancestry, then added:

> It is a long odyssey from that Idaho farm to this Tabernacle, where thousands gather in respect and love to pay him honor and acknowledge the power of God in his life. But with all of the triumph of that life, there also has been much of sorrow, much of struggle, much of adversity, much of disappointment, of frustration, of bitter defeat.
>
> But be it said to his eternal credit that wherever circumstances knocked him down, as they frequently did, he stood again where he

had fallen and then moved on to greater achievement. Perhaps even in this travail there was the molding power of the Lord in his behalf, for out of that chastening process there came a refinement, a patience, a polish, an understanding, a grace beautiful to witness and marvelous in its expression.

Elder Hinckley further told of preparing for this funeral address by looking at a handwritten memorandum from President Lee, and how his initials "HBL" seemed to grow into three words— *Humility, Benevolence,* and *Loyalty:*

Ours was the rare privilege of traveling with President and Sister Lee many thousands of miles in the British Isles, in Europe, in Israel, and in other lands. No one could have that experience without coming to know that here was a humble man—a man without arrogance, void of officiousness, never haughty or noisy or offensive. His was not a groveling humility, but rather that of which the Master spoke when he declared on the Mount: "Blessed are the meek: for they shall inherit the earth." (Matthew 5:5.)

In 1972 we walked together in the Holy Land. . . . On that sacred occasion, when moonlight filtered through the leaves of the olive trees [at the Garden Tomb meeting], he whom we sustained as prophet spoke in humble, quiet testimony. We felt something of heaven and I saw that night President Harold B. Lee as a man of true humility, with the faith of a child, standing in the stature of a prophet who bore witness of the living reality of the Lord Jesus Christ.

Man of benevolence. Legions are those who could testify of his kindness. Much has been written of his great service in the Church welfare program.

But there have been other more intimate expressions of love. I know of no man who went more frequently to the hospital to visit the sick, to comfort, to bless. There sits a man in this hall today who could testify of his coming in the hours of the night in a time of desperation; and in the authority of the holy priesthood in him vested, he laid his hands upon that man's head and rebuked the very powers of death.

Loyalty to God and his Son, the resurrected Lord. This was the flawless gem in the crown of his life. He was wont to say, "Never think of me as the head of this Church. Jesus Christ is the head of this Church. I am only a man, his servant." Of him, the Lord, he testified with a persuasiveness almost irresistible. A business leader said to him one day, "I believe in the Lord, but I do not have a testimony of the living Lord." President Lee replied, "Then you lean on my testimony while you study and pray until your own is strong enough to stand alone."

The magnificent tributes and testimonies borne by his fellow General Authorities and the beautiful music of the Tabernacle Choir subdued the aching hearts and brought much comfort. Outside the Tabernacle the elements and atmosphere were much less soothing.

THE BURIAL

Leaden skies above Salt Lake City produced a downpour of cold rain after the funeral. The day, gray and dreary, had begun with a brief sprinkling of snow turning to occasional drops of rain during the funeral, but a heavy storm erupted just as family members and friends of the late President of the Church began to surround the grave high in the hillside overlooking a fog-shrouded valley at the Salt Lake City Cemetery.

At least one hundred persons attended the graveside rites, many of whom were waiting as the funeral cortege entered the cemetery. Graveyard attendants had shoveled snow from the site and mourners stood on soggy grass or on the canvas that was spread on the winter ground. Besides the General Authorities and family members, those gathered at the grave included children, elderly persons, and others who wished to pay their last respects to the prophet who had led the Church for only one year, five months, and nineteen days.

Private and public interest mingled at the gravesite. Banks of microphones broadcasting the proceedings to radio listeners necessitated a maze of electronic wiring. Floral offerings were arranged at the scene, providing a bank of color to the otherwise gloomy black-and-white backdrop at the graveside service.

President Spencer W. Kimball presided at the brief service, sharing an umbrella with L. Brent Goates, who later pronounced the dedicatory prayer.

This was the scene as, under a sea of black umbrellas and in a drenching rain, President Harold Bingham Lee was buried at the side of his first wife, Fern Lucinda Tanner Lee, who died September 24, 1962. Under the adverse circumstances the dedication of the grave lasted only a few minutes, but some mourners had stood for more than half an hour in the rain awaiting the arrival of the funeral cortege.

At dedication of grave

L. Brent Goates, a Regional Representative of the Twelve, began his dedicatory prayer:

> It is not unfitting that the heavens should weep today, because we, the Church membership worldwide, weep too—for ourselves—at the sudden passing of President Lee. . . .
> The loved ones and leaders of the Church take comfort in the assurance which has come that President Lee's work here on earth is done, knowing that only thy summons can release a prophet from his life's mission, and that he has undoubtedly gone on to a much more glorious and important assignment in the world beyond. . . .
> In the authority of the Holy Priesthood, I thus dedicate this grave as the final resting place of President Harold Bingham Lee's mortal remains until the time of the resurrection of the just, when body and spirit will again be reunited, to clasp the loved ones here reposed, in the morning of the glorious resurrection attending the coming of thy Son, Jesus the Christ.

IN MEMORY OF A PROPHET OF GOD

A prophet died, and at his grave
Stood mourning Saints of God;

We wept, and heaven wept; her tears
Splashed on the winter sod.

Some lived and died and never knew
The value of his word
Because they never knew he was
A prophet of the Lord.

Some found their comfort far away
And never saw his face,
Nor touched his hand, nor heard his voice;
Still knew his gentle grace.

Some lived near the prophet's heart
And knelt with him in prayer;
Acquainted with a noble man,
They knew his kind watch-care.

I bless his name because I knew!
And know! And shall remember
The day I wept, and heaven wept,
One sad day in December.

—Jo M. Shaw

GONE, BUT NOT FORGOTTEN

Who can measure the loss of their living Prophet as felt by thousands of loyal, faithful Saints? What was the significance of the passing of President Harold B. Lee to innumerable individuals who suffered from this separation? A glimpse of an answer comes from these few, selected responses after the funeral.

From far-off Tokyo, Japan, the patriarch of the Japan Tokyo Stake, Ken Watanabe, wrote to the widow of the President:

> As I pause and reflect upon the life of President Lee I am saddened and new tears roll down, for he was not only my Prophet, Seer and Revelator, but also my father, teacher, brother, and friend.
>
> His passing was the greatest shock of my life. As many others, I shed tears of love for him. I think I wept for him more than anybody here in Asia. Oh, how I loved him. But, now he has gone . . .
>
> I do not know the will of the Lord fully, however, I know that the President has finished his mission here on the earth and was called home for the greater assignment. I also feel that the best way to pay my tribute to him is to become like him and to keep all the commandments of the Lord and to have a privilege to meet him

when the Savior comes. Till that time, I hope to be a good son to you, Sister Lee, as John the Beloved was to the Savior's mother.

The youth of the Church felt bereft, too. When Elder James E. Faust spoke at Brigham Young University early in January, 1974, he made some remarks and bore his testimony about the passing of President Lee. Afterwards he received a letter from a young lady that said, "I felt very close to President Lee, although I never knew him." Elder Faust added his concurrence to the Lee family, saying, "I think this statement is indicative of how thousands and thousands of people felt toward him."

Perhaps representing all the youth of the Church is Connie Holton of Salt Lake City, who came to the Lee home with a loaf of bread on Christmas, 1973, and also left an endearing note which stated in part:

> One of the strongest spiritual experiences that I've received has been when I felt the Holy Ghost testify to me that you are a prophet of God. This I have felt whenever I've been in the sound of your voice. My prayers are with you always, for I realize, although I'm sure in only a small way, that your responsibilities are great.
>
> I deeply love you and know that you are a spokesman for Jesus Christ. Hopefully I will be found worthy to be with you and the prophets of the ages and all the righteous when Christ comes again. I promise to sustain you in all things for I know that in doing so I will be following our Savior.

Even nonmembers of the Church who had had only a brushing acquaintance with President Lee felt so moved by his sudden passing that they were compelled to write of the loss they too felt. Here is one such comment from a journalist, Tammy Tanaka, of the Religious News Service of New York City. Her expression came in a letter dated January 11, 1974, addressed to Wendell J. Ashton.

> President Lee is one of the most beautiful human beings I have ever met—whose inner light and love I will always remember as a goal toward which we should all strive. I cannot find words to properly describe him, but President Lee made a permanent and deep impression on me, as I know he did on others.
>
> I have the profoundest love and respect for this great man, whose power and closeness to God is indisputable!

From Seattle, Washington, F. Arthur Kay, then a Regional Representative of the Twelve and later the President of the Seattle

Temple and a General Authority, wrote this letter of bereavement on January 3, 1974:

> We, of the Great Northwest, were stunned and unbelieving at the first news releases, hoping and praying they would prove to be false. Few, if any men, in my time, have left a greater void or a greater sense of profound loss at their passing. Few, if any, have had a greater impact on the Church and its programs designed to meet the needs of the individual member, and few, if any, have inspired a greater response for good in the lives of all who knew him the world over.
>
> President Lee left so many lasting and profoundly moving effects on my life and those of my family that we shall revere his life and labors forever, and because of this great love and respect, we extend it to you, his family.

A previously unknown departing missionary, who was befriended by President Lee at the Missionary Training Center when his mother passed away, wrote from the Italy South Mission to Sister Lee on January 1, 1974, to return the gift of faith which he had received from the President of the Church. Elder Gary W. Gerhard wrote:

> I loved President Lee very much and I know that he loved and continues to love every person on this earth with every fiber of his soul. . . . You see, President Lee thought of me and my family four months ago, when I was in the Missionary Home, when my mother passed from this earthly existence. He bore a solemn testimony to me that I cannot deny of this plan of salvation, and now I have been moved by the Spirit to write to you, and leave you my testimony and love that this Church is the kingdom of God on earth.

The personal ministrations President Lee rendered to so many friends and the loss they felt, is represented by a letter to Sister Lee from Lenore (Mrs. George) Romney of Bloomfield Hills, Michigan. She wrote:

> We love him, too! Your loss is incomparable because you had so much, but we share with you deep sorrow that your beloved Harold's magnificent spirit and personality cannot again shine upon us in this life. Yet always I have what he brought to my soul: renewal in every way and faith in my own worth and mission. In fact, his influence upon me was greater than that of any other man, save that of my own father and my husband.
>
> Every moment, every glimpse of him, I treasure, for I was warmed and blessed by his every word. As you know, he restored

me to life and health while in our home, blessing our family with his prophetic insight and inspiration, and restored me anew with his magnificent blessing in the Oakland Temple with you at his side. Later he helped me have the courage to stand firm in the bruising political arena, knowing, through his loving counsel, what was required of me. Later, our visit together in St. George at the commencement exercises of Dixie College was another peak experience. I shall always feel the glow of his tender, compassionate consideration of me.

I still see President Lee standing before us in the Salt Lake Tabernacle with prophetic vision and personal revelation pouring forth from his countenance that shone with the light of heaven upon us all, thrilling and stirring our souls.

The same sentiments were being expressed in his most intimate circle, too. From the office staff who daily worked with him and saw him under all situations and pressures came a tribute from Francis M. Gibbons, secretary to the First Presidency, written to Helen and Brent Goates on the night of his death.

All of us share the great loss which you and your lovely family have suffered this day. God bless you in this sad hour.

Without exception, we all reached out to President Lee as if to a father. His unfailing concern for our welfare and his constant reaching out to help us and ours made us all feel that we were part of his family, while the concrete achievements of his ministry will hardly be exceeded by any of his predecessors except Joseph, and, perhaps, Brigham. I believe that the thing that will make his memory endure was his great capacity for love and compassion and his ability to make everyone feel needed and loved.

REASON IN A PARABLE

The meaning and purpose of the tremendous loss of President Lee is nowhere better understood nor more beautifully and expertly explained than in these words of Elder Boyd K. Packer of the Council of the Twelve, excerpted from his remarks at the conclusion of the Coordinating Council meeting of January 30, 1974:

Harold B. Lee—prophet, seer, and revelator. All of us have been close to him and worked closely with him over the last few years. He, of course, could properly be titled, "the architect of priesthood correlation." Under assignment from President David O. McKay he served as chairman of the Correlation Committee for many years. As a counselor to President Joseph Fielding Smith, and as President of the Church, he directed what is known as Priesthood Correlation. We have visited with him, sometimes in intimate conversations, in travel, or in his office, or in meetings such as this. We've looked back with him to his junior years as a member of the Council of the Twelve.

He saw some drifting and felt some anxiety, and he carried that concern with him for years. There is no question but what he saw today, for he was a seer; or that he understood and saw what was out in the world. He saw the narrow places that we must navigate as a Church. And, over the years, as he grew in stature, there came, as he often expressed, ideas that met their day.

Now, as we were jolted by the death of President Lee and sat up and took note of what happened, all of us, I think, asked ourselves the question and asked one another the question, "Well, what does it mean? Harold B. Lee has gone. What does that mean?"

Imagine a group of people who are going on a journey through a territory that is dangerous and unplotted. They have a large bus for transportation, and they are making preparations. They find among them a master mechanic. He is appointed to get their vehicle ready, with all of us to help. He insists that it be stripped down completely, every part taken from the other part and inspected carefully, cleaned, renewed, repaired, and some of them replaced.

Some of the gears are not efficient. They are not producing the power they should for the amount of fuel they use. And so they are replaced. This means a change in linkage, a change in the pattern of connections and delivering the power. So they go to work, with this master mechanic directing the retooling and refitting of this vehicle.

There are steep inclines that must be made and there has to be sufficient power. There will be curves and switchbacks, there will be places where control will have to be perfect, where the braking will have to be perfect.

So, painstakingly and deliberately, without undue pressure, the bus is disassembled, and ultimately is put together again.

Then comes the time when there has to be a shakedown, a test run, if you will. The signal comes that this master mechanic will also be appointed the driver. He will head the journey.

So the test is run. It is not a very long one, but there are some very difficult obstacles in it so that it is a full test. All of us, as we stand by, are delighted with the result. It is roadworthy! Now we know that it will make every hill and it will go over, and if necessary through, any obstacles in our way.

We see the master mechanic, pleased with his work, step down and say that it's ready. He dusts a little dust off the radiator cap.

Then comes the signal that Spencer will drive. And the protest comes, "Oh, but not another! We need Harold to drive. There's never been anyone who has seen so much and knows so much about the vehicle we are going to use. No man in all history has so completely gone through this vehicle and no one knows as much as he knows. No one is so thoroughly familiar with it!''

But the command is definite. Spencer will drive! Some protest that the new driver isn't so much a mechanic. "What if there is trouble along the way?" And the answer comes back, "Perhaps that's all to the good that he may not be a mechanic. It may well be, for should there be a little grinding of the gears, he won't be quite so inclined to strip it down, take out all the gears, and start to overhaul it again. He'll try first a little lubrication perhaps, a little grease here and there, and that will be all it needs.''

We must now move forward and move out. The signal comes to all of us who are on the crew. "Climb aboard. Spencer's been appointed to drive!" We obediently and with acceptance move out into that journey.

The death of a prophet is never accidental. A prophet cannot be taken, save his ministry is complete. Those of us who were present in that first meeting that first morning after that night of shock, came to know by that sacred power of communication that *He* is in charge. This is *His* work and *He* will do as *He* will do. We of the Twelve were reminded in those meetings as the reorganization was effected, that "my thoughts are not your thoughts, neither are your ways my ways" (Isaiah 55:8).

The work of President Harold B. Lee will have effect just as long as this Church endures; until the Lord himself says, "It is finished," until *His* work is done. Never through all generations can it be minimized or mitigated.

Never will the Church be the same, always it will run with more precision, more power, so that as we are on the hills, we will make the grade. When we are on the switchbacks, we will have the control. The brakes are intact so that they can be applied if we move too quickly or stray too closely to the edge of safe travel.

And so the question, then, What about those of us of the crew? What's ahead, then? What's our signal?

We must do things in order with moderation and dignity and restraint.

Those feelings have been on my mind constantly. I can confess sleepless nights as I have prayed and wondered and pondered over "Why?" I thought, when we needed President Lee the most, he who was familiar and conversant as no man ever had been with the programs of the Church, he was taken from us. But the peace was there immediately. There is no question, the Lord is in charge.

Epilogue

Epilogue

MAN MEASURE

Here and there, and now and then
    God plants a giant among men
That such as you and I may see
    The height of true nobility;
A giant spurring lesser men
    To polish up their dreams again;
A giant calling smaller souls
    To dredge up long-forgotten goals;
A giant men may look upon,
    As men have looked upon the dawn—
The weak, the bitter, the oppressed,
    With new hope rising in their breasts—
A measure of what man can be
    Who prizes human dignity. *

On the last day of 1973, five days after the passing of President Lee, a letter from Torrington, Wyoming, came to Sister Lee from a Church member named Carla Kelly. She related how one of the missionaries working in Wyoming told her of an experience

---

* Reprint of poem "Man Measure" from the book *Hold to Your Dream* by Helen Lowrie Marshall, published by Doubleday in 1965. Used with permission.

another Elder had had across the mission in Nebraska. He and his companion were tracting and came upon an elderly woman who told them she had been contacted many years before by the missionaries. She then naively asked the young Elder: "By the way, whatever became of that missionary named Elder Lee?"

What became of Elder Lee! If only she knew! He rose from poverty and obscurity, during a long odyssey from a humble farm home in Idaho to become the most important man on earth, God's spokesman to the inhabitants of this world.

How this transformation took place has been unfolded in the foregoing pages. Only a final testament summary remains to be told.

Harold B. Lee was always ahead of his years in accomplishment. He started school a year earlier than was the practice in his community because he could already write his name and knew the alphabet. He was ordained a deacon at ten years of age because he was large for his size and all his friends were being ordained. He became a school teacher at seventeen, and a school principal at eighteen, all before his full-time mission for the Church. He spent most of the time on his mission as the Denver Conference president. At age thirty-one he was the youngest stake president in the Church, and two years later was a Salt Lake City commissioner, a community leader. He was a very junior Apostle at age forty-two among a quorum of white-haired Brethren. This caused President J. Reuben Clark, Jr., his tutor, to affectionately refer to him as "Kid." He was ready ahead of time with his ideas for Church organizational innovation, but found he had to first learn the virtue of patience through a long wait.

He was a prodigious worker. He never put off until tomorrow what could be done today. He attacked every challenge with uncommon vigor, in his Church responsibilities as well as in his personal life.

In his years as Church President he demonstrated a remarkable transparency. He opened to view the office of prophet, seer, and revelator as it had never been exposed since the days of the Prophet Joseph Smith. He allowed all interested to look into the heart of a prophet. As a result, most Saints wanted to be near him. It was wearying just to keep pace with their unintended demands.

Harold B. Lee had an amazing faculty for making people feel important. He had a remarkable memory for names and faces, recalling incidents with clarity even after twenty or thirty years had passed. He challenged many to be better than they were by telling them they already were what he knew they could become. His "as if" approach was effective, yet it was not a contrived style, but merely an indigenous human relations magic which he possessed.

Being a very sensitive man, he had a genius to identify with people and their problems. He moved instinctively to the rescue of someone in danger. It was not done in a sense of duty; his natural reflex was to simply care for other people.

Since 1941, after his call to the apostleship, President Lee worked quietly but steadily to prepare for his destiny. He set himself an ideal which few men aspire to achieve: the learning of all wisdom and intelligence from the scriptures, and the learning of all secular knowledge. Elder Neal A. Maxwell described it in these words:

> He was at home in the world of ideas. For instance, his brief experience in politics and government permitted him to distill from that period what other men would have taken years to learn. Being secure spiritually and intellectually he could be eclectic in gathering in ideas, concepts, and truths which would be helpful to the work of the kingdom. Though he had not had the opportunity for extensive education in the secular sense, he could cope with and even use ideas which his remarkable spiritual education encouraged him to reach out for.

He never compromised his ideals of a spiritual kingdom and a personal relationship with Deity, despite encounters along his Church career with an environment that featured the sophisticated learning of men. As a result he was consistently a worker of miracles and brought heaven closer to thousands.

Spirituality thus became his greatest leadership tool. He took direction from the heavens. He knew how to talk with God and how to obtain answers to his prayers for the Saints.

Organizational conceptual skills were innate to him. The welfare program emerged under his leadership, born out of his own creativity in meeting the problems of presiding over a stake of poor people during the Great Depression. Using the scriptures as his guide in the creation of the correlation program, he completely restructured the Church in the 1960s. An epitomizing picture was to see President Lee at his desk, his scriptures opened, with a massive *Webster's Dictionary* on a table at his side. He was the scholar in these activities.

He was a revelator. The new programs he implemented were boldly labelled "revelations"—the welfare program; the correlation program; the cyclical curriculum program of the Church;

home teaching and family home evening; Regional Representatives as a new layer of Church leadership; Aaronic Priesthood-MIA and its correlation with the Boy Scouts of America; and many others.

President Lee expanded the Church abroad; his administration will be remembered for further internationalizing the Church. Area conferences were taken to overseas soil for the first time, helping remove the "Utah/America" label from the Church. He wanted the Church members abroad to have close association with their prophet and other General Authorities, as was common in the United States.

President Lee widened the channels of communication among the General Authorities so that all had a participative role in approving and understanding new programs and the creative thinking of the First Presidency. The monthly meetings in the Salt Lake Temple for all General Authorities became the new mechanism for this accomplishment.

Among the many strengths that President Lee possessed was his unwavering, uncompromising devotion to what the Lord promised and expected in the revelations. He believed with refreshing candor that the Lord meant what he said in the scriptures. With a simple faith and understanding based on personal testimony President Lee would say, "If he said it, he expects us to do it." The Lee administration was noted for fully accepting the Lord's statements at face value, thus producing among the membership an assurance that the Church was moving ahead confidently.

He had the total admiration and respect of the Brethren. They had sat with Elder Lee in the temple, traveled on planes with him, and surrounded tables in committee meetings for years. Universally, they admired his wisdom. After everyone had spoken in a meeting, President Lee had the genius for going right to the heart of the matter under discussion. He could get to the very kernel by asking the penetrating questions at the right moment. His timing was superb. In a simple statement of inquiry he could bring the discussion back into focus. This leadership was revered.

One of his greatest accomplishments as President was to move out among the people. He went to conference after conference, going thousands of extra miles to meet the members. After a long period of time when the leadership of the Church remained unseen due to age and illness, he closed the gap. He went to conferences in England, Mexico, and Germany in his first year as President, with two or three other tours abroad and scores of youth conferences. This helped the prophetic image to return to young people, whom he served by taking time out of his busy life to be with them at scores of youth conferences and firesides.

Several General Authorities speak of sacred public meetings with President Lee as being the most spiritual experiences of their lives. He had the ability to throw away the script and to teach by the Holy Ghost. Elder Paul H. Dunn described it in this way: "We got about as close to heaven as you can on earth. I saw Elder Lee in a heavenly light as he spoke and bore witness that night in the Salt Lake Temple." He was a conduit for personal revelation, and pentecostal experiences were possible through him.

President Lee possessed deep compassion for people and their problems. Endlessly he called on the sick, blessing people who needed help in their lives. He listened patiently to their problems, went to their homes, preached at their funerals, made right the wrongs in their lives. He listened and served like the Master who had called him.

His counsel was valued by the mighty men of the earth. Millionaires, politicians, educators, and business tycoons sought him, but he belonged indigenously, emotionally, and psychologically to the poor. They were his people, for he came from among them and never lost his common touch.

No one was his equal, according to some associates, in comprehending the role of priesthood and Church government.

Especially after becoming President of the Church his manner was gentle, compassionate, gracious, hospitable, and always thoughtful of others. He was always the gentleman, impeccably dressed.

Yet, President Lee was a complex personality. There were times when he seemed withdrawn and uncommunicative. His silence during a conversation was the signal to those who knew him to put aside the issue for another day. He was capable of enjoying good humor but didn't engage in or appreciate levity, especially in Church buildings. Very few persons addressed him by his first name. There was a respectful aura of dignity about him which one penetrated only at his invitation. Even close friends and associates usually approached him with caution to await clues as to whether he was then available.

He was an inveterate teacher. One of the marks of his genius was that he was always teaching whenever he was talking, even in casual conversations. Whether in giving a blessing, counseling, or talking as a father, he was always teaching the gospel. He never wasted a minute. Like the Savior, his teaching was often skillfully mixed with interesting experiences and anecdotes that caused many persons, content with the obvious, to miss the deeper significance of the lesson. He was not one to force his teachings, but they were always there for those who had "eyes to see, and ears to hear."

In private settings he was not averse to giving reproof to others, but this then was followed by that outpouring of redemptive affection which the scriptures call for, along with concrete efforts to help the individual who had been reproved, and counseled, sometimes by stinging rebuke. Yet Elder Lee never held grudges and could overcome earlier perceptions of another person, revising impressions as more and different data came in. Many of those who had been appropriately reprimanded became later his closest and most trusted associates.

It seemed as if by the close of his life President Lee had overcome all enemies and weaknesses; that at the end, he was simply too good, too great for this world; that he had run out of challenges worthy of his amazing talents. It was not by any means an easy triumph, however. Consider these tests, among many, which he faced:

- He had critics who were jealous of his "beyond his years" abilities.

- He was forced to learn patience, to wait behind leaders with more seniority than himself before his ideas could gain acceptance.

- He learned how to control his fiery temper and quick, action-oriented disposition which earlier in his life had offended people.

- He learned tolerance and unselfishness by subduing all personal desires and placing those of others ahead of his own. This is most notably illustrated in his determination to make his second marriage a happy one, even though it required an almost complete reversal of habit patterns for himself.

- He practiced control and finally excelled, as he had in all other aspects of his life, to gain a mellowing Sainthood that the heavens couldn't reject.

When he was taken, so abruptly and most thought prematurely, there was one universal reconciliation in the Church. All seemed to say that his work on earth was finished and he had gone on to a more important labor. What work could have been so important as to claim priority over his presidency among us?

One can only speculate on this, of course. But there could be a clue offered in the prophetic patriarchal blessing given to Harold Bingham Lee by Patriarch James Reid McNiel in Clifton, Idaho, on March 18, 1917, when Harold B. Lee was a lad of just eighteen years of age. A portion of the blessing reads:

> Thou shalt assist in the rearing of temples and labor therein for thy kindred dead, until thou art fully satisfied. Thou shalt read the words and works of the Savior, that he performed among the Ten Tribes of Israel after his resurrection and ascension, even in the congregations of the Saints, and labor with that people in bestowing upon them their blessings that they shall receive under the hands of Ephraim.

This seems to be a calling to a work beyond this earthly sphere. The thought of him laboring amongst the Ten Lost Tribes as an assigned commission brings comfort and consolation to those who felt keenly the loss of President Lee when he was taken in death in 1973. We share him reluctantly in this extra-terrestrial setting. Harold B. Lee now truly belongs to the ages.

Appendix: Summary of First Welfare Regional Meetings Held

Following are Harold B. Lee's notes of his first trip through the Church to organize regions and teach the Church Security Program:

April 21, 1936: Ogden Region, attended by President Grant, Melvin J. Ballard, Mark Austin, and Harold B. Lee.

Stake	Attendance	Stake President	Regional Officers
Weber	23	Browning	Chairman
North Weber	38	Irvine	
Morgan	18	Randall	
Box Elder	31	Lee	

Stake	Attendance	Stake President	Regional Officers
Malad	27	Richards	
Mt. Ogden	27	Reeder	Vice-Chairman
Ogden	36	McKay	
Bear River	38	Smith	
Woodruff	16	Brown	
Total	254		

The first regional council meeting was set for May 12, 1936 at 7:30 p.m. in the Eccles Building, 512.

April 22, 1936 in Heber City, Utah, from 7:30 to 10:30 p.m., the Regional Meeting was held, attended by President Grant and Joseph Anderson (secretary), Melvin J. Ballard, Bishop Cannon, Mark Austin, and Harold B. Lee.

Stake	Attendance	Stake President	Regional Officers
Wasatch	47	Broadbent	Chairman
Uintah	27	Calder	
South Summit	28	Oblad	Vice-Chairman
Summit	15	Wilde	
Roosevelt	11	Colton	
Duchesne		Bennion	
Total	128		

Uintah Stake is in deplorable condition due to the drouth.

———

April 23, 1936, in Provo, Utah, a regional meeting was held from 7:30 to 10:15 p.m. with President Grant, Elder Melvin J. Ballard, Bishop Cannon, Mark Austin, and Harold B. Lee attending.

Stake	Attendance	Stake President	Regional Officers
Utah	29	Taylor	
Palmyra	26	Gardner	
Sharon	13	Watkins	Chairman
Alpine	17	Young	
Carbon	27	-	
Kolob	16	Bird	
Nebo	20	Taylor	
Timpanogos	16	Warnock	Vice-Chairman
Lehi	19	Schow	
Emery	21	Peterson	
San Juan	4	Redd	
Total	208		

Topics discussed: Sugar beet war; sedition against President Grant; what about using old sugar factory for canning?; stimulate garden projects for surplus; what about tunnel project in San Juan?; power, drills, food.

———

April 24, 1936 in Burley, Idaho, from 7:30 to 10:00 p.m.:

Stake	Attendance	Stake President	Regional Officers
Burley	30	Langlois	Vice-Chairman
Blaine	12	Adamson	
Minidoka	27	May	
Boise	17	Brown	
Cassia	12	Clark	Chairman
Raft River	12	Elison	
Curlew	12	Sweeten	
Total	159		

Topics discussed: Possibility of creating a new region at Baker, Oregon, with Union and Boise stakes and portions of the Northwestern States Mission; Kio Ranch, 3,600 acres in Raft River Stake, can be purchased for $20,000 . . . possible colonization of forty acres per family; what about the dissipation of bonuses to produce surpluses for needy?; other possible farm lands near headwaters of Raft River.

———

April 25, 1936, East Idaho Region in Idaho Falls, Idaho, from 7:30 to 10:15 p.m.:

Stake	Attendance	Stake President	Regional Officers
Yellowstone	18	White	
Pocatello	47	Henderson	
North Idaho Falls	23	Smith	Chairman
Rexburg	32	Ricks	
Rigby	35	Call	
Blackfoot	36	Duckworth	
Idaho Falls	16	Ball	Vice-Chairman
Teton	9	Choules	
Lost River	5	-	
Portneuf	29	-	
Total	276		

Topics discussed: Possible to secure sugar company warehouse; Pres. Henderson is on W.P.A. as a tool checker.

April 26, 1936 in Preston, Idaho, from 10:00 a.m. to 12:30 p.m.:

Stake	Attendance	Stake President	Regional Officers
Franklin	98	Barton	Chairman
Oneida	83	Nelson	
Bannock	19	Sorenson	
Montpelier	35	Rich	Vice-Chairman
Idaho	12	Gilbert	
Total	247		

April 26, 1936 in Logan, Utah, from 2:00 p.m. to 4:30 p.m.:

Stake	Attendance	Stake President	Regional Officers
Logan	45	Anderson	Chairman
Cache	40	Cardon	
Bear Lake	24	Robinson	
Hyrum	28	Bickmore	
Benson	40	Pond	Vice-Chairman
Total	177		

Topics discussed: Clothing drive on; beet projects.

April 27, 1936 in Nephi, Utah, from 7:30 to 10:00 p.m.:

Stake	Attendance	Stake President	Regional Officers
Juab	17	Belliston	Vice-Chairman
Gunnison	20	Hansen	
Moroni	12	Christiansen	
North Sanpete	17	Nielson	Chairman
Tintic	10	Birch	
South Sanpete	32	Anderson	
Deseret	31	Finlandson	
Millard	25	Callister (Bushnell)	
Total	164		

Topics discussed: Seventies quorum in Juab has a wheat-growing farm kept up by quorum participation; encourage farmer solidarity by urging purchase of a factory to establish a farmers' cooperative sugar factory.

April 28, 1936 in Richfield, Utah, from 10:00 a.m. to 12:30 p.m.:

Stake	Attendance	Stake President	Regional Officers
Sevier	34	Poulson	Chairman
South Sevier	15	Ware	
North Sevier	11	Williams	
Beaver	12	Farnsworth	
Wayne	12	Webster	
Garfield	17	Twitchell	
Panguitch	18	Hatch	Vice-Chairman
Total	119		

Topics discussed: Project producing commercial fertilizer to beet growers—chemical analysis needed, Mark Austin to investigate; lumber mill project in Panguitch may need some Church financing to get started; building of a flume near Fruita with Church funds would provide for the colony that will be forced out otherwise.

April 28, 1936 in St. George, Utah, from 7:30 to 10:30 p.m.:

Stake	Attendance	Stake President	Regional Officers
Moapa	31	Jones	
Parowan	24	Palmer	Chairman
St. George	28	Bentley	
Zion Park	24	Herschi	Vice-Chairman
Kanab	17	Heaton	
Total	124		

Topics discussed: Pres. Bentley is county manager of W.P.A.; regional council meeting will be held on Tuesday, May 13, at 2:00 p.m.; growing beet seed and reviving farming; active building—sewer, school building; location of old cotton mill; semi-tropical fruits.

———————

May 1, 1936 in Oakland, California, the Northern California region met from 4:00 to 6:00 p.m. with Elder Melvin J. Ballard, Bishop Sylvester Q. Cannon, and Harold B. Lee in attendance:

Stake	Attendance	Stake President	Regional Officers
San Francisco	14	Winter	
Oakland	37	MacDonald	Chairman
Sacramento	12	Cram	Vice-Chairman
Gridley	5	Todd	
Total	68		

Topics discussed: Possible chance to use storehouse here for a distributing point for Utah and Idaho produce; alert men here with Pres. W. Aird MacDonald, Bishop Nalder, A. D. Erickson, and Charles Call. Although the meeting was hurried they seemed to accept the program very well. A number expressed their joy that at last the Church was taking a stand in the relief program. Elder Ballard was disappointed that opposition continued among a few in high places.

———————

May 2, 1936, in Los Angeles region: A special priesthood meeting was held from 7:30 to 10:00 p.m. in connection with stake conference, where the time was devoted to a discussion of the relief program. In attendance were President Grant, Dr. John A. Widtsoe, Elder Ballard, Bishop Cannon, and Harold B. Lee. All but Elder Widtsoe were called to speak.

Stake	Attendance	Stake President	Regional Officers
Los Angeles	61	Muir	Chairman
Hollywood	21	Edling	
Pasadena	31	Cannon	Vice-Chairman
San Bernardino	15	Larson	
Total	128		

Topics discussed: Long Beach Stake was organized with President Jones as president. Circulars failed to arrive in time for distribution. Elder Widstoe characterized the relief meeting as "an epoch-making" meeting and declared the principles explained and the program announced as sound. After the meeting Sister Widstoe told Harold B. Lee that she wanted to learn of the program and promised to visit with him when they returned to Salt Lake City. Harold B. Lee spoke at both Sunday sessions of stake conference before overflowing congregations.

May 4, 1936 in Phoenix and Mesa, Arizona regional meeting, held from 4:00 to 7:30 p.m.:

Stake	Attendance	Stake President	Regional Officers
Maricopa	52	Price	Chairman
St. Johns	14	Udall	
St. Joseph	35	Payne	
Snowflake	24	Smith	Vice-Chairman
Total	125		

Index

About the Author

Born and reared in Salt Lake City, L. Brent Goates earned his degree in business management from the University of Utah. After a dozen years in journalism he moved into the hospital administration field, becoming administrator of the Latter-day Saints Hospital in Salt Lake City and then assistant commissioner for the Church's multi-hospital system, Health Services Corporation. Before retirement he worked in the Church Missionary Department, serving successively as director of exhibits, director of visitors' centers, and director of missionary operations.

The author has held membership and leadership positions in various professional organizations, committees, and service organizations. In addition to a full-time mission when young, he has served in such Church positions as bishop, stake president, mission president, Regional Representative, and on the Church Priesthood Home Teaching Committee. He is now a sealer in the Salt Lake Temple.

Subsequent to this book he authored two other books about President Lee, *He Changed My Life* (1988) and *Modern-day Miracles* (1996). He has also published many articles in professional journals.

Brent Goates was married to the late Helen Lee Goates, President Lee's youngest daughter. The couple had six children.